American Automobile Association

Presents

P9-DWT-788

GUIDE TO THE BEST

WINERIES
OF
NORTH AMERICA

A Discriminating and Practical Guide to Wineries and Wines
from Canada to Mexico and from California to New England

Editor-in-Chief & Publisher
André Gayot

Editorial
Editor & Chief Critic: Edward Guiliano
Contributing Editor & Consultant: Barbara Ensrud
Contributing Editor: Deborah H. Busching
AGP Editor: Jeffrey Hirsch   Associate Editor: Laura Reiley

Special thanks to AAA staff for their invaluable contribution

AAA Geographic Information Systems: Maps
AAA Design Center: Cover Design
Steve Benton: Cover Art

Publishing Director
Alain Gayot

An André Gayot Publication / Gault Millau

Los Angeles • Paris • New York • San Francisco • London

ANDRÉ GAYOT PUBLICATIONS
Bring You

The Best of Chicago	The Best of New England
The Best of Florida	The Best of New Orleans
The Best of France	The Best of New York
The Best of Germany	The Best of Paris
The Best of Hawaii	The Best of San Francisco
The Best of Hong Kong	The Best of Thailand
The Best of Italy	The Best of Toronto
The Best of London	The Best of Washington
The Best of Los Angeles	The Best Wineries of North America

Tastes Newsletter

Published by Gault Millau, Inc.
Los Angeles, California

Please address all comments regarding
The Best Wines of North America to:
Gault Millau, Inc.
P.O. Box 361144
Los Angeles, CA 90036

Page Layout and Design by Stuart/Stephens
141 El Camino Drive
Beverly Hills, California

Library of Congress Cataloging-in-Publication Data

The Best Wineries of North America: a discriminating and practical guide to wineries and wines
from Canada to Mexico and from Califonia to New England /
editor-in-chief & publisher, André Gayot.
p. cm.
"Presented by American Automobile Association"
"An André Gayot publication."
Includes index.
ISBN 1-881066-02-9: $18.00
1. Wine and wine making—United States. 2. Wine and wine making—Canada. 3. Wine and
wine making—Mexico. I. Gayot, André.
II. American Automobile Association.

TP557.B48 1993   93-4463
641.2'2'097—dc20   CIP

Printed in the United States of America

CONTENTS

A Word From

THE mark of a truly satisfying dining experience lies in successfully blending the flavors, presentation and compatibility of the food and drink. These elements must come together to create gustatory pleasure that will long be savored and remembered. Without each ingredient present, a potentially magnificent repast becomes just another meal. Equally as important as the exacting preparation of the food comprising the meal is the knowledgeable selection of the wine, which is, without question, an integral component of the fine dining experience.

Through annual restaurant inspections and ratings, the American Automobile Association (AAA) has for many years provided its members with detailed information about select dining establishments across the United States, Canada and Mexico. This service is but one example of the Association fulfilling its mission to provide its more than 34 million members with the most accurate and current travel information available. Through rigorous evaluations, AAA inspectors assess the quality of each establishment's menu, wine list, service and decor, communicating this information to members in detailed reports, and with trusted diamond ratings.

The Association has, to this point, expected diners to rely on their existing knowledge of wines to guide them in making the crucial selection of a meal's complementary beverage. Now, with this *Guide To The Best Wineries of North America*, AAA presents diners with *all* the information to make the dining experience complete. With the information contained in this volume, members and other readers will gain a better understanding of the complexities of wines and the vinification process, and learn where to locate the best buys. With this new publication to rely on, readers can be more assured when ordering and tasting wine, and feel more confident of the quality and value they have selected.

An enjoyable way to approach this learning experience is to discover, at firsthand, how wine is made. A day trip or long weekend provides the perfect opportunity to explore the many intriguing wine regions of North America. Though most widely associated with California, vineyards of quality abound across our continent. Now a delightfully rewarding winery tour in any region of the United States, Canada or Mexico is within easy reach. One need only plan a journey using this guide—and then take off!

For more than 90 years, the American Automobile Association has enjoyed a preeminent position as the authority on all aspects of motoring, from driving concerns to the more pleasurable aspects of auto travel and touring. With this publication, AAA joins André Gayot, American publisher of the famed Gault Millau travel guide series and an acknowledged expert in all aspects of food and wine appreciation, in an exciting and mutually beneficial relationship. Both organizations, dedicated to best serving the needs of those who place high value on the fine dining experience, now bring together all that is needed to experience epicurean excellence across North America in one complete guide.

— *American Automobile Association*

For Those in the Know and Those Who Want to Be...

W INE is emotion, voluptuousness, euphoria. Or it can be, depending on all sorts of extenuating circumstances, from pearls of frost on grape vines in the hills of a distant state to the degree of sensitivity of each wine drinker's taste buds.

Having published numerous books and articles about wine over the years, we discover, with this new volume, entirely new horizons. A lifetime does not suffice for gaining a mastery of wine. Knowledge of this most inscrutable subject has no limit.

Because of the vastness of the subject, there is always room for additional learning. Among the many good wine books already published, we found that an important one was still missing: one that helps you penetrate and fathom this fascinating universe, that allows you to appreciate this symphony, without requiring you to learn the rudiments of its composition. After all, you need not go through the intense training required to obtain an FAA pilot's license to embark on a 747 jet and enjoy the flight. This book seeks to make of you a satisfied passenger; it does not pretend to be a pilot's training manual.

Don't be daunted by the seemingly esoteric vocabulary of wine. Our glossary in Part Three of this book will help to clear up many semantic mysteries. Take a look at this material and then quickly move on to a consideration of what might be called "the phenomenology of wine." Discover, for instance, that the first savor our tongue detects is sweetness. The reason: the papillae attuned to sweet tastes are located at the front of our tongue. This is why it's so easy to seduce any palate with sugary foods and beverages, and why wines offered to the American public in the past were excessively sweet.

As we explore our palate further, we find that in the back of the mouth, the tongue can easily detect other tastes, like acid and bitterness. With this bit of knowledge,you may naturally come to demand more of your wine and you will likely enjoy it more fully. A balance of sweetness and acidity in a fine wine, you will find, creates a pleasurable sensation in your mouth while revealing, on a more sophisticated level, your body's ability to experience what is offered it.

Making the most of all your senses as you sip a glass of ruby red Cabernet Sauvignon or topaz-colored Chardonnay; investigating some of the extraordinary complexities of the plant life on our planet; appreciating the ingenuity of the artisans and scientists striving to perfect nature and capture its essence in a bottle—this is what this book is about.

Those precious drops filling your glass result from, among a myriad of other variables, the selected grape varietal, the prevailing geology, microclimate and meteorology, the manner of cultivation, the winemaking techniques, and the mode of storing and aging. At every stage in the process, a lot of work—and a lot of luck—also play crucial roles. But let's leave these matters, with the many technical details they imply, to the experts. It is for us to simply enjoy this wonderful and complex elixir.

After the sight of the wine, our exploration continues with our nose, a much more sensitive sensory organ than our tongue. The nose captures many flavors that our palates are destined to be ignorant of forever, for the tongue was not made to discriminate on such a refined plane. Breathe in deeply the scent of the sacred liquid and fill your nostrils with (depending on the variety of wine in your glass) aromas of fruit—cherries, black currants, apples, bananas, raspberries—the perfume of flowers—roses, acacia, violets, peonies, rose hips— and the smell of herbs—fern, mint, hay, licorice.

Following this first wave of olfactory perception, a second tier of aromas will tickle your nose. These new fragrances reflect the wine's alcoholic fermentation (in which sugar is transformed into alcohol) and, when present, its malolactic fermentation (in which malic acid is transformed into lactic acid) and result in a scent with a rounder, creamier note, reminiscent of fresh butter or hazelnut.

And that's not all the wine has to offer your nose: while aging in barrels, wine develops yet another level of aromas. With time, existing scents are polished and refined. Tannins add to the developing taste of the wine: astringency is now a part of the evolving medley of sensations. In that process, new scents are added as well such as wood, leather, sometimes even truffle.

Now, when you run into the word "complexity" being applied to wine, you will have to admit that it is not an exaggeration. All the phases through which a wine develops, all its transformations, must come at precisely the right time, under exactly the right conditions.

Wine is a living, breathing substance. Wine, like a baby, is dependent on its inherited gifts and the care with which it is nurtured. It can develop character of high quality or it may prove undistinguished. And like an infant—like all living things—even the best wines are susceptible to disease. Minor "illnesses" may not be immediately discernable, still they can weaken or render tasteless an otherwise great wine.

Having considered the breadth and depth of the wine world, we now arrive at the Big Question: How to choose from the shelves of our neighborhood wine store, or select from our favorite restaurant's wine list, the right wine for the occasion, the time of day (or of the year) and, of course, for our budget? How do we identify that very bottle that will enhance the conviviality and multiply the pleasure of a celebration with friends, a family reunion, or a romantic rendezvous? Do we want the majesty of a golden Chardonnay, the zestiness of a Sauvignon Blanc, the sensuousness of a Pinot Noir, the exuberance of a sparkling wine? The answers to these and many other questions lie in the following pages. Have no fear: we will not bore you with a highly technical academic treatise. Instead, we invite you to join us in an appreciation of what we believe are some of the best wineries in North America. Many other establishments, in addition to those profiled in this volume, deserve credit and consideration for their efforts. They will understand that to keep this book of reasonable proportions, we could not possibly include *every* winery in North America. We will undoubtedly treat additional vintners in subsequent editions.

In the tasting rooms of many of the wineries discussed in this book and at tastings at restaurants and in homes, with the help of sommeliers, wine lovers, collectors, colleagues, and friends, we have sampled, over a period of two years, thousands of wines. Facing such a profusion, it is almost certain that we have overlooked some fine bottles. We apologize for the unavoidable omissions and errors that may come to light as we publish the results of this huge undertaking.

To guide you through the maze and to make of you a wine connoisseur—or, if you prefer, to simply help you discover, with a minimum of risk and disappointment, some very good wines—we have enlisted the services of Edward Guiliano. The author or editor of eight books, including The *Annotated Dickens,* Mr. Guiliano served as editor and chief critic of Gault Millau's award-winning *The Best of New York.* He is currently a distinguished Professor of English at The New York Institute of Technology, Old Westbury, New York, and finds time to write extensively about food and wine, for which he has developed an abiding passion and penetrating knowledge. Your other guide to the best wines of North America is Barbara Ensrud, the well-known author of several books on wine including *American Vineyards* and *Wine with Food* and a columnist for *The Wall Street Journal* and numerous national magazines.

It is our hope that after reading this book you will have an increased understanding of, and appreciation for, fine wine. When next you raise a wine glass to your lips, many images may come to mind: the pastoral beauty of the rolling hills of the Napa Valley, the joyful faces of vintners celebrating a splendid new release, the serenity of a cavernous cellar lined with old oak barrels. With the very wine you are about to enjoy, you pay tribute to the enormous wealth of knowledge and talent, the arduous effort, and inevitably, the serendipitous circumstances that bring every brand and variety of this special beverage into being.

In North America alone, thousands and thousands of wines are available to you, which may or may not not be fit for your needs and tastes. Or for your wallet. Dozens, if not hundreds of these wines can provide you the kind of satisfaction that adds not only to your sensual enjoyment of life, but also to your spiritual fulfillment. Only if it is misused, will wine induce inebriation. Consumed with food at meals, wine, itself a food, in the moderate quantities in which it is best savored, can enhance your social and intellectual life.

The recent discoveries (or, more properly, rediscoveries) of the dietary virtues of wine drinking and of its impact on our health—most notably in combating arterial disease—add another explanation for the ever-increasing popularity of this most invaluable product. Wine has become a part of life worldwide, and today plays an important symbolic role in peacefully and joyfully unifying people of disparate cultures in a communal celebration of all things good and beautiful.

This book, in the end, is a cordial salute to the vintners of America. (In France, where wine has long been a way of life, there is an old Gallic saying: A meal without wine is like a day without sunshine.) We have observed and admired the rise of American viniculture and viticulture over the last quarter century. Recent progress has been remarkable and is especially conspicuous in regions outside of California. At this point in American wine history—400 years, compared to 4000 years of world wine history—there is still an exciting lot of the great North American wine adventure left to unfold. It is our modest desire to bring to the process of discovery, edification, and building currently in progress, our own little stone.

André

— André Gayot

A Disclaimer

Readers are advised that prices and conditions change over the course of time. The wineries profiled and wines reviewed in this book have been considered over a period of time, and the profiles and reviews reflect the personal experiences and opinions of the reviewers. The reviewers and publisher cannot be held responsible for the experiences of the reader in relation to the wineries or wines reviewed. Readers are invited to write the publisher with ideas, comments, and suggestions for future editions.

PART I

Assessing the Best Wines and Values

Introduction

The Best and Getting the Best Bang for the Buck

B EST is a concept invented to make life easier. It simplifies the establishment of hierarchies within all tribes, societies, and groups. But any way you judge it, even if you attempt to apply the most precise criteria, determination of the "best" remains a subjective exercise.

For instance, we will probably remember the name of the winner of an Olympic gold medal as the "best" athlete in his category. His footsteps have been precisely clocked in a race televised around the globe, but is he truly the best 100-meter runner in the world? He was perhaps the "best" this particular day, under these precise and necessarily limited circumstances. But the day before or the following day, another athlete has or will run a tad faster. Or maybe on a remote country road somewhere, yet another runner, sprinting through the unspoiled landscape for the sheer joy of it (and with no interest whatsoever in competition), will achieve a speed that would leave our Olympic star in the dust. Because we need a "best," we've concocted elaborate but ultimately rather arbitrary methods of singling out a champion.

If it's difficult to determine the "best" athlete, it's harder still to judge the "very best" wine. It is not unusual to find among a jury of seasoned tasters some variations in their ratings of a particular wine. This can be explained by individual preferences and even the state of each juror's health and spiritual well-being at the time of the tasting. Nevertheless, to an educated palate, distinctions among "excellent," "very good," "good," and "poor" can be clearly drawn.

In consequence, we ask that you not take the superlative "the best" contained in the title of our book as absolute, incontrovertible dogma. Remember the old joke about the three competing restaurants on the same block. The first restaurant advertises that it is "The Best in Town." The second boasts of being "The Best in the State." The proprietor of the third restaurant is both a bit more modest and a good deal more clever. He proclaims himself simply "The Best on the Block." So we see just how relative is the concept of the "best."

"Best" is a fickle rubric by nature; it can stay put or disappear. And its applicability will vary from time to time. Certainly with wine, vintage matters a lot. The sun, the rain, the temperature, and the distribution of these and countless other elements over the course of a given growing season may or may not have created the best conditions for the best wines. Of course, human error can later mitigate against even the most ideal of growing conditions. To possess the potential to become the "best" wine and then to actually achieve such great promise—that is a long and tricky road to travel.

We have studied and interpreted a wide range of factors, utilizing all of the available information, to arrive at our choices of the "best" wines and wineries of North America. In all honesty, we believe that the statements contained in this volume offer a fair, sound overview of what is indeed the best currently available to the avid—or the merely curious—wine consumer.

Having measured the difficulties by which we arrived at this voluminous roster of beautiful wines, can anyone explain how their prices have been determined, and what gives them their value?

Wine is not a commodity whose price is dictated by a distant exchange where speculators trade frantically on reports of frost or phylloxera.

First, let us not forget the law of supply and demand applies here as in every market. Then, there are objective considerations to take into account in establishing a particular bottle's price: the cost of capitalizing the vineyard and winery, land value and investment in planting and equipment, and expenditures for labor. The more ambitious or elaborate the wines, the more work required to make them, to say nothing of the necessity of employing qualified (skilled and seasoned) enologists and winemakers.

Inordinate care and attention to detail, naturally, add to the cost. Top-quality products such as dessert wines, for example, demand a lot of hand work: grape clusters must be sorted out individually. Time, too, exacts a toll. Grapegrowers cannot make their vines grow any faster than nature has programmed them to. And the first grapes harvested after several years of cultivating new vines are not usually first-rate. It will take more time for these vines to

---

"Good wine is not a

commodity. The comparison is

frequently made between wine

and works of fine art."

---

reach full maturity and for their yields to allow for the production of premium wine. Every drinker of fine wine pays the price for the time it takes nature to do its work.

Some grape varietals require more care, are more fragile, and yield less than others. Hence another price differential: Chardonnay costs more than Colombard. Vintners can also decide to produce better grapes by pruning some of their vines back. This reduces the yield even as it demands additional labor. And less abundant production justifies a higher unit price.

Hail, frost, untimely rain, as well as mildew and phylloxera can quickly ruin a serious vintner's efforts and expectations of many years. All this explains why good wine cannot come cheaply. If care, time, love, work, work, and more work do not necessarily result in great wines, unfortunately, no great wine can possibly exist without all of these things. Is it any surprise that extraordinary wines requiring so much effort to bring to market are bound to cost more than younger, simpler wines?

Why do some wines otherwise comparable in vintage and quality bear different price tags? This question may be best answered with another question: Why are those of us who wish to drive a Rolls Royce willing to pay ten times the price of a standard, utilitarian car? Yes, the leather is richer in the Rolls, the burled wood more deeply polished, the engine quieter, the craftsmanship altogether superior. But does all this justify such a difference in price? Yes, it does, to one willing and able to pay. The Rolls may not take you to your destination much faster than a generic auto, but you get there in a Rolls!

With superb bottles of wine come famous labels, romantic stories of winemaking dynasties, and associations to the glories of eras long past. And there is the frequently made comparison between wine and works of fine art. As with a wonderful painting the culture has come to value highly, for an exceptional wine there is no other limit to the price it might fetch than what the collector who absolutely must have it is willing to pay.

Like works of art, great wine has long been sought after by collectors. Some of the rarest wines produced in North America never even see the shelves of the wine stores. They are purchased directly from the winery and land in private cellars. This factor skews the simple relationship between supply and demand and sometimes helps to make the matter of wine pricing difficult to comprehend.

Good wine cannot be mass-produced like beer. The volume that a particular vintage's harvest will render cannot be predetermined; it depends entirely on the generosity of nature. But in the end, when all is said and done, it is your satisfaction that constitutes the real determining factor of the value of the wine you will choose to purchase.

If cost is not your primary concern, in the following section titled "Safe Bets and the Best of the Best" we offer, by category, our ratings of some of the finest wines of North America. Regardless of their price, these wines represent, in our estimation, appreciable value. (When we speak of "good value," we are not only thinking of the intrinsic quality of the wine at hand, but also of the relationship between its quality and its price.)

Everyone loves a bargain, and we usually think of bargains as something moderately priced. With wine, as with so many other things in life, perfection comes at a high cost. But goodness—and affordability—are certainly well within reach for all of us. If you wish to spend less for your wine, see our "150+ Best Values for Under $10" section. Here we have endeavored to offer good advice on the best values available in the lower price range. At such a popular and competitive level, of course, you will encounter many good and many bad wines. To avoid disappointment, you'll do well to rely on the wineries included in our "Best Values" listing; their seriousness is confirmed by consistent quality sustained over many years.

The price of wine is not artificially established. You will find quality at every price level. And you can enjoy a Sauvignon Blanc or a Riesling (albeit in a different manner), where a Chardonnay may seem too costly. The same is true of, for example, moderately priced Merlots in comparison to expensive Cabernet Sauvignons.

Think, too, of North American wines in their full geographical range—from Canada to Mexico, via Oregon and Texas. If in addition to the renown star vintners of California, you consider wineries on both sides of the Rockies, you will find some very good, though less well-known, values. Turn the pages, and we will lead you to them.

—A.G.

Ten Steps in Assessing Wines & Wineries

1. When it comes to judging wines and wineries, there are both objective and subjective criteria that come into play. We begin and end with quality, which, paradoxically, is both an absolute and a relative concept. We judge a wine's quality by whether it is well made and appropriately flavorful. There are some fairly objective standards of measurement we can apply, but mostly we rely upon experienced palates: our own and others' ability to assess a wine against a lifetime data base of previously tasted samples. While a wine may be excellent—flawlessly made and filled with the appropriate flavors—we still might not *like* it, and that's okay, because "likes" are subjective responses. There is no right or wrong, no good or bad, when it comes to personal preference. Who's to say we shouldn't enjoy a blush Zinfandel, even though it's easy to show weaknesses in it if compared to more complex and elegant examples of other varietals?

2. There exists a consensus of opinion that, above all, the highest quality wines exhibit concentrated and complex aromas and flavors, harmonious balance of all components, a degree of finesse and fullness, and a long finish. We don't have to look for these qualities; they are simply there and are hard to miss, although in young wines, especially big red wines, it sometimes requires skill with a crystal ball (or a prescient palate) to appreciate what will eventually emerge in the fullness of time. Continuing to assess quality, one can look for the particular presence of the fruit, that is the aromas and flavors associated with a particular varietal. The common denominator of all good wines—the minimum requirement for a wine to be recommendable—is cleanliness and an absence of flaws, unpleasant aromas, and flavors.

3. Consistency is yet another important criterion of whether a wine or winery makes it into this book. An accident of nature can produce a great wine one season, but a record of creating quality wines year in and year out owes a lot to the art of man.

4. All too often in America it appears that all the good wine is produced in one place (California) and from two grapes (Chardonnay and Cabernet Sauvignon). Far and away most of the wine produced in America is made in California, and it seems that all of the more than 800 wineries there do produce a Chardonnay and/or a Cabernet. Focusing exclusively on this area and on these varietals would neglect the compelling variety we delight in, and ignore the successes many wineries from various other regions in North America have achieved, notably in the last couple of years.

5. Some wineries do extremely well with a particular varietal, but not so well with another. Should a winery that consistently produces a terrific Merlot be included in this book even

though that winery's Chardonnay is only average? We think so, as long as we point out that the winery is among the best because of its outstanding Merlot.

6. Young wineries or those in young viticultural areas invariably experiment, making wines from a range of grape varieties. The results are inevitably mixed, but over a decade or more, one or two varietals emerge as best-served by the winery. It is upon these wines that we base our overall assessment, forgiving the failures that will disappear with new plantings.

7. Wineries are always replanting, and young vines do not generally produce the finest wines, though they can display potential greatness. We find no honor in dismissing a winery because its first or second release of a new wine doesn't match the quality and consistency of its most established, standard-bearing bottling.

8. Not only do most wineries continue experimenting to discover which grape varieties are best suited to their vineyards and area, but most are continually refining their vinicultural or viticultural techniques to maximize results in the bottle. In making our selection for this volume, therefore, we looked particularly at the best wines produced by a given winery. The absolute common denominator among the wineries selected for this book is that each produced one—and usually more than one—quality wine we can recommend without hesitation.

9. We've had to face the clear national bias towards the notion that the best wine comes from California and is generally made from either the Chardonnay or Cabernet Sauvignon grape (and, by extension, towards the international yardsticks of white Burgundy and red Bordeaux wines). The American wineries with the top reputations, it seems, earned them through either their Chardonnay or Cabernet bottlings. (A few picked up reputations as high quality Pinot Noir or Merlot specialists.) While there is little question that wineries producing the finest bottles of Chardonnay, Cabernet, Merlot, and Pinot Noir in North America belong in this book, shouldn't we also include wineries distinguished by their Sauvignon Blanc, Zinfandel, Johannisberg Riesling, Sémillon, Sevyal Blanc, Chenin Blanc, Pinot Gris, and other varietals, as well as dessert wines? And what about a winery that consistently produces quality wines at modest prices? Isn't that, in a different but equally important sense, one of the best wineries? We think so.

10. We also had to recognize and accept without prejudice that economics have pushed many wineries, including some of the legendary stars, into marketing relatively low-cost, simple wines as "cash cows," making it possible for them to continue nurturing their outstanding estate offerings.

—E. G.

Safe Bets and the Best of the Best

LET'S get numeric. There are some 1,700 wineries in North America, and with a very conservative average of six different bottlings or types of wine released by each winery (some have more than 20 different bottlings!) and at least two vintages in the marketing pipeline at any given time (one or another on restaurant lists, in shops, at distributors, or just shipped from the winery), there are no less than 20,400 different wines in current release in plus selected back vintages. To definitively survey the wines of North America, one would have to taste all of these wines and preferably in one day. In any event, the survey would be dated the very next day, as new wines were released and old ones evolved in the bottle.

You don't want to sample 20,000 wines; the great majority are less than thrilling. Nor did we open 20,000 bottles, but we did systematically taste thousands of wines during the past year in preparing this book. We conducted blind tastings; we traveled to trade events, competitions and wineries; we purchased wines; and we badgered some out-of-the-way regional wineries to ship us samples (sometimes operating on questionable legal grounds, thanks to the Byzantine laws and taxes involved in shipping wine out of various states).

What follows is a listing, by type, of the best wines we tasted in the 17 months between October 1991 and March 1993. Again, don't take it as the definitive listing, as we undoubtedly missed tasting some great wines. It is simply our way of helping you sort through those 20,000 bottles out there in a reasonable manner. Virtually all of the wines listed come from wineries that are profiled in Part Two of this volume, where descriptions of the style of the wines produced are rendered. That very few wines cited below come from wineries not profiled is understandable: the fact that a particular winery can make a very good bottle of one specific type of wine in one specific vintage did not, after all, move us to automatically declare it one of the best wineries in North America.

We rated the wines using the long-established Gault Millau 20-point international rating scale, which itself is derived from the 20-point system used in French schools. A 13 in a French school is a good grade. Compared with some of the more liberal ranking systems used by publications and panels in North America, our ratings may appear low. They're not.

Key to Our Rating System

13-14/20	Good
15-16/20	Very Good
17-18/20	Excellent
19-19.5/20	Extraordinary
20/20	Unattainable Perfection

Remember: 13 is a good mark, and any wine awarded a rating of 13/20 is one we can recommend without hesitation. Remember, too, that a rating for a Merlot must be seen in the context of, say, a 1985 Pétrus (made from 95 percent Merlot grapes), or a rating for a Pinot Noir against a 1978 Romanée Conti. Gault Millau ratings are world-class ratings. Finally, note that regardless of how good, for example, a Gamay Beaujolais is, the wine simply lacks the depth and majesty ever to be termed a great wine, the way some Cabernet Sauvignons, to take another example, can be. So, a rating of 13 or 14 for a Gamay Beaujolais is a very good rating indeed.

Chardonnay

In America and around the world, we're seemingly awash with Chardonnay, generally recognized as the most esteemed white grape and wine. In its finest expression to date, the masterworks produced in France's Burgundy, the varietal sets the standard in the marketplace and on the palate. Consumers who used to ask for "white wine" now substitute the word "Chardonnay." Hundreds and hundreds of North American wineries covering virtually every geographical region produce the wine. Although some of the best Chardonnays in the world are made in California and at selected wineries elsewhere in North America, there is nevertheless an appalling amount of plonk being passed off as Chardonnay—wines that lack varietal character and are often flawed, unbalanced and sometimes overly lean, angular or sweet. Chardonnays can be found at $5 and $50 a bottle; rip-offs are not restricted to either end of the spectrum.

When a Chardonnay is right, it is delicious. The good, inexpensive "fighting varietal" versions tend to be fairly lean in body but lively, fresh, balanced, and flavorful (along both citrus and apple lines). Oak is generally less pronounced in this category than in the high-end wines, and there tends to be a touch more sweetness at the low end than might be necessary (a disheartening trend). Buttery, smokey, spicy, nutty, leafy, tart, citric, apple- or lime-like, and pineapple-like are the primary adjectives associated with Chardonnays at all levels. The two predominant styles among quality Chardonnays are, roughly speaking, 1) fresh, fruity, flavorful, complex, and lightly-oaked, and 2) toasty (barrel oak), spicy, buttery,

creamy, big, and complex. Naturally, the overall range is full of variations, and one style is not necessarily better than another. Choosing is as much a matter of personal preference as quality. (Each producer's Chardonnay style and philosophy are touched upon in the individual winery's entry in Part Two.)

25 Highly Reliable Chardonnay Producers

Au Bon Climat
Byron Vineyard and Winery (Reserve)
Chaddsford Winery
Chalone Vineyard
Chateau Montelena Winery
Chateau Woltner
De Loach Vineyards
Far Niente Winery
Ferrari-Carano Winery
Grgich Hills Cellar
Gristina Vineyards
Hanzell Vineyards
Kistler Vineyards
Long Vineyards
Matanzas Creek Winery
Robert Mondavi Winery
Peter Michael Winery
Piedmont Vineyards
Robert Talbott Vineyard & Winery
Simi Winery (Reserve)
Sonoma-Cutrer Vineyards (Les Pierres)
Stag's Leap Wine Cellars
Stony Hill Vineyard
Trefethen Vineyards
Woodward Canyon Winery

Ratings of 25 Top Chardonnays Tasted in the Past Year

Chateau Woltner 1988, Titus Vineyard	18 /20
Au Bon Climat 1990, Reserve	17
Chateau Woltner 1990, Estate Reserve	17
Kistler Vineyards 1990, Estate Vineyard	17
Trefethen Vineyards 1990	16.5
Trefethen Vineyards 1985, Library Selection	16.5
Forest Hill Vineyard 1990, Private Reserve	16
Peter Michael Winery 1990, Mon Plaisir, Sonoma	16
Stag's Leap Wine Cellars 1990, Reserve	16
Steele 1991, Sangiacomo Vineyard, Carneros	16
Byron Vineyard & Winery 1989, Reserve	15.5
Far Niente Winery 1990	15.5
Ravenswood 1990, Sangiacomo Vineyard	15.5
Robert Mondavi Winery 1989	15.5
Floréal [Flora Springs] 1990	15
Franciscan Oakville Estate 1990, Cuvée Sauvage Napa	15
Merry Vintners 1990, Private Reserve	15
Olivet Lane Estate 1991	15
Robert Talbott Vineyard & Winery 1990, Diamond Estate	15
Signorello 1991, Founder's Reserve	15
Sonoma-Loeb 1990	15
Chaddsford Winery 1989, Philip Roth Vineyard	14.5
Chalk Hill 1991	14.5
Flora Springs 1990, Barrel Fermented	14.5
Shafer Vineyards 1990, Napa Valley	14.5

Ratings of 10 Top Chardonnays Under $10, Tasted in the Past Year

Hess Collection Winery 1990, Select Napa	14.5
Benziger of Glen Ellen 1990, Sonoma	14
Hawk Crest [Stag's Leap Wine Cellars] 1990, Napa	14
Rodney Strong Vineyards 1990, Chalk Hill	14
Seghesio Winery 1991	14
Beaulieu Vineyards 1990, Beau Tour	13.5
Chateau Souverain 1991	13.5
Estancia Estates 1990, Monterey	13.5
Meridian Vineyards 1990, Santa Barbara	13.5
Montdomaine Cellars 1990, Barrel Select, Virginia	13.5

Sauvignon Blanc (Fumé Blanc)

Often considered an alternative to more expensive Chardonnay, Sauvignon Blanc has steadily evolved over the last decade to become a sought-after wine in its own right. The best wines are dry, with zesty fruit strongly accented with lemon and often a touch of oak. Early versions from the 1970s in California frequently had a pronounced herbaceous character described as "grassy." Vintners tried to make a virtue of this somewhat green, sometimes vegetal, character. New techniques in the vineyard, however—trellising for better ripening, for instance, and the use of less vigorous rootstocks—have led to improved quality and balance. Sauvignon Blanc, in fact, has never been better, and it remains one of the best values in white wines.

Winemaking techniques have also evolved, as winemakers understand the grape better. Some of the best Sauvignons are barrel fermented and left in contact with the lees to gain greater depth of flavor and roundness. Many are aged in oak, though for shorter periods than Chardonnay, usually anywhere from six weeks to three months. Oak softens the wine and adds a touch of spice to the citrus flavors that mark most Sauvignons from California. Sémillon, with its character of green plums or figs, is used in the blend for some wines, adding breadth to the flavor as well as potential for aging. As with Chardonnay, there is the unfortunate trend to make some Sauvignons (or Fumé Blancs) sweetish, either to temper high acidity or to appeal to the American sweet tooth.

15 Highly Reliable Sauvignon Blanc Producers

Carmenet Vineyard
Caymus Vineyards
Dry Creek Vineyards
Duckhorn Vineyards
Flora Springs Winery
Frog's Leap
Grgich Hills Cellar
Hogue Cellars
Kenwood Vineyards
Matanzas Creek Winery
Murphy-Goode Estate Winery
Robert Mondavi Winery
Quivera Vineyards
Simi Winery
Stag's Leap Wine Cellars

Producers aim basically at two styles, 1) with the emphasis on fresh, youthful fruit, similar to wines of the Loire such as Sancerre, and 2) the more complex style, fermented or aged in oak, perhaps with Sémillon added to the blend. Sauvignon Blanc is increasingly grown outside California, and does particularly well in Washington, Virginia, and Texas.

Ratings of 10 Top Sauvignon Blancs Tasted in the Past Year

Stag's Leap Wine Cellars 1991	15 /20
Chateau Ste. Michelle 1991	14.5
Clos du Bois 1990, Barrel Fermented	14.5
Flora Springs Winery 1990, Soliloquy	14.5
Robert Mondavi Winery 1990, Fumé Blanc Reserve	14.5
Simi Winery 1990	14.5
Cap*Rock 1991, Texas	14
Carmenet Vineyards 1990, Reserve, Edna Valley	14
De Loach Vineyards 1990, Fumé Blanc	14
Dry Creek Vineyard 1990, Fumé Blanc Reserve	14

Chenin Blanc

Chenin Blanc, prominent in the Loire Valley of France where it produces Vouvray, Savennières, vins mousseux, and any number of long-lived sweet wines, is a gentle white. In California, where some 40,000 acres of the grape are planted (most of it in the San Joaquin Valley for use in generic whites), Chenin sometimes produces a crisp, lively wine. In the cooler coastal regions, Chenin produces a somewhat racier wine, simple but appealing; these qualities are especially apparent in wines marking the recent trend to drier styles. Good Chenin also comes from the Clarksburg region of the Sacramento Delta and has shown promise in places like Washington, Texas and southeast Arizona. Flavors of citrus, melons and sweet apples characterize the fruit, but good acidity is essential for quality. Sweet Chenin Blanc affected by *botrytis* is occasionally produced, notably by Callaway in Southern California.

10 Highly Reliable Chenin Blanc Producers

Callaway Vineyard & Winery
Chappellet
Dry Creek Vineyards
Fetzer Vineyards
Folie à Deux Winery
Girard Winery
Hacienda Wine Cellars
Kiona Vineyards Winery
Pine Ridge Vineyards
Preston Vineyards

"Chenin Blanc is a gentle white ... simple but appealing."

Ratings of 5 Top Chenin Blancs Tasted in the Past Year

Girard Winery 1990	14.5/20
Llano Estacado 1991, Texas	14
Hacienda Wine Cellars 1991, Dry CB, Clarksburg	14
Preston Vineyards 1990, Dry Creek Valley	13.5
Kiona Vineyards Winery 1990, Yakima Valley	13

Riesling

In America, the true German Riesling is known as White or Johannisberg Riesling to differentiate it from lesser Riesling varieties, such as Sylvaner. This seems odd, since Riesling is the most widely-grown white grape on the North American continent, exceeding even Chardonnay. Other so-called Riesling varieties are a decided minority (Gray Riesling, Emerald Riesling, Franken Riesling, which is actually Sylvaner). In this volume, the name always refers to the noble Riesling of Germany. It does particularly well in cooler areas like Washington, Oregon, New York State and Ontario, but also surprisingly well in warmer regions such as Texas and Virginia, where it is picked early.

Riesling produces attractively crisp, young wines, in North America mostly sweet or off-dry, which are pleasantly fragrant and agreeable to drink. More impressive are late-harvest sweet wines, most made from Riesling grapes infected with *Botrytis cinerea*, the mold known as "noble rot" in Germany and the Sauternes district of Bordeaux in France. Some of the best sweet Rieslings are ice wines (*eiswein* in Germany), made from grapes that have frozen on the vine. Excellent ice wine has been produced in the Finger Lakes region of New York.

Though Riesling performs well in several American wine regions, it rarely achieves the exalted character and complexity of the great Rieslings from the Rhine and Mosel valleys in Germany. The preference for dry wines that prevailed in the seventies and eighties made it difficult for Riesling in the marketplace. It wasn't deemed "stylish" and was largely ignored by serious wine buffs. As a result, a great deal of Riesling went into anonymous jug wines. Recently, however, aided by a generation of new wine drinkers, Riesling is gaining in popularity. Part of the reason is that many young adults who are used to sweet beverages have come along and are as yet unaffected by the snobbery that disdains sweet wines. But probably another part of it is due to the emergence of dry Rieslings, wines with little or no residual sugar. Some very good Rieslings are now coming out of Washington, Oregon and New York. These wines are stylishly dry and fragrant, and are showing more character and nuance than ever before.

15 Highly Reliable Riesling Producers

Amity Vineyards
Chateau Ste. Michelle
Columbia Crest Winery
Elk Cove Vineyards
Fetzer Vineyards
Firestone Vineyard
Hermann J. Wiemer Vineyard
Hogue Cellars
Kiona Vineyards Winery
Meredyth Vineyard
Navarro Vineyards
Rapidan River Vineyards
Renaissance Vineyard & Winery
Trefethen Vineyards
Tualatin Vineyards

Ratings of 10 Top Rieslings Tasted in the Past Year

Elk Cove Vineyards 1990, Willamette Valley	14.5/20
Chateau Ste. Michelle 1991, Dry Riesling	14.5
Trefethen Vineyards 1990, Napa Valley	14.5
Cave Spring Cellars 1990, [Semi-Dry] Indian Summer	14
Tualatin Vineyards 1990, Willamette Valley	14
Firestone Vineyard 1991, Santa Ynez Valley	13
Kiona Vineyards Winery 1990, Yakima Valley	13
Meredyth Vineyard 1989, Virginia	13
Rapidan River Vineyards 1989 [Semi] Dry, Virginia	13
Columbia Crest Winery 1990, Columbia Valley	12.5

Other White Wines

Numerous other white varieties are grown in North America; a selection of some of the more distinctive types is listed below. Among vinifera, Gewürztraminer, Pinot Blanc, Pinot Gris and Muscat are the leading grapes (*see also* Dessert Wines). Gewürztraminer can be attractive with its spicy and distinctive flavors, but thus far in North America is basically simple and no more than pleasant; late-harvest *botrytised* wines are somewhat more impressive. This grape does well in colder climates, including California's Anderson Valley. Pinot Blanc is often made in a fairly full-bodied style and aged in oak. Pinot Gris has evoked considerable interest in Oregon, where acreage is on the increase. Other states, including New York and Virginia are also experimenting with the variety. Muscats are mostly made as dessert wines. Viognier, the white variety that is creating a lot of excitement, is used in the Rhône to make Condrieu. An extremely difficult grape to cultivate, Viognier produces a fragrant, full-bodied, dry white with distinctive character. Though only a few hundred acres exist in the United States, most in California and some in Virginia, new plantings are under way in California and elsewhere. Sémillon is another varietal that is being used more frequently, though it

is still a minor player. While it has never produced a great wine, it is rendering some pleasant wines in California and elsewhere, and has been used successfully in blendings, especially to tame some of the grassier California Sauvignon Blancs.

5 Highly Reliable Producers

Bonny Doon Vineyard
Chateau Ste. Michelle
Llano Estacado Winery
Merryvale Vineyards
Piedmont Vineyards & Winery

In Canada, Pinot Auxerrois and German varieties such as Scheurebe, Müller-Thurgau, Ehrenfelser, Bacchus and Kerner survive the cold winters, as do French hybrids (grown in many regions east of the Rockies), such as Seyval Blanc and Vidal Blanc. Seyval and Vidal often have a Loire-like crispness similar to that of Muscadet. In the midwestern and northeastern U.S., there is increasing interest in Vignoles, which produces flavorful dry wines and quite luscious sweet ones. One of the most widely planted white grapes in California is French Colombard, a simple white with flowery aromas that mostly goes into generic blends, though it occasionally is made into a light, fragrant varietal wine.

Ratings of 10 Top Whites Tasted in the Past Year

Bonny Doon Vineyard 1990, Viognier	16.5/20
Calera Wine Co. 1990, Viognier	16
Merryvale Vineyards 1991, Meritage White	15.5
Rex Hill Vineyards 1991, Pinot Gris	15
Bonny Doon Vineyards 1991, Ca'del Solo Malvasia Bianco	14.5
Chalet Debonné 1990, Vidal Blanc	14
Murphy-Goode Estate Winery 1991, Pinot Blanc	14
Ponzi Vineyards 1990, Pinot Gris	14
Alderbrook Vineyards 1990, Dry Creek Sémillon	13.5
Piedmont Vineyards 1991, Sémillon Reserve	13.5

Ratings of 5 Top Whites Under $10, Tasted in the Past Year

Alderbrook Vineyards 1990, Dry Creek Sémillon	13.5
Chalet Debonné 1990, Vidal Blanc	13
De Loach Vineyards 1991, Gewürztraminer	13
Palmer Vineyards 1990, Gewürztraminer, Reserve	13
Valley Vineyards 1991, [Semi-Dry] Vidal Blanc	13

Sparkling Wines

Sparkling wines are produced in a remarkable number of areas throughout North America, from Canada and the Pacific Northwest to New York, Virginia, Texas, Arizona, and New Mexico. Indeed, it seems that a greater diversity of North American winemakers try their hand at producing a bubbly than any other wine except Riesling and Chardonnay. If any wine is made in a given region, it's a safe bet that some of it is sparkling. The better sparkling wines are made by the classic méthode champenoise using Chardonnay, Pinot Noir, and, in America, a little Pinot Blanc, though Pinot Meunier is lately making a renewed appearance. Riesling, Muscat, and the hybrid Symphony are also used to a lesser extent.

Sparkling wines have steadily progressed in quality in recent years, and the result is some of the best bubbly outside the Champagne region. New York led the develop-

15 Highly Reliable Sparkling Wine Producers

S. Anderson Vineyard
Argyle
Cordoniu Napa
Domaine Carneros
Domaine Chandon
Glenora Wine Cellars
Hermann J. Wiemer Vineyard
Iron Horse Vineyards
Jordan Sparkling "J"
Maison Deutz
Mumm Napa Valley
Piper Sonoma
Roederer Estate
Scharffenberger Cellars
Schramsberg Vineyards

15

ment of sparkling wines in North America and for a long time led in production, too: mostly lesser-quality, bulk-processed plonk made from hybrid grapes. Today, California leads the way, and the French themselves have played a major role in the state. With little room to expand their appellation in France, many of the top Champagne houses have opened facilities in California, mostly in the coolest coastal regions like Carneros, Mendocino, and on the Central Coast. Centuries of experience have given them a distinct edge in terms of finesse and elegance. Nevertheless, it was the efforts of Schramsberg Vineyards of Napa Valley that convinced the first French arrivals, Moët & Chandon, that California had tremendous potential.

Few of the best sparklers are available for $10, unless they manage to sneak under as loss leaders or markdowns. This is likely to occur around the holidays, when competition for bubbly sales is keen. Some real bargains surface from time to time. A good quality bubbly will be clean and crisp with varying degrees of grape, yeast and citrus flavors, and will possess length and depth.

Ratings of 10 Top Sparklers Tasted in the Past Year

Iron Horse Vineyards 1987, Blanc de Noirs	16 /20
Scharffenberger 1988, Blanc de Blancs	16
Iron Horse Vineyards 1989, Brut	15.5
Jordan 1988, "J"	15
Maison Deutz Rosé	15
Schramsberg Vineyards 1985, Blanc de Noirs	14.5
Domaine Chandon NV, Blanc de Noirs	14
Roederer Estate Anderson Valley NV, Brut	14
Mumm 1987, Napa Valley Vintage Reserve	14
Codorniu Napa NV, Brut	13.5

Cabernet Sauvignon

Cabernet Sauvignon is currently king of the reds. The backbone of many of the great Bordeaux clarets, Cabs virtually made Napa Valley's reputation. Stellar examples have been produced by such great old names in Napa as Inglenook, Beaulieu, Beringer, and Louis M. Martini, as well as such newer wineries as Robert Mondavi, Stag's Leap Wine Cellars, Clos du Val, Sterling, and Far Niente, among a host of others. Sonoma has drawn apace in the last two decades with wines from Jordan, Laurel Glen, Simi Reserve, Carmenet, Domaine Michel and others. Outside California, Cabernet production is on the increase, but few regions can match either the concentration of winemakers or the flavor achieved in California—except perhaps for parts of eastern Washington, which in exceptional vintages produces exciting Cabernet from the likes of Quilceda Creek, Woodward Canyon, Columbia, and Chateau Ste. Michelle. Elsewhere, Virginia and New York's Long Island appear to be the most promising regions, but Texas, Georgia, Arizona, Colorado, Idaho, New Mexico, Mexico, Arkansas, and even Mississippi also grow this popular grape.

Cabernet is, arguably, California's best wine. Any disagreement with this opinion that does arise is likely to come from those who would argue in favor of Chardonnay, but they will never convince red wine lovers. California's climate and soils are capable of producing superb Cabernet. Some of the best ones—Caymus, Beaulieu's Georges de Latour Private Reserve, Ridge Monte Bello, Heitz Martha's Vineyard and Bella Oaks, Dunn and Diamond Creek—are 100 percent varietal. Most, however, while predominantly Cabernet Sauvignon (and so labeled), contain varying amounts of Merlot, Cabernet Franc, and occasionally Petit Verdot and Malbec.

Cabernets are redolent of berry flavors, such as cassis and blackberry, or are more herbaceous with hints of olive, black tea, chocolate, mint, and eucalyptus. Aged in oak, as it invariably is for quality bottlings, the wine acquires overtones of cedar, tobacco, and spices. With age, the flavors and aromas meld and evolve, picking up the scent of old leather, faded rose, or dark cherries.

25 Highly Reliable Cabernet Sauvignon Producers

Beaulieu Vineyard
Beringer Vineyards
Caymus Vineyards
Chappellet Vineyards
Chateau Montelena Winery
Diamond Creek Vineyard
Dunn Vineyards
Forman Vineyards
Grace Family Vineyards
Grgich Hills Cellars
Heitz Cellars
Joseph Phelps Vineyards
Jordan Vineyard & Winery
Laurel Glen Vineyard
Leonetti Cellar
Montdomaine Cellars (Reserve)
Opus One
Pine Ridge Winery (Andrus Reserve)
Ridge Vineyards (Monte Bello)
Robert Mondavi Winery
Spottswoode Winery
Stag's Leap Wine Cellars
Sterling Vineyards (Reserve)
Shafer Vineyards
Rodney Strong Vineyards

Ratings of 30 Top Cabernets Tasted in the Past Year

Ridge Vineyards 1990, Monte Bello	18 /20
Chappelet 1987, Napa Valley Reserve	17
Diamond Creek Vineyard 1989, Volcanic Hill	17
Joseph Phelps Vineyards 1988, Insignia	17
Ridge Vineyards 1989, Monte Bello	17
Silverado Vineyards 1987, Stags Leap District	17
Stag's Leap Wine Cellars 1988, SLV	17
Far Niente Winery 1988, Napa Valley	16.5
Caymus Vineyards 1987, Special Selection	16
Flora Springs 1988, Napa Valley	16

Forman Vineyards 1989, Napa Valley	16
Leonetti Cellar 1989, Washington	16
Pine Ridge Winery 1990, Andrus Reserve	16
Spottswoode Winery 1987, Napa Valley	16
Beringer Vineyards 1987, Reserve	15.5
Beaulieu Vineyards 1987, BV Georges de Latour	15.5
Husch Vineyards 1988, Mendocino, La Ribera Vineyard	15.5
Jordan 1989, Alexander Valley	15.5
Laurel Glen Vineyard 1989, Sonoma Mountain	15.5
Long Vineyards 1988, Napa Valley	15.5
Robert Mondavi Winery 1988, Reserve	15.5
Rutherford Hill Winery 1989, XVS	15.5
Benziger of Glen Ellen 1989, Sonoma	15
Groth Vineyards & Winery 1987, Reserve	15
Heitz Wine Cellars 1987, Martha's Vineyard	15
Livingston Vineyards 1989, Stanley Selection	15
Rodney Strong Vineyards 1989, Alexander Crown Vineyard	15
Shafer Vineyards 1987, Stags Leap Hillside Selection	15
Woodward Canyon Winery 1988, Columbia Valley	15
Alexander Valley Vineyards 1989, Wetzel Family Estate	14.5

"Cabernet production is on the increase. This wine is redolent of berry flavors, such as cassis and blackberry."

Ratings of 10 Top Cabernets Under $10, Tasted in the Past Year

Columbia Crest Winery 1987, Columbia Valley	14.5
Villa Mt. Eden Winery 1988, Cellar Select	14.5
Estancia Estates 1989, Alexander Valley	14
Fetzer Vineyards 1988, Barrel Select	14
Hawk Crest [Stag's Leap Wine Cellars] 1989	14
Mont St. John Cellars 1987, Napa Valley	14
Poppy Hill [Mont St. John Cellars] 1988, Napa Founders Sel.	13
Laurel Glen Vineyards 1989, Terra Rosa	12.5
Poppy Hill [Mont St. John Cellars] 1988, California	12.5
Rodney Strong 1989, Sonoma County	12.5

Merlot

Merlot as a varietal has gained ground—literally—in the last decade. Acreage has increased dramatically, mostly in California, but in other states as well. Merlot's traditional role, in Bordeaux as well as in California, was to soften the firmness of Cabernet Sauvignon, to blunt the harsh tannins in young Cabernets, and to offer another dimension of complexity as the wine matures. Increasingly, however, the berryish charms of Merlot have encouraged producers to bottle it on its own as a varietal, not only in California, but elsewhere in North America as well. Merlot does especially well in a place like New York's Long Island, where the maritime climate of the North Fork is hospitable to the variety. It also does well in Virginia, eastern Washington and Colorado and shows promise in Ohio and Maryland.

Merlots are made primarily in two styles: 1) medium-bodied and fruity, with a modicum of tannins, or 2) more concentrated and firm-structured, designed for improving with age. Even the latter style generally matures sooner than comparable Cabernet. Well-balanced Merlot, with its plummy richness and spicy, berrylike flavors, can be excellent, rivaling fine Cabernet in some instances. Extremely tannic wines, however, may lose fruit before the tannins subside. Such wines never really evolve into harmonious reds. Most Merlot is currently made in a lighter style and is best enjoyed within three to five years of the vintage.

10 Highly Reliable Merlot Producers

Bedell Vineyards
Columbia Crest Winery
Duckhorn Vineyards
Gundlach-Bundshu Winery
Hogue Cellars
Jaeger Inglewood Cellars
Markham Winery
Matanzas Creek Winery
Shafer Vineyards
St. Francis Vineyards & Winery

Ratings of 20 Top Merlots Tasted in the Past Year

Matanzas Creek Winery 1989, Sonoma Valley	17 /20
Cafaro Cellars 1989, Napa Valley	16
Shafer Vineyards 1990, Napa Valley	16
Jaeger Inglewood Cellars 1989, Napa Valley	15.5
Bedell Cellars 1988, Reserve, North Fork, Long Island	15
Gundlach-Bundshu Winery 1989, Sonoma Rhinefarm Vyd.	15
Leonetti Cellar 1990, Washington	15
Markham Winery 1989, Napa Valley	15
Neuharth 1990, Washington	15
Ravenswood 1989, Sonoma County	15
Columbia Crest Winery 1987, Barrel Select, Columbia Valley	14.5
Rutherford Hill Winery 1989, Napa Valley	14

St. Francis 1990, Reserve Estate	14
Bridgehampton Winery 1989, Long Island	13.5
Newton Vineyard 1989, Napa Valley	13.5
Bedell Vineyards 1990, North Fork, Long Island	13
Hogue Cellars 1989, Washington	13
Justin 1989, Paso Robles	13
Kendall-Jackson Vineyards 1989, Vintner's Reserve	13
Robert Sinskey Vineyards 1989, Los Carneros	13

Rating of 5 Top Merlots Under $10, Tasted in the Past Year

Chateau Souverain 1990, Sonoma	13
Oliver 1989, Indiana	13
Columbia Crest Winery 1989, Columbia Valley	12.5
Sebastiani Vineyards 1989, Sonoma	12.5
Bel Arbors Vineyards [Fetzer] 1989, America	12.5

Meritage

This new category of reds or whites blended from Bordeaux varieties (Cabernet Sauvignon, Cabernet Franc, Merlot, Petit Verdot and Malbec for red wines; Sauvignon Blanc, Sémillon and Muscadelle for whites) was created in the mid-eighties. As the practice of blending increased over the last decade, the use of varietal names was no longer applicable for wines that contained less than 75 percent of any single variety. Moreover, some vintners wanted to be free to change the blend of their wines from vintage to vintage as quality and style demanded. Thus, the need arose for some new way to designate proprietary blends; the name selected was Meritage. Some producers use the term with the winery name, as in Franciscan Meritage Red or Benziger Meritage White. Others, however, use only proprietary names such as Opus One, Merryvale Profile, or Niebaum-Coppola Rubicon. Whether or not the term is used on the label, Bordeaux blends are increasingly included in listings under the heading Meritage.

There is considerable variation in style among the blends. Prices cover a wide range as well, with some of the most expensive reds

15 Highly Reliable Meritage Producers

Cain Cellars (Five)
Carmenet Vineyard
Clos du Val
Conn Creek (Triomphe)
Dominus Estate
Flora Springs Winery
Franciscan Oakville Estate
Iron Horse (Cabernets)
Joseph Phelps Vineyards (Insignia)
Merryvale Vineyards
Niebaum-Coppola Estate
Opus One
Pahlmeyer
Ravenswood (Pickberry)
Sterling Vineyards (Three Palms)

bottled under proprietary names. The marketplace, attuned to consistent quality and demand, will eventually sort out the hierarchy among these wines.

Ratings of 20 Top Meritages Tasted in the Past Year

Flora Springs Winery 1988, Trilogy	16 /20
Ravenswood 1989, Pickberry	16
Conn Creek 1987, Triomphe	15.5
Niebaum-Coppola Estate 1984, Rubicon	15.5
Benziger 1989, Tribute	15
Clos du Val 1987, Reserve	15
Dominus Estate 1986	15
Franciscan Oakville Estate 1988, Meritage	15
Iron Horse 1988, Cabernets	15
Justin Winery & Vineyards 1989, Reserve Red	15
Niebaum-Coppola Estate 1986, Rubicon	15
Pahlmeyer 1988, Red Table Wine, Caldwell Vineyards	15
Bridgehampton Winery 1990, Grand Vineyard Selection	14.5
Merryvale Vineyards 1987, Profile	14.5
Quivira Vineyards 1989, Cabernet Cuvée	14.5
Golden Creek Vineyard 1989, Caberlot	14
Joseph Phelps Vineyards 1987, Insignia	14
Robert Sinskey Vineyards 1988, Carneros Claret	14
Montdomaine Cellars 1988, Heritage	13.5
Pindar Vineyards 1988, Mythology	13.5

Pinot Noir

Pinot Noir, the sole variety used for red Burgundy, took longer to find its place in the New World than any other European grape. Though the search for the best vineyard sites is not over by any means, choice spots have emerged where Pinot excels: cool regions such as the Carneros in Napa Valley and Sonoma's Russian River, areas along the California Central Coast, and Oregon's Willamette Valley. Good, if not great, Pinot Noirs occasionally pop up in more unlikely places, such as North Carolina and eastern Washington.

The varietal was largely abandoned in the late seventies by all but the most dedicated

10 Highly Reliable Pinot Noir Producers

Au Bon Climat
Calera Wine Co.
Eyrie Vineyards
J. Rochioli Vineyards
Ponzi Vineyards
Rex Hill Vineyards
Robert Mondavi Winery
Robert Sinskey Vineyards
Saintsbury
Williams-Selyem Winery

producers, whose aim invariably was to produce wines with Burgundian style and flavor. An elusive quest, perhaps, but one that increasingly meets with varying degrees of success. Current versions, particularly from California, may be full-bodied and intensely flavored—but without the load of tannins that burdened earlier efforts. Just as often, however, fine Pinots are more graceful in style and lighter in body, with an emphasis on fruit, enhanced with a touch of new oak, as is typical of the wines from Oregon. Oregon Pinots, for all their lighter proportions, frequently surprise the experts by how well they age. The better Pinots are costly, but a few light, appealing styles can be found for $10 or under.

"Fine Pinots are graceful in style with an emphasis on fruit."

Ratings of 20 Top Pinot Noirs Tasted in the Past Year

Au Bon Climat 1989, Benedict Vineyard	16.5/20
Calera Wine Co. 1988, Jensen	16.5
Sanford Winery 1989, Barrel Select	16.5
Calera Wine Co. 1989, Mills	15.5
Elk Cove Vineyards 1988, Reserve	15.5
Eyrie Vineyards 1989, Reserve	15.5
Gary Farrell 1990, Allen Vineyard	15.5
Robert Sinskey Vineyards 1990, Los Carneros	15.5
Williams-Selyem Winery 1989, Russian River	15
Rodney Strong Vineyards 1990, River E. Vineyard, Sonoma	14.5
Robert Stemmler Winery 1988	14
Robert Mondavi Winery 1989, Reserve	14
Salishan Vineyards 1987	14
Sanford Winery 1990	14
Ponzi Vineyards 1989, Reserve	14
Rex Hill Vineyards 1988, Willamette	14
Domaine Drouhin 1990	13.5
Greenwood Ridge Vineyards 1990, Anderson Valley	13.5
Saintsbury 1989, Carneros	13
Hargrave Vineyard 1988, Le Noirien	13

Ratings of 5 Top Pinots Under $10, Tasted in the Past Year

Elk Cove Vineyards 1989, Willamette Valley	13
Buena Vista Carneros 1990	12.5
Christophe 1989, Napa Valley Carneros Reserve	12.5
Parducci 1990, Mendocino County	12.5
Saintsbury 1991, Carneros Garnet	12.5

Zinfandel

Due to its mysterious heritage—its origins are still not known for certain—Zinfandel was until lately a variety unique to California. For most of its New World life, it was used as a principal component for sturdy, generic reds. In the seventies, it became California's powerhouse red, often overripe and densely tannic—virtually undrinkable

> *"From mysterious origins, Zinfandel once unique to California, is now grown in Texas and Mexico."*

in some cases—and so suffered a brief fall from favor. The variety resurfaced as white Zinfandel, a blush-tinted, lightly sweet quaffer that became the fad wine of the mid-eighties. Interestingly, the vast quantities of white Zinfandel produced absorbed most of the mediocre fruit, leaving the best vineyards (including a few highly esteemed plots

with 60- to 100-year-old vines) to more serious producers.

Noted for intense berry flavors and rich texture, top Zins have a loyal following. Some of the best wines come from places like the Dry Creek and Alexander valleys in Sonoma and the Paso Robles region of the Central Coast. Zinfandel has jumped across Californian borders over the last decade and is now grown in Texas, the Southwest, and in Mexico. Many are predicting a relatively bright future for this red, as its price and quality are attractive in today's market.

10 Highly Reliable Zinfandel Producers

A. Rafanelli Winery
Caymus Vineyards
Dry Creek Vineyards
Louis M. Martini
Nalle Winery
Quivira Vineyards
Ravenswood
Ridge Vineyards
Rosenblum Cellars
Storybook Mountain Vineyards

Ratings of 15 Top Zinfandels Tasted in the Past Year

Gary Farrell 1990, Collins Vineyard Russian River	16 /20
Quivira Vineyards 1990, Dry Creek Valley	16
Ravenswood 1990, Napa Valley Dickinson	16
Storybook Mountain Vineyards 1990	16
Rosenblum Cellars 1990, Sonoma	15
De Loach 1990, Russian River Valley	14.5
A. Rafanelli Winery 1990, Dry Creek Unfiltered	14.5
Ravenswood 1990, Sonoma	14.5
Sarafornia [Storybook Mountain Vineyards] 1989	14.5
David Bruce 1990, San Luis Obispo County	14
Louis M. Martini 1989	14
Nalle Winery 1990, Dry Creek Valley	14
Ridge Vineyards 1990, Geysersville	14
Riverside Farm 1989	14
Caymus 1990, Napa Valley	13.5

Ratings of 15 Top Zinfandels Under $10, Tasted in the Past Year

Gundlach-Bundschu 1990, Sonoma	14.5
Sarafornia [Storybook Mountain Vineyards] 1989	14.5
Louis M. Martini 1989	14
Riverside Farm 1989	14
Ridge Vineyards 1989, Sonoma	13.5
Beringer Vineyards 1990	13
Creston Vineyards 1990	13
Dry Creek Vineyards 1990, Old Vines	13
Fetzer Vineyards 1989, Barrel Select	13
Monteviña Wines 1989, Amador County	13
Poppy Hill [Mt. St. John] 1989, Founder's Selection	13
Ravenswood 1989, Vintner's Blend	13
Rosenblum 1990, California Vintners Cuvée	13
Seghesio Winery 1990	13
Villa Mt. Eden Winery 1990, California Cellar Select	13

On a turnout along the Coast Highway

just north of Laguna Beach

there's a place where the talk is usually about water.

They call it the Shake Shack.

Perrier. Part of the local color.

ALL ACROSS EUROPE, AS THE NEW DAY ARRIVES, SO DO WE.

Old City Center, Munich.

It happens in London, Paris
and Madrid just as the cities start to stir.
In Frankfurt, Duesseldorf, Munich
and Berlin. In Zurich and Milan. In Glasgow,
Stockholm, Brussels and Manchester.
As the new day arrives, so do we. So call
your Travel Agent or American at
1-800-624-6262 today. And you could be
landing in Europe tomorrow morning.

AmericanAirlines®
Something special to Europe.

FRANCE   BELGIUM   ENGLAND   SCOTLAND   GERMANY   SPAIN   SWITZERLAND   SWEDEN   ITALY

FOR AWARD-WINNING WORLD-CLASS CAVIAR, CALL 1-800-4-CAVIAR.

Caviarteria
CAVIAR CENTER U.S.A
NEW YORK • BEVERLY HILLS

29 EAST 60TH STREET
NEW YORK, NY 10022
(212) 759-7410

247 NORTH BEVERLY DRIVE
BEVERLY HILLS, CA 90210
(310) 285-9773

*Caviarteria is America's largest importer and distributor
of the finest Russian Caviar and related luxury foods.
We guarantee complete satisfaction and invite you
to try some of our best and most popular products.*

BELUGA PRIME

Top-grade Beluga Caviar
fresh from the Caspian Sea
with a delicate sea spray
flavor. An impressive gift
or a special treat.

SEVRUGA MALASSOL

Your best Caviar value!
An outstanding taste and full

flavor which is sweet and
smokey. Sevruga is the
"reasonable" world-class
caviar.

SMOKED
SCOTTISH SALMON

Indisputably the best authentic
Scottish Salmon! Mild and
delicately smoked, full-textured,

center belly cut and hand
sliced.

FINEST FOIE GRAS

Exclusive with Caviarteria!
Foie Gras from Rougie of
France is the world's most
exquisite meat product at its
best. A runaway favorite
with our customers.

OVERNIGHT DELIVERY • **GIFT CERTIFICATES AVAILABLE**

33 West 55th Street, New York, New York 10019
(212) 586-4252

Rhône Blends

Wines blended from Rhône grapes—mostly such reds as Syrah, Mourvèdre, Grenache and Cinsault—created a big splash in the 1980s. A dozen or so maverick winemakers, corralled under the tongue-in-cheek rubric "Rhône Rangers," now produce dark, sturdy, often earthy reds that are Rhône-ish in spirit, if not always in character. Some are produced as varietals, particularly Syrah and Mourvèdre; often the wines are blends of two or more Rhône varieties and are labeled with proprietary names like Le Cigare Volant, Old Telegram, Les Côtes Sauvages or Terre Rouge. Lighter blends somewhat along the lines of simple Côtes du Rhône can be attractive values. Good, dry vin gris is also made, usually from Grenache and Mourvèdre. Petite Sirah, actually a lesser grape in the Rhône known as Durif, also produces dark, powerful, big-flavored reds, which are occasionally superb. Besides California, Rhône varieties are now being planted in Texas and Colorado.

5 Highly Reliable Rhône Blend Producers

Bonny Doon Vineyard
Cline Cellars
Edmunds St. John
McDowell Valley
Qupé

Ratings of 15 Top Rhône Blends Tasted in the Past Year

Bonny Doon Vineyard 1989, Le Cigare Volant	15.5/20
Concannon Vineyard 1985, Petite Sirah Reserve	15
R. H. Phillips Vineyard 1989, EXP Syrah	15
Foppiano Vineyards 1987, Petite Sirah, Sonoma Reserve	15
Qupé 1990, Syrah	14.5
Bonny Doon Vineyard 1990, Vin Gris de Cigare [Rosé]	14
Concannon Vineyard 1987, Petite Sirah	14
Meridian Vineyards 1990, Syrah	14
Sean H. Thackeray [Thackeray & Co.] 1989, Mourvèdre	14
Cline Cellars 1989, Mourvèdre Reserve, Contra Costa	13.5
Joseph Phelps Vineyards 1989, Vin du Mistral Rouge	13.5
McDowell Valley Vineyards 1988, Les Vieux Cépages Syrah	13.5
Kendall-Jackson 1989, Syrah Durrell Vineyard	13.5
Preston Vineyards 1989, Sirah-Syrah, Dry Creek Valley	13.5
R.H. Phillips Vineyards NV, Night Harvest Cuvée Rouge	13.5

Ratings of 10 Top Rhône Blends Under $10, Tasted in the Past Year

Foppiano Vineyards 1987, Petite Sirah, Sonoma Reserve	15
Cline Cellars 1989, Côte d'Oakley	14
Concannon Vineyards 1987, Petite Sirah	14
Foppiano Vineyards 1990, Petite Sirah, Sonoma	14
McDowell Les Vieux Cépages Grenache Rose 1990	14
Bonny Doon 1990, Grenache California, Clos de Gilroy	13.5
Joseph Phelps Vineyards 1989, Vin du Mistral Rouge	13.5
R.H. Phillips NV, Night Harvest Cuvée Rouge	13.5
Louis M. Martini 1987, Petite Sirah	13
Preston 1990, Faux-Castel	13

Other Red Wines

Grouped here is a selection of superior values from other red varieties. Other vinifera grown in North America include Napa Gamay and Gamay Beaujolais (actually a light clone of Pinot Noir), Barbera, Sangiovese, Nebbiolo, Refosco, and Lemburger. Among French hybrids, the roster includes Chancellor, Chambourcin, Marechal Foch, and Baco Noir. Of the native varieties, the Norton, or Cynthiana, seems to have potential. Many of these are priced under $10.

5 Highly Reliable Producers

Alto Vineyards
Chalet Debonné Vineyards
Louis M. Martini
Kiona Vineyards Winery
Preston Vineyards

Ratings of 10 Top Reds
Tasted in the Past Year

Atlas Peak Vineyard 1988, Sangiovese	14 /20
Louis M. Martini 1989, Barbera	14
Kiona Vineyards Winery 1989, Lemberger	13.5
Palmer Vineyards 1989, Cabernet Franc, North Fork, Long Island	13.5
Robert Pepi Winery 1990, Sangiovese	13.5
Topolos 1990, Alicante Bouschet, Russian River	13.5
Chalet Debonné Vineyards 1990, Chambourcin	13
Meadow Glen NV, Old Vines Claret	13
Preston Vineyards 1989, Barbera Limited	13
Alto Vineyards 1989, Chancellor	12.5

Dessert Wines

Not all sweet wines are limited to serving as accompaniment to dessert; some work well as aperitifs or with appetizers (for example, foie gras), and many people enjoy drinking semi-sweet wines throughout the meal. Nevertheless, the term "dessert wine" is generally accepted for highly sweet wines (in the best cases counter-balanced with acidity). Most often these wines are marketed in half bottles, as a glass or two of these lush "meditation" wines is usually all one desires. Dessert wines are made in every wine region of North America. They include those made from late-harvested, extra-ripe grapes with residual sugar of more than four percent, as well as fortified wines like sweet sherry, Port and some Muscats. Since the early seventies, when the mold affecting some of the grapes was discovered to be the "noble rot," *Botrytis cinerea,* luscious dessert wines have become a specialty of certain regions and producers. *Botrytised* late-harvest Rieslings from California, New York and Washington often achieve the intense sweetness, if not the finesse, of Germany's great *Beerenauslesen* and *Trockenbeerenauslesen. Botrytis* also plays a part in rendering of dessert wines made from Sauvignon Blanc and Sémillon, as well as French hybrid varieties like Vignoles and Vidal Blanc. Less common, but often quite good, are ice wines, made from grapes frozen on the vine (or, in the case of Bonny Doon Vin Glacier, gathered and frozen at the

10 Highly Reliable Dessert Wine Producers

Bonny Doon Vineyard
Freemark Abbey
Hermann J. Weimer Vineyards
Joseph Phelps Vineyards
Kiona Vineyards Winery
Navarro Vineyards
Quady Winery
Renaissance Vineyard & Winery
Robert Mondavi Winery
Wagner Vineyards

winery). American Ports and sherries have not approached the singular character of their prototypes in Portugal and Spain, but some of the domestic efforts are intriguing. The best sweet Muscats are made from Muscat Blanc, orange Muscat and black Muscat.

Ratings of 10 Top Dessert Wines Tasted in the Past Year

Bonny Doon Vineyard 1990, Muscat Canelli	15 /20
Freemark Abbey 1991, J.Riesling Late Harvest Gold	15
Renaissance 1985, Late Harvest Riesling	15
Heitz Wine Cellars 1974, Angelica	14.5
Kiona Vineyards Winery 1990, Chenin Blanc Ice Wine	14.5
Eberle Winery 1990, Muscat Canelli	14
Messina Hof Cellars 1990, Angel Late Harvest J. Riesling	14
Navarro 1989, Anderson Valley Late Harvest Gewürztraminer	13.5
Bonny Doon Vineyards 1989, Gewürztraminer Vin Glacier	13
Dr. Frank's Vinifera 1991, Sereksia	13

150+ Best Values for Under $10

THERE'S something magical about the figure $10. Price something at $9.99 and it sells, at $10.01, and it doesn't. It's called a consumer price point, and in the wine trade, $10 is the most significant retail price point of all, the hottest and most competitive category for wines. Consumers have dictated to wineries, marketing firms, distributors, and retailers that *this* is the price they will pay. It appears the $10 ceiling will be with us for some time: amid so much competition, few are likely to test higher price levels any time soon. Of course many wines are sold for much more than $10, and a large number of them can still be termed excellent values, because of their high quality and added dimensions.

Under $10, we actually find two pricing tiers. Forget anything below $4. In the $4-7 ($3.99 to 6.99) category, there are the "fighting varietals" (generic grape blends, often non-vintage). There are some good wines here with some flavor and depth, but lots of poor excuses for wine too; the real quality and value appears in the $7-10 range and is even more tightly grouped at $8-10 ($7.99-9.99). Often you'll have to go to the next price point, $15 ($14.99), or higher to discern a quality leap. A number of wineries set suggested retail prices at $10.99-12.99, with the understanding that distributors and retailers will periodically discount these wines down below the magical $10. Also, as taxes and market practices vary in the 50 states and three countries that comprise North America, there is far from a standard price for any particular wine from sea to shining sea. The wines listed below can generally be found for less than $10; a few of them are available at that price only when on sale.

Because Chardonnay and Cabernet Sauvignon grapes are the most expensive, it should come as no surprise that some of the best wine values under $10 are in wines made from other grape varieties, such as Sauvignon Blanc or Riesling, or Chenin Blanc for a white and Merlot or Zinfandel for a red. The price for a fine bottle of one of these varietal wines can easily undercut a comparable California Chardonnay or Cabernet. Sparkling wines, which generally contain a significant percentage of Chardonnay grapes in their blends and also involve significant labor and aging costs, are one type of wine where a few more dollars can yield significant rewards. In rare cases, during the year-end holiday period, it may be possible to find a respected *méthode champenoise* bubbly on sale for $9.99.

The wines we've selected and present below represented to us good values year in and year out. Some wineries produce good-value wines in good vintages but not in others. Too many of the low-cost wines tend to be sweeter than they need be, to appeal to a large audience. We've tried not to be "cute" and list lots of wines in very limited supply or distribution. Thus, among regional wines in particular, additional good values can be identified by checking the winery profiles in Part Two. Although most of the wines listed below come from wineries profiled in this book, a few do not. The ability to make one decent wine and sell it for less than $10 is commendable, but in itself does not set a winery apart as one of the best in North America. The wines recommended below are listed alphabetically by type. We have included state abbreviations in parentheses for wineries outside California, and we have provided additional information when we are recommending a specific bottling from a winery.

White Wines

Chardonnay

Alderbrook Vineyards
Beaulieu Vineyard, Beau Tour
Belvedere Winery
Benziger of Glen Ellen
Chateau Souverain
Clos Robert
Estancia Estates
Fetzer Vineyards, Mendocino Barrel Select
Firelands, Lake Erie Barrel Select (OH)
Glen Ellen Proprietor's Reserve
Hawk Crest [Stag's Leap Wine Cellars]
Haywood Winery, Vintner's Select
Hess Collection Winery, Select
Hogue Cellars (WA)
Kendall-Jackson Vintner's Reserve
Latah Creek (WA)
Lolonis Winery
Louis M. Martini
Montdomaine Cellars, Barrel Select (VA)
R.H. Phillips Vineyard, Barrel Cuvée
St. Francis Vineyards & Winery
Seghesio
Silverado Hill Cellars
Stephen Zellerback
Trefethen Vineyards
Villa Mt. Eden Winery, Cellar Select
Waterbrook (WA)
Wente Brothers
Zaca Mesa

Sauvignon Blanc/ Fumé Blanc

Adler Fels Fumé Blanc
Barboursville Vineyards (VA)
Benziger Fumé Blanc, Sonoma
Beringer Vineyards Sauvignon Blanc
Callaway Vineyards & Winery Fumé Blanc
Cap*Rock (TX)
Chateau Ste. Michelle Sauvignon Blanc (WA)
Concannon Sauvignon Blanc
De Loach Vineyards Fumé Blanc
Dry Creek Vineyard Fumé Blanc
Ernest & Julio Gallo
Fall Creek Vineyards (TX)
Geyser Peak Winery Sauvignon Blanc
Hogue Cellars Fumé Blanc (WA)
Kenwood Vineyards Sauvignon Blanc
Konocti Winery Fumé Blanc
Llano Estacado Winery (TX)
Navarro Vineyards, Sauvignon Blanc
Preston Vineyards Sauvignon Blanc, Dry Creek Valley Cuvée de Fumé
Quivira Vineyards
R. H. Phillips Vineyard Sauvignon Blanc, Night Harvest Cuvée
Simi Winery Sauvignon Blanc
Sterling Vineyards Sauvignon Blanc

Riesling / Johannisberg Riesling

Alexander Valley Vineyards
Chateau Grand Traverse, Dry Johannisberg Riesling (MI)
Chateau Ste. Chapelle Winery, Idaho Vineyard Select (ID)
Chateau Ste. Michelle, Columbia Valley (ID)
Claiborne & Churchill Vintners, Central Coast Alsatian Style
Dr. Frank's Vinifera Wine Cellars Dry Riesling (NY)
Fenn Valley Vineyards, Lake Michigan Shore (MI)
Fetzer Vineyards
Firestone Vineyard
Glenora Wine Cellars (NY)

Hagafen Cellars
Hermann J. Wiemer Vineyards (NY)
Hogue Cellars (WA)
Llano Estacado Winery (TX)
Rose Creek Vineyards (ID)
Trefethen Vineyards
Tualatin Vineyards (OR)

Gewürztraminer

De Loach Vineyards
Fetzer Vineyards
Navarro Vineyards, Cuvée Traditional
St. Francis Vineyards & Winery
Sumac Ridge Estate Winery (CAN)
Tualatin Vineyards (OR)

Chenin Blanc

Callaway Vineyard & Winery
Chappellet
Dry Creek Vineyards
Fetzer Vineyards
Grand Cru Vineyards
Hacienda Wine Cellars
Kiona Vineyards Winery (WA)
Llano Estacado Winery (TX)

Pine Ridge Vineyards
Preston Vineyards
Simi Winery

Other Whites

Alderbrook Vineyards, Sémillon
Boordy Vineyards, Semi-Dry Vidal Blanc (MD)
Carmenet Vineyard, "Old Vines" Colombard
Cedarcreek Estate Winery, Pinot Blanc (CAN)
Chalet Debonné Vineyards, Vidal Blanc (OH)
Chateau Elan, Summer Wine (GA)
Chateau Ste. Michelle, Sémillon (WA)
Gehringer Brothers Estate, Pinot Auxerrois (CAN)
Hermannhof, Vignoles (MO)
Hogue Cellars, Sémillon (WA)
Linden Vineyards, Riesling-Vidal (VA)
Rivendell Winery, Seyval Blanc, New York Sarabande Sur Lie (NY)
Sakkonet Vineyards, Vidal Blanc (RI)

Red Wines

Cabernet Sauvignon

Beaulieu Vineyards, Beau Tour
Castoro Cellars
Chateau Souverain
Columbia Crest Winery (WA)
Ernest & Julio Gallo
Estancia Estates
Fetzer Vineyards, California Barrel Select
Hawk Crest [Stag's Leap Wine Cellars]

Haywood Winery, Vintner's Select
J. Lohr Winery, Seven Oaks
Laurel Glen, Sonoma Terra Rosa
Monterey Vineyards, Classic
Mont St. John Cellars
Poppy Hill [Mont St. John Cellars], Napa Founders Selection
Rodney Strong
Rutherford Estate, California Valley Oaks
Villa Mount Eden, Napa Cellar Select

Merlot

Bel Arbors Vineyards [Fetzer]
Chateau Julien
Chateau Souverain
Columbia Crest (WA)
Geyser Peak
Hahn
J. Lohr, California Cypress
Konocti Winery
Mill Creek Winery
Monterey Vineyard, Classic
Ravenswood, North Coast Vintners Blend
Sebastiani Vineyards
Stone Creek
Stratford Winery

Zinfandel

Beringer Vineyards, North Coast
Canterbury
Castoro Cellars
Caymus Vineyards
Fetzer Vineyards, California Barrel Select
Franciscan Oakville Estate
Louis M. Martini
Rabbit Ridge Vineyards Winery
Ravenswood, Vintners Blend North Coast
Ridge Vineyards, Sonoma
Riverside Farm
Robert Mondavi Winery, Woodbridge
Seghesio Winery
Sarafornia Cellars [Storybook Mountain Vineyards]
Villa Mt. Eden Winery

Pinot Noir

Buena Vista Carneros
Christophe, Napa Valley Carneros Reserve
Elk Cove Vineyards (OR)
Knudson-Erath Winery, Vintage Select (OR)

Monterey Vineyard
Mont St. John Cellars
Saintsbury, Carneros Garnet
Seghesio Winery

Other Reds and Blends

Beringer Vineyards, Gamay Beaujolais Method Carbonique
Ca'del Solo [Bonny Doon], Big House Red
Chalet Debonné Vineyards, Chambourcin (OH)
Cline Cellars, Côte d'Oakley
Fenn Valley Vineyards, Chancellor (MI)
Foppiano Vineyards, Petite Sirah
Kiona Vineyards Winery, Lemberger (WA)
Latah Creek Wine Cellars, Red (Lemberger) (WA)
Louis M. Martini, Barbera
Newton Vineyard, Claret
R. H. Phillips Vineyard, Midnight Cuvée
Sumac Ridge Estate Winery, Chancellor (CAN)
Trefethen Vineyards, Eschol Cabernet/ Merlot

Pinks / Rosés

Cap*Rock, Cabernet Royal (TX)
Hagafen, Pinot Noir Blanc
Joseph Phelps Vineyards, Grenache Rosé Vin du Mistral
Kenwood Vineyards, White Zinfandel
Louis M. Martini, White Zinfandel
Robert Mondavi Winery, Woodbridge White Zinfandel
Saintsbury, Vincent Vin Gris
Sanford Winery, Vin Gris
Simeon Vineyards, Vin Gris de Pinot Noir (VA)
Simi Winery, Rosé of Cabernet

IF YOU THINK OF AAA AS "THE MAP MAKER"...

YOU'RE *RIGHT!*

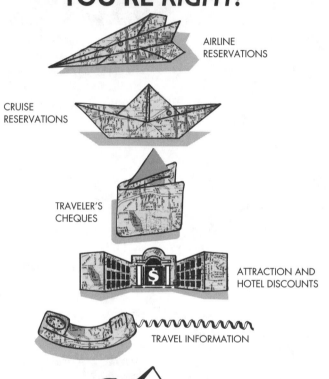

AIRLINE RESERVATIONS

CRUISE RESERVATIONS

TRAVELER'S CHEQUES

ATTRACTION AND HOTEL DISCOUNTS

TRAVEL INFORMATION

AND, of course... TOWING SERVICE

Let AAA assist you in mapping out your travel plans.
Whether you need traveler's cheques, reservations, insurance,
international driving permits, TourBooks® or a map - one phone call does it all.

TO JOIN AAA TODAY CALL
1-800-AAA-4357

More than maps...much more

PART II

The Best Wineries of North America

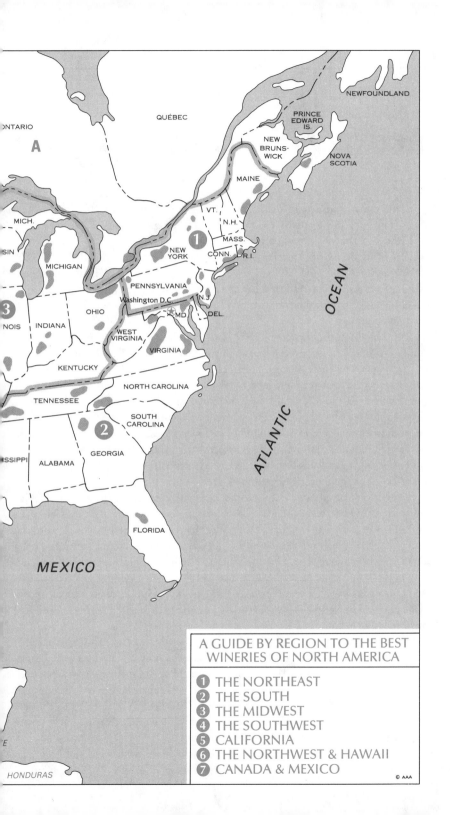

A

ONTARIO

QUÉBEC

NEWFOUNDLAND

PRINCE
EDWARD
IS.

NEW
BRUNS-
WICK

NOVA
SCOTIA

MAINE

MICH.

SIN

MICHIGAN

VT.

N.H.

NEW
YORK

MASS.

CONN.

R.I.

3

NOIS

INDIANA

OHIO

PENNSYLVANIA

Washington D.C.

N.J.

MD.

DEL.

WEST
VIRGINIA

VIRGINIA

KENTUCKY

OCEAN

TENNESSEE

NORTH CAROLINA

2

SOUTH
CAROLINA

SSIPPI

ALABAMA

GEORGIA

ATLANTIC

MEXICO

FLORIDA

E

HONDURAS

A GUIDE BY REGION TO THE BEST WINERIES OF NORTH AMERICA

1 THE NORTHEAST
2 THE SOUTH
3 THE MIDWEST
4 THE SOUTHWEST
5 CALIFORNIA
6 THE NORTHWEST & HAWAII
7 CANADA & MEXICO

© AAA

Introduction

America as Natural Vineyard

W INE may conjure up an image of the Old World, North Americans may drink 30 times more soft drinks and 15 times more beer than wine, and California may contain the only truly well-recognized winemaking region in America. These facts, however, paint a greatly distorted picture.

The world of wine in North America is old, rich, broadly-distributed and vibrant. The so-called North American wine "industry" is itself more than 400 years old. A natural continuation of the great wine tradition begun in Europe and the Middle East thousands of years ago, it was brought to our native shores from countless countries by immigrants who settled here long ago.

Grapes grow seemingly everywhere on the North American continent, and have done so for thousands—probably millions—of years. The Old Norse sagas tell us that in A.D. 1001, when Leif Erikson and his men (among them was a German named Tyrker) set off on their voyages of discovery, they arrived in a land filled with vines. Tyrker identified the fruit on these vines as wineberries, and the land became known as Wineland or Vinland. That the place was probably Newfoundland, too far north for wild grapes to thrive, and therefore the vines were presumably wild cranberries, is of no real import. Because when explorers crossed the ocean in the fifteenth, sixteenth and seventeenth centuries, virtually every place they landed contained wild grapes. Indeed, one is tempted to say the New World seemed then— and seems still—one big natural vineyard.

Today, wines are produced from vines planted in several provinces of Canada and Mexico and in 44 of the United States. In the U.S., winemaking is hardly confined to California and New York. Ohio has 50 wineries. Ditto Virginia, ditto Pennsylvania. Oregon and Washington State have close to 100 each. Although California is by far the largest and most important wine-producing region, fewer than than one-half of the North American wineries we identify in this volume are in that state. It may come as a surprise to some to learn that the greatest grape-growing region in North America outside of California is near the shores of Lake Erie and encompasses parts of Canada's Ontario province, Ohio, New York and even a small touch of Pennsylvania.

North Americans may drink lots of soft drinks, but nevertheless they drink a lot of wine, too. Some 500 million gallons, in fact, are consumed annually in North America. Consumption is pronounced in, and spread throughout, all major metropolitan areas, with the East and West coasts about equal in the volume of their wine drinking. The United States is currently the sixth largest wine producer in the world. California alone out-produces France's famed Bordeaux and Burgundy regions combined. Wine is both a popular beverage and at the heart of a prosperous industry across America.

Wine was first produced commercially in North America in Mexico and the American Southeast, then the Southwest. Cortez had Spanish grapevines planted in Mexico around

1523, though in 1595 further plantings were forbidden. There's reason to believe that French Huguenots may have made wine from the native Scuppernong grape near Jacksonville, Florida as early as 1564, but it's well-documented that a vineyard was planted at a Spanish settlement on Parris Island, South Carolina in 1568. Around the turn of the seventeenth century, Spanish missionaries traveling north from Mexico produced wine in Texas and New Mexico. Not long thereafter, the first permanent British settlers in Jamestown, Virginia were much taken with the profusion of native vines and grapes, and the potential to produce wine for export to England became one of the more compelling arguments for the colonization of America. Still, it was not until the nineteenth century that winemaking became an industry, first and foremost in New York and then in California, but also throughout the East and Southwest.

Key

$ 750-ml bottle of wine costing less than $10.

$$ Bottle priced between $10 and $20.

$$$ Bottle costing more than $20.

$-$$$ In red indicates excellent value in its class;
       good relationship between quality and price.

As waves of new immigrants arrived, the young industry thrived. Then, in 1919, Prohibition hit and lasted until 1933. Only a hundred wineries survived Prohibition, selling medicinal and sacramental wines and juice concentrate. Though a thousand more were established in the year following the repeal of Prohibition, only later, in the 1960s and especially in the 1980s, did the industry become really healthy and wineries proliferate, fueled in part by the exposure Americans were gaining to the wines of the world through relatively inexpensive international travel.

In the regional introductions that follow, we look at some local winemaking history and, perhaps more to the point, current geographical trends in production, especially as they relate to grape varieties and improved winemaking techniques. Then in individual profiles, we look at the best of the regional wineries, describing their history and the scale of their operations today, and detailing the range and style of their winemaking (we also offer specific recommendations). We further provide key facts about each winery and the wines it produces, highlighting in red those wines that consistently represent good value.

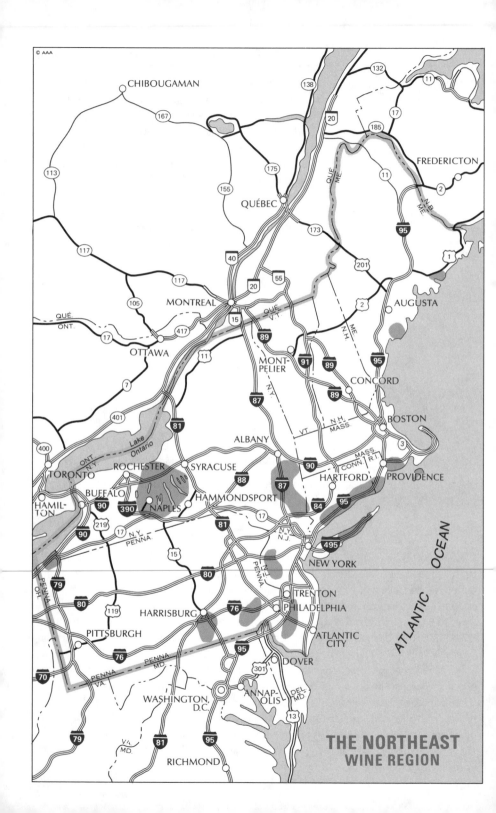

THE NORTHEAST
WINE REGION

The Northeast

Planting a New Tradition

THE Northeast, with its long and not infrequently severe winters, has never been an easy place to grow grapes, except for such native species as Concord, Catawba, Niagara (*vitis labrusca*), and a dozen other types best suited to fruit juice, jams, and jellies. Yet throughout the eighties, this long-established commercial wine-producing region has evolved dramatically. Led in part by the establishment of premium wineries on the eastern end of Long Island, New York, in particular, made considerable strides to overcome its traditional image as the home of "jelly-jar" wines. And who would have predicted that in rival New Jersey there would one day be 17 wineries, all within 50 miles of Manhattan's Times Square, or that Philadelphia would come to have an equal number of wineries located less than an hour away from its City Hall? Make no mistake about it: With its excellent Merlots, Cabernets, Rieslings, and Chardonnays, one of America's oldest wine regions is today making its mark worldwide as among the very finest regions, and one just beginning to realize its full potential.

New York State boasts America's oldest wine industry, established in the early 1800s in the Finger Lakes region of western New York and in the Hudson Valley, an hour or so north of New York City. The vineyards were planted mostly to labrusca species until the 1950s and 1960s, when cold-resistant French hybrids made significant inroads. Viticulture scientists had always maintained that the climate made it impossible to grow vinifera grapes, not only here, but virtually anywhere east of the Rockies. By the late seventies and early eighties, however, increasing numbers of venturesome growers shifted to cool region varieties such as Riesling and Chardonnay. Today, vinifera varieties are at least surviving in the Northeast, struggling in some areas, and doing quite well in other areas.

More importantly, winemaking skills have improved significantly in this region, as is evident not only in the attractive Chardonnay, Riesling, Merlot, Cabernet Sauvignon and the occasional Pinot Noir or Gamay produced here, but in French hybrid varieties as well. Some of the whites from this region, such as Vidal Blanc, Cayuga, Seyval Blanc, and Ravat, can be similar in style to Muscadet or Sauvignon Blanc. Well-made and reasonably priced, they've more than found a niche in the local marketplace. Dessert wines from the Northeast, including some traditional ice wines, have improved greatly, and some are now consistently excellent. And the long-established sparkling wine industry here has made great advances with vinifera-based wines, effectively exploiting the region's relatively high-acid, lean Chardonnay juice to produce clean, crisp bubblies.

New York has the largest vineyard acreage in the region—over 100,000 acres total (only a third of it in vinifera grapes)—and produces by far the largest volume of wine, 30 million gallons annually. In the U.S., it ranks second only to California in total production. Vineyard acreage is limited elsewhere: well under a thousand acres in each of the other northeastern states, including Pennsylvania, which contains a few relatively large estates and many smaller ones.

Pennsylvania has achieved a reputation for its Chardonnay. New Jersey wineries have produced creditable Gewürztraminer and Riesling, and a few stylish hybrids such as Vidal Blanc. In the New England states, where winter's cold is most severe, winegrowing is a daunting challenge. Still, Connecticut has nine wineries producing a mix of vinifera wines (mostly Chardonnay and Riesling) and French hybrids; Rhode Island has five; Massachusetts about the same. Northernmost Maine, Vermont, and New Hampshire produce primarily fruit wines, though table wines made from local grapes are in evidence as well. Maine blueberry and Vermont apple wines (dry versions as well as semi-dry and sweet) are well worth a try. Rhode Island, which enjoys a climate moderated by the Atlantic Ocean, produces vinifera varieties such as Chardonnay, Gewürztraminer, and Pinot Noir. Sakonnet, founded in 1974, is the state's most successful winery. Years of struggle here have paid off in stylish wines that are among the best in the Northeast.

Connecticut's small wineries feel safest with French hybrids, bred to handle cold and sudden freezes. A couple of wineries, notably Crosswoods, near Stonington, also grow vinifera varieties such as Chardonnay, Merlot, Riesling, and Gamay; the generation of wineries that came of age in the eighties, such as Chamard Vineyards (founded in 1983), are planted over completely to vinifera. Chardonnay has been the most successful so far in this area. These and other wineries meet consumer tastes and market demand by buying additional grapes (most often Chardonnay) from Long Island and Finger Lakes vineyards.

New Jersey rediscovered its winegrowing potential in the 1980s. The Garden State's best wines now come from small operations such as Alba, but growers and vintners across the state have lately organized to work for greater quality and increased recognition.

Efforts at grapegrowing in Pennsylvania go back to 1683, when William Penn, founder of Philadelphia, tried to grow vines imported from France and Spain; the attempt failed. Penn's gardener, James Alexander, subsequently domesticated America's first wild grapes for cultivation. Prior to Prohibition, Pennsylvania was a leading producer of bulk wine. Today, the state has more than 50 wineries, but only a handful produce wines worth recommending. Acreage planted in vinifera varieties, particularly Chardonnay, Riesling, and Cabernet Sauvignon, is on the increase in the eastern part of the state and also on its far western edge, on the shores of Lake Erie.

New York's Regions: The Promise of the Empire State

New York has five officially-designated wine regions. The three largest are around the eastern end of Lake Erie, on the Niagara Peninsula, and in the Finger Lakes area. Chardonnay and Riesling attract the most attention here; some white hybrids (Seyval, Vidal) also do well. The biggest acreage is still planted in Concord, Catawba and other native grapes that are now used more for juice and jam than for wine, though significant quantities of wine continue to be made from these varieties to meet existing demand.

The Hudson River region, with vineyards and wineries situated east and west of the Hudson River some 50 to 75 miles north of New York City, is smallest in production and acreage. The river here offers some protection from frost and cold. Millbrook Vineyard, east of the Hudson near Millbrook, has proved that vinifera varieties can succeed in this region when planted in an appropriate spot. West Park Vineyards is devoted exclusively to Chardonnay; Seyval Blanc, however, is the most widely-planted white grape in the Hudson River region at the moment. But that is fast changing.

New York's youngest wine region, on the eastern reaches of Long Island, has done the most to combat New York's comparatively low profile with consumers. This area was planted almost exclusively to vinifera from its beginnings in the early seventies. Most vineyards here are on the North Fork; a few are in the Hamptons to the south. Taking their cue from Bordeaux, where the maritime climate and soils are similar, Long Island growers have concentrated on Merlot, Cabernet Sauvignon, Cabernet Franc, and Sauvignon Blanc, though Chardonnay has proven more consistently successful in yielding good white wines. Reds from this region can be lean and rather hard, but they are well structured and some improve with age. Lately, they've shown significant improvement. Indeed, as Long Island's vines have matured, the quality and concentration of fruit in the wines made here has increased markedly. Barrel-fermented Chardonnay, Sauvignon Blanc, and Riesling are often flavorful and polished. This region is only now beginning to hit its stride with these varieties, and promises to one day become the source of some of the finest wines made in North America—and beyond.

Connecticut

Chamard Vineyards

115 Cow Hill Road
Clinton, Connecticut 06413
tel. (203) 664-0299; fax (203) 664-0297
Open to the public by appt.; est. 1983

This 40-acre estate, two miles from the Long Island Sound, comprises twenty acres of vineyards, all planted with vinifera (Chardonnay 70 percent, Merlot 12 percent, Cabernet Sauvignon 8 percent, Cabernet Franc 6 percent and Pinot Noir 4 percent). Owner Bill Chaney and winemaker Larry McCulloch have nurtured these vines since 1983 and are convinced that the area's microclimate, with its favorable temperatures and lengthy growing season, offers a fine environment for premium vinifera. They built a modern winery in 1988—a classic New England design utilizing fieldstone from the property, as well as wooden beams milled from trees which once stood where there are now vineyards—and employ a state-of-the-art approach to winemaking. In recent years, they've returned to fermenting some of their wine in French oak barrels.

The winery's Chardonnays are its biggest success in volume and quality. In fact, Chamard buys grapes from across the Sound on eastern Long Island to produce a Suffolk County Chardonnay. The winemakers here are proudest, however, of their Estate Reserve Chardonnay. The 1990 Connecticut Estate Reserve Chardonnay, indeed a very good bottle, could easily slip into a tasting of some of the better known Chardonnays in the U.S. It's big, buttery, and earthy with good varietal fruit, and a distinctive and attractive mild tea aroma and finish. The Long Island Chardonnay from the same vintage is lighter and less attractively flavored and balanced, though still crisp and serviceable. The estate-grown Merlot and Cabernet Franc grapes are blended into the Cabernet Sauvignon, which with the Pinot Noir, is in extremely limited supply and for sale at the winery only.

Wines/Varietals: Suffolk County Chardonnay ($), Estate Reserve Chardonnay ($$), Cabernet Sauvignon ($$), Pinot Noir ($).

Stonington Vineyards

Taugwonk Road
Stonington, Connecticut 06378
tel. (203) 535-1222; fax (203) 535-2182
Open to the public; est. 1986

Situated near the picturesque former whaling ports of Stonington and Mystic on the Connecticut coast, Stonington Vineyards' 14 acres of vinifera and hybrid grapes enjoy the moderating influence of the Atlantic Ocean. Purchased by Nick and Happy Smith in 1986, the expanded vineyard is planted with Chardonnay, Pinot Noir, Riesling, Vidal Blanc and Seyval Blanc. To supplement annual production of 6,500 cases, the Smiths buy roughly 40 percent of their grapes from vineyards in Connecticut and on Long Island in New York. This small, high-quality operation is to be encouraged.

Stonington's two most popular wines are Seaport White (27 percent of production) and Seaport Blush (15 percent), both attractive, off-dry blends. The estate-bottled Chardonnay (15 percent) is barrel fermented and aged in French oak, as is the Connecticut-grown Pinot Noir (13 percent). Both varietals are on the lean side but cleanly made. The Smiths also produce an appealing off-dry rosé of Pinot Noir (14 percent). Stonington wines are sold throughout Connecticut, Rhode Island and Massachusetts. A unique dessert wine labeled Chapel Hill, a Vignoles/Riesling blend, is available only at the winery. We especially like the barrel fermented and oak-aged on the lees Suffolk County Chardonnay; Nick is partial to his 1990 Estate Bottled Chardonnay.

Wines/Varietals: Chardonnay ($$), Suffolk County Chardonnay ($), Pinot Noir Indian Neck Farms ($$), NV Seaport White ($), NV Seaport Blush ($), Rosé of Pinot ($).

Maine

Bartlett Maine Estate Winery
RR #1, Box 598
Gouldsboro, Maine 04607
tel. (207) 546-2408
Open to the public; est. 1983

Most people think "sweet" when fruit wines are mentioned, but the Bartlett family's dry blueberry wine is something like a medium-bodied, well-balanced claret. The faintly herby, berryish flavors make the wine a palatable, if seemingly unlikely, match with lamb or beef. Winemaking skills here are state-of-the-art: Robert Bartlett is an enthusiast and experimenter. He even bottles a Nouveau Blueberry made by a carbonic maceration process that results in a Beaujolais-style quaffer.

The Bartletts make wines from a variety of mostly Maine-grown fruits, including apples, pears, strawberries and raspberries. But it's their blueberry wines that are unique and especially distinctive. The dry, claret-style blueberry ages in French and American oak, as does the pear (the NV French Oak Pear is a quality surprise), which gives both wines an added degree of complexity. A rather delightful summer blush is also made here from 96 percent apple and 4 percent blueberry. Semi-dry pear and sweet raspberry and blueberry wines (the latter quite good with apple pie) and a sparkling pear-apple round out this winery's roster.

Wines/Varietals: Dry Blueberry ($$), French Oak Blueberry ($$), French Oak Pear ($$), Apple Dry ($), Apple Blush ($), Coastal White ($), Semi-dry Pear and Blueberry ($), Sweet Blueberry ($), Raspberry ($), Coastal Red ($).

Massachussetts

Westport Rivers Vineyard & Winery
417 Hixbridge Road
Westport, Massachusetts 02790
tel. (508) 636-3423; fax (508) 636-4133
Open to the public by appt.;
est. 1989 (vineyards planted 1986)

An hour away from Boston between New Bedford and Narragansett Bay, Carol and Bob Russell have transformed a seventeenth-century farm into the largest *vitis vinifera* vineyard in New England. Since the late 1800s, the Russells' 110 acres had been used primarily to grow potatoes and turnips and have earned recognition as one of Massa-

43

chusetts' most profitable farms. When the Russells acquired the land in 1982, it was with the understanding that a vineyard would be established. Their efforts on the farm combined interests in viniculture, viticulture and land preservation. They have planted the 43 acres (of the 65 they hope to eventually plant), which currently yield the fruits of Chardonnay, Riesling, and Pinot Noir vines. Also growing here are some 3,000 vines of Seyval and Gruner Veltliner, along with a number of experimental varieties. The winery's annual production of 4,000 cases is steadily increasing with a goal of 12,000 cases set for century's end.

Temperatures in the Westport area approximate those of France's Burgundy region, except in the extreme cold of February. A training system for keeping the vines planted here small in diameter helps reduce the threat of extreme winter temperatures. The Russells hand-harvest their Pinot Noir and about eight acres of Chardonnay to minimize grape/skin contact for the *méthode champenoise* sparkling wines they produce, which are due for release in 1994 or 1995. Rieslings are also hand-harvested in order to select *botrytized* grapes for their distinctive flavor and high sugar content. Son Bill Russell, who apprenticed at Frog's Leap and elsewhere, makes the wines here. Try his 1990 Chardonnay: Aged in French oak, it is crisp, buttery, and full-bodied with a long, dry finish. Chardonnay accounts for a bit more than a third of this winery's production.

Wines/Varietals: Chardonnay ($$), Johannisberg Riesling ($), Evensong (Pinot Noir & Pinot Blanc, $).

New Jersey

Alba Vineyard

269 Route 627
Milford, New Jersey 08848
tel. (908) 995-7800; fax (908) 995-7155
Open to the public; est. 1983

Owner-winemaker Rudolf C. Marchesi's 35 acres of vineyards, producing 4,000 cases of wine annually, are planted in Vidal Blanc (20 percent), Foch (20 percent), Cayuga (30 percent), Chardonnay (5 percent), Baco Noir (5 percent), De Chaunac (15 percent) and Landot Noir (5 percent).

We are taken with Alba's fortified vintage port, which is everything it should be. It displays a classic nose, good plummy fruit, medium body, sweetness without being cloying, and good acidity. Most important: It drinks well. The blended estate wines are light and occasionally seem a tad too herbal.

Wines/Varietals: Proprietor's White Reserve ($), Mainsl White ($), Cayuga White ($), Vidal Blanc ($), New Jersey Blush ($), Blush ($), Proprietor's Red Reserve ($), Captain's Red ($), Vintage Port ($$), Alba Brut ($), Red Raspberry Dessert Wine ($).

Tomasello Winery

225 White Horse Pike
Hammonton, New Jersey 08021
tel. 1-800-666-WINE or (609) 561-0567;
fax (609) 561-8617
Open to the public; est. 1933

We confess a certain admiration for this New Jersey winery that opened right after Prohibition and is still going strong today, producing 40,000 cases a year, all essentially from grapes grown on its own 65 acres of vineyards. The Tomasello family likes to say they cater to all wine lovers— and they do by producing 27 different still wines and eight types of sparkling wines (all *méthode champenoise*). They are beginning to progress with vinifera (15 percent), but what interests us most at present are a half dozen of the winery's finest offerings.

The Tomasellos are proudest of their estate Chardonnay (1990 was their best effort to date, fruitier and less oaky than in the past). Their 1990 Chambourcin is an interesting wine, and, at $8, well worth the risk. This winery has just started releasing a promising Vidal Blanc. It comes from viticulturist Dante Romanini's Panther Branch Vineyard and is dry and crisp, with a hint of apples. Speaking of fruit, if you enjoy drinking your dessert, Tomasello offers raspberry wine that is sweet, but not without a good dose of underlying acidity.

Wines/Varietals: Chardonnay ($$), Chambourcin ($), NV Raspberry Wine ($), Cabernet Sauvignon ($$), Seyval Blanc ($), Vidal Blanc ($), Mulled Spice (Concord, $), NV Niagara ($), NV Blush ($), NV Cape May White ($), American Almonique (sweet, $), Smithville Rosé (Noah grape, $), Rhine ($), Blueberry Wine ($), Vintage Chardonnay Sparkling Wine ($$), Blanc de Blancs Natural Sparkling ($$), Blanc de Blancs Brut ($$), Spumante ($), Pink Champagne ($), Sparkling Rkatziteli ($).

For the convenience of the reader, we have kept this book to reasonable proportions. We were unable to profile every quality winery. This volume contains descriptions of hundreds of the best establishments producing wine; others probably deserve to be included. Those omitted will understand our space limitations.

New York

Bedell Cellars
Route 25, Main Road
Cutchogue, New York 11935
tel. (516) 734-7537
Open to the public; est. 1985 (vineyards planted 1980)

Hurricane Gloria struck Long Island in 1985, during the harvest of Bedell Cellars' first grapes destined for commercial wines. This auspicious beginning—though the event might have proved catastrophic, there was, fortunately, little destruction—provided a fitting test for the nascent winery's informing philosophy of winemaking: "A community of people working in partnership with nature." Owners Kip and Susan Bedell planted the initial 15 acres of their vineyard in 1980. Acreage has since doubled, with Chardonnay and Merlot sharing 60 percent of the vineyard, and the rest planted in Cabernet Sauvignon, Cabernet Franc, Riesling and Gewürztraminer. The Bedells produce about 5,500 cases annually and purchase about 20 percent of the grapes they need for production.

Bedell's early wines, a stylish Chardonnay, and well-balanced, firmly-structured Cabernet and Merlot, met with immediate praise. Consistent quality has made Bedell one of the North Fork's leading wineries in a very short time. While the winery's 1988 Merlot was a benchmark (in an exceptional vintage year), Bedell Chardonnays have a restrained elegance that improves with age, particularly the 1990 Chardonnay Reserve with its rich accent of oak and fine balance. The excellent 1988 Merlot Reserve (plum,

45

chocolate) was almost matched by a fine 1988 Cabernet (tannic, leathery/ tarry). The 1990 Merlot is also a good bottle, though not up to the 1988.

Wines/Varietals: Chardonnay ($$), Chardonnay Reserve ($$), Merlot ($$), Merlot Reserve ($$$), Cabernet Sauvignon ($$), Cygnet (NV Riesling/ Gewürztraminer blend, $), Late Harvest Riesling ($), NV Raspberry Wine ($).

Benmarl Wine Company, Ltd.
156 Highland Avenue,
PO Box 549
Marlboro, New York 12542
tel. (914) 236-4265
Open to the public; est. 1971 (vineyards planted 1780)

Former illustrator Mark Miller is undoubtedly the locomotive driving the resurgence of Hudson River Valley wines. A tireless and imaginative promoter (and the father of Eric Miller of Pennsylvania's top winery, Chaddsford), Miller has some great vineyards and a surefire marketing touch. The Benmarl vineyards, considered the oldest continuously operating vineyard in eastern America (since 1780!), comprise 72 acres planted to major vinifera and hybrids and produce virtually all the grapes necessary for the annual production of 10,000 cases. These wines are mostly sold in advance privately to members of Benmarl's Societé des Vignerons, a Hudson River area group, formed to provide for agricultural and enological research and to stimulate public awareness of local wines. Members are entitled to "vine" rights, which means that they can purchase a case of wine each year with a personalized label and are invited to participate in winery activities, including the crush and social events (Talk about cutting labor and marketing costs!). As a result, only a small portion of Benmarl wines ever make it into commercial channels.

Among the vinifera and many hybrids produced here, the winemakers have had the most success with their reds, which tend to be rich and intense, as well as long-lived. Baco, Chelois, Chancellor, and a Foch blend stand out. Among the whites, the Seyval Blanc is fine, the Chardonnay okay.

Wines/Varietals: Riesling ($), Chardonnay ($$), Cabernet Sauvignon ($$), Pinot Noir ($$), Seyval Blanc ($), Ravat ($), Chelois ($), Chambourcin ($), Villard Noir ($), Chancellor ($), Foch ($).

Bidwell Vineyards
Route 48
Cutchogue, New York 11935
tel. (516) 734-5200; fax (516) 734-6763
Open to the public; est. 1983

The Bidwell family purchased 40 acres on Long Island's North Fork in 1982. Twenty-five are now planted (Chardonnay 5 acres, Sauvignon Blanc 4, White Riesling 8.5, Cabernet Franc 1, Merlot 3, and Cabernet Sauvignon 3.5). And the Bidwells still buy 10 to 40 percent of their grapes, so it's safe to call their winery both successful and ambitious. From a first crush of 6,000 cases in 1986, they've increased production to 15,000 cases annually, and, with their first sparkling wine now on sale, are projecting production of 30,000 cases in the near future. Unusual for Long Island wineries, which generally sell all their production in the New York Metropolitan area, Bidwell thinks big, and has some 17 distributors in 10 U.S. states, Canada, and abroad.

In general, Bidwell seeks an elegant style, lean and tightly-structured. We remember with fondness their impressive 1987 Cabernet Sauvignon (24 percent Merlot) with its herbal, leathery character and good structure. Yet over the years, the whites, especially the Riesling (floral, some sweetness, but backed up with good acidity) and the Chardonnays, especially the reasonably-priced, barrel fermented Chardonnay, have earned the winery its good reputation and strong sales.

Wines/Varietals: Chardonnay ($), Barrel Fermented Chardonnay ($$), White Riesling ($), Pinot Noir Blanc ($), Merlot ($$), Cabernet Sauvignon ($$).

The Bridgehampton Winery

Sag Harbor Turnpike, PO Box 979
Bridgehampton, New York 11932
tel. (516) 537-3155; fax (516) 537-5440
Open to the public; est. 1982 (vineyards planted 1979)

In the real estate business the talk is location, location, and location. Well, Bridgehampton Winery's got location. (It has an address in the Hamptons, where land is as precious—and relatively costly—as Romanée Conti wine). The growing Long Island wine industry has now mostly settled on the North Fork, but Bridgehampton, the second winery to open on Long Island, was the first on the South Fork and is still one of the very few located there. You can find a bottle or two of Bridgehampton's good wine in the upscale restaurants there (on the same lists as Romanée Conti); it is enjoyed by the movers and shakers who dominate the local scene. Adman-owner Lyle Greenfield has niftily designed his winery to look like a Long Island potato barn, a sight that once

dominated the Hamptons' landscape as much as mega houses do today.

About 80 percent of the 5,000 cases of wines produced here annually are estate bottled from 25 acres of vineyards (20 acres Chardonnay, 3 Merlot, and 2 Cabernet Franc). Obviously Chardonnay is this winery's calling card. The 1991 Estate Reserve Chardonnay is simple and pleasant. Cornell-educated winemaker Richard Olsen-Harbich is especially compelling when it comes to Merlot. The 1988 was excellent; the big and spicy 1989, almost as good. A treat is the Meritage "Grand Vineyard Selection" Red Reserve (in 1988, 65 percent Cabernet, 32 percent Merlot and 3 percent Cabernet Franc), which impressed us mightily. The 1989 was leaner, but still a quality offering.

Wines/Varietals: Long Island Chardonnay ($), Estate Reserve Chardonnay ($$), Grand Vineyard Chardonnay ($$), Merlot ($$), Cabernet Sauvignon ($$), Meritage Reserve ($$).

Brotherhood Winery

35 North Street
Washingtonville, New York 10992
tel. (914) 496-9101; fax (914) 496-8720
Open to the public; est. 1839

You get points in our book for longevity. Brotherhood lays claim to being America's oldest winery in continuous operation—and no one has stepped forward to dispute the claim. Not surprisingly, the winery has had several owners and endured many ups and downs in its long history. European emigré John Jaques founded the winery and later sold it to a local religious commune known as the Brotherhood. After a few years, the Brotherhood moved west, transporting its organizational and winemaking skills to California's Sonoma County. Under different ownership, the Hudson Valley winery remained in operation, producing sacramental wines throughout Prohibition. Today, Brotherhood has no vineyards of its own, but buys grapes from New York appellations, including Long Island (Cabernet Sauvignon), the Finger Lakes and the Hudson Valley (mostly labruscas and French hybrids). Annual production is currently up to 50,000 cases, including specialty wines and alcohol-free wines.

In 1987, the current owners, a partnership headed by Cesar Baeza, modernized the winery, renovated its facilities and improved grape quality and winemaking techniques. The results are promising, particularly for efforts with vinifera that include a Cabernet/Chardonnay blend known as "Mariage" (fairly light with leathery/vegetal varietal character) and a good Chardonnay. We also enjoyed the semi-dry 1990 Johannisberg Riesling (and the rare 1988 Riesling Eiswein) and were taken with the Grand Monarque Méthode champenoise sparkling wine made from Chardonnay (30 percent) and Pinot Noir (70 percent). The quality of the winery's other offerings, however, is all over the place.

Wines/Varietals: Chardonnay ($), Seyval Blanc ($), Johannisberg Riesling ($), Chelois ($), Cabernet Sauvignon ($$), Mariage ($$), Pinot Noir ($), Rhineling ($), Sauterne ($), Harvest Blush Catawba ($), NY Chablis ($), NY Blush Chablis ($), NY Burgundy ($), Ruby Port ($$), Holiday Spice Wine ($), Charval (Chardonnay-Seyval Blanc, $), White Zinfandel ($), Blanc de Blancs Champagne ($), Grand Monarque Méthode Champenoise ($$), Late Harvest Riesling Eiswein ($$), Cream Sherry ($), Tawny Port ($$).

Casa Larga Vineyards, Inc.

2287 Turk Hill Road
Fairport, New York 14450
tel. (716) 223-4210; fax (716) 223-8899
Open to the public; est. 1979

Andrew Coloruotolo, a successful builder in the Rochester area, purchased land intended for a housing development and established this Finger Lakes region winery on it. (Though the winery is actually in suburban Rochester, in sight of the climatically-influential Lake Ontario, it still qualifies as a Finger Lakes operation.) Originally from Italy, where his family owned the Casa Larga Vineyards, Coloruotolo initially planted native and hybrid grapes, believing that was all he could grow in the location. Later he met Dr. Konstantin Frank, the New York vintner known for having made the first successful attempt at growing vinifera grapes in the Finger Lakes region. The meeting resulted in Coloruotolo tearing out almost all of his original vines and replanting to vinifera. Of Casa Larga's 30 acres, approximately 90 percent are vinifera plantings today; the remainder are French hybrids. Average annual production is 10,000 cases.

Andrew and son John have produced a wide range of wines and earned a solid reputation for their Riesling and Chardonnay. They pride themselves on their 1988 Chardonnay Reserve; the 1989 Johannisberg Riesling is also a winner. Recently we've been impressed with the improved quality of this winery's reds, notably the 1987 Cabernet Sauvignon and the 1990 Estate Red.

Wines/Varietals: Estate White ($), Vidal Blanc ($), Vineyard Hill Chardonnay ($), Johannisberg Riesling ($), Chardonnay Reserve ($$), Gewürztraminer ($$), Pinot Blanc

($$), Blanc Brut ($$), Blanc Naturel ($$), Brut D'Ottonel ($$), Estate Rosé ($), Delaware ($), Blush ($), Petite Noir ($), Estate Red ($), Cabernet Sauvignon ($$), Pinot Noir ($$), Muscat Ottonel ($).

Cascade Mountain Vineyards
Flint Hill Road
Amenia, New York 12501
tel. (914) 373-9021
Open to the public; est. 1977

Novelist and freelance writer William Wetmore purchased this 10-acre vineyard in 1972. Four years later, he and his son, Charles, built the wooden winery structure on the property as a project for Charles' senior high school class. Situated on 70 acres of Dutchess County woods and fields, Cascade Mountain is planted to Baco Noir (2 acres), Aurora (2), Chancellor (1), Foch (2.5 acres), and Léon Millot (2.5). Sixty percent of the required grapes are purchased to produce 4,000 cases annually.

It has been with the purchased grapes that the winery has had the most success. The dry Seyval Blanc (20 percent of production), fresh with apple-like overtones, and the late-harvest Vignoles have been impressive. The Private Reserve White (a blend of Chardonnay and Seyval Blanc) is usually the winery's top offering.

Wines/Varietals: Private Reserve White ($$), Seyval Blanc ($), Summertide ($), Harvest Rosé ($), Private Reserve Red ($$), Dry Red ($), Vignoles ($$).

Chateau Frank, Inc.
9683 Middle Road
Hammondsport, New York 14840
tel./fax (607) 969-4884
Open to the public; est. 1982

In 1982, Willy Frank and his wife, Margrit, purchased land on Seneca Lake, just down the road from his father's highly-influential Dr. Frank's Vinifera Wine Cellars, and established Château Frank to produce sparkling wine.

There are 35 acres of the traditional Champagne grape varieties here: Chardonnay, Pinot Noir, Pinot Meunier and Pinot Blanc. Currently the Franks produce the only New York State sparkler made from all four. On tirage (time spent on the yeast for second fermentation) for five years, Château Frank Brut Champagne is briskly fruity, well balanced, and bone dry. This house's vintage New York State Champagne can be counted on to win its share of awards every year. Château Frank lends support to the claim that, owing to the striking similarities between the Champagne district in France and the Finger Lakes region, New York vineyards have the potential to yield outstanding sparkling wines. Current production is 4,000 cases, all from estate grapes.

Wines/Varietals: Vintage Brut Sparkling Wine ($$).

Dr. Frank's Vinifera Wine Cellars
9749 Middle Road
Hammondsport, New York 14840
tel. (607) 868-4884
Open to the public; est. 1963

Russian-born Konstantin Frank came to New York in 1951. A trained viticulturalist and enologist, he headed for the nearest grapegrowing area—the Finger Lakes region. He spoke no English at the time and the only job he could get was hoeing blueberries at the agricultural experiment station in Geneva, NY. Within two years, however, he met Charles Fournier of Gold Seal Vineyards who hired him as vineyard manager. In those days it was believed that only native grapes (Concord, Catawba, Dutchess, and others) could thrive in the cold region. (French hybrids were just beginning to come in.) But based on his experience growing grapes in Russia, Dr. Frank believed that vinifera could not only survive in the area, but would do well. He convinced Fournier to plant Chardonnay at Gold Seal and proved it could succeed. In 1962, he purchased land above Lake Keuka and over the next several years planted some 60 varieties of *vitis vinifera*. Chardonnay, Riesling, and Muscat proved the most successful. Dr. Frank died in 1985, but his son Willy Frank had come aboard the year before.

While Dr. Frank made some interesting wines, notably Riesling, his main interest was the cultivation of his vineyard. Willy concentrated on the wines, hiring winemakers trained in California and Europe and importing French oak for aging. Today Chardonnay makes up 40 percent of the winery's production, Riesling 30 percent; the rest is a mix of Pinot Noir, Cabernet Sauvignon, Gewürztraminer, Muscat Ottonel and Rkatsiteli and Sereksia, two Russian grapes. The 70-acre vineyard produces 10,000 to 13,000 cases annually. The most successful wines here are Riesling, Gewürztraminer and Chardonnay. The 1990 semi-dry Johannisberg Riesling is representative of the winery's best efforts. While the Cabernet shows promise, it has yet to achieve the ripeness to balance its acidity. The Pinot

Noir, on the other hand, has been a quiet success. The 1991 Sereksia, a dessert wine, is most impressive.

Wines/Varietals: Chardonnay ($$), Dry Johannisberg Riesling ($), Semi-Dry Johannisberg Riesling ($), Gewürztraminer ($$), Pinot Noir ($$), Premiere Blush ($), Cabernet Sauvignon ($$$), Rkatsiteli ($), Muscat Ottonel (375 ml, $$), Sereksia (375 ml, $$).

Glenora Wine Cellars, Inc.

5435 Route 14
Dundee, New York 12837
tel. (607) 243-5511; fax (607) 243-5514
Open to the public; est. 1977

By all accounts, this Finger Lake winery is consistently one of New York's finest. On the west side of Lake Seneca, Glenora's winery and vineyards overlook the water and attract 35,000 visitors annually. While the winery owns only 20 acres outright, it farms an additional 125 under contract (50 acres Chardonnay, 10 Pinot Noir, 20 Riesling, the rest divided into small parcels). The winery has lately taken to buying some grapes from Long Island as well (especially to use in its sparkling wine blend). The annual production of 30,000 cases is achieved with an admirable dedication to quality and innovation. No question: Glenora is a New York viticultural and vinicultural trendsetter, which has won award after award for its wide range of wines.

A major expansion (including a changeover to vinifera plantings) was undertaken here in 1987; the sparkling wines, of which people at the winery, led by President Gene Pierce, are now so justly proud, was introduced in that year. The 1988 Blanc de Blancs is excellent—bone dry, crisp, light, elegant.

The 1989 is its equal. Winemaker David Munksgard does well with Chardonnay in its still wine incarnation as well: the 1989 Chardonnay is a winner. As could be predicted of a top Finger Lakes producer, Glenora also handles Riesling well; the 1991s are fine examples.

Wines/Varietals: Chardonnay ($), Chardonnay Reserve ($$), Chardonnay Sur Lie ($$), Johannisberg Riesling ($), Dry Riesling ($), Gewürztraminer ($), Cabernet Sauvignon ($), Vintage Blanc de Blancs Sparkling Wine ($$), Vintage Brut Sparkling Wine ($), Vintner's Select Riesling (dessert wine 375 ml, $$).

Gristina Vineyards
Main Road, PO Box 1009
Cutchogue, New York 11935
tel. (516) 734-7089; fax (516) 734-7114
Open to the public for sales, tours by appt.; est. 1984

Planted on Long Island's North Fork in 1984, Gristina's 30 acres of vineyards (10 acres each of Chardonnay, Merlot and Cabernet Sauvignon) have begun to come of age and deliver quality grapes that are really putting this winery on the map. This family-run vineyard, with its Bordeaux-style sandy loam soil, was built at a relatively high elevation and has, in its brief history, been worked by three generations of Gristinas. Winemaker Larry Fuller-Perrine barrel-ferments the Chardonnay (currently 2,000 cases annually) and ages the Merlot (1,500 cases) in the barrel for about a year; Cabernet (1,000 cases) is aged for more than a year.

The 1988 Cabernet (good tight structure, deep fruit with pronounced tannins) was, to our mind, this winery's breakthrough wine, though the Merlot probably has greater long-term potential. The superbly balanced 1989 Cab (which contains 15 percent Merlot) was in the same style as its immediate predecessor and is as good, if not better. The 1991 Chardonnay with wonderful fruit, buttery, pear-like, and slightly vanilla/oaky flavors is Gristina's best effort to date and confirms that this winery can be expected to deliver consistently top-quality wines for years to come.

Wines/Varietals: Chardonnay ($$), Merlot ($$), Cabernet Sauvignon ($$).

Hargrave Vineyard
Box 927, Route 48
Cutchogue, New York 11935
tel./fax (516) 734-5111
Open to the public; est. 1973

Alex and Louisa Hargrave willed the Long Island wine region into being. Or, at any rate, they created the first winery in the area on what was once a 66-acre potato farm. Today that acreage is planted over to Chardonnay (50 percent), Merlot, Cabernet and Cabernet Franc (30 percent), Pinot Noir (15 percent) and Sauvignon Blanc (5 percent). With some additional purchased grapes, the Hargraves currently produce 8,000 to 10,000 cases of wine annually. As the story goes—and Alex Hargrave loves to tell it—the Hargraves, after searching on the East and West coasts for the right place to settle down as back-to-the-earth farmers, became convinced that Long Island is perfectly suited for growing vinifera. They cited the North Fork's microclimate (moderated by surrounding ocean and bay waters) and geographical similarities to Bordeaux's Médoc, in convincing lots of people (including the owners of more than a dozen wineries) that their dream could come true. To

51

make Alex's rather lengthy story short, they were right.

The Hargraves will always enjoy a preeminent place among American vintners for their historic pioneering efforts. They have, of course, the oldest vines on Long Island, and the proof is often in the bottle. Their Pinot Noir "le Noirien," for example, is excellent—the best of the region—and in 1988, a strong competitor nationwide. Over the years we've enjoyed this winery's creditable Cabernet Sauvignon and Merlot, and at times its deep Cabernet Franc. The Hargraves take pride in their Chardonnay; we prefer the Blanc Fumé—powerful and pleasant, if not abundant with Sauvignon Blanc varietal character.

Wines/Varietals: Chardonnay ($$), Blanc Fumé ($), Merlot ($$), Cabernet Sauvignon ($$), Cabernet Franc ($$), Pinot Noir, Le Noirien ($$$).

Hermann J. Wiemer Vineyard

Route 14, Box 38
Dundee, New York 14837
tel. (607) 243-7971; fax (607) 243-7983
Open to the public by appt.; est. 1979

Hermann Wiemer comes from a line of German winemakers stretching back 300 years. Curious about winemaking in the United States, he traveled to the Finger Lakes area in 1968, a time when very little vinifera was being grown in the region. But Wiemer saw the area's potential and eventually purchased land on Seneca Lake to start his own vineyard. Ever since, he has been an influential force in furthering the expansion of vinifera vineyards, not only in the Finger Lakes, but also elsewhere east of the Rockies. Though he today produces some of New

York's finest Riesling, Chardonnay, and sparkling wine, perhaps Wiemer's most significant contribution is the nursery he operates, grafting vinifera onto suitable rootstock and then selling the vines throughout the United States. The Weimer winery is housed in a huge Victorian barn on a slope overlooking Seneca lake. Surrounding it are 60 acres of vineyard that provide 85 to 90 percent of Wiemer's production of 12,000 to 15,000 cases a year.

Wiemer's Rieslings are, not surprisingly, Germanic in style and superbly balanced. They range from the dry Riesling made in a *Kabinett* style, consistently one of this winery's best efforts (notably excellent in 1991), to the lightly sweet Riesling that is comparable to a Rheingau *Spätlese*, to the luscious Individual Bunch Select Late Harvest Riesling that is Wiemer's version of a *Trockenbeerenauslese*. Also produced here is an Alsatian-style, late-harvest Riesling that exhibits distinctive richness and *botrytized* fruit without intense sweetness (Wiemer recommends serving it with lobster or foods served in heavy cream sauces). Wiemer Chardonnays are often equally impressive; they are barrel fermented but made in a lean style that is rather Chablis-like, though the Reserve Chardonnay is somewhat oakier and more full-bodied (both 1990s were top efforts). Wiemer also produces an appealing Pinot Noir that certainly makes a strong argument for growing more Pinot grapes on Seneca Lake. The 1990 Pinot Noir has vibrant garnet color and dark cherry flavors with a hint of smokiness about it. A streak of tannin provides structure for aging. Sparkling wines also receive meticulous attention here. The Naturale, made from 100 percent Riesling, is crisp and bone dry. The Blanc de Noirs is made from mostly Pinot

Noir and a modicum of Chardonnay. Both are excellent.

Wines/Varietals: Chardonnay ($$), Reserve Chardonnay ($$), Dry Riesling ($), Semi-Dry Riesling ($), Late-Harvest Riesling ($$), Bunch Select Late Harvest Riesling (375 ml, $$), Pinot Noir ($$), Vinifera White ($), Vintage Blanc de Noirs Sparkling Wine ($$), Vintage Naturale Sparkling Wine ($$).

Heron Hill Vineyards, Inc.

8203 Pleasant Valley Road
Hammondsport, New York 14840
tel. (607) 868-4201
Open to the public; est. 1977

Madison Avenue advertising copy writer Peter Johnstone visited the Finger Lakes region in 1968 and liked it so much he decided to stay. He is now co-owner and winemaker at Heron Hill. His partner, John Ingle, is a grape grower on Canandaigua Lake. The 50 acres of vineyards at Heron Hill are planted to Chardonnay (17 acres), Riesling (23), Pinot Noir (5), and Seyval (5). As good as the wine here can be, especially the German-style Rieslings, it can't top the views of Keuka Lake that can be seen from the chalet-like winery on Bully Hill.

In his wines, Johnstone seeks to achieve high acid content balanced with natural sugars to bring out good fruit flavors. Specializing in white varietals, this winery produces 15,000 cases a year, 60 percent from purchased grapes. The well-made, clean, and simple Heron Hill White Table Wine, produced from a blend of grape varieties, is the best-seller here, though the "Simply New York's Best White Table Wine" bottling (a blend of 5 varieties) wins the biggest hype award. Both the Dry Johannisberg Riesling and the Dessert Riesling deserve

recognition for their high quality. The winery's second labels (bottles containing perhaps even higher quality wines) are Otter Spring (using only free-run juice) and Little Heron (more French- or American-style than the Germanic-style Heron Hill label).

Wines/Varietals: Heron Hill White Table Wine ($), Cayuga White ($), Chardonnay ($$), Seyval Blanc, Ingle Vineyard ($), Chardonnay, Ingle Vineyard ($$), Johannisberg Riesling Ingle Vineyard ($$), Otter Blanc, Spring White Table Wine ($), Otter Spring Seyval Blanc ($), Otter Spring Chardonnay ($$), Little Heron Johannisberg Riesling ($), Little Heron Chardonnay ($), Eye of the Heron (blush, $), Heron Hill Red Table Wine ($), Otter Spring Claret ($), Heron Hill Apple Wine ($), Muscat Dessert Wine (375 ml, $$$).

Hunt Country Vineyards

4021 Italy Hill Road
Branchport, New York 14418
tel./fax (315) 595-2812
Open to the public (off season by appt. only); est. 1981

Owned since 1987 by Arthur and Joyce Hunt, this winery overlooking the shores of Keuka Lake, focuses on specialty (especially late-harvest) wines. The 60 planted acres here, comprising native American hybrids and some vinifera, are abetted by 30-60 percent purchased grapes, to achieve an annual production averaging 12,000 cases. Hunt Country is especially proud to have been the first vineyard in these cold climes to perform a successful experiment in field grafting (a common procedure in California and other warm climates, as well as in temperature-controlled nurseries) with Cooperative Extension grape specialist Thomas Zabadel.

The semi-dry 1.5 liter, non-vintage, Classic White here is relatively clean and fruity. It's the winery's best-seller, and a genuinely winning wine for the price ($6.99 for a 1.5 liter bottle). The house's vintage Cayuga White is in the same class. The elegant 1990 Chardonnay shows soft flavors. In the end, Hunt Country Vineyards makes our cut based on its recent efforts with Vidal, Seyval Blanc and Vignoles. The 1989 Vidal Ice Wine is a real treat.

Wines/Varietals: Chardonnay ($$), Johannisberg Riesling ($), Seyval Blanc ($), Cayuga White ($), Classic White ($), Foxy Lady Blush ($), Vignoles ($), Late Harvest Vignoles ($), Classic Red ($), Vidal Ice Wine ($$).

Knapp Vineyards

2770 County Road 128
Romulus, New York 14541
tel. (607) 869-9271; fax (607) 869-3212
Open to the public; est. 1982 (vineyards planted 1971)

Douglas and Susanna Knapp planted their first grapes in the seventies and learned winemaking, as they put it, "from the ground up." Their 70-acre vineyard is planted to vinifera—largely Chardonnay and Pinot Noir—and to hybrids like Seyval Blanc, Vignoles and Cayuga. (The Knapps are in the process of removing some of the vines planted in 1971 and replacing them with red vinifera.) About 8,000 cases of estate wines are produced here annually.

Currently, Knapp white wines are crisp and well balanced, particularly the Seyval and Cayuga. Doug Knapp, who is wine-

maker (as well as owner and president), is proudest of his Chardonnay, which, though somewhat austere in style, is balanced with appley fruit. The Seyval Blanc produced here (and also labeled as Seashore White), is a good bottle of dry, modestly-priced white wine that reflects the Knapps' philosophy of producing affordably priced wines that don't overwhelm, but rather enhance a meal. Knapp also produces sparkling wines using the traditional *méthode champenoise.*

Wines/Varietals: Chardonnay ($), Seyval Blanc ($), Lady's Shipper (blush, $), Dutchman's Breeches (blend, $), Vignoles ($), Riesling ($), Pinot Noir ($$), Cabernet Sauvignon ($$), Vintage Blanc de Blancs Sparkling ($$).

Millbrook Vineyards

Wing Road
R.R.#1, Box 1670
Millbrook, New York 11525
tel. (914) 677-8383; fax (914) 677-6186
Open to the public; est. 1983

In 1983, former New York State Commissioner of Agriculture John Dyson purchased a run-down dairy farm in the Hudson River Valley that is today Millbrook Vineyards. Initially interested in protecting the land from developers, Dyson converted the old barn on the property into the winery where he currently produces 5,000-plus cases of wine annually. Chardonnay now accounts for 60 percent of production and 30 of the 50 acres in vine. Pinot Noir accounts for another 15 percent of the acreage, Cabernet Sauvignon, Cabernet Franc, and Merlot, 5 percent each. There are also experimental plantings of a wide range of varieties, including some promising Italian grapes: Nebbiolo, Teroldigo, Tocai Friulano.

Millbrook claims to be the first New York winery planted exclusively in vinifera. Dyson's recently-deployed trellising system allows his grapes greater exposure and extends his growing area to the north. Millbrook Vineyards' Chardonnay, Cabernet Franc, and Pinot Noir have all been praised and have received awards. The winery's 1990 Reserve Chardonnay demonstrates the quality being realized here with each successive vintage. It is a standout: very crisp with apple and melon flavors and a touch of vanilla.

Wines/Varietals: Chardonnay ($$), Pinot Noir ($), Cabernet Sauvignon ($$), Cabernet Franc ($$), Claret (Merlot-based, $$), Sparkling Wine ($$).

North Salem Vineyard

R.R.#2, Hardscrabble Road
North Salem, New York 10560
tel. (914) 669-5518 or (800) 564-6905
Open to the public; est. 1979

Retired M.D. George Naumberg began planting his vineyard in 1965. Of the 36 grape varieties he tried, including Chardonnay, Riesling and Cabernet Sauvignon, Naumberg determined that the hybrids produced the best wine. By 1979, confident about which grapes were suited to his soil, he established a commercial winery on the premises.

Seyval Blanc comprises 13 of Naumberg's 18 acres and almost 80 percent of wine production. The other five acres here are planted in De Chaunac, Foch, and Chancellor. Average production is 2,500 cases annually. The Reserve White is North Salem's flagship wine and the reason the winery is included in this book. It is 85 percent Seyval Blanc, with 10 percent Vidal and 5 percent

Ravat added to yield more complex aromas and flavors than most Seyval Blanc varietals. Now long gone, the 1988 was a winner, and the 1990 is a fresh and pleasant example of its kind. We've found that these wines hold up well, two to five years for certain, and generally up to 10 years without problems.

Wines/Varietals: Reserve White (Seyval, $), Rosé ($), Preview ($), Sweet Red Table Wine ($), Reserve Red ($), New York State Champagne (Seyval Blanc-based, $$).

Palmer Vineyards

PO Box 2125
Aquebogue, New York 11931
tel. (516) 722-9463; fax (516) 722-5364
Open to the public; est. 1986

Palmer is emerging as one of Long Island's strongest wineries in terms of quality—especially its reds—and in terms of marketing. Robert Palmer began converting a typical East End 60-acre potato and pumpkin farm into a vineyard in 1983 and established the winery in 1986. The modern facility was built to resemble the weather-aged barn on the property; with his wife, Lorraine, Palmer also restored the eighteenth-century farmhouse and furnished it with local antiques. Today 50 acres of vineyards are planted over to Chardonnay (about one-third), Merlot, Cabernet Franc, Cabernet Sauvignon, Gewürztraminer, White Riesling, and Pinot Blanc. With about 20 percent purchased grapes, the winery produces 10,000 or so cases annually, and ships its product all over the place—from Disney World in Florida to Japan to Canada to Great Britain and, of course, within New York.

Palmer and current winemaker, Dan Kleck, are seeking a lean and elegant style: crisp whites and Bordeaux-like reds. The

Chardonnay and Gewürztraminer are appealing achievements (the 1990 Winemaker's Reserve Gewürztraminer impressed us with its classic varietal character and good acid and balance). But we're most taken with a few of the reds that set this winery apart as one of the best. The 1988 Merlot is long and deep, with balanced dark fruit and wood, and with tannins that suggest the wine won't fully emerge until 1995. Even more noteworthy is the 1988 Cabernet; it possesses elegant, medium-full bodied, tight Cabernet flavors and, again, tannins hinting that it will benefit from a couple more years in the bottle. Most impressive of all in our many tastings of Palmer wines was the 1989 Cabernet Franc. Now this is a bottle for which you won't easily find a worthy competitor (as can always be done with Merlots and Cabernets)—unless it's the 1987 Palmer Cabernet Franc.

Wines/Varietals: Chardonnay ($$), Chardonnay, Barrel Fermented ($$), Pinot Blanc ($), Gewürztraminer, Winemaker's Reserve ($), NV Pinot Noir Blanc ($), Merlot ($$), Cabernet Sauvignon ($$), Cabernet Franc, Proprietor's Reserve ($$), Late Harvest White Riesling ($).

Peconic Bay Vineyards
Box 709, Main Road
Cutchogue, New York 11935
tel. (516) 734-7361; fax (516) 734-7173
Open to the public, by appt.; est. 1980

Ray Blum founded Peconic Bay Vineyards in 1980 on the site of yet another East End potato farm-turned-vineyard. The vineyards here have deep, sandy loam with excellent drainage, and enjoy mild winters and moderate summers with plenty of rain. The winery grows all of its own grapes: 36 acres are divided among Chardonnay, Cabernet Sauvignon, Merlot, Riesling, and Cabernet Franc. (Additional acres in several selected sites in the North Fork are also farmed by Peconic Bay). Total production: 6,000 cases annually, 35 percent of which is Chardonnay.

A good and representative bottle (and much better than the previous year's effort) is Peconic Bay's 1990 Chardonnay—barrel fermented in French oak, a nice balance of fruit and oak. Both the Merlot and Cabernet Sauvignon have also proved sound efforts in the past. The Bordeaux-style Cabernets, with 20 percent Merlot in the blend, are elegant and medium-bodied. The 1988 Cab is the best we've tasted from Peconic.

Wines/Varietals: Dry White Riesling ($), Chardonnay ($$), Petite Chardonnay ($), Vin de l'Ile-Blanc (Late Harvest Riesling, $), Peconic Bay Blush ($), Merlot ($$), Cabernet Sauvignon ($$).

Pindar Vineyards
PO Box 332
Peconic, New York 11958
tel. (516) 734-6200; fax (516) 734-6205
Open to the public; est. 1978

Dr. Herodotus Damianos, an internist from Stony Brook, owns Long Island's largest winery, which produces 50,000 cases of wine annually. In honor of his Greek heritage, Dr. Damianos named the winery after the Greek lyric poet Pindar, who lived during the golden age of Greek culture in 500 B.C. Pindar's 245 acres of vineyard is planted to 16 varieties of vinifera, 70 percent in white grapes.

Chef Antoin Bouterin of Le Perigord

"★ ★ ★   from the New York Times, Bryan Miller"

"A seldom stated fact of life about the best French restaurants of New York is that both chef and host of Le Perigord are among the most respected men at what they do..."

(Bob Lape, Agenda New York, April 1992)

Two private rooms accommodating 15-130

405 East 52nd Street (212)755-6244

Nowhere But New York.
Nowhere But The Pierre.

Even in a city as remarkable as New York, there is only one hotel that reaches beyond the standards of every other renowned hotel—because of the way it completely adapts to you. That hotel is The Pierre.

We anticipate your needs with a singlemindedness born of decades of tradition. It's a standard that means no request is too small or too large. That's what a grand hotel is all about. And it means your stay here will leave you feeling The Pierre is exactly where you belong.

We invite you to experience this legendary feeling for yourself at The Pierre. Everything you'd expect from a Four Seasons Hotel.

For information and reservations call 212-838-8000, 1-800-743-7734 or the Leading Hotels of the World.

Four Seasons
The Pierre
NEW YORK
Fifth Avenue at 61st Street
New York, NY 10021
Fax: 212-940-8109

one of
The Leading Hotels of the World®

Gault Millau Guide and The Wine Spectator agree on the same Italian restaurant's wine list.

Tony May's

SANDOMENICO

The most acclaimed Italian restaurant
in America

240 Central Park South in New York City
(212) 265-5959 • Open Seven Days a Week

To those of you who know us only for our caviar...

Tsk. Tsk.

Sixty percent of Pindar's output is Chardonnay, produced in a simple, fruity version and a richer, oak-aged Reserve. Both of the 1991 Chards are equally impressive. Pindar's is best known, however, for Merlot, which is often the most impressive wine made here: firmly structured with herby, berryish flavors and the potential to age well. Pindar was the first Long Island winery to produce a Meritage red, "Mythology," blended from estate-grown Bordeaux varieties and consisting of varying amounts of Cabernet Sauvignon, Cabernet Franc, Merlot, Petit Verdot and Malbec. The 1988 Mythology (33.5 percent Cabernet Sauvignon, 27 percent Merlot, 22 percent Cabernet Franc, 12.5 percent Petit Verdot, 5 percent Malbec) is a dark, dense, still somewhat tannic wine, noteworthy for its concentration and weight and in need of several more years of bottle age (probably at least until 1995 or 1996) for its balanced underlying fruit to emerge fully. The regular Merlot tends to be drinkable sooner. In 1985, Pindar made its first *méthode champenoise* sparkling wine, a blend of Chardonnay, Pinot Noir and Pinot Meunier. The winery now produces two sparkling wines, the vintage Premier Brut and the Cuvée Rare, which is 100 percent Pinot Meunier, rare indeed, and not the one-dimensional wine one might expect. In some vintages, Pindar also produces a port; the 1989 is made entirely from November-harvested Cabernet Sauvignon.

Wines/Varietals: Chardonnay ($), Chardonnay Reserve ($$), Johannisberg Riesling ($), Gewürztraminer ($), Gamay Beaujolais ($), Cabernet Sauvignon ($$), Merlot ($$), Merlot Reserve ($$), Mythology ($$$), Premier Cuvée Brut Sparkling Wine ($$), Cuveé Rare Sparkling Wine ($$$), Port ($$).

Rivendell Winery

714 Albany Post Road
New Paltz, New York 12561
tel. (914) 255-0892; fax (914) 255-0894
Open to the public; est. 1984 (vineyards planted 1980)

This lower Hudson River Valley winery, owned by the Ransom family, quickly earned a reputation for consistently producing fine wines and has already made a big impact in its short life. Today it is one of the most important wineries in New York. (Located only 75 miles from New York City, the winery attracts 30,000 visitors a year.) With only 15 acres of vines (10 acres of Vidal and 5 of De Chaunac) on its 55-acre property, this winery purchases approximately 60 percent of the fruit it requires in New York's Finger Lakes region and another 30 percent from the North Fork of Long Island. In addition, very small quantities of red vinifera grapes come from Oregon, Washington, or California. Annual production here is 20,000 cases, 80 percent of it from vinifera grapes. Great care is taken in the winemaking: careful attention is paid to such matters as yeast and barrel selection and individual vineyard lots are fermented separately. Very little filtering is done here and some of the house's best wines are unfined and unfiltered. Rivendell's handcrafted wines have been exceptionally well received by critics and in national wine competitions.

There's no question but that the 1990 Barrel Select Chardonnay is a very fine effort (more buttery and lush than fruity), but, of course, there are lots of good Chardonnays in the marketplace. The New York Sarabande Sur Lie, on the other hand, doesn't have much competition. This wine stands out as an affordable dry white with fruit (melon) and spice flavors, good body and butteriness, crispness, and elegance; it resembles a Sauvignon Blanc, but is made primarily from Seyval Blanc with some Vignoles in the blend. The 1990 is even better than the multiple award-winning 1989. The straight Seyval Blanc was also very good in 1989. Merlot is this winery's best red, but production is so small it sells out in a couple of weeks. Look to Rivendell's excellent dessert wines as well. "Tear of the Clouds" is a lush, honey and fruit-flavored late-harvest Vignoles, and "Apres" is a lighter-style wine with tropical flavors, also made from Vignoles.

Wines/Varietals: Chardonnay ($), Barrel Select Chardonnay ($$), Reserve Chardonnay ($$), Sarabande Sur Lie ($), Vidal ($), Merlot ($$), Apres (375 ml dessert wine, $), Tear of the Clouds (375 ml late-harvest dessert wine, $), Northern Lights (white blend, $), Interlude (blush, $), NV Vintner's Blend White ($), NV Vintner's Blend Red ($).

Wagner Vineyards
9322 Route 414
Lodi, New York 14860
tel. (607) 582-6450; fax (607) 582-6446
Open to the public; est. 1978

Wagner Vineyards was one of the first wineries to call attention to the fact that New York could produce stylish wines of real quality that don't have the traditional "jelly-jar" taste. The handsome octagonal-shaped winery, designed by founder-owner Bill Wagner, overlooks Seneca Lake, one of the five Finger Lakes. Wagner owns 200

acres of French hybrids and vinifera, and produces 33,000 cases of estate-grown wines annually. Though the winery is best known for its opulent, oaky, barrel fermented Chardonnay, Wagner has also gained recognition for being the first winemaker to barrel ferment Seyval Blanc, which results in a rich, full-bodied style white that has since been emulated by other Seyval producers. Overall, Wagner's record for consistent quality is one of the best in the state.

Chardonnay and Seyval are the leading varietals produced here, but Wagner also grows and makes Riesling, Gewürztraminer, Pinot Noir, and Ravat. During the eighties, John Herbert and Ann Raffetto, winemakers since 1983, produced the first of Wagner's superb ice wines from Riesling and Ravat. The 1989 (or 1990) Ravat Ice Wine is a star, and the 1989 Riesling Ice Wine is as appealing. Wagner's next major venture will be to produce red wines from some of the first Cabernet Sauvignon and Merlot to be planted in the Finger Lakes region, despite the fact that the region has always been considered too cool for these varieties. Bill Wagner believes his microclimate will provide ample time for these grapes to ripen.

Wines/Varietals: Grace House Chardonnay ($$), Barrel fermented Chardonnay ($$), Reserve Chardonnay ($$), Pinot Noir ($), Pinot Noir Blanc ($), NV Vintner's Pinot Noir ($), NV Alta Blanc ($), Delaware ($), Niagara ($), Reserve Red ($), De Chaunac ($), Barrel fermented Seyval Blanc ($), Gewürztraminer ($), Gewürztraminer, Semi-Dry ($), Johannisberg Riesling ($), Johannisberg Riesling Ice Wine (375 ml, $$), Ravat Blanc ($), Ravat Ice Wine (375 ml, $$), Brut Sparkling Wine ($$).

West Park Wine Cellars
Burroughs Drive
West Park-on-Hudson, New York 12493
tel. (914) 384-6709
Open to the public; est. 1979

Common wisdom about putting all one's eggs in a single basket notwithstanding, Louis Fiore grows and produces only Chardonnay. Situated in the Hudson River Valley, his 15 acres of vines (on a 100-acre site) produce an average of 2,500 cases annually, all fermented and aged in French oak. An early, rainy spring in 1990, when poor fruit and extended wet and dry spells produced an inferior grape crop, proved a setback to this one-product vineyard. Fiore and wine consultant, Jim Gifford, decided not to release the 1990 Chardonnay rather than risk the winery's reputation, which speaks volumes about the commitment to quality here.

The 1989 Chardonnay, in turn, speaks well of the house style, which is light- to medium-bodied, in the Burgundy manner, with excellent balance, trim fruit, and slight overtones of oak.

Wines/Varietals: Chardonnay ($$).

Pennsylvania

Allegro Vineyards
R.D.#2, Box 64
Brogue, Pennsylvania 17309
tel. (717) 927-9148
Open to the public; est. 1980

This small winery was formally established with its 1980 release and now produces 2,000 cases annually. Winemaker and co-owner John Crouch is very serious about his wines, and the high level of quality he has achieved has earned much respect. This south-central Pennsylvania winery has 16 acres of vineyards (6 acres Seyval Blanc, 1 Vidal Blanc, 1 Chambourcin, 3 Chardonnay, 2 Cabernet Sauvignon, 2 Riesling, one miscellaneous) and buys about 10 percent of its grapes.

Allegro's Seyval Blanc is a nice bottle, but if you can get your hands on one of this winery's wines, go for the Cadenza, a Bordeaux-style Meritage. Crouch has always done well with Cabernet: the 1988 Cadenza (85 percent Cabernet) and the 1989 Cabernet Sauvignon were good efforts, though they are decidedly in a vegetal style.

Wines/Varietals: Premium White ($), Vidal Blanc ($), Seyval Blanc ($), Riesling ($), Reserve Chardonnay ($$), Pennsylvania Blush ($), Celeste ($), Premium Red ($), Cabernet Sauvignon ($$), Cadenza ($$), Brut Sparkling Wine ($$).

Chaddsford Winery

Route One, PO Box 229
Chaddsford, Pennsylvania 19317
tel. (215) 388-6221; fax (215) 388-0360
Open to the public; est. 1982

Eric Miller, co-proprietor of Chaddsford with his wife Lee, is one of the stars of East Coast winemaking; he's widely recognized for his well-balanced, nicely oaked Chardonnays. Miller grew up on a farm in Burgundy where his family lived during the fifties. When the family returned to America, they settled in the Hudson Valley of New York, and Miller's father started his own winery: Benmarl. Eric was winemaker there for a time, then struck out on his own. He and his wife, Lee, who has written extensively about winegrowing in the east, went in search of the right combination of climate and soil that would allow them to produce world-class wines. In 1982, the Millers moved to Pennsylvania's Brandywine Valley—Andrew Wyeth country—where they converted an eighteenth century barn into a winery and tasting room.

Though the couple own a 19-acre vineyard, Miller works closely with other Pennsylvania growers who provide him with grapes. His vineyard-designated Chardonnays have made two properties nationally-known: Roth Vineyard and Stargazer Vineyard. The rich, buttery Stargarzer Chardonnay is particularly appealing (equally in 1988 and 1989). The 1989 Philip Roth Vineyard Chardonnay (no connection to the novelist) was, for us, one of the best North American Chardonnays in that year, possessing a luscious, earthy character with all the right varietal signals. Simple quaffing wines are best-sellers at Chaddsford, the most popular being the young, fruity Spring Wine and the Proprietor's Reserve White (a blend of Seyval Blanc, Vidal and Vignoles). In wintertime, around the holidays, the Spiced Apple Wine, with its sweet-tart apple flavors, is a big hit. Miller's Cabernet Sauvignon and Pinot Noir don't yet have the intensity of character and balance of his Chardonnays, but they bear watching. Chaddsford's total annual production is 15,000 to 20,000 cases.

Wines/Varietals: Stargazer Vineyard Chardonnay ($$$), Philip Roth Vineyard Chardonnay ($$$), Johannisberg Riesling ($$), Moorhead Vineyard Cabernet Sauvignon ($$$), Pinot Noir ($$$), Spring Wine ($), Nouveau ($), Proprietor's Reserve White (Seyval Blanc/Vidal/Vignoles, $), Proprietor's Reserve Red (Chambourcin, $), Spiced Apple Wine ($), NV Blanc de Blancs et Noirs Sparkling Wine ($$$).

Naylor Wine Cellars, Inc.

R.D.# 3, Box 424 Ebaugh Road
Stewartstown, Pennsylvania 17363
tel. (800) 292-3370 or (717) 993-2431
Open to the public; est. 1978

Dick and Audrey Naylor purchased one acre of land in hilly southern York County in 1975, and adding yearly to their vineyard, today own 27 planted acres (on a 90 acre site) and have plans for continued expansion. Naylor firmly believes that the area is particularly well-suited to grape growing—so much so that he envisions southern York County becoming a primary wine-producing region in the U.S. (In the early nineteenth century, the area did support the second oldest commercial winery in America, but is perhaps better known for being the first capital of the United States—for nine months in 1777.)

Naylor grows and produces wine—28 varieties in all from Pinot Gris to Vidalweiss to Pinot Noir—from native American, classic European, and French hybrid grapes. While this may seem to be a little-bit-of-this-and-a-little-bit-of-that approach, Naylor has achieved success with both hybrids and vinifera, as well as some fruit wines. He ages all his red wines and some of the whites and rosés in oak and strives to produce wines that, in general, reflect the nature of the local soils and the effect of climate on the grapes, while recalling to the seasoned palate a classic European essence. In general, his wines are low in alcohol (11 percent or less), are well-made and reasonably-priced. The Chambourcin 1989, dry, full-bodied, plum flavored, and nicely oaky, is a worthy example of the Naylor style. The lighter-style Chardonnay produced in 1990 is pleasant and easy drinking. This winery's output amounts to 6,000 cases annually.

Wines/Varietals: Chambourcin ($), First Capital (red, $), White Rosé ($), Rhinelander ($), Niagara ($), Vidalweiss ($), Catawba ($), Concord ($), Cabernet Sauvignon ($$), Chardonnay ($), Dry Riesling ($), Blush ($), Pinot Gris ($), Pinot Noir ($), Fruit Wine ($), Ekem (Vignoles-based, $$).

Nissley Vineyards and Winery Estate

R.D.#1, Box 92-B
Bainbridge, Pennsylvania 17502
tel. (717) 426-3514
Open to the public; est. 1978

The Richard Nissley family moved to the hills of Lancaster County in 1972 and established this winery in 1978. The 35-acre vineyard, on a 300-acre parcel of rolling Pennsylvania farm and woodlands, is planted mostly to French hybrid varieties such as Vidal Blanc, Aurora, Ravat, Seyval Blanc, Chambourcin, and De Chaunac, with a smattering of hardy Concord and Niagara.

The winery here, a renovated tobacco barn, produces about 15 different wines: moderately-priced varietals and blends (read: under $10), as well as fruit wines (apple and cherry) that are sold mostly at the winery and in markets in eastern Pennsylvania. Over the years, the Seyval Blanc, De Chaunac, and Niagara have probably earned this winery its highest honors. The proprietary "Candlelight" is a also notable achievement.

Wines/Varietals: Seyval Blanc ($), Aurora ($), Vidal Blanc ($), Montmorency Cherry ($), Niagara ($), De Chaunac ($), Chambourcin ($), Candlelight (blend, $), Bainbridge White ($), Apple ($).

Presque Isle Wine Cellars

9440 Buffalo Road
North East, Pennsylvania 16428
tel. (814) 725-1314; fax (814) 725-2092
Open to the public; est. 1964

With 160 acres of vineyards planted in vinifera and French-American hybrids, Presque Isle, in the northwestern part of the state near Lake Erie, is one of Pennsylvania's largest vineyards, and that earns points. So does the fact that it is the state's oldest continuously operated winery. Winemaker Robert Green only produces 1,600 cases annually, however, as most of the grapes grown here are sold off.

Nevertheless, Green produces a full range of estate wines. Over the years, the vineyard's Cabernet Sauvignon grapes have earned a very good reputation, but the estate Chardonnay is currently the winery's best offering. We also recommend Presque Isle's Cabernet Franc or Vidal Blanc.

Wines/Varietals: Chardonnay ($), Riesling ($), Pinot Gris ($), Aligote ($), Petite Sirah ($), Vidal ($), Vignoles ($), Cabernet Sauvignon ($), Cabernet Franc ($).

Rhode Island

Sakonnet Vineyards
PO Box 197
Little Compton, Rhode Island 02837
tel. (401) 635-8486; fax (401) 635-2101
Open to the public; est. 1975

The oldest surviving New England winery, Sakonnet is perched on a hill above Rhode Island Sound, where the maritime climate makes it viable for growing vinifera and hybrid grapes. The Mitchell family laid the groundwork here in the 1970s and early 1980s, but the winery was in danger of going out of business until it was rescued by Earl and Susan Samson in 1987. Earl, formerly an investment analyst in New York, and Susan, an actress, took up winegrowing with gusto, replanting and expanding the 44-acre vineyard and increasing annual production to 22,000 cases. About a quarter of the grapes required are purchased and of the Samson's own grapes, 30 percent are Vidal and 20 percent Chardonnay.

Sakonnet's Chardonnay Barrel Select is quite good (the 1989 was full of fruit and spice flavors with classic buttery overlay); the Gewürztraminer is fruity and appealing. The Vidal Blanc has the brisk, dry fruit of Loire Valley wines. The winery's Pinot Noir

is light and tart. It's shy in flavor but perhaps will show potential as the vines mature. Over 70 percent of production here goes into moderately-priced proprietary blends with appropriately seaworthy names like America's Cup White (30 percent), Eye of the Storm (33 percent), Compass Rosé (2 percent) and Spinnaker (5 percent), but the Samsons are proudest of their varietals, especially the Chardonnays.

Wines/Varietals: Chardonnay Barrel Select ($$), Chardonnay ($), Vidal Blanc ($), America's Cup White ($), Gewürztraminer ($$), Eye of the Storm ($), Spinnaker White ($), Compass Rosé ($), Pinot Noir ($$), Rhode Island Red ($).

Key

$ 750-ml bottle of wine costing less than $10.

$$ Bottle priced between $10 and $20.

$$$ Bottle costing more than $20.

$-$$$ In red indicates excellent value in its class; good relationship between quality and price.

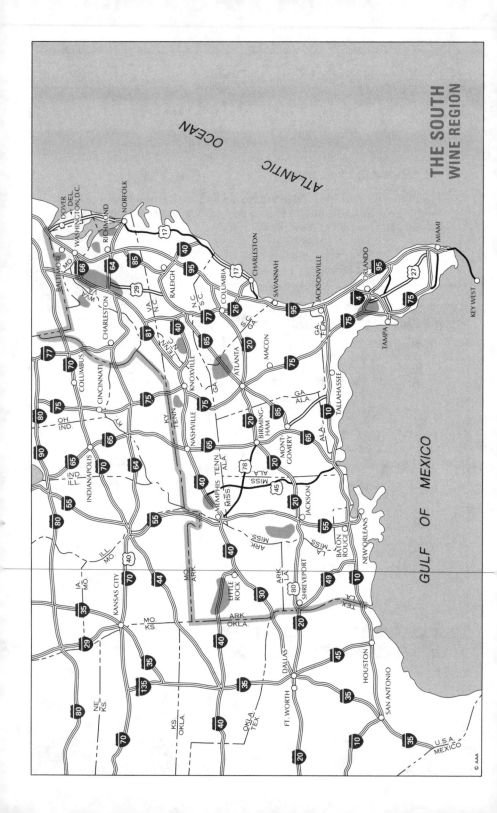

THE SOUTH
WINE REGION

The Vines of Thomas Jefferson

AMERICA'S first efforts at winemaking occurred in the South: not only at Jamestown (even earlier, French Huguenots made muscadine wine on the gulf coast of Florida), but in the colony of Maryland, where Lord Baltimore tried to establish European vines, and in Georgia, where James Oglethorpe made a similar attempt. Later in Virginia at Monticello, Thomas Jefferson made serious and extensive efforts at grape growing, planting 20 or so different varieties, including native hybrids as well as vinifera such as Cabernet Sauvignon, Pinot Noir, Muscat, Nebbiolo, and Chardonnay. Jefferson fervently hoped the young republic could develop its own wine industry so that Americans would be free to choose wine over rum and whiskey. His experiments with vinifera, however, were thwarted by the prevailing climate—warm, humid summers that promoted powdery mildew, and devastating spring frosts that killed off young vines—and by phylloxera, the root louse that a century later would destroy the vineyards of Europe, and today is wreaking havoc in California.

Modern technology and advanced viticultural practices can now overcome most such problems; nevertheless, successful winegrowing in the South is quite a recent phenomenon. The most dramatic progress has been achieved in Virginia, which could claim only six wineries in 1979, and today is home to over fifty. This state currently has the region's largest number of acres planted in vinifera varieties, concentrated mainly in Chardonnay, Merlot, Cabernet Sauvignon, and Riesling.

Elsewhere in the South, interesting wines of steadily improving quality are also being produced, but usually only in very limited quantities. Maryland has a handful of wineries achieving good results with French hybrids and vinifera grapes, notably Merlot and Cabernet Franc. Georgia growers are successfully bringing to market Cabernet Sauvignon, Chardonnay, and Riesling. However unlikely it may seem, the red soil of northern Georgia is perfectly capable of producing supple reds from Cabernet Sauvignon, Merlot, and perhaps other varieties as well.

Growers in the Lafayette, Lakeridge and Chautauqua areas in northern Florida have taken a different tack, choosing to develop native muscadine varieties that are not troubled by high humidity or frost. Some grapes, such as Stover, Blanc DuBois, and Noble produce wines that are off-dry, clean, and crisp, if somewhat neutral in character; muscadine flavors, though, are quite different from vinifera and are something of an acquired taste. North Carolina winery owners have gone in both directions: the Biltmore Estate in Asheville grows vinifera exclusively (and very successfully) and also imports grapes from California and elsewhere. Duplin Cellars in the southeastern part of the state produces all muscadine wines in semi-dry, sweet, and sparkling styles. And in West Virginia, Robert Pliska does a very creditable job with French hybrids, particularly reds such as Maréchal Foch.

Other states in the Deep South—Tennessee, Alabama, and Mississippi—grow a mix of mostly French hybrids and muscadines, with a smattering of courageous effort being applied to cultivating vinifera, notably Cabernet Sauvignon and Sauvignon Blanc. Viticultural conditions in Tennessee's central valleys have encouraged limited efforts with French hybrids and some tentative experimentation with late-ripening vinifera such as Cabernet Sauvignon. The best results to date seem to revolve around careful blends that emphasize fruit in light-bodied, drinkable wines like the Gamay-style red from Laurel Hill in Memphis.

Even the Mississippi Delta can today lay claim to being the site of some serious winegrowing: tiny Claiborne Vineyards cultivates French hybrids such as Vidal, as well as (amazingly) Cabernet Sauvignon. As in other regions, one of the biggest problems confronting Southern wineries in the 1990s is the flat—or shrinking—wine market and the increasing availability of wines from California and abroad at competitive prices. Locally produced wines that cannot measure up in terms of style and quality will likely have a very rough go of it. At the same time, acceptance of wines produced in this region appears to be growing, especially in Virginia and Maryland.

Virginia: A Spectacular Expansion

The dramatic expansion in vineyard acreage in Virginia, from 286 acres in 1979 to some 1,400 acres in 1991, represents an increase of nearly 400 percent. About 65 percent of the acreage today is planted to vinifera varieties (Chardonnay, Cabernet Sauvignon, Riesling, Merlot), 28 percent to French hybrids (Seyval Blanc, Vidal Blanc, Maréchal Foch) and the rest, about 7 percent, to native varieties such as Concord and Delaware. Most of the industry's growth has been in northern and western Virginia, the Piedmont region west of Washington, D.C., Charlottesville (with its Monticello appellation in Albemarle County) and in the Shenandoah Valley. Recently, the tidewater plains of eastern Virginia have proved accommodating to Cabernet and Merlot.

Virginia's greatest success to date is with Chardonnay. Several wineries are now producing good, appealing wines from this grape; they are medium-bodied, leaner than California Chardonnays, but graceful, well-balanced, and flavorful. There is good potential for reds, too, but as yet it has only been realized in isolated areas. Cabernet Sauvignon, Merlot, and Cabernet Franc made in Virginia often achieve vivid depth of color, but high acidity can overpower the fruit in these wines—and all too frequently it does. Skillful chaptalizing would probably help, but many Virginia winemakers feel reluctant to do it. In sum, Virginia wines have improved significantly over the last decade. There is every indication that additional experience on the part of the state's winemakers will ultimately result in wines of greater finesse.

Arkansas

Wiederkehr
Wine Cellars, Inc.
Route 1, Box 14
Altus, Arkansas 72821
tel. (501) 468-2611 or 468-9463;
fax (501) 468-4791
Open to the public; est. 1880

Al Wiederkehr, president and winemaker at the mid-south's oldest winery, represents the fourth generation of a German-Swiss family that came to America in the 1870s. Wiederkehr's great grandfather, Johann Andreas, settled in the Arkansas Ozarks at the foot of St. Mary's Mountain. He first made wines from wild grapes, blackberries, and persimmons, and eventually planted American grapes such as Catawba and Niagara along with other varieties. Arkansas is the only U.S. state to commercially produce all five species of wine grapes: vinifera, rotundifolia, labrusca, aestivalis and French hybrids. All five are represented at Wiederkehr.

The 260-acre vineyard here supplies 60 percent of Wiederkehr's production of 65,000 to 70,000 cases annually; the remaining 40 percent is purchased from other Arkansas vineyards. Vinifera grapes are a recent addition to the winery's roster, with the Johannisberg Riesling currently the best and most consistent. In some years, the Cabernet has also been respectably drinkable, possessing good, medium-weight fruit and balance. The Arkansas version of Cynthiana is sweet, rather than dry as in Missouri. While wines from native grapes remain among Wiederkehr's best-sellers,

several French hybrids (notably Verdelet Blanc, Vidal Blanc, and the Extra Dry sparkler) are made into wines that are crisp, fruity, and well-balanced. Altus Spumante, a sparkling Muscat, is sweet but clean and crisp, with appealing Muscat aromas and flavors reminiscent of a good Asti. To our palate, this is arguably Wiederkehr's best wine, though the Johannisberg Riesling is becoming a contender.

Wines/Varietals: Johannisberg Riesling ($$), French Colombard ($), Verdelet Blanc ($), Gewürztraminer ($), Vidal Blanc ($), Muscat di Tanta Maria ($), Rhine ($), Chablis Blanc ($), Edelweiss ($), Niagara ($), Alpine Chablis ($), Seyval Blanc ($), Vin Rosé Sec ($), Pink Catawba ($), Alpine Rosé ($), Blanc de Noirs ($), Blush Chablis ($), Blush Niagara ($), White Zinfandel ($), Cabernet Sauvignon ($), Baco Noir ($), Cynthiana ($), Burgundy ($), Sangria ($), Cabernet Sauvignon Vintage Port ($$), Chateau du Monte Extra Dry Champagne ($$), Chateau du Monte Pink Champagne ($), Hanns Wiederkehr Extra Dry Sparkling Wine ($), Altus Spumante ($), Blanc de Noirs Champagne ($).

Florida

Lafayette/Lakeridge
19239 U.S. Highway 27 North
Clermont, Florida 34711
tel. (904) 394-8627
Open to the public; est. 1983

Lafayette Winery, originally founded in Tallahassee by partners Gary Cox and Gary Ketchum, opened Lakeridge in central Florida in 1989. The plan was to operate the two wineries as separate facilities, but the wine market near Orlando (and Disney World, 30 minutes from Clermont) proved so much better than the one in Tallahassee that the partners moved the Lafayette operation to the Lakeridge facility. Jeanne Burgess, Lafayette's winemaker since 1983, now makes all the wines at Lakeridge and bottles them under both labels. The better wines are bottled under the Lafayette label and the everyday, supermarket-style wines bear the Lakeridge label. Lakeridge, the name of the winery at Clermont, draws on about 60 acres of vineyard, owned or under long-term contract, for half of its production. Other Florida growers furnish additional grapes to meet production of about 12,500 cases.

The grape varieties used are either muscadine hybrids such as Carlos, Magnolia, Welder, and Noble, or Florida bunch grapes, Stover, Suwannee, and Blanc DuBois, varieties developed at the Florida research center in Leesburg. Lakeridge has also begun working with Miss Blanc, a bunch grape variety developed at Mississippi State. These are the only species resistant to subtropical diseases that will grow reliably in Florida's warm, humid climate. Most go into blends with proprietary names, but a couple are made as varietals, such as the Stover Special Reserve, which is aged in oak, giving it a curious but attractive flavor: sweet but well balanced and quite drinkable. One of Lafayette's most popular labels is Noble Nouveau, made from whole grape clusters in the nouveau style, and available from Valentine's Day to September. Sparkling wines are made under both labels. Among the generally well-made and distinctive wines produced here, the sparkling wine (in the sweeter, flower/pear dessert style) is perhaps the most successful, though the others are pleasant drinking once one gets used to their somewhat different

grape flavors (the most notable taste difference is in the sweet muscadines, markedly different from vinifera or hybrids).

Wines/Varietals: Lafayette label: Stover Special Reserve ($), Cuvée Blanc Reserve ($), Blanc de Fleur Sparkling Wine ($$), Semisweet Red ($), Semisweet White ($), Noble Nouveau ($); Lakeridge label: Suwannee ($), Cuvée Blanc ($), Sun Blush ($), Southern Red ($), Southern White ($), Crescendo Sparkling Wine ($$).

Georgia

Chateau Elan

7000 Old Winder Highway
Braselton, Georgia 30517
tel. (800) 233-9463 or (404) 658-9463;
fax (404) 867-8714
Open to the public; est. 1982

Donald Panoz respects both tradition and technology. When this pharmaceutical company executive and his wife, Nancy, came to Atlanta, his background in chemistry and their appreciation of fine wine coalesced into a vision of a high-quality vineyard and winery to be created on an unlikely site an hour out of Atlanta. Panoz soon created something of a showplace. The Chateau, modeled after the architectural style of sixteenth century France, offers shops, cafés, art galleries, entertainment—and, of course, winetasting—reflecting Panoz's belief that wine is meant to be appreciated in combination with the other fine things life has to offer. Six *vitis vinifera* grape varieties (Chardonnay, Riesling, Sauvignon Blanc, Cabernet Sauvignon, Merlot, and Cabernet Franc) and two American hybrids (Chambourcin and Seyval Blanc) are cultivated on the 185 acres at Chateau Elan. Panoz also imports grapes from California to produce wines under an American appellation. He professes to be more interested in making wines that are good to drink than in pursuing an estate-grown appellation.

He hired French winemaker Jean Courtois in 1985; their stated objective is to produce wines that go well with food. Current annual production is 35,000 cases. Chateau Elan's most popular wines are southern in heritage: flavored muscadines such as the Summer Wine—simple, sound and surprisingly pleasing with good peach flavors and balance—and Autumn Blush, with raspberry. The Georgia-grown varietals are still evolving in style, though in recent vintages the Chardonnay has been sound and appealing. The Cabernet Essence isn't the concentrated red that the label suggests; it is a mild but decently-drinkable Cab. The sparkling wines produced here show promise, too.

Wines/Varietals: Founders Reserve Chardonnay ($), Founders Reserve Cabernet Sauvignon Essence ($$), Founders Reserve White Cabernet Sauvignon ($), Founders Reserve Sauvignon Blanc ($), Johannisberg Riesling ($), Summer Wine (Peach and Muscadine, $), Autumn Blush (Raspberry and Muscadine, $), Sparkling Wine ($$).

Chestnut Mountain

PO Box 72
Braselton, Georgia 30517
tel. (404) 867-6914
Open to the public; est. 1988

Chestnut Mountain proves that Georgia's red clay soil can produce surprisingly good—and varietally-sound—Cabernet Sauvignon, Chardonnay, and Merlot. Owner-founder Jim Laikam, a former Californian, is committed to cultivating solely Georgia-grown vinifera. He has planted 11 acres, mostly in Cabernet and Cabernet Franc, with an acre and a half of Nebbiolo as an experiment, in the red hills, half an hour northwest of Atlanta in northern Georgia. Some 250 acres of vinifera are grown in this part of the state. To date, Chestnut Mountain has bought fruit from half a dozen growers, awaiting the time when its own vineyards will be fully bearing.

Winemaker David Harris, a native Georgian trained in enology at Fresno State in California, has a deft hand with Chardonnay (40 percent of production) in particular, but his Cabernet Sauvignon (40 percent) and Merlot (20 percent) also have good varietal character, appealing fruit and balance. The winery also makes Cabernet Blanc and in some years, Chenin Blanc. The 1991 Chardonnay surely qualifies as one of the South's best Chardonnays, and we were also impressed with the well-made 1989 Cabernet Sauvignon Georgia Mossy Creek Vineyard, which bursts with varietal character, including cherries and eucalyptus. The lean, good 1990 Merlot points up the potential of this fine operation and the potential of red wines from this region.

Wines/Varietals: Chardonnay ($$), Cabernet Sauvignon ($$), Merlot ($$), Dry Chenin Blanc ($), Cabernet Blanc ($).

Maryland

Boordy Vineyards

12820 Long Green Pike
Hydes, Maryland 21082
tel. (410) 592-5015; fax (410) 592-5385
Open to the public; est. 1945

The founders of Boordy Vineyards, Philip and Mary Wagner, were among the original latter-day pioneers of winegrowing east of the Rockies. It was Philip Wagner who introduced French-American hybrid varieties to eastern vineyards, enabling vintners in the region to produce table wines without the foxy taste of such native American grapes as Concord and Catawba. Wagner provided rooted cuttings of dozens of hybrid varieties and made his own wines at his country home outside Baltimore. In 1980, the Wagners sold Boordy to the DeFord family. Robert B. DeFord III currently presides over the nearly 7,000-case-a-year winery, housed in a nineteenth century barn with massive stone walls, hand-hewn beams, and dark, cool cellars; it is decidedly old world. The 14-acre vineyard is planted to hybrids such as Seyval Blanc, Vidal, Foch and Chambourcin, as well as Chardonnay and Cabernet Sauvignon vinifera.

Winemaker Thomas Burns produces well-balanced, appealing wines, particularly crisp, off-dry hybrid whites like Vidal Blanc and Seyval. Boordy is proud of its Cabernet, which to date is pleasantly fruity but mild in Cabernet character. We give our nod to the house's semi-dry Vidal with simple, refreshing, almost spritzy character and peachy overtones.

Wines/Varietals: Semi-Dry Vidal Blanc ($), Seyval Blanc ($), Seyval Blanc Sur Lie Reserve ($), Chardonnay ($), Maryland White ($), Cabernet Blanc ($), Maryland Blush ($), Maryland Red ($), Nouveau ($), Cabernet Sauvignon ($$), Wassail ($), Sparkling Wine ($).

Catoctin Vineyards

805 Greenbridge Road
Brookeville, Maryland 20833
tel. (301) 774-2310
Open to the public; est. 1983

Named for the mountain range in the foothills of the Appalachians, Catoctin produces some of Maryland's most stylish wines, largely from vinifera grapes grown on its 32-acre vineyard. To meet production of 3,500 cases, about 20 percent of the required grapes are purchased. All of the grapes are Maryland grown. Founded by a partnership (Robert Lyon, Shahin Bagheri, Jerry and Ann Milne), Catoctin has plans to expand production to 10,000 cases over the next few years. Winemaker Bob Lyon received a degree in enology from the University of California at Davis and worked at several California wineries, including Chateau Montelena, Domaine Chandon, Inglenook and Sebastiani, before coming east.

Chardonnay and Cabernet Sauvignon, the primary focus here, result in balanced wines with good varietal character and clean, attractive flavors. Aged in French oak barrels, they offer good value, especially the 1990 Chardonnay and the 1985 Reserve Cabernet Sauvignon, with its dry berry and cedar flavor. Mariage is a pleasantly drinkable everyday red; Eye of the Oriole, an appealing semi-dry blush.

Wines/Varietals: Chardonnay ($), Chardonnay Oak Fermented ($), Cabernet Sauvignon ($), Cabernet Reserve ($$), Johannisberg Riesling ($), Mariage ($), Eye of the Oriole ($), Eye of the Beholder ($).

Wines/Varietals: Sauvignon Blanc ($$), Cabernet Sauvignon ($$), Seyval Blanc ($), Villard Blanc ($), Bayou Rouge ($).

Mississippi

Claiborne Vineyards
PO Box 350
Indianola, Mississippi 38751
tel. (601) 887-2327
Open to the public by appt.; est. 1984

Claiborne's postage-stamp sized vineyard—five acres set in a corner of a cotton plantation on the Mississippi Delta—was planted in 1982 with one acre each of Cabernet Sauvignon and Sauvignon Blanc and three acres equally divided French hybrids, Seyval Blanc and Villard Blanc. Owners E. Claiborne and Marion Barnwell named the vineyard in honor of beloved uncle and American cookbook author Craig Claiborne, who was born nearby in Sunflower, Mississippi. The hot, humid Delta region seems an unlikely spot for wine grapes, but the vineyard here is thriving, due to the Barnwells' meticulous care.

Claiborne white wines are crisply dry; the Seyval is the freshest and most appealing, but the Sauvignon Blanc holds promise and is currently the producer's favorite. In 1988, this varietal's soft honey, pears, and herbal flavors came together successfully. The house Cabernet, light and tart, is drinkable. The blended table red, Bayou Rouge, is fruity and agreeable, and the winery's best value.

North Carolina

Biltmore Estate Winery
One North Pack Square
Asheville, North Carolina 28801
tel. (800) 543-2961 or (704) 255-1700;
fax (704) 255-1139
Open to the public; est. 1985 (vineyards planted in 1979)

Several American wineries use the name "chateau" on their labels, but only Biltmore Estate in North Carolina compares in grandeur to Europe's fabled vineyard estates. Biltmore, a 250-room mansion, was built in 1880 by George Washington Vanderbilt. Set on a high plateau in the Blue Ridge Mountains near Asheville, this property consists of 8,000 acres still owned by the family. Vanderbilt's grandson, William Amherst Vanderbilt Cecil, planted the first vineyards here in 1979. Today, 77.5 acres of vinifera grow at an elevation of 4,500 feet. The elevation provides a cooler environment than that of most southeastern regions, but can occasionally pose a problem to the grapestock's achieving full ripeness. Cabernet Sauvignon, Chardonnay, and Riesling make up the majority of the plantings with smaller plot devoted to Pinot Noir, Merlot, Cabernet Franc, and Sauvignon Blanc.

The estate vineyards supply a quarter of the grapes needed to achieve an annual production of 36,000 cases. Additional grapes are purchased from California. French-trained winemaster Philippe Jourdain was hired in 1979. He or winemaker Bernard de Lille (also French) travel to California each harvest to select grapes which are then shipped back to North Carolina in refrigerated trucks. Wines made all or in part from purchased grapes are produced under the Biltmore Estate label with American appellations, including Cabernet Sauvignon, Sauvignon Blanc, and sparkling Blanc de Blancs. Chateau Biltmore brand wines are made exclusively from grapes grown on the estate. Several, particularly barrel fermented Chardonnay, Pinot Noir, and Riesling, have proven North Carolina's capabilities with vinifera. The 1990 Chateau Biltmore Chardonnay North Carolina is a very fine bottle indeed: crisp, good fruit with citrus flavors—altogether the match in quality for Chardonnays produced anywhere. Biltmore sparkling wines have been good in some cuvées; at their best, they are light and lively, impressively clean and refreshing. Table wines, particularly Chardonnay and Riesling, have been of reliable quality, with crisp, clean lines. Though somewhat light in character, they are well-balanced and steadily gaining in quality and consistency.

Wines/Varietals: Chateau Biltmore Barrel fermented Chardonnay ($$), Biltmore Chardonnay Sur Lies ($$), Cabernet Sauvignon ($$), Chateau Biltmore Riesling ($), Blanc de Noirs (Cabernet and Zinfandel, $), Vintage Blanc de Blancs Méthode Champenoise ($$$).

Tennessee

Cordova Cellars
9050 Macon Road
Cordova, Tennessee 38018
tel. (901) 754-3442; fax (901) 755-9612
Open to the public; est. 1989

Randy and Mary Birks, founders of Cordova Cellars, fell in love with wine while stationed abroad in the military. Returning to Tennessee, Randy planted an experimental plot on the Dutcher family farm in Cordova (half an hour east of Memphis) and later studied viticulture and enology at Mississippi State University. Today, the Birks and Jane Dutcher operate Tennessee's youngest winery, housed in an attractive brick and redwood barn, and farm 4.5 acres of Vidal Blanc and Chardonnay, which studies suggest are the two grapes best suited to this area. The vineyard here supplies half of the grapes for an annual production of 2,000 cases; the Birks buy the rest of the fruit they need, a mix of vinifera grapes, French hybrids, and native grapes like Niagara and Venus. (Cabernet and Chardonnay grapes come from Washington State; Niagara, Vidal Blanc, and Vignoles from New York.)

The American Cabernet Sauvignon (from purchased grapes) and the American Chardonnay (with estate and purchased grapes) are both sound, displaying competent winemaking technique and a good future. Try Cordova's estate grown Vidal Blanc if you'd like to have a taste of Tennessee. The 1990 Shelby County Vidal Blanc Barrel Reserve did not display a lot of fruit in the nose, but the mild, greenish character vintage that followed was pleasant. Its dryness carried through to a crisp finish—a promising effort.

Wines/Varietals: American Chardonnay ($$), American Cabernet Sauvignon ($$), Shelby County Vidal Blanc ($), American Gewürztraminer ($), American Niagara ($), Fayette Red ($), White Table Wine ($), Cordova Rosé ($).

are sweet. The semi-dry Royal White is a skillfully-made blend that sells well, and the sweet Muscadine is favorite in the South. Of their kind, these wines are strong efforts.

Wines/Varietals: Chardonnay ($), Royal White ($), Cayuga White ($), White Riesling ($), Southern Blush ($), Royal Rosé ($), Muscadine ($), Highland White ($), Highland Red ($).

Highland Manor Winery, Inc.
Highway 127, Box 33B
Jamestown, Tennessee 38556
tel./fax (615) 879-9519
Open to the public; est. 1980

This Tudor-style winery rises out of the Cumberland Plateau west of the Smoky Mountains in northern Tennessee. "Most people are surprised to learn you can grow wine grapes here," observes winemaker Irving Martin, "but the intense, seasonal climate is what makes it possible." Varieties that do well here are mostly hybrids, like Cayuga and Vidal, and native grapes such as Catawba, Niagara, and Muscadine. Highland Manor has 21 acres of vineyards planted to these and other varieties, including golden Muscat, De Chaunac, Seyval Blanc, and Cynthiana.

Growing vinifera here has proved much tougher. Martin's vinifera vines were killed by a severe winter freeze, so he now buys Chardonnay and Riesling from Washington State, and produces attractively crisp wines; the Chardonnay is dry and the Riesling lightly sweet. The winery produces about 5,000 cases annually, 60 percent of it from estate-grown grapes. Most of Highland Manor's white wines, but for its Chardonnay,

Laurel Hill Winery
1370 Madison Avenue
Memphis, Tennessee 38104
tel. (901) 725-9128
Open to the public; est. 1984

Laurel Hill bills itself as "a small farm winery in the heart of Memphis." And indeed, Ray Skinner's wines—all 900 cases annually—are made in downtown Memphis, though the grapes come from the Cumberland Plateau in middle Tennessee. Skinner owns 7.5 acres there, planted in a mix of French hybrids, vinifera (Chardonnay), and native grapes such as Scuppernong, Lenoir and Herbemont. He also purchases grapes from other growers in the mid-South.

Skinner's Chardonnay is light in character and fairly austere, but clean and crisp; the dry Vidal is a more appealing white. The most drinkable wine produced here is the simple, fruity blend labeled Central Gardens Red, made from five or six varieties including Cabernet Sauvignon.

Wines/Varietals: Central Gardens Red ($), Chardonnay ($), Vidal Blanc ($), Avalon ($), Magevney House Old Memphis Scuppernong ($).

Virginia

Autumn Hill Vineyards

Route 1, Box 199C
Standardsville, Virginia 22973
tel. (804) 985-6100
Open to the public by appt.; est. 1986

Autumn Hill's lovely setting overlooking the Blue Ridge Mountains in northwestern Virginia includes 8.5 acres planted only to vinifera varieties: Cabernet Sauvignon, Chardonnay, and Riesling. Owner-winemaker Ed Schwab, who once ran an interior design firm on Long Island, but whose "mid-life crisis" propelled him to Virginia and into winegrowing, buys about 30 percent of the grapes he needs to produce 1,700 cases annually.

Sixty-five percent of the output here is Chardonnay, which has shown considerable promise in recent vintages, particularly 1989 and 1991 (Schwab shuns oak, so lean fruit and crispness are at the fore of these wines; they work well with food). Autumn Hill Cabernets may improve. The 1991 Riesling, semi-sweet in style, is well-balanced and appealing.

Wines/Varietals: Chardonnay ($), Cabernet Sauvignon ($$), Riesling ($), Montage (blush, $).

Barboursville Vineyards

Route 777, PO Box 136
Barboursville, Virginia 22923
tel. (703) 832-3824; fax (703) 832-7572
Open to the public; est. 1976

Barboursville occupies a splendid site some 17 miles north of Charlottesville. Set in the foothills of the Blue Ridge Mountains, the estate was once the property of Virginia governor James Barbour. An imposing manor, designed by the governor's neighbor, Thomas Jefferson, was destroyed by fire in 1884. But picturesque ruins of the house, with its columned facade, are today a registered historic landmark and are rendered on the label of Barboursville wines. The estate is now owned by the Zonin family of Northern Italy, who recognized the potential for winegrowing in Virginia in the mid-seventies. At a time when most Virginia wineries were hedging their bets by planting hybrids along with vinifera, Gianni Zonin planted all vinifera. Today there are some 14 different varieties planted on 65 acres, the bulk of the land devoted to Chardonnay, Cabernet Sauvignon, and Pinot Noir. The vineyard also contains lesser quantities of Sauvignon Blanc, Merlot, Cabernet Franc, Riesling and Gewürztraminer, as well as Italian varieties such as Malvasia, Barbera, and the latest addition, Pinot Grigio, planted in 1992.

Winemaker Luca Paschina annually produces 10,000 cases of well-balanced, fruity wines that have gained character as the vines here have matured. Particularly good are Barboursville Chardonnay, dry, racy Sauvignon Blanc and lightly spicy Gewürztraminer. The Cabernet is much improved in recent years: more concentrated than earlier versions, which were pleasant enough but rather thin. Most of the reds lean to the lighter side. (Paschina is excited about the prospects for producing Pinot Grigio.) Malvasia is a late-harvest dessert wine, amber in color and richly sweet. Top marks here go to the 1989 and 1990 Virginia Monticello Reserve Chardonnay: crisp and lively, citrus- and pear-flavored with vanilla and oak richness in strong harmony.

Wines/Varietals: Chardonnay ($), Chardonnay Reserve ($$), Sauvignon Blanc ($), Riesling ($), Cabernet Blanc ($), Gewürztraminer ($$), Pinot Noir ($), Merlot ($), Barbera ($), Vin Rosé ($), Malvasia ($$).

Burnley Vineyards

Route 1, Box 122
Barboursville, Virginia 22923
tel. (703) 832-2828 or (703) 832-3874;
fax (703) 832-2828
Open to the public; est. 1984

Colonel C.J. Reeder purchased 40 acres near Barboursville as a retirement haven and planted grapevines in 1976. The property now has 25 acres of vineyard planted to both vinifera and hybrid grapes; purchases of additional grapes provide for annual production of 7,000 cases. Family members fill most of the winery positions here and serve up samples of the house wines in a handsome, cathedral-ceilinged tasting room, which has a 30-foot balcony offering wonderful views of the Virginia countryside.

Hybrids are used primarily in blends such as Rivanna Red (Chambourcin, De Chaunac, Maréchal Foch, and Baco Noir), Rivanna White (primarily Vidal Blanc), and Rivanna Sunset (Chambourcin), an attractively fruity, blush wine. Among varietals, Burnley makes Chardonnay, Riesling, and Cabernet Sauvignon. Chardonnay has earned the winery the most respect over the years, though there is consistent quality across the board

here, and a commitment to marketing at modest prices that has earned the winery a devoted following.

Wines/Varietals: Chardonnay ($), Riesling ($), Rivanna White ($), Rivanna Sunset ($), Rivanna Red ($), Daniel Cellars Somerset ($), Cabernet Sauvignon ($$).

Ingleside Plantation Vineyards

Hwy 638, PO Box 1038
Oak Grove, Virginia 22443
tel. (804) 224-8687; fax (804) 224-2032
Open to the public; est. 1980

Carl Flemer, Jr., owner of the 2,500 acre Ingleside Plantation Nursery near Chesapeake Bay, between the Potomic and Rappahannok rivers, planted grapevines experimentally in 1976. When Belgian winemaker Jacques Recht arrived on the scene three years later, having sailed across the Atlantic, he and Flemer met and were encouraged by their first efforts at making wine from Flemer's grapes. Recht stayed on and has since served as consultant to several Virginia wineries. He introduced the first Virginia sparkling wines, made mostly from Pinot Noir and Chardonnay. The Ingleside vineyard today comprises 75 acres, mostly planted to vinifera, but a few given over to hybrids. Annual production here is 20,000 cases, which requires the purchase of up to 80 percent of the necessary grapes; all are Virginia-grown.

Ingleside has produced some very good Cabernet Sauvignon and Chardonnay (each 20 percent of total production), as well as attractive everyday blends known as Chesapeake White (made from Seyval Blanc) and Chesapeake Claret. The Cabernets and the

Chesapeake Claret seem to be a little more consistent than the white blends. The *méthode champenoise* Virginia Brut sparkling wine, vintage in some years, is generally light and brisk in character, and just off-dry.

Wines/Varietals: Cabernet Sauvignon ($), Cabernet Sauvignon Barrel Select ($$), Chardonnay ($), Chardonnay Reserve ($$), Chesapeake Claret ($), Chesapeake Blanc ($), Le Blanc ($), Le Blush ($), Le Rouge ($), George Washington Red ($), Pinot Noir ($$), Virginia Brut ($$), Fréulein (Gewürztraminer, $).

Linden Vineyards
Route 1, Box 96
Linden, Virginia 22642
tel. (703) 364-1997
Open to the public; est. 1987

Jim and Peggy Law spent two years searching for just the right spot to grow grapes, settling, in 1983, on a steep slope that rises over 1,300 feet in the Blue Ridge Mountains range. After clearing the land, they planted their first vines, a mix of vinifera and hybrids that today covers 18 acres. The elevation and northeastern exposure of the vineyards offers a longer growing season than elsewhere in Virginia, pushing the harvest into October for some varieties. The Laws also grow rare varieties of apples such as Gala, Black Twig, and Seek No Further, as well as blueberries on their property. The small, modern winery, with its wraparound deck, perches at the top of the slope, providing a panoramic view of the hills and woods surrounding the vineyard.

Jim, the winemaker, excels at white wines, producing stylish, well-balanced Sauvignon Blanc, Chardonnay, and an appealing blend of Riesling-Vidal that is one of Linden's most popular "picnic wines." The Cabernet here is a blend of Cabernet Sauvignon and Cabernet Franc, with the emphasis on fruit, though a firm underpinning of tannins gives the wine structure and hints that more richness and character may develop as the vines mature. Current production: about 3,800 cases, with plans to reach 5,000 within a few years. The 1990 Chardonnay is one of the winery's best efforts to date—clean, crisp, and tightly focused with apple and pear flavors, but with a hint of herbal highlights. The 1988 Cabernet (24 percent Cabernet Franc in the blend) is the most impressive Linden wine we've tasted: big and tannic, but balanced, with deep blackberry and varietal flavors.

Wines/Varietals: Sauvignon Blanc ($$), Chardonnay ($$), Riesling-Vidal ($), Cabernet Sauvignon ($$), Seyval Blanc ($).

Meredyth Vineyards
Route 628, PO Box 347
Middleburg, Virginia 22117
tel. (703) 687-6277
Open to the public; est. 1972

Archie Smith, Jr. is Virginia's first winegrower of the modern era. In 1972, he was advised against planting vinifera, so instead began cultivating French hybrids on his farm at Middleburg, about an hour west of Washington, D.C. Today the 60-acre vineyard includes one-third vinifera varieties, among them Cabernet Sauvignon, Chardonnay, Riesling, Merlot, and Cabernet Franc. Archie Smith III, formerly an instructor in philosophy at Oxford, came home from England to serve as winemaker here, honing his craft through trial and error as he discovered what Virginia's soil and climate could do.

Meredyth has long produced lively, quaffable wines from hybrids, particularly the barrel fermented Seyval Blanc and an off-dry blush. Recent vintages have shown improved quality in reds, with moderated tannins in the Cabernet, Merlot and Maréchal Foch. Archie III has adopted the Bordeaux method with Cabernet, giving it an extended period on the lees following fermentation, to soften the tannins. The 1987 and 1989 Cabs, however, will still seem a bit light in style to those most familiar with California Cabernets. We prefer the 1989 Merlot, though the winemaker is partial to his Cabernets. Smith seemed to hit his stride with Chardonnay in the 1991 vintage, the winery's best to date and one of Virginia's best ever. Meredyth's most expensive wine, in very limited production, is the 1990 Merlot (around $25), with firm, somewhat tart fruit.

Wines/Varietals: Chardonnay ($$), Seyval Blanc ($), Sauvignon Blanc ($), Riesling ($), October Harvest ($), Delaware ($), Premium White ($), Cabernet Sauvignon ($$), Merlot ($$), De Chaunac ($), Maréchal Foch ($), Premium Red ($), Blush ($), Harvest Red ($).

Misty Mountain Vineyards, Inc.
Route 698, S.R.#2, Box 458
Madison, Virginia 22727
tel. (703) 923-4738; fax (703) 923-4069
Open to the public; est. 1986

Dr. Michael J. Merceo (primarily a defense software contractor) planted 12 acres of vinifera in the hills of the Blue Ridge Mountains in the mid-eighties. He planted over his vineyards equally to Chardonnay, Cabernet Sauvignon, Riesling, and Merlot and plans to significantly increase plantings on the 1,250-foot elevation hillsides, which enjoy long growing seasons. Son and manager, Michael, and winemakers, Jacques Recht and Phillipe DeLoume, currently purchase about 30 percent of the grapes

required to supplement production of around 4,000 cases annually; nearly half is Chardonnay. And the wines here demonstrate that classy Chardonnays of the highest quality can be made in Virginia. (The winery has recently been put up for sale. We hope that its new owners will continue to show the way.)

One of the first Chardonnays Misty Mountain produced won the state's 1990 Governor's Cup competition, thanks to good grapes and the skill of Recht, a European-born student of Emile Peynaud. This winery's barrel fermented Chardonnays, all well balanced and elegant in structure, have a toasty, oak character that does not overwhelm the rather simple fruit. The 1990 vintage, however, was not as generous in flavors as the 1989 and 1991. Misty Mountain shows good potential for producing red wines, too, especially its Cabernet, which has a good thrust of sturdy fruit. The 1988 is a rich, deeply-flavored bottle.

Wines/Varietals: Chardonnay ($$), Barrel Fermented Chardonnay ($$), Riesling ($), Gewürztraminer ($), Virginia Chablis (Riesling, Seyval, and Vidal, $), Seyval Blanc ($), Cabernet Sauvignon ($$), Merlot ($$).

Montdomaine Cellars
Route 6, Box 188A
Charlottesville, Virginia 22902
tel. (804) 971-8947
Open to the public by appt.; est. 1984

The original partners in Montdomaine were inspired by Thomas Jefferson, whose efforts at nearby Monticello took root in the same red soil and eastern exposures as those of Montdomaine's 50-acre vineyard. Planted in 1977, the vineyard appears to have developed distinctive character, particularly for red varieties like Merlot, Cabernet

Sauvignon, and Cabernet Franc. Earlier versions of these wines tended to toughness and astringency, but recent vintages have shown greater intensity of fruit and better balance. In 1989 and 1990, owner Dennis Horton planted Rhône varieties, including Grenache, Syrah, Mourvèdre, and 15 acres of Viognier. He has very high hopes for the Viognier, which will be produced for the first time in 1992.

Heritage, the Bordeaux-style blend made here, is quite good, with plummy fruit and firm structure. A blend of predominantly Merlot, with Cabernet Franc and Cabernet Sauvignon added, it is a more handsome wine than the house's straight varietals, Merlot and Cabernet Sauvignon, though both of these reds have potential for aging. We enjoyed the 1987 Merlot Reserve, a rich example with lively, plentiful fruit. Montdomaine also makes elegant Chardonnay: the 1990 Barrel Select has fine varietal character, good body and length, with a nice touch of oak. With winemaker Shep Rouse at the helm and Tony Bieda as general manager, Montdomaine's future looks very bright.

Wines/Varietals: Chardonnay ($), Chardonnay Barrel Select ($), Heritage ($$), Merlot ($), Merlot Monticello Reserve ($$), Cabernet Sauvignon ($), Cabernet Sauvignon Reserve ($$).

Naked Mountain Vineyard and Winery

PO Box 131
Markham, Virginia 22643
tel. (703) 364-1609
Open to the public; est. 1981

When Robert and Phoebe Harper moved to the mountainside in Virginia, Robert did a little home winemaking before getting serious about quality. In pursuit of excellence, he planted his own vinifera, concentrating mainly on Chardonnay grapes, which today make up 11 of the 13 acres in his vineyard. He also grows small amounts of Riesling, Sauvignon Blanc, and Cabernet Sauvignon. Annual production is 3,500 cases.

Harper barrel ferments the Chardonnay to get a fairly rich and well-balanced wine that has the length to age three or four years. His 1989 Chard represents well the winery's style and quality.

Wines/Varietals: Barrel Fermented Chardonnay ($$), White Riesling ($$), Sauvignon Blanc ($), Cabernet Sauvignon ($$).

Oakencroft Vineyard & Winery Corp.

Route 5, Box 429
Charlottesville, Virginia 22901
tel. (804) 296-4188
Open to the public; est. 1983

Felicia Warburg Rogan, a New Yorker accustomed to drinking good wine, became intrigued with Virginia's history in grapegrowing when she married a Virginian and moved to Charlottesville in the late seventies. The state's wine industry was just gearing up then, and the dynamic Rogan diverted much of her considerable energy to starting her own vineyard at Oakencroft and to founding the Jeffersonian Grapegrowers Society of Albemarle County. (She was also instrumental in obtaining the Monticello appellation for vineyards around Charlottesville.) Oakencroft started with a couple of rows of Merlot and Seyval Blanc vines in 1981, and released its first wines in 1983. Rogan and her husband, John (since deceased), then built a handsome wood and stone winery, appropriately barnlike in keeping with the setting—a farm on which registered cattle are raised. With the aid of vineyard manager Philip Ponton, the Rogans expanded the vineyard, on a site with good drainage above the winery, to 15 acres. The fresh, lively Countryside White, made from Seyval Blanc and Vidal, has been a consistent medal winner in competitions, but the winery's future may lie more with Cabernet Sauvignon.

Wines/Varietals: Chardonnay ($$), Countryside White ($), Blush ($), Cabernet Sauvignon ($$).

Oasis Vineyards

Route 1, Box 116
Hume, Virginia 22639
tel. (703) 635-3103; fax (703) 635-4653
Open to the public; est. 1980

When Dirgham Salahi and his wife, Corinne, planted an all-vinifera vineyard back in 1975, people thought, "those Salahis are crazy," the Jerusalem-born Salahi recalls.

In its handsome, French Provincial-style winery, Oasis produces 10,000 cases of wine per year, one-third of it sparkling wines made in the traditional Champagne method. Oasis buys Pinot Noir grapes for its Brut and Extra Dry Virginia champagnes. The Extra Dry is excellent, just off-dry, clean, and very well balanced. The barrel fermented Chardonnay here is aromatic and flavorful, with good length. Oasis Cabernets are a little on the pale side and a bit astringent, but the Riesling and Gewürztraminer are lightly sweet and quite appealing.

Wines/Varietals: Chardonnay ($), Gewürztraminer ($), Riesling ($), White Cha-

blis ($), Blush ($), Cabernet Sauvignon ($$), Merlot ($$), Red (Chelois, $), Virginia Champagne Brut ($$), NV Extra Dry Virginia Champagne ($$).

Piedmont Vineyards

Route 626, PO Box 286
Middleburg, Virginia 22117
tel. (703) 687-5528
Open to the public; est. 1973

In 1973, Elizabeth Furness planted Virginia's first vinifera since colonial times. She was 75 when she embarked upon a new course as a winegrower. Waverly, her Middleburg estate, was a dairy farm until the successful new venture was established. Then, the century-old dairy barn was converted to a winery. The original 15 acres of vineyard has now expanded to 36 acres, 60 percent of it Chardonnay, and 20 percent devoted to Sémillon. Near the end of her life, Furness persuaded her daughter, Elizabeth Worrall, to come back from California and help with the winery. Worrall took over after her mother's death in 1986 and has maintained Piedmont's status as one of Virginia's top wineries. Production has now reached 6,000 cases annually and will gradually increase to about 10,000, though Worrall is not in any hurry. While its great success to date has been in producing white wines, Piedmont will introduce its first red in the fall of 1992.

Piedmont pioneered cultivating Sémillon in Virginia, and its 1991 Sémillon, containing 15 percent Sauvignon Blanc, is the winery's best yet. Piedmont has also produced some of Virginia's best Chardonnay: round and flavorful, elegantly structured with a fine balance. The 1991 Reserve is a real winner. These wines age quite well: Piedmont's 1985 Chardonnay is still lively and appealing, and the 1990 Special Reserve is every bit as good. The regular Chardonnay here tends toward a Mâcon style, reflecting, perhaps, the influence of French winemaker Eric Brévart, who came aboard in 1989. Piedmont makes several fresh, simple white wines from purchased grapes, including Hunt Country White, Little River White, a barrel fermented Seyval Blanc, and a popular blush labeled Virginia Scarlett. The 1991 Piedmont Claret, an attractive blend of Cabernet Sauvignon and Cabernet Franc, is aged in French and American oak. It marks a strong beginning with reds for this winery.

Wines/Varietals: Chardonnay Winemaker Select ($), Chardonnay Special Reserve ($$), Sémillon ($$), Hunt Country White ($), Little River White ($), Seyval Blanc ($), Virginia Scarlett ($), Piedmont Claret ($).

Prince Michel Vineyards

Route 29, H.C.R.#4, Box 77
Leon, Virginia 22725
tel. (703) 547-3707; fax (703) 547-3088
Open to the public; est. 1983

Prince Michel Vineyards is Virginia's largest winery, with 130 acres under vine near Culpeper, Virginia (an additional 25 acres are owned in California's Napa Valley). The winery's owner, French industrialist Jean Leducq, has made a major commitment in Virginia; the corporation he established also owns Rapidan River (*see* separate entry). Prince Michel is planted entirely to vinifera varieties, 45 percent of it in Chardonnay, 25 percent in Cabernet Sauvignon, the rest in Riesling, Merlot, and Pinot Noir. The winery purchases up to 45 percent of its grapes annually to meet its needs for production of 65,000 to 70,000 cases—a level that makes it a major locomotive in the Virginia wine world.

Prince Michel's Meritage red, bottled as "Le Ducq," is a blend of Bordeaux varieties from Virginia and the Napa Valley, blended in unspecified proportions. Big and deeply colored, spicy with new oak and a lot of extract, the wine is priced at $50 a bottle! (To be fair, the 1987 fared well more than once in our blind tastings.) Jean Leducq brings consultant Jacques Boissenot over from Bordeaux several times a year to supervise the crush and winemaking here. Prince Michel also makes good Chardonnay, particularly evident in the 1991 vintage, which sports fine varietal character, following the 1990 Virginia Chardonnay, which showed reasonably well. The winery turns out a nouveau red called "Vavin," and blush and sparkling wines, too.

Wines/Varietals: Chardonnay ($), Chardonnay Barrel Select ($$), White Burgundy ($), Vavin Nouveau ($), Blanc de Michel ($), Blush de Michel ($), Cabernet Barrel Select ($$), Le Ducq ($$$), Blanc de Blancs Sparkling Wine ($$), Blanc de Noirs Sparkling Wine ($$).

Rapidan River Vineyards

H.C.R.#4, Box 77
Leon, Virginia 22725
tel. (703) 547-3707; fax (707) 547-3088
Not open to the public; est. 1981

Founded by physician Gerhard Guth, Rapidan River, with Joachim Hollerith at the helm as winemaker, gained an early reputation for turning out fine, German-style Riesling. Trained at Geisenheim on the Rhine, Hollerith produced some of Virginia's best Riesling in a range of styles, from dry to late-harvest. The winery was acquired by Jean Leducq of Prince Michel Vineyards (a half-hour away) in 1985; Hollerith returned to Germany in 1990. Chris Johnson is the current winemaker , and Jacques Boissent the consulting oenologist. Today, the estate's 50 acres of vineyards are planted over to vinifera: Riesling (30 percent), Chardonnay (35 percent), Gerwürztraminer (5 percent), Merlot (10 percent) and Cabernet Sauvignon (20 percent).

Rapidan continues to make appealing Riesling and Gewürztraminer. The 1990 Semi-Dry Riesling was without flaws: a fine bottle, with clear varietal characteristics, altogether one of the best North American Rieslings we tasted from that year. The 1990 Virginia Gewürztraminer was also a quality effort, with a floral nose and grapefruit and varietal flavors. Other varietals—Merlot, Chardonnay, and Cabernet—are agreeable.

Wines/Varietals: Dry Riesling ($), Riesling Semi-Dry ($), Gewürztraminer ($), Chardonnay ($), Merlot ($), Méthode Champenoise Sparkling Wine ($$).

Shenandoah Vineyards

Route 2, Box 323
Edinburg, Virginia 22824
tel. (703) 984-8699
Open to the public; est. 1977

The family of founder James Randel still owns and operates Shenandoah, one of Virginia's oldest modern wineries. Emma Randel, now president of the winery, returned from New Jersey to her native Shenandoah Valley with her late husband, James, and together they bought a modest vineyard. The rest, as they say, is history. Today, 40 acres of Shenandoah vineyards are planted to vinifera, including Riesling and Chardonnay, and several French hybrids.

Shenandoah wines are, for the most part, quite fruity, notably the dry, attractive Seyval Blanc and the lightly sweet Vidal. The win-

ery produces several blends ranging from off-dry to quite sweet. Shenandoah merits recognition for its consistent work with Chambourcin and for its pioneering efforts in the Shenandoah Valley, long known for agricultural abundance but not for high-quality winemaking.

Wines/Varietals: Vignoles ($), Chardonnay ($$), Seyval Blanc ($), Johannisberg Riesling ($), Shenandoah Blanc ($), Vidal Blanc ($), Sweet Serenade ($), Blushing Belle ($), Shenandoah Rosé ($), Shenandoah Rouge ($), Shenandoah Ruby ($), Fiesta ($), Chambourcin ($).

Simeon Vineyards

R.F.D.#9, Box 293
Charlottesville, Virginia 22902
tel. (804) 229-0999
Open to the public by appt.; est. 1983

Stanley Woodward, a state department official and former ambassador to Canada, started Simeon Vineyards in the early eighties. Woodward died in the summer of 1992, leaving the winery to his son, Stanley, Jr. The 750-acre farm is set on the outskirts of Charlottesville and is part of the tract of land near Monticello that Thomas Jefferson gave to Filippo Mazzei in 1774. Mazzei, an Italian, planted a vinifera vineyard here, but it was destroyed by troops during the Revolutionary War. Simeon's winemaker today comes from Italy: Gabriele Rausse, who was the first winemaker at Barboursville Vineyards. Rausse made Simeon's first wines in 1983; the winery has since grown to an annual production of about 4,500 cases.

The wines made here are mostly clean and fruity; the Chardonnay is light and crisp, the Merlot berryish, the Vin Gris dry and appealing.

81

Wines/Varietals: Chardonnay ($$), Chenin Blanc ($), Vin Gris de Pinot Noir ($), Merlot ($$), Pinot Grigio ($$), Pinot Noir ($$), Cabernet Sauvignon ($$).

Tarara

13648 Tarara Lane
Leesburg, Virginia 22075
tel. (703) 771-7100; fax (703) 771-8443
Open to the public; est. 1989

As owners of one of Virginia's youngest wineries, Ralph (Whitie) Hubert and his son, Michael, have already made their presence felt with lively Chardonnays. Their sizeable estate near Leesburg has 42 acres planted with vinifera and some hybrids, as well as an ornamental nursery, orchards, and vegetable gardens. The Huberts dug a cave to house their 3,000-square-foot winery, which is large enough to handle growing production. Production here, 3,000 cases at present, is projected to eventually reach full capacity at 40,000 cases.

Currently the winery produces Cabernet Sauvignon, Terra Rouge, a semi-dry blend of Chambourcin and Seyval, quite pleasant when served chilled, and Charval, a lively blend of Chardonnay and Seyval Blanc. The 1990 Virginia Barrel fermented Chardonnay put Tarara on the wine map of North America. It's a fine round wine with overtones of butter, pears, and almonds and perfect balance—as the winery's motto proclaims, a "uniquely Virginian wine of outstanding quality." Winemaker Debbi Dellinger, who has worked at Virginian and other East Coast wineries since 1978, is one to watch.

Wines/Varietals: Chardonnay ($$), Cabernet Sauvignon ($$), NV Charval ($), NV Terra Rouge ($), NV Cameo ($).

The Williamsburg Winery, Ltd.

Lake Powell Rd., PO Box 3592
Williamsburg, Virginia 23187
tel. (804) 229-0999; fax (804) 229-0911
Open to the public; est. 1984

Patrick Duffeler felt that historic Williamsburg had everything but a winery, and filled the gap by founding an eponymous operation in 1984. Duffeler and his wife, Peggy, started small, turning out only 3,000 cases annually, but have been so successful that production already nears 40,000 cases. Duffeler draws on 76 acres of vineyard planted primarily to vinifera, more than a third of it in Chardonnay. All the red Bordeaux grape varieties are also in production here, and their prospects for the future bode well. In some years, Duffeler supplements his estate-grown fruit with grapes from other Virginia growers.

Williamsburg has excelled with Chardonnay, due in part to the expertise of California-trained winemaker Steve Warner. Warner makes more than one Chardonnay: his consistently best, labeled "Acte 12 of 1619," is named for a statute enacted by the Jamestown Settlement that required all colonists to plant 10 grape vines. With its well-defined Chardonnay character and toasty flavors, Acte 12 is one of Virginia's best Chardonnays. The 1990 holds its own with Chardonnays from anywhere in North America; it's lean in style, crisp with citrus and apple flavors, and a hint of oak. The barrel fermented Vintage Reserve Chardonnay is the pick of best grape lots, and is also impressive. Reds are now getting more attention here, as well. Williamsburg produces a Meritage red, labeled Gabriel Archer Reserve. The winery also makes an attractive everyday white blend, James River White.

Wines/Varietals: Chardonnay ($), Acte 12 Chardonnay ($$), Vintage Reserve Chardonnay ($$), James River White ($), Plantation Blush ($), Governor's White (Riesling and Vidal, $), Merlot ($$), Cabernet Sauvignon ($$), Gabriel Archer Reserve (Meritage red, $$$).

West Virginia

Robert F. Pliska and Company Winery

101 Piterra Place
Purgitsville, West Virginia 26852-0101
tel. (800) 841-3652 or (304) 289-3493
Open to the public; est. 1983

Who would have thought a Pliska wine from West Virginia would show up on the dinner table at the American Embassy in Paris? It was a Maréchal Foch and very well received, indeed. (Subsequently, a Burgundian winery owner, on a visit to America, made a detour to West Virginia to see how they had produced such an impressive wine.) And who would have thought Julia Child would have used—and recommended—a Pliska wine on her TV cooking show, or that Lech Walesa would have been served one at a luncheon in Chicago, or that the U.S.S. West Virginia would be christened with a bottle of Pliska's sparkling wine? Impressive as these credentials are, they are perhaps topped by the fact that the Pliska Winery is operated for the benefit of, and to provide employment for, mentally-handicapped adults, many of whom live on

the estate. Founded by Robert Pliska, a professor of management philosophy, and a winemaker with a master's degree in enology, and his wife, Dr. Ruth E. Haley-Pliska, the winery's president and an expert in the care of the mentally retarded, the winery today produces 1,400 cases annually. The 14 acres of vineyards here are planted over to Foch (4), Seyval Blanc (5), Aurora (4), and Chancellor (1). The winery is well-situated in the Potomac Highland; four other West Virginia wineries are neighbors.

Wines produced at this winery are released under two labels: 101 Piterra Place and Assumption. An apple wine is also bottled and labeled "Mountain Mama Apple Wine." The 101 Piterra Place Foch is arguably the top wine made here: dry, balanced, and full flavored, as evidenced in the 1990 bottling. With the exception of the semi-dry Ridge Runner Red, all Pliska-made wines are vinified dry. A tiny amount of sparkling wine is also produced.

Wines/Varietals: St. Vincent Seyval ($), 101 Piterra Place Foch ($), Assumption Aurora ($), 101 Piterra Place Chancellor ($$), Quincentennial Cabernet ($$$), 101 Piterra Place Ridge Runner Red ($).

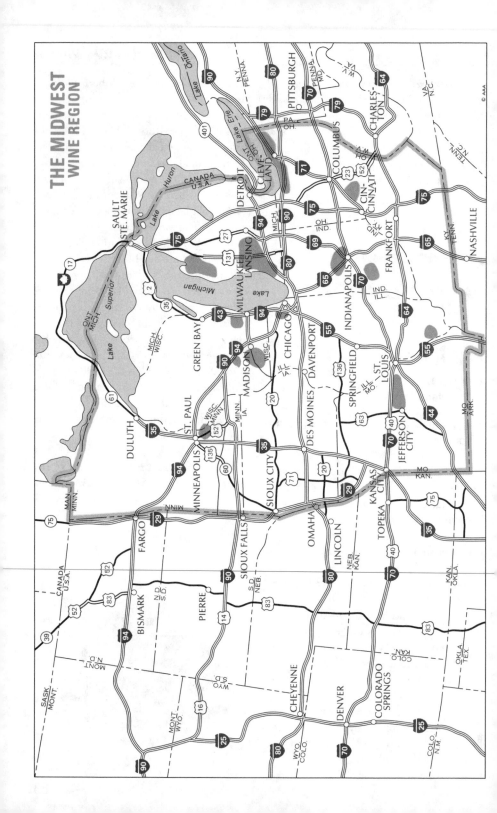

THE MIDWEST
WINE REGION

The Midwest

The Big Chill Factor

AS the American wine industry comes of age, the trend everywhere—including in the nation's midsection and on its broad prairies and plains—is toward *vitis vinifera*. In the Midwest, however, vinifera faces its toughest test. The severe winter cold here has wiped out many a dedicated effort at grapegrowing. Arctic storms sweep down from Canada and across the unprotected plains, bringing subzero temperatures that can linger for days or even weeks. A persistent winter freeze will kill primary and secondary grape buds, destroying a year's crop and inevitably damaging all but the very strongest vines.

Despite this hazard, a few growers have succeeded with vinifera, particularly in microclimates where moderating conditions exist. On Michigan's upper peninsula (the Leelanau viticultural area), which juts into Lake Michigan, for example, Riesling, Chardonnay, and other vinifera are grown successfully. Vinifera vineyards also flourish in the well-established fruit belt of southwestern Michigan, south of Grand Rapids. And the Lake Erie escarpment in Ohio, east of Cleveland, supports vinifera, too (as, incidentally, to a limited extent, do the Ozark plateaus in Arkansas).

Native grape varieties such as Concord and Catawba, mostly used for grape juice (though some is made into Cold Duck—invented in Michigan—and some into sweet and fortified wines), still make up the bulk of the vines cultivated in the Midwest. French hybrids such as Vignoles, Seyval Blanc, Vidal,

Chancellor, Chambourcin, and Maréchal Foch are more viable as wine grapes than vinifera at present, though efforts with the latter persist. Kansas' three small wineries all work with French hybrids, and Iowa's wineries (with a regional wine heritage dating far back into the 1800s) are better known today for their fruit wines than for their French hybrids. Minnesota's handful of young wineries falls into the same category: some hybrids are produced, along with fruit wines, and, it should be added, sparkling wines. One of the most intriguing native grapes, the Norton, or Cynthiana, which produces a sturdy, firm-structured red wine that might be called "the claret of the Ozarks," receives serious attention in the Ozark highlands of Missouri and Arkansas.

Wisconsin claims an especially noble vinous heritage. Count Agoston Haraszthy, the nineteenth century Hungarian nobleman and adventurer who founded Buena Vista Winery in Sonoma, California, established his first North American winery in Wisconsin, across the Wisconsin River from what is now Sauk City. Remnants of the old stone winery and storage caves still exist on the property now owned by Wollersheim Vineyards. Though Wollersheim has a consistent record of producing sound reds, it doesn't seem to have inspired others to grow grapes in Wisconsin—and even Wollersheim buys grapes, especially vinifera, from out of state. Fruit wines are still the most interesting wines produced in Wisconsin.

Purchasing grapes from California, Washington, New York, or Michigan, is the preferred supply route for Illinois' handful of wineries. Tiny Alto Vineyards, however, produces very appealing, quite stylish wines from such homegrown hybrid varieties as Vignoles and Chambourcin.

Michigan: In Quest of Resistant Varieties

As noted, Michigan's two principal growing regions are in its southwest corner and on its northern peninsula; the climate in both areas is moderated by the vast, deep waters of Lake Michigan. Michigan's largest winery, St. Julian, started out cultivating native grapes such as Concord and Catawba, which are capable of withstanding severe cold. During the 1960s and 1970s, French hybrids (known locally as "resistant" varieties) were planted, and today produce some of the state's best wines, particularly from such white varieties as Seyval, Vidal, and Vignoles, the latter made in both sweet and late-harvest versions. Among red grapes, Chambourcin has shown an interesting versatility in this state, producing quite fruity wine (some say Burgundian), when whole-cluster fermentation is employed, and a firmer red that takes well to barrel aging when other fermentation techniques are used. Chancellor and Maréchal Foch are the other reds widely planted in Michigan.

Lately, vinifera plantings are expanding here as they are in regional vineyards elsewhere. Riesling and Gewürztraminer have done well for some time, and more recent experiments with Chardonnay, Pinot Gris, Pinot Blanc, and Pinot Noir have proven equally successful and will undoubtedly increase in the years to come. A new hybrid developed in New York (with considerable input from Michigan grape scientists), the Chardonnel, a cross between Chardonnay and Seyval Blanc, has also shown promise. It yields a dry, full-bodied white that takes well to barrel fermentation and *sur lie* techniques. And it withstands cold better than Chardonnay. Chardonnay and Pinot Noir are used for making sparkling wine here in most years, though in exceptional vintages these varietals make good, ageable still wines. Wineries located in Michigan's fruit belts also make good fruit wines.

Missouri: In the German Style

It is Missouri that bears the brunt of those blasts of frigid air known as "Albert Clippers" that zing down from Canada, soundly defeating local efforts with vinifera varieties. Perhaps the cold-resistant Chardonnel will perform well here, but currently the greatest success is with French hybrids like Vignoles, Vidal Blanc, Seyval, Chambourcin and natives like the Cynthiana, or Norton. Most local wineries call the grape Cynthiana, but Missouri's oldest winery, Stone Hill Vineyards in Hermann, prefers the name Norton, for Dr. Daniel Norton, the eighteenth-century grape breeder from Virginia who developed what he dubbed "Virginia seedling." The grape, *vitis rotundifolia cynthiana,* produces a sturdy red, quite dry with rustic fruit, but no hint of the wild grapey flavors that characterize concord and other native American varieties. It is aged in wood for up to two years, and when well-balanced, will keep for five to seven years. As growers and winemakers gain experience with Cynthiana, it may indeed live up to its potential as a claret-style red.

The Ozark highlands of Missouri were settled largely by German immigrants. Even today, the best wines produced here are Germanic in style: crisp, white wines mostly, that range from lightly sweet to quite sweet dessert wines. The most stylish whites made in this area are Vidal Blanc, Seyval Blanc, and Vignoles. A few new winegrowers are presently gearing up to give an added boost to Missouri's growing wine industry.

Ohio: Pioneering Vintners

One of the nation's oldest wine industries—predating California's by half a century—took root in Ohio in the 1820s. Nicholas Longworth, a Cincinnati lawyer and financier, envisioned the banks of the Ohio River becoming the "Rhineland of America." He planted the native hybrid grape, Catawba, which is hardy enough to withstand Ohio winters, on the river banks near Cincinnati. In 1845, Ohio produced some 300,000 gallons of wine, and by 1860 led the nation in wine production. Within a decade, however, Ohio vineyards lay in ruins, wiped out by black rot and mildew. Late in the century, cultivation of the vine shifted north to small islands off the southern shores of Lake Erie, which were blessed with favorable climates, the northern cold tempered by the lake. Vineyards of mostly native labrusca varieties were planted largely by German immigrants. By the turn of the century, a wine renaissance was underway, only to be foiled by Prohibition.

After Repeal in 1933, it was another three decades before the industry turned the corner into the modern era of grape growing. In the mid-1960s, a few Ohio growers began to plant French-American hybrids such as Seyval Blanc, Vignoles, Vidal, and Chambourcin. In the 1970s and 1980s, vinifera varieties began to prosper in the state, pioneered by small wineries such as Markko Vineyard, Firelands and Chalet Debonné. In 1965, there were 20 wineries in Ohio; today there are 50, including some of the largest in the U.S., such as Meier's. As in most other states, however, it is the small wineries that aim for quality and that have done pioneering work with vinifera, including Chardonnay, Riesling, and Cabernet Sauvignon.

Illinois

Alto Vineyards
Highway 127
Alto Pass, Illinois 62905
tel. (618) 893-4898
Open to the public weekends, weekdays
by appt.; est. 1988

Tiny Alto Vineyards, a 1,600-case-a-year winery in southwestern Illinois, has only produced wine a few years, but its output is already impressive. Guy Renzaglia, a retired university professor, started growing grapes in 1982 on a site very near the Mississippi River. The first plantings were a mix of Chardonnay, Riesling, and French hybrids. The vinifera could not survive the extreme cold of the Illinois winter, so Renzaglia concentrated on French hybrids.

The 10-acre vineyard produces appealing, well-balanced whites such as dry Vidal Blanc and Vignoles, and attractive, fruity, big reds from Chambourcin and Chancellor. We enjoyed the 1989 Chambourcin's good balance, surprising softness for a big wine, and its characteristically mild vegetal character, good grape flavors and long finish. The dry Vidal in particular has crisp, stylish fruit with clean lines very suitable for pairing with fish and other light foods. The 1990 Vidal bore marked acidity and some vegetal flavors as well as good balance. The reds produced here are fruity and well-balanced with none of the hard bitterness often associated with hybrid reds.

Wines/Varietals: , *Vignoles ($$),* , *Chancellor ($),* *Autumn Rosé ($), Heartland Blush ($).*

Lynfred Winery
15 South Roselle Road
Roselle, Illinois 60172
tel. (708) 529-9463; fax (708) 529-4971
Open to the public; est. 1977

Fred Koehler was more interested in making good wine than in trying to buck the odds against successfully growing grapes in Illinois. When he decided to become a winemaker, he imported grapes from California and Michigan; he continues to do so today. Fred and his wife, Lynn, renovated a 1912 residence in Roselle, converting the basement into a fermentation and storage cellar, and the upstairs area into a tasting room. They now produce 10,000 cases annually from purchased grapes and other fruit.

Lynfred wines, particularly the Chardonnay, have won a number of medals in competition. The Koehlers produce over 20 wines, including vinifera, hybrids, and fruit wines. Though Koehler favors his Chenin Blanc made of California grapes from Ventana Vineyards in Monterey, we prefer simple Fred's Red. A spicy and deep American blend, it's a good pizza wine. We also recommend the vintage fruit wines, especially the raspberry and the rhubarb.

Wines/Varietals: Chenin Blanc ($), Chardonnay ($$), Vintner's Reserve Chardonnay ($$), White Riesling ($$), Vidal Blanc ($$), Fumé Blanc ($$), Gewürztraminer ($), Villard Blanc ($), Cabernet Sauvignon Knight's Valley ($$), Merlot ($$), Chambourcin ($$), Chancellor ($$), Carignane ($), Pinot Noir ($$), Zinfandel ($$), Fred's Red ($), Fruit Wines (Pear, Strawberry, Rhubarb, Raspberry, Red Currant, Blackberry, Apple, $), Select Harvest Muscat Blanc (375 ml, $$), Semi-Dry Johannisberg Riesling ($).

Dinner guests who thrive on a tumultuous environment and faddish overpriced cuisine won't thrive at Adrienne. However, those who prefer haute to hot will. For classic cuisine and impeccable service, in a setting of timeless elegance, join us for dinner. Things are popping here five nights a week. For reservations Tuesday through Saturday, please call 212-903-3918 or 800-262-9467.

OUR VERSION OF POP CULTURE.

NEW YORK

HÔTEL PLAZA ATHÉNÉE

37 East 64th Street
New York, New York 10021
(212) 734-9100
Telefax: (212) 772-0958
Telex: 6972900

one of

The Leading Hotels of the World®

NEW YORK

For an extraordinary culinary experience for Lunch or Dinner with reasonable prices, any connoisseur will tell you that Le Cirque is the place. Here you will find one of the most exciting, elegant and cheerful atmospheres in New York.

Le Cirque restaurant is owned and managed by the flamboyant and famed restaurateur Sirio Maccioni. Every day the Chef and his crew create extraordinary dishes ranging from classical french cuisine to the variations of contemporary french haute cuisine.

Excellent service and an awarded wine list make Le Cirque one of the most cherished and renowned restaurants in the world.

LE CIRQUE
58 E. 65th Street • New York
(212) 794-9292

FRENCH RESTAURANT

★ ★ ★

New York Times–May 1st, 1992
Forbes–Gourmet

- Parties up to 100
- Discount Parking after 5:30 PM
- Within walking distance to Theatre District

4 West 49 St. (West of 5th Ave.)
247-2993
Rockefeller Center

Indiana

Oliver Wine Company, Inc.
8024 North State Road 37
Bloomington, Indiana 47404
tel. (800) 25-TASTE or (812) 876-5800;
fax (812) 876-9309
Open to the public; est. 1972

Chateau Thomas Winery
501 Madison Avenue
Indianapolis, Indiana 46225
tel. (800) 899-8466 or (317) 635-WINE
Open to the public; est. 1984

Dr. Charles R. Thomas, an Indianapolis physician, loves and collects wine. With a palate attuned to the tastes of European wines, he strives to make the kind of wines he likes to drink. Instead of trying to grow grape varieties suited to the Midwest, he imports fruit from some of California's best growing regions: Merlot and Sauvignon Blanc from Oakville, Cabernet Sauvignon from Rutherford, Chardonnay and Pinot Noir from Carneros.

Dr. Thomas produces eight varietals at his 6,000-case-a-year winery. They are well-made and quite drinkable wines, available at the winery in Indianapolis and at local restaurants. Over 50 percent of production is Chardonnay and Cabernet Sauvignon, with Chenin Blanc amounting to 28 percent. Merlot, Sauvignon Blanc, Zinfandel, and Pinot Noir round out the production. The 1988 Chardonnay and the 1987 Cabernet Sauvignon proved the merits of Thomas's efforts; his Merlot is also promising.

Wines/Varietals: Merlot ($$), Cabernet Sauvignon ($$), Pinot Noir ($$), Chardonnay ($$), Sauvignon Blanc ($), Zinfandel Late Harvest ($$).

William Oliver, a professor of law at the University of Indiana, and his wife, Mary, established one of Indiana's first farm wineries since Prohibition. Oliver, who turned out homemade wine as a hobby, persuaded state lawmakers to pass a farm winery law in 1971; the following year he planted his own vineyard a few miles north of Bloomington. Growing grapes, however, proved difficult in this part of Indiana: midwinter thaws, followed by severe freezes, often killed the vines. After two or three disastrous winters in a row, Oliver gave up the vineyard, but continued to make wine, purchasing grapes from eastern Washington, California, and the Finger Lakes region of New York.

Oliver now makes 12,600 cases a year from vinifera varietals and semi-dry and sweet hybrids; he also produces native wines from Niagara, Catawba and Concord grapes, and fruit wines like Hummingbird (a semi-dry, peach-raspberry-honey blend) and Camelot Mead (made from Indiana honey). The winery's 1989 Merlot, made from Washington State grapes, is an especially pleasant bottle with a big, peppery yet sweet nose and a fruity, light body that drinks well young. The 1990 Sauvignon Blanc, a good and complex wine, fares well in any comparison tasting.

Wines/Varietals: Sémillon ($), Sauvignon Blanc ($), Merlot ($), Chenin Blanc ($), Gewürztraminer ($), Seyval Blanc ($), Hummingbird ($), Riesling ($), Champagne Brut ($$).

Michigan

Château Grand Traverse

12239 Center Road
Traverse City, Michigan 49684
tel. (616) 223-7355; fax (616) 223-4105
Open to the public; est. 1974

Edward O'Keefe went up against the skeptics when he decided to grow wine grapes on the Old Michigan Peninsula, where winter temperatures can drop to 38 degrees below zero. His choice of a microclimate moderated by the deep waters of Lake Michigan, which surrounds the peninsula on three sides, is key to the survival of the 55 acres of vinifera grapes he now has planted. O'Keefe purchased grapes from California growers to supplement production until his own vines began to thrive. The winery continues to buy about 15 percent of the fruit needed for production of 20,000 cases annually, but only Michigan-grown grapes are used for the house's primary label, Château Grand Traverse.

Riesling, made in a variety of styles from dry to late-harvest to sparkling, is the most successful wine produced here, particularly the dry and semi-dry versions and a Cherry Riesling (a blend of cherry wine and Riesling). We also enjoyed the 1990 Dry Johannisberg Riesling Old Mission Peninsula, which is crisp and floral with underlying minerals. The 1991 Sur Lie Chardonnay is fresh and attractive. Among Grand Traverse's reds, the Gamay Nouveau has fruity appeal. The Cherry Wine, a natural for this cherry-growing region, is a worthy best-seller.

Wines/Varietals: Riesling Dry ($), Dry Select Harvest Riesling ($$), Semi-Dry Riesling ($), Late Harvest Riesling ($$), Ice Wine ($$$), Chardonnay Sur Lie ($), Barrel Fermented Chardonnay ($$), Merlot ($$), Pinot Noir ($$), Cherry Wine ($), Cherry Riesling ($), Spiced Cherry Wine ($).

Fenn Valley Vineyards, Inc.

6130 122nd Avenue
Fennville, Michigan 49408
tel. /fax (616) 561-2396
Open to the public; est. 1973

Fenn Valley Vineyards' 50 acres of vinifera and French hybrid grapes are planted on a sandy ridge just five miles from Lake Michigan in Michigan's southwestern fruit belt. William Welsch bought this 230-acre farm in 1972 and selected a site for his vineyard after reviewing weather, climate, and soil maps. The site, which provides good sun, air, and drainage for a longer growing season, was cleared of fruit trees in 1973 and planted to French hybrids such as Seyval Blanc, Chancellor, Foch, and Chambourcin. Later experiments with vinifera varieties proved successful; the Welsch family has now added Riesling, Chardonnay, Gewürztraminer, Pinot Gris, and Pinot Noir vines. Fenn Valley also grows the new hybrid Chardonnel, a cross of Seyval Blanc and Chardonnay, which shows great promise for growing in colder regions.

The vineyard supplies all the required fruit for the winery's 4,000-case annual production. Welsch's son, Doug, is the winemaker here and his daughter, Diana, is office and marketing manager. Doug makes a point of never employing pasteurization or using preservatives in making Fenn Valley wines. His best red is a robust Chancellor, rather angular in youth with dark, plummy fruit and tannins, that needs a few years in bottle to drink well. Fenn Valley Chardonnel is lightly Chablis-like in character. The off-dry Riesling has lively green-apple flavors and is quite appealing (the 1989 was the best effort to date), and a late harvest Vignoles is luscious. Recent efforts with Pinot Gris and Pinot Noir show promise, too.

Wines/Varietals: Chardonnay ($), Chardonnel ($), Pinot Gris ($$), Pinot Noir ($$), Johannisberg Riesling ($), Late Harvest Vignoles ($$), Lakeshore White ($), Lakeshore Sunset ($), Lakeshore Red ($), Chancellor ($).

Madron Lake Hills

14387 Madron Lake Road
Buchanan, Michigan 49107
tel. (616) 695-5660
Open to the public by appt.; est. 1982

This young winery in southwestern Michigan's fruit belt is devoted exclusively to vinifera varieties—unusual in this northerly region. Madron Lake's principals, founder James Eschner, and partners Franz-Bernard Lickteig and James Lester, are convinced that this is the only way to go. They planted their 23-acre vineyard primarily to Chardonnay and White Riesling, but there are over five acres of red grapes, too, including two acres of Pinot Noir. Eschner has particularly high hopes for Pinot and is expanding planting of this grape as a result of its success in his experimental vineyard. Eschner also experiments with Barbera, Gamay, Pinot Gris and other grapes. Currently, the 4,000-case-a-year winery purchases anywhere from 25 to 60 percent of the grapes it requires from Michigan, the Lake Erie region of Ohio, Pennsylvania and New York.

Madron Lake Chardonnay, with its light touch of oak and crisp acidity, is an attractive wine. This winery's Riesling and Gewürztraminer are floral in character, with high acidity balancing a light sweetness. Late-harvest styles are also made here; the 1990 Late Harvest Semi-dry Riesling shows the winery at its best. And if you want to try a Michigan Chardonnay, you won't be displeased with the 1988 vintage produced here. (The 1990 was almost as good.) Madron Lake Hills HeartLand Vineyards Claret, a blend of Bordeaux grapes, is light and taut. The future looks bright for this winery's Pinot Noir and Gamay.

Wines/Varietals: HeartLand Vineyards Chardonnay ($$), White Riesling ($), Estate White Riesling Selected Late Harvest ($$), Estate Pinot Noir ($$), Estate Gewürztraminer Selected Late Harvest ($$), HeartLand Vineyards Claret ($$).

L. Mawby Vineyards

4561 South Elm Valley Road
Suttons Bay, Michigan 49682
tel. (616) 271-3522
Open to the public; est. 1978

Larry Mawby's 12 acres of French hybrids and vinifera were first planted in 1973. Mawby makes only about 2,500 cases of wine a year and plans to remain small; he will add perhaps four to six acres of grapes in the coming years and may increase production to 3,000 cases. The winery here is best known for producing dry, barrel fermented Vignoles and sparkling wines made by the *méthode champenoise,* and for several proprietary wines with punny names (Shard O'Neigh, for instance, is a barrel-aged red made from De Chaunac, and Turkey Red is a nouveau-style red made from Maréchal Foch).

Mawby is now growing several of the Pinot varieties thought to be particularly suited to colder climes, including Pinot Noir, Pinot Gris, Pinot Blanc, Pinot Auxerrois and Pinot Meunier. Most are used for the house's Brut sparkling wines, but can also be expected to do well as table wines. We enjoyed the 1988 Estate Reserve Vignoles.

Wines/Varietals: Vignoles ($), P.G.W. Pun ($), Big Two Heart ($), Brut Méthode Champenoise Sparkling Wine ($$), Blanc de Très Blancs Sparkling Wine ($$), Sandpiper (white, $).

St. Julian
Wine Company, Inc.

716 Kalamazoo Rd., PO Box 127
Paw Paw, Michigan 49079
tel. (616) 657-5568; fax (616) 657-5743
Open to the public; est. 1921

One of Michigan's largest wineries, St. Julian is owned by the Braganini family and named for the patron saint of the Italian town where the winery's founder was born. Fifty thousand cases of wine a year are produced here; the company owns no vineyards, but buys its grapes under contract from growers in the Lake Michigan Shore appellation on the Lake's eastern coast. St. Julian's broad spectrum of labels includes wines made from both vinifera and hybrid grapes.

The winery's most interesting white is its barrel fermented Vignoles, actually richer in flavor and texture than the Chardonnay made here, which is somewhat lighter in structure and taste. St. Julian's best red is Chancellor Reserve, which is fairly firm, but

attractive in vintages that yield ripe fruit. The Chambourcin is a fruitier red, also appealing, as is the oak-aged Village Red, a hearty Italian-style red wine, which we found a tad sweet. We especially admire the 1990 Chambourcin for its good balance and good fruits, with jam and some berry presenting themselves, as well as underlying tannins and a firm acid backbone. St. Julian is particularly proud of its solera-aged cream sherry, a very creditable effort and easily among the very finest produced in North America. Riesling and sparkling wines are also made here.

Wines/Varietals: Vignoles Barrel Fermented ($), Seyval Blanc Reserve ($), Vidal Blanc Reserve ($), Chardonnay ($), Punctual Harvest Riesling ($), Chancellor ($), Chambourcin ($), Solera Cream Sherry ($$), Ice Wine (375 ml, $$$), Brut Champagne ($), Raspberry Champagne ($), White Champagne ($), Van Buren Port ($).

Minnesota

Alexis Bailly Vineyard

18200 Kirby Avenue
Hastings, Minnesota 55033
tel. (612) 437-1413
Open to the public; est. 1976

This 12-acre vineyard owned by Nan Bailly bears the distinction of having produced the first wine ever from 100 percent Minnesota-grown grapes—and every vintage bottled has won national awards. To combat the effects of Minnesota winter temperatures that can plummet to 40 degrees below zero, vines here are laid beneath six to ten inches of soil and covered with a protective layer of snow. Sixty percent of the 12 acres of this winery's Upper Mississippi River Valley vineyards is devoted to Maréchal Foch vines, 30 percent to Léon Millot, and the rest to Seyval Blanc and other hybrids. Buying about 25 percent of the required grapes, Bailly produces about 2,000 cases annually.

The winery's best wine is, not surprisingly, its Maréchal Foch, which in 1990 was distinctive, with smokey, earthy yet soft varietal flavors and light to medium body. The regular Country Red table wine is also a nicely blended effort: medium-bodied, with a range of flavors from vegetables to cherries.

Wines/Varietals: Maréchal Foch ($), Léon Millot ($), Seyval Blanc ($), NV Country Red ($), NV Country White ($), NV Country Rosé ($), NV Hastings Reserve (dessert, $$).

Missouri

Hermannhof
330 East First Street
Hermann, Missouri 65041
tel. (314) 486-5959; fax (314) 486-3311
Open to the public; est. 1978

Grapes were first planted in the town of Hermann in 1843 by Jacob Fugger, a German immigrant, and the local wines have been German in style ever since. Hermannhof, owned by James Dierberg, draws on 40 acres of vineyard planted mostly to French hybrids (Seyval, Vidal, Chambourcin, and Cayuga) and to the na-

tive red grape, here called Norton (elsewhere known as Cynthiana). Annual production is 8,000 cases.

The Germanic style whites made here, especially the barrel fermented Vidal Blanc and off-dry Vignoles, are lightly sweet, clean, crisp, and much improved in recent vintages. Hermannhof's Norton is a firm red, with the added fruitiness of 10 percent Chambourcin. The winery is proudest of its Brut and Blanc de Blancs sparkling wines.

Wines/Varietals: Brut Sparkling Wine ($$), Blanc de Blancs Sparkling Wine ($$), Vignoles ($), Vidal Blanc ($), Vidal Barrel Fermented ($), Norton ($$), Spring Blush ($), White Lady ($), Seyval ($).

Montelle Winery at Osage
Highway 94, Osage Ridge
Augusta, Missouri 63332
tel. (314) 228-4464
Open to the public; est. 1970

Thirty-five miles west of St. Louis, in Daniel Boone country, lies historic Augusta, Missouri, a little town settled by German immigrants on the Lewis and Clark Trail. Just east of town, Montelle Winery sits atop Osage Ridge, a 400-foot bluff overlooking the Missouri River. Founded in 1970 by the late Clayton Byers, Montelle is now owned by Byers' partners, Robert and Judith Slifer and Joanne and William Fitch. The winery here draws on 30 acres of French hybrids and native vines, and buys about 25 percent of the fruit required to produce 6,500 cases annually. About 70 percent of production is white wine, including Vignoles, Vidal Blanc, and a Private Ridge Reserve estate-grown white, aged in French oak.

Winemaker Bob Slifer has won considerable recognition for dry, appealing Vignoles and Vidal Blanc as well as for Montelle's fruity native red, Cynthiana, a medium-bodied and well-balanced example of the "claret of the Ozarks." In addition to table wines, Montelle also produces fruit wines made from fermented fruits such as raspberries.

Wines/Varietals: Cynthiana, Coyote Crossing Vineyard ($$), **Private Ridge Reserve (white, $$), Dry Vignoles ($$),** *Vidal Blanc ($)*, *Chancellor ($), Lewis and Clark (red, $), Red Raspberry ($), Sweet Brier (dessert white, $).*

Mount Pleasant Vineyards

5634 High Street
Augusta, Missouri 63332
tel. (314) 228-4419; fax (314) 228-4426
Open to the public; est. 1881 (in continuous operation since 1967)

Wine buff Lucian Dressel revived a nineteenth-century vineyard and winery in the late sixties. In 1983, on behalf of Augusta growers, he applied for—and was granted—the first official Viticultural Area designation in the U.S. Dressel's 49-acre vineyard is presently planted to Vidal Blanc (25 percent), Cabernet Sauvignon, Merlot, and Cabernet Franc (10 percent), Seyval Blanc (15 percent), St. Vincent (15 percent), and half a dozen other hybrids. Production is up to 15,000 cases annually.

By the mid-eighties, Mount Pleasant was producing a Vintage Port and other wines that garnered several medals in national competitions. Mount Pleasant has produced some attractive wines, including well-balanced, clean-flavored Vidal Blanc, a sweet ice wine (1989 is a good effort), light but pleasant Chardonnay, a native red Cynthiana and the acclaimed Vintage Port. The 1988

Port is a nice one in a stewed prunes, ripe, soft style that's a fine finish to a supper of Southern cooking.

Wines/Varietals: Vintage Port ($$), Ice Wine ($$), Chardonnay, Les Copain Vineyard ($$), Private Reserve Red (Bordeaux blend, $$), Vidal Blanc ($), Seyval Blanc ($), Brut Imperial ($$), Augusta Village (red ,$), Mead ($).

Stone Hill Winery

Route One, Box 26
Hermann, Missouri 65041
tel. (314) 486-2120; fax (314) 486-3828
Open to the public; est. 1847 (in continuous operation since 1965)

Missouri's oldest winery was closed down during Prohibition; its handsome, vaulted, stone cellars were then used for growing mushrooms. But in its heyday, Stone Hill helped put Missouri on the map as a major wine producer. On display today in the winery's tasting room are colorful historic labels and medals awarded at various world fairs, including the 1900 Paris Exposition. In 1965, local farmers Jim and Betty Held re-opened the winery. Though it took several years to renovate the cellars and establish the 61-acre vineyard, Stone Hill has steadily grown in size and quality to its current position as Missouri's foremost winery.

The Held family is fully involved in all aspects of the operation here. Three of the four Held children hold degrees in enology and/or viticulture: viticulturist Jon is Stone Hill's general manager and enologist Patty is sales manager. The Helds experimented briefly with vinifera, but now focus exclusively on hybrids and the native red variety, Norton. To meet growing production (now 41,000 cases annually), the Helds purchase additional grapes to supplement the yield of their own vineyard. Winemaker David Johnson produces a firm-structured red from the Norton grape (he is especially proud of the 1988, which is a good choice for someone wanting to experience this variety), and stylish whites from Vignoles and Vidal.

Wines/Varietals: Norton ($$), Vignoles ($), Vidal ($), Seyval ($), Barrel Fermented Seyval ($), Hermanner Steinverg ($), Hermannsberger ($), Missouri Riesling ($), Pink Catawba ($), Blush ($), Harvest Peach ($), Rose Montaigne ($), Golden Rhine ($), Concord ($), Spumante Blush ($), Golden Spumante ($), Missouri Champagne ($$).

Ohio

Chalet Debonné Vineyards

7743 Doty Road
Madison, Ohio 44057
tel. (216) 466-3485; fax (216) 466-6753
Open to the public; est.1971

In 1916, Anton Debevec planted his first grape crop in the Grand River Valley, in Madison, along the south shore of Lake Erie. Four generations of Debevecs have now worked in the vineyards here: the current winery, established in 1971, is very much a family affair. Tony Debevec, who holds a degree in horticulture and is president of the winery, made a crucial decision in 1984, when he hired Tony Carlucci as winemaker. Carlucci brought with him a degree in enology, California winemaking experience, and the ability to produce premium varietal wines utilizing advanced vinification techniques. The winery subsequently moved

further away from the labruscas it had become known for in the early 1970s, and now produces a wide range of styles and types of wines: American and French/American hybrid and vinifera grapes are currently made into red, white, rosé, and sparkling wines. Currently, 18,000 cases are produced annually (making this the third largest winery in the state) from 65 acres of estate grapes and additional grapes purchased from Ohio, Pennsylvania, and New York .

Judging by the bottles we've tasted, this is a top midwestern winery. Chalet Debonné's satisfying and intriguing Chardonnay is barrel fermented, *sur lie*, eight to ten months in white oak barrels made from trees grown on the Debevec Farm, and is then assembled in Higbee, Missouri. The 1991 is their best Chardonnay to date, nicely fruity with appley and butter flavors, and superb balance and finish within a lighter style. The Grand River Valley Johannisberg Riesling reflects well this winery's philosophy and noteworthy achievement in quality; yet, we were more impressed with the Vidal and the Chambourcin, the latter put through malolactic fermentation and aged six months in oak barrels. The best of this house's many wines are marketed as the Debonné Vineyards Premium Line. The 1990 Chambourcin—medium-light body, well-made with grapey fruit flavor—provides very easy drinking. The 1990 Vidal Blanc stands out strongly among examples of this variety made in North America. It possesses a beautiful floral nose and balanced body, semi-dry sweetness, and a long finish.

Wines/Varietals: Seyval ($), Chardonnay ($), Chardonnay Private Reserve ($$), Vignoles ($), Johannisberg Riesling, American ($), Johannisberg Riesling, Ohio ($), Vidal Blanc ($), Cabernet Sauvignon ($), Chambourcin

*($), Classic White ($), Niagara ($), Reflec-
tions (Vidal Blanc, $), Seyval ($), Vignoles
($), Erie Shores Chablis ($), Delaware ($),
Pink Catawba ($), Rosé ($), Classic Red ($),
River Rouge ($), Debonné Blush ($), Brut
(méthode champenoise, $$).*

Firelands Winery
917 Barshar Road
Sandusky, Ohio 44870
tel. (800) 548-9463 or (419) 625-5474
Open to the public; est. 1880

Firelands occupies the site of the original
Mantey Vineyards, founded by Edward
Mantey in 1880. The property was bought
in 1980 by Paramount Distillers of Cleve-
land, which also own Meier's Wine Cellars
on Isle St. George in Lake Erie. Under
president Robert Gottesman, a part of this
estate's 22-acre vineyard was replanted dur-
ing the eighties to vinifera and French hy-
brids. The winery also draws upon 170 acres
of vineyards on North Bass Island, 100 of
which are planted to Catawba. (The grapes
travel to the mainland via a three-hour boat
ride.) About 40,000 people a year visit the
winery, which is on the north coast of Ohio.
Firelands produces about 30,000 cases of
wine annually, turning out over 20 different
wines under two labels. Hybrids and vinifera
appear under the Firelands label; native
labruscas under the Mantey label. This is
without a doubt one of the leaders in Ohio's
wine industry.

Firelands makes a truly stylish
Chardonnay: brisk and somewhat Chablis-
like in its austere, minerally character—
kudos to Italian-trained winemaker Claudio
Salvador! The 1990 Barrel Select, with oak
adding depth and complexity to its citrus
flavors, did well in our tastings—and in the
company of some renowned California

Chardonnays. The winery also does a nice
job with Riesling and Gewürztraminer. The
sound, peppery Cabernet Sauvignon pro-
duced here provides proof that Firelands
does a good job growing and vinifying vinif-
era. The house's two sparkling wines are also
worthy of note. Using the traditional Cham-
pagne method, Firelands produces a Brut
from Chardonnay and Pinot Noir grapes,
and a semi-dry sparkler from Riesling. Both
are well made, and the Riesling is one of the
best of its kind. Firelands' quite drinkable
blush, called White Baco Noir, is Ohio's
answer to white Zinfandel.

*Wines/Varietals: Barrel Select Estate
Chardonnay ($), Estate Gewürztraminer ($),
Estate Johannisberg Riesling ($), White Baco
Noir, Lake Erie ($), Vidal Blanc, Lake Erie
($), Brut Champagne American ($$), Riesling
Champagne, Lake Erie ($), Cabernet
Sauvignon, Lake Erie ($), Country Estate
White ($), Country Estate Red ($), Country
Estate Blush ($).*

Harpersfield Vineyard
6387 Route 307 West
Geneva, Ohio 44041
tel. (216) 466-4739
Open to the public by appt.; est. 1986

We applaud owners Wes and Margaret
Gerlosky for creating this tiny boutique
winery dedicated to producing Ohio wines
of the highest quality, all from vinifera, and
all estate grown. Their 12 acres are planted
to Chardonnay (8 acres), Riesling (3), and
Gewürztraminer (1). Annual production
does not exceed 1,200 cases, but they are
1,200 cases of the very best white wines
produced in the state.

Acting as winemaker, Wes Gerlosky emphasizes traditional winemaking techniques
such as barrel fermentation (*sur lie*) and

minimal interference with the wine through-out its development. The excellent results are in the bottle. Harpersfield's medal-winning Chardonnay is perhaps the state's best: bigger in body and flavor than what one has come to expect of Ohio vintners.

Wines/Varietals: Chardonnay ($$), Riesling ($), Gewürztraminer ($).

Klingshirn Winery, Inc.

33050 Webber Road
Avon Lake, Ohio 44012
tel. (216) 933-6666
Open to the public; est. 1935

A surplus grape crop in 1935 inspired Albert R. Klingshirn to roll 20 barrels into the cellar of his home and begin commercial wine production, thus establishing this now third-generation family farm in Avon Lake as a noteworthy winery. Present owner Allan Klingshirn, son of the founder, took charge in 1955, and later expanded to four times its original size. The winery today contains complete production facilities from which 4,000 cases of wine are shipped yearly. Sixty percent of production derives from 18 acres of estate grapes; plantings here include White Riesling and Vidal Blanc (14 percent), Seyval Blanc, Delaware, and Concord (40 percent), and miscellaneous vinifera and hybrids.

Klingshirn's youngest son, Lee, now the winemaker here, received his bachelor's degree in viticulture and enology from Ohio State in 1986. His fruity Lake Erie Vidal Blanc is a notable semi-dry effort: light-bodied, perhaps overly sweet, but not without some elegance. Overall, the Klingshirn wines well serve a clientele who prefer semi-dry wines. Even the house's well-regarded White Riesling is vinified semi-dry.

Wines/ Varietals: Niagara ($), Catawba ($), Delaware ($), Vidal Blanc ($), Seyval Blanc ($), Chancellor ($), Concord ($), White Riesling ($), Country Blush ($), Pink Catawba ($), Champagne ($$).

Markko Vineyard

4500 South Ridge Road, R.D.#2
Conneaut, Ohio 44030
Open to the public; est. 1968

Markko may be small, but its influence in Ohio is large. In 1968, Arnulf Esterer and partner Tim Hubbard broke with the more than one hundred-year-old Ohio winemaking tradition of working with native and French-hybrid grapes. Under the guidance of New York's Dr. Konstantin Frank, they boldly planted European vinifera on the shores of Lake Erie. Today their 14 acres of vineyards are planted exclusively in vinifera: Chardonnay (45 percent), Riesling (35 percent), and the rest Cabernet Sauvignon, Pinot Noir, and Pinot Gris. (Okay, there's a speck of Chambourcin grown here as well.) Fifty percent of the 2,000 cases Markko produces annually are Chardonnay.

As can be deduced from the plantings, Chardonnay and Riesling have proved the most successful grapes here. Markko's pioneering efforts with these varietals have influenced virtually the entire Ohio winemaking community, and given rise to several fine boutique wineries. The 1988 Chardonnay, aged two years *sur lie*, is one of this winery's better efforts, though four years after being bottled, it was showing its age in fading fruit and a deep honey color. The lighter 1989 has a more citrus character. The Cabernet Sauvignon is coming into its own lately, especially when blended with Chambourcin, Cabernet Franc, and Merlot

97

(the 1989 was medium-light, somewhat tannic, and lean, with some raspberry overtones, but clearly acceptable on a dinner table). The 1989 Pinot Noir is light and mildy berryish but definitely well-made and acceptable. This winery also produces a blend called Underridge White and a series of non-vintage varietals under the Covered Bridge label.

Wines/Varietals: Chardonnay ($$), Johannisberg Riesling ($), Johannisberg Riesling Reserve ($$), Late Harvest Riesling ($$), Cabernet Sauvignon ($$), Pinot Noir ($$$), Vintage Excelsior Champagne ($$$).

Valley Vineyards Winery

2276 East U.S. 22-3
Morrow, Ohio 45152
tel. (513) 899-2485
Open to the public; est. 1969

Ken Schuchter (aided by brother Jim) planted his first 20 acres of grapes, a mix of French hybrids and a few labruscas like Catawba, Niagara, and Concord, in the late sixties. Since then, Schuchter has been joined by his wife, Beth, daughter, Angela Roosa, son, Kenny, Jr., and daughter-in-law, Dodie. The vineyard has grown to 41 acres, mostly planted to French hybrids with an acre or two of vinifera varieties such as Merlot, Chardonnay, Cabernet, Riesling, and Siegfried. Currently the Schuchters produce about 6,000 cases annually in their chalet-like brick, wood, and stucco winery, which is surrounded by rolling hills and well-landscaped grounds in western Ohio's Little Miami River area.

The Schuchters' personal favorite among their products is a mead, or honey wine. They also make a big-bubble, floral, *méthode champenoise* Blanc de Blancs Sparkling Wine

that's quite palatable. But this operation and its winemaker, Greg Pollman, particularly earn our respect (and a place in this book) for their very fine Vidal Blanc. The 1991, with an attractive bouquet and fresh varietal fruit flavors and balance, is described as semi-sweet, but it's really only slightly sweet and surely a table rather than dessert wine.

Wines/Varietals: Seyval ($), Chablis ($), Niagara ($), Vidal Blanc ($), Valley Blush ($), Valley Rosé ($), Pink Concord ($), Pink Catawba ($), Hillside Red ($), Blue Eye ($), De Chaunac ($), Sangria ($), Honey Wine ($), Valley Champagne ($), Blanc de Blancs Sparkling Wine ($$).

Wisconsin

Cedar Creek Winery

N70 W6340 Bridge Road
Cedarburg, Wisconsin 53012
tel. (800) 827-3020 or (414) 377-8020;
fax (414) 375-9428
Open to the public; est. 1972

Situated 15 miles north of downtown Milwaukee, Cedar Creek Winery is located in an old wool mill that was in operation from 1864 right up until 1969. The building was converted to a winery in 1972, and its cool, limestone cellars are today used for storing the fruit wines and the small production of grape wine made here. In 1990, Robert and JoAnn Wollersheim, owners of the important Wollersheim Winery (*see* below), purchased Cedar Creek and converted it to premium grape wine production under the direction of their French-born winemaker, Philippe Coquard. All of the required grapes are purchased—from Michigan, New York, and Oregon—for the production of 4,500 cases annually.

Both vinifera and French-American hybrids are vinified here; beginning with the 1992 harvest, the winery also makes sparkling wines. The most popular (30 percent of production) and most interesting wine turned out here—probably the best, too—is a curious Cranberry Blush. It's made from New York State grown Seyval Blanc grapes with cranberry juice added. Best served chilled, it is fresh, fruity, spicy and relatively sweet (3.1 percent residual sugar). The mouth-filling flavors are pleasant: more in the watermelon Seyval Blanc zone than strongly cranberry. The Cedar Creek Chardonnay and Cabernet Sauvignon, both made from Oregon grapes, age in French oak. In 1991, good results were had with Vidal made from 100 percent Michigan grapes, vinified in an off-dry fashion. In recent years, the Vidal has won several medals in national competitions.

Wines/Varietals: Cranberry Blush ($), Semi-Dry American Vidal Blanc ($), Riesling ($), Chardonnay ($), Cabernet Sauvignon ($$), Cedar Creek Gold (dessert Seyval Blanc, $).

Wollersheim Winery

Hwy. 188, PO Box 87
Prairie du Sac, Wisconsin 53578
tel. (800) VIP-WINE or (608) 643-6515;
fax (608) 643-8149
Open to the public; est. 1858 (in continuous operation since 1972)

Wollersheim, certainly Wisconsin's most important winery, occupies a significant place in the wine history of North America. Its pedigree was established by Count Agoston Haraszthy in the 1840s. Count Haraszthy planted the first vineyards on this property and his German steward, Peter Kehl, took over the vineyards and constructed the house and winery on a hillside overlooking the Wisconsin River when the Count moved on to California. Kehl used limestone from the hill to craft a big, European-style winery with two-foot thick stone walls and arched underground wine cellars. Things went more or less well for Kehl until 1899, when the vineyards froze. Thereafter, the property was returned to traditional Wisconsin agricultural crops. Enter Robert and JoAnn Wollersheim in 1972. They restored the land and buildings here and replanted the vineyards with French-American hybrids. Today they have 23 acres planted, including some to vinifera (Maréchal Foch 50 percent, Seyval Blanc 20 percent, Léon Millot 15 percent, Pinot Noir 10 percent, and Chardonnay 10 percent). About 50 percent of the grapes required to produce nearly 11,000 cases annually are purchased from outside sources.

Philippe Coquard, a French winemaker from Beaujolais, joined Wollersheim in 1984. He makes dry wines from the vinifera and semi-dry whites from the hybrids by stopping the fermentation process. Among the whites made here, the 1990 and 1991 Prairie Fumé (100 percent Seyval Blanc) are good, simple bottles, not too sweet, with pleasant melon flavors. The 1991 Dry Riesling is also a good bottle in the German *trocken* style, with hints of apricots. Among the reds, the Domaine du Sac Wisconsin Dry Red Wine is a good one, full of dark berry flavors, that drinks well. In 1991, it was made from 80 percent Maréchal Foch and 20 percent Léon Millot estate-grown grapes aged in French and American oak.

Wines/Varietals: Prairie Fumé ($), Riesling ($), Dry Riesling ($), Chardonnay ($), Domaine du Sac ($), Domaine Reserve ($$), Pinot Noir ($$).

99

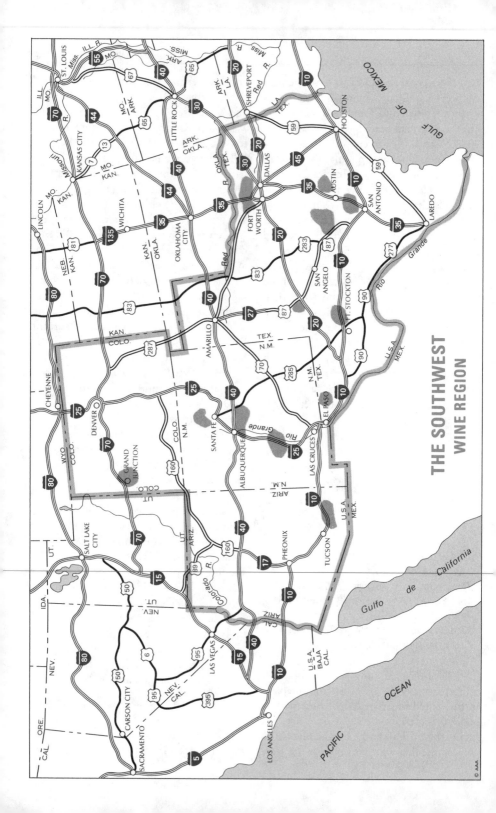

THE SOUTHWEST
WINE REGION

The Southwest

Back in Action

D ESPITE playing a notable role in the early history of winegrowing in North America—New Mexico was the fifth largest wine-producing state prior to Prohibition—the Southwest is one of the newer players in the modern U.S. wine industry. The action today is in the four states: Texas, New Mexico, Arizona, and Colorado. Areas in the Southwest are the most arid in the country, for here are the high desert plateaus of New Mexico and Texas, where rainfall can dwindle to as little as eight inches a year during drought. Green patches of vineyard are often the only touches of color in the dusty landscapes of West Texas: vast stretches of mesquite and tumbleweed are broken only by table-topped mesas and oil rigs. Reliable water sources are vital to agriculture here and vineyards are always situated near rivers, lakes, or reservoirs that can be tapped for irrigation.

The Southwest is also the hottest part of the country: summer temperatures commonly reach 115 degrees in Tucson and Albuquerque. The heat would pose a real obstacle to winegrowing, were it not for the elevation of high desert regions like the Texas hill country and the *llano estacado*, as the high desert plains of northwest Texas are known, the plateaus and valleys along the Rio Grande in New Mexico and southeastern Arizona, and the mountain valleys west of the Rockies in Colorado. In such places, the altitude—more than 5,000 feet in some areas—ameliorates the high temperatures and cools the earth at night. Correspond-

101

ingly, however, these areas can experience severe cold in winter. Most vinifera cannot survive the cold in, for example, the Sangre de Cristo mountains of northern New Mexico.

Currently, the best and most consistently interesting southwestern wines, almost exclusively from vinifera grapes, come from Texas: sound reds from Merlot and Cabernet Sauvignon, and stylish whites from Chardonnay, Sauvignon Blanc, Gewürztraminer, Riesling, and Chenin Blanc. The Southwest is also producing some very good sparkling wines. The region even boasts its own *Southwest International Wine & Food Review*, a bimonthly newsletter published in Sapello, New Mexico.

New Mexico is perhaps the most problematic of the Southwest regions' winegrowers. Out of some 20 wineries, only a handful produce wines of a quality sufficiently consistent to recommend. This is curious, because even French and Swiss concerns have invested in the state, clearly believing that the potential for producing good, palatable wine exists here. One of New Mexico's largest vineyards, in fact—the 250-acre St. Clair Vineyard in the Mimbres Valley near Deming—was planted in the early eighties by a family of vintners from Switzerland. A number of wineries in the state, though they seem to lack consistency, nevertheless produce occasionally interesting bottles. Anderson Valley Vineyards near Albuquerque, one of the state's more accomplished wineries, produces a good Cabernet that hints at the potential here. That more can be achieved is proven by tiny La Chiripada Vineyards. This winery, tucked away in a small valley between Santa Fe and Taos, produces several charming wines, mostly blends made from French hybrids. Currently, New Mexico's biggest success is with sparkling wine, notably from two French-owned and run wineries: Devalmont (the Gruet label) and Domaine Cheurlin.

Colorado's best vineyards are in the valleys west of the Great Divide around Grand Junction, the principal town in the region; there are also a few on the plains east of Denver. In microclimates favorable to red varieties such as Merlot and Cabernet Sauvignon, wineries like Plum Creek Cellars, Colorado Cellars and Pike's Peak (at Colorado Springs, east of the Great Divide) produce flavorful, well-balanced reds as well as attractive whites, notably Chardonnay and Riesling. Though few in number, Colorado wineries are producing some of the Southwest's best Merlot: plummy, well balanced, and flavorful with some aging potential.

Wine production in the state before Prohibition was noteworthy, but Arizona's wine industry today comprises only six wineries, all situated in the southern part of the state below Tucson. The high, fertile valleys around Elgin possess a combination of soil and climate capable of producing good wine. As yet, however, Arizona wines are uneven in quality, reflecting perhaps the youthfulness of the industry in the state. The potential for red wines made from Pinot Noir and Cabernet Sauvignon, whites from Sauvignon Blanc and dry Chenin Blanc (in the style of Vouvray), as well as for sparkling wines, seems promising. There is currently little to recommend without qualification, but this part of the Southwest region bears watching.

Texas: The Home of Native American Rootstock

Texas has a significant history in winemaking, as well as a claim to international fame for having saved European vineyards from the scourge of phylloxera in the late 1800s. Much of the native American rootstock that proved resistant to the dread plant louse was shipped to France from Texas by viticulturalist T.V. Munson of Dennison. Vinifera vines were grafted onto American rootstocks, regenerating the great vineyards of Bordeaux, Burgundy, and Champagne, as well as those of the Rhine and Mosel valleys, the Piedmont, Tuscany, and virtually all other wine regions of Europe (with a few exceptions such as the Rioja and southern Portugal).

Numerous varieties of wild grapes have always grown in Texas. For a long time, the territory of Texas, decades before achieving statehood, was credited with producing America's first wine—in 1662, in the El Paso Valley of West Texas, at a mission established by Spanish padres who had ventured there from Mexico. (Earlier records have now surfaced, indicating that the very first American wine was made on the west coast of Florida by a group of Huguenots sometime in the 1560s.)

Texas can boast of containing one of the country's oldest surviving wineries: Val Verde, situated on the Rio Grande bordering Mexico. Founded in 1883, this winery grew such native wild species as Lenoir and Herbemont, but lately has earned something of a reputation for producing port-like reds. Younger wineries, started in the late seventies and early eighties, have played the largest part in proving Texas to be a viable region for cultivating wine grapes.

Vineyards are today clustered in several areas of the Lone Star State—in the hill country west of Austin, on the plains surrounding the Dallas-Fort Worth area, on the high desert plains in west Texas around Lubbock, in the extreme west near El Paso, and in the Fort Davis Mountains. A little over a decade ago, the University of Texas Land Extension Project experimented on the western plains with several crops as alternatives to cattle ranching. With demand for beef declining, the cost of raising cattle (and supplying them with large amounts of precious water) on vast acres of open grassland had become prohibitive. Wine grapes proved to be one of the crops that offered the best return on investment per acre, so the University planted a thousand acres near Fort Stockton (south of Midland-Odessa) on a trial basis. At one time, the aim was to produce some 600,000 cases of table wine a year. The decline in wine consumption during the late eighties, however, nearly destroyed that pipe dream. Now part of a joint venture between the University and Cordier, one of the largest wine producers in France, production here is scaled to a few hundred thousand cases annually, with wine produced under two labels, Domaine Cordier and Ste. Geneviève.

The best Texas wines to date have come from a handful of small wineries devoted to quality, notably Llano Estacado, Fall Creek Vineyards, and Oberhellmann. Recent comers include Slaughter-Leftwich, Schoppaul-Hill, and Cap*Rock. Due to maturing vines and more skillful winemaking, Texas wines can now be compared favorably with those of California and the Northwest, and have proved themselves winners in national competitions.

Arizona

Callaghan Vineyards
PO Box 530
Sonoita, Arizona 85637
tel. (602) 455-5650
Open to the public by appt.; est. 1991

The Callaghan family, Harold, Karen and son Kent, have bold plans for their young, 18-acre vinifera vineyard. Planted to Bordeaux varieties, plus Pinot Gris, Syrah, Mourvèdre, Marsanne, Zinfandel, and Nebbiolo, most of the vines were just beginning to bear useable fruit in 1993. The Callaghans' vineyard benefits from its high elevation (4,000 to 5,000 feet), which provides cool temperatures at night and the rich, red earth of southeastern Arizona. The focus here is on unfiltered red wines, mainly Cabernet Sauvignon, fermented in small, open-top containers with extended maceration, then aged six to 24 months in oak, 50 percent of which is new. Whites, including Sauvignon Blanc, are partially barrel fermented, and kept on the lees for six months. The first releases in 1992 (approximately 1,500 cases) were varietals, but the Callaghans feel that with blends they are more likely to achieve their goal of producing full-flavored, complex wines capable of aging 10 to 12 years. The barrel samples we tasted encouraged us to select Callaghan for this volume ahead of some more established Arizona wineries.

Wines/Varietals: Sauvignon Blanc ($), Sauvignon Blanc Reserve ($), Cabernet Sauvignon ($$).

Sonoita Vineyards
Canello Rd., HCR Box 33
Elgin, Arizona 85611
tel. (602) 455-5893
Open to the public weekends or by appt.; est. 1983

Professor Gordon Dutt, a soil scientist at Arizona State University, is convinced that the *terra rossa* (red earth) of southeastern Arizona will one day produce some of the country's best Pinot Noir and Cabernet Sauvignon. He and a group of partners established Sonoita's 40-acre vineyard on a high plateau (4,000- to 5,000-foot elevation) and planted exclusively to vinifera. Half of this winery's annual production of 3,000 cases is Cabernet Sauvignon, made in a full-bodied, rugged style.

Sonoita makes white wines from Sauvignon Blanc and Chenin Blanc, the latter in a dry style that aims at Vouvray. It may not quite hit the mark, but in some years, this wine has shown an interesting richness very unlike the simple fruitiness of most American Chenin Blanc. Dutt is also keen to cultivate Pinot Noir, which he believes can achieve Burgundian style in this region. Indeed, Dutt is waging a good fight to deliver on his promise of making excellent wine in Arizona, where there once was a thriving wine industry. Sonita's wines are already more than drinkable. The 1987 Cabernet Reserve has an earthy appeal and is the best we've tasted of this house's wines.

Wines/Varietals: Fumé Blanc ($), Cochise County Colombard ($), Arizona Sunset ($), Sonora Blanca ($), Cabernet Sauvignon Private Reserve ($$), Pinot Noir ($$), Sonora Rossa ($).

Colorado

Plum Creek Cellars

3708 G. Road
Palisade, Colorado 81528
tel. (303) 464-PLUM; fax (303) 399-8073
Open to the public; est. 1984

When the wine bug bit a group of six enthusiasts in Denver, they began making wine at home, and, in the early eighties, formed a business partnership. One of the group, geologist Erik Bruner, was put in charge of making the wine. In 1986, the group had 300 cases of wine to sell. The following year, the Colorado grape harvest was so large (and the partners so committed), that Bruner quit his job and became Plum Creek's winemaker full time. He and his partners soon received affirmation of their venture: their 1987 Merlot won a gold medal at the International Eastern Wine Competition. The winning wine surprised a lot of people with its Colorado roots. It is excellent: dark and full of the berryish flavors typical of good Merlot. In 1990, the partners built a winery in Palisade, a few miles outside of Denver, close to their source of grapes in Mesa and Delta counties. The winery draws on 53 acres of vineyard owned by three of the partners. Planted to Chardonnay (31 acres), Pinot Noir, Riesling, and Merlot, this vineyard supplies about 75 percent of the fruit required for production; the rest is purchased from other Colorado growers. All of Plum Creeks' wines are made from Colorado grapes. The vineyard company also manages additional acreage; there's plenty of room for increased production here in the future.

Over half of Plum Creek's current 2,000-case annual production consists of Chardonnay, including the barrel fermented Redstone Chardonnay introduced in 1991, a lovely, elegantly-balanced wine—rich and complex but not heavy. Grapes for the Redstone come from one of the partners' vineyards on Sunshine Mesa, which at an elevation of 5,800 feet is the highest site of any vineyard in the state. The 1988 Mesa County Chardonnay, also barrel fermented, is very good, too. Merlot remains the principal red produced here, along with a premium blend, made from superior lots of red wines, labeled Grand Mesa. One of Plum Creek's most popular wines is Festival, a fruity blend of Chardonnay and Gewürztraminer. Plum Creek also makes appealing Riesling, in dry and sweet versions.

Wines/Varietals: Redstone Chardonnay ($$), Chardonnay, Mesa County ($), Merlot ($$), Sauvignon Blanc ($), Gewürztraminer ($), Festival ($), Dry Riesling ($), Sweet Riesling ($), Pinot Noir Blanc ($).

New Mexico

Anderson Valley Vineyards
4920 Rio Grande NW
Albuquerque, New Mexico 87107
tel. (505) 344-7266; fax (505) 345-7748
Open to the public; est. 1984

Along the famed Rio Grande River, adjacent to the Andersons' Arabian horse farm and amid reminders of the family's passion for hot air ballooning, sits this 10,000-case-a-year winery. Kris Anderson and his mother, Patty, founded the winery in 1984, after the death (in a ballooning accident) of the clan's patriarch, Maxie Anderson. The vineyard Maxie began as a hobby has today grown to 15 acres; the family leases another 100 acres in southern New Mexico.

The emphasis here is on vinifera, the assumption being that hybrids have no market so close to California. In Anderson Valley's tasting room—a veritable museum recounting New Mexico's rich winemaking history—you can sample Sauvignon Blanc, Cabernet Sauvignon, Johannisberg Riesling, Muscat Canelli and the like. We enjoyed this winery's 1987 New Mexico Cabernet Sauvignon Reserve, a highly creditable bottle, strong in fruit flavors along cassis and raspberry lines, with a hint of herbs and vegetables in the finish. The Sauvignon Blanc is surely drinkable and moderately priced, though it lacks as clear a varietal character as the Cab.

Wines/Varietals: Chardonnay ($), Chenin Blanc ($), White Cabernet ($), White Zinfandel ($), Balloon Blush ($), Johannisberg Riesling ($), Muscat Canelli ($), Burgundy ($), Claret ($), Reserve Cabernet Sauvignon ($), Red Zinfandel ($).

Domaine Cheurlin
PO Box 506
Truth or Consequences, New Mexico 87901
tel. (505) 894-7083; fax. (505) 744-5418
Open to the public weekdays, weekends by appt.; est. 1981

The Cheurlin family has grown grapes in the Champagne region of France for four generations. In the late seventies, Jacques Cheurlin began looking for suitable vineyard land in the U.S. He found it on the high plateaus of New Mexico, where warm days and cool nights provide what he considers optimum conditions for cultivating Chardonnay and Pinot Noir grapes. Domaine Cheurlin's 75 acres are currently planted to 85 percent Chardonnay and 15 percent Pinot; the winery produces about 6,000 cases of sparkling wine annually.

Winemaker Patrice Cheurlin, Jacques' son, produces Domaine Cheurlin Brut and Extra Dry in strict accordance with the *méthode champenoise*. These wines, both non-vintage, are crisp and well balanced; the Extra Dry is perceptibly sweet. The New Mexico Brut, with light toast and pear flavors, is attractive in its well-made simplicity.

Wines/Varietals: NV New Mexico Brut ($$), NV American Brut ($$), NV New Mexico Extra Dry ($$).

See color labels
adjacent to
page 249 for
Southwest wineries

Gruet Winery
3758 Hawkins N.E.
Albuquerque, New Mexico 87109
tel. (505) 344-4453; fax (505) 344-2310
Open to the public weekdays, weekends
by appt.; est. 1987

The Gruet family hails from France's Champagne region, where they founded their first Champagne house in 1952. Faced with little possibility of expanding their operations at home, they set out to establish a second winery outside France. (The Gruet & Fils label in France is employed by a cooperative of 60 growers who specialize in cultivating blanc de blancs grapes and selling directly to the public.) The Gruets looked first in California and then in New Mexico, where they were impressed by the state's history of grapegrowing, dating back to the seventeenth century. Like their fellow Champenois at Domaine Cheurlin, the Gruets determined that New Mexico's soil, altitude, and climate conditions—especially its warm days and cool nights—would present the potential for realizing the very specific aromas they wished their sparkling wines to possess. In 1984, Laurent Gruet and Farid and Natalie Himeur moved from France to New Mexico.

Today this winery produces 10,000 cases annually from 12 acres of vineyards. Chardonnay reigns supreme here, and with the 1991 vintage, the house began producing a still Chardonnay (only 600 cases) to accompany its sparkling wines. The NV Brut is Gruet's flagship wine. On the lighter side, with 75 percent Chardonnay, it is well made, crisp, and lightly toasty. The Blanc de Noirs reverses the blend of Chardonnay and Pinot Noir to 75 percent Pinot; proof of the winery's greater success with the Chardonnay grape is in the bottle. Gruet plans to release its first vintage-dated sparkling wine, the 1990 Blanc de Blancs, in the fall of 1993.

Wines/Varietals: NV Brut ($$), NV Brut Blanc de Noirs ($$), Chardonnay ($$).

La Chiripada Winery and Vineyards
PO Box 191
Dixon, New Mexico 87527
tel. (505) 579-4434
Open to the public; est. 1981

Michael and Patrick Johnson, former Californians, have been swimming against the prevailing tide, favoring vinifera production and winning awards along the way. This small, highly-regarded winery specializes in French hybrids capable of withstanding the freezing temperatures in the 6,100 foot elevation of the Rio Embudo Valley. Like many of their cold weather cousins in the Northeast, Midwest and Canada, these vintners also grow Johannisberg Riesling. The 10 acres of vineyards here are planted over to Léon Millot (30 percent), White Riesling (30 percent), Seyval Blanc (10 percent), Vidal Blanc (10 percent) and De Chaunac (20 percent). About half of the grapes required for production are purchased from other growers.

Quality is high here (the wines go well with New Mexican cuisine), so it's not surprising that most of La Chiripada's annual output of 2,500 cases is sold straight out of its white adobe winery. The top-seller, Rio Embudo Red (60 percent Léon Millot and 40 percent De Chaunac), is a fine, earthy, vintage premium red. The vintage white counterpart, called Primavera, is made from Vidal Blanc.

Wines/Varietals: Vidal Blanc Reserve ($), Special Reserve Riesling ($$), Primavera ($), Rio Embudo White ($$), Rio Embudo Red ($$).

fruit. The 1990 Chardonnay similarly shows a simple, light style.

Wines/Varietals: Chardonnay ($), Sémillon ($), Cabernet Sauvignon ($$), Pinot Noir ($).

Texas

Bell Mountain/ Oberhellman Vineyards

Llario Rd. (Highway 16), Box 22
Fredericksburg, Texas 78624
tel. (512) 685-3297
Open to the public; est. 1983

Though Robert Oberhellman bought the land on which to build Oberhellman Vineyards in 1976, he took his time about gearing up to produce his own wines. Bucking the prevailing trend in Texas to the cultivation of French hybrids, he eventually planted only vinifera varieties in his 55-acre Texas Hill Country vineyard. Since 1986, the vineyards (at an elevation of 2,000 feet) have been classified with the surrounding area as the Bell Mountain Viticultural Area. Oberhellman has focused primarily on Cabernet Sauvignon, which makes up 36 percent of the vineyard, with additional emphasis on Pinot Noir and Chardonnay. Sémillon and Riesling are also among the plantings here.

Bell Mountain Cabernets have won a number of medals in competition and are among the state's best Cabs: firm in structure with the flavors of currant and oak, they are drinkable young, but have the potential to age. The 1989 Cabernet, a fine bottle in this house style, repeatedly scored well in our blind tastings. Bell Mountain Pinot has the briery character of Pinot but is a little thin on fruit, lacking the flesh that may come in time. The Sémillon that Oberhellman produces here is lightly sweet but with decent acid to enhance its figlike

Cap*Rock Winery

Route 6, Box 713K
Lubbock, Texas 79423-9744
tel. (806) 863-2704
Open to the public; est. 1992

The winery now known as Cap*Rock is in its second incarnation: this handsome, modern structure of Southwestern design was built by Teysha Cellars in 1988. The vineyards and winery of the defunct Teysha were bought in 1992 by The Plains Capital Corporation, a partnership formed by a group of Texas businessmen. Kim McPherson, originally at Llano Estacado and later employed by Teysha, remained aboard as Cap*Rock's winemaker. (Tony Soter of the Napa Valley now serves as consultant to McPherson.) Cap*Rock's grapes come from a 98-acre vineyard acquired with the winery, as well as from other Lubbock vineyards under contract. There are plans afoot to plant experimental plots of Rhône and Italian varieties, both red and white. Production currently averages 25,000 to 30,000 cases a year.

The wines produced here continue to reflect McPherson's style. Whites are clean, crisp, and a little on the sweet side. "Dry" to McPherson means at least .4 percent residual sugar—or higher, as in the case of the 1990 Tapestry, a Sauvignon Blanc-Sémillon-Melon de Bourgogne blend which is described as dry but measures .85 percent residual sugar. Good acidity, however, typical of the Lubbock area, gives the white wines a lively balance. The 1991 Sauvignon

Blanc, currently Cap*Rock's best white, is quite dry, zesty, flavorful, and well balanced. Reds from this area can be lean and tannic with high acidity, but McPherson's skill enables him to restrain these qualities, so that the fruit shows to best advantage. The 1990 Reserve Cabernet, just under 12 percent alcohol and a good example of the style, is intended for current consumption. The 1991 Cabernet Royale, however, is not a red wine but a cherry-colored rosé; its off-dry berryish fruit is suitable for a variety of foods including spicy Tex-Mex.

Wines/Varietals: Chardonnay ($), Reserve Chardonnay ($), Chenin Blanc ($), Sauvignon Blanc ($), Tapestry ($), White Table Wine ($), Cabernet Sauvignon ($), Reserve Cabernet Sauvignon ($), Cabernet Royale ($), Blush ($), Red Table Wine ($).

Fall Creek Vineyards

111 Guadalupe Street
Austin, Texas 78701
tel. (512) 476-4477; fax (512) 476-6116
Open to the public; est. 1979

Austin lawyer Ed Auler raised prize cattle at his Fall Creek Ranch in the Texas Hill Country. Then, in 1973, he and his wife, Susan, traveled to France. They enjoyed the fine wines of Burgundy, and Ed noted that Burgundian soil and terrain were similar to those on his ranch. He decided to further explore the similarities by planting hybrid varieties of grapes in Austin. His 65-acre vineyard, situated on the shores of Lake Buchanan, enjoys warm days and is cooled at night by winds off the lake. In 1975, his vines having proved themselves by yielding high-quality fruit, Auler converted to vinifera. Today, Fall Creek Vineyards, named for

the 100-foot waterfall that pours into Lake Buchanan from an upper ridge on the ranch, is the best-known winery in Texas. Demand for wines made here currently outstrips supply, not only in Texas, but in several markets outside the state as well, including some beyond U.S. shores. The handsome Fall Creek winery, surrounded by vineyards, produces 16,000 cases a year. The Aulers plan to expand both the vineyards and production in the near future.

Most of the Aulers' wines are simple, fruity whites, including the very quaffable Texas Grande Reserve Chardonnay, the popular Emerald Riesling, and the Sauvignon Blanc. The 1990 Texas Grande Reserve Chardonnay is the finest effort yet released, with superb balance and silky varietal character. We've also been impressed of late with Fall Creek's reds, most notably the 1989 Cabernet Sauvignon: firmly structured with good berry and cedar flavors. Auler acknowledges that his best wines are yet to come. "From the beginning," he says, "I set an ambitious goal for Fall Creek Vineyards that I knew would take years, perhaps generations, to fully accomplish." The Aulers' ambitions are well on the way to being realized.

Wines/Varietals: Chardonnay ($$), Texas Grande Reserve Chardonnay ($$), Sauvignon Blanc ($), Emerald Riesling ($), Sémillon-Sauvignon Blanc ($), Chenin Blanc ($), Granite Blush ($), Carnelian ($), Cabernet Sauvignon ($$).

Llano Estacado Winery, Inc.

FM 1585, PO Box 3487
Lubbock, Texas 79452
tel. (806) 745-2258; fax (806) 748-1674
Open to the public; est. 1976

Llano Estacado, the first winery to succeed on the High Plains of West Texas, has won more medals, including many golds, than any other winery in the state. The winery's name is the old Spanish word for the vast, grass-covered plain that conquistador Francisco Coronado traversed in the sixteenth century. The grass reportedly grew so high that a man on horseback was not visible. The conquistadors were said to have placed tall stakes to mark trails through the territory, which became known thereafter as the *llano estacado*, or "staked plain." The handsome stone and concrete winery here, built in the traditional Texas Alamo style, hugs the flat terrain under endless, ever-changing skies. A partnership, comprising businesspersons and professionals with a shared interest in wine, founded Llano Estacado. The group owns only eight acres of vineyard; over 95 percent of the grapes required to produce 73,000 cases annually are purchased from vineyards around Lubbock and elsewhere in Texas.

Llano Estacado's earliest successes were with white varietals like Riesling and Gewürztraminer, but more recently the focus here has been on Chardonnay, Sauvignon Blanc, Cabernet Sauvignon, and Merlot. In fact, the winery was about to phase out production of Gewürztraminer when the wine won a gold medal and the best-of-show award in the Lone Star competition. The clean, crisp white wines made here have grown steadily better over the years, gaining in flavor and fruit intensity as Texas vineyards have matured. This is particularly so for the house's Sauvignon Blanc, Chardonnay, and Riesling, which are consistently well balanced, somewhat light in body, but flavorful. This is also true of the winery's Cabernet and Merlot, but these reds will undoubtedly achieve more with time and benefit from the new emphasis now being placed on their production here. Llano Estacado's beautifully balanced, off-dry 1991 Chenin Blanc is one of the country's best Chenins. The 1990 Sauvignon Blanc is a good value and a classic, lean, crisp, grassy bottle. We are particularly impressed by the consistent quality running across this winery's entire range of bottlings—unusual for any winery and altogether rare outside of California.

Wines/Varietals: Sauvignon Blanc ($), Johannisberg Riesling ($), Chenin Blanc ($), Chardonnay ($$), Cabernet Sauvignon ($$), Merlot ($$).

Messina Hof Wine Cellars

Route 7, Box 905
Bryan, Texas 77802
tel. (409) 778-9463; fax (409) 778-7984
Open to the public; est. 1983

The mixed heritage suggested by the name Messina Hof has classic American melting-pot significance. Owner Paul Bonnarigo's Italian-American family came to the Southwest from Messina, Italy, via New York City; his wife Merrill's forebears came to

Texas from Germany. The Bonnarigos were growers for several years before they decided to make their own wines. Today, they own 40 acres of vineyard in East Texas and purchase 60 percent of the grapes they require to produce some 20 wines in a volume of 23,000 cases. The vineyard here is all vinifera (nearly 20 percent is planted to Chardonnay), except for a six-acre patch of Lenoir, a traditional American red variety from which the winery makes port. Zinfandel, Cabernet Sauvignon, and Johannisberg Riesling are the other leading varietals cultivated here, along with smaller quantities of Sauvignon Blanc, Chenin Blanc, and Cabernet Franc.

Messina Hof gained national attention with a late harvest Riesling called "Angel," a honeyed wine with peach and apricot flavors. The 1990 is a fine example and one of the top dessert wines produced in North America that we tasted in the past year. As silken and delicious as it was upon release, it will age well and probably continue to improve for a few more years. The Bonnarigos make a range of Chardonnays and Cabernets that reflect varying styles. So far, the Reserve versions have more flavor from oak than fruit, though the blend of Cabernet Sauvignon, Cabernet Franc, and Merlot, called "Reflections," is promising.

Wines/Varietals: Traditions Chardonnay ($), Private Reserve Chardonnay ($$), Barrel Reserve Chardonnay ($$), Chenin Blanc ($), Fumé Blanc ($), White Zinfandel ($), Traditions White ($), Traditions Blush ($), Traditions Cabernet Sauvignon ($), Barrel Reserve Cabernet Sauvignon ($$), Private Reserve Cabernet Sauvignon ($), Reflections ($$), Zinfandel ($), Cabernet Franc ($$), NV Papa Paulo Port ($$), Vintage Private Reserve Papa

Paulo Port ($$), Angel, Johannisberg Riesling Late Harvest ($$)

Moyer Winery
3939 IH 35 South, Suite 209B
San Marcos, Texas 78666
Winery location: 1941 Interstate Highway 35E, New Braunfels
tel. (512) 396-1600; fax (512) 396-1605
Open to the public; est. 1980

Ken Moyer of Ohio founded Moyer Winery exclusively for the production of sparkling wine. The Texas operation was sold in 1986 to Henri Bernabé, a Frenchman whose family has been in wine for more than five generations. Bernabé, an original partner in Ste. Geneviéve in Fort Stockton, Texas, is currently Moyer's president and winemaker. He purchases Texas grapes to achieve a production of 5,000 cases annually.

Non-vintage blends are produced here in two styles, Brut and Extra Dry, from Chenin Blanc and Chardonnay in the traditional *méthode champenoise*. Both are well-made sparkling wines; the Brut is toasty, but off-dry rather than bone dry. The Extra Dry is appealingly fresh and fruity, slightly melony in flavor. Moyer's top wine, Cuvée T.V. Munson, a non-vintage blend of 85 percent Pinot Noir and 15 percent Chardonnay, is quite fruity and simple but crisp. The label honors T.V. Munson, the Texas grape breeder who supplied France with phylloxera-resistant rootstocks in the late nineteenth century. All three sparkling wines are good efforts and are recommended.

Wines/Varietals: NV Star Brut Texas ($$), NV Brut Texas ($), NV Brut Especial ($), Extra Dry Texas ($), Cuvée T.V. Munson ($$$), Rosé ($).

111

Pedernales Vineyards

HC 12, Box 70AA
Fredericksburg, Texas 78624
tel. (512) 997-8326
Open to the public; est. 1986

Owners Karl and Judy Koch, who are active in the soft drink and bottled water business in South Texas, established this boutique estate winery in 1986. They own 22 acres of vineyards in the Texas Hill Country Viticultural Area, planted over to Cabernet Sauvignon (40 percent), Merlot (10 percent), Sauvignon Blanc (40 percent), Cabernet Franc (3 percent), and Chardonnay (7 percent). The area produces good grapes, and though winemaker Vernon Gold is still feeling his way, there's good potential here, especially as the vines mature. Current production is 2,000 cases.

Fifty percent of production is Cabernet Sauvignon, and the first release from this young winery worthy of assessment was the 1988. We found the 1988 (after getting over an odd nose) to be balanced, distinctive, with lean but clear fruit. The 1989 shows even further improvement, which suggests to us that this well-situated winery is one to watch. Winemaker Gold also works with Sauvignon Blanc, which should, in time, develop as well as the Cabernet has.

Wines/Varietals: Sauvignon Blanc ($), Cabernet Sauvignon ($).

Pheasant Ridge Winery

Route 3, Box 191
Lubbock, Texas 79401
tel. /fax (806) 746-6750
Open to the public the second Saturday of the month, or by appt.; est. 1982

Robert and Jennifer Cox were among the first to grow vinifera grapes in the Lubbock area of High Plains, alongside cotton and soybean crops. Their vines, first planted in

Key

$ 750-ml bottle of wine costing less than $10.

$$ Bottle priced between $10 and $20.

$$$ Bottle costing more than $20.

$-$$$ In red indicates excellent value in its class; good relationship between quality and price.

1978, have now grown to 48 acres, 20 percent of which are in Cabernet Sauvignon, Merlot, and Cabernet Franc. Total average annual production here is 12,000 cases.

Pheasant Ridge has produced a couple of soundly-made Cabernet Sauvignons and reasonably good Chardonnay. Following years of some inconsistency, recent vintages are more on track. The Cabernet's plummy fruit, sometimes overweighted with tannins, is nevertheless generally satisfying. The Lubbock area produces excellent quality white grapes with distinctive flavors; if a less heavy hand is employed in making the barrel fermented Chardonnay (less oak, livelier acid), a more elegant wine should result. The 1988 Cabernet Sauvignon shows the winery at its best, and the 1989 Chardonnay is a sound effort as well.

Wines/Varietals: Chardonnay ($$), Dry Chenin Blanc ($), Sauvignon Blanc ($), Cabernet Sauvignon Lubbock Reserve ($$), Cabernet Sauvignon Vintner's Cuvée ($).

Ste. Geneviève
(Cordier Estates, Inc.)
Interstate 10, PO Box 607
Fort Stockton, Texas 79735
tel. (915) 395-2417; fax (915) 395-2431
Open to the public by appt.; est. 1987

French-owned Domaine Cordier is Texas' largest winery, producing the equivalent of nearly 300,000 cases annually. Half is sold under the Ste. Geneviève label; the rest is sold in bulk, with sizeable quantities going to Canada. The wines are made at a huge, state-of-the-art winery in the West Texas desert near Fort Stockton. A mile or so east of the winery is a 1,000-acre vineyard planted entirely to vinifera varieties. Sauvignon

Blanc makes up nearly a quarter of the vineyard, with Chardonnay a close second (23 percent). Other varietals grown here include Chenin Blanc (21 percent), Merlot (3 percent), Cabernet Franc (3 percent), Barbera (5 percent), and smaller quantities of Pinot Noir, Muscat, Zinfandel, and Ruby Cabernet. The vineyard was planted by the University of Texas Department of Soil and Conservation. Seeking the most profitable use for the University's vast land holdings, the department planted test plots of several different crops in the mid-seventies. The experiment demonstrated that wine grapes bring the highest return per acre, a result that gave a big boost to the winegrowing industry in Texas. The winery project originated in the early eighties as a joint venture by a group of French and Texan businesspeople. Their plan involved leasing the vineyard from the University and producing wine under the Ste. Geneviève label. When the partnership was subsequently dissolved, one of the partners, Etablissement Cordier, acquired the winery and maintained the leasing arrangement with the University.

Jean-Louis Haberer, an enologist and viticulturalist from France, came to Ste. Geneviéve in 1987, when the young vineyard was still struggling to become established. He is particularly pleased with the performance of Chardonnay and Cabernet Sauvignon grapes here. The house's Chardonnay Grand Reserve is crisp and well-balanced. The Cabernet Grand Reserve is the most noteworthy red produced here, with good color and concentration. The 1991 Sauvignon Blanc displays clear and pleasing varietal character. We actually prefer the very nice non-vintage Sauvignon Blanc Texas Varietal, which has clean, grassy character with a more lush, medium-body, and is a good value. The house's character-istic "light" style can be found in the Texas Cabernet Sauvignon as well, which is spicy and nicely balanced.

Wines/Varietals: Sauvignon Blanc Texas Varietal ($), Fumé Blanc ($), Chenin Blanc Varietal ($), Chardonnay Varietal ($), Chardonnay Grand Reserve ($), Texas White ($), Texas Blush ($), Cabernet Varietal ($), Cabernet Sauvignon Grand Reserve ($), Merlot Varietal ($), Texas First Blush ($), American White Zinfandel Varietal ($), Texas Red ($).

Schoppaul Hill Winery
PO Box 77
Ivanhoe, Texas 75447
tel. (903) 583-2846
Open to the public by appt.; est. 1988

In 1984, Schoppaul Hill's owner, Denton orthopedist Dr. John R. Anderson, planted his 12.5-acre vineyard on a hill, adjacent to the family farm in Ivanhoe, just north of Dallas and an hour or so away from the Red River Valley. He chose mostly white variet-ies such as Chardonnay, Sauvignon Blanc, and French Colombard, but also laid in a few acres of Cabernet Sauvignon, Cabernet Franc, and Merlot.

Dr. Anderson's small vineyard supplies about 15 percent of the 4,500 cases pro-duced annually at the winery; the rest of the required grapes are purchased. Schoppaul Hill turns out an attractive, lightly-sweet Chenin Blanc (a strong example was bottled in 1990), a pleasant Muscat, and a curiously rich-style Sauvignon Blanc. The Chardonnay made here is lively and shows promise; ditto for the estate-bottled Cabernet Sauvignon.

Wines/Varietals: Chardonnay ($), Barrel fermented Chardonnay ($$), Sauvignon Blanc

($), Chenin Blanc ($), Muscat Canelli ($), Johannisberg Riesling ($), Cabernet Sauvignon Red River Reserve ($$).

Sister Creek Vineyards
FM 1376
Sisterdale, Texas 78006
tel. (512) 324-6704
Not open to the public; est. 1988

This young and tiny (1,400 case) winery has started to release some reds that have caused us—and others—to take note. About half of the grapes currently used are pur-chased; the other half comes from five acres of vineyards (2 acres of Chardonnay, 1 of Pinot Noir, 1.5 Cabernet Sauvignon, .25 Merlot, .25 Cabernet Franc).

Winemakers Danny Hernandez and Vernon Friesnhahn (also president of the winery) released a 1988 Cabernet Blend of 50 percent Cabernet Sauvignon and 50 per-cent Cabernet Franc, modified in 1989 to 38 percent Cabernet Sauvignon, 36 percent Cabernet Franc, and 26 percent of a grape called Ruby Cabernet. The result is a me-dium-bodied wine with lean fruit and no flaws, that is easy drinking and suggests there is more good to come from this winery. Already this red is the equal of some low-priced California blends; if another layer of complexity can be added to it, Sister Creek will make its mark in Texas' premium wine industry. A little more time could make a big difference at so new a winery. We're taking a little leap of faith in recommending this winery, but its quality is already evident, and its potential quite apparent.

Wines/Varietals: Chardonnay ($$), Cabernet Blend ($$).

Slaughter Leftwich Vineyards
107-R.R. 620, Box 22F
Austin, Texas 78734
(512) 266-3331
Open to the public; est. 1986

The Slaughter-Leftwich family—six-generation Texans—planted the first vineyards in the state's High Plains region (3,300 ft. elevation) near Lubbock in 1979. The first Texas Chardonnay produced in 1982 by Llano Estacado Winery used Slaughter-Leftwich. June Leftwich Head and her son, Scott Slaughter, partners in the fledgling Llano Estacado operation, decided to establish their own winery in 1986. Slaughter Leftwich Vineyards' native stone winemaking facility was built on the outskirts of Austin in the Hill Country, overlooking Lake Travis.

The 50-acre vineyard near Lubbock supplies about 90 percent of the fruit needed for production of 11,000 cases. Slaughter-Leftwich has earned something of a reputation for making fine, crisp Chardonnay and Sauvignon Blanc; their best wines are moderately priced and good values. The 1990 Sauvignon Blanc is easy drinking with citrus and pineapple flavors, a hint of vanilla, and light acidity. Nearly half of the production here is of an attractive, lightly-sweet, pale pink wine known as "Austin Blush." The winery also makes Cabernet Sauvignon.

Wines/Varietals: Texas Chardonnay ($), Texas Sauvignon Blanc ($), Texas Cabernet Sauvignon ($), Austin Blush ($).

A Disclaimer

Readers are advised that prices and conditions change over the course of time. The wineries profiled and wines reviewed in this book have been considered over a period of time, and the profiles and reviews reflect the personal experiences and opinions of the reviewers. The reviewers and publisher cannot be held responsible for the experiences of the reader in relation to the wineries or wines reviewed. Readers are invited to write the publisher with ideas, comments, and suggestions for future editions.

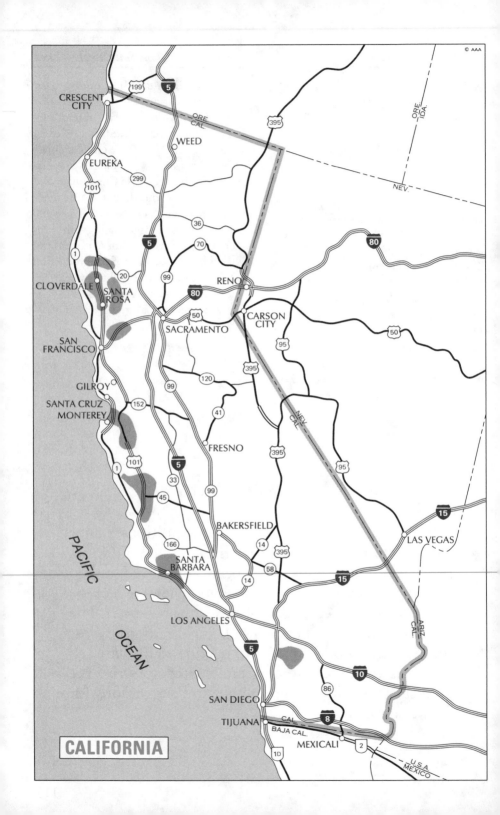

CALIFORNIA

CALIFORNIA and grape vines seem a natural marriage. Immigrants to America's westernmost shores recognized it: almost the moment Europeans set foot on Pacific Coast soil, they started vineyards. First came the Spanish padres, who established Franciscan missions from San Diego to Sonoma in the latter part of the eighteenth century, planting a variety that became known as the "Mission" grape. Around 1833, a Frenchman, Jean Louis Vignes, brought vine cuttings from Bordeaux and other parts of France to the New World and planted them in what is now downtown Los Angeles. And a few decades later, Count Agoston Haraszthy of Hungary, convinced the best foreign grapes could grow in California, traveled through Europe's top vineyards and delivered to America crates full of choice cuttings. He planted first, in 1851, in the San Diego area, and later at his Buena Vista vineyard in Sonoma. Eventually, these European stock vines were distributed to winegrowers throughout the state of California. Beginning in the late 1880s and up through the early years of this century, French, Italian, and German immigrants settled in the Golden State's coastal valleys and hillsides, bringing with them a heritage of grape growing and winemaking. It seemed that bountiful California, with its agreeable climate and fertile soil, was the only place in America where *vitis vinifera* grew easily and well.

Though the young wine industry in California suffered periods of starts and stops throughout its early history, it grew and flourished until 1919. Prohibition, enacted that year, lasted for 14 years and virtually destroyed the state's wine economy. When Prohibition was repealed in 1933, the wine industry had to start all over again. And it proved pretty slow going until around 1960 when, prompted by the exposure to wine which increasing numbers of Americans gained while traveling abroad, interest in domestic table wine was sparked. In the following couple of decades, growth was phenomenal. Only when the state's economy hit the skids in the early 1990s did the wine industry's forward momentum slow down.

Few wine regions have changed as rapidly over the last three decades—or as dramatically from decade to decade—as California. In the 27 years between 1965 and 1992, vineyard acreage here jumped from 130,000 acres to more than 327,000; total production went from some 40 million cases to more than 200 million; and the number of wineries operating in the state leaped from perhaps 150 to well over 700.

Dramatic as these numbers are, however, they do not tell the most interesting part of the story. The real revolution here has been in style and quality. Since the mid-seventies, when California Cabernet Sauvignon and Chardonnay began to achieve international recognition, new winegrowing regions have emerged; fresh styles of winemaking have evolved; and the quality of the state's very best wines has taken a quantum leap forward. While there is still tremendous diversity of wine types—and practically as many different styles of each particular type of wine as there are wineries in the state—California wines have, in the main, never been better. The rich but overbearing Chardonnays of the seventies have given way to wines that are still opulent but better balanced and more elegant. Intensely tannic and concentrated red wines, notably Cabernet, Pinot Noir, and Zinfandel, are more supple today but have the structure to age longer and more gracefully than the blockbusters of 15 to 20 years ago.

The seventies in California were a decade of experimentation that often resulted in highly alcoholic, over-extracted, over-oaked wines. The eighties were a period of fine-tuning, with more experienced winemaking being brought to bear and fruit from more mature vineyards finding its way into the hands of a growing legion of serious-minded vintners. The nineties will undoubtedly see further refinements, not only with Cabernet Sauvignon and Chardonnay, but also for such other, increasingly popular wines as Sauvignon Blanc, Merlot, Riesling, and Rhône varieties like Syrah, Mourvèdre, Grenache, Viognier and Petite Sirah.

The best California wines have, until quite recently, gone exclusively by varietal names, i.e., the name of the principal grape variety contained in each wine. California's leading grapes comprise most of the well-known vinifera varieties: Cabernet Sauvignon, Chardonnay (the two most widely planted), Zinfandel, Sauvignon Blanc, Pinot Noir, Merlot, Cabernet Franc, Riesling, Chenin Blanc, Pinot Blanc, Barbera, Petite Sirah, Gewürztraminer, Grenache and Muscat. More recently, Syrah, Mourvèdre, Viognier, Marsanne, Sangiovese, Nebbiolo and Dolcetto grapes have begun to be harvested here. (*See* Glossary of North American Wine Grapes).

Blends, however, were the big news of the eighties. In particular, two new categories— Meritage and Rhône-style blends—were created. Prior to 1983, when varietal wines were required by U.S. Bureau of Alcohol, Tobacco & Firearms (BATF) regulations to contain only 51 percent of their namesake grape, many varietals were blended with lesser grapes. The "filler" sometimes accounted for fully 49 percent of what went into the bottle. For a wine to be 100 percent varietal was a true mark of quality in the sixties and seventies. In 1983, the U.S. law changed to require that a varietal contain a minimum of 75 percent of the grape for which it is named.

By this time, however, winemakers—especially producers of Cabernet Sauvignon—were taking another look at the art of blending. They discovered that adding Merlot or Cabernet Franc to Cabernet Sauvignon moderates the toughness of young wines and often provides an extra note of flavor or complexity. (Classic Bordeaux wines, of course, are a blend of at least two, and more commonly three or four, varieties.) As winemakers experimented, they came to need a name for wines that could no longer be referred to as varietals by virtue of their consisting of less than 75 percent of the predominate grape variety. The name selected for blends utilizing the red Bordeaux varieties is "Meritage" (rhymes with heritage).

Interest in Rhône-style wines erupted in the late eighties when wineries such as Bonny Doon, McDowell, Joseph Phelps, Qupé, and perhaps a dozen others—admirers of the great Rhône reds which include Hermitage, Côte-Rotie and Châteauneuf-du-Pape—began producing domestic wines from grapes traditionally grown in France's Rhône Valley. This new category of wines is not yet large: California vineyards contain only a relatively few scattered acres of the true Syrah grape (as opposed to the lesser Petite Sirah) and Mourvèdre (a grape which was widely planted a century ago as Mataro.) Vineyards in the northern and central coastal regions are expanding plantings of these grape varieties, however, as demand for Rhône-style wines increases.

Another significant development of the eighties was the emergence of more narrowly defined appellations—sub-regions with distinctive microclimates—designated by the BATF as American Viticultural Areas (AVAs). Sonoma County, for example, has several such appellations, among them Alexander Valley, Dry Creek Valley, Sonoma Mountain, and Russian River Valley. The bulk of California's wine grapes continues to come from the 300-mile-long San Joaquin Valley that runs from Lodi to just south of Bakersfield. San Joaquin is the state's warmest region and has always been the source of enormous quantities of wine for the jug trade. California's best wines, however, come from the cool coastal regions, from Mendocino (less than two hours north of San Francisco) to Temecula (just southeast of Los Angeles).

The new story for the California wine industry in the nineties is, in fact, the frightening old story of phylloxera. Tiny lice that eat away at a grapevine's roots, phylloxera were a vineyard plague in the late nineteenth century in both California and Europe. A native American root stock seemingly resistant to the bugs solved the problem back then, but only after a huge, extraordinarily costly replanting effort. A different strain of phylloxera is back in the 1990s, this one apparently only too happy to feast on native vines. As a result of this destructive menace, during the current decade, many of California's most celebrated vineyards will have to be replanted at great expense with existing root stocks of a different variety proven resistant to the microscopic scourge.

Top California Appellations

North Coast

Napa Valley The most densely planted of California's wine regions and the most famous, though not the largest. Slightly northeast of San Francisco, the Napa Valley runs south to north some 35 miles between two ranges of the Coast Range Mountains. (The hills to the west are part of the Mayacamas range; the least important hills in terms of viticulture on the eastern side contain Howell Mountain.) Some of the most famous and venerated California names are here: Beringer, Charles Krug, Christian Brothers, and Inglenook, as well as the modern classic houses of Robert Mondavi, Beaulieu, Chappellet, and Chateau Montelena. There are also a hundred newer wineries here, including some of the currently hottest names in California wine. The southern end of the valley has the most exposure to Pacific fog and breezes and is coolest, particularly the Carneros area. Among other Napa Valley sub-appellations are the Stags Leap District, best known for Cabernet Sauvignon, Merlot, and Meritage reds, and Howell Mountain on the east side of the valley overlooking St. Helena.

Sonoma County Larger in area than Napa Valley, Sonoma has the most Viticultural Areas of any region in California: Alexander Valley, Dry Creek Valley, Russian River Valley (and a sub-region, Green Valley), Carneros-Sonoma, Sonoma Mountain, Bennett Valley, and Sonoma Valley. The Spanish established vineyards here well before Napa was settled. Count Haraszthy founded Buena Vista Winery near the town of Sonoma in the 1860s; much later, the well-known wineries of Korbel, Simi, and Sebastiani were established here. The leading wines produced in the region are Cabernet Sauvignon, Chardonnay, Sauvignon Blanc, Zinfandel, Merlot, Pinot Noir, Chenin Blanc, and Petite Sirah.

Mendocino The northernmost coastal region in California, with cool temperatures and, in western areas such as the Anderson Valley, generally more rainfall than in other winegrowing regions in the state. Anderson Valley is the source of very good sparkling wines, Chardonnay, Gewürztraminer, and late-harvest Riesling. Eastern Mendocino is drier and well-suited to red varieties and good Riesling, Chenin Blanc, and lighter Chardonnays.

Lake County A small area north of the Napa Valley, Lake County is growing and becoming well known for Sauvignon Blanc, and in the rich soils at higher elevations, Cabernet Sauvignon and Merlot. Guenoc Winery in eastern Lake County has its own AVA: Guenoc Valley.

Livermore Valley Southeast of San Francisco, this arid valley with its gravelly soil was home in the late nineteenth century to such pioneering vintners as the Wente brothers and Charles Wetmore, who imported cuttings from Château d'Yquem to make his own version

VITA NOVA
P.O. Box 822
Los Olivos, CA 93441

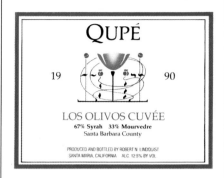

QUPÉ
P.O. Box 440
Los Olivos, CA 93441

Guided tours and tastings hosted by a knowledgeable staff are available daily from 10:00 am to 4:00 pm. Groups of ten or more are requested to make an appointment in advance.

Located just north of Santa Barbara, near Solvang. Take Highway 101 to Zaca Station Road.
Proceed 2.5 miles to winery.

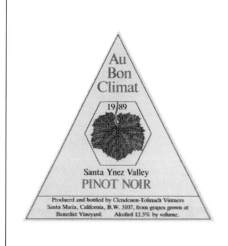

AU BON CLIMAT
P.O. Box 113
Los Olivos, CA 93441

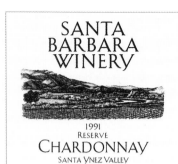

SANTA BARBARA WINERY

1991
RESERVE
CHARDONNAY
SANTA YNEZ VALLEY

PRODUCED AND BOTTLED BY SANTA BARBARA WINERY
SANTA BARBARA, CALIFORNIA   ALCOHOL 13.1% BY VOLUME
PIERRE LAFOND, PROPRIETOR   BRUCE McGUIRE, WINEMAKER

*Making Award-winning
wines in the heart of
Santa Barbara
202 Anacapa Street
Two blocks from the beach
10 to 5 daily
800.225.3633*

"Occasionally Eccentric, Always Exciting Wines"

Babcock Vineyards
Located 9.5 miles west of Buellton
5175 Highway 246
Lompoc, CA 93436

Tasting Room Hours:
Weekends — 10:30 am to 4:00 pm
Weekdays by Appointment
805.736.1455

*Visitors are always welcome at
Sanford Winery
tasting room and picnic area.
Located just outside Buellton,
4.7 miles west of Highway 101
at
7250 Santa Rosa Road.
Open Daily from 11-4 pm.
805.688.3300*

*Brander
Estate-Grown
Sauvignon Blanc Specialist*

*Tasting Room Hours:
Monday-Sunday 10:00-5:00
2401 Refugio Rd.
Los Olivos, CA 93441*
805.688.2455

In a world where bigger is usually considered better, we at Hotel Sofitel would like to remind you that true contentment is most often found in the smallest of details. Like our big, plush towels. Our overstuffed chairs that are as soft and comfortable as they are beautiful. And a staff that's trained to accomplish nothing less than the impossible. You'll find us at La Cienega and Beverly boulevards. Just steps from

Many hotels are so large, you could get lost in them. We suppose the same could be said of our towels.

countless shops and incredible dining possibilities. For your reservations, simply call (310) 278-5444 or 1-800-SOFITEL. We'll happily keep **✦ Hotel Sofitel** — LOS ANGELES — *your towel fluffed.*

Ma Maison

of Sauternes. The leading wines produced here are Chardonnay, Sauvignon Blanc, Sémillon, Petite Sirah, and Merlot.

Santa Cruz Mountains There is limited but choice acreage in this range of hills about an hour south of San Francisco. Ridge Vineyards grows superb Cabernet Sauvignon at a 2,000-foot elevation on Monte Bello Ridge. Bonny Doon, Mount Eden, and David Bruce are other top names here, and another handful of small wineries are also scattered about the hills.

Central Coast

Monterey The vast Salinas Valley is one of California's coolest regions, producing good Chardonnay and Riesling in its northern areas and good Cabernet Sauvignon in warmer areas to the south. Wente, Mirassou, and Monterey Vineyard are among the influential players here. Some of the largest coastal vineyards in the state are planted here; their grapes are sold to wineries in Napa and Sonoma. Pinot Noir is another leading wine produced in this region and recent plantings of Italian varieties (Sangiovese, Malvasia, Barbera, and Nebbiolo) show promise.

San Luis Obispo County The best-known appellation here is Edna Valley, home of big, richly flavored Chardonnays. Part of the Santa Maria Valley is in this region as well. Up and coming Paso Robles, in the northern part of the county, has gained a reputation for intensely flavored reds, particularly Zinfandel and more recently Syrah and other Rhône varieties. The Rhône varieties currently being planted here will undoubtedly gain greater recognition during the nineties.

Santa Barbara County Acreage planted here in the cool coastal Santa Ynez and Santa Maria valleys is expanding dramatically. The climate, considerably cooler than in much of Napa and Sonoma, produces impressive Chardonnay, Pinot Noir, and Syrah, as well as some of California's finest Riesling and Gewürztraminer.

Southern California

Temecula This desert-like area east of Los Angeles and Palm Springs supports a green oasis of vines, thanks to successful irrigation and cooling Pacific breezes which sweep through the region every afternoon. It is best suited to white varieties such as Chardonnay, Riesling, and Chenin Blanc, and to Pinot Noir for sparkling wines.

There are also vineyards planted north of San Diego near Escondido in the AVA known as San Pasqual Valley.

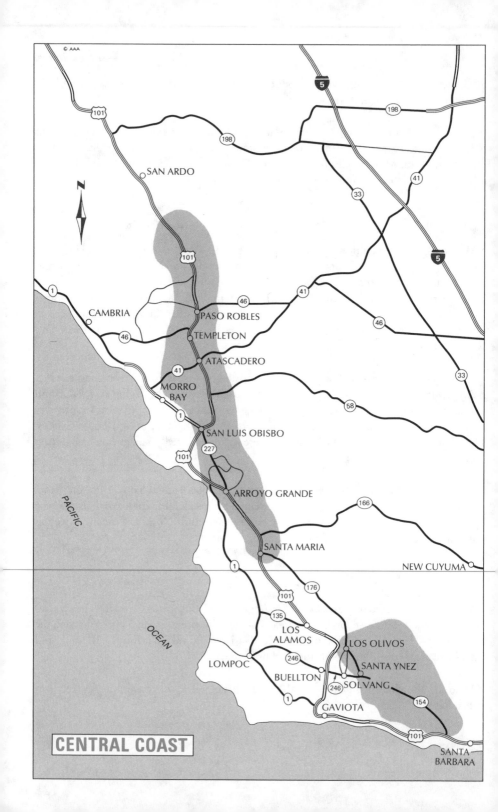

CENTRAL COAST

Central Coast & Santa Barbara

Adelaida Cellars

2170 Adelaida Road (winery at 5805 Adelaida)
Paso Robles, CA 93446
tel. (805) 239-0190; fax (805) 239-4671
Open to the public; est. 1983

This 5,000-case winery is the work of John Munch, who, using purchased grapes and the fruit from his couple of acres of Syrah vineyards, produces good wines, primarily Chardonnay and Cabernet Sauvignon.

Both tend to be forward and to display typical varietal flavors. The 1988 Paso Robles Chardonnay is the best of the Adelaida Cellars wines we've tasted. The Cabernet was also very good in 1988—spicy with ripe flavors of currants and berries, a generally elegant bottle that will not peak before the mid-1990s. Good progress is also being made here with Zinfandel. The 1989 is fairly big, tannic, spicy, and untamed, but the fruit and balance should continue to emerge, as an already good bottle becomes even better in the next few years.

Wines/Varietals: Chardonnay ($$), Cabernet Sauvignon ($$), Zinfandel ($).

Au Bon Climat

Box 113
Los Olivos, CA 93441
tel. (805) 688-863 or 937-9801;
fax (805) 686-1016
Not open to the public; est. 1982

Au Bon Climat is synonymous with sole owner (since 1991) and winemaker, Jim Clendenen, and is undisputedly one of the brightest stars in the North American winery firmament. Clendenen, born in Akron, Ohio "to gastronomically impoverished parents during the culinary dark ages of the 1950s," found himself, as a student at U.C. Santa Barbara, spending a junior year abroad in France. Following graduation, he returned to Europe and spent a month each in Champagne and Burgundy before entering law school. But he was already smitten. In 1978, he took a job as assistant winemaker at Zaca Mesa. With a few harvests there under his belt, and with additional experience gained at wineries around the world (especially in Australia), Clendenen set up his own shop in Santa Barbara County in 1982. He still purchases his grapes from a few top estates as he did back then, and over the past decade has, through careful re-investment from its own production, developed this Burgundian-school winery to an output 10,000 cases. The winery's Pinot Noir, and increasingly its Chardonnay, have received the highest accolades and are generally vineyard designated. ABC (as the winery is known colloquially) has an outstanding track record for quality. It also has a second label, Il Podere Dell'Olivos, that Clendenen uses for wines made from Italian grape varieties such as Nebbiolo and Sangiovese. These "Italian" wines are not yet up to Au Bon Climat's level of quality.

Seventy percent of production here is Chardonnay, and the 1990 Bien Nacido Reserve Chardonnay is the winery's finest effort to date: rich and creamy with butterscotch flavors, toasty-oaky, in the French style, vinified in new oak barrels, aged 18 months in barrel, and bottled unfiltered. The highly extracted Santa Ynez Pinot Noir is as good as Central Coast Pinot gets, which is very good indeed.

Wines/Varietals: Chardonnay, Santa Barbara County ($$), Reserve Chardonnay, Bien Nacido ($$$), Reserve Chardonnay, Talley ($$$), Pinot Blanc ($$), Pinot Noir/Pinot Blanc Pink Wine ($), Pinot Noir, Santa Maria Valley ($$), Pinot Noir, Santa Barbara, Bien Nacido ($$), Pinot Noir, Santa Ynez Valley Sanford & Benedict ($$$).

Babcock Vineyards

5175 Highway 246
Lompoc, CA 93436
tel. (805) 736-1455; fax (805) 736-3886
Open to the public weekends, weekdays
by appt.; est.1984

Walt and Mona Babcock own the eponymous vineyard and winery established in 1984, but it is their son, Bryan, who is most closely identified with Babcock Vineyards as winemaker, spokesperson, and exuberant impresario. Located on the western edge of the Santa Ynez Valley Appellation in Santa Barbara County, Babcock has 50 acres under vine, 31 of which are Chardonnay. The winery's early focus was on estate grown Chardonnay, Johannisburg Riesling, Sauvignon Blanc, and Gewürztraminer. Such Italian varieties as Sangiovese and Vernaccia have now been added to the mix, as well as five acres of Pinot Noir. Annual production is 8,000 cases, about a third from purchased grapes.

Earliest success here came with intense and dry Gewürztraminers. Next the Sauvignon Blancs, especially under the 11 Oaks Ranch designation, earned raves. The big volume Chardonnays are sound, too, with ample fruit and plenty of oak in the balance. The 1990 is a good effort—lean and crisp with citrus and acid bite. Babcock's regular Chardonnay and its late-harvest

Rieslings are also noteworthy. The Italian-style wines are promising. The Pinot Noir, with its unusual delicacy, may yet prove the operation's top achievement. The 1990 is well balanced with a depth of flavors that should continue to emerge for several years. Fathom is a table wine of blended varieties—in 1990, 50 percent Sauvignon Blanc, 35 percent Gewürztraminer, and 15 percent Chardonnay. A second label, Riverbreak, is used for declassified wines.

Wines/Varieties: Chardonnay ($$), Chardonnay, Grand Cuvée ($$$), Sauvignon Blanc ($), Sauvignon Blanc, 11 Oaks Ranch ($$), Gewürztraminer ($$), Riesling ($$), Fathom ($), Pinot Noir ($$).

The Brander Vineyard

2401 Refugio Road, PO Box 92
Los Olivos, CA 93441
tel. (805) 688-2455; fax (805) 688-4881
Open to the public; est.1980 (vineyards
planted in 1975)

Young Fred Brander planted his first vineyards in 1975, dreaming of producing good Bordeaux-style wines in an area better known for Burgundy-type wines. He made his first estate wine in 1979, and in the early years produced mostly Sauvignon Blanc (with Sémillon in the blend). In the late 1980s, he at last realized his dream and saw a sharp rise in the quality of his line overall. This winery now produces a small quantity of Chardonnay—hardly a Bordeaux-style wine—but Sauvignon Blanc still ranks as its calling card. Out of a 6,400-case annual production, 3,500 is Sauvignon Blanc and 2,000 a Bordeaux blend labeled Bouchet

(Cabernet Sauvignon, Cabernet Franc, and Merlot). The grapes all come from the winery's 40 contiguous acres of vineyards, bought in the 1970s for Brander by his parents, who emigrated from Argentina to Santa Barbara with little C. Frederic in 1962. C. Frederic, now Fred, is active in all sorts of local food and wine promotions for his and other wines, including the annual Santa Barbara Bouillabaisse Festival held at the Brander winery.

When making his wines, Fred keeps *terroir* in mind—but in the back of his mind—and "beverage" very much in the forefront of it. His much-awarded Sauvignon Blanc is also released in a flagship Tête de Cuvée bottling (2,800 cases) that is half barrel fermented and half cold fermented in stainless steel and aged *sur lie* for five months. In 1990, the blend of 78 percent Sauvignon Blanc and 22 percent Sémillon is dry, clean, and crisp with good varietal character and with lemony and herbal highlights that will soften with some bottle age. Its modest price is right. The Chardonnay usually tends to be big, toasty, buttery and floral in style; the 1990 was not up to the 1989 (which also had a Tête de Cuvée release). The red blend in its 1989 Tête de Cuvée rendering (1,400 cases) is composed of 53 percent Cabernet Sauvignon, 34 percent Cabernet Franc, and 13 percent Merlot, and is aged in 100 percent French oak (70 percent new barrels). The vines here are beginning to show their maturity, and this attractive medium-bodied bottle of wine is full of classic flavors—cassis, plum, spices, oak.

Wines/Varietals: Estate Sauvignon Blanc, Santa Ynez Valley ($), Sauvignon Blanc, Tête de Cuvée ($), Estate Chardonnay, Estate ($$), Bouchet, Santa Ynez Valley ($$), Bouchet, Tête de Cuvée ($$$).

Byron Vineyard & Winery

5230 Tepusquet Road
Santa Maria, CA 93454
tel. (805) 937-7288; fax (805) 937-1246
Open to the public; est. 1984

Winemaker Byron "Ken" Brown, a self-proclaimed Pinot Noir nut, established his winery in 1984 to produce world-class Burgundian-style wines in the very cool foothills of northern Santa Barbara County's Santa Maria Valley. He succeeded so well with Chardonnay and Pinot Noir that he attracted the interest of the Robert Mondavi family, which purchased Byron from its partners in 1990 and are allowing the winery to operate independently under Ken Brown's direction. So far, so very good. Production is up to 27,000 cases, with 70 percent made from the winery's 650 acres of vineyards. Some 97 of those acres comprise the Nielson Vineyard, purchased in 1989, the oldest post-Prohibition vineyard in the county with vines (planted in 1964) that should provide excellent fruit in the years ahead. Chardonnay is the quantity leader here at 60 percent of production and with 371 acres of vineyards. Cabernet accounts for 166 acres of vines, Pinot Noir another 100, and there are small plots devoted to Rhône varieties. Ten percent of Byron's total production is Sauvignon Blanc made from purchased grapes.

Out of an isolated winery surrounded by sycamore trees along Tepusquet Creek, Brown and enologist Julie Guffy are producing some excellent wines. The Chardonnay comes in two versions. The reserve is 100 percent barrel fermented in French oak and undergoes malolactic fermentation and *sur lie* aging (including weekly hand stirring). The Santa Barbara County Chardonnay is partially barrel fermented and aged eight to 12 months in French oak, but the emphasis here is on fruity, floral components. We especially liked the 1989 Reserve, tasted in 1992, which has a caramel nose, classic flavors, lushness, and dense concentration— a very fine bottle. The 1990s are good as well, with the regular Santa Barbara County bottling showing fresh fruit along exotic tropical fruit flavor lines, a creamy texture, buttery aromatics, and barrel pepper. The 1990 Pinot Noir is good, medium-bodied with spicy flavors over varietal fruit. The 1989 unfiltered Reserve Pinot Noir is excellent; the 1990 Reserve is good, but needs time for its fruit to emerge over a tight, leathery flavor base. The Reserve Pinot here is a blend from two vineyards, vinified using old-world techniques, including long skin contact, open vat fermentation, and punching down the caps by hand three or four times daily. We found the 1989 deep, silky, complex, and young. Byron also produces Sauvignon Blanc and Cabernet Sauvignon (the 1989 is blended with other grapes and is nice, soft, and easy drinking), both of which usually show regional vegetalness.

Wines/Varietals: Sauvignon Blanc ($), Pinot Blanc ($), Chardonnay, Santa Barbara County ($$), Reserve Chardonnay, Santa Barbara County ($$), Cabernet Sauvignon ($$), Pinot Noir, Santa Barbara County ($$), Reserve Pinot Noir, Santa Barbara County ($$), NV Sparkling Brut Reserve ($$).

Cambria Winery & Vineyard

5475 Chardonnay Lane, PO Box 5957
Santa Maria, CA 93456
tel. (805) 937-8091; fax (805) 934-3589
Not open to the public; est. 1987

The keys to the success of this young winery are location, vineyards, and seasoned executives. The Santa Maria Valley area in northern Santa Barbara County was originally inhabited by American Chumash Indians, but a Mexican land grant ceded 8,900 acres of the Tespesqu*[sic]* Rancho to the Olivera family who retained the property until 1900. In the nineteenth century, English and Welsh settlers named the area Cambria, the Roman word for Wales. But only in the 1970s was the south-facing slope, soil, and microclimate of the area recognized as ideal for vineyards. The Tepusquet vineyard grew to 1,200 contiguous acres and became a choice grape source for key California wineries, including Kendall-Jackson. When the property became available in 1987, Kendall-Jackson's Jess Jackson and his wife, Barbara Banke, headed up an investment team that purchased it. The vineyards are now planted 95 percent to Chardonnay and five percent to Pinot Noir. Different microclimes within the vineyard have led to several vineyard designations: Katherine's, Cambria, and Tepusquet Vineyards for Chardonnay, and Julia's Vineyard for Pinot Noir.

Winemaker Signe Zoller's offerings have already met with critical acclaim and have received many awards. Zoller, who came from Kendall-Jackson in 1989, produced very fine wines here in 1989 and 1990. (A Katherine's Vineyard Chardonnay, a Reserve Chardonnay made from special lots from the best part of the vineyard, and a Julia's Pinot Noir are produced.) All the wines generally show the area's intense fruit character. The 1990 Katherine's Vineyard Chardonnay, which is barrel fermented, put through 100 percent malolactic fermentation and aged in barrels on the lees for about four months, is excellent: smooth with apple, fig, and complex spice flavors and a long, balanced finish. The good 1989 Pinot is soft and elegant with a cedar, tobacco, and cherry flavor character. Cambria's capacity is 100,000 cases; it is probably now about halfway there.

Wines/Varietals: Chardonnay, Katherine's Vineyard ($$), Reserve Chardonnay ($$$), Pinot Noir, Julia's Vineyard ($$).

Carey Cellars
1711 Alamo Pintado Road
Solvang, CA 93463
tel. (805) 688-8554; fax (805) 688-5327
Open to the public; est. 1978 (under current ownership since 1987)

In 1987, Kate and Brooks Firestone (of Firestone Vineyards and tire connections) purchased this small winery from their neighbors, the Carey family. With Kate at the helm as general manager (joined in 1990 by son Adam) and Kent Barthman as winemaker, the new proprietors of Carey Cellars set out on an ambitious course. Their stated intention is "to produce rich, fruity, long-lived Chardonnays and intense, yet balanced, Cabernets." They are in the midst of a four-year development plan that will upgrade quality and bring production to the 10,000 case level from its current 7,000 cases. Carey Cellars buys in about 25 percent of its grapes; currently the winery's 25 acres of vineyards are planted to Sauvignon Blanc (3.5 acres), Cabernet Sauvignon (18 acres) and Merlot (3.5). Estate vineyards, located 40 miles north of Santa Barbara and bearing the Santa Ynez Valley appellation, are neatly split into two distinct parcels, half "Alamo Pintado Vineyard" and half "La Cuesta," just over the crest above the rustic red barn winery.

We've liked the Cabernet Sauvignon from La Cuesta. The 1987 is firm, deep, yet supple with blackberry and peppery overtones. In the 1989 offering, a little more flesh would have better covered the bell-pepper, tannic, and tart structure. We expect even better things from this vineyard in the years to come. The winery's most consistent performer to date has been its Chardonnay with a pronounced oaky flavor.

Wines/Varietals: Sauvignon Blanc ($), Chardonnay ($$), Muscat ($), Arabesque (Bordeaux blend, $$), Merlot ($$), Cabernet Sauvignon ($$), Cabernet Sauvignon, La Cuesta ($$).

Castoro Cellars
1480 N. Bethel Road
Templeton, CA 93465
tel. (805) 238-0725; fax (805) 467-2004
Open to the public; est. 1983

"Castoro" is Italian for beaver, hence the creature's portrait on this winery's label. As a child, owner Niels Udsen was known as "Beaver" and as an adult, he continued to manifest the tenacious character of his nicknamesake. Determined to become involved in the wine industry following college, Niels and his wife, Berit, knocked on the doors of many California wineries. They received one rejection after another until Berit, responding to an advertisement for harvest help, found both of them work at Estrella River Winery. Niels spent five years there learning the ropes of grapegrowing and winemaking. In 1983, he founded Castoro, where he has five acres planted in Zinfandel. Purchasing additional grapes from

Paso Robles or within San Luis Obispo County, he produces 18,000 cases annually.

The emphasis here is on Cabernet and Zinfandel (both white and red) and on good value, though the winery produces a full range of white and red wines. The Cabernets, aged for a year in American oak, are reasonably big with earthy and varietal flavors. Over the years, we've enjoyed the Zinfandels—berryish, black pepper, and modestly priced—that come from the winery's 60-year-old dry-farmed vineyards. At under $10, the 1989 Cabernet Sauvignon Paso Robles is an attractive bottle, solidly medium-full body in weight and complexity, with ripe berries and plum flavors, a touch of oak, and a lacing of bracing tannins.

Wines/Varietals: Chardonnay ($), Fumé Blanc ($), White Zinfandel ($), Vintage Sparkling Wine ($$), Cabernet Sauvignon ($), Reserve Cabernet Sauvignon ($$), Gamay (nouveau-styled, $), Zinfandel ($)

Chansa Cellars
900 E. Stowell Road
Santa Maria, CA 93454
tel. (805) 928-9210
Not open to the public; est. 1988

Sometimes it's in the genes, and this tiny winery certainly has them. We think it could have a bright future. Owner and winemaker Kim McPherson—who graduated from Texas Tech University and then studied at U.C. Davis and worked at Trefethen Vineyards—is the son of Dr. Clinton McPherson, a leading figure as grower and winery owner in the Texas wine renaissance. (Kim's brother, Jon, is the winemaker for Culbertson Winery, the California sparkling wine operation in Temecula.) Kim is also winemaker at

Cap*Rock in Texas and is a consulting enologist for a few other Texas outposts. His dream is to make a go of it in California, thus "Chansa," Spanish slang for "a chance." He has set up shop in the Central Coast area and is currently buying all his grapes from a couple of choice local vineyards.

Production is currently under 1,000 cases of Chardonnay and Pinot Noir. Some Rhône varieties may be on the horizon. The Chardonnay is special: barrel fermented in large puncheons rather than small oak barrels and left on its lees for nearly a year. Also, a small percentage of Pinot Blanc is added. The result is a balanced, harmonious Chardonnay with a butterscotch nose and rich varietal flavors.

Wines/Varietals: Chardonnay, Santa Barbara County ($$), Pinot Noir ($$).

Claiborne & Churchill
860 E. Capitolio Way, PO Box 12742
San Luis Obispo, CA 93406
tel. (805) 544-4066; fax (805) 544-7012
Open to the public by appt.; est. 1983

This small winery specializing in white wines is owned and operated by the husband and wife team of Claiborne Thompson and Fredrika Churchill. Thompson, the winemaker, initially leased space from Edna Valley Vineyard before establishing his own facility. The five acres of vineyards owned by Claiborne & Churchill are to be planted in 1993; currently the 4,000 cases produced here annually are made from purchased Central Coast grapes.

Inspired by the wines of Alsace, Claiborne & Churchill currently produces a dry Riesling, a dry Gewürztraminer, a Muscat Canelli, and a proprietor's blend Edelzwicker (Riesling and Gewürztraminer with a touch of the Muscat) that's a fruity, flowery, everyday light wine. In the 1990 vintage, they also produced a standard Chardonnay and Pinot Noir. The Riesling and Gewürztraminer have proven consistent and appealing. The 1991 Gewürztraminer is an enjoyable, well-made bottle with floral and grapefruit varietal flavors.

Wines/Varietals: Dry Gewürztraminer ($), Dry Riesling ($), Chardonnay ($$), Pinot Noir ($$), NV Proprietor's Blend, Napa Valley (Edelzwicker, $), Dry Muscat ($).

Eberle Winery

Highway 46 East, PO Box 2459
Paso Robles, CA 93447
tel. (805) 238-9607; fax (805) 237-0344
Open to the public; est. 1982

U.C. Davis grad Gary Eberle came to Paso Robles in 1973 to put his study of enology and viticulture into practice. After supervising the development of a large vineyard for his stepbrother, Eberle and his wife, Jeanie, became convinced that only a smaller winery permits the kind of quality control that produces the best wines. They established their own operation, limiting production to 10,000 cases annually. The Eberles now have 42 acres, half planted in Cabernet Sauvignon, the remainder in Chardonnay (40 percent) and Muscat (10 percent).

Eberle and his team are proudest of their unblended estate Cabernets. The 1985 and 1987 are drinking especially well and display the winery's characteristic full-bodied style with flavor overtones of deep cherry, dried herbs, and coffee. The sweet-finish Muscat Canelli is notable for its crispness and classic Muscat flavors. We also liked the 1990 Paso Robles Sauret Vineyard Zinfandel with ripe raspberry and plum grace notes on a spicy, toasty oak base.

Wines/Varietals: Estate Chardonnay ($$), Estate Cabernet Sauvignon ($$), Zinfandel ($$), Estate Muscat Canelli ($).

Edna Valley Vineyard

2585 Biddle Ranch Road
San Luis Obispo, CA 93401
tel. (805) 544-9594; fax (805) 544-0112
Open to the public; est. 1980

A joint venture between Chalone Wine Group and Paragon Vineyard, Edna Valley Vineyard produces 58,000 cases of Chardonnay (90 percent) and Pinot Noir (10 percent) annually. The winery is located in the Central Coast region in the Edna Valley Viticultural Area. Of Edna Valley Vineyard's 700 acres, one-third are used for production; planned expansion will take production up to 80,000 cases. The quality to price ratio here is good: sound, flavorful wines are made and marketed at prices well below those of big brother Chalone.

We prefer the barrel fermented Chardonnays, which are characterized by ripe fruit and a good balance of acidity, to the Pinot Noir, produced here in smaller amounts. Very small quantities of Pinot Noir (briary), Vin Gris of Pinot Noir (dry, copper-colored, and full flavored), and Brut sparkling wine are also produced for sale only at the winery. The 1989 Chardonnay is a widely admired, elegant wine with peach and pear lushness. The 1991, released early in 1993, is dry, somewhat lean, and definitely crisp. It may round out nicely.

Wines/Varietals: Estate Chardonnay ($$), Reserve Chardonnay ($$$), Pinot Noir Vin Gris ($), Estate Pinot Noir ($$), Reserve Pinot Noir ($$).

Ficklin Vineyards

30246 Avenue 7-1/2
Madera, CA 93637
tel./fax (209) 674-4598
Open to the public by appt.; est. 1946

Firestone Vineyard

PO Box 244
Los Olivos, CA 93441
tel. (805) 688-3940; fax (805) 686-1256
Open to the public; est. 1973

Why not a place in this book for California's ranking producer of Port-like wines? In 1918, Walter and Mame Ficklin purchased the land that is now Ficklin Vineyards to grow fruit and raisin grapes. During the 1930s and 1940s, U.C. Davis experimentation indicated promise for the cultivation in the San Joaquin Valley of the varietals used to produce Portugal's premium red dessert wines. This study influenced the Ficklins' decision to grow wine grapes and produce wines following World War II. Walter and his sons committed themselves to producing only Port wine from top-quality Portuguese varietals, and to keeping production small enough to be completely overseen by the family—a commitment Ficklin Vineyards continues to honor today.

Ficklin's 31 planted acres comprise Tinta Madeira (19 acres), Tinta Cao (1 acre), Touriga (7 acres), and Souzao (4 acres). There's a Tinta NV (9,000 of the 10,000 cases produced annually) that's like a cross between a Ruby and a Vintage-character Port: smooth, sweet, and flavorful. And there's a vintage Port, done in the traditional manner, that's spicy, big, and rich.

Wines/Varietals: California NV Port ($$), Vintage Port ($$$).

Brooks Firestone is grandson of the founder of Firestone Tire and Rubber Company. After earning a degree in economics at Columbia University, he spent 11 years in the family business preparing to assume a top management position. But in the mid-seventies, his father, former Ambassador to Belgium Leonard K. Firestone, purchased a large parcel of land in Northern California and suggested that Brooks investigate the possibility of turning the property into a vineyard. Brooks' research led to his forming a three-way partnership with his father and Suntory Limited Company of Japan. In 1987, the Firestones acquired Carey Cellars (*see* separate entry), which is also located in the Santa Ynez Valley and is overseen by Kate Firestone, Brooks' wife.

With an additional 10 percent of purchased grapes, the 260 acres of vineyards here currently produce a total of 75,000 cases. Firestone's Cabernet Sauvignon and Merlot have greatly improved in recent years. One of the winery's best offerings is its Johannisberg Riesling—well-balanced with good fruit flavors. The 1991 is crisp with green apple flavors and sound balance. Among the reds, the 1990 Cabernet Sauvignon Reserve Santa Ynez Valley with its big Cab/blackberry nose, tight fruit, toasty oak, and chocolate flavors is the one to try— a good bottle that may develop into an excellent one. The Merlot, too, is likely to improve with time.

Wines/Varietals: Chardonnay ($$), Sauvignon Blanc ($), Johannisberg Riesling ($), Johannisberg Riesling, Selected Harvest (375 ml, $$), Dry Riesling ($), Gewürztraminer ($), Merlot ($$), Cabernet Sauvignon ($$), Cabernet Sauvignon, Vintage Reserve ($$).

The Gainey Vineyard

3950 Highway 246, PO Box 910
Santa Ynez, CA 93460
tel. (805) 688-0558; fax (805) 688-5864
Open to the public; est. 1984

Daniel Gainey produces about 15,000 cases of wine yearly on his 1,800-acre Santa Ynez Valley Arabian horse ranch. From the 62.5 planted acres here, as well as from purchased grapes (50 percent), The Gainey Vineyard makes European-styled wines that are marketed directly to consumers, and occasionally sold in exclusive wine shops.

Like all good winemakers, Gainey's Rich Longoria stresses "balance and varietal integrity" in his winemaking style. He emphasizes the importance of identifying quality vineyards producing grapes that can be used for limited bottlings of vineyard-designated wines. The 1990 Sauvignon Blanc is a good Central Coast rendering, but for razzmatazz, we prefer the Gainey Chardonnay with its Sanford & Benedict Vineyard grapes, and to a somewhat lesser degree, the Pinot Noir from the same vineyard. Look, too, for the 1990 Pinot Noir. And take note: the winery is high on the prospects for its 1991 reds.

Wines/Varietals: Sauvignon Blanc ($), Johannisberg Riesling ($), Chardonnay ($$), Late Harvest Johannisberg Riesling ($$), Cabernet Sauvignon ($$), Merlot ($$), Pinot Noir ($$$).

Justin Winery & Vineyard

11680 Chimney Rock Road
Paso Robles, CA 93446
tel. (805) 238-6932; fax (805) 238-7382
Open to the public; est. 1981

Former investment banker Justin Baldwin loves Bordeaux wines (his favorite is Château Margaux), and in 1981 he bought a 160-acre property in Paso Robles to produce the kind of wine he loves. One of the pioneering growers of premium wines in the Paso Robles area, he planted 70 acres of vineyards with the classic red grapes of Bordeaux—Cabernet Sauvignon, Merlot, and Cabernet Franc—as well as some Chardonnay. His 12-year-old vines afford him the luxury of producing as one of the few 100 percent estate wineries in the Central Coast region. Eight thousand cases of wine a year are turned out here; Justin does not expect that production will ever exceed 10,000 cases.

Justin used to make his own wine with the help of a consultant (his wife, Deborah, runs the small winery with him), but he recently hired Tim Spear as winemaker. The emphasis here is on low yields to produce a rich varietal character and on extended aging in oak barrels for the Cabs. Justin Winery produces a Paso Robles Cabernet that is 100 percent varietal and an Isosceles Reserve that reflects the three components of its blend: Cabernet Sauvignon, Merlot, and Cabernet Franc. Both are good in 1989 with a balance of the ripe fruit favored here and cedary characteristics in a big-bodied package. A

131

good Cabernet Franc is also produced. The 1988 Paso Robles Chardonnay (100 percent barrel fermented) is a rich, buttery, flavorful, Burgundy-style wine of distinction.

Wines/Varietals: Chardonnay, Paso Robles ($$), Cabernet Franc, Paso Robles ($$), Merlot, Paso Robles ($$), Cabernet Sauvignon, Paso Robles ($$), Isosceles Reserve ($$$).

Maison Deutz

453 Deutz Drive
Arroyo Grande, CA 93420
tel. (805) 481-1763; fax (805) 481-6920
Open to the public; est. 1985

Maison Deutz has leaped to prominence among California sparkling wines, proving itself one of the best in respect of balance, elegance, and finesse. Co-owned by Champagne Deutz of France and Wine World Estates, parent company of Beringer Vineyards in the Napa Valley, Maison Deutz is the state's only premium sparkling wine producer situated in the cool Central Coast region, south of San Luis Obispo. The winery's 150 acres of Pinot Noir, Chardonnay, and Pinot Blanc supply up to 70 percent of its grape needs; the remaining 30 percent is purchased from other Central Coast growers.

André Lallier-Deutz of Champagne Deutz established the style for this California sparkler and remains in close touch with winemaker Christian Rougenant. Of the roughly 29,000 cases now being produced here, most is non-vintage Brut Cuvée, an equal blend of Pinot Noir, Chardonnay, and Pinot Blanc. It's a briskly dry, crisp, and well-balanced wine. The Brut Rosé (princi-

pally Pinot Noir), also very dry but longer in the finish and with greater depth, has a faint coral hue. A small amount of Brut Reserve is made from exceptional lots and aged *en tirage* (on the yeasts) for three years. It is very French in nose, lightly toasty, clean, and more complex than either of the other bruts.

Wines/Varietals: Brut Cuvée ($$), Brut Rosé ($$), Brut Reserve ($$$).

Meridian Vineyards

7000 Highway 46 E., PO Box 3289
Paso Robles, CA 93447
tel. (805) 237-6000; fax (805) 239-5715
Open to the public; est. 1988

The "new" Meridian will be interesting to watch. Wine World Estates (Nestlé's California wine group) purchased a bankrupt winery with 560 acres of Paso Robles vineyards in 1988 and then bought the Meridian label from Charles Ottman, bringing the experienced, high-tech winemaker into the new venture. Meridian can draw upon 3,500 acres (560 at the winery and the rest in Santa Barbara County) planted to Cabernet Sauvignon, Chardonnay, Syrah, and Pinot Noir. This winery gets its first pick of the fruit and the rest is sold to other wineries. A lot of money has been poured into the operation: the winery is state-of-the-art, and 5,000 French oak barrels are already being used (you can taste them across the line), with more on the way.

Good quality and fine value are already in evidence here. The trick now will be to sustain this early success in the face of growing production (Meridian does not disclose production numbers). Winemaking is the thing here, and especially generating high-end Chardonnays at moderate prices. The Chardonnays show bright and focused fruit characteristic of this region—mostly along tropical flavor lines for the Santa Barbara designation and more melony lines for the Edna Valley bottling. The 1990 Chards are good ones. The reds drink easily as well—the Cabs are not overpowered by the vegetal quality so prevalent in this area. The 1989 is a fine wine, tight and tannic. It will likely take until, say, 1994 to start showing its best stuff. For us, Meridian's most interesting wine is the Syrah made from Paso Robles estate grapes cultivated on vines grown from Chapoutier cuttings planted in 1972. The 1989 Syrah is bursting with the taste of strawberry and raspberry on top of black pepper barrel flavors.

Wines/Varietals: Chardonnay, Santa Barbara County ($$), Chardonnay, Edna Valley ($$), Pinot Noir, Santa Barbara County ($$), Cabernet Sauvignon, Paso Robles ($$), Syrah, Paso Robles ($$).

The Ojai Vineyard

10540 Encinco Drive, PO Box 952
Oak View, CA 93022
tel. (805) 649-1674 or (805) 687-4967;
fax (805) 687-2342
Not open to the public; est. 1984

Owners Adam Tolmach (who was also co-owner of Au Bon Climat until 1991) and Helen Hardenbergh are the dynamic duo behind this 5.5-acre Central Coast mini-winery. Though small in size, Ojai is big on quality: Old world winemaking is spoken here. Tolmach and Hardenbergh take pride in growing their grapes without the use of herbicides or fertilizers. They stress the vines by means of limited watering practices, sacrificing higher yields for better results at harvest. Two-thirds of Ojai's fruit is pur-

chased to supplement estate grown Syrah (50 percent of the vineyards), Sauvignon Blanc (33 percent), and Sémillon (17 percent). Production here is 3,000 cases annually.

Ojai's white grapes are hand-picked and pressed without crushing. After initial aging in French oak, the white wines here undergo secondary malolactic fermentation and remain on their lees from December until they are racked in the spring. Ojai Syrah is made with some of the grapes added as whole clusters during fermentation to increase tannin and complexity. The wine completes malolactic fermentation in the fall, but is not racked until spring. After the following autumn's harvest, the wine is fined with egg whites and bottled—always unfiltered. What's in the bottle of the 1989 Syrah is pretty special: this wine is lush and intensely flavored with a long finish. Also rather remarkable is the 1990 Cuvée Spéciale, Sainte Hélène, Santa Ynez Valley, Buttonwood Farm (67 percent Sauvignon Blanc, 33 percent Sémillon), which shows a decided improvement over the 1989.

Wines/Varietals: Chardonnay, Bien Nacido Vineyard, Santa Barbara County ($$), Sauvignon Blanc ($$), Cuvée Spéciale, Sainte Hélène, Buttonwood Farm, Santa Ynez Valley ($$), Syrah, California Vineyards (50 percent Ojai, 50 percent Bien Nacido Vineyards, $$).

Qupé

PO Box 440
Los Olivos, CA 93441
tel. (805) 688-2477; fax (707) 688-4470
Not open to the public; est. 1982

Owner/winemaker Bob Lindquist started making Chardonnay in a temporary winery

133

in 1982—classic, full-blown, California Chardonnay. He has subsequently toned down his style a bit and moved in spectacular fashion to producing wines in the Rhône manner. Since 1989 Lindquist has shared a new winery facility in the Santa Maria Valley with Jim Clendenen of Au Bon Climat (they were once co-workers at Zaca Mesa Winery). The owners of Bien Nacido Vineyard, both vintners' principal grape source, built the winery for them. Qupé (a Native American word for poppy) is presently working up to a 10,000 case annual production.

Some 2,000 of the cases are of superb Syrah, arguably the finest and most authentic Rhône-style wine currently being made in America. The 1989 Bien Nacido Vineyard is terrific: full of robust flavors with cherry at the core and all sorts of spicy flavors buzzing around, from pepper to oak to cedar. The regular Central Coast Syrah is good, too, well balanced and flavorful but smoother and not quite as big. The regular Santa Barbara Syrah is in between the other two. It's spicy and has plenty of plum character and depth. Lindquist was among the first of the contemporary Californians to bottle Mourvèdre, Viognier, and Marsanne, the latter yielding a pleasant and, thus far, mild and fruity red wine. The Chardonnay here is easy to like. It's consistently crisp and clean, with citrus and apple flavors and a touch of oak and honey. Lindquist also co-produces Vita Nova wines with Jim Clendenen. (*See* Vita Nova)

Wines/Varietals: Chardonnay, Sierre Madre, Santa Barbara ($$), Chardonnay, Sierre Madre Reserve ($$$), Marsanne ($$), Syrah, Los Olivos, Santa Barbara ($$), Syrah, Central Coast ($$), Syrah, Bien Nacido ($$$).

Sanford Winery

7250 Santa Rosa Road
Buellton, CA 93427
tel. (805) 688-3300; fax (805) 688-7381
Open to the public; est. 1981

Sanford's award-winning flower labels are beautiful, and lately the wines inside the bottles are beautiful, too—especially the Pinot Noir and increasingly the Chardonnay. Richard Sanford was half of the Sanford and Benedict Winery, before he and partner Mike Benedict agreed to go their separate ways in 1980. The Sanford way led to the launch of Sanford Winery with wife Thekla. They first set up shop in leased space at Edna Valley Vineyards and are currently working out of a Buellton industrial complex. A new winery of their own is currently under construction on a 730-acre property that is part of the original Santa Rosa Land Grant. (It's being built of adobe brick for the material's insulating qualities as well as for its natural beauty.) Sanford's 113 acres of Santa Barbara County vineyards, planted to Chardonnay (60 percent) and Pinot Noir (40 percent), are supplemented by additional purchased fruit (60 percent), to produce 34,000 cases annually.

Winemaker Bruno D'Alfonso takes a traditional approach: whites are fermented in 60-gallon French oak barrels, Pinot Noir in open-top stainless steel tanks, and Sauvignon Blanc is partially fermented in American oak. A vegetal, herbal varietal and regional character is prominent in some vintages of the Sauvignon Blanc, though we find it recedes with a couple of years in the bottle. The Chardonnay here is of the big, buttery, spicy, oaky sort. The regular bottling shows more tropical fruit than the Barrel Select—a highly-reputed, top-class wine. We highly recommend the 1988, 1989, and 1990.

Sanford's Pinot Noir keeps getting better and better. The 1989 and 1990 Santa Barbara County Pinot Noir is lovely stuff, with lush strawberry and cherry fruit flavors.

Wines/Varietals: Chardonnay, Barrel Select ($$$), Chardonnay ($$), Sauvignon Blanc ($), Pinot Noir, Vin Gris ($), Pinot Noir ($$), Pinot Noir, Barrel Select ($$$).

Santa Barbara Winery
202 Anacapa Street
Santa Barbara, CA 93101
tel. (805) 963-3646; fax (805) 962-4981
Open to the public; est. 1962

This is the oldest of the few downtown Santa Barbara wineries. About a decade after it was established, owner Pierre Lafond became quite serious about Santa Barbara County's potential to produce premium wines. Purchasing land in the lower end of the Santa Ynez Valley, he planted 72 acres of vines in 1972. The wines made here have always had beautiful labels done by local artists; more and more, the wines themselves are making good impressions. In the past few years, president and winemaker (since 1981) Bruce McGuire has been producing some well-priced wines of high quality which are demanding of attention.

The 1990 Chardonnay from the Lafond Vineyard convinced us that Santa Barbara Winery should be counted among those in this book. It's a lovely medium-bodied wine

with plenty of tropical fruit and toasty oak flavors, well balanced and with good acidity—a quality performance. There is a range of Chardonnays done here, and the least expensive one, the 1990 Santa Barbara County, is a sound, serviceable wine with pleasing, full, and true flavors. McGuire puts his whites through extended lees contact. His dry Chenin Blanc made from barrel fermented Santa Ynez Valley grapes is a good buy, and with its barrel aging, a surprisingly complex wine. For Pinot Noir and Zinfandel, he uses whole cluster fermentation to bring out the spiciness, intense fruit flavors, and tannins in the wine. The Pinot Noir here is fine, generally soft, fruity, and simple; the Reserve draws 60 percent of its fruit from the highly regarded Bien Nacido Vineyard in Santa Maria. Also noteworthy is "Beaujour," a light, fruity, Beaujolais-style Zinfandel that's an agreeable quaffer. The 1992 Beaujour made from Central Coast grapes is a good, inexpensive value. At the other end of the spectrum, Santa Barbara Winery offers a line of reserve wines of increasing quality.

Wines/Varietals: Chardonnay, Santa Barbara County ($$), Chardonnay, Santa Ynez Valley Reserve ($$$), Chardonnay, Lafond Vineyard ($$$), Dry Chenin Blanc ($), Sauvignon Blanc, Santa Ynez Valley ($), Sauvignon Blanc, Santa Ynez Valley Reserve ($$), Paradis (Riesling, $), Johannisberg Riesling ($), Zinfandel Beaujour ($), Pinot Noir, Santa Barbara County ($$), Reserve Pinot Noir ($$), Cabernet Sauvignon, Santa Ynez Valley ($$), Cabernet Sauvignon, Santa Ynez Valley Reserve ($$$), Zinfandel, Saucelito Canyon ($$), Late Harvest Sauvignon Blanc ($$), Late Harvest Johannisberg Riesling ($$), Late Harvest Zinfandel Essence ($$).

Vita Nova

Box 822
Los Olivos, CA 93441
tel. (805) 688-2477 or 688-8630; fax (805) 686-1016
Not open to the public; est. 1986

Bob Lindquist of Qupé and Jim Clendenen of Au Bon Climat, co-workers since their days together at Zaca Mesa Winery in the late 1970s, have shared a winery facility since they went off on their own, separately, in 1982. In 1986, they decided to make a Bordeaux-style wine together, and so was born "Vita Nova" (New Life) of which Lindquist and Clendenen are co-owners and co-winemakers. Some 3,000 cases of Vita Nova wine, including a Chardonnay, are now made each year out of the modern Santa Maria Valley winery on the Bien Nacido Vineyard that the two men have worked in together— producing their own brands—since 1989.

All of Vita Nova's grapes are purchased. Those for the Cabernet blend generally come from the Santa Barbara and Central Coast regions, with Cabernet Franc and Merlot very prominent components in the wine. The proprietary wine now goes by the name "Reservatum" and tends to show both the area's and the Cabernet Franc grape's strong herbal character, though the wine is otherwise well-balanced. The Chardonnay, made from grapes from the Rancho Viñedo Vineyard, is a good one with an earthy character and plenty of toasty, buttery and apply flavors. A barrel fermented Sauvignon Blanc-Sémillon blend from Santa Ynez Valley grapes has recently been added to the line, and in 1990 was tart but rich in flavor.

Wines/Varietals: Chardonnay, Santa Barbara ($$), Sauvignon Blanc, Chien Méchant ($$), Reservatum ($$).

Wild Horse Winery

1484 Wild Horse Winery Court
Templeton, CA 93465
tel. (805) 434-2541; fax (805) 434-3516
Open to the public by appt.; est. 1982

This Santa Barbara County winery is closely identified with its owner and winemaker, Ken Volk, who built operations here up to the 30,000 or so case level by producing winning, moderately priced wines year after year. His vineyard-designated Pinot Noirs, in particular, were early successes with the wine-loving pubic. Adjacent to the winery, Volk has 38 acres of vineyards in the Paso Robles district, planted mostly to Chardonnay. He buys most of his additional grapes from Santa Maria Valley growers.

Chardonnay, the volume leader here, is a good wine and most impressive in 1990 with plenty of fresh fruit and spice flavors with pear and fig components notable. But it is its range of Pinot Noirs that still distinguishes Wild Horse. All have attractive flavors, displaying cherries and spices, and all are fairly meaty wines. The 1987 Paso Robles Pinot Noir is a memorable one. The regular Santa Barbara bottling is fine, though the Barrel Select is even finer—for twice the price.

Wines/Varietals: Chardonnay, Central Coast ($$), Pinot Noir, Santa Barbara ($$), Pinot Noir, Barrel Select ($$$), Merlot, Central Coast ($$), Cabernet Sauvignon, Paso Robles ($$).

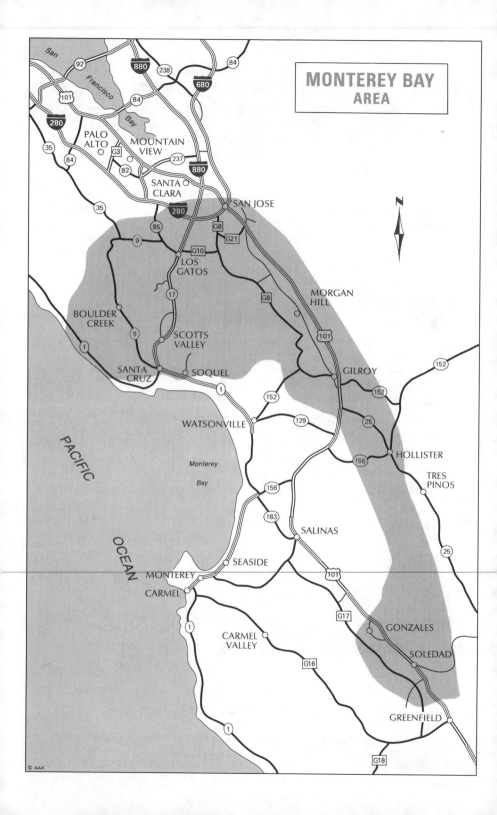

Monterey

Bonny Doon Vineyard
PO Box 8376
Santa Cruz, CA 95061
Winery: 10 Pine Flat Road, Bonny Doon,
CA 95060
tel. (408) 425-3625; fax (408) 425-3856
Open to the public; est. 1983

This much-admired and influential, maverick winery is the expression of its bright, irreverent, and driven owner and winemaker, Randall Grahm. He writes: "Like Columbus who sought a trade route to Asia, I set out in search of the great American Pinot Noir, foundered on the shoals of astringency and finesselessness and ended up running aground in the utterly unexpected New World of Rhône and Italian varietals." (The latter are now bottled under the Ca' del Solo label.) A charter member of the so-called Rhône Rangers, Grahm produces 32,000 cases annually, utilizing mostly purchased grapes to augment fruit from his 64 acres of Santa Cruz Mountains and Monterey County vineyards.

Quality is very high here. Grahm describes his winemaking imperatives thus: "1) having as much fun with the wine as the relevant governmental agencies will allow; 2) producing wines and wine labels that will scintillate the sensibilities of the most jaded imbiber; 3) retaining as much of the natural qualities of grapes (especially fragrance) through careful handling and minimal cellar treatment. Limpidity, for its own sake, is eschewed; 4) paying particularly close attention to the 'chestnut' of wine being pro-

duced in the vineyard." We're fans of his Châteauneuf-du-Pape blend (Grenache, Mourvèdre, Syrah, Cinsault) called Le Cigare Volant and recommend the 1989 vintage. The 1990 Le Sophiste (a Roussanne/Marsanne blend) also tickles our white Rhône-fancying heart. The Vin Gris de Cigare, a dry, fruity blush wine, is consistently pleasing and versatile as is the Clos de Gilroy, a nouveau-styled Mourvèdre blend. Don't miss the Muscat Canelli "Vin de Glacière," which in the 1990 vintage is probably the best North American dessert wine we tasted all year.

Wines/Varietals: Vin Gris de Cigare ($), Chardonnay, La Reina, Monterey ($$), Chardonnay, Santa Cruz Mountain Estate ($$$), Le Sophiste ($$$), Ca' del Solo Malvasia Bianca ($), Ca' del Solo Moscato del Solo ($), Ca' del Solo, Il Pescatore ($$$), Clos de Gilroy ($), Syrah, Santa Cruz Mountains Estate ($$$), Le Cigare Volant ($$$), Ca' del Solo Big House Red ($), Muscat Canelli, Vin de Glacière ($$), NV Framboise, Infusion of Raspberry ($).

Calera Wine Company
11300 Cienega Road
Hollister, CA 95023
tel. (408) 637-9170; fax (408) 637-9070
Open to the public by appt.; est. 1975

A few feet from the San Andreas fault amid isolated limestone hills in the western San Benito County (hardly a chichi wine area), Josh Jensen set out in 1975 to prove that a top-flight Burgundy-style Pinot Noir could be produced in America. Eschewing some of the prevailing U.C. Davis-promulgated views on how to do things, Jensen looked to the soil and kept intervention during winemaking to a minimum to achieve his goal. The results have been splendid and trendsetting. The question now for Jensen and his low-frills winery is: Where do we go from here? In the 1980s, Calera started producing Central Coast Chardonnay and Pinot Noir from purchased grapes to support the small quantity of estate wines it could produce. Now these lesser, though still good, wines account for approximately 16,000 of the winery's 19,000 case annual production.

Calera's flagship wines come from its own 42 acres of chalky mountaintop vineyards. Pinot Noirs come from Jensen, Reed, and Selleck estates. Five acres of estate vineyards are planted in Viognier (resulting in a lush and overpoweringly fragrant wine) and six in Chardonnay (producing a big, toasty, barrel fermented wine). In general, all the estate grapes go through slow, whole cluster maceration, are fermented with natural yeasts, and are rarely racked. The Central Coast wines produced here are sound and somewhat simple; nearly the antithesis of the ripe, rich, and elegant estate Pinots with their layers of complexity and potential for aging. The 1987 Jensen Pinot Noir is a classic bottle to be sought out, and the more recent 1989 Mills Pinot Noir is already seductive, with a medium-full body and lovely dark and deep flavors. In 1992, Jensen's long-time winemaker, Steve Doerner, took off for the Pacific Northwest, so we await new developments at Calera in the next few years.

Wines/Varietals: Estate Pinot Noirs ($$$), Estate Chardonnay ($$$), Estate Viognier ($$$), Chardonnay, Central Coast ($$), Pinot Noir, Central Coast ($$).

Chalone Vineyard

Stonewall Canyon Road, PO Box 855
Soledad, CA 93960
tel. (408) 678-1717; fax (408) 678-2742
Open to the public weekends; weekdays by appt.; est. 1961 (in continuous operation since 1965)

Through much of the late 1970s and the 1980s, Chalone, with its single-vineyard appellation, stood apart from the rest of California's premium wine industry as a monument to quality. It produced incredibly rich, Burgundy-style Chardonnays and Pinot Noirs that are world-class in every dimension. Other wineries have now achieved similar levels of quality, yet Chalone's wines remain distinctive, owing their special character to the soil (rich in limestone) and microclimate (arid) of the winery's 187 acres of vineyards. Chalone wines have what is admired in Burgundy as *goût de terroir*. The winery is distinctive as well for being the namesake of a publicly traded group of wineries (the Chalone Wine Group). One of the group's key investors is the Château Lafite concern in Bordeaux.

Michael Michaud has been making the wine here since 1979. All 35,000 cases produced annually are from estate grapes (excepting a few thousand cases of Gavilan, a somewhat irregularly produced, lower priced, second label made of grapes from various appellations). Fifty-seven percent of production is Chardonnay and we won't soon forget the great Chardonnays made here in 1982 and 1985. They resemble a Montrachet—big, oaky, fruity, impressively powerful, yet elegant and truly profound. They require bottle age. The 1990, tasted on numerous occasions, is fine: crisp and medium-big in body with apple and honey flavors. The 1991 is right on target as a classic. We've also enjoyed the barrel fermented Pinot Blanc as a good, clean, superbly balanced, and refreshing wine with toast and pear flavors—the best of this varietal made in the U.S.: The 1991 is fabulous. As with all of Chalone's wines, this one's price gives one pause. But with quality like this, these bottles provide value nevertheless. As for the house's Pinot Noirs, the 1990 is a good one. The reserve Pinot Noir is a tough bottle to come by; it goes almost exclusively to Chalone stockholders, who, as a perquisite of ownership, receive special buying privileges.

Wines/Varietals: Chardonnay ($$$), Reserve Chardonnay ($$$), Gavilan Chardonnay ($$), Chenin Blanc ($$),* Pinot Blanc *($$), Pinot Noir ($$$), Reserve Pinot Noir ($$$), Gavilan Pinot Noir ($$).

David Bruce Winery

21435 Bear Creek Road
Los Gatos, CA 95030
tel. (408) 354-4214; fax (408) 395-5478
Open to the public; est. 1961

Physician David Bruce's winery in the Santa Cruz mountains above the community of Los Gatos is a pioneering, quintessential California boutique winery that helped put the state's wine industry back on the world map in the 1960s and 1970s. Bruce was a bold experimenter, producing white Zinfandel, toying with Rhône varietals, and turning out powerhouse Pinot Noir in the 1960s. His full-blown Chardonnays and Zinfandels of the 1970s were state-of-the-art then and are still representative, classic, California-style wines. Bruce has recently returned to making highly-extracted Zinfandels, and his Chardonnay is a bit tamer, though still good. Making a great

Pinot Noir has been his long-held dream, and today, at last, Pinot is Bruce's best wine. Production here averages 25,000 cases.

Bruce likes to boast of his commitment to using the best techniques available—no matter the cost. As his own winemaker, he combines labor-intensive traditional methodology with what, in his view, are very untraditional, independent ideas of winemaking. He's known, for example, for working with very ripe grapes and going for high extract. He barrel ferments his Chardonnays, puts them through malolactic fermentation, and then adds a lot of oak from new barrels. The 1990 Estate Chardonnay is a good bottle with lots of oak and pear power. A lighter hand is used in making the Pinot Noir. The 1989 Estate Pinot Noir is very good: strawberries, violets, and cedar on the nose and on the palate with added vanilla and cherry highlights, good balance, acidity, feel, and finish. Bruce's 1989 Cabernet shows good perfume and balance, and reflects the winemaker's philosophy of building Cabs by freely blending vineyards and varietals. Bruce also produces a Petite Sirah and other blends on occasion.

Wines/Varietals: California Chardonnay ($$), Estate Chardonnay ($$$), Petite Sirah, Vintner's Select ($$), Cabernet Sauvignon ($$), California Pinot Noir ($$), Estate Pinot Noir ($$$).

Jekel Vineyards

40155 Walnut Avenue
Greenfield, CA 93927
tel. (408) 674-5522; fax (408) 674-3769
Open to the public; est. 1972

In 1972, Bill Jekel planted 140 acres of grapes on the sloping Arroyo Seco alluvial fan just west of Greenfield in Monterey's Salinas Valley. Marina winds from the Monterey Bay dominate the summer climate here, making this one of coolest winegrape regions in California. In 1983, Jekel planted an additional 187 acres abutting the Arroyo Seco river, convinced that the cool microclimate, longer growing season, and rocky soil would serve to showcase his Johannisberg Riesling, Chardonnay, and Cabernet Sauvignon. Jekel was a tremendously successful promoter of his good wines and their *terroir* in the early 1980s. In recent years, this winery has built up to a 65,000 case annual production and added Merlot and Cabernet Franc to its line. All wines here are currently made from estate-grown grapes.

In 1992, the Brown-Forman spirits concern purchased the winery. Some organizational changes have been made and Jekel's former assistant, Joel Burnstein, was named winemaker, so it's too early to say in which direction Jekel may now move (though an increase in production to 100,000 cases is planned). There are, nevertheless, several Jekel wines currently available that are worthy of note. The 1990 Estate-Grown Chardonnay is 60 percent barrel fermented with extended *sur lies* time that together give the wine a rich mouthfeel and appealing tropical fruit characteristics. The 1991 Johannisberg Riesling, not harvested until almost November, is a pale gold wine with flavors of apricot and kiwi; the residual sugar is balanced by decent acidity and a slight spritz on the finish. Over the years, Jekel's Johannisberg Riesling has proven to be the winery's most consistently appealing wine. The 1989 Cabernet Sauvignon (blended with 20 percent Merlot and 5 percent Cabernet Franc), along raspberry-cherry lines with moderate tannins, is a very drinkable wine.

Wines/Varietals: Johannisberg Riesling ($), Chardonnay ($$), Merlot ($$), Cabernet Sauvignon ($), Cabernet Franc ($$).

J. Lohr Winery
1000 Lenzen Avenue
San Jose, CA 95126
tel. (408) 288-5057; fax (408) 993-2276
Open to the public; est. 1974

It's getting better all the time for Jerry Lohr. Wishing to move beyond his home construction business, Lohr and his then-partner, Bernie Turgeon, purchased a 280-acre vineyard in Monterey County in the early 1970s. They converted an old San Jose brewery site into a winery and tasting room and began producing a good, if somewhat inconsistent, line of wines. Now the sole owner of 1,100 acres of vineyards, divided nearly equally between Arroyo Seco in Monterey County and Paso Robles, Lohr is accumulating accolades from noted connoisseurs for his revamped line-up of good-value wines. With the addition of 15 to 20 percent purchased grapes, this winery's production is now at 250,000 cases annually.

Winemaker Jeff Runquist joined Lohr in 1990. The best of the wines made here is certainly the Monterey County Riverstone Vineyard Reserve Chardonnay, amply proportioned and full-flavored along tropical fruit lines, and impressively consistent from 1987 to 1990. Among the reds, we've enjoyed the 1988 J. Lohr Estates "Seven Oaks" Paso Robles Cabernet. Smooth, with ripe raspberry-style fruit, oak, sweet vanilla flavors and a medium finish, it's a good wine, and at $13 (with discounts perhaps even less), a fine value. In addition to the J. Lohr Estates brand, which includes "Riverstone," "Seven Oaks," "Wildflower," and "Bay Mist" label designations, Lohr also produces a "Cypress" brand that is priced even more affordably. Happily, the lower cost does not reflect any notable compromise in quality: Cypress wines are solid, everyday wines.

Wines/Varietals: J. Lohr Estates brand: Chardonnay, Riverstone, Monterey ($$), Cabernet, Seven Oaks, Paso Robles ($$), Gamay, Wildflower, Monterey ($); Johannisberg Riesling, Bay Mist, Monterey ($); Cypress brand: Chardonnay ($), Chenin Blanc ($), White Zinfandel ($), White Table Wine ($), Fumé Blanc ($), Napa Valley Blush Table Wine ($), Cabernet Sauvignon ($), Merlot ($), Red Table Wine ($).

Mirassou Winery

3000 Aborn Road
San Jose, CA 95135
tel. (408) 274-4000; fax (408) 270-5881
Open to the public; est. 1854

Thwarted in his quest for gold, Pierre Pellier settled in the eastern foothills of the Santa Clara Valley in the early 1850s and planted grapes. For over a century, these vineyards have been carefully tended by the Mirassou family: they certainly get points for longevity. In 1961, brothers Ed and Norm Mirassou (fourth generation family vintners) became the first growers to plant vines in Monterey. The Mirassous today own 750 acres of vineyard in Monterey. Their winery produces 250,000 cases of wine annually, requiring the purchase of some additional fruit (25-30 percent).

Mirassou wines are widely distributed throughout the U.S. The winery's most interesting current offering is the 1991 Harvest Reserve Pinot Blanc. Winemaker Tom Stutz's effort (80 percent barrel fermenta-tion, 100 percent malolactic fermentation) exhibits a fresh, pear/appley varietal charac-ter, buoyed by a toasty vanillin richness. The 1990 Brut (69 percent Pinot Noir, 19 per-cent Chardonnay, 12 percent Pinot Blanc) suggests that some appealing sparklers are now being made here. While the Bruts have tended toward off-dry, we had our eyes opened to Mirassou's renewed quality by the winery's 1988 Au Naturel Cuvée, a fairly crisp and clean wine with underlying citrus and spice flavors. This house's reds tend to be simple, drinkable wines. The 1990 Cabernet Sauvignon (blended with 8 per-cent Caberent Franc and 7 percent Merlot) has forward berry fruit and a bit of chocolate in the nose, and moderate tannins on the palate. The 1990 Merlot is typically light in classic cherry and herb flavors, but balanced and easy drinking.

Wines/Varietals: Chardonnay ($), Chardonnay, Harvest Reserve ($$), Sauvignon Blanc ($), Riesling ($), Chenin Blanc ($), White Burgundy ($), White Zinfandel ($), Pinot Blanc, Harvest Reserve ($$), Cabernet Sauvignon ($), Cabernet Sauvignon, Harvest Reserve ($$), Zinfandel ($), Pinot Noir ($), Pinot Noir, Harvest Reserve ($$), Petit Sirah ($), Cru Gamay ($), Merlot ($), Blanc de Noirs Sparkling Wine ($$), Brut Sparking Wine ($$), Brut Reserve Sparkling Wine ($$), Au Naturel Sparkling Wine ($$).

Morgan Winery

526 Brunken Avenue
Salinas, CA 93901
tel. (408) 422-9855; fax (408) 422-9880
Not open to the public; est. 1982

Daniel Morgan Lee originally set out to be a doctor but moved into winemaking after taking enology courses at U.C. Davis. He and his wife Donna, a loan officer for Wells

143

Fargo Bank, met at a Monterey Winegrowers Association meeting. They started making wine at home, working nights and weekends, while Dan gained experience in day jobs at such wineries as Jekel and Durney. In 1984, the Lees moved their operation to a new building in the town of Salinas. They currently buy all of their grapes for the 20,000 cases of varietals produced at Morgan.

This winery made its name with rich, oaky Chardonnays that wine enthusiasts became enamored of early on. Morgan Chardonnay is an excellent example of all that Chardonnay from Monterey can be. Barrel fermented, this wine undergoes 100 percent malolactic fermentation and is one of the few California Chards that actually benefit from such treatment, because the acidity of the Monterey grape is initially so high (most Chardonnays don't have enough natural acidity to warrant the technique). Through it all, this wine remains crisp but full and rich with lots of upfront fruit and nice toasty vanillin oak, as in the 1990 Reserve, a good wine that will likely be even better in 1994 or 1995. Morgan Sauvignon Blanc, from the Alexander Valley, is slightly grassy but nicely rounded by the addition of Sémillon (averaging 10 percent) and a brief stay in oak. The winery's rather earthy Cabernet Sauvignon, somewhat muscular in structure, is from a vineyard in the Carmel Valley. Lee is now in working with Pinot Noir and has made a couple that show genuine promise. We quite like his 1989 Pinot with its pretty, slightly tart but smokey fruit.

Wines/Varietals: Chardonnay ($$), Chardonnay Reserve ($$$), Pinot Noir ($$), Sauvignon Blanc ($), Cabernet Sauvignon ($$).

Ridge Vineyards
17100 Monte Bello Road,
PO Box 1810
Cupertino, CA 95014
tel. (408) 867-3233; fax (408) 867-2986
Open to the public; est. 1892 (in continuous operation as Ridge since 1962)

One of California's top wineries, Ridge Vineyards was started in 1959 when a group of engineers from Stanford Research Institute purchased a tract of abandoned hilltop land for camping and other amusements. They discovered that the property included the old Monte Bello vineyard (first planted in 1892), situated 2,300 feet up, on a ridge overlooking the Santa Clara Valley. Back then there were only 60 wineries in California; today Ridge is one of nearly 800 or so. Formally established in 1962, this was the first winery of the modern era to focus on appellations, buying grapes from carefully selected regions or vineyards and designating the source on the label. Ridge made its name in the seventies with Zinfandels labeled "Geyserville" (from Lytton Springs Vineyard), "Fiddletown" (Amador), "York Creek" (Spring Mountain in Napa Valley), "Jimsomare" (on Monte Bello ridge), and "Paso Robles," and a consistently stunning Cabernet Sauvignon, referred to simply as "Monte Bello." "Our approach," says Paul Draper, winemaker since 1969 and CEO, "is to begin with the most flavorful, intense grapes and intrude as little as possible on the natural process." The vineyards, all planted in well-drained soils and often at high elevations, are harvested block by block as they ripen. The wines here are fermented with natural yeasts, aged in a combination of American and French oak, and left largely unfiltered to retain maximum fruit and flavor. In 1986, Ridge was purchased by A. Otsuka, a Japanese wine enthusiast and owner of a large pharmaceutical company in Japan. Continuity here remains unbroken, however. Even the old winery, built into the mountainside in the 1880s, has not changed since it was restored—in an unobtrusive, rustic fashion—in the sixties.

Production nears about 45,000 cases, half from Ridge's 150 acres on Monte Bello (82 percent in Cabernet Sauvignon, the rest in Merlot, Cabernet Franc, and Chardonnay), plus the 50 acres of the Ridge owned Lytton Springs Vineyard in Sonoma, and 20 acres on Howell Mountain in the Napa Valley (100 percent Chardonnay). Ridge purchases grapes for half its production from growers under long-term contract. Though the Monte Bello Cabernet represents only 10 percent of production, it is indisputably the signature wine here. Densely textured with complex flavors—ripe berries, herbs, olive, cedar—the 1990 Monte Bello is a classic, probably the equal of the legendary 1970 (still intense and profound). The 1989, more forward in fruit, immediately engages, though it will easily see out a decade or two. Ridge Zinfandels are big, juicy, berry-flavored wines, released young and readily drinkable, though they, too, are capable of aging several years, often becoming rather claret-like as they do. Ridge's hallmark Zin is the Geyserville, which contains grapes from 100-plus year old Alexander Valley vines. Others Zins, including the Lytton Springs, the York Creek (this vineyard also produces Cabernet and Petite Sirah), and the Paso Robles, are all jammed with berryish fruit in varying degrees of intensity. The Sonoma appellation is the lightest. All the Zinfandels age in American oak, which Draper feels works best with the wine's fruit. Ridge has increased its production of Chardonnay in recent years, producing one from vineyards on Monte Bello with a Santa Cruz Mountains appellation, and a second one from Howell Mountain. Both are good, but the 1990 Santa Cruz has the edge for sheer flavor excitement: crisp but buttery with long, lingering flavors that can only deepen over the next year or so. Ridge's labels provide the equivalent of a wine course, offering as much detail as possible about vineyard origin, harvest conditions, winemaking techniques, and proportions of grapes in the blend.

Wines/Varietals: Cabernet Sauvignon, Monte Bello ($$$), Cabernet Sauvignon, Santa Cruz ($$), Cabernet Sauvignon, Jimsomare ($$), Cabernet Sauvignon, York Creek ($$), Zinfandel, Geyserville ($$), Zinfandel, Lytton Springs ($$), Zinfandel, Paso Robles ($$), Zinfandel, York Creek ($$), Zinfandel, Howell Mountain ($$), Zinfandel, Sonoma ($), Merlot, Bradford Mountain ($$), Chardonnay, Santa Cruz Mountains ($$), Chardonnay, Howell Mountain ($$), Petite Sirah, York Creek ($$).

Robert Talbott Vineyards

1380 River Rd., PO Box 776
Gonzales, CA 93926-0776
tel. (408) 675-3000; fax (408) 675-3120
Not open to the public; est. 1982

From their garage in Carmel, Robb Talbott's parents launched a necktie company in 1950 that eventually grew to be an international success. But the Talbotts had always wanted to own a winery, and in the early 1980s, they at last saw their dream come true. Following his father's retirement from the clothing business, Robb Talbott decided to turn the family's Diamond T Ranch into a vineyard. Robert Talbott Vineyard's first release in 1983 made good on the family's promise to produce top-quality Chardonnay. The subsequent 1984 vintage, however, was below the high standards the Talbotts set for themselves, so Robb and his father poured all 3,000 cases of the wine down the drain. They've never had to do that again: today Talbott Chardonnay are among the most esteemed (and costly) on the market.

The vineyard here totals 134 acres, and buying in 70 percent of their grapes, Robb and winemaker Sam Balderas now produce 12,000 cases a year. Seven percent of Talbott's vineyards are devoted to Pinot Noir; this varietal will surely figure in the winery's future. There are currently three Chardonnays produced here: Monterey, Diamond T Estate, and Logan Chardonnay, a second label bottling. All three are good; the Monterey and Diamond T are generally very good, with layers of fruit and mineral characteristics laced with a crisp acidity that invites cellaring and suggests a long life. Top vintages are 1990 and 1989, and if you can find a bottle of Talbott's 1986 Monterey Chardonnay, drink it to see why people are eager to pay the price to own a Talbott wine. "Commitment to quality" is much more than a glib slogan here.

Wines/Varietals: Chardonnay, Monterey ($$$), Chardonnay, Diamond T Estate ($$$), Logan Chardonnay ($$).

Sarah's Vineyard

4005 Hecker Pass Highway
Gilroy, CA 95020
tel. (408) 842-4278; fax (408) 848-3895
Open to the public by appt.; est. 1978

Marilyn and John Otteman own this tiny eight-acre vineyard and winery in the Santa Cruz Mountains that have earned a strong following and sound reputation. Marilyn, the winemaker here, has experimented with a variety of grapes, and settled on Chardonnay as the primary focus of her efforts (90 percent of production). Ten percent of the Ottemans' fruit is purchased to supplement the estate-grown Chardonnay (98 percent of production) and Pinot Noir (2 percent). Sarah's Vineyard also produces a small amount of Merlot from the fruit of the John Radike Vineyard in San Luis Obispo County. The redwood-clad winery on a hill overlooking the town of Gilroy in the Heck's Pass region ferments and stores its wine in stainless-steel tanks (8,000-gallon capacity) and ages them in a mixed age assortment of French oak barrels. Average annual production here is 2,000 cases.

Quality, we find, has become ever more dependable here of late as prices have also stabilized. Naturally, because production is so small and demand so high, there is still a pretty price to be paid for both the Chardonnay and Merlot, which tend to be soft wines. The Chardonnay is clean and shows ripe fruit, as in 1988, and the Merlot shows dark fruit, such as blackberries.

Wines/Varietals: Estate Chardonnay, Lot 2 ($$$), Estate Chardonnay ($$$), Merlot ($$$).

If this is what you think when you think 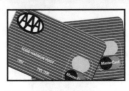 ...

Think again!

You may be surprised to know that AAA is more than a towing company – much more. One stop at AAA takes care of ALL your travel-related needs.

No more trips to the bank, insurance company & travel agency to prepare for your travels. One phone call is all that it takes to plan your trip with AAA's worldwide professional travel service.

Whether it's for arranging airline or cruise reservations, or discounted car rental; securing an international driving permit or traveler's cheques, AAA is at your service!

Need assistance while traveling? Just stop into one of AAA's more than 1,000 clubs and offices for emergency check cashing or on-the-spot travel counseling using our famous maps and TourBooks®.

You don't even have to leave home to apply for personal accident insurance or a AAA credit card.

And, of course, if you get a flat, you know who to call...

 and again...

 and again...

 and again...

 and again...

 and again...

TO JOIN AAA TODAY CALL
1-800-AAA-4357

 and again.

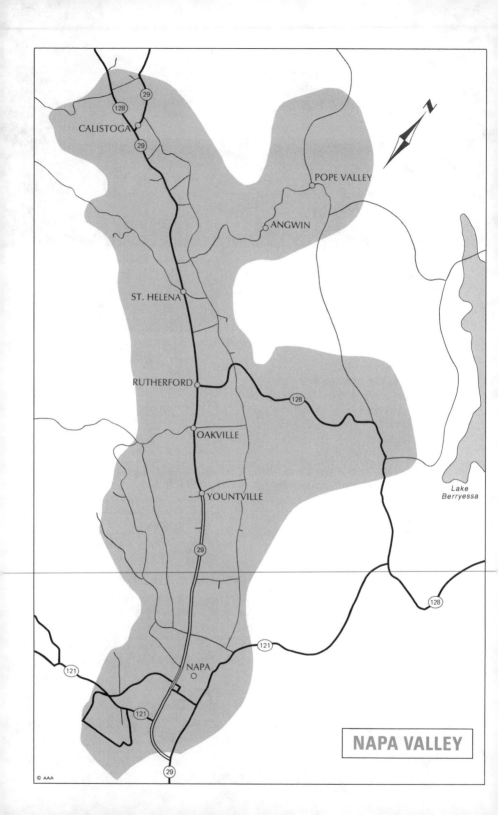

NAPA VALLEY

Napa

Acacia Winery

2750 Las Amigas Road
Napa, CA 94559
tel. (707) 226-9991; fax (707) 226-1685
Open to the public by appt.; est. 1979

This 47,000-case winery in the Carneros district of southern Napa has an enviable record of consistency. Larry Brooks has been the winemaker since Acacia was founded in 1979, and after the winery became part of the Chalone group in 1986, the philosophy here remained constant: to produce top-quality Burgundian varietals, Chardonnay and Pinot Noir. The winery's 50-acre Marina Estate Vineyard is planted solely in Chardonnay. Additional grapes are purchased, generally from the same growers who were there at the winery's first crush.

The winery, a model of modern technology and traditional Burgundian winemaking techniques, including small lot fermentation, vineyard designation, and extensive use of toasted new French oak barrels for aging, opened a lot of eyes in the early 1980s with its high-quality Chardonnays and Pinot Noirs. The competition has now caught up, so the wines no longer stand out quite as much, but the quality and consistency are still there. The Chardonnay (about 65 percent of production) and the Pinot Noir are noted for their oaky/woody flavors. The 1988 Pinot Noir Carneros, medium-full-bodied with clear varietal flavors, is very good indeed. The 1990 struck us as lighter and simpler, with sweeter fruit. The 1990 St. Clair is more substantial, with deep cherry flavors and a depth that promises potential for complexity. The 1990 Chardonnay is a good one—stylishly crisp with pear, melon, and oak flavors.

Wines/Varietals: Chardonnay, Carneros ($$), Chardonnay, Marina Vineyard ($$), Pinot Noir, St. Clair Vineyard ($$$), Pinot Noir, Carneros ($$), Vintage Brut Sparkling Wine ($$$).

S. Anderson Vineyard

1473 Yountville Crossroad
Yountville, CA 94599
tel. (800) 428-2259 or (707) 944-8642; fax (707) 944-8020
Open to the public; est. 1971

This 10,000-case Napa winery, with a very good reputation among the cognoscenti for its sparkling wines, faces a lot of competition from the increasingly large number of high-powered sparkling wine producers in California—especially those with European affiliations— that have raised quality standards appreciably in the past few years. S. Anderson has two important things going for it that continue to keep it a top winery: its vineyards and its still wines. The Anderson family (led by Stanley, a dentist by profession) started up the winery in 1971 by planting 20 acres of Chardonnay. Plantings of Chardonnay and Pinot (half-and-half) now total 120 acres and supply the largest portion of the grapes that go into both the sparkling and still wines. The addition in 1988 of 68 acres of Pinot Noir and Chardonnay vineyards in Carneros should help to maintain consistent quality. Nowadays about a quarter of the winery's production is Estate Chardonnay from the Stags Leap District, always pleasant and sometimes more than that.

All of the sparkling wines made here are good, though the winery's reputation rests principally on its vintage blanc de noirs *méthode champenoise* sparkling wine. Produced from 100 percent Pinot Noir grapes (a blend of fruit from four vineyards: S. Anderson Vineyard in Stags Leap, C.V.I. in Carneros, Beard on the Yountville Crossroad, and Hoffman on Big Ranch Road), it is a big, creamy, and complex wine with a lively toasty/yeasty character and a hint of fruit. The Estate Chardonnay (which was great in 1985) in 1989 and 1990 was crisp, somewhat lean, and fresh with citrus and pear flavors. It is a bit tart with pronounced acids that will make the wine long-lived, and is seemingly much less toasty/oaky than in the past.

Wines/Varietals: Estate Chardonnay ($$), Cabernet Sauvignon, Richard Chambers Vineyard ($$$), Vintage Brut Sparkling Wine ($$), NV Tivoli Sparkling Wine ($$), Vintage Rosé Sparkling Wine ($$$), Vintage Blanc de Noirs ($$$).

Beaucanon Winery

1695 St. Helena Highway
St. Helena, CA 94574
tel. (707) 967-3520; fax (707) 967-3527
Open to the public; est. 1987

This young one is here on faith: most of the variables are in place for a real quality surge. For starters, the vineyards and the winery are first-rate. Founded in 1987 by Jacques de Coninck of France, Beaucanon released its first wines in 1988. It operates 240 acres of Napa Valley vineyards, 88 currently in production. When the other 135 acres of prime vineyard land (all in proven regions of Napa) are fully developed, they will no doubt add harmonizing elements and greater levels of complexity that may well lift this winery to new heights. General Manager Jean-Marie Mauréze envisions kicking production up from the current 25,000 cases to two or three times that number when all the vineyards are yielding fruit.

Production here is divided into three varieties: Chardonnay, Cabernet Sauvignon, and Merlot. All see plenty of aging in new oak barrels. The 1988 Merlot gives testimony to the real quality that can be expected from Beaucanon. The 1989 Merlot will take some years to evolve. It's full of ripe, spicy flavors with cherry-plum highlights and lots of French oak (Allier/Nevers) in evidence. The 1988 Cabernet, on the other hand, does not have quite the same strength in body and style. The good 1991 Chardonnay displays some toasty oakiness with European butter, vanilla, and banana Chardonnay flavors overlaying the expected pear/citrus component base—just like it does in the 1990 vintage. In 1991, the winery also produced a Late Harvest Chardonnay.

Wines/Varietals: Chardonnay ($), Merlot ($$), Cabernet Sauvignon ($$), Late Harvest Chardonnay (375 ml, $).

Beaulieu Vineyard

1960 St. Helena Highway, PO Box 219
Rutherford, CA 94573
tel. (707) 963-2411; fax (707) 967-3190
Open to the public; est. 1900

The history of the Napa Valley and the history of wine in America are knit up with the history of this winery. Frenchman Georges de Latour founded BV, as it has come to be known, in 1900, and named it Beaulieu—"beautiful place." Great care was taken from the beginning: rootstocks were imported, and the vineyards gradually expanded. A 128-acre site next to Latour's Rutherford property became known as Beaulieu Vineyard No. 1. Several years later an Oakville vineyard site was dubbed Beaulieu Vineyard No. 2. BV survived Prohibition by producing and selling sacramental wines (its owner's deep pockets also helped), and in the 1930s and 1940s, its international reputation for producing fine wines helped put the Napa Valley on the map. In 1938, French-trained enologist André Tchelistcheff came aboard here and began the most influential career yet of any winemaker in America. He introduced a range of quality controls and production practices at BV that raised the quality of its wines to new levels, and went on to train a couple of generations of young winemakers, Joe Heitz, Theo Rosenbrand, Mike Grgich, and Richard Peterson among them. Heublein (part of the Grand Met-IDV British drinks conglomerate) purchased BV in 1969.

Purchasing about 50 percent of its grapes to supplement 736 acres—some 300 in Carneros—of estate grapes (371 acres of Cabernet Sauvignon, 180 of Pinot Noir, and 185 of Chardonnay), BV produces a wide assortment of wines, including a low-priced Beautour Cabernet and a line of generic wines that are sold in magnums. The top-of-the-line wines are very sound. The BV Private Reserve (Georges de Latour) has been made for over half a century from grapes from the original Beaulieu Nos. 1 and 2 vineyards. A 100 percent Cabernet, aged in American oak, that is big, powerful, well-structured, classy, and that ages extremely well, the Reserve is a leading item for collectors of California wines. The 1978 was thrilling; the 1984-1987 are fine bottles; the 1986 and 1985, in particular, are great. The

1987, typically smokey and herbal, contains complex plum-like fruit and has a silky texture. The Beautour Cabs, which contain some blended Merlot, are consistently fine values within their price range.

Wines/Varietals: Chardonnay, Beaufort ($), Beautour Chardonnay ($), Chardonnay, Carneros Reserve ($$), Dry Sauvignon Blanc ($), Beautour Fumé Blanc ($), Estate Chablis ($), Gamay Beaujolais ($), Pinot Noir ($), Pinot Noir, Carneros Reserve ($$), Estate Burgundy ($), Beautour Cabernet Sauvignon ($), Cabernet Sauvignon, Rutherford ($$), Cabernet Sauvignon, Georges de Latour Private Reserve ($$$).

Beringer Vineyards

2000 Main Street, PO Box 111
St. Helena, CA 94574
tel. (707) 963-7115; fax (707) 963-5054
Open to the public; est. 1876

Some legends simply fade away; others, of which this pre-Prohibition winery is an excellent example, hang right in there, achieving new fame and fortune. Jacob and Frederick Beringer, who built the landmark Rhine House stone winery into the hillside here, would recognize little else about Beringer today. In 1969, Nestlé, the Swiss-based food and drinks conglomerate, purchased the winery; today is it the anchor of the corporation's American Wine World Estates, Inc. division.

Aggressive investment and expansion have led to huge, prime vineyard holdings: 2,855 acres are owned overall, of which at least 2,098 acres are in the Napa Valley and Knights Valley, including 1,043 planted over to Chardonnay and 641 to Cabernet Sauvignon. Correspondingly huge production here is estimated at about 1.5 million cases a year, which requires buying lots of grapes. A great deal of the output is in white Zinfandel and Chenin Blanc. Beringer and Wine World Estates operate a moderately-priced second label, Napa Ridge, whose production is included in these figures.

Among Beringer's classic front-line varietals, overall quality ranges from good to very good. This is also the case with the special Cabernets and some of the limited release library wines available only at the winery. The Napa Valley Reserve Cabernets are dependably great, as in 1984-88. Among the more widely available Cabs, the 1988 Knights Valley bottling is also a good one, with black cherry, spice, and plummy flavors with a classic tea-leaf and tannic edge. The 1989 is similar but with more fruit. The Private Reserve always ranks among the top Cabernets in the market and is noted for its concentrated fruit, complex flavors, and fine balance. The 1990 Chardonnays are all very good: the Napa Valley release is fresh and fruity along softer pear and peach lines with an agreeable touch of vanilla.

Wines/Varietals: Chardonnay, Napa Valley ($$), Chardonnay, Napa Valley Private Reserve ($$), Sauvignon Blanc, Knights Valley ($), Fumé Blanc, Napa Valley ($), Dry French Colombard, Napa Valley ($), Grey Riesling, North Coast ($), Gewürztraminer, North Coast ($), Chenin Blanc, Napa Valley ($), Johannisberg Riesling, North Coast ($), White Cabernet, North Coast ($), White Zinfandel, North Coast ($), Premier Nouveau Gamay Beaujolais ($), Gamay Beaujolais, North Coast ($), Zinfandel, North Coast ($), Cabernet Sauvignon, Knights Valley ($$, older vintages $$$), Cabernet Sauvignon, Napa Valley Private Reserve ($$$), Cabernet Sauvignon, Chabot Vineyard ($$$), Late Harvest

Johannisburg Riesling (375 ml, $$), Cabernet Sauvignon Port, Napa Valley ($$).

Bouchaine Vineyards

1075 Buchli Station Road
Napa, CA 94559
tel. (707) 252-9065; fax (707) 252-0401
Open to the public by appt.; est. 1981

This 15,000-case Chardonnay and Pinot Noir specialty winery in Napa's relatively cool Carneros region is dedicated to producing premium Burgundian varietal wines. Winemaker John Montero preaches the Burgundian "let the *terroir* speak" gospel, even though he blends his regular wines from several growers, arguing that it gives him flexibility to choose vineyards with distinctive characteristics. This winery possesses 31 acres of vineyards (25 acres of Chardonnay and 6 acres of Pinot Noir). Owned since 1986 by a group of quality-minded, hands-on investors led by Chairman Gerret Copeland, Bouchaine Vineyards is the oldest continuously operated winery in the Carneros district. Its vineyards were established in 1899 and have a colorful history of various owners, including, in the 1920s, immigrant Johnny Garetto. While Chardonnay production currently exceeds that of Pinot Noir, the winery is headed to a 50-50 balance.

For his Pinot Noirs, winemaker Montero uses partial whole berry fermentation and manual punchdown of the cap. In recent vintages, the quality has been sound and consistent. The regular Pinot Noir is fairly light and soft in style, as in 1989, with some pleasing cherry and smokey flavors, and much pronounced sweet fruit. The Reserve has a little more depth and complexity, notably in the 1988 release. The

WHEN IT'S THAT IMPORTANT, ONLY THE BELAGE WILL DO.

The BelAge Hotel de Grande Classe evokes the essence of the "Bel Epoch".

In the plush, four-star, Diaghilev Restaurant, sumptuous nouvelle-Russe cuisine is served. Just next door, the informal Brasserie, with its spectacular view of the city, known for its phenomenal Sunday Brunch, creates its own innovations of California cuisine. La Brasserie has the exclusive Michel Montignac Menu in Southern California. At nights, Club Brasserie is a vibrant jazz supper and lounge rendezvous.

With such culinary delights, it's no wonder that The BelAge Hotel is the site for over 400 weddings, charity fund-raisers, holiday parties and special celebrations each year. The result? Besides making you look marvelous, we make your event memorable and affordable.

LA BRASSERIE

CLUB BRASSERIE

DIAGHILEV

CATERING

310/854-1111
800/424-4443

THE BELAGE

1020 North San Vicente Blvd., W. Hollywood, CA

© 1992. L'ERMITAGE HOTELS. A COLLECTION OF ORIGINALS.   SMART

Eberle Winery

Tasting Room Open daily
10:00 am to 5:00 pm
Summer Hours till 6:00 pm

Picnic on the patio with panoramic
views of Estate Vineyards.

Hwy 46 East, 3.5 miles from Paso Robles
P.O. Box 2459
Paso Robles, CA 93447
805.238.9607

Maison Deutz Winery
Open daily except Tues.
Retail Sales
Tastings – 11 am-5 pm
453 Deutz Drive
Arroyo Grande, CA 93420
805.481.1763

Byington Winery & Vineyard, Inc.
21850 Bear Creek Road
Los Gatos, CA 95030
408.354.1111

MERIDIAN

Open daily, except Tues.
Retail Sales
Tastings & Self-guided Tours
Winter Hrs. – 10 am-5 pm
Summer Hrs. – 10 am-6 pm
7000 Hwy 46 East
Paso Robles, CA 93446
805.237.6000

THE TRUE JAPAN IS...
SUSHI AND KAISEKI

SAISAI
彩菜

BILTMORE HOTEL, 501 South Olive Street, Los Angeles, California 90013
Telephone: 213-624-1100

Quady Winery
Specializing in
Dessert Wines & Port
13181 Road 24
Madera, CA 93637
209.673.8068

*Visit & Join Our Private
Cellar Club*

*Tasting room open noon to 5:00 pm
Wednesday – Sunday*

*See the beautiful & dangerous
Santa Cruz Mountains
from our picnic facilities.*

David Bruce Winery
21439 Bear Creek Rd.
Los Gatos, CA 95030
800.397.9972

1991

R E S E R V E
Chardonnay
ALEXANDER VALLEY

ALCOHOL 13.2% BY VOLUME

*Award Winning Chardonnays.
Tasting and Picnicking.
Unique Gift Items.
Open Daily.*
101 Adobe Canyon Road,
Kenwood, CA 95452.
707.833.1144

Chardonnays go through partial malolactic fermentation and have a somewhat lush body over tropical fruit flavors. The regular release, consistent from year to year and especially fine in 1990, has lively acidity but is still a Chardonnay to drink young (the balanced and sound 1990 might evolve more, coming from such a good harvest). The Estate Reserve can use some bottle age. The 1988 has a big, buttery nose, a tart, balanced, and appealing body and a long finish. Bouchaine also produces a small amount of Alsatian-styled Gewürztraminer from Russian River Valley grapes. In 1992, the winery began releasing moderately priced Pinot Noir and Chardonnay under the whimsical label, "Q.C. Fly," named for a forgotten turn-of-the-century local.

Wines/Varietals: Chardonnay, Napa Valley ($$), Chardonnay, Carneros Estate Reserve ($$$), Gewürztraminer, Russian River Valley ($), Pinot Noir, Carneros ($$), Pinot Noir, Carneros Reserve ($$$).

Buehler Vineyards, Inc.
820 Greenfield Road
St. Helena, CA 94574
tel. (707) 963-2155; fax (707) 963-3747
Open to the public by appt.; est. 1978

When father and son both changed careers to begin this tiny winery, they initially produced just 800 cases of wine. John Buehler, Sr., a retired vice president of Bechtel Corporation, and John, Jr., a former advertising copy writer, have gradually expanded Buehler Vineyards to an annual level of 50,000 or so cases, which are distributed all over the U.S. and in Switzerland. White Zinfandel accounts for 44 percent of production here and Chardonnay accounts for 40 percent of the rest of the output. Cabernet Sauvignon

(34 acres), Zinfandel (28), and Pinot Blanc (3) make up the 65 acres of vineyards nestled in the mountains along the eastern edge of the Napa Valley. The Buehlers purchase 70 percent of their fruit.

They used to produce and promote an attractive Pinot Blanc along fig and pear lines, but gave up the fight for recognition and acceptance with a last release in 1988. Too bad. The estate Cabernet Sauvignon and the estate Zinfandel are now this winery's most distinctive wines. Though produced only in small quantities, both are big statement wines. The 1989 Cabernet, 100 percent varietal from Buehler's 26-acre vineyard in the Vaca Mountains, is powerful with oak over some concentrated sunny fruit flavors. The estate Zinfandel is perhaps more consistently attractive; we're not sure if the lighter 1990 indicates a new direction in winemaking here. A commercial line of low-priced varietals has been introduced, called Bon Marché (French for "inexpensive"), and are proving to be serveable bottles.

Wines/Varietals: White Zinfandel ($), Sauvignon Blanc ($), Bon Marché Chardonnay ($), Zinfandel ($), Bon Marché Cabernet Sauvignon ($), Estate Cabernet Sauvignon ($$), Bon Marché Pinot Noir ($).

Burgess Cellars
1108 Deer Park Road, PO Box 282
St. Helena, CA 94574
tel. (707) 963-4766; fax (707) 963-8774
Open to the public by appt.; est.1972 (on the site of an 1875 winery)

Tom and Linda Burgess have had admirable success with the winery they purchased in 1972 (it was then known, from 1942 to 1972, as Souverain Winery and back in 1875 as Rossini Winery). Located on the

153

hillside of western Howell Mountain, Burgess has 110 acres under vine, divided between the winery's vineyards and another larger Triere vineyard plot south of Yountville. For a number of years, the winery has been operating at its optimal 30,000-case level, and in the late 1990s, when all the vines planted come into production, all of its wine will come from estate grown grapes (currently 25 percent are purchased).

While there has been a continuity of winemakers here—Bill Sorenson has been the one and only since 1972—some years ago there was a fairly dramatic change in winemaking style. In the 1970s, like so many other Napa wineries, Burgess produced major-league, heavyweight whites and reds. In the 1980s, there was a sharp move toward more elegant wines with greater breeding; the quality here has been consistently higher since the change. Burgess currently produces three wines, a Triere Vineyard Chardonnay (60 percent of total output), a Napa Valley Zinfandel (15 percent), and a Napa Valley Vintage Selection Cabernet Sauvignon (25 percent). The Cab is made from non-irrigated, low-yielding hillside grapes with estate Merlot and Cabernet Franc grapes blended in. The Chardonnay is highly reliable and, in its excellent 1990 rendering, is welcomingly dramatic indeed: simultaneously delicate and full flavored, displaying unusually pronounced vanilla and nutmeg flavors with full buttery and pear complexities. We enjoyed the 1989 Zinfandel, which has a medium-to-full body, good, clear berry flavors, some oakiness and moderately strong tannins that will soften in three or four years. The Cabs, full of cherry and plum flavors and plenty of tannin, also need time. Thankfully, Burgess Cellars is one of the few wineries with an excellent release program of properly aged library selections of Cabernet and Chardonnay.

Wines/Varietals: Chardonnay, Triere Vineyard ($$), Zinfandel, Napa Valley ($$), Cabernet Sauvignon, Napa Valley Vintage Select ($$$).

Cafaro Cellars

1591 Dean York Lane
St. Helena, CA 94574
tel. (707) 963-7181; fax (707) 963-8458
Not open to the public; est. 1986

Joe Cafaro, owner and winemaker here, made wine at Chappellet, was founding winemaker at Keenan, and later worked at Acacia. Since 1985 he has been a leading consultant in Napa, working for Jaeger Family Winery, Dalla Valle Vineyards, Oakville Ranch Vineyard, Niebaum-Coppola, and Robert Sinskey Vineyards. Here at Cafaro Cellars, he does his own thing, producing about 1,500 cases of Cabernet Sauvignon (60 percent) and Merlot from purchased grapes (fine hillside selections from a handful of producers). "No compromises, because my name is on the label," he asserts.

Both the Cabernets and Merlots are vinified traditionally, pumped over the cap to extract the fruit and made in stainless steel fermenting tanks. After malolactic fermentation and two rackings, the wines are put in French oak barrels (50 percent new), bottled after two years and then aged another year in the bottle before release. We prefer the 1988 Cabernet to the 1989; both have deep blackberry and cherry fruit flavors, new oak, smoothness, and balance. The Merlots all have a spicy, herbal quality with plenty of tannins on top of packed fruit, which in the very good 1988 had plum and cherry overtones and real elegance. The complex flavors of this wine need time to emerge.

Wines/Varietals: Merlot, Napa Valley ($$$), Cabernet Sauvignon, Napa Valley ($$$).

Cain Cellars

3800 Langtry Road
St. Helena, CA 94574
tel. (707) 963-1616; fax (707) 963-7952
Open to the public by appt.; est. 1980

Situated at the crest of Spring Mountain above the Napa Valley, Cain Cellars occupies a commanding 540-acre site with views of both Napa and Sonoma counties. In recent years, its wines have risen to the heights as well. Established by Jerry Cain with partners Jim and Nancy Meadlock, the Meadlocks became sole owners here in 1991. Their architecturally ambitious winery has some 100 acres planted to Bordeaux varieties: Cabernet Sauvignon (75 acres), Merlot (20 acres), Cabernet Franc (4), Malbec (3), and Petit Verdot (2). Although there were plans to increase production to 25,000 or 30,000 cases, the winery has now settled into a 10,000-15,000 case annual output. All the reds made here are from estate grapes with relatively small amounts of Sauvignon Blanc and Chardonnay produced from purchased fruit.

This winery is best known for its pioneering Cain 5, a top-of-the-line Bordeaux blend of superior quality. It begins with hillside grapes with great concentration, which are harvested by hand, destemmed, and put through a prolonged maceration with the free run wine drawn off. The best grape lots are used for Cain 5. The remaining fruit "pommace" is manually placed in the press to be gently coaxed one additional time,

then discarded. The 1987 Cain 5 is typically complex with deep, dark fruit extract, ripe and sweet but laced with spice and cedar flavors. Opulent, elegant, and long. Cain Cellars' winning Merlot, which we hadn't seen for a while, appears to be back in limited 1990 release. In whites, this winery produces two Chardonnays, one from Napa Valley grapes and the other from Carneros grapes—both are fine, clean, toasty-oaky—and a Sauvignon Blanc that is oak-accented and pleasant with soft fruit tones.

Wines/Varietals: Chardonnay, Napa Valley ($), Chardonnay, Carneros ($$), Sauvignon Blanc, Napa Valley Musqué ($$), Cain 5 ($$$).

Cakebread Cellars

8300 St. Helena Highway, PO Box 216
Rutherford, CA 94573
tel. (707) 963-5221; fax (707) 963-1067
Open to the public by appt.; est. 1973

This 45,000-case family winery—Jack and Dolores Cakebread, and their sons, Bruce and Dennis, all work here—has a solid reputation for quality and continuity. Since its founding in 1973, Cakebread Cellars has been a solid citizen of the Napa Valley, helping to lead the area, with Cakebread's wines and marketing efforts, to the great recognition it has today. The Cakebreads make user-friendly wines from three vinifera: Chardonnay (50 percent of production), Sauvignon Blanc (30 percent), and Cabernet Sauvignon (20 percent). They draw upon 75 acres of vineyards on their Napa Valley property (60 percent Cabernet

155

Sauvignon, 40 percent Sauvignon Blanc) and buy 60 percent of their grapes, including all of the Chardonnay, from Napa Valley suppliers they have been working with for many years.

Winemaker Bruce Cakebread's Sauvignon Blancs are on the herbaceous side but have typical melon and grapefruit flavor highlights. As evidenced by the 1990, they are fairly round and ripe with just an accent of oak. The Chardonnay, too, was fine in 1990 with a nice balance of fruit (pears and melons), vanillin, and acid. About a quarter of this wine is barrel fermented, approximately a third is put through malolactic fermentation, and all of it sees seven or eight months in the barrel. The 1989 Reserve is a good effort in a problematic year for Napa Valley Chardonnay, with a clear toast underpinning from an increased percentage of barrel fermenting and slightly increased barrel aging. The reserves here are also given a few years of bottle age before release. The Chardonnays are cleanly made and perhaps not as strong as the Cabernets. The 1989 Cab is medium-soft with lots of varietal character in a slightly herbal style with cedar and ripe, firm plum and dark cherry fruit lying low beneath the oak tannins. Grapes from an older section of the Cabernet vineyard at the winery are used as the primary source for the Rutherford Reserve release, which is given a lot of wood and bottle aging before it is put on the market (in 1992, the vintage available was the 1986). It's sound, but carries a big price tag.

Wines/Varietals: Sauvignon Blanc ($$), Chardonnay, Napa Valley ($$$), Reserve Chardonnay ($$$), Cabernet Sauvignon, Napa Valley ($$$), Cabernet Sauvignon, Rutherford Reserve ($$$).

Carneros Creek Winery

1285 Dealy Lane
Napa, CA 94558
tel. (707) 253-9463; fax (707) 253-9465
Open to the public; est. 1972

This family-run winery specializing in Pinot Noir (it also produces Chardonnay) has played an important role in improving Pinot Noir in America and establishing the Carneros region as a top growing area for the varietal. Francis Mahoney, founder, president, and lover of great Burgundy wines, has worked on an important Pinot Noir clonal selection research project with the University of California at Davis since 1974. The winery has 45 acres of vineyards and purchases about 40 percent of its grapes.

Sixty percent of the winery's 25,000 cases produced annually are Pinot Noir, 40 percent Chardonnay. At one end of the Pinot spectrum, the winery produces a lighter-bodied, early maturing "Fleur de Carneros" Pinot Noir that seems to change some of its distinguishing characteristics and flavors with each vintage. At the other end is the standout "Signature Reserve," a limited-edition wine that, judging from the good 1989, is rich, medium deep, oaky, cherryish, sometimes with plummy overtones and with medium aging potential. The 1990 "Los Carneros" Chardonnay is Carneros Creek's finest effort to date and a very good one indeed: soft fruit flavors, hazelnut overtones, and plenty of creamy complexity soothe the underlying vibrant acidity.

Wines/Varietals: Chardonnay, Los Carneros ($$), Pinot Noir, Fleur de Carneros ($), Pinot Noir, Los Carneros ($$), Pinot Noir, Signature Reserve ($$$).

Caymus Vineyards

8700 Conn Creek Road, PO Box 268
Rutherford, CA 94573
tel. (707) 963-4204; fax (707) 963-5958
Open to the public; est. 1972 (property
purchased in 1943)

Cabernet Sauvignon is arguably Napa Valley's finest wine, and Napa-based Caymus is unquestionably among a handful of the finest producers of Cabernet Sauvignon in America. Caymus is a superstar when it comes to Cabernet, and this family winery shines with other varietals, too. Over the decades, Charlie Wagner developed a grand reputation as a grape grower, and then in 1972, he converted an old barn into a winery. Randy Dunn helped establish the house's Cabernet pedigree and now Charlie's son, Chuck, serves as the red winemaker and sets the benchmark standard other vintners strive to reach. Of the winery's 73 acres of vineyards, 80 percent are planted with Cabernet, the rest with Sauvignon Blanc. Including the winery's low-cost, Chardonnay-driven second label, Liberty School, about 80 percent of the required grapes are purchased each year to make 71,500 cases of wine. About half of it is Cabernet.

The Caymus "Special Selection" Cabernet Sauvignon is as good (and as expensive) as it gets. Year in and year out it earns the very highest accolades. The great 1987 is a typical powerhouse: rich, complex, yet velvety and displaying a range of spices and oak over very supple fruits. The 1988 is nearly as good. The regular estate Cabernet is only slightly less rich and a good value for a top wine—the 1989 is a fine California Cab. The Caymus Sauvignon Blanc-based proprietary white wine called "Conundrum" is an especially flavorful quaff, with Chardonnay, Muscat, and Sémillon sending flavor signals

all over the place. Both the 1989 and 1990 are classy efforts, the 1991 a bit less so, but still sound. Caymus Zinfandel is a good value.

Wines/Varietals: Conundrum ($$),* Cabernet Sauvignon, Napa Valley Special Selection *($$$),* Estate Cabernet Sauvignon, Napa Valley *($$), Zinfandel, Napa Valley ($), Pinot Noir, Special Selection ($$), Sauvignon Blanc ($).

Chappellet Vineyard, Inc.

1581 Sage Canyon Road
St. Helena, CA 94574
tel. (707) 963-7136
Open to the public by appt.; est. 1967

Over the years, the Chappellets—Donn and Molly and son Cyril, the operation's marketing director—have earned a loyal following for the wines generated from their 110 acres of terraced vineyards at elevations of up to 1,700 feet. Employing a tiny percentage of purchased grapes, the handsome and rustic winery here, with its dramatic view overlooking Lake Hennessy east of Rutherford Peak, produces 20,000-25,000 cases annually. The Chappellet vineyards are planted to 35 percent Chenin Blanc, 25 percent Chardonnay, 25 percent Cabernet, 5 percent Merlot, and 10 percent Sangiovese.

Chappellet wines are sound and consistent. The Chardonnay is in the lean and austere style. It is marked by barrel flavors (it's barrel fermented), and ages with real distinction in some vintages such as the 1986 and probably the well-balanced 1990. The Cabernet Sauvignon is a bit fleshier with strong tannins and varietal flavors. The 1987 Signature Reserve is one of Chappellet's best Cabernets since the 1970s and among the top ones produced anywhere in North America that excellent year. This winery continues to produce significant amounts of Chenin Blanc, especially notable for its bone-dry, oak-aged character.

Wines/Varietals: Chenin Blanc ($), *Chardonnay ($$), Merlot ($$), Cabernet Sauvignon ($$$).*

Charles Krug

2800 Main Street
St. Helena, CA 94574
tel. (707) 963-2761; fax (707) 963-7913
Open to the public; est. 1861

Charles Krug is the oldest winery in the Napa Valley, and its history reads like the script for an episode of TV's "Falcon's Crest." Founded by a Prussian immigrant in 1861, the winery has been owned by the Mondavi family for the past fifty years. A family squabble in 1966 led eldest son Robert to break from the family business to start his own highly acclaimed winery. While Charles Krug played a large part in the history of the Valley, the winery has stood by stoically as a generation or two of upstart operations have stolen the spotlight of media and consumer attention. Charles Krug currently owns or controls 1,200 acres of vineyards and produces approximately 125,000 cases of wine annually.

Charles Krug was known in the 1950s and 1960s for its excellent Cabernets. In the 1980s, the winery became better known for effective marketing and distribution of generally low-cost offerings. Lately, there is more than talk of a rededication to quality here. The wines of Charles Krug currently include several notable for their quality as well as for their reasonable prices. The 1992 Chenin Blanc is a good quaffer, with a green/gold color, melon and fresh pear on the nose, and clean apple and pear fruit, and refreshing acidity on the palate. The regular Cabernet Sauvignon is light in 1989, but not disagreeable. It shows hints of mint in the nose, some currant and plum flavors on the palate, and supple tannins. We're looking for Charles Krug to do good things in the 1990s.

Wines/Varietals: White Zinfandel ($), Chenin Blanc ($), Sauvignon Blanc ($), Gewürztraminer ($), Johannisberg Riesling ($), Grey Riesling ($), Chardonnay ($$), Chardonnay, Carneros Reserve ($$), White and Red Table Wine ($), Gamay Beaujolais ($), Pinot Noir ($), Merlot ($$), Zinfandel ($), Cabernet Sauvignon ($$$), Cabernet Sauvignon, Vintage Selection ($$$), Muscat Canelli (375 ml, $).

Chateau Montelena Winery

1429 Tubbs Lane
Calistoga, CA 95415
tel. (707) 942-5105; fax (707) 942-4221
Open to the public; est. 1882 (reopened 1972)

If you're looking for quality and consistency—and who isn't?—then Chateau Montelena is a name to remember. Year in, year out, with the old winemaker or the new one, the admirable, classic style of Montelena Chardonnay, Cabernet, Zinfandel, and (off-dry) Johannisberg Riesling remains the same. The winery produces 30,000 cases annually with grapes from its own 95 acres and from supplementary purchased lots. The grand, medieval-style, stone chateau carved in the hillside north of Calistoga, with its formal Chinese gardens, is a landmark site.

The 1987 Estate Cabernet Sauvignon reminded us just how good the wines from Chateau Montelena can be. It was among the very finest made that year—deep, exuding extract and classic varietal flavors, and possessing the stuff to go on for years. The 1988 is sound, as are all the other wines. Their classic American Chardonnays are unfussy and drink well young or old.

Wines/Varietals: Chardonnay, Napa Valley ($$$), Estate Cabernet Sauvignon ($$$), Estate Zinfandel ($$), Johannisberg Riesling ($).

Chateau Woltner

150 South White Cottage Road
Angwin, CA 95408
tel. (707) 963-1744; fax (707) 963-8135
Open to public by appt.; est. 1886 (in continuous operation since 1981)

A number of things are coming together at Chateau Woltner to make it a top-class winery. Francis and Françoise DeWavrin-Woltner, former owners of France's prestigious Chateau La Mission Haut Brion in Bordeaux, bought this property, which had been a winery before Prohibition, in 1980. They started planting vineyards in 1982 and began releasing wine in 1985. All of it is Chardonnay and all of it is extremely Burgundian in style. Until recently, the wines of Chateau Woltner (five separate Chardonnay labels, including small vineyard designations within the contiguous 56-acre plot) had been high priced—and with such young vineyards, the quality has just begun to reach the highest levels—but with some market pressure and some price adjustment, the Woltner Chardonnays are now more price-competitive. And the quality of the Chardonnay made here equals that of the best Chards produced in America or anywhere else for that matter. Indeed, Woltner wines are comparable to the top white Burgundies they so much resemble. Overall, this winery produces 8,000-10,000 cases.

Chateau Woltner's wines are big and lush. Its vineyards at elevations of 1,600-1,800 feet up on Howell Mountain yield very small quantities of concentrated fruit and provide different growing conditions from those on the Napa Valley floor. The 1990s and the 1991s (tasted in barrel) promise great things. These are wines that will be longed-lived and luscious. Superb winemaker Ted Lemon, an American who trained for five years in Burgundy, has produced a 1989 Estate Reserve (2,500 cases) that is firm, balanced, deep, round, and long with flavor overtones of butter, vanilla, peppery wood, citrus, and nuts. Drinking well now and likely for several years to come, this bottling is a fine value among quality Chardonnays. The same can be said for the follow-up 1990 Estate Reserve. The single vineyard designation wines produced here deliver greatness, but at a price. In the Burgundy style, Woltner's Titus and Frédérique Vineyard Chardonnays are about as good as it gets in North America.

Wines/Varietals: Chardonnay, Howell Mountain ($), Chardonnay, Estate Reserve ($$), Chardonnay, St. Thomas Vineyard ($$$), Chardonnay, Titus Vineyard ($$$), Chardonnay, Frédérique Vineyard ($$$).

Chimney Rock Winery

5350 Silverado Trail
Napa, CA 94558
tel. (707) 257-2641; fax (707) 257-2036
Open to the public; est. 1984

Hack Wilson is no stranger to the beverage industry, having spent years as an executive for Pepsi and as president of Rheingold Breweries. In 1980, he turned his attention to the wine industry and fixed his sights on the Stags Leap District in the Napa Valley. Wilson purchased the former Chimney Rock Golf Course and an adjacent mountain. He bulldozed nine holes on the course and planted 75 acres of Cabernet Sauvignon, Merlot, Cabernet Franc, Sauvignon Blanc, and Chardonnay. All of Chimney Rock's wines are estate grown and over half of its annual production of 20,000 cases is Cabernet Sauvignon.

Winemaker Doug Fletcher has built this winery's reputation for consistency on good Cabernet Sauvignon from the always reliable Stags Leap-area Cabernet vineyards. The Cabernet vines here, planted on southwestern-facing hillsides of volcanic soil in the Stags Leap District, are subject to warm days and cool nights, allowing the grapes to reach optimal maturity. Chimney Rock's 1989 Cabernet (blended with 16 percent Merlot and 5 percent Cabernet Franc) is a good effort: medium-dark with a slight herbal tone and intense cassis and black cherry fruit aromas, good depth and concentration with excellent acidity and moderate tannins. The 1990 Chardonnay is also a notable wine. It underwent 100 percent malolactic fermentation and was mostly barrel aged, imparting a spicy, honeyed vanilla character with tropical fruit and pear overtones. Chimney Rock Fumé Blanc is vinified in a much lighter style, fermented in stainless steel, and bottled without any wood aging within three months of fermentation. The 1990 is a crisp, fresh offering with a slight sweet peas Sauvignon Blanc varietal note.

Wines/Varietals: Chardonnay ($$), Fumé Blanc ($), Cabernet Sauvignon ($$).

Clos Du Val

5330 Silverado Trail, PO 4350
Napa, CA 94558
tel. (707) 252-6711; fax (707) 252-6125
Open to the public; est. 1972

Owned by John Goelet, Clos du Val is closely associated with Bernard Portet, a Frenchman whose father was the technical director at Chateau Lafite-Rothschild. Portet became convinced of the potential of Napa Valley vineyards, urged Goelet to establish a winery here, and has been the winemaker at Clos du Val since its inception. Today he is also the winery's president. (Portet's brother, Dominique, plays a similar role at another Goelet-owned property, the Taltarni Winery in Australia.) The estate's 265 acres of vineyards (34 percent Cabernet Sauvignon, 4 percent Cabernet Franc, 8.5 percent Merlot, 3.5 percent Zinfandel, 6 percent Pinot Noir, 41 percent Chardonnay, and 3 percent Sémillon) are divided between Napa's Stags Leap District and Carneros (the latter mostly Chardonnay and Pinot Noir). Additional grapes are purchased to achieve the annual production of 60,000 cases.

With the help of co-winemaker Krimo Souilah, who joined Portet in 1990, this winery's early success with Merlot, Cabernet, and Zinfandel has been maintained. The Carneros Chardonnay, combined with the Cabernet, amount to 75 percent of production here, including a second line of Cabernet and Chardonnay named "Joli Val" made from non-estate grapes. Lower-priced white and red blends are labeled "Le Clos." The reds turned out here are reliable and sometimes outstanding, as was the 1987 Cabernet Sauvignon: big, rich, concentrated, yet smooth and lush with plum, blackberry, chocolate and oaky vanillin flavor extracts. The 1988 and 1989 Cabs are fine; the recent Merlots even better. Clos du Val Reserve, produced only in exceptional vintages, is the winery's premier red. Portet pointedly avoids revealing the blend, but it is clearly mostly Cabernet. The 1987 is dark and currant-like with cedary overtones and a firm grip of tannins. We recommend cellaring it until past the turn of the century.

Wines/Varietals: Chardonnay ($$), Joli Val Chardonnay ($$), Sémillon ($$), Le Clos White ($), NV Le Clos Red ($), Joli Val Cabernet Sauvignon ($$), Cabernet Sauvignon ($$), Pinot Noir ($$), Merlot ($$), Zinfandel ($$), Clos du Val Reserve ($$$).

Clos Pegase Winery

1060 Dunaweal Lane
Calistoga, CA 94515
tel. (707) 942-4981; fax (707) 942-4993
Open to the public; est. 1985

Jan Shrem's twin passions for art and wine are immediately evident to anyone visiting this huge, post-modern, Michael Graves-designed winery in Calistoga. Further establishing the art/wine connection, Shrem introduced a line of wines under the "Hommage" rubric to recognize contemporary artists (the labels depict works from Shrem's private collection). Two hundred and sixty-nine acres (out of 435 overall), divided among several Napa Valley locations, are currently in production. Mostly planted to Chardonnay, Merlot, and Cabernet Sauvignon, these vineyards provide 75 percent of the grapes necessary for the production of 35,000 cases annually.

Bob Masyczek, formerly assistant winemaker at Cuvaison, became Clos Pegase's winemaker in 1992. His current focus here is to integrate the fruit from a new Carneros vineyard in the winery's offerings. He believes that the job of a winemaker is to bring out an appellation's inherent fruit character. Of note is the extensive work and experimentation being done in Clos Pegase's vineyards to produce grapes of greater complexity—no fewer than seven different Chardonnay scion clones have been grafted, along with four Merlot clones and two Cabernet Sauvignon clones. The quality of the winery's Chardonnays, including those from its Napa-Carneros vineyards, has been consistently high, perhaps highest in the 1988 bottling with its crisp citrus and apple flavors. The reds are getting better; the 1986 Napa Valley Cabernet Sauvignon remains the house's finest moment.

Wines/Varietals: Chardonnay, Napa Valley ($$), Hommage Chardonnay ($$$), Sauvignon Blanc, Napa Valley ($), Cabernet Sauvignon, Napa Valley ($$), Merlot, Napa Valley ($$), Pegaso Red ($$), Hommage Red ($$$).

161

Codorniu Napa

1345 Henry Road
Napa, CA 94558
tel. (707) 224-1668; fax (707) 224-1672
Open to the public; est. 1991

First, the leading French Champagne companies all had to have their own California sparkling wine operations, then so did the two leading Spanish sparkler makers. This is Codorniu's, Spain's number two producer of sparkling wines, effort, and it is an impressive one. Annual production here started off at 30,000 cases; the winery is capable of producing 180,000 cases. Unlike the Champagne houses whose California sparklers are half the price of their parent brand's import, Codorniu's California sparkling wine—which aims for the same quality level—is twice as expensive as Spanish *cava*. The parent company has made a huge investment here in establishing a high-quality operation (including an architecturally arresting winery framed against the background of Milliken Peak in the Carneros district of the Napa Valley), and has also invested heavily in 250 acres of vineyards currently planted half-and-half to Chardonnay and Pinot Noir.

Janet Pagano functions in the dual role of Codorniu Napa's winemaker and general manager. Her first release of *méthode champenoise* Brut struck us as a balanced, dry sparkler of honorable quality with much citrus and melon flavor, a touch of hazelnut and a medium-long, medium-crisp finish. The wine is well made, perhaps a bit lean and acidic. We'll be curious to see if a stronger personality emerges in future bottlings.

Wines/Varietals: Brut Napa Valley Sparkling Wine ($$).

162

Conn Creek

8711 Silverado Trail
St. Helena, CA 94574
tel. (707) 963-9100; fax (707) 963-7840
Open to the public; est. 1974

Stimson Lane Wine & Spirits (owners of Chateau Ste. Michelle, Columbia Crest, and Villa Mt. Eden) purchased Conn Creek in 1986 and recently began reshaping its profile, reducing the number of wines offered and lowering prices as well. Quality, on the other hand, is now on the way up. Essentially a Cabernet house with only three acres of adjoining vineyards, the bulk of Conn Creek's grapes come from two growers who sell exclusively to this winery and also from the 55-acre Collins vineyard that once belonged to the winery. Annual production here is 35,000 cases.

Jeff Booth, winemaker since 1986, and Bob Pepi, general manager, have led the remaking of the Conn Creek's wine line. Booth looks for lots of fruit extract and uses six to seven-year-old barrels so the oak won't dull the fruit. The last reserve wines that will be made here will be from the 1989 vintage. Then it'll be a single Cabernet, a single Merlot, and "Triomphe," a Bordeaux-style blend (there may still be a few additions to line, including perhaps a white Meritage). The 1987 Private Reserve Cabernet has lovely color and ripe flavors along Merlot lines, nice, silky harmonious structure and a pleasant finish. The 1987 Triomphe (16 percent Merlot, 14 percent Cabernet Franc, 70 percent Cabernet Sauvignon), tasted on several occasions, is Conn Creek's most impressive bottle: concentrated, elegant, accessible with cherry and spice flavors with hints of mint and oak all lingering well. First produced from very fine 1987 grapes, subsequent vintages should tell the tale of this winery's future.

Wines/Varietals: Merlot ($$), Cabernet Sauvignon ($$), Triomphe ($$$).

Corison Wines
PO Box 344
Oakville, CA 94562
tel. (707) 963-7357; fax (707) 963-5776
Not open to the public; est. 1987

Cathy Corison, who formerly served a decade as winemaker at Chappellet Vineyards, is the artisan at this Napa Valley Cabernet Sauvignon specialist. She buys grapes here and there mid-Valley to produce about 2,000 excellent cases annually that collectors invariably covet.

Her Cabs tend to be lush with rich fruit and good structure. In the 1989 vintage, her wine is lovely, dark, and deep with herbal and ripe cherry/currant flavors and lots of tannins that will need plenty of time to soften. The 1990 release should be even better.

Wines/Varietals: Cabernet Sauvignon, Napa Valley ($$$).

Cosentino Winery
7415 St. Helena Highway, PO Box 2818
Yountville, CA 94599
tel. (707) 944-1220; fax (707) 944-1254
Open to the public; est. 1980

Back in 1980, in rented quarters in Modesto, Mitch Cosentino started to produce small amounts of wine from San Joaquin and Sacramento Valley grapes. He bottled his line of table wines under the Crystal Valley Cellars label. Things changed, though, around 1985 when Costentino commenced work with Bordeaux grapes, including Cabernet Franc. These new wines were very enthusiastically received and Cosentino Winery, as the winemaker called his new enterprise, soon achieved preeminence. (It's the old story: putting your name on the bottle means *you* are the wine, so it better be good. In this case it was—so long Crystal Valley!) Matters improved again in 1990 when the vintner settled in Yountville in a proper Cosentino Winery facility. Most of the red grapes for production here now come from Napa, Sonoma, and Lake County. Annual output is about 12,500 cases.

While there's consistent quality across the Cosentino line, most of the excitement here is in the big, gutsy reds that can stand up to plenty of oak, a case in point being the 1988 Zinfandel. Both regular and a reserve Chardonnay are usually produced and they have found eager admirers. The 1991 Chard shows balance through its spicy flavor and is a good bottle. The reserve Chardonnay, from Napa grapes, is called "The Sculptor;" a premium Bordeaux blend is labeled "The Poet." The 1989 Meritage Cos "Cosentino" is now tight, but it could emerge with boisterous, deep black cherry and chocolate flavors. The regular 1990 Cab is much more straightforward. Could it be Mitch is lightening up? The 200 cases of Zinfandel he made in 1991 are good ones.

Wines/Varietals: Chardonnay, Napa Valley ($$), Chardonnay, North Coast ($$, discounted to $), Chardonnay, The Sculptor ($$), NV Francesca D'Amore ($), Merlot ($$), Pinot Noir ($$), Cabernet Franc ($$), Cabernet Sauvignon, Napa Valley ($$), Reserve Cabernet Sauvignon ($$$), Meritage Cos, Napa Valley ($$$), Zinfandel, Russian River ($$), The Poet (red, $$$).

163

Cuvaison Winery

4550 Silverado Trail, PO Box 384
Calistoga, CA 94515
tel. (707) 942-6266; fax (707) 942-5732
Open to the public for tasting, winery by
appt.; est. 1969

Cuvaison calls itself "a focused winery." It produces Chardonnay, Merlot, and Cabernet Sauvignon almost exclusively from estate grapes grown on its 300 acres of vineyards in Carneros. In 1979, Swiss investors Stephan and Alexander Schmidneiny purchased the winery and in 1986, when they took full control, Manfred Esser was appointed president. Today, things are looking up. Cuvaison's quality is good and so is its marketing. The winery's international connections have resulted in its wines being sold in 21 countries. In 1992, Cuvaison entered a joint marketing agreement with Schramsberg for the U.S. outside California. Set on the Silverado Trail just south of Calistoga, Cuvaison (the name is the French word meaning "the fermenting of red wines on the skins") is currently producing 55,000 cases annually.

Seventy-seven percent of Cuvaison's production is Chardonnay, 5 percent of that is reserve. Two-thirds of the regular Chardonnay blend goes through barrel fermentation. Racking off the lees is limited and individual lots are aged in oak three to eight months before blending, bottling, and release. These wines are well balanced, crisp with appley fruit and toasty oak overtones. The reserve wines are 80 percent barrel fermented, the bulk of it in new oak. Additionally, 50 percent undergoes malolactic fermentation. The 1990 Chardonnay (a fine Napa vintage) is good at the moment and structured to improve over the next few years. The 1987 Cabernet Sauvignon is something remarkable to remember.

Wines/Varietals: Chardonnay, Carneros, Napa Valley ($$), Reserve Chardonnay ($$$), Cabernet Sauvignon, Napa Valley ($$), Merlot, Napa Valley ($$$).

Dalla Valle Vineyards

7776 Silverado Trail
Napa, CA 94558
tel. (707) 944-2676; fax (707) 944-8411
Not open to the public; est. 1982

This 3,000-case star Cabernet producer is situated south of Howell Mountain on the eastern side of the Napa Valley, almost in the center of the Vaca foothills overlooking the Silverado Trail. In 1982, Gustav Dalla Valle moved here with his sixth wife Naoko (whom he married at age 74) and set out to make great wine. Scion of a wealthy Italian family, he'd already had a highly successful career as a scuba diver and worked in Hollywood filmmaking (especially underwater films) and other ventures.

Employing Cabernet grapes from 25 acres of estate vines (an additional 10 percent of the grapes are purchased), winemaker Heidi Barrett produces dense, powerful Cabernets and a splendid proprietary wine (55 percent Cabernet Sauvignon and 45 percent Cabernet Franc) named "Maya," after Dalla Valle's young daughter. These wines need lots of age to show themselves to best advantage. The 1988 Cabernet is richly packed with layers of chocolate, cassis, and spice flavors over tense tannins. The huge bouquet promises much that the wine may eventually deliver.

Wines/Varietals: Cabernet Sauvignon ($$$), Maya (red, $$$).

Diamond Creek Vineyards
1500 Diamond Mountain Road
Calistoga, CA 94515
tel. (707) 942-6926; fax (707) 942-6936
Not open to the public; est. 1972

This tiny, top-end Cabernet specialist has earned a strong following among collectors eager for the 3,000 or so cases of wine produced here from four separate estate vineyards each year. Situated at a high altitude, Diamond Creek is also high-quality—and high-priced. L.A.-expatriate Al Brounstein purchased 79 acres of forested land on a 660-foot high ridge on Diamond Mountain, southwest of Calistoga. He was able to establish only 21 acres of vineyards (all Cabernet Sauvignon, save for a dose of mellowing Merlot) on the steep site; each block of vines yields wines with distinct personalities.

Brounstein developed a reputation in the 1980s for producing consistently excellent Cabernets that are rustic in character, with a rich earthiness and depth of flavor, and that require time for any real grace to emerge. Wines made here are bottled separately by vineyard. The largest plot is the eight-acre Volcanic Hill, so named for its volcanic soil, which produces wines that are usually dry, austere, tannic, and earthy in flavor. The Red Rock Terrace vineyard (the soil here is rich in iron oxide) bottling is fruitier. The third vineyard bottling, Gravelly Meadow, is often, though not always, blended with grapes from the single acre Lake Vineyard, alongside an artificial pond. This is the earthiest of all the bottlings and the most forward. The quality here is consistent: this is, after all, one of California's finest Cabernet producers. We feel that the Volcanic Hill vineyard is the leading light here each year. Wine under this label is excellent in 1990 (as

is the Red Rock Terrace), good in 1989. By 1998, the raspberry and currant-flavored fruit of the power-packed and spicy 1990 Volcanic Hill should have emerged from behind the tannins. Figure $50 a bottle for each Diamond Creek Cab upon release. When a separate Lake Vineyard wine is bottled in some years, it has the distinction, at $150 a bottle upon release, of being California's most expensive wine.

Wines/Varietals: Cabernet Sauvignon, Volcanic Hill ($$$), Cabernet Sauvignon, Red Rock Terrace ($$$), Cabernet Sauvignon, Gravelly Meadow ($$$).

Domaine Carneros
1240 Duhig Road
Napa, CA 94581
tel. (707) 257-0101; fax (707) 257-3020
Open to the public; est. 1987

Driving along the Carneros highway in Northern California, you can't miss the striking French chateau rising out of the hills near Napa. Built by Taittinger, the French Champagne house, the design of the winery here was inspired by the eighteenth century Château de la Marquetterie, owned by the Taittinger family in Champagne. The new winery is the grandest, most opulent, and most Gallic of any sparkling (or other) wine facility in California. Domaine Carneros extends over 138 acres, with 120 planted to classic Champagne varieties (60 percent Chardonnay, 35 percent Pinot Noir, 5 percent Pinot Meunier, and a smattering of Pinot Blanc). Aiming at complexity and nuance, five clones of Chardonnay were included in the vineyard, and four clones of

165

Pinot Noir. Claude Taittinger is president of Domaine Carneros; Eileen Crane serves as managing director and winemaker.

The *méthode champenoise* sparkling wines are aged in the winery's cellars, which are carved into the hillside beneath the structure, maintaining cool temperatures year-round. The first release of Domaine Carneros Brut was from the 1987 vintage (released in late 1990 as non-vintage); the second cuvée released was crisp, briskly dry, and elegantly balanced, with clean fruit, ranking it among the good sparkling wines of California. The promising third cuvée, released in 1993, shows the winemaker making minor adjustments to the still-evolving house style. We expect that in the years to come, things will settle down agreeably at this young winery.

Wines/Varietals: Domaine Carneros Brut ($$).

Domaine Chandon

1 California Drive, PO Box 2470
Yountville, CA 94599
tel. (707) 944-8844; fax (707) 944-0902
Open to the public; est. 1973

This outpost of Möet & Chandon, the French Champagne giant, revolutionized the sparkling wine industry in America and spurred a host of domestic winery investments by other leading French Champagne firms. It's also chiefly responsible for a sharp rise in the quality of sparkling wines produced on this side of the Atlantic. Using French know-how and purchased grapes (at least at first) to produce only *méthode champenoise* sparkling wines, Domaine Chandon has grown from an initial release of 10,000 cases to about 400,000 cases today. Though it now owns 2,100 acres of vineyards, including a large hillside plot in Carneros, large quantities of grapes are still purchased. In 1977, Domaine Chandon opened a showcase winery, restaurant, and tourist center in Yountville, and this too set a precedent many other vintners have followed.

Under the direction of Dawnine Dyer, vice president and winemaker, Domaine Chandon produces four wines: Chandon Brut (a blend of Pinot Noir, Chardonnay, Pinot Blanc, and Pinot Meunier, which accounts for 63 percent of total production), Chandon Blanc de Noirs (a 100 percent Pinot Noir Brut), Chandon Reserve (a select blend, aged longer), and Etoile (a top blend made from older cuvées). Overall these wines are good and consistent, fruity and admirable—indeed impressive for the volume in which they are made. The winery also produces lower-priced Shadow Creek sparkling wines from non-Napa grapes. We prefer the Brut Reserve, which is toasty and crisp and very well focused, fleshy, complex, smooth, and balanced, to the higher-priced Etoile with its toasty, woody nose and simple fruit with sweetish highlights. The Blanc de Noirs is also attractive with fine balance, fruit, and acidity.

Wines/Varietals: Brut Sparkling Wine ($$), Blanc de Blancs Sparkling Wine ($$), Reserve Sparkling Wine ($$), Blanc de Noirs Sparkling Wine ($$), Etoile Sparkling Wine ($$$).

Domaine Napa

1155 Mee Lane
St. Helena, CA 94574
tel. (707) 963-1666; fax (707) 963-5471
Open to the public; est. 1986

Born and raised on the French Riviera, but from a Burgundian family which still tends grapes in the village of La Roche-Vineuse, Michel Perret owned a winery in the Côte de Provence where he produced rosé wines for the tourists and red wines for the locals. Fed up with French government regulations, he moved his family to California in 1977 and for five years raised sugar beets, cotton, alfalfa, and corn. His love of winemaking eventually led him to the Napa Valley, where he purchased 11 acres south of St. Helena. Today, Perret farms an additional 200 acres of Rutherford and Rutherford Bench grapes for use in his own wines, and tends vineyards atop Mt. Veeder and in Carneros for other vintners. With the help of Grant Taylor, a New Zealand-born and American-educated winemaker, Perret is now producing 10,000 cases of wine annually under the Domaine Napa label. Up to another 10,000 cases of wine are produced out of the winery here for custom-crush customers.

The wines made here are consistently easy drinking and moderately priced. Perret and Taylor subscribe to two guiding principals: 1) control the wine grapes from pruning to crush, and 2) emphasize balance over all other factors in creating wines that drink well upon release but that can bear up to some aging. Among Domaine Napa's whites, the Sauvignon Blanc is more distinguished than the Chardonnay. The 1987 Cabernet is typical of this house's current wines: it's a good quaffer with cherry and varietal fruit on the nose, medium-light body with good balance but little depth. The Proprietal Vintage Red, first produced in the 1990 vintage

(50 percent Cab, 30 percent Merlot, 20 percent Cabernet Franc), will easily be their best wine yet released.

Wines/Varietals: Chardonnay ($$), Sauvignon Blanc ($), Merlot ($$), Cabernet Sauvignon ($$).

Dominus Estate
PO Box 3275
Yountville, CA 94599
tel. (707) 944-8954; fax (707) 944-0547
Not open to the public; est. 1982

First, there was Möet & Chandon's investment in Domaine Chandon, then Château Mouton-Rothschild's partnership with Robert Mondavi in Opus One, and finally, the arrangement between Christian Moueix, of Château Pétrus fame, and Robin Lail and Marcia Smith, the daughters of John Daniel, which created Dominus Estate—collectively these three joint ventures signalled the Napa Valley's unassailable eminence in the wine world. In 1982, Moueix began producing Bordeaux-style red wines under the Dominus Estate label, employing grapes from the renowned Napa Valley vineyard west of Yountville called Napanook. The 125-acre vineyard, currently planted to Cabernet Sauvignon (69 percent), Cabernet Franc (15 percent), Merlot (14 percent), and Petit Verdot (2 percent), supplies grapes for about 6,500 cases of wine annually.

The wines here have been priced at $45 since the release of the initial 1983 vintage (released after the softer 1984 bottling). These blended wines are clearly excellent: some critics and consumers believe they are the finest reds ever produced in America. Most of the releases to date will start showing off their best stuff in the years to come. The wines are distinctive with an atypical aromatic set for the Napa Valley—complex, elegant, profound, deep but in a total Bordeaux style generally unmatched in America. There's no problem slipping this wine harmoniously into a blind tasting of top classified growths from Bordeaux with which the Dominus Estate bottlings share some very traditional French winemaking procedures. Christian Moueix clearly thinks very highly of these wines: he endorses them with his portrait on every label. The 1987 is opulent, full of power and strength, with meaty, spicy, cedar, and vanillin flavors, and lots of tannins. The 1988, released in 1993, is a big, tight, tannic wine with great balance; its quality is impressive. The 1989, 1990, and 1991 are reported to be even better.

Wines/Varietals: Dominus ($$$).

Duckhorn Vineyards

3027 Silverado Trail
St. Helena, CA 94574
tel. (707) 963-7108; fax (707) 963-7595
Open to the public weekdays for sales only; est. 1976

This partnership of 10 families is ever-so-ably managed by one of them: Dan Duckhorn (president) and Margaret Duckhorn (vice president, sales & marketing). Their daughter Kelly also works at the winery. The Duckhorns buy 80 percent of the grapes needed to turn out 25,000 cases a year. They nevertheless produce greatness: superb Merlot (and the Duckhorns' tireless and highly effective promotional work) have earned this winery high regard. The celebrated Merlot accounts for 40 percent of production, Cabernet Sauvignon 20 per-

cent, and Sauvignon Blanc 40 percent (Cabernet Franc and Sémillon are also crushed and used in blending).

Winemaker Tom Rinaldi (at Duckhorn since 1978) produces two Merlots, a Napa Valley Merlot and the acclaimed vineyard-designated Three Palms Merlot (the vineyard is in Calistoga). The 1989 Three Palms Merlot is lush and lovely with dense layers of fruit, plum, currant and blackberry flavors; it's easy drinking but has plenty of bottle life. The Sauvignon Blanc, made from estate grapes, about 50 percent barrel fermented, and blended with 20 percent Sémillon, is an increasingly impressive wine. The 1990 is an excellent example with crisp citrus and banana flavors as well as a classic touch of varietal herbaceousness. The 1991, almost as good, has lots of lively fruit flavors including pears and grapefruit. While the Cabernets would seem to take a back seat here, these, too, have been stellar in some vintages. In short, quality and consistency across the board are a Duckhorn trademark. A small amount of light, second-label "Decoy" wines are also produced, notably a Pinot Noir and a Sémillon.

Wines/Varietals: Sauvignon Blanc ($), Cabernet Sauvignon ($$$), Merlot, Napa Valley ($$), Merlot, Three Palms ($$$).

Dunn Vineyards

805 White Cottage Road
Angwin, CA 94508
tel. (707) 965-3642
Not open to the public; est.1982

The saga of Dunn Vineyards is one of the biggest American wine success stories of the 1980s, the tale of a great winemaker and one of this generation's true superstar wines.

While working as winemaker for Caymus, Randy Dunn and wife, Lori, decided to rehabilitate an old Cabernet Sauvignon vineyard on the property surrounding their out-of-the-way home on Napa's Howell Mountain. They successfully nurtured the vines, brought the fruit back and, in 1979, produced 600 cases of eye-opening wine: big, delicious, and loaded with complex berry flavors. Encouraged by friends and the owners of Caymus, Dunn established his own little winery in 1982 and has been turning out wine that has a cult following ever since. Total production is about 4,000 cases (2,000 with the revered Howell Mountain designation from 14 acres of estate grapes—the original 6, plus 8 adjacent that are leased—and another 2,000 with a Napa Valley designation from purchased grapes); demand far outstrips supply. In 1991, Dunn purchased the 47-acre Park-Muscatine Vineyard close to his winery and planted it entirely to Cabernet Sauvignon.

These are wines with personality and breeding. Dunn did a fine job with Cabernet at Caymus and as a consultant for La Jota, Grace Family, Livingston, Pahlmeyer et al.; he makes wines for the long haul, with plenty of distinctive fruit flavors. The excellent Napa Valley bottling is a tad softer and rounder than the famed Howell Mountain bottling. The wines here are great every year, perhaps a bit less so in 1988. The 1987 Howell Mountain Cabernet Sauvignon is massive, dynamically concentrated with cedar, mineral, and briary flavors to go along with its currant and berry character. Of course the law of supply and demand makes these wines platinum priced—if you can get them. Our only reservation about these wines is that there isn't yet a sufficient track record of older vintages to determine if all the promise in the bottle will come to full fruition. But we're more than willing to wait and see.

Wines/Varietals: Cabernet Sauvignon, Napa Valley ($$$), Cabernet Sauvignon, Howell Mountain ($$$).

El Molino Winery
Lyman Canyon Road, PO Box 306
St. Helena, CA 94574
tel. (707) 963-3632; fax (707) 963-1647
Open to the public by appt.; est. 1871 (in continuous operation since 1981)

Reg Oliver's 1,000 cases of good Pinot Noir and Chardonnay are much sought after, but because a few top retailers around the country receive an allocation and sell the wines, we're happy to tip the reader off about this tiny winery. El Molino is better known as a vineyard planted with 35 acres of Chardonnay, 16 of Cabernet Sauvignon, and two of Pinot Noir. It sells off most of its grapes and buys in 50 percent of the fruit required to make its 1,000 cases annually.

Two-thirds of the wine made here is Pinot Noir. The 1988 Napa Pinot Noir is velvety with plum and cherry flavors, a toasty oakiness, and a somewhat distracting herbaceousness. The 1990 Chardonnay is excellent, very much in the Burgundian style, with a buttery, smokey nose and a richly evocative and complex body.

Wines/Varietals: Chardonnay ($$$), Pinot Noir ($$$).

Estancia Estates

PO Box 407
Rutherford, CA 94573
tel. (707) 963-7111; fax (707) 963-7867
Not Open to the public; est. 1985

Estancia is often thought of as the second label of Franciscan Vineyards in Napa Valley. In fact, it is a separate operation of the same owner, Augustin Huneeus. The moderately priced Estancia wines, largely varietals that sell for under $10 a bottle, offer excellent value. Estancia owns 250 acres of vineyard in the Alexander Valley and 500 in Monterey County east of Soledad. In Alexander Valley, where the climate is better suited to reds, the property is planted to Cabernet Sauvignon, Merlot, and Sangiovese. Estancia's white wines— Chardonnay, Sauvignon Blanc, and Sémillon—come from the Monterey vineyard.

Annual production here is about 130,000 cases, nearly 70 percent Chardonnay, 20 percent Cabernet Sauvignon, and 5 percent Sauvignon Blanc. Estancia's 1990 Chardonnay from Monterey is crisp and rather stylish, not quite as varietal in character as the 1989 Cabernet Sauvignon with its warm, berryish fruit typical of the Alexander Valley. Estancia produces both red and white meritage wines. The 1990 white, a blend of Sauvignon Blanc and Sémillon, is good, if a little severe, well-balanced and likely to be very elegant at three or four years of age. The red Meritage 1989 is excellent, with firm Cabernet structure and vigorous fruit. It, too, should age quite nicely, which makes it a fine value at $12 (or less) a bottle. Quality is agreeably consistent across the line here making the moderate pricing even nicer.

Wines/Varietals: Chardonnay ($), Sauvignon Blanc ($), Cabernet Sauvignon ($), White Meritage ($$), Red Meritage ($$).

Etude Wines

PO Box 21
Oakville, CA 94562
tel. (707) 963-7357
Not open to the public; est. 1985

Star winemaker and consultant Tony Soter (Spotteswood, Chappellet, Niebaum-Coppola, etc.) has been making about 2,000 cases of Pinot Noir and Cabernet Sauvignon from purchased Napa grapes in rented digs here since 1985. Under his own label, he makes wines the way he wants—winemaker's wines. Generally he succeeds, sometimes splendidly.

For his Cabernet Sauvignon, Soter blends in about 12 percent Merlot and another 10 percent Cabernet Franc. These are fairly bold wines, big and tannic but of the iron-fist-inside-a-velvet-glove variety. The 1987 is a fine bottling. Though Etude's Cabs used to outshine its Pinot Noirs, recently the big, supple Pinots have taken on quite a luster. The 1990 is first rate; its superior quality is no doubt the result of the addition of Carneros fruit.

Wines/Varietals: Pinot Noir, Carneros ($$$), Cabernet Sauvignon, Napa Valley ($$$).

Far Niente

Off Oakville Grade, PO Box 327
Oakville, CA 94562
tel. (707) 944-2861; fax (707) 944-2312
Not open to the public; est. 1885 (in continuous operation since 1982)

In 1978, Gil Nickel set out to restore this stone winery founded in 1885 and abandoned during Prohibition. When he began the project, only the shell of the original structure remained. Today, the original design has been given new life; state-of-the-art facilities have been added; and the building is listed on the National Register of Historic Places. In 1990, 15,000 square feet of man-made aging caves were excavated, completing the restoration. All the impressive work undertaken here notwithstanding, the winery's name is Italian for "without a care."

Of Far Niente's 150 acres of vineyards, two-thirds are planted to Chardonnay, one-third to Cabernet Sauvignon. As annual production here has grown to 35,000 cases, quality has steadily improved. We especially like the Chardonnays, which in many years are excellent in an oaky, full-bodied, fruity manner. Far Niente's is certainly one of the best 1989 Napa Chards available, and the 1990, with its honey and pear flavors, tightness, and crisp acidity is very nice as well—one of the finest in that vintage; it will likely continue to get better until perhaps 1994. The 1986 and 1987 Cabs—firm and flavorful—were great.

Wines/Varietals: Chardonnay ($$$), Cabernet Sauvignon ($$$).

Flora Springs Wine Company

1978 W. Zinfandel Lane
St. Helena, CA 94574
tel. (707) 963-5711; fax (707) 963-7518
Open to the public by appt.; est. 1978

This family affair began when Jerry Komes retired from Bechtel Industries, seeking a new challenge as well as a lifestyle change in his golden years. He bought an abandoned winery dating from the nineteenth century and his son, John, (now Flora Spring's president) rebuilt it. Daughter Julie and her husband, Pat Garvey, soon joined the team—Pat as vineyard manager and Julie as director of marketing and sales. Vineyards are Flora Springs convincing claim to fame: four hundred acres spread over five excellent sites in the Napa Valley. The largest plantings are in Cabernet Sauvignon (119 acres), Chardonnay (75 acres), Sauvignon Blanc (69 acres), and Zinfandel (62 acres); there are also lesser amounts of Merlot, Cabernet Franc, Petit Verdot, Sangiovese, and Pinot Noir. In addition, the family owns two vineyards in Carneros that are not yet supplying grapes to Flora Springs. Indeed, the Komes' vineyards provide more grapes than required for the 35,000 cases produced annually by their winery, making Flora Springs an important commercial grape grower. Like so many others growers, however, Flora Springs is facing a major replanting due to phylloxera infestation. This, along with a desire to market wines at a lower price point, led to the introduction of a second line labeled "Floréal." The new label also serves as a hedge since it is not committed to using 100 percent estate-grown grapes as is the Flora Springs line.

Winemaker Ken Deis has been producing consistently excellent wines across the board here since his arrival in 1980. He makes two Chardonnays: a barrel fermented bottling is the winery's best known offering. It's very good in 1990, probably the winery's best ever, with toasty, peppery barrel components adding to silky pear, honey, mango, pineapple, and vanilla flavors and aromas. The regular Chardonnay, which is fermented in stainless steel then finished in small oak barrels (no malolactic fermentation), is fruitier in a clean, tropical style and now is released under the Floréal label. We loved the 1990 with floral character and luscious, juicy fruit. To our taste, Flora Springs' Sauvignon Blancs are well-made stars: crisp, French-style, with appealing fruit and only modest grassiness and no flawed "green" character in the Floréal release. "Soliloquy" is a Flora Springs bottling that is racked with the fermentation lees into oak where it is aged *sur lie*. Judging from the 1990, it is crisp, fruity with floral and toast overtones, and far more complex and elegant than almost any other California Sauvignon Blanc. While this winery's reds aren't credited with being as outstanding as its whites, both the Merlots and the Cabernets we've tasted recently are fine wines (the 1988 Cab is wonderful). "Trilogy," touted as "a thinking person's Bordeaux blend" (about a third each of Cabernet Sauvignon, Merlot, and Cabernet Franc), is superb. We've repeatedly enjoyed the 1988 with its core of rich fruit and layers of flavors that come at you in an easygoing, balanced, and harmonious way that completely seduces you without your noticing. Overall, the style of Flora Springs wines is fruity, accessible, and complex without being overly firm with the angular proportions that are fashionable in some wine circles.

Wines/Varietals: Floréal Sauvignon Blanc ($), Soliloquy ($$), Floréal Chardonnay ($$), Chardonnay, Barrel Fermented ($$$), Floréal Merlot ($$), Floréal Cabernet Sauvignon ($$), Cabernet Sauvignon, Cellar Select Reserve ($$$), Trilogy ($$$).

Forest Hill Vineyard
PO Box 96
St. Helena, CA 94574
tel. (707) 963-7229 or (415) 386-2559
Not open to the public; est. 1987

San Francisco plastic surgeon E. David Manace knows something about aesthetics and about putting things right. The good doctor and Kathryn Cole Manace, his wife, have made Forest Hill Vineyard Chardonnay a fully rewarding aesthetic experience—from the superb label on the outside of the bottle to the opulent Burgundy-style Chardonnay inside. They only produce 650 cases annually, all Chardonnay marked "Private Reserve," from grapes purchased from two, 10-acre Napa Valley plots under long-term contract.

Their 1989 Chardonnay opened our eyes. In a watery Napa Valley vintage full of disappointments, Forest Hill's Chardonnay stood out in our tastings with its medium body and depth of citrus and nut flavors. When we tasted their efforts with the excellent 1990 vintage, all was confirmed: once again, what was concocted here was among the fairest of the fair—a truly super-premium American Chardonnay. Winemaker Robert Jay Levy, working with hand-picked, whole-cluster pressed grapes, ferments and ages the wines in small Nevers oak barrels and follows the labor-intensive practice of stirring the lees weekly. The 1990 possesses a rich honey, nut, and toasty nose; it has big, rich fruit flavors along apple lines, a lush, medium-to-full body, with a firm oak backbone and good acid structure gracefully balanced. It finishes long and elegantly with honey and butter overtones and should drink well for years.

Wines/Varietals: Private Reserve Chardonnay ($$$).

Forman Vineyard
1501 Big Rock Road, PO Box 343
St. Helena, CA 94574
tel. (707) 963-0234; fax (707) 255-6873
Open to the public by appt.; est. 1983

This one-man winery produces 4,000 cases annually of very fine reds and Chardonnays. The one man is Ric Forman, a highly regarded winemaker, who trained at U.C. Davis, and has worked at Stony Hill, Robert Mondavi, Sterling, and Charles Shaw wineries. He now operates on the western slopes of Howell Mountain, where he controls 21 acres of Cabernet Sauvignon. He has an additional 41 acres in Rutherford, split evenly between Cabernet and Chardonnay grapes. Overall the vineyard package is 90 acres and includes 10 acres of Merlot, nine of Cabernet Franc, and one of Petit Verdot, all of which are blended into Foreman's Cabernet. A small percentage of the grapes for his Chardonnay are purchased. Limited production and consistent quality put Forman's wines into the cult, hard-to-get category on the West Coast; oddly enough they're easier to find in the East.

Forman's wines tend to be sleek and classy. His Chardonnay is barrel fermented and lean, focused, and ripe, with enough underlying power and flavor so as not to have to announce itself with "in your face"

oppulence. The 1990 is a fine example with real authority and fine fruit. The 1991 is a bit leaner and tart but lively with lemon, oak, and honey flavors. The celebrated Cabernets made here are similar, with much substance. We admire the 1989 in particular (supple, spicy, with attractive fruit) and have fond memories of the 1986. Forman sometimes uses a second label, Chateau La Grande Roche, for Grenache and any other lower-priced varietals he wishes to bottle.

Wines/Varietals: Chardonnay ($$$), Cabernet Sauvignon ($$$).

Franciscan Oakville Estate
1178 Galleron Road, PO Box 407
Rutherford, CA 94573
tel. (707) 963-7111; fax (707) 963-7867
Open to the public; est.1985

Production here under current owners Peter Eckes and Augustin Huneeus is going strong at 48,000 cases annually. (The partnership also owns Estancia, and Huneeus owns Mount Veeder Vineyards.) Two hundred forty acres of Franciscan vineyards are planted to Cabernet Sauvignon (40 percent), Chardonnay (35 percent), Merlot (20 percent), and Zinfandel (5 percent). All of the wines produced here are from estate-grown grapes.

All of Franciscan's wines represent good, appreciable quality and fine value, with the reds finishing a nose ahead of the Chardonnay. The 1990 Reserve Chardonnay is the house's best Chard to date—big and toasty, with peach and honey flavor tones. The owners are proud of their 1988 Oakville Estate Meritage, and we're fans too: it's a big child, firm with cedar and currant flavors, careful balance, and good depth and complexity. It should be lovely on its eighth, ninth, or tenth birthday.

Wines/Varietals: Chardonnay ($$), Zinfandel ($$), Cabernet Sauvignon ($$), Merlot ($$), Meritage ($$).

Freemark Abbey

3022 St. Helena Highway N.,
PO Box 410
St. Helena, CA 94574
tel. (707) 963-0554; fax (707) 963-0554
Open to the public; est. 1886

The original winery at Freemark Abbey dates back to 1886 (it was given its current name in 1939) and was continuously operated until the late 1950s. The present owners, a seven-member partnership headed by Chuck Carpy, had the winery restored (resuscitated might be a better word) in 1967. The revitalized Freemark Abbey quickly gained recognition for its quality wines, especially its Cabernets. With the exception of Cabernet Bosché from the Rutherford Bench, all of the winery's grapes come from Napa Valley estate vineyards. Totaling 300 acres, plantings here include Cabernet Sauvignon, Chardonnay, Merlot, Johannisberg Riesling, Sauvignon Blanc, Cabernet Franc, and Pinot Noir.

The 40,000 cases made here each year speak of their soil. They are good, straightforward Napa Valley wines. The Cabernet from the Sycamore Vineyards, for example, with a little bottle age—say the 1986—has personality and style. Then there's the late-harvest Riesling "Edelwein Gold." It's terrific: sweet but firm, with a rich buttery layer over fig, pineapple, and pear flavors. Drink it now or age it as its avid collectors do; this is consistently one of the very top American-made dessert wines.

Wines/Varietals: Chardonnay ($$), Chardonnay, Carpy Ranch ($$$), Johannisberg Riesling ($), Cabernet Sauvignon ($$), Cabernet Sauvignon, Sycamore Vineyards ($$$), Cabernet Bosché ($$$), Merlot ($$), Edelwein Gold ($$$).

Frog's Leap

3358 St. Helena Highway
St. Helena, CA 94574
tel. (707) 963-4704; fax (707) 963-0242
Open to the public by appt.; est. 1981

The name's not all that goofy. It derives from the fact that this one-time farm formerly supplied frogs to San Francisco restaurants (and, of course, it's also a bit of tongue-in-cheek nod toward famed Stag's Leap Wine Cellars). This rustic, creek-side winery remains truly "natural" in character, relying on natural acidity, native yeasts that need no nutritive supplements, and the absolute minimal sulfur required to protect the wine. Indeed, Frog's Leap doesn't wish to be any more high-tech than...a frog farm. Physician Larry Turley bought the old farm over a decade ago, and when his "home winemaking" experiments with Sauvignon Blanc captured people's imaginations (could it have been the name?), he brought in a then-young, ex-New Yorker named John Williams as winemaker and partner. Now friends as well as partners, the men, and their wives, Julie Williams and Suzanne Turley, form a foursome that is fun-loving and serious about what they are doing at the same time. (Hey, if some of the big decisions around here are made in the hot tub, so what? They've proven sound.) The winery owns 15 acres of vineyards (11 planted to Zinfandel), and purchases about 70 percent of its grapes (via 10 long-term contracts with

Napa Valley grape growers) to produce 24,000 cases annually.

Fifty percent of production is Sauvignon Blanc from organically grown grapes; it's generally crisp and lively with lemony and grapefruit citrus flavors and subdued herbaceousness. The good 1990 proffers some of its barrel oak (10 percent was barrel fermented in new oak). The Carneros Chardonnay is barrel fermented and goes through a natural malolactic fermentation. The fine and harmonious 1990 is easily the best Frog's Leap Chardonnay yet (pears, yeast, toasty oak, and crisp acidity are character highlights). The reds—Merlot, Zinfandel, and Cabernet Sauvignon—are good, fairly intense, and a bit rustic. Sometimes the Cabernet is glorious, as in 1987.

Wines/Varietals: Sauvignon Blanc ($), Chardonnay, Carneros ($$), Merlot ($$), Zinfandel ($$), Cabernet Sauvignon ($$).

Girard Winery

7717 Silverado Trail, PO Box 105
Oakville, CA 94562
tel. (707) 944-8577; fax (707) 944-2828
Open to the public; est. 1980

The Girard family, looking for a project that would bring the clan together on a regular basis, settled on winegrowing in the Napa Valley. Stephen Girard, Jr., a self-confessed "wine geek" back in the seventies, instigated the venture. In 1974, the family purchased a choice vineyard near Oakville along the Silverado Trail and put Steve in charge of running things. For a time, the Girards sold grapes to Robert Mondavi; they established their own winery in 1980. The senior Girards now live on the property and Steve's three sisters fly in from Ohio,

New Jersey, and San Francisco for family conferences and board meetings. Virtually all Girard wines are made from the family's 80 acres of vineyards in Oakville and Yountville, planted to Chardonnay (50 percent), Cabernet Sauvignon (38 percent), Sémillon (5 percent), Merlot (5 percent) and Cabernet Franc (5 percent). Production of 20,000 cases includes about 15 percent Chenin Blanc that's made in a crisp, dry style from purchased grapes and which we rate highly. A small amount of stylish Sémillon is also made here.

Girard is best known for its Chardonnay and Cabernet Sauvignon, both estate grown, with reserve wines produced in vintages yielding exceptional fruit. The 1989 Reserve Chardonnay we find outstanding: tautly balanced fruit with flavors of citrus and pear, and toasty vanillins that come together in a long finish that bodes well for the next three to five years. The 1990 Chardonnay is lighter but delicious—we like its elegant balance and creamy fruit. The Cabernets are also tautly structured and can be lean and tannic in some years, as in 1989, though the 1988 was supple and appealing. The 1989 Reserve Cabernet is closer to the mark, concentrated and intense with a tannic grip nicely set off by luxuriant berry fruit, as in the highly successful 1986 and 1985 Reserves. In keeping with Steve Girard's interest in Pinot Noir and his belief that Oregon is the place to grow it, this winery has produced an Oregon Pinot since 1987. Steve is now co-owner of a 75-acre vineyard in the southern Willamette Valley of Oregon. He's aiming to plant another 75 acres in the near future and ultimately to start a winery there.

Wines/Varietals: Chardonnay ($$), Reserve Chardonnay ($$$), Sémillon ($$), Dry Chenin Blanc ($), Cabernet Sauvignon ($$), Reserve Cabernet Sauvignon ($$$).

Grace Family Vineyards

1210 Rockland Road
St. Helena, CA 94574
tel. (707) 963-0808
Open to the public by appt.; est. 1987

Grgich Hills Cellar

1829 St. Helena Highway, PO Box 450
Rutherford, CA 94573
tel. (707) 963-2784; fax (707) 963-8725
Open to the public; est. 1977

Dick Grace's claim to viticultural fame derives from a two-acre vineyard of 100 percent Cabernet Sauvignon. The retired stockbroker and his wife, Ann, made their move to the country in 1974, initially planting a single acre from which their first wine was produced at Caymus Vineyard in 1978. The high-quality result brought almost instant demand from collectors. Grace now produces about 250 much sought-after cases a year at his own tiny winery, built in 1987.

An important aspect of Grace's grape-growing philosophy requires that vines be planted close together to achieve flavor intensity. The 100 percent varietal Grace Family Cabernet is aged in French oak for three years and sells—to a fortunate few—for $125 to $150 a bottle. (At the 1990 Napa Valley Wine Auction, a bottle of the 1987 vintage went for $20,000, one of the highest prices ever paid for a bottle of American wine.) The 1987 Cabernet is certainly the winery's finest effort to date and an altogether extraordinary bottle with layers of flavors—cherry, currant, *terroir*, oak, and anise—and much suppleness and finesse. Quality here has been high in all vintages, perhaps a bit less so in 1989. Good luck finding a bottle of this wine—see if you can get on the winery's mailing list.

Wines/Varietals: Cabernet Sauvignon ($$$).

In 1977, Miljenko "Mike" Grgich (pronounced GUR-gitch) formed a partnership with coffee magnate Austin Hills and became co-owner and winemaker of Grgich Hills Winery. The year before, Grgich's 1973 Chateau Montelena Chardonnay placed first in a 1976 Paris tasting that pitted American Chardonnays against white Burgundies. It wasn't a one-shot success: Grgich Hills Chardonnays are always among the top wines of the vintage, and are consistently sought after for their silky texture and outstanding fruit. Diminutive Mike, with his ebullient personality, is a lively embodiment of the American dream and one of the most colorful figures in the California wine industry. He left Croatia, then part of communist Yugoslavia, in 1956, and arrived in Canada, barely able to speak English, with little money. His real destination was America; two years later he came to the Napa Valley. He worked for Souverain, Beaulieu Vineyards, and Robert Mondavi before joining Chateau Montelena in 1972. The white stucco, vine-covered Grgich Hills winery on Highway 29 in Rutherford now produces 50,000 to 60,000 cases of wine annually (65 percent Chardonnay, 20 percent Cabernet Sauvignon, 10 percent Fumé Blanc and 5 percent Zinfandel). The Grgich partnership owns 200 acres of vineyards scattered around the southern part of the Napa Valley, from Rutherford to Carneros, which supply two-thirds of the winery's grapes. The rest are purchased from growers in these same districts.

The taut structure and beautifully integrated flavors of Grgich Chardonnay come from the artful blending that Grigich consistently achieves. His Chard is particularly notable in the 1990 vintage, with its pear-citrus fruit and long finish. This is a wine we expect to blossom more fully in its third or fourth year. Chardonnays produced here are noted for their longevity; in fact, wines from the early seventies, including the 1973, are amazing for their fresh fruit and vibrant flavor—partly, perhaps, because they did not undergo malolactic fermentation as do so many California Chardonnays. Though Grgich is most famous (and deservedly so!) for Chardonnay, the estate-bottled Cabernet Sauvignon, exclusively from the Yountville Vineyard, also reveals the winemaker's deft touch. It is full of ripe currant and dark cherry fruit with a moderate influence of French and American oak. Convinced that California Zinfandel is related to the hearty Dalmatian Plavac grape, Grgich makes a small quantity of highly regarded Zinfandel, with ripe but well-defined berryish fruit. Grgich Hills also produces excellent Fumé Blanc, which is classic in structure, faintly herbacious in character, and softly rounded with a brief stint in oak.

Wines/Varietals: Chardonnay ($$$), Fumé Blanc ($$), Zinfandel ($$), Cabernet Sauvignon ($$$).

Groth Vineyards & Winery

750 Oakville Cross Road, PO Box 390
Oakville, CA 94562
tel. (707) 944-0290; fax (707) 944-8932
Open to the public by appt.; est. 1982

Dennis and Judy Groth purchased Oakcross Vineyard, now 121 acres smack in the middle of the Napa Valley, in 1981. The following year, Dennis left a successful corporate career in marketing and finance to become a full-time vintner. Also in 1982, the Groths purchased the Hillview vineyard, 43 acres along Highway 29 south of Yountville planted to Sauvignon Blanc and Merlot. Dennis, Judy, and their three children are now all actively involved in the winery's operation. In 1985, the Groths produced the Reserve Cabernet Sauvignon that put them on the wine map. It's a vigorous, earthy wine, packed with ripe berry flavors, that probably won't reach its peak for another five years, perhaps more.

The 87-acre Oakcross vineyard (100 percent Cabernet), delivers the concentrated fruit typical of Groth Cabernets. Gifted winemaker Nils Venge translates the best of the Oakcross fruit into the sensuous, richly textured wines that have become his signature. (He was formerly winemaker at Villa Mt. Eden, where he made reds of similar intensity and depth from a vineyard adjacent to Oakcross.) The 1987 Reserve Cabernet is an excellent example of Venge's art: reminiscent of the powerful 1985, it has perhaps less complexity but even greater elegance. Groth Cabernets typically include a percentage of Merlot from Hillview Vineyard. Forty acres of Chardonnay at Oakcross Vineyard yield well-balanced, lemon-fruited Chardonnays, with rich, oaky overtones, on a consistent basis. In one of the winery's better efforts with this grape, we found the pear and citrus flavors of the 1990 Chardonnay neatly poised to develop interesting complexity by 1993-94. Groth also makes attractive, consistently crisp and flavorful, oak-aged Sauvignon Blanc—it's the Groth white to seek out.

Wines/Varietals: Cabernet Sauvignon ($$), Reserve Cabernet Sauvignon ($$$), Chardonnay ($$), Sauvignon Blanc ($).

Guenoc Winery

21000 Butts Canyon Road,
PO Box 1146
Middletown, CA 95461
tel. (707) 987-2385; fax (707) 987-9351
Open to the public; est. 1981

So what's all the fuss here about Lillie Langtry? About 4,000 acres on this vast estate, now owned by the Magoon family, once belonged to the famous Victorian actress, who lived here from 1888 to 1906. In the 1960s, Orville and William Magoon restored Langtry's quaint farmhouse about 20 miles north of St. Helena and planted vineyards on the property where Miss Lillie first introduced vines in the nineteenth century. In the 1980s, the Magoons established their own winery and used Langtry's name and likeness everywhere possible, including on the wine labels and in print ads. Currently 320 acres of winery-owned vineyards supply most of the grapes needed for the 100,000 or so cases produced here annually; additional fruit is brought in from Lake County and the North Coast. Some of the Magoon's Guenoc vineyards fall into the Lake County part of the Guenoc Valley other plots are in Napa County. What's unusual about this is that the Magoons successfully won a viticultural area designation (AVA status) for the Guenoc Valley in 1982, and theirs is still the only winery producing from this appellation.

The good news is that in the 1990s, Guenoc is producing some very fine wines, and winning a good deal of critical praise for them. As it happens, the non-estate wines are the ones to look for first as they represent good quality *and* good value: the 1989 North Coast Cabernet Sauvignon and the 1989 North Coast Petite Sirah are our leading choices. The 1989 Cabernet Sauvignon Reserve Napa Valley Beckstoffer Vineyard is a fine bottle, with coffee, smoke, leather, spice, and plenty of dark, ripe berry fruit. The 1989 Langtry Meritage Red (73 percent Cabernet Sauvignon) is equally good, with tight structure and lovely fruit waiting to emerge. From the Guenoc property, the 1990 Chardonnay Reserve Genevieve Magoon Vineyard is a top offering and probably this house's best wine ever: rich, focused, and complex with ripe flavors highlighted by pear, pineapple, spices, and a touch of oak. Guenoc also releases wines, notably Sauvignon Blanc, under the Domaine Breton label.

Wines/Varietals: Chardonnay ($), Chardonnay, Genevieve Magoon Vineyard Reserve ($$$), Sauvignon Blanc ($), Langtry Meritage White ($$), Petite Sirah ($$), Zinfandel, California ($), Cabernet Sauvignon, Lake County ($$), Cabernet Sauvignon, Beckstoffer Vineyard Reserve, Napa Valley ($$$), Langtry Meritage Red ($$).

Harrison Vineyards

1527 Sage Canyon Road
St. Helena, CA 94574
tel. (707) 963-8271; fax (707) 963-4552
Not open to the public; est. 1988

Situated in the eastern hills of the Napa Valley, this young, 17-acre vineyard, owned by Lindsay and Michael Harrison, has recently attracted attention for its Cabernets and Chardonnays. Consulting winemaker Bob Long of neighboring Long Vineyards was behind a move to have Harrison Vineyard's first vintages custom made by Pecota Winery. In 1989—a year that was hardly the best for a first-time Napa Valley Chardonnay—Harrison nevertheless came out with a noteworthy wine. The winery followed up with a strong 1990 bottling.

All of Harrison's grapes are estate grown; half of the total annual production of 2,000 cases is Cabernet, the other half is Chardonnay. The barrel fermented Chardonnays made here undergo complete malolactic fermentation and are aged with lees contact. Indicative of Harrison Vineyards' winemaking philosophy and the quality it achieves is the 1989 Cabernet Sauvignon. As black as the stripes on the winery's distinctive zebra-print logo, this intense mountain wine has black pepper, cherry, and raspberry flavors, enhanced by just enough oak and tannins. The 1990 is just as good.

Wines/Varietals: Chardonnay ($$$), Cabernet Sauvignon ($$$).

Heitz Wine Cellars

500 Taplin Road
St. Helena, CA 94574
tel. (707) 963-3542; fax (707) 963-7454
Open to the public by appt.; est. 1961

The Heitz family developed a passion for wine in their native Ohio, but figured that California was a more likely place to realize their dream of becoming winemakers. So in 1961, Joe and Alice established a Napa Valley winery. Their children, David, Kathleen, and Rollie, now hold key positions at this 40,000 case operation with its 300 acres of vineyards. Together, the Heitzes have earned a place among the first families of American wine. While their name is synonymous with California Cabernet Sauvignon, including the legendary "Martha's Vineyard," the family also produces a full range of other varietals because, as they observe, "one cannot live on Cabernets alone."

For many, the 1968, 1970, and 1974 Cabernets made by Joe Heitz with minty-tasting grapes from Tom and Martha May's vineyard—thus the Martha's Vineyard designation—are some of the greatest, if not *the* greatest, bottles of wine ever produced in North America. Today Heitz Wine Cellars produces a range of Cabernets in each vintage (five or more), and a good Chardonnay. One of the winery's more unusual offerings is "Angelica," a traditional (and now rarely produced) sherry-like dessert wine. Made from Mission grapes, this attractive wine was first produced by the Franciscan missionaries in the early 1800s. As for the Cabernets, the 1987s here are excellent choices: the Martha's Vineyard is great, the regular Napa Valley is excellent, and the "Bella Oaks" is good to excellent.

Wines/Varietals: Cabernet Sauvignon ($$), Cabernet Sauvignon, Bella Oaks ($$), Cabernet Sauvignon, Martha's Vineyard ($$$), Chardonnay, Trailside ($$), Chardonnay, Heitz Vineyards ($$), Grignolino ($), Grignolino Rosé ($), Angelica ($$$), Zinfandel ($), Pinot Noir ($$), Ryan's Red Table Wine ($), Alicia (Botrytized Chardonnay, $$).

The Hess Collection

4411 Redwood Road, PO Box 4140
Napa, CA 94558
tel. (707) 255-1144; fax (707) 253-1682
Open to the public; est. 1986

Swiss entrepreneur Donald Hess, whose family has been in the brewing business for nine generations, acquired his first U.S. vineyard property on Mt. Veeder in the Napa Valley in 1978. Hess' estate vineyard acreage has since expanded to 320 acres, and is today planted to Cabernet Sauvignon (210 acres), Merlot and Cabernet Franc (30 acres), and Chardonnay (80 acres). In 1989, Hess purchased 300 additional acres of Chardonnay in Monterey County. The original Mt. Veeder property contained Mount La Salle, a stone winery built at the turn-of-the-century by the Christian Brothers. Renovated and modernized for wine production in 1986, the handsome structure now also houses Hess' extensive art collection, selections from which are displayed in the winery's visitors' center. Though Hess resides in Bern, Switzerland, he spends a good part of the year here, in his home on Mt. Veeder. His fine wines are at home anywhere.

There are currently three excellent wines, all estate-bottled from the Mt. Veeder vineyards, produced under The Hess Collection label: Cabernet Sauvignon, Chardonnay, and Merlot. The owner's commitment to quality has been evident from the beginning. Under winemaker Randle Johnson, the wines made here exhibit the concentration and intensity of fruit typical of mountain-grown grapes. The 1987 Hess Collection Cabernet, for instance, is a classic: beautifully balanced, deep and long, and promising great complexity as it matures. The 1988 Cabernet also has concentrated ripe berry flavor, hinting of raisins, with an overlay of spicy oak. It's not quite as finely structured as the 1987, but is every bit as intense. The 1989 Merlot, of limited production and available only at the winery, is softer than the Cabs but has concentrated red currant flavors that are appealing. The Hess Collection 1990 Chardonnay is the winery's best to date, with crisp citrus-and-pear fruit countered with oak and clove accents in a creamy texture braced by just the right acidity. With an eye to providing good value, this winery launched the "Hess Select" second label line of moderately priced varietals in 1989. At under $10 a bottle, the Hess Select Chardonnay, mostly from the Monterey vineyard, has been a hit with consumers. The Hess Select 1990 Cabernet Sauvignon is also a good value, with robust fruit and ready drinkability.

Wines/Varietals: The Hess Collection: Cabernet Sauvignon ($$), Chardonnay ($$), Merlot ($$); Hess Select: Chardonnay ($), Cabernet Sauvignon ($).

Husch Vineyards

4400 Highway 128,
PO Box 189, Talmage, CA 95481
Philo, CA 95466
tel. (707) 895-3216 or (707) 462-5370;
fax (707) 462-5374
Open to the public; est. 1971

Husch Vineyards is the Anderson Valley's oldest winery. The Oswald family purchased a Mendocino vineyard from Tony Husch in 1979, and combined it with their own 110-acre "La Ribera" (The Riverbank) estate on the Russian River in the Ukiah Valley. The two vineyards, planted to Chardonnay, Sauvignon Blanc, Gewürztraminer, Chenin Blanc, Cabernet Sauvignon, and Pinot Noir, now total 200 acres and provide fruit for an annual production of 30,000 cases. Husch wines are exclusively estate-bottled. Warmer climate varietals (Sauvignon Blanc, Cabernet Sauvignon, Chenin Blanc) are grown at La Ribera; Chardonnay from both vineyards is blended to combine the characteristics of the two microclimates.

Ken Oswald and other members of his family of third generation farmers combine their experience with the skills of winemaker Mark Theis, a U.C. Davis enology school grad, and assistant winemaker Fritz Meier, a graduate of Germany's Geisenheim University. The Gewürztraminer and the Mendocino Chardonnay, combining crisp, green apple Anderson Valley Chard flavors with lusher Ukiah Valley Chardonnay grape flavors, are the most consistent wines made here. The 1990 Chardonnay is quite good. The 1991, at around $11, is a strikingly good value and a complex wine with a bit creamier flavors (honey, figs, pears, toasty oak) and textures than in past releases. The

Select La Ribera Cabernet is only made in years when grape conditions dictate that softer, younger wines be produced. The 1985, 1986, and 1989 vintages are lovely with soft, ripe, plum and cherry-flavored fruit with some barrel spices and vanilla aromas. We were also impressed with the 1988 Mendocino La Ribera Vineyard Cabernet. Tasted in 1992, it has a strawberry nose, and is big-bodied with berry fruit and just a hint of herbal character, good balance, lots of tannins, attractive structure, and a long, distinguished finish. The more expensive North Field Select Cab from the La Ribera Vineyard 1988 vintage is sound, too.

Wines/Varietals: Chardonnay, Mendocino ($$), Sauvignon Blanc, La Ribera Vineyards ($), Gewürztraminer, Anderson Valley ($), Chenin Blanc, La Ribera Vineyards ($), Pinot Noir, Anderson Valley ($$), Cabernet Sauvignon, La Ribera Vineyards ($$), Cabernet Sauvignon, North Field Select Estate Bottled, La Ribera Vineyards ($$$).

Inglenook-Napa Valley

PO Box 391
Rutherford, CA 94573
tel. (707) 967-3362; fax (707) 967-3190
Not open to the public; est. 1879

Based on its extraordinary Cabernets (especially those from a half century ago), this 114-year-old winery belongs in any guide to the finest wineries in America. Founded by Gustave Niebaum, and operated by his grandnephew, John Daniel, Jr., until 1964, when the Heublein-Grand Met-IDV concern assumed ownership, this pioneering winery's place in history is secure.

In recent years, this winery has produced about 150,000 cases annually, covering a wide range of varietals. Cabernet Sauvignon leads the way here today, followed by Chardonnay. In 1992, we tasted greatness from Inglenook in the form of the 1966, the 1955, and especially the 1941 Cabernet Sauvignons. This last had a deep, rich, plummy nose and a powerful fruit body; it is lush and excellent, a remarkable wine, fully alive at 50-plus years. Among current release wines, the 1987 Reserve Cask Cabernet Sauvignon is the best, with roses, violets, berries, and some mint aromas and flavors in a medium body with soft qualities. The winery also produces a jug wine under the name "Navalle Selections."

Wines/Varietals: Chardonnay ($), Chardonnay, Gustave Niebaum ($$), Sauvignon Blanc ($), Gravion Estate Premium White Blend ($$), Gewürztraminer ($), Gewürztraminer, Late Harvest ($), Cabernet Sauvignon ($), Reserve Cask Cabernet Sauvignon ($$), Reserve Merlot ($), Reserve Pinot Noir ($), Zinfandel ($), Reunion Red Table Wine ($$$), Vintage Port ($).

Jaeger Inglenook

Inglenook Avenue, PO Box 322
St. Helena, CA 94574
tel. (707) 963-1875; fax (707) 963-1904
Not open to the public; est. 1979

Bill and Lila Jaeger became Merlot fans while visiting Pomerol in Bordeaux during the 1960s. Surrounding the Jaeger home in St. Helena today are Merlot vineyards. First planted in 1968, the grapes from these vineyards initially went to Rutherford Hill, where the Jaegers are co-owners and managing

partners. The home vineyard produced grapes of such quality, that when their four children came of age and showed an interest in the business, Bill and Lila created the separate Inglewood estate, with Bill as managing partner and his three sons, Jeff, Jack, and William III, as general partners.

Jaeger Inglenook's 28 acres at the upper end of the Rutherford Bench are comprised of 75 percent Merlot, 13 percent Cabernet Sauvignon, and 12 percent Cabernet Franc, and produce 6,000 cases of highly regarded Merlot. Winemaker Joe Cafaro's Merlot is consistently one of the richest in California. Ripe with dark berry fruit, it is boldly structured to age well for at least a decade, considerably longer in exceptional vintages like 1987 (and probably 1990). The wine gets extended maceration after fermentation: blended with varying amounts of Cabernet Sauvignon and Cabernet Franc, it spends two years in French oak barrels, and another two years in bottle before release.

Wines/Varietals: Merlot ($$).

Joseph Phelps Vineyards

200 Taplin Road, PO Box 1031
St. Helena, CA 94574
tel. (707) 963-2745; fax (707) 963-4831
Open to the public by appt.; est. 1973

Joe Phelps was a building contractor in Denver before he came to the Napa Valley in the early seventies and started his own winery and vineyard. He bought a ranch in the rolling hills off the Silverado Trail, known as Spring Valley, and built a handsome winery, notable for its striking architecture. The 175 acres around the winery are planted to a dozen premium varieties; Phelps owns additional vineyards in other parts of Napa, including Yountville and the Stags Leap

District. His largest plantings are devoted to Chardonnay (98 acres) and Cabernet Sauvignon (82 acres). The Spring Valley estate around the winery contains 12 acres of some of the earliest stands of Syrah planted in California. Phelps's 340 acres of vineyard supply about 70 percent of production here for a total of 85,000 cases annually. The other 30 percent of the required fruit is purchased, much of it from such distinguished growers as Eisele, Backus, and Sangiacomo, to make wines that consistently exhibit a strong vineyard signature.

While Joseph Phelps Vineyards made its early reputation with white wines, notably German-style late harvest Rieslings, today it is its red wines that make the strongest statements. The Backus Cabernet, for example, is dark and dense, and massively concentrated (remarkably so in 1989, an uneven vintage). The 1989 Backus, typically thick in texture, tastes like a fistful of ripe blackberries flavored with mint and spicy oak. The Eisele (pronounced EYES-lee) Cabernet is equally intense, but a little more complex due to the mature, dry-farmed vineyard (planted in 1964) from which it originates. Both wines need years in bottle to tame their tannins. Phelps "Insignia," a blend of Cabernet, Merlot, and Cabernet Franc in proportions that vary dramatically from year to year, is the most complex red made here. Since 1983, it is, in our view, also the most interesting, with more elegant structure than the Cabernets. The 1987 Insignia (70 percent Cabernet, 20 percent Cabernet Franc, 10 percent Merlot) has the edge over the less intense 1988 for longevity. Phelps Sangiacomo Chardonnay, from Carneros, has impressive richness and excellent balance, particularly the elegant 1990 version. This winery also shows real finesse with Gewürztraminer, increasingly made in the drier style of Alsace but with a rich fruit underpinning. Recent emphasis here is on Rhône varieties bottled under the "Vin du Mistral" label, including Syrah, Viognier, an off-dry rosé (Grenache and Mourvèdre), and "Le Mistral," a red blend of Syrah, Mourvèdre, and Grenache that is simple and fruity, best served chilled. Phelps' late harvest Rieslings, its occasional Scheurebe, and its Sauternes-like "Delice du Sémillon" are honeyed sweet wines, noted for their lusciousness. Phelps also makes a moderately-priced Cabernet and Chardonnay under the "Innisfree" label.

Wines/Varietals: Napa Valley Chardonnay ($$), Innisfree Chardonnay ($$), Chardonnay, San Giacomo ($$), Sauvignon Blanc ($), Vin du Mistral Viognier ($$$), Johannisberg Riesling ($$), Johannisberg Riesling, Late Harvest ($$), Gewürztraminer ($), Delice du Sémillon ($$), Vin du Mistral Syrah ($$), Vin du Mistral Grenache Rosé ($), Vin du Mistral Le Mistral ($$), Cabernet Sauvignon, Napa Valley ($$), Innisfree Cabernet Sauvignon ($$), Cabernet Sauvignon, Backus Vineyard ($$$), Cabernet Sauvignon, Eisele Vineyard ($$$), Insignia ($$$).

Konocti Winery

Highway 29, PO Box 890
Kelseyville, CA 95451
tel. (707) 279-8861; fax (707) 279-9633
Open to the public; est. 1979

Konocti Winery is an agricultural cooperative of 18 independent Lake County grape growers. (Three investor partners joined the association in 1982.) Named for Mt. Konocti, the inactive volcano that is a landmark in the region, this winery began producing wines with the 1975 vintage. Konocti produces 45,000 cases of wine annually, with 90 percent of the required fruit coming from the 300 acres of vineyards owned by co-op growers. Konocti, together with Kendall-Jackson and Guenoc, the region's other wineries, has helped bring recognition to Lake County. The region's volcanic soils seem to be particularly well-suited to Sauvignon Blanc (40 percent of Konocti's production) and such reds as Cabernet Sauvignon, Merlot, Cabernet Franc, and Zinfandel.

Konocti produces consistently drinkable, moderately-priced red and white wines. The emphasis here is on clean, bright fruit and well-balanced flavors. This winery is best known for its Fumé Blanc, produced in a crisp, dry, zesty style that is fresh and appealing. The 1991 is an excellent example, following on the heels of good 1990 and 1989 releases. The reds, while well structured, are immediately drinkable. Though rarely complex, they are straightforwardly fruity, yet well balanced and ageworthy, particularly the Cabernet Sauvignon and the Merlot. Whites, such as Riesling, are lightly sweet but high in acidity, and possess a certain delicacy. The Chardonnay is off-dry and has high acidity that renders it crisp.

Wines/Varietals: Fumé Blanc ($), Chardonnay ($), White Cabernet ($), White Riesling ($), Meritage White ($$), Merlot ($), Cabernet Sauvignon ($), Cabernet Franc ($).

La Jota Vineyard

1102 Las Posadas Road
Angwin, CA 94508
tel. (707) 965-0320; fax (707) 965-0324
Open to the public by appt.; est. 1982

Howell Mountain, looming on the east side of the Napa Valley at St. Helena, is fast becoming one of the hottest of Napa appellations. Just over the mountain is the town of Angwin, where La Jota Vineyards planted vines in the iron-rich volcanic soil in 1976. Nineteen of the winery's 28 acres are in Cabernet Sauvignon, and there are five in Cabernet Franc, one in Merlot, and three in Viognier. Total production here is 3,600 cases annually; 70 percent is Cabernet Sauvignon.

The mountain-grown grapes used here can really stand out in years when the valley floor's fruit is less than stellar, as in 1988. It was a modest year in Napa Valley overall, but La Jota's 1988 Cabernet (100 percent varietal) is dark and rich and, though less tannic than previous vintages, well-structured and definitely ageworthy. The follow-up 1989 and 1990 are major league as well, with occasionally overpowering rough tannins on top of cherry fruit flavors. La Jota's most impressive wine, however, may be its Viognier, a gorgeous wine, scented with hints of locust blossom and honeysuckle. Trouble is, there is just too little of it—700 cases max, and that's in a bountiful vintage. Some years owners Bill and Joan Smith have produced under a hundred cases. La Jota also makes a Cabernet Franc blended with up to 25 percent Merlot, quite limited, too, at about 400 cases annually.

Wines/Varietals: Viognier ($$$), Cabernet Sauvignon ($$), Cabernet Franc ($$).

Lamborn Family Vineyards

1475 Powell Street, # 107
Emeryville, CA 94608
tel. (510) 547-4643 or (707) 965-2811;
fax (510) 547-4643
Not open to the public; est. 1987

All that Bob Lamborn wanted was a hideaway where he could escape the pressures of his work as a private eye. He didn't have a clue that the Howell Mountain property he

Open Daily
Retail Sales
Tours & Tasting
3522 Silverado Trail
St. Helena, CA 94574
707.963.5170

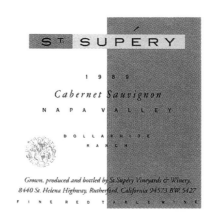

St. Supéry Vineyards & Winery
8440 St. Helena Highway
Rutherford, CA 94573

"An Art, A Passion, A Tradition"

Conveniently located off Hwy 29...just off the
beaten path. Producing Sauvignon Blanc,
Chardonnay, Merlot and Cabernet Sauvignon
selected from 200 acres of outstanding vineyards.

1155 Mee Lane, St. Helena
Open daily 10-5
707.963.1666

Beringer Vineyards
Open daily – Retail Sales,
Tours & Tastings – 9:30 am-5:00 pm
2000 Main Street
St. Helena, CA
707.963.7115

**Beaulieu Vineyard
Rutherford, CA**

PRODUCE OF CALIFORNIA

1990

CHATEAU WOLTNER

FREDERIQUE VINEYARD

*Napa Valley Chardonnay
Appellation Howell Mountain*

**CHATEAU WOLTNER
3500 Silverado Trail
St. Helena, CA 94574**

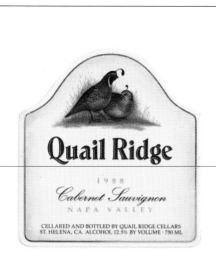

**Quail Ridge Cellars
St. Helena, CA**

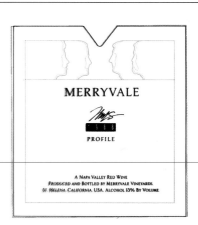

**Merryvale Vineyards
1000 Main Street
St. Helena, CA 94574**

**Tasting Room
Open daily 10:00-5:30.
707.963.2225**

Inglenook-Napa Valley
St. Helena, CA

Groth Vineyards & Winery
750 Oakville Crossroad
Oakville, CA 94562
Call for appointment
707.944.0290

Napa Beaucanon Co.
707.967.3520

purchased had once been the site of a famous vineyard. After he made the discovery, though, Lamborn began planting Zinfandel, and by 1979, he produced 100 cases of wine with the help of neighbor and winemaking magician Randy Dunn. Today Lamborn's ten acres of Zinfandel produce 2,000 cases annually, and he may one day use the other ten plantable acres he owns to add other grape varieties.

There's some greatness in these Zins. We especially like the 1989 Howell Mountain/Napa Valley release, which is fresh and lively with spices and rich fruit. The "Autumnal Harvest" releases tend to be much richer in an almost Port style, with sweet, prune-like fruit.

Wines/Varietals: Zinfandel, Howell Mountain, Napa Valley ($$), Autumnal Harvest Zinfandel, Howell Mountain, Napa Valley ($$).

Livingston Wines

1895 Cabernet Lane
St. Helena, CA 94574
tel. (707) 963-2120; fax (707) 963-9385
Not open to public; est. 1984

Cabernet Sauvignon is the sole product of this small winery in the Napa Valley owned by John and Diane Livingston. Located on the Rutherford Bench between the high profile Inglenook and Louis Martini estates, Livingston Wines' 10-acre vineyard is planted to Cabernet Sauvignon, Merlot, and Cabernet Franc. Half of the winery's 3,000 case annual output is estate-bottled "Moffett Vineyard" Cabernet, named after Diane's family. The "Stanley's Selection" Cabernet is produced from grapes grown in three separate areas of the Napa Valley, all of which are recognized for their outstanding

Cabernet vineyards. Both wines are aged in French oak for 20 to 30 months.

Careful pruning and dry farming of the hillside Moffett Vineyard result in a low-yield grape crop with high acid content. The 1988 Napa Valley Cabernet Sauvignon Moffett Vineyard is an especially good bottle—rich with black currant and cedar flavors, spicy overtones, complex and well-balanced with firm tannins and a long, oaky finish. The earlier 1987 is great and the 1990 promises to be another fine wine. We are also most impressed with the 1989 Stanley's Selection, a wine overflowing with dark berry fruit and laced with smokey oak flavor overtones. In all, this is a winery with a fine and consistent record of quality.

Wines/Varietals: Cabernet Sauvignon, Stanley's Selection, Napa Valley ($$), Cabernet Sauvignon, Moffett Vineyard, Napa Valley ($$).

Long Vineyards

1535 Sage Canyon Road, PO Box 50
St. Helena, CA 94574
tel. (707) 963-2496; fax (707) 963-5016
Open to the public by appt.; est.1977

Long Vineyards, established on Pritchard Hill, east of St. Helena, in the late seventies by Zelma Long and her former-husband, Robert, specializes in highly flavorful, limited-quantity varietals. This 4,000-case winery is best known for a luscious, well-structured Chardonnay that ages well and for sweet late harvest Riesling. The 20-acre mountain vineyard supplies about two-thirds of production.

Long Chardonnays are opulent in fruit and highly scented with prominent oak influence, qualities fully in evidence with the 1989 bottling. Cabernet here comes from an experimental vineyard planted 30 years ago by the University of California at Davis. It has rich, spicy fruit, faintly cedary in flavor, and is firm and solid with a tannic backbone that requires time in bottle to mellow. Very little is made. The 1988 Cab is an elegant bottle, not too big, but firm, long and slightly herbal on top of classic flavors. Long Vineyards' Sauvignon Blanc is also rather on the rich side, as this house's wines are traditionally, but very well balanced. The late harvest Riesling is, again, rich but well balanced and will live long and well in the bottle.

Wines/Varietals: *Chardonnay ($$$), Johannisberg Riesling ($$), Sauvignon Blanc ($$), Cabernet Sauvignon ($$$)*.

Louis M. Martini

PO Box 112,
254 South St. Helena Highway
St. Helena, CA 94574
tel. (707) 963-2736; fax (707) 963-8750
Open to the public; est. 1922

This venerable family winery was founded in 1922 by Italian immigrants as the L. M. Martini Grape Products Co., and began producing table wines under its present name after Prohibition, in 1933. Among the first to release vintage-dated varietal wines and a leader in identifying and propagating vinifera clones, Martini produces 200,000 cases of wine annually and is known for its sound wines and honest prices. The family currently owns 2,850 acres of land in Napa, Sonoma, and Lake counties and has 1,300 under vine. Recognized for its red wines, this winery has an agreement with the Buena Vista/Racke USA Group to market Martini wines.

Martini makes a highly agreeable Barbera worth seeking out. Blended with about 15 percent Zinfandel and 8 percent Petite Sirah, it is medium-bodied with lovely cherry and blackberry aromas and constitutes a balanced mouthful of medium-intense, well-made wine. The top bottle from Martini in recent years has been the first-rate 1987 Monte Rosso Vineyard Selection Cabernet Sauvignon. Also in 1987, the Petite Sirah Reserve was big, tannic, powerfully-flavored, and inviting. Among the whites, we found the 1990 Chardonnay (24 percent of production, and made with 79 percent Napa and 21 percent Sonoma grapes) to be pleasant, with soft and fleshy body, some citrus flavors in the finish, and just a touch of oak. Zinfandels, from old vines, also star in some vintages and are excellent values.

Wines/Varietals: Sauvignon Blanc ($), Chardonnay ($), Reserve Chardonnay ($$), Chardonnay Vineyard Selection, Las Amigas Vineyard ($$), Gewürztraminer ($), Gamay Beaujolais ($), Pinot Noir ($), Pinot Noir Vineyard Selection, La Loma Vineyards ($$), Merlot ($), Merlot Vineyard Selection, Los Vinedos del Rio Vineyards ($$$), Barbera ($), Zinfandel ($), Cabernet Sauvignon ($), Reserve Cabernet Sauvignon ($$), Cabernet Sauvignon Vineyard Selection, Monte Rosso Vineyard ($$$), Reserve Petite Sirah ($$).

Marcassin Wines

PO Box 332
Calistoga, CA 94515
tel. (707) 942-6828,
c/o All Seasons Wine Shop
Not open to the public; est. 1989

Helen Turley, sister of Larry Turley, Frog's Leap Winery's co-owner, made some very good wines in the 1980s at the B. R. Cohn Winery and some great wines at the Peter Michael Winery. Now she's producing a few hundred cases a year of her own wines. So far only a Chardonnay is being marketed, but a Pinot Noir is also part of the plan here. Turley's Marcassin label wines are about as hard to get and about as highly coveted by those "in the know" as any in California.

She's a terrific winemaker seeking to raise the vineyard, the vintage, and the varietal character of her grapes up to their highest possible collective expression. Using traditional methods and with minimal intervention, she makes two Chardonnays: one from the Hyde Vineyard in Carneros and the other from the Lorenzo Vineyard along the Sonoma coast. Both are solidly in the Burgundian camp and both are reportedly great in the 1990 vintage. The 1990 Lorenzo we tasted was crisp and a bit leaner than we expected, but distinctively flavorful and multi-dimensional. It should evolve into a splendid wine.

Wines/Varietals: Chardonnay, Hyde Vineyard, Carneros ($$), Chardonnay, Lorenzo Vineyard, Sonoma ($$).

Markham Vineyards

2812 St. Helena Highway N.,
PO Box 636
St. Helena, CA 94574
tel. (707) 963-5292; fax (707) 963-4616
Open to the public for sales, tours by appt.; est. 1978

This is a Napa Valley winery in transition. A multi-million dollar renovation of the winery here will double its size and production capacity in 1993. Early in 1992, Paterno Imports in Chicago was assigned all the national sales, public relations, and marketing responsibilities for the winery. And late in 1992, Robert Hunter, III, was appointed Markham's new winemaker. Currently the winery is producing 30,000 cases of good to very good quality wines from its 230 acres of fine vineyards.

The reds have traditionally been the strength here, but in the past few years the whites have improved so dramatically that quality is now sound and consistent across the line. The 1990 Chardonnay (100 percent barrel fermented) is a very good one: well made with floral, fruit, and oak aromas and soft, citrus flavors. We also recommend highly the 1991 Sauvignon Blanc. At just $9, it's a polished wine with lots of smooth flavor complexities, including pears, figs, citrus, and spices. Perhaps the best value here is the moderately priced Merlot, which in 1989 is lovely with dark cherry and blueberry flavors and a seductive, smooth body. Cabernet remains the star, though, especially the concentrated and supple estate-grown Markham Vineyard wines. The 1989 Cab is a good release. Markham also produces some inexpensive wines under the "Glass Mountain" label.

Wines/Varietals: Sauvignon Blanc ($), Chardonnay, Napa Valley ($$), Muscat Blanc ($), Merlot ($$), Cabernet Sauvignon ($$).

Mayacamas Vineyards

1155 Lokoya Road
Napa, CA 94558
tel. (707) 224-4030; fax (707) 224-3979
Open to the public by appt.; est. 1889 (in continuous operation since 1968)

Robert and Elinor Travers bought Mayacamas in 1968. Their vineyard, 50 acres now, is nestled high against the mountains of the Mayacamas range that straddles the Napa and Sonoma valleys. The emphasis here is on Cabernet Sauvignon and Chardonnay, and to a lesser extent, Sauvignon Blanc and Pinot Noir. Occasion-

187

ally other varietals, most often Zinfandel, are produced if a special lot of grapes comes the Travers' way. Nevertheless, Mayacamas' excellent reputation rests with its Cabernet.

Bob Travers, president and winemaker, makes big, flavorful, concentrated wines. His Chardonnays are rich and oaky and, in a sense, old-fashioned; his reds, especially the Cabernet, are densely tannic, and in need of at least a decade, usually more, to become truly drinkable. "We make wines to age," Travers declares, and the winery's annual library releases of bottles of each vintage, aged at the winery and released when they approach their peak potential, proves the point (prime examples are the 1979 Cabernet Sauvignon and the 1985 and 1986 Chardonnays). Travers has lately focused on Sauvignon Blanc, which he makes in a rich, aromatic style capable of aging several years. Production here is limited, about 5,000 cases annually, and the wines have a loyal following.

Wines/Varietals: Cabernet Sauvignon ($$$), Cabernet Sauvignon, Library Selection ($$$), Chardonnay ($$), Chardonnay, Library Selection ($$$), Sauvignon Blanc ($$), Sauvignon Blanc, Library Selection ($$), Pinot Noir ($$), Pinot Noir, Library Selection ($$).

Merryvale Vineyards

1000 Main Street
St. Helena, CA 94574
tel. (707) 963-2225; fax (707) 963-1949
Open to the public; est. 1983

In 1983, Napa Valley real estate investment partners William Harlan, John Montgomery, and the late Peter Stoker joined forces with Robin Lail (of the family that founded Inglenook Napa Valley) and her husband, Jon. Together they established Merryvale Vineyards and engaged U.C. Davis-trained enologist Robert Levy as winemaker. Merryvale's 16,000 cases of wines are produced and bottled each year at the Sunny St. Helena Winery, which is also owned by the partnership. All of Merryvale's fruit is purchased from Napa Valley vineyards. Its wines are marketed under three labels: Merryvale (Profile and Reserve), Merryvale Vineyards, and Sunny St. Helena.

The Chardonnays made here have earned top ratings in international wine tastings, including one conducted by Gault Millau in Paris, and established this winery's excellent reputation. These Chards have notably clean flavors: the 1990 Napa Reserve shows pears and spices. The fine 1990 Napa "Starmount" has nice and appealing fruit aromas, good balance and some oak. With aging, more complexity may evolve. We are even more taken with "Profile," Merryvale's meritage blend. In 1987 it is a rich, concentrated wine (89 percent Cabernet Sauvignon and 11 percent Cabernet Franc) with highly attractive currant-cassis, cherry, and vanilla flavors, and fine balance, though high acid. It's chewy, with hints of raspberry and mint. Another good blend is the flavorful white Napa Valley Meritage (63 percent Sauvignon Blanc and 37 percent Sémillon, 100 percent barrel fermented in 1990). We are also impressed with Merryvale's Cabs, especially the lovely 1988 (tasted in 1992), which has excellent fruit along black cherry lines with vanilla, clove, mint overtones, fine balance, and a velvety character. The 1990 Merlot is another winner—big and bold with blackberry and plum flavors—that will evolve nicely in the firm tannic and oak structure.

Wines/Varietals: Reserve Chardonnay ($$$), Chardonnay, Starmont ($$), Meritage White ($$), Cabernet Sauvignon ($$), Profile ($$$).

Mount Veeder Winery

1999 Mount Veeder Road
Napa, CA 94558
tel. (707) 963-7111; fax (707) 963-7867
Open to the public by appt.; est. 1972

Mount Veeder was among the first small, Napa Valley estates to make a statement in the early seventies with its intense, pungent, deep-structured Cabernet from mountain-grown grapes. The winery's 45 acres of vineyard on Mount Veder produce 8,000 cases annually, all estate-bottled.

Under the ownership of partners Augustin Huneeus and Peter Eckes of Germany (also owners of Franciscan Oakville Estate and Estancia Estates) since 1989, Mount Veeder remains dedicated to producing intense, concentrated wines from its mountain vineyards. Peter Franus, winemaker here since 1983, produces three wines: Cabernet Sauvignon (50 percent of production), Chardonnay (30 percent), and a red Meritage (20 percent). The 1988 Meritage is impressive, with dark currant-like fruit and a firm spine of tannin that will need until 1998 or so to soften. The Chardonnay can also seem oaky, though the fruit from Mount Veeder's volcanic soil is characteristically earthy, laced with mineral flavors and thickly layered. The good 1988 and 1990 Chardonnays are this winery's best efforts to date, though it is likely to continue to be known primarily as a Cabernet specialist. In recent vintages, both of the reds show more polish and strong Mount Veeder identities.

Wines/Varietals: Cabernet Sauvignon ($$), Chardonnay ($$), Meritage ($$$).

Mumm Napa Valley

8445 Silverado Trail, PO Drawer 50
Rutherford, CA 94573
tel. (707) 942-3300; fax (707) 942-3326
Open to the public; est. 1986

There are those who say that the best sparkling wines produced by the French Champagne house of Mumm are the domestic sparklers from Mumm Napa Valley. We tend to agree. Since its inception under Chef de Caves Guy DeVaux (recently retired) and winemaker Greg Fowler (formerly at Schramsberg), Mumm Napa Valley has become one of the front-runners in the ever more hotly contested California sparkling wine race. With the powerful Seagram wines and spirits company (owner of Champagne Mumm and Seagrams Classics Wine Co.) behind it, Mumm Napa Valley is a big commercial success, rapidly leapfrogging older premium sparkling wineries to an annual production of approximately 150,000 cases. The handsome green-gabled facility, with its dashing racing stable design, purchases 100 percent of the grapes (exclusively Chardonnay, Pinot Noir, and Pinot Meunier) used for its four cuvées.

The basic nonvintage Cuvée Napa Brut Prestige is dry, crisp, and fruity, and a good value. The Winery Lake Cuvée from the Winery Lake Vineyard in Carneros has bolder character and a bit more elegance, as in the 1988. The newest addition to the line is the Blanc de Noirs, a little weightier but seemingly with a slightly sweeter dosage. It's not as dry, at any rate, as the Brut Prestige or the Vintage Reserve, which are produced when the vintage is above average—in most years, in fact. While this winery's best value is the Cuvée Napa Brut Prestige, followed by the Vintage Reserve, its best wine is the Winery Lake Cuvée.

Wines/Varietals: Cuvée Napa Brut Prestige ($$), Cuvée Napa Vintage Reserve ($$), Winery Lake Cuvée ($$$), Cuvée Napa Blanc de Noirs ($$).

Newton Vineyard

2555 Madrona Ave., PO Box 540
St. Helena, CA 94574
tel. (707) 963-9000; fax (707) 963-5408
Not open to the public; est. 1978

Englishman Peter Newton and his Eurasian wife, Su Hua, an associate professor at the University of San Francisco, have created a unique estate on the slopes of the Mayacamas Mountains above St. Helena. The 560-acre ranch reflects the passions of its owners, with a superb rose garden, a formal Japanese temple garden, impeccable decor, and 103 acres of vineyard dramatically terraced on elevations up to 1,800 feet.

Winemaker John Kongsgaard's wines are often as dramatic as the setting in which they are made, particularly the reds: a Cabernet blended of all four varieties grown here, an impressively structured Merlot (combined with a small amount of Cabernet Franc for extra fruit thrust), arguably Newton's best wine, and the house's Claret, a supple red with nice balance and plummy flavors. The 1988 Cabernet is firm and solidly built on layers of fruit and tannin that promise complexity by the late nineties. The 1989 Merlot is fairly concentrated for this lighter year, and has punchy flavors typical of hillside grapes held to low yields. The 1990 Unfiltered Chardonnay, first of a limited production, has powerful and intense fruit, with clove and vanilla accents.

Wines/Varietals: Cabernet Sauvignon ($$), Merlot ($$$), Claret ($$), Chardonnay ($$), Unfiltered Chardonnay ($$$).

Niebaum-Coppola Estate Winery

PO Box 208
Rutherford, CA 94573
tel. (707) 963-9099; fax (707) 964-9084
Open to the public by appt.; established 1978 (on the site of a 1879 winery)

Gustave Nybom (later Niebaum), a Finnish sea captain, came to the Napa Valley in the late 1870s and founded Inglenook, one of Napa's earliest wine estates. Situated on the Rutherford Bench at the foot of Mount St. John on the west side of the valley, the property was among the first California vineyards to produce distinctive red wines (they won recognition at the Paris Exposition of 1889). Filmmaker Francis Ford Coppola and his wife, Eleanor, purchased the 1,600-acre estate from Inglenook in 1975; included in the deal were Niebaum's Victorian home and the hillside cave where the vintner made wines from his first crush in 1882. Renamed Niebaum-Coppola, the estate currently has 110 acres under vine, mostly Cabernet Sauvignon, Cabernet Franc, and Merlot. There are also smaller amounts of Zinfandel and Chardonnay (which are made into house wines) and recently planted experimental plots of Viognier and Nebbiolo.

Mindful of the long tradition of fine Cabernets established here by Niebaum and maintained, following Prohibition, by Niebaum's great nephew, John Daniel, Coppola sought to make a single, claret-style red "capable of aging a hundred years." He released his first wine, a 1979 blend of top lots of Cabernet and Merlot and a dollop or so of Cabernet Franc, in 1985, dubbing it "Rubicon." Subsequent vintages established Rubicon as one of California's most distinguished reds. Richly textured and packed with dark, cassis-like fruit, Rubicon spends three years in French oak (new and used) and three in bottle before release; it's aged longer before being sent to market than nearly any other domestic red we can think of. Only 20 percent of the grapes grown here (Cabernet Sauvignon is dominant) are used for Rubicon and the rest are sold to Inglenook. Early versions of Rubicon were extremely concentrated and tannic, the way California winemakers once thought wines had to be to age for decades. The 1982 Rubicon, one of the best, is still too tannic to drink but will indeed be a wine for the ages. Since 1986, the tannins in the new releases are a little more restrained, but the wine is no less impressive. It's more so, in fact: rich in flavor with enormous depth but greater finesse. The 1986 Rubicon, leaner than the chewy 1985, is more classic in structure (68 percent Cabernet Sauvignon) and has tremendous aging potential. Less than 5,000 cases of Rubicon are produced annually, but in some vintages, such as 1982 and 1990, the winery also makes a Cabernet Franc. With a new winemaking team comprised of Scott McLeod and consultant Tony Soter in place since 1990, the Coppolas seem set to welcome the millennium with panache.

Wines/Varietals: Rubicon ($$$).

Opus One
1144 Oakville Cross, PO Box 6
Oakville, CA 94562
tel. (707) 944-9442; fax (707) 944-9357
Open to the public by appt.; est. 1979

Robert Mondavi scored a brilliant coup in taking up the offer of the dynamic Baron Phillipe Rothschild and the unquestionably great French winery, Château Mouton-Rothschild, to become a full partner in this joint venture. The forging of the Franco-American alliance that led to the creation of Opus One benefited the entire California premium wine industry, adding instantly and immeasurably to its international credibility. In a sense, Opus One has given America its first accepted first-growth red wine. Nowadays, though, it's hard to think of this winery or its wine without feeling some sadness. A heavy case of phylloxera infestation has required that the vineyards here be torn up and that expensive replanting be undertaken. The wine, which was made for most of its existence at the Robert Mondavi winery from Mondavi-grown and additional purchased local grapes, recently got a new home in Oakville, comprising 110 acres of vineyards and a striking, spare-no-expense show-place winery.

A blend of Cabernet Sauvignon, Cabernet Franc, and often also Merlot, the wine has been consistently good from the start, sometimes exceedingly good. Opus One is the real thing; we are hopeful that it will hold up with time and recover from the setback in the vineyard. We found Opus One lovely in 1984, 1985, and 1987—firm, flavorful, and dynamic with deep black cherry and currant flavors with over-riding creamy oak. The 1989 is similar in style and flavors but lacks the resonances of the very top vintages.

Wines/Varietals: Opus One ($$$).

Pahlmeyer
PO Box 2410
Napa, CA 94558
tel. (707) 255-2321; fax (707) 255-6786
Not open to the public; est. 1985

Trial lawyer Jayson Pahlmeyer began development of this 25-acre vineyard in the Coombsville area of Napa's cool Carneros district in the early 1980s. Annual production here is 2,000 cases, split evenly between red wine and Chardonnay. All of Pahlmeyer's grapes are estate-grown in the terraced hillside Caldwell Vineyard (named for vineyard manager John Caldwell) at an elevation of 500 feet.

Randy Dunn of Dunn Vineyards is the highly regarded winemaker here. He utilizes traditional winemaking methods, racking the reds in French Nevers oak after fermentation and aging them for two-and-a-half years. Pahlmeyer Chardonnay is barrel fermented and it is good. The red wine made here is even better. The 1988 Pahlmeyer Estate Bottled Caldwell Vineyard (a blend of the five red Bordeaux varietals) is a graceful wine with blackberry fruit and attractive cedar tones. The early success of this winery and its terrific vineyards make Pahlmeyer one to watch closely.

Wines/Varietals: Chardonnay, Napa Valley Estate Bottled ($$$), Red Table Wine, Napa Valley Estate Bottled ($$$).

Pine Ridge Winery

5901 Silverado Trail; PO Box 2508
Yountsville, CA 94558
Winery: 5901 Silverado Trail, Napa
tel. (707) 253-7500; fax (707) 253-1493
Open to the public for tasting, tours by appt.; est. 1978

Gary Andrus bought a 50-acre site partly planted to Chardonnay (dating from 1964) in the Stags Leap District on the Silverado Trail in 1978. He has since grown the winery to 159 acres and an annual production of 50,000 cases. Cabernet is king in Andrus' world, and most of his are outstanding. Top-flight Cabernets amount to 25 percent of production here, and a simpler Chenin Blanc (off-dry, fruity-citrus style) amounts to another 35 percent. It seems Andrus wants it both ways—red *and* white—and he

more or less succeeds. His Chardonnays, crisp, bone dry, toasty-oaky French, are still being perfected, yet they are already admirable. Estate fruit accounts for 65 percent of this winery's needs.

Among recent releases, the winery prides itself particularly on the fine, rich, and supple 1987 Cabernet Sauvignon, Stags Leap District (smoke and violets). For us, the Rutherford Cuvée is nearly a match, with its Rutherford Bench flavor markings apparent and its pricing making it a sound buy. We also much enjoyed the splendid 1988 Cabs from Howell Mountain and from Diamond Mountain, both of which carry the Andrus Reserve label. All have lots of oak and a compact structure with deep underlying fruit; it's hard to go wrong with a Pine Ridge Cabernet.

Wines/Varietals: Chenin Blanc, Yountville ($), Chardonnay, Knollside ($$), Chardonnay, Stags Leap District ($$$), Merlot ($$), Cabernet Sauvignon, Rutherford Cuvée ($$), Cabernet Sauvignon, Stags Leap District ($$$).

Plam Vineyard & Winery

6200 Washington Street
Yountville, CA 94599
tel. (707) 944-1102; fax (707) 963-1727
Open to the public by appt.; est. 1984

This 10,000-case winery in the southern Napa Valley was the old Hopper Creek Vineyards when Bay Area engineer Ken Plam purchased it in 1984. Plam's renovations and vineyard expansion (currently 26 acres devoted to Cabernet Sauvignon, Chardonnay, and Merlot) have paid off. With good and consistent quality, Plam represents very much an honest bottle of wine.

The Chardonnays here won early praise for their buttery, appley fruit and balance, and have been consistently attractive. Perhaps a touch less consistent, yet excellent nonetheless, the Plam Cabernet was at its best in 1986—enormously full-bodied, lush, complex, with black currant and plum flavors and classic hints of cedar and chocolate on the long finish. The winery also makes a crisp Fumé Blanc from purchased grapes.

Wines/Varietals: Chardonnay, Napa Valley ($$), Fumé Blanc, Napa Valley ($), Cabernet Sauvignon, Napa Valley ($$$).

Raymond Vineyard & Cellar

849 Zinfandel Lane
St. Helena, CA 94574
tel. (707) 963-3141 or (707) 963-8511;
fax (707) 963-8498
Open to the public; est.1974

Roy Raymond, Sr., went to work for Beringer Vineyards in the Napa Valley in 1933, and three years later married Martha Jane Beringer, whose grandfather and uncle had emigrated from Germany and founded Beringer in 1876. Roy spent 30-plus years at Beringer before he and sons, Roy, Jr., and Walt, established their own 80-acre vineyard in 1971. Roy, Jr. now manages the vineyard here and Walt makes the wine. Though officially retired, Roy, Sr., is still active in the business. In 1989, the Raymonds formed a partnership with Kirin Brewery of Japan, and now are managing partners with a minority interest in the property. Production is currently 150,000 cases annually.

Raymond makes accessible, generally moderately priced wines of consistently sound quality. Fermentation usually takes place in jacketed stainless-steel tanks (white wines are fermented at cool temperatures to retain

fruitiness), and aging occurs in 60-gallon French barrels of Allier, Limousin, and Nevers oak. In the early 1980s, the Raymonds had a string of successes with Cabernet, which they haven't been quite able to match since. The Raymond Cabs generally need time in the bottle to evolve and emerge. The Private Reserve Napa Valley, with jam and plum flavors but also a somewhat leafy, minty character, is better and bigger than this winery's regular Napa Valley Cab. The best Raymond wine we've tasted recently is the 100 percent barrel fermented 1990 Private Reserve Chardonnay, an elegant wine with classic Chardonnay flavors of apple and pear, which are blended with soft vanilla and toasted almond aromas in a harmonious balance between fruit, acid, and oak. Raymond's other 1990 Chardonnays are straightforward, along crisp and citrusy lines.

Wines/Varietals: Sauvignon Blanc ($), Chardonnay, California ($$), Chardonnay, Napa Valley ($$), Private Reserve Chardonnay ($$), Cabernet Sauvignon ($$), Private Reserve Cabernet Sauvignon ($$$).

Ritchie Creek Vineyard

4024 Spring Mountain Road
St. Helena, CA 94574
tel. (707) 963-4661
Not open to the public; est. 1974

Napa Valley dentist Richard Minor planted vines on the steep slopes of Spring Mountain as early as 1964, but he didn't have a crop worthy of producing wine until a decade later. Today he has 8 acres planted (4 Cabernet Sauvignon/Merlot, 3 Chardonnay, 1 Viognier) and has built a small winery capable of handling the 1,200 cases a year the estate currently produces.

We could have passed over such a small winery, but we admire the consistent quality and style of Minor's wines as well as his pioneering efforts with the difficult Viognier grape. The Cabs, true to their Napa hillside origin, are dark and firm. The Chardonnay, which makes up most of the winery's production, is a good one, generally polished and complex, as in 1989. First released in 1986, the Viognier is succeeding with tart bright flavors and classic floral overtones.

Wines/Varietals: Chardonnay ($$), Viognier ($$), Cabernet Sauvignon ($$).

Robert Keenan Winery

3660 Spring Mountain Road,
PO Box 142
St. Helena, CA 94574
tel. (707) 963-9177 or (707) 963-9178;
fax (707) 963-8209
Open to the public by appt.; est. 1904 (in continuous operation since 1974)

Formerly the Conradi Winery (defunct since Prohibition), Robert and Ann Keenan's 180-acre estate (62 acres of vineyard) is situated on top of Spring Mountain at 1,700 feet. The Keenans bought the property in the early 1970s, and built a stone winery into the hillside here. Production is 10,000 cases. This winery is better known for its big boy reds than for its whites, but both have been quality wines ever since their first release in 1977. Nonetheless, keeping up with the competition has seemingly led to nice advances in quality and accessibility here in recent years. Two Chardonnays are currently produced. The estate Chardonnay, "Ann's Vineyard," is fermented in stainless steel. The Napa Valley Chardonnay, a blend of estate-grown and Carneros grapes, is partially barrel fermented. Both have fruit and charm along somewhat austere lines. The

Napa Valley Chardonnay has always been a pleaser, particularly since the 1987 vintage. The 1991 Napa Chard is a good one, with lemon and pear flavors with some oak highlights. The 1988 Cabernet is representative of this winery's current style: rich in deep, fairly intense, berry flavors and currants, the wine had a little tannic bitterness upon release, requiring four or five years of aging. Keenan's 1989 Merlot is a superb one.

Wines/Varietals: Chardonnay, Napa Valley ($$), Chardonnay, Ann's Vineyard ($$), Cabernet Sauvignon, Napa Valley ($$), Cabernet Franc, Napa Valley ($$), Merlot, Napa Valley ($$).

Robert Mondavi Winery

7801 St. Helena Hwy., PO Box 106
Oakville, CA 94562
tel. (707) 963-9611; fax (707) 963-1007
Open to the public; est. 1966

Robert Mondavi, the man, merits his own entry in this and every other book on North American wine. He is easily deserving of all the praise we can heap on him for his brilliant leadership of the California wine industry over the past 25-plus years. His story—of blood feuds and dogged independence, of breaking away from an established family enterprise and opening this winery in 1966, of building his own concern into an icon of the American wine industry—surely are due a special chapter. The winery and wine group Mondavi's sons, Michael and Tim, now direct as managing partners are, of course, entities separate from the remarkable man. What has made the Mondavi Winery so extraordinary over the years is, certainly, the high quality of its Napa Valley wines (especially the Reserve wines), but also its unexcelled ability to fascinate the world with the culture and all of the activity that has grown up around it. Nowadays, the Robert Mondavi Winery in Oakville owns 2,000 acres of vineyards and buys about two-thirds of its grapes to produce an unspecified amount of premium wine. It is, however, a little guy compared with the million cases of modestly-priced wines produced at Mondavi Oakbridge. A recent joint venture with big-volume Cambria Winery, some downsizing at Mondavi-owned Vichon Winery, and a public stock offering suggest a modified course and reconceived identity for the Mondavi winery network of the 1990s.

The Napa winery produces a full range of varietals and is renowned for its technical innovation. Not to take anything away from pioneering Hanzell Vineyards, but it was Robert Mondavi who really put the French barrels into the American wine business (which resulted in the wines attaining new levels of quality and complexity) and built one of the first and most influential high-tech winemaking operations (which resulted in clean, and consistently reliable wines). Lately, Tim Mondavi has made great strides towards putting some of the fruit's natural flesh back into the wines here—the Reserve Chardonnay, Reserve Fumé Blanc, Reserve Pinot Noir, and of course the famous Reserve Cabernet Sauvignon have rarely been better. The Fumé Blanc, early on the winery's flagship varietal, remains a good value. When Robert established his winery, he was obliged to purchase the entire harvests of certain suppliers. He found himself the owner of Sauvignon Blanc grapes, which were not much admired at the time. By leaving the juice of the grapes in contact with the skins for a period after crushing, fermenting in temperature-controlled stainless steel, and

aging in French oak barrels, he was able to produce a pleasing and complex wine he dubbed Fumé Blanc. Many vintners across the country have since followed in his footsteps. This winery's other whites, notably its Chenin Blanc and Riesling, are generally nicely balanced but on the sweet side. Recent bottles of special merit include the 1988 and 1990 Chardonnay Reserve, the 1991 Fumé Blanc, the 1990 Fumé Blanc Reserve, the 1988 and 1990 Pinot Noir Reserve, and the 1987 and 1989 Cabernet Sauvignon Reserve. The regular 1989 Napa Cab will be ready for drinking in a few years.

Wines/Varietals: Chardonnay ($$), Reserve Chardonnay ($$$), Fumé Blanc ($), Reserve Fumé Blanc ($$), Reserve Brut Sparkling Wine ($$$), Reserve Brut Chardonnay ($$$), Chenin Blanc ($), Johannisberg Riesling ($), Johannisberg Riesling Botrytis (375 ml, $$$), Moscato d'Oro ($), Sauvignon Blanc Botrytis ($$$), Pinot Noir ($$), Reserve Pinot Noir ($$$), Cabernet Sauvignon ($$), Reserve Cabernet Sauvignon ($$$).

Robert Pecota Winery

3299 Bennett Lane, PO Box 303
Calistoga, CA 94515
tel. (707) 942-6625; fax (707) 942-6671
Open to the public by appt.; est. 1978

An ex-Beringer Vineyards exec, experienced in land acquisition, Robert Pecota acquired his own vineyard at the foot of Mount St. Helena in 1978. His 45 acres of vineyards, some of the valley's northernmost acreage, are devoted to Merlot (20 acres), Cabernet Sauvignon (14 acres), and Sauvignon Blanc (11 acres). Buying in about 50 percent of his grapes, Pecota currently produces 20,000 cases a year. In recent years, he has ambitiously diversified his line beyond Cabernet and Chardonnay. And the wines have become very good.

Pecota is especially fond of his dessert wine, which he calls "Moscato di Andrea, Napa Valley Muscat Blanc." The Andrea in question is the winemaker's daughter. The wine, with 10 percent residual sugar, is intensely perfumed with characteristic apricot and citrus flavors. In some years, such as 1988 and 1990, Pecota also bottles "Sweet Andrea," a late-harvest wine with 21 percent residual sugar. This winery merits kudos for turning out a nouveau-style Gamay Beaujolais that is vivid and well focused with plenty of the exuberant fruit one expects from a wine with the word "Beaujolais" on the label. The Sauvignon Blanc here is soft and not too herbaceous, and the Merlot is sound, too. The Cabernet, from Kara's Vineyard, has really improved. It is a multidimensional wine with cinnamon, cherry, plum, chocolate, and cedar flavor complexities, beautifully balanced, that from 1987 onwards has been consistently more than good.

Wines/Varietals: Sauvignon Blanc ($), Gamay Beaujolais ($), Moscato di Andrea, Napa Valley Muscat Blanc (375 ml, $), Sweet Andrea, Napa Valley Muscat Blanc (375 ml, $$), Merlot, Steven Andre ($$), Cabernet Sauvignon, Kara's Vineyard ($$).

Robert Pepi Winery

7585 St. Helena Highway
Oakville, CA 94562
tel. (707) 944-2807; fax (707) 944-5628
Open to the public; est. 1981

The descendants of generations of Tuscan winemakers and grapegrowers, Bob and Aurora Pepi purchased 70 acres in the Napa

Valley in 1966 and planted them to Sauvignon Blanc, Sémillon, Chardonnay, and Cabernet Sauvignon. For years they sold all the fruit they grew, but in 1980 they decided to try their hand at winemaking. Sauvignon Blanc has historically dominated production at this 26,000 case-a-year winery; some 17,000 cases of a regular Sauvignon Blanc are bottled, along with an additional 1,100 cases of a reserve bottling.

John Engelskirger, the new winemaker here as of 1991, has continued to work well with Sauvignon Blanc, supplementing estate grapes with an increasing quantity of purchased fruit. His new focus, however, has been on Sangiovese Grosso, the traditional grape of Tuscany. A total of 1,766 cases of the Sangiovese were made here in 1990 (the Pepi version blends in a bit of Petite Sirah and Cabernet Sauvignon). The result—a wine with violet and spice nose, ripe cherry fruit, firm tannins, and velvety finish—though still subdued compared with what we expect will eventually be done here with Sangiovese, nevertheless bodes well for the future of this varietal in California, and for Pepi. The Sauvignon Blanc continues to be a nice offering. In 1991 it is blended with 17 percent Sémillon, and shows fruit and jalapeño peppers on the nose and ripe melon, pineapple, and a bit of varietal grassiness on the palate. It makes a statement that lingers. The 1990 Puncheon Fermented Napa Valley Chardonnay is a good one, with intensity and toasty almond and fruit flavors.

Wines/Varietals: Sauvignon Blanc ($), Reserve Sauvignon Blanc ($$), Chardonnay ($$), Cabernet Sauvignon ($$), Colline di Sassi Sangiovese Grosso ($$$).

Robert Sinskey Vineyards

6320 Silverado Trail
Napa, CA 94558
tel. (707) 944-9090; fax (707) 944-9092
Open to the public; est. 1986

Physician Robert Sinskey and his son, Rob, built a handsome stone winery on the Silverado Trail just above the town of Napa. Their 90-acre vineyard in Carneros produces 8,000 cases annually.

Joe Cafaro, Sinskey's first winemaker, produces wines—especially Merlot—with intense flavor and sensuous texture; both qualities are evident in the 1986 and 1987 Merlot bottlings, slightly less so in the 1989. Sinskey's Carneros Claret is also Merlot-based. The 1990 contains 50 to 60 percent Merlot blended with Cabernet Sauvignon and Cabernet Franc. Well balanced and complex, it already boasts toothsome flavors but will likely reward cellaring for a decade. The richness in Sinskey wines also extends to its Pinot Noir, particularly the RSV 1989 Reserve. With its dark berry flavors and accent of new oak, this is perhaps the winery's best release to date. We are eager to see how it fares with five or six years in the bottle. We recommend, too, the 1990 Los Carneros Pinot Noir—among the very best we've tasted in the past year. It's a medium-bodied wine with lots of underlying fruit that emerges in the glass and will do so in the bottle over the next few years. Sinskey Chardonnays are fairly big but tightly structured; the Reserve is oakier and more intense. Cafaro is only peripherally involved here now, mostly at blending time; Jeff Virnig is now winemaker.

Wines/Varietals: Pinot Noir, Los Carneros ($$), Pinot Noir, RSV Reserve ($$),* *Chardonnay, Los Carneros ($$), Merlot, Los Carneros ($$), Carneros Claret ($$$).

Round Hill Cellars

1680 Silverado Trail
St. Helena, CA 94574
tel. (707) 963-5251; fax (707) 963-0834
Open to the public by appt.; est. 1977

The wines of Round Hill will wash down foods and tickle your palate simply and agreeably while safeguarding your wallet. Round Hill produces a lot of wine, probably very near the winery's 300,000-case capacity level each year. These wines are priced modestly, and some of them—the Napa Valley Cabernet Sauvignon and the Napa Valley Zinfandel, for example—are quite high-quality for their price. Over the years this winery has evolved into a large negociant-style operation. Round Hill currently owns 50 acres of vineyard and buys additional grapes to produce several lines of wine: some house California generics, a line of Napa appellation varietals, and a line of reserve wines, also from the Napa Valley and drawn from vineyards that Round Hill owns or farms.

Its reserve wines are agreeable, but more likely to attract our attention are Round Hill's well-priced Napa Valley wines: Chardonnay, Gewürztraminer, Merlot, Cabernet Sauvignon, and Zinfandel. We find their quality sound and consistent. The 1990 Zinfandel is a fine bottle with rich plum, cherry, spice, and oak flavors and a $6 price tag that makes its nearly irresistible.

Wines/Varietals: Fumé Blanc, Napa Valley ($), Fumé Blanc, California ($), Chardonnay, California ($), Chardonnay, Napa Valley ($),

Chardonnay, Napa Valley Reserve ($$), House Chardonnay ($), Gewürztraminer, Napa Valley ($), White Zinfandel, California ($), House NV White ($), Merlot, California ($), Merlot, Napa Valley ($), Merlot, Napa Valley Reserve ($$), Zinfandel, Napa Valley ($), Cabernet Sauvignon, Napa Valley ($), Cabernet Sauvignon, Napa Valley Reserve ($$), Cabernet Sauvignon, California ($), House NV Red ($).

Rutherford Hill Winery
200 Rutherford Road (Rutherford),
PO Box 410
St. Helena, CA 94574
tel. (707) 963-1871 or (707) 963-7194;
fax (707) 963-1904
Open to the public; est. 1976

Rutherford Hill's combined vineyard holdings, all located in the Napa Valley, total more than 600 acres. Formerly owned by Pillsbury, this winery was operated under the name Souverain of Rutherford for a brief period. Members of the current limited partnership (who also jointly own Freemark Abbey) include managing partner Bill Jaeger. Among this concern's holdings is the 55-acre Jaeger Ranch, the largest single block of Merlot in the Napa Valley, and one of the first tracts of Merlot planted there.

Between the 1988 and 1989 vintages, the partnership doubled its production of Merlot, which now represents more than 50 percent of production here. Merlot is the "varietal of the future" according to Jaeger, who expects Rutherford Hill to become the leading quality producer of Merlot in the United States (With this end in mind, the partnership signed a marketing agreement with Chicago-based Paterno Imports in December of 1992). Rutherford Hill also makes two Cabernet Sauvignons, three

Chardonnays, Sauvignon Blanc, Gewürztraminer, and Vintage Zinfandel Port. Annual production is already at 110,000 cases; 200,000 is the target with Paterno distribution. The generally ripe, fleshy, and relatively deep Merlot is, of course, Rutherford Hill's signature wine. It does very nicely at the dinner table, and when it is at its best is attractive in body and price. Contrary to some critical estimates, we enjoyed the 1989 Napa Merlot, which has good balance and fruit. The 1986 "XVS" Cabernet Sauvignon and the 1987 Cabernet Sauvignon, however, are the most impressive Rutherford Hill wines we've tasted recently.

Wines/Varietals: Chardonnay, Jaeger Vineyards ($$), Chardonnay, XVS ($$), Sauvignon Blanc, Napa Valley ($), Gewürztraminer, Napa Valley ($), Merlot, Napa Valley ($$), Cabernet Sauvignon, Napa Valley ($$), Cabernet Sauvignon, XVS ($$$), Cabernet Sauvignon, Library Reserve ($$), Vintage Zinfandel Port ($$).

St. Clement Vineyards
2867 St. Helena Highway; PO Box 261
St. Helena, CA 94574
tel. (707) 963-7221; fax (707) 963-9174
Open to the public; est. 1878 (in continuous operation as St. Clement since 1975)

The winemaking history of St. Clement, located on a landmark Napa Valley estate, dates back to 1878, when wines were first vinified here from estate grapes. The property hosted a century-long succession of vintners producing wines under a variety of labels; Dr. William Casey bought the site in 1975 and renamed it after a Chesapeake Bay island where his family owned property. Sapporo, USA, the U.S. subsidiary of the

Japanese brewery and drinks company, purchased it from Casey in 1987 and also bought the Abbott Vineyard in Carneros. Annual production: 12,000 cases.

Dennis Johns, St. Clement's winemaker since 1979, handles grape lots separately in order to study various factors (soil, climate, enological techniques, etc.) affecting the wines. He made his mark here first with top-quality Sauvignon Blanc and later with first-rate Cabernet Sauvignon. Of the wines in production currently, the Chardonnay, Sauvignon Blanc, Merlot, and Cabernet all bear the Napa Valley appellation. All are recommended. The Sauvignon Blanc, highly aromatic in 1990, can in some years, such as 1989, be rather herbal. The regular Chardonnay (blended from Abbotts Vineyard and Vine Hill Ranch grapes) is lovely in 1990. The 100 percent Abbott's Vineyard bottling gets extra time in wood and is released about a year later than the regular Chardonnay. It may evolve into something outstanding. The small amount of Merlot produced by this winery can also be special. The cherryish 1988 drinks well enough, but look for the 1985—it's superb. The 1985 Cabernet offers something extra, too. The more widely available 1989 is good; the 1987 is clearly a winner.

Wines/Varietals: Chardonnay ($$), Chardonnay, Abbotts Vineyard ($$), Sauvignon Blanc ($), Merlot ($$), Cabernet Sauvignon ($$).

Saintsbury

1500 Los Carneros Avenue
Napa, CA 94558
tel. (707) 252-0592; fax (707) 252-0595
Open to the public by appt.; est. 1981

Although Saintsbury produces Chardonnay, and a good one at that, Pinot Noir is its *raison d'être*. In 1981, partners Richard Ward and David Graves made their first 3,000 cases of Pinot Noir and Chardonnay in rented space in the middle of the Napa Valley. When their wines met with success, Ward and Graves established a permanent home in Carneros where they now own 53 acres of vineyard. The name Saintsbury pays homage to George Saintsbury, the English wine connoisseur and author of *Notes on a Cellar Book*, published in 1920. The winery continues to purchase some grapes, mostly in Carneros; production here has grown to 41,000 cases.

Saintsbury currently produces three Pinot Noirs: the light, fruity and appealing Garnet, the berry jam-flavored Carneros Pinot Noir, which bears more concentrated fruit and is consistently elegant and well-balanced, and, in most years, a Carneros Reserve. The 1990 Reserve, superb, deep, and full-bodied with spicy berry fruit and a rich texture, should become velvety as the tannins soften: we look for it to develop distinctive complexity by the end of the century. The Carneros Chardonnay is reliably good; the Reserve Chardonnay is distinctive, rich, and creamy. We found the 1990 Carneros Reserve to be one of the winery's best, with intense fruit and oaky vanillin flavors that will undoubtedly be at their best in 1994 or 1995. Saintsbury also makes a delightful dry blush wine, a vin gris of Pinot Noir, bottled under the whimsical sobriquet "Vincent Vin Gris."

Wines/Varietals: Chardonnay ($$), Chardonnay, Carneros Reserve ($$), Pinot Noir, Garnet ($$), Pinot Noir, Carneros ($$), Pinot Noir, Carneros Reserve ($$$), Vincent Vin Gris ($).

St. Supéry

8440 St. Helena Highway
Rutherford, CA 94573
tel. (800) 942-0809 or (707) 963-4507;
fax (707) 963-4526
Open to the public; est.1989

St. Supéry is owned by Skalli, a large French food corporation and negociant. In the early eighties, Robert Skalli, head of Skalli Enterprises, decided to invest in California and met Greg and Michaela Rodeno, who owned a small vineyard in Pope Valley, an area east of Howell Mountain but within the Napa Valley appellation. The Rodenos had a great deal of experience in the California wine world: Skalli liked the Rodenos and he liked the Pope Valley area. He purchased the Dollarhide Ranch, (1,500 acres of cattle land) in 1982, and began planting grapes the following year on the Pope Valley property. Today there are 400 acres planted there, most devoted to Bordeaux varieties such as Sauvignon Blanc, Cabernet Sauvignon and Merlot, plus a plot of Chardonnay. In 1986 Skalli bought a second property mid-valley—Main Street Napa Valley—at Rutherford, where he built a large winery the next year. Flying both French and American flags, the structure has something of a modern look; inside it is handsomely appointed. Skalli and Michaela Rodeno (president and CEO) have created an atmosphere that reflects their shared desire to make people feel comfortable with wine. The emphasis is on education at St. Supéry's Wine Discovery Center, which provides an in-depth look at winegrowing in the Napa Valley. There's a display vineyard, a "Smell-O-Vision" and tasting area, and self-guided tours of the winery. The Rutherford property was once owned by French immigrant Edward St. Supéry, hence the winery's name.

The wines here, made to be supple and accessible on release, are as consumer-friendly as the winemaking facility. St. Supéry's first releases were simple and clean; lately there has been a sharp improvement in quality. At the same time, this winery's commendable value-oriented pricing philosophy keeps its products at attractive price points. St. Supéry considers itself a red wine house, though Sauvignon Blanc dominates production at the moment. The 1991 Sauvignon Blanc is dry and well balanced with racy citrus flavors and a hint of wood. St. Supéry Chardonnay is clean, dry and fruity, well made and attractive. The 1991 Chard pleased us with its compact honey, vanilla, pear, and spice flavors and its tight structure. This wine should evolve agreeably. As the Cabernet and Merlot vines mature, production of these wines will increase. Both 1989 reds are good and highly drinkable, particularly the 1989 Cabernet with its cherry-blackberry flavors. The Merlot also has good berry flavors as well as good structure. A 35-acre vineyard at the winery in Rutherford is planted entirely to Cabernet Sauvignon and may one day result in a vineyard-designated addition to St. Supéry's line.

Wines/Varietals: Sauvignon Blanc ($), Chardonnay ($$), Cabernet Sauvignon ($$), Merlot ($$), Moscato ($$).

Schramsberg Vineyards

1400 Schramsberg Road
Calistoga, CA 95415
tel. (707) 942-4558; fax (707) 942-5943
Open to the public by appt.; est.1862 (in continuous operation since 1965)

Bravo Schramsberg. Congratulations Jack and Jamie Davies. Thank you for proving that ultra-premium *méthode champenoise* sparkling wines could be made in North America. Now will you consider lowering your prices just a bit? There are perhaps a half-dozen lower-priced California sparkling wines currently vying for a spot in the top-quality niche you once occupied by yourself. Give us some of the old excitement. In 1965, the Davies purchased the old dilapidated Schramsberg winery on an isolated mountainside, and set about bringing it back to life. Working with purchased grapes, they began releasing premium sparkling wines of hitherto unequaled quality, pioneering an industry in California that many French Champagne and Spanish *cava* producers have subsequently rushed to invest in. By the mid-to-late 1970s, they had built considerable prestige and excellence into their bottles. Sixty acres of vineyard now supply some of the grapes here, but Schramsberg still purchases 85 percent of the fruit required to produce 40,000 cases annually.

The Davies and winemaker Alan Tenscher have traveled every conceivable road to quality in producing their six vintage sparkling wines. The wines made here are probably better today than they've ever been. (It's also true, of course, that the competition has become keener.) Schramsberg Blanc de Blancs (40 percent of production) is fairly citric, austere, and sound. We prefer the Blanc de Noirs (30 percent of production) with its layers of toasted almond, caramel, cherry, and spice in a crisp base. To us, the house's best wine is the Brut Reserve. It receives a higher proportion of barrel fermentation and longer aging on the lees than either the Blanc de Noirs or Brut Reserve, and has added complexity, aristocratic breeding, and fine acid and flavor balance. In fall 1992, Schramsberg—thinking, perhaps, that

it was giving birth to an American Dom Pérignon—released a prestige cuvée called "J. Schram" in honor of Jacob Schram, the winery's 19th-century founder. It is prudent to reserve judgment on this pricey bottle until we can taste it at various stages of its evolution and sample subsequent releases. At any rate, we applaud the four-and-a-half years of extended aging on the yeasts this vaunted wine is receiving.

Wines/Varietals: Blanc de Blancs ($$$), Blanc de Noirs ($$$), Cuvée de Pinot ($$$), Crémant Demi-Sec ($$$), Brut Reserve ($$$), J. Schram ($$$).

Shafer Vineyards

6154 Silverado Trail
Napa, CA 94558
tel. (707) 944-2877; fax (707) 944-9454
Open to the public by appt.; est. 1979

In 1972, Chicago publishing industry veteran John Shafer turned a daydream into reality: he moved his family to a 210-acre Napa Valley estate to grow grapes. By 1978 the Shafers ventured into winemaking, and today, with 135 acres under vine, they produce 20,000 cases annually. Over 75 percent of the grapes used here come from Shafer's hillside vineyards, which are entirely devoted to red grapes. (They also purchase Stags Leap District grapes for their Cabernet and fruit from the Stags Leap District, Oak Knoll, and Carneros—all in the Napa Valley—for their Chardonnay.) While vineyards are at the core of the Shafer quest for quality, family is the true heart of this operation. It is truly a hands-on family business: John and Bett Shafer, along with their children, Doug (the winemaker here) and Libby, work side-by-side managing the vineyard, making the wines and marketing them. They are doing a first-rate job all around.

We like the fine Shafer Chardonnays, medium-to-full bodied wines, crisp, and flavorful without being too bold. They're 100 percent barrel fermented and aged *sur lies* for 8 months, so there's some toasty oak to go with the clean tropical fruit flavors. The 1990 is very good. The reds, though, are delicious. The 1987 Stags Leap Hillside Selection Cabernet is a big winner in a Bordeaux style—elegant yet intense with dark berry, chocolate, and pepper flavors, and superb balance and structure. The 1988 Hillside Cab is also a quality release. First offered in 1993, it is plenty stylish, supple, and silky. The regular 1989 Stags Leap Cab is good, too. The excellent 1989 Merlot is rich, firm, fruity, and well structured. The 1990 Merlot is great. Packed with cherry and berry flavors, it opens with floral and spice aromas, and finishes generously.

Wines/Varietals: Chardonnay, Napa Valley ($$), Merlot, Napa Valley ($$), Cabernet Sauvignon, Napa Valley Stags Leap District ($$), Cabernet Sauvignon, Hillside Select Napa Valley Stags Leap District ($$).

Signorello Vineyards

4500 Silverado Trail
Napa, CA 94558
(707) 255-5990; fax (415) 346-2609
Open by to the public by appt.; est. 1980

San Francisco-born Raymond Signorello bought a vineyard in 1980 on the Silverado Trail just north of the town of Napa in the Stags Leap/Oak Knoll area. He sold grapes for a few years before plunging into producing his own wines. With nearly a hundred acres planted to eight varieties, he still sells about 80 percent of his grapes to other wineries. (He buys Pinot Noir from a local grower on long-term contract.) Signorello, with son Ray, Jr., currently produces some 4,000 cases annually of highly esteemed wines.

Signorello released its first wines—Chardonnay and Sauvignon Blanc—in 1985. With Ray, Jr. as winemaker, recent vintages exhibit a combination of lush fruit and commendable structure. The reds are lusty and rich, both Pinot Noir and Cabernet Sauvignon (the 1988 Reserve is superb). They see little or no fining or filtering, especially in the case of the Founder's Reserve. But it's the Chardonnay that reaps the most attention for this winery: it has buttery, spicy, bright fruit, powerful oak flavors, and is in perfect balance in the outstanding 1990 bottling. The 1991 Chardonnay Founder's Reserve, 100 percent barrel fermented and unfiltered, is also remarkably good. Signorello also produces an attractive barrel fermented Sémillon and a fruity, florid Sauvignon Blanc. The 1991 Sémillon is recommended. This is definitely a winery to watch.

Wines/Varietals: Chardonnay ($$$), Cabernet Sauvignon ($$$), Pinot Noir ($$$), Sauvignon Blanc ($$), Sémillon ($$).

Silver Oak Wine Cellars

915 Oakville Cross Rd., PO Box 414
Oakville, CA 94562
tel. (707) 944-8808; fax (707) 944-2817
Open to the public; est. 1972

When Ray Duncan needed someone with experience to plant and manage his 750-acre Napa Valley vineyard, he sought out Justin Meyer. A former Christian Brother with a master's degree in viticulture and enology from U.C. Davis, Meyer had the expertise to turn this operation (in which he is a partner) into a winning enterprise. It was Meyer's idea to produce only one great wine: Cabernet Sauvignon. Initially the grapes all came from the Alexander Valley, but in 1979 Silver Oak introduced bottlings from the Napa Valley and from Bonny's Vineyard (named for Meyer's wife) in Oakville. The 200 acres of estate vineyards, with the addition of some purchased grapes, today yield 30,000 cases annually. All of Silver Oak's Cabernets are aged for three years in fire-bent American oak, then bottle-aged two more years.

This winery has the proven ability to produce good to great Cabernets every year, regardless of vintage characteristics. You can almost close your eyes and choose a bottle here: going back at least as far as 1984 you're certain to select a winner. Of course, there are some definite stylistic differences among the three Cabs produced in each vintage. The Alexander Valley wine is always highly regarded with its ripe, fresh, very complex fruit flavors, including olive, in harmony with the distinct barrel components. The Bonny's Vineyard is somewhat controversial. Certainly the biggest and most profound of the three, its explosive flavor extracts tend toward black currants and vegetables. Some people passionately love it and others do not. The Napa wine is consistent and very good, but displays a less flamboyant personality than either the Alexander Valley or Bonny's Vineyard wines. The 1987 and 1988 Alexander Valley Cabs are excellent. The 1987 shows berry and cherry fruit aromas with plenty of chocolate, herbal, and smokey oak tones. The 1987 Bonny's Vineyard, more lavishly oaked and strikingly herbal, is a fine wine, too, with lots of broad flavors—pepper, anise, olive—laced in deep currant and black cherry fruit. It has excel-

lent balance, a long finish, and a sky-high price ($50+).

Wines/Varietals: Cabernet Sauvignon, Alexander Valley ($$$), Cabernet Sauvignon, Napa Valley ($$$), Cabernet Sauvignon, Bonny's Vineyard ($$$).

Silverado Vineyards

6121 Silverado Trail
Napa, CA 94558
tel. (707) 257-1770; fax (707) 257-1538
Open to the public; est. 1981

Lillian Disney, wife of the late Walt Disney, and Ron and Diane Miller (Lillian's daughter) own Silverado's 328 acres. They sold their grapes for a few vintages, then built a winery in the Stags Leap District overlooking the Silverado Trail and took to producing their own wine. Grape varietals planted at Silverado Vineyards (spread out over four locations) include Sauvignon Blanc (24 acres), Chardonnay (109 acres), Cabernet Sauvignon (114 acres), Merlot (67 acres), Cabernet Franc (9 acres), Sémillon (1 acre), and Sangiovese (5 acres). Fifty percent of Silverado's Chardonnay and 20 percent of its Sauvignon Blanc are produced from purchased fruit. Average annual production is 100,000 cases.

Jack Stuart has been the winemaker and general manager here from the beginning, so through all the steady growth in vineyard acreage and production, there has been a consistent approach and style. Silverado's white wines are very good, often deliciously fruity. Its reds are often great, the Cabs among America's very best. We find the 1987 to be one of the finest California wines we tasted in the past year or two: elegant and superbly structured with round and appealing flavors of deep, dark fruit, with strawberry overtones and spicy accents.

*Wines/Varietals: Sauvignon Blanc ($),
Chardonnay ($$), Chardonnay, Limited Reserve ($$$), Cabernet Sauvignon, Stags Leap
District ($$), Cabernet Sauvignon, Stags Leap
District Limited Reserve ($$$), Merlot ($$).*

Sky Vineyards

1500 Lokoya Road
Napa, CA 94558
tel. (707) 935-1391
Not open to the public; est. 1979

This postage stamp-sized vineyard sits on
a Mt. Veeder ridgetop in the Mayacamas
Mountains. Indeed, the sky must appear
quite near from the vantage point of this 12-
acre parcel at an elevation of 2,000-foot,
planted to top-quality Zinfandel. Owners
Lore Olds and Linn Briner use only estate-
grown grapes to produce 1,500 cases annually of Zinfandel table wine and a late harvest
Zin.

Though there is some fluctuation in quality from vintage to vintage, Sky Vineyards
has developed an almost cult following for
its generally ripe and opulent wines. The
1987 and 1989 are both impressive. The
1987 is intensely and complexly flavored
with cherry, raspberry, and peppery flavors
that will take till the mid-1990s to fully
emerge. It has a long and promising finish.

*Wines/Varietals: Zinfandel ($$), Zinfandel,
Late Harvest ($$).*

Spottswoode Winery

1401 Hudson Avenue
St. Helena, CA 94574
tel. (707) 963-0134; fax (707) 963-2886
Open to the public by appt. only; est.
1982

Spottswoode produces one of California's
most distinctive and outstanding Cabernets,

entirely estate-grown on the benchlands
nestled against the Mayacamas Mountain
range in St. Helena. This 46-acre estate was
founded in 1882 by George Schonewald
and acquired in 1910 by the Spotts family
who gave the winery its name. It was purchased in 1972 by Mary Weber Novak and
the late Dr. Jack Novak who restored the
estate's handsome Victorian residence and
its vineyard. Beth Novak Milliken, the
Novak's daughter, is now general manager
and marketing director here. The 40-acre
vineyard, planted to Cabernet Sauvignon
(37 acres) and Cabernet Franc (3 acres),
currently produces 7,000 cases annually.
Sauvignon Blanc from purchased grapes is
also made.

Consultant Tony Soter has been involved
with Spottswoode since its first vintage in
1982, which instantly established the
winery's Cabernet as a collector's dream. In
vintage after vintage this dark, richly textured wine—brilliantly focused and finely
balanced— proves its mettle. None have yet
reached their peak; the 1982 has a decade
ahead of it and it's be hard to predict when
great vintages such as 1985 and 1987 will
become fully mature. The 1988 and 1986
Cabernets are lighter but no less impressive,
perhaps more elegant in structure. The
plummy, spicy, ripe berry flavors of
Spottswoode's 1989 Cab belie the overall
vintage's somewhat lackluster reputation.
Enlivened with the bright thrust of Cabernet
Franc fruit (4 to 6 percent has been added to
the Cabs here since 1984), the 1989 is
concentrated and complex with enormous
potential. A firm grip of tannin interwoven
with seductive cassis-like fruit and spicy oak
provides backbone. Pam Starr has been
Spottswoode's winemaker since 1992; Soter
continues as consultant. This winery also
produces well-made Sauvignon Blanc, partially barrel fermented in new oak.

Wines/Varietals: Cabernet Sauvignon ($$$), Sauvignon Blanc ($$).

Stag's Leap Wine Cellars
5766 Silverado Trail
Napa, CA 94558
tel. (707) 944-2020; fax (707) 257-7501
Open to the public by appt.; est. 1972

With the second Cabernet produced at this winery in the mid-seventies, the name "Stag's Leap" became assured of a place in the wine history books. At the prestigious Paris Tasting of 1976, Stag's Leap Wine Cellars' 1973 Cabernet Sauvignon bested several top Bordeaux in the blind tasting to become toast of the town. Warren and Barbara Winiarski planted their estate vineyard, SLV, in 1970; two years later they founded Stag's Leap Wine Cellars. Situated below the dramatic promontory of jagged rock known as "Stag's Leap" (which lends its name to the "Stags Leap District" appellation), the 44-acre estate vineyard produces one of this winery's three Cabernets. In 1986 Winiarski purchased the adjacent Nathan Fay Vineyard, first planted in 1961 and now consisting of Cabernet Sauvignon (55 acres), Merlot (10 acres), and Petit Verdot (1.5 acres) The winery also produces Chardonnay, Sauvignon Blanc, and occasionally Riesling from purchased grapes. Total annual production here reaches 30,000 cases, with another 60,000 cases produced entirely with purchased grapes under a second label, "Hawk Crest."

The reserve-style Cabernet produced from best lots of a given vintage is designated "Cask 23," which, since the outstanding 1985 vintage, has been among California's most expensive Cabs at $75 a bottle. This wine is not produced every year; the 1990

Cask 23 will be released in 1994. In 1989 and 1990, fruit from SLV and the Fay Vineyard was blended into a dual vineyard-designated Cabernet Sauvignon. The 1989 version is not up to the usual concentration that either vineyard typically yields, though it must be noted that overall this was a lesser vintage. We expect this usually rich blackberry-cassis-flavored wine to be back on track with the upcoming 1990. Though Stag's Leap is best known for its reds, in recent vintages two whites have practically stolen the show. In 1990, the winery's Chardonnay, particularly the Reserve, had fabulous fruit cloaked in spicy clove-accented oak. The Sauvignon Blanc, now one of the best made in the Napa Valley, has brisk citrus-melon flavors and a nice touch of oak. The 1991 Sauvignon Blanc is excellent, too. The winery's second label, Hawk Crest, offers consistent value in readily drinkable varietals, particularly Cabernet Sauvignon and Chardonnay.

Wines/Varietals: Chardonnay ($$), Reserve Chardonnay ($$), Chardonnay, Hawk Crest ($), Sauvignon Blanc ($), Sauvignon Blanc, Hawk Crest ($), White Riesling ($), Petite Sirah ($$), Cabernet Sauvignon, SLV-Fay Vineyard ($$), Cabernet Sauvignon, Cask 23 ($$$), Cabernet Sauvignon, Hawk Crest ($).

Stags' Leap Winery, Inc.
6150 Silverado Trail
Napa, CA 94558
tel. (707) 944-1303; fax (707) 944-9433
Not open to the public; est. 1972

This other Stags Leap enterprise, also opened in 1972, produces good wines. It took a while for this to be proved, though, as the Carl Doumani family was long caught up in a trademark battle with its better-known neighbor. Following their initial releases, not until 1979 and the resolution of their trademark conflict were the Doumanis again able to crush the fruit from their own vineyards under their Stags' Leap label (note the position of the apostrophe). The Doumanis' vineyards, part of the historic 240-acre Stags' Leap Manor, now total about 100 acres planted mostly to Cabernet Sauvignon (two-thirds), and, in order of decreasing quantity, Merlot, Petite Sirah, Cabernet Franc, and Chardonnay. This house's red wines are all estate-grown; some grapes are brought in for the whites. Total production is approximately 20,000 cases annually.

Stags' Leap Winery is best known for its Petite Sirah, and to a lesser degree, its Chenin Blanc. Cabernet Sauvignon, though, is its biggest wine by volume. Moderately priced and from a top vineyard site, the Cab is a good value. The Petite Sirah, a big, rustic, bold, flavorful, tannic wine, is long-lived and quite Rhône-like in some vintages, such as 1987. The Cabernet, on the other hand, is much more restrained, lean even, with well-defined fruit flavors. It's consistently pleasant and in 1987 has attractive plum and cassis flavors in a soft, smokey body. The Merlot is particularly good in 1989, with opulent plum and spice flavors as well as chocolate highlights and substantial tannins that will need until, say, 1994-1995 to recede. The last Stags' Leap Chardonnay we tasted, the 1989, is good—clean, crisp, and smooth with plenty of citrus flavors.

Wines/Varietals: Chardonnay ($$), Chenin Blanc ($), Cabernet Sauvignon ($$), Merlot ($$), Reserve Merlot ($$$), Petite Sirah ($$), Reserve Petite Sirah ($$$).

Steltzner Vineyards

5998 Silverado Trail
Napa, CA 94558
tel. (707) 252-7272; fax (707) 252-2079
Open to the public by appt.; est. 1977

Dick Steltzner bought this 100-acre Stags Leap District vineyard in 1966, having already earned a solid reputation as a grower. Beginning in 1977, he made wines in others cellars. But in 1983, Steltzner established a modest winemaking facility at the vineyard which he and his wife, Christine, have recently expanded with the addition of a new storage cave.

Acting as his own winemaker, Steltzner strives to produce wines with excellent aging potential to accompany fine food. All of his wines are aged 18 to 22 months in French oak. The Cabernet Sauvignon, accounting for 60 percent of production here, is currently vitified on vines averaging 24 years old. Steltzner's excellent 1986 Cab, with rich, ripe currant, black cherry, and cassis flavors, is full-bodied, with overtones of cedar and oak. More recently, the 1990 is very fine, too, and it may yet prove to be outstanding. The 1990 Claret, a Bordeaux blend from Stags Leap area grapes, is also highly recommended. The 1989 is the Merlot to look for: it's very good. The 1990 Sauvignon Blanc from the Oak Knoll Ranch in Napa shows considerable improvement over previous efforts.

Wines/Varietals: Sauvignon Blanc ($), Merlot ($$), Cabernet Sauvignon ($$), Claret ($$).

Sterling Vineyards

1111 Dunaweal Lane; PO Box 365
Calistoga, CA 95415
tel. (707) 942-3300; fax (707) 942-3464
Open to the public; est. 1969

One of California's most striking wineries, the gleaming white villa-like Sterling is built on a 300-foot knoll near the crest of the Napa Valley between St. Helena and Calistoga. Visitor access to the winery is by cable car, affording a spectacular view of the valley below. Sterling was founded by a partnership that sold the winery to Coca-Cola in 1977; Joseph E. Seagram & Sons acquired it in 1983. It is now the flagship of Seagram's winery holdings, which include Mumm Napa Valley and The Monterey Vineyards. Sterling owns 1,200 acres of vineyard, including such stellar properties as Winery Lake Vineyard in Carneros, Diamond Mountain Ranch on steep hillsides in the Mayacamas Mountain range, and Three Palms Vineyard on the Napa Valley floor. Production is 220,000 cases annually.

Bill Dyer, winemaker here since 1985, considers Sterling Reserve, produced from selected lots of Cabernet, Merlot, and Cabernet Franc, to be the wine that best reflects this winery's style and aim. The 1987 Reserve was a benchmark bottle, more on the mark than the recently released 1989. We actually feel that Sterling's "Three Palms," a meritage-type blend, shows more interesting character and complexity, with its spicy oak and cedary black-currant flavors that linger nicely in the 1988. The Diamond Mountain Cabernet has impressively concentrated fruit, yet lacks definition or distinctive character. Sterling Merlot is a stalwart red of plummy fruit and firm structure, recommended for aging five years or longer to be at its best. All of the reds made here are ageworthy; in fact, there are Sterling Cabernets from the seventies that are still developing, particularly the fine 1978. The Winery Lake Vineyard in Carneros produces highly regarded Chardonnay and Pinot Noir—both are quite concentrated though the Chard shows greater finesse. Sterling Sauvignon Blanc is reliably dry and

crisp, the 1991 more elegant than most on the market, with citrus-melon-fig flavors.

Wines/Varietals: Cabernet Sauvignon ($$), Cabernet Sauvignon, Diamond Mountain ($$), Three Palms ($$$), Sterling Reserve ($$$), Merlot ($$), Chardonnay ($$), Chardonnay, Winery Lake ($$), Chardonnay, Diamond Mountain ($$), Pinot Noir, Winery Lake ($$), Sauvignon Blanc ($).

Stony Hill Vineyard

3331 N. St. Helena Hwy, PO Box 308
St. Helena, CA 94574
tel. (707) 963-2636
Open to the public by appt.; est. 1952

There must be a place in this book for what connoisseurs consider one of California's legendary wineries. Stony Hill was founded by Eleanor and Fred McCrea of San Francisco as something of a mom-and-pop operation at the summer home they purchased in 1943, north of St. Helena. The McCreas planted vines in 1946 (with northern hillside exposure) and released their first wine in 1952. Chardonnay was always their predominant grape, and the superbly balanced, remarkably long-lived wines they produced are acknowledged reference points for California Chardonnay. Today, the wines are the McCreas' legacy: Fred died in 1977 and Eleanor in 1991. The vineyard and winery continue under family ownership (Willinda McCrea is an active participant), with Mike Chelini, winemaker here since 1972, maintaining continuity and forward momentum. Though Stony Hill's vineyards total 42 acres (27 devoted to Chardonnay), their yield is extremely low. Some grapes must be brought in from Howell Mountain even to produce a few thousand cases of Chardonnay. This winery has never made more than 3,500 cases in a year.

Fred believed in not intervening in the winemaking process and letting the vineyards and grapes speak with a full and distinctive voice. Probably it is the Chardonnay clone that McCrea selected in combination with the soil, microclimate, and low yield that contributes most to the unique style, structure, and quality of Stony Hill's Chardonnays. They are not put through a malolactic fermentation and are 70 percent barrel-aged in new and old barrels. Upon release the wines are clearly backward and austere, but they have superb balance and depth of flavor that blossoms with full-blown pear, honey, spice, and oak flavors after 5 years and continues to flourish for another 10. The 1988 and 1985 are excellent among the recent vintages; the 1964 is the stuff of legend. The winery produces a little Riesling as well. It's reliably excellent, as in 1989.

Wines/Varietals: Estate Chardonnay ($$$), White Riesling ($$).

Storybook Mountain Vineyards
3835 Highway 128
Calistoga, CA 94515
tel. (707) 942-5310; fax (707) 942-5334
Open to the public by appt.; est. 1882 (in continuous operation since 1976)

Jerry Seps takes Zinfandel very seriously. A former university professor of European history, Seps changed careers in order to grow and produce wine from the not-so-widely-respected grape that California introduced to the world. No pedestrian pinkish stuff here—only red Zinfandel, which Seps believes is capable of competing with the currently more fashionable Cabernet. Seps has 38 acres, planted 100 percent to Zinfandel, in the hills near Calistoga. He purchased the property, formerly Grimms Brothers Winery, in 1978, and renamed it "Storybook Mountain." He buys in 20 percent of his grapes, and produces an average of 9,000 cases annually. Considering he has won more medals for his Zinfandels than

any other producer, this man—and his wine—are deserving of respect.

Seps is consistently successful in producing rich, full-flavored wines that are tight, tart, and firm in their youth but open up well after a few years. The Reserves here have a booster stage of complexity and require more aging. Among recent offerings, the 1987 Storybook Mountain Vineyards Estate Reserve is highly recommended, with lots of fruit with big raspberry flavor components, as well as spices and tannins, adding to its power. The 1990 Estate is good; we'd choose it over the 1989 wines. Storybook also produces "Serafornia," a second label of moderately-priced wines.

Wines/Varietals: Estate Zinfandel, Napa Valley ($$), Estate Reserve Zinfandel, Napa Valley ($$$).

Swanson Vineyards
1271 Manley Lane, PO Box 459
Rutherford, CA 94573
tel. (707) 944-0905 or (707) 944-1642; fax (707) 944-0955
Open to the public by appt.; est.1985

As a student at Stanford University in the early sixties, Swanson Foods heir Clarke Swanson frequently spent his weekends visiting Napa Valley wineries, mainly interested, at the time, in doing some tasting. During school vacations he worked for the family food business, and after graduation, spent some time in banking; he later become involved in developing businesses in the communications and media industries in Florida. He made annual visits back to the Napa Valley, though, and his fascination with the world of wine continued to grow. He purchased his first vineyard here in the early 1980s, and between 1986 and 1989 he bought a small winery and 165 acres of vineyards in the Oakville and Rutherford districts. Drawing on his earlier experience in business, Swanson made marketing contacts in the U.S., Europe, Australia, and the

Far East. Outside of the U.S., his main target market today is the United Kingdom, where he is principal owner and chairman of Averys of Bristol, Ltd., a 200-year-old wine merchant. Principal vineyard plantings here are Merlot (42 percent), Cabernet Sauvignon (25 percent) and Chardonnay (20 percent), with the remaining acreage planted to Cabernet Franc, Sangiovese, and Syrah. With the addition of some purchased grapes (20 percent), Swanson Vineyard's annual output is 12,000 cases.

Winemaker Marco Cappelli, an '84 U.C. Davis grad, joined the Swanson team in 1986, having gained experience in Tuscany and Bordeaux. Swanson puts its label on wines vinified from only about 25 percent of the fruit harvested in its vineyards—the rest of the grapes are sold to other wineries. What's put in the bottle here continues to impress us in blind tastings; we believe this relatively young winery is one to watch. The Napa Valley Estate Merlot, for example, shows fine potential. We enjoyed the 1990, a big, supple wine that could evolve. It has an attractive nose, a deep berry and wood-flavored body, and hard tannins but good balance. The 1988 Zinfandel is also a big wine, inviting both in its nose and on the palate, with plenty of peppery oak and currant flavors. It suggests a Bordeaux-style claret. And the 1987 Cabernet Sauvignon is indeed a quality Bordeaux-style wine with lush, ripe, plum-like fruit and good structure. The Swanson Chardonnays we've tasted are showing laudable growth. The regular Napa Valley bottling is bright, clean, and crisp with citrus flavors, and the Reserve, first released in 1988, is more complex and toasty-oaky. The 1990 regular Napa Chardonnay is recommended. It's elegant and full of finesse, with lots of soft fruit (as opposed to citrus) flavors, pear in particular, and a touch of vanilla oak.

Wines/Varietals: Estate Chardonnay ($$), Reserve Chardonnay ($$), Late Harvest Sémillon, Napa Valley ($$$), Zinfandel, Howell Mountain ($$), Estate Merlot ($$), Cabernet Sauvignon ($$$).

The Terraces

PO Box 511
Rutherford, CA 94573
tel. (707) 963-1707
Not open to the public; est. 1985

Wayne Hogue, now in his late sixties, purchased a five-acre vineyard off the Silverado Trail in 1977. The quality of his Cabernet and Zinfandel grapes were impressive enough that he wanted to put his own name on bottles of wine made from them. However, the Hogue Winery in Washington State already laid claim to the name, so Hogue looked over the landscape of his vineyards and labeled his wines "The Terraces." Only estate reds are produced from Hogue grapes—about 1,000 cases a year—and the winemaking has been handled until now by Caymus Vineyards. The grower has plans to move operations to his own, new winery, currently under construction.

There's no doubt that the quality of these wines is consistently excellent. Hogue produces reds that are redolent with unusually complex fruit flavors laced with plenty of toasty oak. He keeps the Cabs in barrel for 36 months, far longer than most producers. The 1987 Cabernet is superb, oozing oak and accented with currant, herb and fruit flavors along an iron fist-in-a-velvet glove line. Hogue's Zins are profoundly varietal and infused with spicy oak. The 1989 is a good one in the oaky Terraces cherry/berry style.

Wines/Varietals: Cabernet Sauvignon ($$$), Zinfandel ($$).

Trefethen Vineyards

1160 Oak Knoll Ave., PO Box 2460
Napa, CA 94558
tel. (707) 255-7700; fax. (707) 255-0793
Open to the public for tasting, winery by appt.; est. 1973 (vineyard planted in 1968)

One of the driving forces of the Napa Valley wine renaissance in the 1970s and

1980s, Trefethen Vineyards, in the cool Oak Knoll region of the southern Napa Valley, has roots that extend back into the nineteenth century. The winery building here, in fact, is a registered national landmark. In 1968, Gene Trefethen, a top Kaiser Aluminum executive, purchased an old ranch and vineyard named "Eshcol Estate" ("Eshcol" is the Biblical name of the large cluster of grapes found by Moses) and set about restoring it and establishing a retirement home for himself and his wife, Katie. When Trefethen's son, John, and daughter-in-law, Janet, started working here, the family graduated, in 1973, from grape growers to winemakers. A 1976 Trefethen Chardonnay placed first in the widely publicized 1979 Gault Millau *Grand Marathon des Vins du Monde* in Paris. Trefethen owns extensive valley floor and hillside vineyards and produces far more grapes than it can use in its own wines. It has long been a grape supplier to some of the best-known wineries in the Napa Valley. Trefethen's 650 acres of vineyards include 237 acres of Chardonnay, 184 of Pinot Noir (though the winery no longer produces a Pinot Noir of its own), 89 of Cabernet Sauvignon, 38 of White Riesling, and 25 of Merlot. An ongoing replanting program will change these totals gradually, and see an increase in acreage devoted to Merlot. Annual production is currently 75,000 cases, all from estate-grown grapes.

Peter Luthi, winemaker here since 1985, strives for a pure expression of the estate's Chardonnay fruit, which is along apple, pear, and citrus flavor lines with good acid. All Trefethen Chardonnays age in French oak and some Eschol lots are put through malolactic fermentation. The house's style is elegant and emphasizes ripe fruit and ageworthiness. The Library Selection Chardonnays, though ripe and good upon release, are luscious after 4 or 5 years in the bottle. Trefethen holds back its wines, giving them extra aging before release. The 1990 Trefethen Chardonnay is superb. This winery's Cabernets were overshadowed until recently by its Chardonnays, but the great

hillside fruit from around John and Janet's home on the estate has added a noteworthy level of new complexity, and a 100 percent Hillside Select Cab has now replaced the Reserve as Trefethen's top offering. The Trefethens also deserve credit for producing one of California's best dry Rieslings, which age well. The easy-drinking and moderately-priced non-vintage Eshcol white and red (now labeled Eschol Chardonnay and Eschol Cabernet/Merlot).

Wines/Varietals: Chardonnay ($$), Chardonnay, Library Selection ($$$), Eshcol Chardonnay ($), White Riesling ($), Cabernet Sauvignon ($$), Cabernet Sauvignon, Hillside Selection ($$$), Eshcol Cabernet/Merlot ($).

Vichon Winery

1595 Oakville Grade
Oakville, CA 94562
tel (707) 944-2811; fax (707) 944-9224
Open to the public; est. 1980

Launched by an association of restaurateurs, Vichon got its name from two letters of the surnames of each of the three original managing partners, George Vierra, Peter Brucher, and Doug Watson. The trio built a winery just off the Oakville Grade, not far from the Robert Mondavi Winery. In 1985 Vichon was purchased by Robert Mondavi's children, Tim, Marcie and Michael. Under Tim Mondavi's management, Vichon has become successful as a producer of Chardonnay, Chevrignon (a blend of Sauvignon Blanc and Sémillon that from the winery's start was its best offering), Cabernet Sauvignon, and Merlot. Today, 85 percent of the grapes used here come from outside sources.

Vichon's winemaking philosophy is "less is more." Michael Weis, director of winemaking, explains: "Less handling, less filtering, less processing in general allows for the fullest expression of the fruit." In 1992 a "Coastal Selection" line targeted at the under $10 market was introduced. Overall, the Vichon wines are sound and well made. We especially like the Cabernet Sauvignon from Stags Leap District grapes. The 1988 and 1989, made by winemaker Karen Culler, are fine Cabs, smooth and balanced with attractive berry, currant, spice, cedar and vanillin flavor tones.

Wines/Varietals: Chardonnay, Napa Valley ($$), Chardonnay Coastal Selection ($), Chevrignon, Napa Valley ($), Merlot, Napa Valley ($), Cabernet Sauvignon, Coastal Selection ($), Cabernet Sauvignon, Napa Valley ($$), Cabernet Sauvignon, Stags Leap District ($$).

Villa Mt. Eden

620 Oakville Crossroads
Oakville, CA 94562
tel. (707) 944-2414; fax (707) 944-9657
Open to the public; est. 1881

Most people are surprised to learn that Villa Mt. Eden is one of the Napa Valley's oldest properties. It wasn't until the seventies that the winery, under winemaker Nils Venge (now at Groth Vineyards), became noted for producing rich, powerful Cabernets. Purchased by Stimson Lane Wine & Spirits in 1986, Villa Mt. Eden is on a new course set by Mike McGrath, winemaker here since 1983, and consultant Jedediah Steele, who came aboard in 1991. The winery's 48 acres midway up the center of the Napa Valley are planted to Chardonnay (13 acres) and Cabernet Sauvignon (25 acres) with 10 acres scheduled for replanting. Villa Mt. Eden buys 90 percent of its grapes in

keeping with Jed Steele's philosophy of blending from different areas to obtain style and complexity. Annual production averages 30,000 cases.

Villa Mt. Eden now produces two lines of varietals, "Grande Reserve" and the moderately-priced "Cellar Select." Both lines are quite good. The Grande Reserve Cabernet typically shows concentrated cherry-black currant fruit, and is more supple and accessible than earlier Villa Mt. Eden Cabernets. It's almost as ageworthy, though: certainly the 1988 is so. The 1990 barrel fermented Grande Reserve Chardonnay has lush tropical fruit and toasty vanilla flavors. The 1991 is leaner but still good with pear and pineapple flavors over spicy oak. The Cellar Select line—Cabernet, Chardonnay, and Zinfandel—offers excellent value for under $10 a bottle, particularly, in our view, the reds. The berryish 1989 Cabernet is drinkable, and the spicy, intensely fruity 1990 Zinfandel is good, too. The Chardonnay, simple but crisp and fresh, is fairly full-bodied.

Wines/Varietals: Grande Reserve Chardonnay ($$), Chardonnay, Cellar Select ($), Grande Reserve Cabernet Sauvignon ($$), Cabernet Sauvignon, Cellar Select ($), Zinfandel, Cellar Select ($).

Villa Zapu

3090 Mt. Veeder Road
Napa, CA 94558
tel. (707) 226-2501; fax (707) 226-1429
Not open to the public; est. 1988

The name's catchy and the place has to be seen to be believed. Swedish-born Tom Lundstrum, heir to a bread baking fortune, bought this 130-acre estate on Mount Veeder in 1984 and set out to build himself a striking mansion and winery "fortress," complete with white tower adorned with red pennants. In 1993, he put the estate up for sale. The wine label and brand are not being offered for sale, so there will likely be brand stability for at least a few years at any rate. This winery is very young, but recent releases suggest that the good times are already here—and that they're getting better. Villa Zapu's production is up to about 10,000 cases annually.

The 1989 Chardonnay was one of the best anyone turned out of a poor Napa vintage. In fact, it is a good bottle for any vintage, lush with fruit, creamy with toasty overtones. The 1988 and 1990 are also good, proving that the fine 1989 was no fluke. The 1990 is livelier—spicy with a splash of oak over attractive apple and pear Chardonnay flavors—than the round, attractive 1988. Villa Zapu's 1988 Cabernet shows promise. It's a good wine with plenty of firm, rustic flavor embracing a core of berry and smokey oak taste components.

Wines/Varietals: Chardonnay, Napa Valley ($$), Cabernet Sauvignon, Napa Valley ($$$).

White Rock Vineyards
1115 Loma Vista Drive
Napa, CA 94558
tel. (707) 257-0170
Not open to the public; est. 1870

Henry and Claire Vandendriessche have brought new life to this 35-acre vineyard and winery established in 1870. They purchased the vineyard in 1977, and for a decade sold their grapes to a small number of Napa Valley wineries. They eventually dug their own underground winery with 6,000 square feet of storage caves. The 3,000 cases currently produced here annually are cave-aged until an order for them is received.

White Rock is situated in the southern foothills of the Stags Leap District above the Napa Valley floor. Its vineyard is planted to Chardonnay (13 acres), Cabernet Sauvignon (18 acres), and Cabernet Franc, Merlot, and Petit Verdot (5 acres combined). The winery's red grapes are blended into a Bordeaux-style claret. The juice of hand-picked and hand-sorted Chardonnay grapes is fermented and aged with lees contact in French oak. The Vandendriessches pride themselves on farming without the aid of insecticides or herbicides; each of their vines is hand-hoed. Their 1990 Chardonnay is very attractive, crisp and lively with floral and fruit (peach, pineapple) flavors and a long, satisfying finish. We also recommend the 1988 Claret.

Wines/Varietals: Chardonnay ($$), Claret ($$).

Whitehall Lane Winery
1563 St. Helena Highway
St. Helena, CA 94574
tel. (707) 963-9454; fax (707) 963-7035
Open to the public; est. 1979

Brothers Art Finkelstein and Alan Steen decided to get into the wine business in 1979. Art was an architect who wanted to design a winery; Alan, a plastic surgeon, planned to manage the vineyard. Whitehall Lane's original 26-acre vineyard (it is now 38.5-acres) had to be pulled and replanted. After almost a decade of ups and downs, the brothers sold the vineyard to Hideaki Ando of Japan in 1988. Then, in 1993, it was sold to San Francisco wine-shop owner Tom Leonardi, who plans to upgrade the facilities some and to replant the phylloxera-infested vineyards. Sixty percent of Whitehall Lane's fruit is purchased from multiple sources to complement its estate-grown Cabernet Sauvignon (15 acres), Merlot (7 acres), Chardonnay (16 acres), and Cabernet Franc (.5 acre). Production here is currently at 20,000 cases annually.

Some of Whitehall Lane's red wines are superb and the recent purchase included 50,000 cases of 1990, 1991, and 1992 Cabernets. The reserve Cabernet, which like the regular Cab contains both Merlot and Cabernet Franc in the blend, is a good one—nice in 1988. Even better is the 1987, notably minty with concentrated dark berry and currant fruit and a smooth silky texture. The regular 1989 Cab is attractive, too, showing the same minty style with spices and fruit in a lean and sound structure. The recently added Moriosoli Vineyard Cab is most promising; the 1990 possesses the stuff of greatness. The Merlot made from Knights Valley grapes is consistently good. The Pinot Noir here is decidedly fruity in style and reliable. With its Cabernet Franc and Chardonnay (barrel fermented), Whitehall Lane has yet to hit its stride. "Primavera," a dessert wine, accounts for 10 percent of production here; Whitehall also does a Late Harvest Riesling.

Wines/Varietals: Reserve Chardonnay ($$), Cabernet Sauvignon ($$), Reserve Cabernet Sauvignon ($$$), Cabernet Sauvignon, Moriosoli Vineyard ($$$), Merlot, Knights Valley ($$), Cabernet Franc ($$), Pinot Noir ($$), Primavera ($$), Late Harvest Riesling ($$).

ZD Wines

8383 Silverado Trail
Napa, CA 94558
tel. (707) 963-5188; fax (707) 963-2640
Open to the public; est. 1969

ZD was established in the Sonoma Valley in 1969 by two Sacramento aerospace engineers, Gino Zepponi and Norman de Leuze. Relocation to the present site along the Silverado Trail took place in 1979, when the business outgrew its former facility. Now owned by Norman and Rosa Lee De Leuze and family, the 3.5 acres here are planted to Cabernet Sauvignon. With a 90 percent complement of fruit purchased from other vineyards, ZD's total output is 18,000 cases a year. Son Robert is the winemaker here, son Brett marketing director, and daughter Julie administrative director.

ZD's Chardonnay is barrel fermented and then aged in 50-gallon oak barrels for ten months. For years these have been good, reliable Chardonnays of the "if it ain't broke, don't fix it" sort. This winery uses purchased grapes from up and down the coast (it was among the first to buy Chardonnay from the Tepusquet Vineyard in Santa Barbara County) and produces Chards that exhibit exotic fruit flavors and plenty of oak. The 1990 is a good one—clean and crisp with characteristically creamy tropical fruit and oak flavors. Red wines here are hand punched and oak aged for 22 months. The Cabernet (deep, tannic, and ageworthy) is good, and like all ZD wines, it is consistent in style and quality. The Pinot Noir is even more impressive. The 1990 Napa Valley-Carneros is quite good, displaying a rich nose of deep berries, cherries, violets and cinnamon that continue on to the palate in a deep, sound, complex wine with added pepper and oak overtones.

Wines/Varietals: Chardonnay, California ($$), Pinot Noir, Carneros, Napa Valley ($$), Cabernet Sauvignon, Napa Valley ($$).

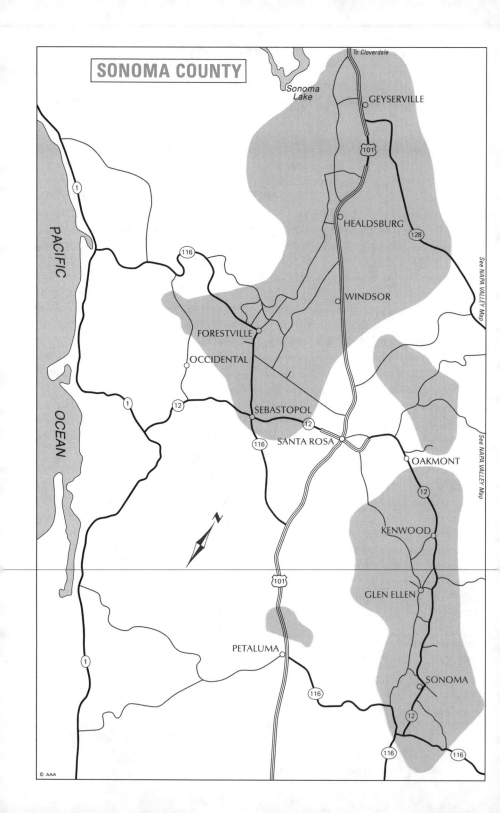

Sonoma

Adler Fels

5325 Corrick Lane
Santa Rosa, CA 95409
tel. (707) 539-3123; fax (707) 539-3128
Open to the public by appt.; est. 1980

This Sonoma winery, positioned high up on the northwestern side of the Mayacamas Mountains, has become a reliable producer of a range of primarily white wines. Purchased grapes yield Fumé Blancs (the volume leader here), Gewürztraminers, Chardonnay, and "Mélange à Deux," a curious sparkling wine made from Gewürztraminer and Riesling. Annual production is around 15,000 cases.

The style here is full-throttle flavor. The Fumé (Sauvignon) Blanc (half of production) has won lots of medals in competition. It is what is called "intensely varietal;" its grassiness announces itself clearly on the nose. When it rains at harvest, a delightful late-harvest Sauvignon Blanc is produced. Adler Fels' Gewürztraminer is off-dry and probably the best of its kind in Sonoma.

Wines/Varietals: Chardonnay ($), Chardonnay, Colman Reserve ($$), Fumé Blanc ($), Gewürztraminer ($), Mélange à Deux Sparkling Wine ($$).

Alderbrook

2306 Magnolia Drive
Healdsburg, CA 95448
tel. (707) 433-9154; fax (707) 433-1862
Open to the public, tours by appt.; est. 1981

A textbook example of a modern California winery: specializing in white whites made from mostly purchased grapes, Alderbrook produces clean-tasting wines with good varietal character at low prices. Partners John Grace, Philip Staley, and Mark Rafanelli got together in 1981 and transformed an old barn and the surrounding orchard in Sonoma's Dry Creek Valley into a successful business operation. They currently manage 55 acres of vineyards around the winery (some labels carry an "estate bottling" designation), and buy grapes in Dry Creek and the Russian River Valley to produce 24,000 cases annually. Chardonnay accounts for 72 percent of the winery's output; reliable quality and good value makes this an underrated winemaker.

The 1990 releases from Alderbrook were impressive. The Dry Sémillon was among the best of its kind produced that year, floral, crisp, and filled out with melon and butter highlights (it is aged in oak). The 1991 is a worthy follow up. The Sauvignon Blanc is a bit less stylish; it's is nevertheless easy drinking—simple, soft with a light body, grapefruit and melon flavors, and an added touch of classic grassiness. The winery prides itself on the quality of this bottle and recommends it as an example of the style its winemakers are striving to achieve. The 1990 Chardonnay, a tad sweet, is a good value.

Wines/Varietals: Chardonnay ($), Chardonnay, Estate Bottled ($$), Sauvignon Blanc ($), Sémillon ($), Gewürztraminer ($), Petite Sirah ($$).

215

Alexander Valley Vineyards

8644 Highway 128
Healdsburg, CA 95448
tel. (707) 433-7209; fax (707) 431-2556
Open to the public by appt.; est. 1975

This approximately 50,000-case operation produces wines from eight vinifera. At one time or another all of them have been good and reasonably priced. The winery makes our recommended list, though, on the strength of its Cabernet. Harry Wetzel and his family (particularly son Hank, who is the winemaker) are the force behind this concern with its 120 acres of estate vineyards in the Alexander Valley (the family is a partner in another 120-acre vineyard next door).

The 1990 Chardonnay is a good issue: clean, crisp, with some elegance and oak, honey, and pear flavors as well as the potential to improve in the bottle. The highly reliable Cabernet, which contains a touch of Merlot, is a big boy: deep, complex, with dark berry flavors, yet supple.

Wines/Varietals: Chardonnay ($$), Dry Chenin Blanc ($), Gewürztraminer ($), Johannisberg Riesling ($), Cabernet Sauvignon ($$), Merlot ($$), Pinot Noir ($$), Zinfandel ($$).

Arrowood Vineyards & Winery

14347 Sonoma Highway,
PO Box 987 Glen Ellen, CA 95442
tel. (707) 938-5170; fax (707) 938-5196
Open to the public, tours by appt.; est. 1985

Dick Arrowood is one of California's, and therefore one of America's, best-known winemakers. He may go to the grave described as "the former winemaker at Chateau St. Jean" (when the winery was at its peak), but in reality he is Sonoma-born and began working as a winemaker in 1965. At the new winery that bears his name—a stylish New England house-like affair on a hillside looking out over the Sonoma Valley—Arrowood and his wife, Alis, hope to write a new chapter in California wine history and, perhaps, earn Dick a more up-to-date epitaph. About 20,000 cases are being produced here annually, virtually all from purchased grapes. Arrowood's philosophy is to blend grapes from excellent vineyards and produce relatively small amounts of handcrafted wines. The blends he makes draw from several viticultural areas in Sonoma. The Cabernet and Merlot, for example, are produced by blending various selections of Cabernet Sauvignon, Merlot, Cabernet Franc, Malbec, and Petit Verdot. The Chardonnay is a blend of various clones from various estates. Arrowood ages in both American and French oak barrels as part of his quest to achieve balance and breeding in his wines.

The results to date have been encouraging. We've liked the reds more than the Chardonnays, which in their regular bottling we find to be clean, appley, and tart. The very limited Reserve Chardonnay is more attractive to us. The 1988 Cabernet is

Ferrari-Carano
Vineyards and Winery

Located at the north end of the picturesque Dry Creek Valley in Sonoma County, the winery is open daily from 10-5. Beautifully landscaped gardens, a friendly tasting room staff, and the elegant winery facility, beckon guests who are always welcome to visit.

8761 Dry Creek Road
Healdsburg, CA
707.433.6700

Jordan Sparkling Wine Company
Healdsburg, CA
707.431.5200

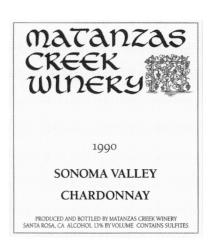

Matanzas Creek Winery
6097 Bennett Valley Road
Santa Rosa, CA 95404
707.528.6464

Jordan Vineyard & Winery
Healdsburg, CA
707.431.5250

Rodney Strong Vineyards
welcomes guests seven days a week
between 10 and 5 o'clock.
Tasting is complimentary, and balcony
tours to view and learn about the phases
of winemaking are scheduled daily.
Groups may visit by appointment. And "The
Green," a great picnic spot, may also be reserved
for weddings, receptions or large events.

11455 Old Redwood Hwy
Healdsburg, CA 95448
707.431.1533

Olive Hill Estate
Home of Award Winning
Wine & Olive Oil
Sales Daily, 10 to 4:30
15140 Sonoma Hwy
Glen Ellen, CA 95442
707.938.4064

Chateau Souverain
Open daily except
Tues & Wed.
Retail sales & Tastings
707.433.8281

Café At The Winery
Open Fri, Sat & Sun
Lunch – Noon-4 pm
Dinner – 4 pm-8 pm

GEYSER PEAK WINERY

Tasting Room Hours
10 to 5 daily
Picnic facilities available
22281 Chianti Rd.
Geyserville, CA 95441
(800) 255.9463

CAMPTON PLACE HOTEL
Kempinski San Francisco

Just off Union Square, there is a small European style hotel that strives to create an atmosphere of unparalleled luxury and elegance. It's Campton Place—where the china is Wedgwood, the flowers are cut fresh daily, and the gracious, personal service is an obsession. Less than an hour from California's famed wine country, Campton Place is the only choice for the sophisticated traveler.

(415) 781-5555
340 Stockton Street, San Francisco, CA 94108

"One of the top 25 restaurants in America."
Food & Wine Magazine

EXPERIENCE CALIFORNIA'S KEMPINSKI HOTELS.

CHECKERS HOTEL
Kempinski Los Angeles

There is a tranquillity about Checkers Hotel that makes it difficult to imagine that the great business and cultural centers of Los Angeles are just steps away. Checkers, the only European-style luxury hotel downtown, provides an experience of understated elegance… an experience distinguished by 24 hour room service, a sumptuous restaurant, tasteful decor, and dedicated personal service. And that is why our discriminating guests return to us time and again.

(213) 624-0000
535 South Grand Avenue, Los Angeles, CA 90071

The Los Angeles skyline from the oasis of the Checkers' rooftop garden.

KEMPINSKI
HOTELS

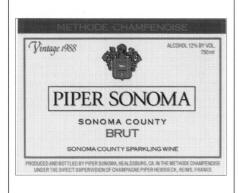

Piper Sonoma
11447 Old Redwood Hwy
Healdsburg, CA 95448

Open daily 10-5
707.433.8843

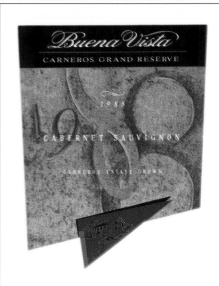

Buena Vista
P.O. Box 182
Sonoma, CA 95476
707.252.7117

Matanzas Creek Winery
6097 Bennett Valley Road
Santa Rosa, CA 95404
707.528.6464

Jordan Vineyard & Winery
Healdsburg, CA
707.431.5250

pleasant and fruity—round with a backbone of acid and tannin. Other years it has been a bit deeper. The Merlot is also in the ripe style, with sweet fruit, as in the 1989 offering. Arrowood's late-harvest Riesling is sound, though a bit too sweet for our taste (we seek a bit more acidity.) More than half of the winery's production is Cabernet Sauvignon.

Wines/Varietals: Chardonnay ($$), Cabernet Sauvignon ($$$), Merlot ($$$), Late Harvest Riesling ($$$).

Bellerose Vineyard
435 West Dry Creek Road
Healdsburg, CA 95448
tel. (700) 433-1637; fax (707) 433-7024
Open to the public; est. 1978

In 1978, Charles and Nancy Richard purchased a Dry Creek Valley property (72 acres, 45 currently under vine) that had been the site of a nineteenth-century winery and vineyard. An earlier owner brought stones from the nearby Mill Creek area to build a winery in 1887; it was operated until destroyed by fire in 1937. The Richards built their own winery on the foundation of the old one. The Bellerose approach to winemaking relies on the Richards' deep commitment to organic farming and sustainable agriculture—no herbicides, insecticides, or artificial fertilizers have been used here since 1984. Indeed, Richard can often be found out in the vineyards behind Rowdy and Chuck, a team of Belgian draft horses, working the land.

The guiding winemaking philosophy here is to exploit the potential of the finest grapes that can be grown on the estate with as little intervention as possible, thus there is hardly any filtering or fining. Sulfur dioxide levels are kept to a minimum, below 100 parts per million. The product mix is exclusively Bordeaux-style wines and blends, and the results have been most encouraging. Cuvée Bellerose, a blend of Cabernet Sauvignon, Merlot, Cabernet Franc, Petit Verdot, and Malbec is a relatively big but elegant wine with plenty of fruit and classic flavors and complexity. The 1985, which we tasted in 1992, was still a bit tannic and acidic, but sound with a medium body and plummy-berry nose and flavors. The Reserve Cabernets seem to need time, too. The 1988 is a bit tart and tannic, but has interesting stemmy, menthol, and fruit flavors that may open up into a more complex and interesting wine. The 1987 is a tad better and promises even more over time if its big berry flavors emerge as its dry tannins recede. The Sauvignon Blanc is simple with some pronounced grassy and lesser melon varietal flavors as evidenced in the barrel fermented 1990 from Dry Creek Valley grapes. Of the Merlots we've tasted, we prefer the 1987 Reserve to the 1988 Reserve. The 1987 is still tight, but could evolve greater depths of flavors. It is already a good wine with sound fruit. The winery's annual production is 7,000 cases.

Wines/Varietals: Reserve Sauvignon Blanc ($), Reserve Merlot ($$), Reserve Cuvée Cabernet Sauvignon ($$$), Cuvée Bellerose ($$).

Benziger of Glen Ellen
1883 London Ranch Road
Glen Ellen, CA 95442
tel. (707) 935-3000; fax (707) 935-4049
Open to the public; est. 1981

Talk about success: it doesn't get much better than at Benziger. After selling his New

York wine and spirits distributorship, Bruno Benziger moved out West to join his son, Mike, who founded the Benziger Winery in 1980. One thing (mainly Bruno's marketing skill) led to another, and with purchased grapes, low prices, and more than acceptable quality, one of California's greatest wine success stories was written. Today the company's four labels (Benziger of Glen Ellen Wines, Glen Ellen Wines, M.G. Vallejo Wines and Imagery & Estate Wines) account for 4.2 million cases annually. The Glen Ellen Estate wines and those labeled Benziger of Glen Ellen are by far the quality leaders here and are worthy of respect. The Benziger family spun off the Benziger of Glen Ellen label in 1988 to serve the high end of the market

The wines bearing this label are all made with Sonoma County grapes, including some from the 85 acres of Benziger vineyards adjacent to the Glen Ellen winery (planted in Cabernet Sauvignon 40 percent, Sauvignon Blanc 20 percent, Merlot 20 percent, Sémillon 10 percent, Cabernet Franc 5 percent, and Malbec 5 percent). These are labeled with the Sonoma Mountain appellation; others bear Sonoma County or Carneros designations. Benziger Fumé Blanc is creditably dry with attractive citrus/pear fruit and is a good value. The 1990 Premiere Vineyard Chardonnay from Carneros promises to be the winery's best effort yet with this varietal—rich and spicy, elegantly balanced. Look for the "Tribute Red" (a Merlot-based Bordeaux blend named in tribute to the late Bruno Benziger) or the Cabernet Sauvignon, a firm, well-defined, and accessibly fruity wine of which the 1989 was exemplary.

Wines/Varietals: Vintage Blanc de Blancs Sparkling Wine ($$), Fumé Blanc ($), *Chardonnay ($$), Chardonnay, Premiere Vineyard ($$), Pinot Noir, Sonoma County ($$), Cabernet Sauvignon, Sonoma County ($$), Muscat Canelli ($), Tribute White ($$), Tribute Red ($$$).*

Buena Vista Carneros

1800 Old Winery Road, PO Box 1842
Sonoma, CA 95476
tel. (707) 938-1266 or (707) 252-7117;
fax (707) 252-0392
Open to the public; est.1857 (continuously operated since 1940)

The cornerstone of the Racke USA enterprise, Buena Vista is a 230,000 case winery on the Napa-Sonoma border in Carneros. It is the decendent of the pioneering winery of the same name established by Count Agoston Haraszthy with European vinifera in the mid-19th century. Though it had ceased operation by Prohibition, the winery was revived in 1940 and then was purchased in 1979 by the German firm, A. Racke, and brought to its current vibrancy by Chairman Marcus Moller-Racke, his wife, Anne Moller-Racke, and Jill Davis, the head of winemaking here since 1983. The 935 acres under vine currently provide about 80 percent of the winery's needs. In 1989, Buena Vista began converting its Carneros vineyards to organic farming and by late 1992 it had 770 acres free of any synthetic treatments—one of the largest certified organic vineyards in the U.S.

The wines here across the board are sound and well made along clean, high-tech lines. The most merit can be found in the series of small quantity Private Reserve wines, though we've also regularly liked the Sauvignon Blanc made from purchased Lake County grapes. In a good year, such as 1990, the regular Carneros Chardonnay is a pleasing wine, too, and a good value; it has plenty of forward tropical fruit flavors combined with some deeper spicy/woodsy complexities. The house's Cabernets often surprise with their intense, herby, currant-like fruit, as in the 1987 Private Reserve. "L'Année," a red blend, is made only in exceptional years.

Wines/Varietals: Chardonnay, Carneros ($$, discounted to $), Chardonnay, Carneros Private Reserve ($$), Sauvignon Blanc, Lake County ($), White Pinot Noir, Steelhead Run ($), Gamay Beaujolais, Carneros ($), Pinot Noir, Carneros ($), Pinot Noir, Carneros Private Reserve ($$), Merlot, Carneros ($$), Merlot, Carneros Private Reserve ($$), Cabernet Sauvignon, Carneros ($$, discounted to $), Cabernet Sauvignon, Carneros Private Reserve ($$$), L'Année, Carneros (red, $$$).

Carmenet Vineyard

1700 Moon Mountain Drive
Sonoma, CA 95476
tel. (707) 996-5870; fax (707) 996-5302
Open to the public by appt.; est. 1981

North of the town of Sonoma and high up on Mount Pisgah, Carmenet Vineyard & Winery, a member of the Chalone Group, is producing quality Bordeaux-style wines and living up to the tradition implied by its name, which in classical French signifies the grape varieties of the Bordeaux region. With 70 acres of vineyards planted on steep terraces in the Mayacamas Mountains (69 percent Cabernet Sauvignon, 10 percent Merlot and 21 percent Cabernet Franc), Carmenet supplies about half of the grapes it requires to produce approximately 30,000 cases of red and white wines annually.

Carmenet Estate Red is a classic Bordeaux blend and the winery's proudest achievement. The 1987 is a big and fragrant wine with lots of smokey, herbal and ripe blackberry/cassis fruit flavors. The 1989 meritage (79 percent Cabernet), with its Moon Mountain Estate Vineyard grapes, is a sound bottle with deep flavors. The winery produces two Sauvignon blends: Carmenet White Reserve, Edna Valley Appellation (grapes from a Chalone Group vineyard near San Luis Obispo are blended with 24 percent Sémillon) and Sauvignon Blanc, Sonoma (with 5 percent Sémillon). Both wines are fermented and aged in barrels. The white meritage blend with Edna Valley grapes is more herbal and fig-like than the tropical fruit style Sauvignon from Sonoma. The winery also produces an unusual and attractive "Old Vines" Colombard with grapes from the Napa Valley that's rich in texture and bears flowers and green apple flavors.

Wines/Varietals: Carmenet Estate Red ($$$), Carmenet White Reserve, Edna Valley Appellation ($$), Sauvignon Blanc, Sonoma ($$), Old Vines Colombard ($).

Chalk Hill Winery

10300 Chalk Hill Road
Healdsburg, CA 95448
tel. (707) 838-4306; fax (707) 838-9687
Open to the public by appt.; est. 1980

This family-owned and operated estate winery with 278 acres of vineyards planted (on a 650+ acre ranch) took a major turn in the right direction when owner Fred Furth hired David Ramey, formerly of Matanzas Creek Winery, as winemaker in 1990. The wines at Chalk Hill were always sound and pleasant but now the full potential of its fine vineyards (150 acres planted in Chardonnay) is beginning to be realized.

In addition to Chardonnay, which is about half of production and is of the fruity-style Chardonnays, this winery splits the rest of its output between Sauvignon Blanc and Cabernet Sauvignon (not up to the whites yet). The 1991 Sauvignon Blanc (50 percent barrel fermented, 80 percent put through malolactic fermentation) is extremely impressive in an elegant and restrained style. In the dessert category, Chalk Hill produces a late-harvest Sémillon, and, when conditions are right, a *botrytis*-affected Sauvignon Blanc. The 1986 Late Harvest Sémillon is a great bottle of sweet wine with unctuous fig-like flavors. We thought the 1990 Chardonnay easily the winery's finest effort to date: round and complex, it is packed with buttery pear, apple, and nutty flavors. Then we tasted the 1991, every bit its equal but with rounder fruit and flavors. This is certainly a winery beginning to probe the stratosphere of American winemaking with its Chardonnay and dessert wine. And with Ramey doing the "cooking," there could be a delectable Merlot in the offing as well.

Wines/Varietals: Chardonnay ($$), Sauvignon Blanc ($), Cabernet Sauvignon ($$), Late Harvest Sémillon (375 ml, $).

Chateau St. Jean

8555 Sonoma Highway
Kenwood, CA 95452
tel. (707) 833-4134; fax (707) 833-4200
Open to the public; est. 1973

This 250,000-case winery, now owned by the Japanese company Suntory, has been a leader in establishing American vineyard-designated wines. Adhering to the belief that wine is the vineyard (there are 117 acres under vine here), Chateau St. Jean, located at the foot of Sugarloaf Ridge in Sonoma Valley, aims for the premium market and generally hits the mark.

Fifty percent of production here is Chardonnay, and the Alexander Valley Chardonnay, Robert Young Vineyards is the winery's finest effort. The 1990 does not disappoint. The winery also produces some very fine late harvest wines including *botrytis*-affected Rieslings and Gewürztraminers. In 1980 the first of Chateau St. Jean's *méthode champenoise* sparkling wines were produced at a separate location in western Sonoma County.

Wines/Varietals: NV Brut Sonoma County Sparkling Wine ($$), NV Blanc de Blancs Sonoma County Sparkling Wine ($$), Grand Cuvée Brut Reserve Sonoma County Sparkling Wine (vintage, $$$), Vin Blanc Sonoma County (white table wine, $), Gewürztraminer, Sonoma County ($), Johannisberg Riesling, Sonoma County ($), Fumé Blanc, Sonoma County ($), Fumé Blanc, La Petite Etoile Russian River Valley ($$), Chardonnay, Sonoma County ($$), Chardonnay, Estate Selection ($$), Chardonnay, Belle Terre Vineyards ($$), Chardonnay, Robert Young Vineyards ($$$), Select Late Harvest Gewürztraminer, Frank Johnson Vineyards (375 ml, $$), Select Late Harvest Johannisberg Riesling, Alexander Valley (375 ml, $$), Special Select Late Harvest Johannisberg Riesling, Hoot Owl Vineyard (375 ml, $$$), Cabernet Sauvignon, Sonoma County ($$), Cabernet Sauvignon, Alexander Valley Reserve ($$$).

Chateau Souverain

400 Souverain Road, PO Box 528
Geyserville, CA 95441
tel. (707) 433-8281; fax (707) 433-5174
Open to the public; est. 1973 (under
current ownership since 1986)

Under Wine World Estates (Nestlé) ownership, there's a lot going on here. Much land is under development as this operation moves toward its goal of becoming a 250,000-case, broad-spectrum Sonoma winery. Even with 135 acres already in production, Chateau Souverain buys additional grapes to produce 100,000 cases annually.

Overall, the Chardonnays (40 percent of production) seem headed in a very good direction and currently represent good values. Both the 1990 Sonoma County Barrel Fermented Chardonnay and the 1990 Carneros Sonoma County Sangiacomo Vineyard Chardonnay merit kudos. The former is solid, fruity, and fresh with vanilla and melon highlights. The latter is smokey and spicy but round and pearlike in texture and flavor. Chateau Souverain Zinfandel is consistently good: the intensely berryish 1990 is particularly well balanced and outstanding.

Wines/Varietals: Sauvignon Blanc, Alexander Valley ($), Chardonnay, Sonoma County ($$, discounted to $), Reserve Chardonnay, Sangiacomo Vineyard, Carneros ($$), Chardonnay, Allen Vineyard Reserve ($$), Chardonnay, Durell Vineyard Reserve ($$), Cabernet Sauvignon, Alexander Valley ($), Cabernet Sauvignon, Alexander Valley Winemaker's Reserve ($$), Zinfandel, Dry Creek Valley ($), Pinot Noir, Carneros ($).

Cline Cellars

24737 Arnold Drive
Sonoma, CA 95476
tel. (707) 935-4310; fax (707) 935-4319
Open to the public; est. 1982

In the early part of this century Contra Costa County (40 miles east of San Francisco) was booming with thousands of acres of healthy vineyards—but the consequences, first of Prohibition, and later of the deadly phylloxera epidemic, virtually wiped out the local wine industry. Fred and Matt Cline are doing their best to change all that. In 1982, Fred took over Firpo Winery and changed the name to Cline Cellars. Matt, his younger brother, came on board four years later as winemaker. After a slow start—the brothers recall days when they couldn't afford to bottle the wines they made—this winery is now producing 22,000 cases annually and marketing its wares in 47 U.S. states, Canada, and Japan. In 1989 Fred and his wife, Nancy, purchased 350 acres in Sonoma Valley and moved the family winery facility there. They made their first crush in Sonoma in 1991. The Clines were and still are in the vanguard of the American Rhône-style wine movement. Our hats are off to them; these Rhône Rangers are doing a great job. Though 40 acres of vineyards in Sonoma are planted over to mostly Rhône varieties (Roussanne, Syrah, Marsanne, Viognier—plus a little Chardonnay, Merlot, and Pinot Noir for good measure), the vines are still too young to provide quality fruit. So all of Cline Cellars grapes are purchased or come from a vineyard on the family ranch in Oakley.

Mourvèdre grapes grown in the 100-year-old Oakley vineyard (dry farmed in sandy soil) provide some of this winery's biggest fireworks. The 1989 Mourvèdre Reserve is superb: deep garnet color, intense, herbal

221

and black plum flavors with hints of to-bacco, and a long, smooth finish. We were also much taken with the 1990 Carignane made from 35-year-old vines; it's a dead on taste-alike for a fine Côte du Rhône-Village. The reasonably priced and more widely avail-able Côtes d'Oakley has evolved into a reli-able Côte du Rhône quaff as well, with rustic herb and berry flavor highlights, as evi-denced in the 1990 (a blend of Carignane, Mourvèdre and Zinfandel). Very high marks go to the 1990 Contra Costa Zinfandel with its appealing soft fruit but medium-big style. The bigger and oakier 1989 Reserve may well settle into something special.

Wines/Varietals: Sémillon, Barrel Fermented ($$), Zinfandel, Reserve Zinfandel, Zinfandel, Late Harvest ($$), Côtes D'Oakley ($), Oakley Cuvée ($$), Angel Rosé ($), Carignane ($), Mourvèdre ($$), Reserve Mourvèdre ($$$).

Clos du Bois

19410 Beyserville Ave., PO Box 940
Geyserville, CA 95441
tel. (707) 857-1651; fax (707) 857-1667
Not open to the public; est. 1974

What started as a modest little winery, with 100 acres of vineyards in the Dry Creek Valley and a first release in 1974 of 2,000 cases, has grown a good deal over the years. It grew and grew and was acquired by the Hiram Walker Group in 1988; then it grew some more to its current 350,000 case level, where it enjoys the leadership position in the production of barrel fermented Chardonnay. Acreage under vine is up to 590 acres; addi-tional grapes are purchased to turn out so large a volume of premium wine.

Margaret Davenport was named winemaker here in 1990, and she has kept on a steady course producing six varietals:

Chardonnay, Sauvignon Blanc, Gewürztraminer, Pinot Noir, Merlot, and Cabernet Sauvignon. Vineyard designations are used for two of the Chardonnays (Calcaire and Flintwood), and one of the Cabernets (Briarcrest). Clos du Bois' top red wine usually is "Marlstone," a Bordeaux blend. Across the board the wines here are good—and occasionally outstanding, an impressive showing for a winery of this size. Of the top Chardonnays, the Calcaire is slightly leaner with smokey pear flavors (though it is 100 percent barrel fermented in Limousin oak), than the Flintwood which gets a heavier dose of Nevers oak. The 1987 Marlstone is a dense wine packed with berry and choco-late flavors covered with enough tannins to suggest aging until, say, 1996 for peak plea-sure. The 1988 Marlstone is not as big or complex, but the 1989 was again closer to the top mark, with concentrated plum-berry fruit and graceful balance.

Wines/Varietals: Chardonnay, Barrel Fer-mented ($$), Chardonnay, Calcaire ($$), Chardonnay, Flintwood ($$), Sauvignon Blanc, Barrel Fermented ($), Gewürztraminer ($), Pinot Noir ($$), Merlot ($$), Cabernet Sauvignon ($$), Cabernet Sauvignon, Briarcrest ($$), Marlstone ($$).

B. R. Cohn Winery

15140 Sonoma Highway
Glen Ellen, CA 95442
tel. (707) 938-4064; fax (707) 938-4585
Open to the public by appt.; est. 1984

Former rock group manager Bruce Cohn owns this 64-acre Olive Hill Vineyard which is planted mostly to Cabernet Sauvignon. Cohn purchases thirty percent of the grapes required to produce 13,000 cases annually;

70 percent of the wine made here is Cabernet Sauvignon.

Cohn's Chardonnays are full-flavored, though the ripe fruit is somewhat overpowered by excessive oak. Winemaker John Speed promises better balance in future, with no sacrifice of the wine's personality. Overall, the Cabernet Sauvignons have rich, ripe fruit flavors and are well-balanced with a good mix of oak and tannin. Two are offered: a "Napa County Silver Label" and, at twice the price, a vineyard-designated Olive Hill Cabernet. The 1989 Olive Hill Cab has luxurious flavors without being a big wine; vanilla and toast components lace plum and currant-style fruit. The 1989 Silver Label is similar and smooth, with slightly diminished dimensions overall. Cohn's Olive Hill Cab already has a following; his Merlot could be a comer.

Wines/Varietals: Chardonnay ($$), Cabernet Sauvignon, Olive Hill ($$$), Cabernet Sauvignon, Silver Label ($$), Merlot, Silver Label ($$).

Davis Bynum Winery

8075 Westside Road
Healdsburg, CA 95448
tel. (707) 433-5852; fax (707) 433-4309
Open to the public; est. 1965

Former *San Francisco Chronicle* newspaperman Davis Bynum made wine at home for 15 years before his father, author of a book on California wine, talked him into starting a professional winery. In 1965 Bynum purchased a former wholesale plumbing warehouse in Albany, California, and established his first winery. He moved to the Russian River Valley in 1973, and purchased 82 acres, in the middle of which sits

an old hop kiln. This is the Davis Bynum Winery of today.

Gary Farrell is the distinguished winemaker at this 22,000 case-a-year winery, which recently sold off its old Barefoot Bynum label to devote all of its efforts to producing high quality Russian River Valley wines—Pinot Noir, Merlot, Cabernet Sauvignon, and Zinfandel. The Chardonnay drinks agreeably and we are mightily impressed with the 1990 Russian River Valley Zinfandel. We also enjoyed the 1990 Pinot Noir Russian River Valley Limited Release, elegant and intense with all sorts of welcome black cherry and strawberry flavors with a dry dose of tea and spice. Among the white wines, the Alsatian-style 1991 Gewürztraminer with its dry grapefruit and lychee tones is refreshing. So, too, is the 1991 Fumé Blanc made with grapes from two Russian River Vineyards. It's a wine with varietal grassiness, well balanced with melon and fruit flavors, and nice complexity and relative power—the best Bynum Fumé Blanc in years, perhaps ever. The 1990 Merlot has charm, with bright, berry flavors and graceful balance.

Wines/Varietals: Chardonnay, Russian River Valley ($$), Chardonnay, Sonoma County ($), Fumé Blanc, Russian River Valley ($), Gewürztraminer, Russian River Valley ($), Cabernet Sauvignon, Sonoma County ($$), Pinot Noir, Russian River Valley ($$).

Dehlinger Winery

6300 Guerneville Road
Sebastopol, CA 95472
tel. (707) 823-2378
Open to the public; est. 1976

This might be called a winemaker's winery. Everything made here is good and shows off the merits of the 50 acres under carefully cultivated vine (20 of Pinot Noir, 15 Chardonnay, 7 Cabernet Sauvignon, 5 Cabernet Franc, and 3 Merlot). The vineyards and winery, located in the Forestville quadrant of the Russian River Valley, produce about 10,000 cases annually. But few consumers are aware of what Tom Dehlinger is achieving here.

Dehlinger, a biochemist who went on to study enology at U.C. Davis, makes wines that benefit from aging, though in the vintages dating from the late 1980s they are medium-bodied and graceful. His Pinot Noirs and Chardonnays are increasingly the wines to seek out. The 1990 Chardonnay is good and lean with plenty of flavors—apple, citrus, and spicy oak. Dehlinger also made 150 cases of a Montrachet Cuvée in 1990 that is bigger than his regular Russian River Valley Chardonnay.

Wines/Varietals: Chardonnay, Estate Bottled ($$), Chardonnay, Montrachet Cuvée, Russian River Valley ($$), Pinot Noir, Sonoma County Selection ($$), Cabernet Franc, Estate Bottled ($$), Cabernet Sauvignon, Estate Bottled ($$).

De Loach Vineyards

1791 Olivet Road
Santa Rosa, CA 95401
tel. (707) 526-9111; fax (707) 526-4151
Open to the public; est. 1970

Cecil and Christine De Loach were among the first to call attention to the Russian River Valley as a source of scintillating Chardonnay and other white varieties. De Loach has grown to nearly 100,000 cases in the last two decades, largely due to the success of its full-bodied, opulent Chardonnays. They are ripe, with hints of sweetness in some versions,

notably the reserve-style OFS Chardonnay. De Loach also does extremely well with several other varieties, including Pinot Noir, Zinfandel (both fat and ripe in fruit), an off-dry Gewürztraminer, and a crisp white Zinfandel. Two hundred and seventy acres of vineyards (84.5 planted to Zinfandel) provide 70 percent of the winery's grape supply.

Recent vintages of Fumé Blanc have been particularly good—dry, somewhat steely, more to our taste than the slightly sweeter-styled Sauvignon Blanc. The 1990 De Loach Zinfandel is lovely, rich in berries and intense flavor; the 1991 is lighter. The 1990 Chardonnay is very good: lush, opulent, full of citrusy, vanilla flavors—one to drink and enjoy immediately. De Loach also produces OFS (Our Finest Selection) bottlings of both Pinot and Chardonnay.

Wines/Varietals: Chardonnay ($$), Chardonnay ,OFS ($$$), Fumé Blanc ($), Sauvignon Blanc ($), Gewürztraminer, Early Harvest ($), Gewürztraminer, Late Harvest ($$), White Zinfandel ($), Pinot Noir ($$), Pinot Noir, OFS ($$$), Zinfandel ($$).

Domaine Michel

4155 Wine Creek Road
Healdsburg, CA 95448
tel. (707) 433-7427; fax (707) 433-0444
Open to the public by appt.; est. 1979

Inspired by the way Tom Jordan created a wine estate in Sonoma, Swiss financier Jean Jacques Michel purchased land in nearby Dry Creek Valley to establish an estate of his own. With the support of partners Ridgeley Bullock and Jacques Schlumberger, Domaine Michel has evolved into one of Sonoma's most promising operations. The winery, tucked away in the hills of

Healdsburg, is a handsome mission-style, white stucco, red tile-roofed structure, with arcades, a lushly landscaped courtyard and a reflecting pool. The facility's tranquil Moorish setting, reminiscent of Andalusia, is in keeping with the property's history as part of a Spanish land grant. Drawing on 51 acres of vineyard, Domaine Michel produces 20,000-25,000 cases of only Cabernet Sauvignon (60 percent) and Chardonnay (40 percent). Thirty-five percent of the required grapes are purchased to supplement the estate-grown Chardonnay (26.6 acres), Cabernet Sauvignon (14.7 acres), Merlot (6.6 acres), and Cabernet Franc (2.6 acres)

Domaine Michel regards as of utmost importance maintaining consistent quality of fruit from vintage to vintage, and to that end pays careful attention to environmental factors and to the nurturing of its vines. Winemaker Fred Payne produced Domaine Michel's best Chardonnay to date in 1990; it's a wine rich in fruit and oak but very well balanced. The 1989 red, a blend of Cabernet Sauvignon, Cabernet Franc, and Merlot was blended in spring following the vintage, in the manner of Bordeaux, and aged about 14 months in French oak. Its dark berry flavors are wrapped in layers of tannin and oak that should ultimately develop intriguing complexity.

Wines/Varietals: Chardonnay ($$), Cabernet Sauvignon ($$).

Dry Creek Vineyard

3770 Lambert Bridge Road, PO Box T
Healdsburg, CA 95448
tel. (707) 433-1000; fax (707) 433-5329
Open to the public; est. 1972

David S. Stare founded this winery in 1972—the first in the Dry Creek Valley

since Prohibition—and is still its president, though he has lately made it a family affair: eldest daughter Kim Stare Wallace is now the winery's dynamic vice president/director of marketing. Dry Creek Vineyard is best known for its pioneering efforts in the Sonoma Valley with Sauvignon Blanc (called Fumé Blanc here). This varietal constitutes just under half of the 75,000 cases of wine produced here annually from estate grapes (Dry Creek has 105 acres of vineyards) and from purchased grapes. Chenin Blanc is also a noteworthy wine here. This winery's wares are marketed in all 50 U.S. states and 16 foreign countries.

The flagship Fumé Blancs tend to be full-blown with lots of grassy, melon, mango, and citrus flavors that are nice complements to some foods. The 1990 is 100 percent Sauvignon Blanc grapes harvested 89 percent from the Dry Creek, Alexander, and Russian River valleys, 7 percent from Mendocino County, and 4 percent from Napa County with the blend aged about 5 months in French oak barrels. Spicy oak and citrus flavors figure, too, in the Reserve Chardonnays. The regular release is almost as good, especially the 1991 100 percent barrel fermented Sonoma County Chardonnay with its apple and spicy flavors. We also admire the Dry Chenin Blanc, which in 1990 and 1991 is a very clean bottle of inexpensive wine with varietal aromas of pears, peaches, citrus, and pineapple—it is indeed vinified dry. The reds, which include old vines Zinfandel, a Cabernet Sauvignon, increasing amounts of Merlot, and a Meritage, all show good fruit focus. To our taste, though, they still take a back seat to the whites—except perhaps the Zinfandel, which in 1990 is excellent. Stare may have a mordant sense of humor: In 1992 he released a "Bug Creek Rosé" made from Cabernet Sauvignon out of weakened phylloxera-infested vines. "Phil Awksira Cellars" is credited as winemaker.

Wines/Varietals: Chenin Blanc, Dry Creek ($), Fumé Blanc ($), Reserve Fumé Blanc ($$), Chardonnay ($$), Reserve Chardonnay ($$), Rosé of Cabernet Sauvignon ($), Merlot ($$), Zinfandel ($$), Cabernet Sauvignon ($$), Meritage Red ($$$).

Ferrari-Carano Vineyards
8761 Dry Creek Road, PO Box 1549
Healdsburg, CA 95448
tel. (707) 433-6700; fax (707) 431-1742
Open to the public; est. 1981

Ferrari-Carano's Chardonnay and Fumé Blanc found immediate favor with consumers and critics when its first wines were released in the early 1980s. Owners Don and Rhonda Carano parlayed their winnings in Reno at the El Dorado Casino and Hotel (as the owners, not at the gaming tables) into choice vineyard land in Sonoma, now 500 acres at four different sites, and a winery complex near the Russian River Valley. The Caranos' enthusiasm for Italian cooking is manifested in the addition here of Villa Fiore, a state-of-the-art kitchen designed for cooking demonstrations and culinary extravaganzas.

Winemaker George Bursick has proven expert with white wines, notably an immediately engaging, rich, tropical fruit Chardonnay and a citrus-flavored Fumé Blanc. The 1991 versions of these wines are excellent, particularly the Chardonnay, with its rather enticing clove and citrus aromas. It seems these Chards give great pleasure at competitive prices every year. If Ferrari-Carano's reds are still somewhat overshadowed by its showier whites, the Cabernet and Merlot, both agreeable and approach-

able young, stand to gain in stature as some of the winery's mountain vineyards mature and develop more character. The 1989 late-harvest Sauvignon Blanc/Sémillon is deep golden in color with honeyed apricot/pineapple flavors. The small production 1990 Dry Creek Zinfandel is a big winner.

Wines/Varietals: Fumé Blanc ($$), Chardonnay ($$), Reserve Chardonnay ($$), Cabernet Sauvignon ($$), Merlot ($$), Zinfandel, Dry Creek Valley ($$), Eldorado Gold, Late Harvest ($$$).

Fisher Vineyards
6200 St. Helena Road
Santa Rosa, CA 95404
tel. (707) 539-7511; fax (707) 539-3601
Open to the public by appt.; est. 1973

"Body by Fisher" has taken on new meaning since the founding of this winery by a descendant of the automotive manufacturing family known for this trademark. Fred Fisher and his wife, Juelle, purchased two vineyards of Chardonnay and Cabernet Sauvignon in the Mayacamas Mountains in 1973. Three years later they added a third vineyard, situated on the Napa Valley floor. Merlot and Cabernet Franc vines have been added to the vineyards, which now total 90 acres. With a supplement of 20 percent purchased grapes, annual production here is at 7,000 cases.

Both Fisher's Chardonnays and its Cabernets have earned substantial critical praise. The Chardonnays tend to be highly stylized, lean, and crisp wines with nice flavor aromatics. The "Coach Insignia" bottling in 1989 is a pleasant one. The Cabernets draw grapes from two estate sources: the Wedding Vineyard, adjacent to the winery at 1,200 feet in the Mayacamas Mountains, and the Lamb Vineyard at the northern end of the Napa Valley. Both the 1989 and 1990 Cabs are intensely flavored and elegant.

Wines/Varietals: Chardonnay, Coach Insignia ($$), Chardonnay, Whitney's Vineyard ($$), Chardonnay, Napa-Sonoma ($), Cabernet Sauvignon, Coach Insignia ($$).

Foppiano Vineyards

12707 Old Redwood Hwy., PO Box 606
Healdsburg, CA 95448
tel/ (707) 433-7272; fax (707) 433-0565
Open to the public; est. 1896

This grandaddy of Russian River Valley wineries produces nearly 200,000 cases of wine annually under three different labels. One bears the family name, Foppiano Vineyards, and another, Fox Mountain, is a small prestige line. The third, Riverside Farms, is a low-priced line of varietals and generics. Both of the premium labels earn Foppiano this entry. The 1970s and 1980s saw the family modernize its operations and enter the varietal market. The Foppianos now own 200 acres of vineyards in the Russian River Valley; their estate-grown wines carry this appellation.

Foppiano Petite Sirah and Fox Mountain Cabernet both win our admiration. The Petite Sirah, which draws from Foppiano's 20 acres of old vines and is offered in regular and reserve bottlings, is quite good. The superb 1987 Petite Sirah Reserve is deep, dark, and sturdy, with lush cherry and dark berry fruit flavors. The 1990 Sonoma Petite Sirah is also a winner. The Foppiano 1989 Sonoma County Cabernet Sauvignon is a good, representative wine: low priced, showing fresh fruit and the somewhat herbal character of all the Foppiano and Fox Mountain Cabs, and easy drinking.

Wines/Varietals: Chardonnay ($), Chardonnay, Fox Mountain Reserve ($$), Sauvignon Blanc ($), Cabernet Sauvignon ($), Cabernet Sauvignon, Fox Mountain Reserve ($$), Petite Sirah ($), Reserve Petite Sirah ($$).

Garric-Langbehn

5400 Alpine Road
Santa Rosa, CA 95404
tel. (707) 539-2078; fax (707) 538-4502
Not open to the public; est. 1986

The "Garric" half is Lynn Garric; the "Langbehn" half is Lynn's husband, Larry. This 50/50 partnership produces 50 percent Chardonnay and 50 percent Cabernet at a small (1,200 case) winery situated on a hillside of the Mayacamas Mountains in Sonoma County. Larry was the winemaker at Freemark Abbey from 1976 to 1985, and subsequently a consultant to the Lamborn Family Winery and other producers. Lynn's French heritage, combined with her Sonoma County upbringing, have given her a serious interest in the wine industry, and led her to establish a tour company aimed at introducing California winemakers to their French counterparts. (This winery's logo is the Occitane Cross, symbol of the Languedoc, France, and of Lynn's ancestry.) All of the wine produced at Garric-Langbehn is from purchased grapes.

We like the 1988 Chardonnay with its soft, restrained Sonoma fruit. The 1990 is a worthy follow-up. The Cabernet is a bigger deal in style, however, and is the owner's favorite. The 1988 is recommended.

Wines/Varietals: Chardonnay ($$), Cabernet Sauvignon ($$).

Gary Farrell Wines

PO Box 341
Forestville, CA 95436
tel. (707) 433-6616
Not open to the public; est. 1982

It's pretty much indisputable: Gary Farrell is one of the most talented winemakers in California. Farrell began as winemaker at Davis Bynum in 1978, later made wine at Rochioli, and eventually launched his own label in 1982. His limited production— 5,000 cases—is always in demand and quickly sells out, particularly the Pinot Noir and the Zinfandel, two perennial standouts.

Farrell owns no vineyards but buys from some of Sonoma's best growers, including the Allen Vineyard, Rochioli, and Bacigalupi. He goes in for rich, chewy, generous fruit, and holds it in check by providing his wines excellent structure. Despite a firmness in the reds that offers tremendous potential for aging, these wines are immediately engaging, particularly the popular Pinot Noir and Zinfandel. This is not intended as a slight to either the Merlot or Cabernet, nor to the appealing, well-balanced Chardonnay. Farrell's 1990 Zinfandel won the top "Sweepstakes Red" prize in the Sonoma County Harvest Fair competition, distinguishing itself in field full of gold medal-winning wines. The winemaker's 1990 Pinot Noir, which he considers his *chef d'oeuvre,* has dark, smokey, berryish flavors, with rich, seductive texture. It is an outstanding effort. The sound 1991 Chard is a bit more upfront with pear and citrus fruit flavors over a touch of oak and sound acidity.

Wines/Varietals: Chardonnay, Russian River ($$), Pinot Noir ($$), Pinot Noir, Allen Vineyard ($$$), Merlot ($$), Cabernet Sauvignon ($$), Zinfandel ($$).

Geyser Peak Winery

22281 Chianti Rd., PO Box 25
Geyserville, CA 95441
tel. (707) 857-9463; fax (707) 857-3545
Open to the public; est. 1880

Augustus Quitzow, the founder of this, one of California's oldest wineries, built his first winemaking facility on a hillside in the northern reaches of the Alexander Valley in 1882. That imposing vine-covered stone structure still occupies the site, overlooking Highway 101 near the town of Geyserville. Current owner Henry Trione and his sons, Victor and Mark, purchased Geyser Peak, including 500 acres of vineyard, in 1982. Today they own 1,000 acres of prime vineyard land, most in the Alexander Valley and the Russian River area, with some 200 acres in Lake County and 130 in Mendocino's Redwood Valley. Annual production here is up to 375,000 cases.

Geyser Peak's wines have lately begun to show new quality and finesse; we were frequently pleasantly surprised by how well they fared in our blind tastings. Winemaker Daryl Groom (he was formerly with Penfolds of Australia) has added a few Australian touches to the line like his crisp, fruity Semchard, a blend of Sémillon and Chardonnay that accentuates the fruit of both varieties with only a touch of oak influence. He has also produced an inky, berryish Shiraz (Syrah) that is likely to be a hit following its 1993 debut. The 1990 Merlot is very approachable, with appealing fruit and soft contours. The rich, full-bodied 1990 Reserve Cabernet, made from best lots of Cabernet Sauvignon, has a bit of Cabernet Franc adding to its complexity. The 1987 Reserve Cab was also a good one.

The "Reserve Alexandre," Geyser Peak's proprietary blend consisting of the five Bordeaux varieties (Cabernet Sauvignon, Cabernet Franc, Merlot, Malbec, and Petit Verdot). is aged only in French oak, most of it new. The 1990 Reserve Alexandre is the winery's best to date, deep and complex with good aging potential. We were impressed, too, with the full-flavored 1990 Sonoma County Chardonnay, the 1991 Reserve Chardonnay (lively, attractively creamy and fairly oaky), and the 1991 Sauvignon Blanc (clean, somewhat grassy, but not entirely dry). Geyser Peak also bottles a small line of varietals under its second label, "Canyon Road."

Wines/Varietals: Chardonnay ($), Reserve Chardonnay ($$), Semchard ($), Soft Johannisberg Riesling ($), Gewürztraminer ($), Sauvignon Blanc ($), Cabernet Sauvignon ($), Reserve Cabernet Sauvignon ($$), Merlot ($$), Gamay Beaujolais ($), Reserve Alexandre ($$$).

Gloria Ferrer
Champagne Caves

23555 Highway 121, PO Box 1427
Sonoma, CA 95476
tel. (707) 996-7256; fax (707) 996-0720
Open to the public; est. 1982

The Spanish firm of Freixenet, whose popular *cavas* are well known in the U.S., built the Gloria Ferrer Champagne Caves in the Carneros district of Sonoma County in 1982. The winery is named for the wife of José Ferrer, Freixenet's president. The couple are active in promoting their California sparkling wines and spend a good deal of time in the state. From the first, Gloria Ferrer sparkling wines offered good value. We, in fact, find them much superior to the owner's Spanish sparklers—perhaps because they are made entirely with the classic Champagne varieties, Chardonnay and Pinot Noir. The Ferrers have now planted 180 acres of their 245-acre property, 59 acres in Chardonnay, the rest to Pinot Noir. The grapes are hand-picked and brought to Ferrer Champagne Caves' handsome California mission-style winery, where they are fermented in stainless steel refrigerated tanks. Secondary fermentation takes place in bottles. Total annual production here averages 65,000 cases.

Ferrer's first non-vintage cuvée was introduced in 1983. Two more vintage cuvées have since been added. Gloria Ferrer Brut is a blend of 80 to 90 percent Pinot Noir, and 10 to 20 percent Chardonnay. Dry and lean, it is well-balanced, with brisk, clean fruit. Gloria Ferrer Royal Cuvée, named in honor of Spain's King Juan Carlos I and Queen Sofia, is made solely from a first pressing of Carneros fruit, roughly 70 percent Pinot Noir, 30 percent Chardonnay. The 1987 appears to have a slightly sweeter dosage. The Gloria Ferrer Carneros Cuvée, this house's top cuvée, is actually a more traditional blend at 60 percent Pinot Noir and 40 percent Chardonnay. We found the 1987 lively and crisp, with good balance and acid, the extra Chardonnay component shining through to give it a little more gloss. In 1993, this winery released two still wines, a 1991 Carneros Pinot Noir and a 1991 Carneros Chardonnay.

Wines/Varietals: Sonoma County Brut ($$), Royal Cuvée ($$), Carneros Cuvée ($$$), Pinot Noir, Carneros ($$), Chardonnay, Carneros ($$).

229

Golden Creek Vineyard

4480 Wallace Road
Santa Rosa, CA 95404
tel. (707) 538-2350
Open to the public by appt.; est. 1983

Golden Creek, producing barely 2,500 cases annually from 12 acres in Sonoma County, quietly stole on the scene in the late 1980s with rich, fruity, well-structured Cabernet Sauvignon and Merlot. The wines went largely unnoticed until they began cropping up among the gold and silver medal winners in a number of competitions. Owner Ladi Danielik, who emigrated from Czechoslovakia in 1968, planted his small vineyard in the hills above Rincon Valley east of Santa Rosa in the late seventies.

Golden Creek's Cabernet and Merlot are full-flavored wines; the Merlot, plummy and rich, is drinkable sooner than the slightly leaner, cassis-flavored Cabernet. Danielik gives both wines a certain glossy finesse that has immediate appeal. The 1989 "Caberlot," Golden Creek's meritage blend, is a much tighter, firmer wine, clearly in need of aging to meld and become harmonious, though already drinking acceptably. Made half-and-half of Cabernet Sauvignon and Merlot, it bears watching. Danielik's Merlot Reserve has already arrived. In 1990, the regular and the reserve Merlots are both fine bottles.

Wines/Varietals: Caberlot ($$), Cabernet Sauvignon ($$), Merlot ($$), Reserve Merlot ($$$).

Gundlach-Bundschu

2000 Denmark Street
Sonoma, CA 95487
tel. (707) 938-5277; fax (707) 938-9460
Open to the public; est. 1858 (in continuous operation since 1973)

In a number of ways Gundlach-Bundschu is the real thing: it relies on little hype and has lots of substance. Its vineyards were planted in 1858 and have been owned and looked after ever since by the same family that purchased the land in 1855. The winery here operated from 1858 to Prohibition, and was revived in 1973. For well over a century, the "Rhinefarm" grapes grown here have gone into very fine bottles of wine; some of the estate's grapes are still sold off today. The Rhinefarm vineyards extend west and south from the lower slopes of the Mayacamas Mountains separating the Napa and Sonoma valleys and roll towards the San Pablo Bay. Two other vineyards contribute to a total of 350 Bundschu family-owned acres under vine.

Jim Bundschu and Lance Cutler have been winemaking partners here since 1985 (their working association goes back to 1978). Cutler also produces his own Cutler Cellars wines in association with the winery. The focus at Gundlach-Bundschu is on estate wines, 15 in all. Only the winery's Sangiacomo Ranch Chardonnay is made from purchased grapes. With output now reaching 50,000 cases annually, and so many varietal wines in the line, there is an understandable variation in the quality of production here. But the big name grapes—Chardonnay, Cabernet Sauvignon, and Merlot—are reliably good, the rich reds sometimes outstanding. The whites tend to be clean and simple and attractively priced. The dry Gewürztraminer certainly has its appealing aspects. The reds share good pricing with the whites and exhibit a bit more personality and complexity. We are most impressed by the 1989 Rhinefarm Merlot: with pronounced cherries on the nose, good balance, and deep fruit with a touch of woody flavors and a hint of eucalyptus, this is a top quality wine to look for. The Rhinefarm Cabs are also consistently good. We like the 1988, and the 1989 is even better.

Wines/Varietals: Chardonnay, Sonoma Valley ($$), Chardonnay, Sangiacomo Ranch ($$), Riesling, Sonoma Valley ($), Gewürztraminer, Sonoma Valley ($), Kleinberger, Sonoma Valley ($), Sonoma White ($), Gamay Beaujolais ($), Pinot Noir, Rhinefarm Vineyards ($$), Cabernet Franc, Rhinefarm Vineyards ($$), Zinfandel, Sonoma Valley ($), Zinfandel, Rhinefarm Vineyards ($$), Merlot, Rhinefarm Vineyards ($$), Cabernet Sauvignon, Rhinefarm Vineyards ($$), Sonoma Red ($).

Hacienda Winery

1000 Vineyard Lane, PO Box 416
Sonoma, CA 95476
tel. (707) 938-3220; fax (707) 938-2663
Open to the public; est. 1973

The Cooley family first settled in California during the gold rush in 1849, and by the 1860s had begun growing grapes on their Cloverdale farm. In 1973 Crawford Cooley acquired the historic 50-acre Hacienda Vineyard, once a part of Buena Vista Winery, and established Hacienda Winery in the Sonoma Valley utilizing grapes from the Cooley vineyard as well as other top area vineyards. Early in 1993, the winery was sold to the giant Bronco Wine Co. of Central California (primarily a big-volume wine producer owned by the Franzia family).

Drawing on a wide variety of grape sources, winemaker Eric Laumann gives special attention to blending techniques, fermenting each lot separately and tasting every barrel or tank several times before putting it all together. Hacienda specializes in Chardonnay, Dry Chenin Blanc, Sauvignon Blanc, and Cabernet Sauvignon, and is currently producing an average of 30,000 cases annually. The Chenin Blanc made here is one of the best in the country. The 1991 Clarksburg Dry Chenin Blanc has a floral and apple nose and a light, balanced body with melony flavors. We like this house's Chardonnay, too. The 1990 "Clair de Lune" has sweet Chardonnay flavors on the nose and plenty of oak barrel and varietal fruit on the palate. Among the reds, we prefer the Cabernets to the Pinot Noir. The Cabs are at their best in a Bordeaux blend called "Antares Sonoma County," which in 1989 (70 percent Cabernet Sauvignon, 25 percent Merlot, 5 percent Cabernet Franc) has good berry flavors on the nose and peppery barrel tones added to the palate. The high acid and tannins suggest this wine won't show its true character for some years.

Wines/Varietals: Dry Chenin Blanc ($), Chardonnay, Claire de Lune ($$), Cabernet Sauvignon ($$), Pinot Noir ($$), Antares Proprietary Blend ($$$).

Hanna Winery

5345 Occidental Road, PO Box 6003
Santa Rosa, CA 95401
tel. (707) 575-0563; fax (707) 575-0563
Open to the public by appt.; est. 1985

Heart surgeon Elias Hanna established this Sonoma County winery in 1985 on an estate with 35 acres of vineyards. Now he owns 272 acres at various sites, including a

100-acre plot in the Alexander Valley. Not all of Hanna's vines are producing fruit yet, so some Sonoma County grapes are still purchased. But as more estate grapes come on line and the vines mature, prospects for this already highly reliable winery look very good. Christine Hanna, as vice president of sales and marketing, works to sell the increasing number of cases being produced here.

Dean Cox became Hanna's winemaker and general manager in 1991. He has continued to produce what we've always found to be good quality wines across the board—from Sauvignon Blanc and barrel fermented Chardonnay (in the Burgundian style) to Cabernet Sauvignon (blended with Merlot). The most impressive Hanna wine we tasted recently is the 1988 Cabernet Sauvignon, which is lush and deep with plum and cassis flavors.

Wines/Varietals: Sauvignon Blanc ($), Chardonnay ($$), Merlot ($$), Cabernet Sauvignon ($$).

Hanzell Vineyards

18596 Lomita Avenue
Sonoma, CA 95476
tel. (707) 996-3860
Open to the public by appt.; est. 1957

Tiny Hanzell Vineyards has made a monumental contribution to the modern era of winemaking in California. With its 1957 Chardonnay, aged in imported Burgundian oak barrels, Hanzell dramatically influenced the style of California Chardonnay. The following year, the winery added a Pinot Noir. Hanzell's founder, millionaire James Zellerbach (head of Crown Zellerbach paper company), had lived in France following World War II, where he became a devotee of

Burgundy wines—specifically Montrachet and Romanée-Conti. In 1952 he planted Chardonnay and Pinot Noir on his 200-acre estate on slopes above the town of Sonoma. He also built a showcase winery, though relatively few wine lovers have ever seen it. Perched above the vines overlooking the area of Sonoma Jack London referred to as "Valley of the Moon," Hanzell's winery is a miniature replica of the famed chateau at Clos de Vougeot on Burgundy's Côte d'Or. Following Zellerbach's death in 1963, Douglas and Mary Day bought the winery. In 1965, the Days resumed production here: it has continued ever since. In 1975, Hanzell was acquired by the Countess Barbara de Brye of Great Britain, who added Bordeaux varieties (Cabernet Sauvignon, Merlot and Cabernet Franc) to the vineyard. At her death in 1991, ownership of the winery passed to her son, Alexander, for whom it is being managed by trustees until he comes of age.

The 33-acre vineyard here yields fruit for only 3,000 cases annually, sometimes less. Traditionally, Hanzell wines were not made exactly like Burgundy—the Chardonnays, for instance, were (and largely still are) fermented in stainless steel rather than in oak, and the wines did not undergo malolactic fermentation. (Many feel this fact accounts for the proven longevity of the early wines: the 1968, 1969, 1972, and 1975 Chardonnays still contain magnificent fruit.) Remarkable continuity in the production of Hanzell wines, particularly its Chardonnay, has been maintained through the years by winemaker Robert Sessions. Little has changed of late. A small portion of the majestic Chardonnay is barrel fermented now and some undergoes malolactic fermentation, but these are still firmly structured wines, profoundly complex and deep, in need of a good four or five years to show their goods, as the 1989 version confirms. Hanzell's Pinot Noir is perhaps less Burgundian than its Chardonnay. The Pinot is earthy and powerful with intense briar and wood flavors mingled with the fruit. It is much more interesting with seven or eight years in bottle, where it develops opulent aromas and a roundness that is heady but appealing. The Cabernet Sauvignon is also a powerful red; the 1988 is concentrated and tannic now, but we expect its rich berry fruit to eventually emerge quite impressively.

Wines/Varietals: Chardonnay ($$$), Cabernet Sauvignon ($$$), Pinot Noir ($$$).

Haywood Winery

27000 Ramal Rd., PO Box 182
Sonoma, CA 95476
tel. (707) 252-7886; fax (707) 252-0392
Not open to the public; est.1980

This 90-acre Sonoma Valley winery, founded by one-time contractor Peter Haywood, produces 75,000 cases yearly. Its vineyard is planted to Zinfandel (24 acres), Cabernet Sauvignon (19 acres), Merlot (7 acres), Sauvignon Blanc (7 acres), and Chardonnay (33 acres). Haywood, who was the first winemaker here (Sara Steiner now does the job), purchases 80 percent of his grapes. In 1991, majority ownership of the winery went to the Racke USA concern, with Haywood remaining as managing partner. Racke now handles sales and marketing.

Quality and prices are good here. The Zinfandel is truly distinguished and some of the older Cabernets have shone well, too. Harrison's Chardonnays are consistently better these days, but estate wines from the mountainous Los Chamizal vineyards are

the ones to look for. Best bets here are the elegant, spicy, and raspberry fruity 1988 and 1990 Los Chamizal Vineyard Zinfandels. For two worthy under $10 values, look for Haywood's 1990 Vintner's Select Cabernet Sauvignon (spicy and complex, with an acid edge), or the 1991 Vintner's Select California Chardonnay (fairly lush with apple and oak flavors and lively acidity).

Wines/Varietals: Chardonnay, Vintner's Select ($), Chardonnay, Los Chamizal Estate ($$), Zinfandel, Estate ($$), Cabernet Sauvignon, Vintner's Select ($), Cabernet Sauvignon, Los Chamizal Estate ($$).

Iron Horse Vineyards

9786 Ross Station Road
Sebastopol, CA 95472
tel. (707) 887-1507; fax (707) 887-1337
Open to the public by appt.; est. 1978

This is the very model of a premium California winery: a beautiful estate with extraordinary flower gardens and rolling vineyards on the property, a handsome Victorian house, and a small, state-of-the-art winery. A tight-knit family produces and promotes the sparkling and the still wines made here; both are of enviable quality. This was once only a railway stop in Sonoma's Green Valley, but winemaker Rodney Strong and a young vineyard manager named Forrest Tancer began to develop vineyards here in 1971. In 1976 corporate attorney Barry Sterling and his wife, Audrey, purchased the property and retained Tancer as winemaker-partner. Much more recently Tancer married the Sterlings' daughter, Joy, and the two couples now live on the estate as one big, happy—and very busy—family. Today Joy and Forrest take the lead in day-to-day operations and development of the winery (they are also very active and effective spokespersons for the California wine industry, especially its Sonoma County constituents). With the Tancer family vineyards (located elsewhere in Sonoma) that Forrest brings to this operation, Iron Horse has 194 acres under vine and is a fully estate-bottled winery. Annual production here hovers around 35,000 cases, split about evenly between sparkling and still wines. (In fact, the volume edge probably goes to the still wines, but the quality edge goes to the sparklers.)

Because it also produces high quality still wines, Iron Horse is perhaps unique among top California sparkling wine producers. Its sparkling wines consistently rank among, say, the top three produced in America. Quality is consistent across the line of Brut, Blanc de Blancs, Blanc de Noirs, and Rosé bottlings, but the late-disgorged brut is the offering that most excites us. The 1986, a special blend of 60 percent Pinot and 40 percent Chardonnay, aged for 4.5 years *en tirage*, is one of the best American sparklers we've ever tasted: medium to full flavors with classic, almost sweet California fruitiness melded with rich, yeasty highlights and a creamy mouthfeel. We like the 1987 almost as much, and think the 1989 Blanc de Noirs is excellent, too. The regular 1989 Brut, released in 1993, is a beautifully balanced, stellar bottling. Of Iron Horse's still wines, Sauvignon Blanc was an early hit with the public, but phylloxera has, for the time being, all but put an end to production of this varietal here. Chardonnay remains the quality and volume leader of the house's still wines and the 1990 is the best release to date. It displays very crisp acidity and buttery barrel, citrus-apple fruit flavors. It is pleasing, and with no malolactic fermentation in this vintage, the wine should have an inter-esting and long evolution in the bottle. Since 1984, the Cabernet Sauvignon made from Tancer Alexander Valley grapes has been called "Cabernets" and blended with Cabernet Franc. It is of consistently good quality (as in 1988), and occasionally is excellent (as in 1986 and 1989). Now and again, Iron Horse produces a Pinot Noir and special cuvée sparkling wines.

Wines/Varietals: Fumé Blanc ($$), Chardonnay ($$), Cabernets ($$), Vintage Brut ($$), Vintage Blanc de Blancs ($$$), Vintage Blanc de Noirs, Wedding Cuvée ($$$), Vintage Rosé ($$$), Vintage Brut, Late Disgorged ($$$).

Jordan Sparkling Wine Company

150 North St., PO Box 1919
Healdsburg, CA 95448
tel (707) 431-5200; fax (707) 431-5207
Not open to the public; est. 1986

This is the daughter, quite literally, of the Jordan Winery (*see* below). Tom Jordan established this operation with his daughter, Judy, co-owner and general manager of the business. As a separate entity at a separate location, we've given this winery its own entry, though its wines are marketed by Jordan Vineyard & Winery's sales force. The "J" (as both the sparkling wine and the winery are known) Ranch is a 120-acre property in the Russian River Valley purchased by the Jordans in 1989. Eighty acres are valley land and 40 acres are rolling hillside. On the red loam soil of the hills, Jordan is growing 24 acres of small-clustered Pinot Noir clones. On the valley floor, where the alluvial soil is bale loam, 55 acres of Chardonnay and 20 acres of a variety of

Pinot Noir clones are planted. The first harvest here took place in August 1992 and the estate's vineyards will soon provide a steady supply of grapes for sparkling wine production.

Winemaker Oded Shakkled hit a home run with his first release of "J," quickly establishing the Jordan sparkler among the handful of top California *méthode champenoise* sparkling wines. (It ranks among the most expensive domestic sparklers as well, with a $21.50 suggested retail price upon release of the inaugural 1988 bottling; the 1989 bottling was released in mid-1993.) The packaging is handsome, and inside the bottle there's a fine bubbly. Blended of 50 percent Chardonnay and 50 percent Pinot Noir, this wine is somewhat lean, dry, elegant, yeasty, beautifully balanced, and classically fashioned but with lengthy citrus and California fruit flavors. The jury is still out on this very young company, but all of the early indications are most favorable.

Wines/Varietals: J Sparkling Wine ($$$).

Jordan Vineyard & Winery

1474 Alexander Valley Road
Healdsburg, CA 95448
tel. (707) 431-5250; fax (707) 431-5266
Open to the public by appt.; est. 1972

Founded, in the manner of a traditional French chateau, as a family estate, by Tom and Sally Jordan, this winery is set on a high knoll in the Alexander Valley. Tom Jordan, who earlier made a fortune in oil and gas exploration, spared no expense in creating this winery, which boasts a state-of-the-art kitchen and private dining room, and lavishly appointed guest rooms adjacent to the winery. After 20 years, the imposing ochre-colored chateau, with its arched doorways and French dormer windows, has settled into its California setting handsomely. The stone facade, now softened by a covering of vines, is nicely set off by groves of citrus and plane trees, and surrounded by venerable native live oaks. Jordan's 275 acres of vineyard on valley land near the Russian River are planted 150 acres to Cabernet, 45 to Merlot, 5 to Cabernet Franc and 75 to Chardonnay.

Initially the plan here was to produce only a Bordeaux-style red, but in 1979 Jordan added a Chardonnay. Winemaker Rob Davis produces a supple-style Cabernet, softened with Merlot and a little Cabernet Franc. Individual lots age in French Nevers oak for two years before selections are made for the final blend, which is then aged another two years in barrels, employing a mix of new and used oak. The fruit is generously lush with jammy highlights, and structure and balance are consistently good, allowing the wines to age well and often with real distinction, as in 1987 and 1989. The 1979 and the 1985 Jordan Cabernets tasted in 1992 were both delicious in their not overpowering but classy Bordeaux manner. The Chardonnay has prominent oak and good acidity. Year in and year out, Jordan wines are big sellers in restaurants, drinking well young, holding their charm, and reaffirming this winery's position in the public eye as one of the California premium wine industry's solid leaders. Annual production here is about 75,000 cases of exclusively estate-bottled wines, with Cabernet accounting for two-thirds of the output.

Wines/Varietals: Chardonnay, Alexander Valley ($$), Cabernet Sauvignon, Alexander Valley ($$$).

Kenwood Vineyards

9592 Sonoma Highway, PO Box 447
Kenwood, CA 95452
tel. (707) 883-5891; fax (707) 833-1146
Open to the public; est. 1906 (under
current ownership since1970)

Brothers Michael and Martin Lee
(winemaker and vice president, marketing
and promotion, respectively), in partnership with brother-in-law John Sheela (president), have developed Kenwood into one of
Sonoma's top wineries. They conceived of
the winery while in college and subsequently
acquired an old jug winery in Sonoma in
1970. They've now transformed the business into a quality, 165,000-case-a-year operation which offers a full range of varietals
and is especially notable for its Sauvignon
Blanc (44 percent of production). Kenwood
owns 140 acres of Sonoma vineyards and
purchases about two-thirds of its grapes.
The winery is housed in the original Sonoma
barn buildings; the varietal wines produced
here are still made "small lot-style" with a
variety of vineyard designations.

Kenwood made its reputation with a racy,
stylish Sauvignon Blanc that's noted for its
crisp structure and grassy flavors and aromas. In recent vintages, Marty Lee has moderated the grassiness somewhat, and the result is a more elegant, balanced wine, with
richer fruit and rounder flavors. The 1990,
characteristically crisp and fruity, is a sound
purchase. Two vineyard-designated
Chardonnays, Yulupa and Beltane Ranch,
consistently rank among the winery's best
wines, especially the toasty Beltane Ranch.
The Cabernet labeled "Jack London Ranch"
(made from grapes grown at London's vineyard in Glen Ellen) is dark and chocolatey.
Kenwood's "Artists Series" Cabernet
Sauvignon, a blend of the finest barrels of

Cabernet from each particular vintage, is
consistently excellent, and much sought after. It is this winery's best Cabernet: firm-
structured and elegant, well-balanced and
ageworthy. The 1989 Kenwood Cabernets,
in particular, are great. And the Zinfandels
here can be quite good, too. The Jack London Vineyard Zinfandel is a deep, well-
structured Zin with intense but lively fruit
and zesty flavors. Like the winery's regular
Sonoma Zinfandel, the Jack London Zin is
a classic and consistently well-favored bottle
of wine.

*Wines/Varietals: Sauvignon Blanc ($),
Chenin Blanc ($), Chardonnay, Sonoma
Valley ($$), Chardonnay, Beltane Ranch ($$),
Chardonnay, Yulupa Vineyard ($$), White
Zinfandel ($), Vintage White ($), Vintage
Red ($), Cabernet Sauvignon, Sonoma Valley
($$), Cabernet Sauvignon, Jack London Ranch
($$), Cabernet Sauvignon, Artist Series ($$$),
Zinfandel, Sonoma Valley ($), Zinfandel, Jack
London Ranch ($$).*

Kistler Vineyards

2207 Morningside Mountain Drive
Glen Ellen, CA 95442
tel. (707) 938-0168; fax (707) 996-7061
Not open to the public; est. 1979

Kistler Vineyards, producing 17,000 cases
annually, is one of California's small but
bright stars. Tucked up in the Mayacamas
Mountain range, between the Napa and
Sonoma valleys, this winery has 22 acres
planted in Chardonnay and 12 in Cabernet
Sauvignon. Kistler also owns vineyard acre-
age planted mostly to Chardonnay and a
little Pinot Noir in the Russian River Valley.
This concern was founded by Stephen Kistler,
a Stanford graduate who caught the wine

bug working at Ridge Vineyards during his student days.

Kistler has built a formidable reputation for Chardonnay, which winemakers Stephen Kistler and Mark Bixler produce in five versions. All are eagerly sought after and disappear from the market within weeks of shipment; each one is as profound and complex as Chardonnay gets in North America. Perhaps the best known is the Dutton Ranch Chardonnay, from the Green Valley area of the Russian River Valley, which consistently exhibits lush, appley fruit with a generous mantle of oak; it is finely-balanced and ageworthy. The other Kistler Chardonnays are as good. Most concentrated and deep is the Estate Vineyard, produced in a big, well-structured style that can be very long-lived. The Durrell Vineyard Chardonnay, from a vineyard on the edge of Carneros, has superb balance, its creamy fruit suspended in a toasty oak frame. The McCrea Vineyard Chardonnay, also grown at hilltop elevations, is extra ripe and powerful. We were much taken with the 1990 bottlings, especially the Estate Vineyard Chardonnay from Sonoma. Vine Hill Road Vineyard, the newest addition to the Chardonnay list here, was inaugurated with the 1991 vintage. Kistler also makes a concentrated, richly textured Cabernet Sauvignon, notable for its suppleness, but with underlying structure that gives it aging potential.

Wines/Varietals: Chardonnay, Dutton Ranch ($$$), Chardonnay, Durrell Vineyard ($$$), Chardonnay, McCrea Vineyard ($$$), Chardonnay, Estate Vineyard ($$$), Chardonnay, Vine Hill Road ($$$), Cabernet Sauvignon ($$$).

Kunde Estate Winery

10155 Sonoma Hwy., PO Box 639
Kenwood, CA 95452
tel. (707) 833-5501; fax (707) 833-2204
Not open to public; est. 1990

For five generations the Kunde family has lived and worked on the same land in the Sonoma Valley, and for five generations the Kundes have produced award-winning wines. Their winery stayed open during Prohibition but was closed during World War II. Subsequently the vineyards were replanted and farmed, but only in 1990 was a new winery established. Originally planted over 100 years ago, the vineyard here was formerly owned by James Shaw and James Drummond, among the Sonoma Valley's first grape growers. Drummond, recognized as having produced the first varietal Cabernet Sauvignon in the world, imported cuttings from France's Château Margaux and Château Lafite-Rothschild to his Northern California vineyard. Today, Kunde's "Drummond Cabernet Sauvignon" is derived from these vines. All Kunde wines are produced from estate-grown grapes. The 650 acre vineyard here is devoted mainly to Cabernet (40 percent), and Chardonnay (40 percent). The winery produces 34,000 cases annually.

The 1990 Chardonnay Reserve, which underwent complete malolactic fermentation, is 100 percent barrel fermented and aged in French oak. It's crisp, with rich, ripe fruit flavors, complex and well-balanced—a very fine bottling. The 1989 Sonoma Valley Louis Kunde Founder's Reserve Cabernet has comparable star quality and is an impressive first release. It's packed with earthy, tar, and deep currant-like fruit extracts and is surely a wine that will evolve for years to come. Look, too, for the 1990 first release of

237

Kunde Zinfandel from 112-year-old vines. This is a rich, deep wine from fruit grown in the Shaw Vineyard in the Sonoma Valley. It's drinking well now, opening with intense fruit and closing with relatively soft tannins, and it should evolve splendidly. The 1991 Sauvignon Blanc is certainly an enjoyable quaff. It's simple and balanced with light strokes of grass and the soft fruit characterisitic of the varietal. As a newly independent winery, this is one to follow.

Wines/Varietals: Chardonnay ($$), Reserve Chardonnay ($$$), Sauvignon Blanc ($), Claret ($$), Cabernet Sauvignon, Louis Kunde Founder's Reserve ($$), Zinfandel ($$).

La Crema Winery

4940 Ross Road
Sebastopol, CA 95472
(707) 829-2609 or (310) 536-0831; fax (310) 536-9237
Open to the public by appt.; est. 1979

The quest for Burgundian-style Pinot Noir and Chardonnay led to the founding of La Crema Vinera in 1979. When its original owners ran into financial problems in the mid-eighties, a group of investors headed by Jason Korman bought the winery. With the help of consultant Jim Olsen and winemakers Tom Milligan and Dan Goldfield, La Crema is back on its feet and producing 80,000 cases annualy, mostly Chardonnay in various styles and Pinot Noir. The winery, now located in Green Valley near Sebastopol, occupies a remodeled building that was formerly an apple-processing plant. Sixty-eight acres of vineyard here supply up to half of La Crema's production; additional fruit is purchased from cool coastal regions such as Santa Barbara County and Mendocino.

In addition to Chardonnay and Chardonnay Reserve (the latter rich and fairly oaky), La Crema produces "Crème de Tête," which it calls "California's answer to Mâcon." Like Macon, it is moderate in price, but unlike Mâcon it is blended with Sémillon and Chenin Blanc and comes across as slightly sweet. La Crema Pinot Noir is somewhat light but pleasant, and generally a good value. The Reserve Pinot is often a big, deeply colored wine with vivid flavor, though it is not typically Burgundian. La Crema also makes an unusual Sauvignon Blanc that is aged for a time on Chardonnay lees, giving the finish a toasty vanilla flavor with citrus accents. Overall, the wines made here are pleasant, and in the cases of the 1990 Reserve Chardonnay and the 1988 Reserve Chardonnay, they are excellent.

Wines/Varietals: Chardonnay ($), Reserve Chardonnay ($$), Sauvignon Blanc ($), Crème de Tête Select White ($), Pinot Noir ($), Reserve Pinot Noir ($$), Crème de Tête Select Red ($).

Landmark Vineyards

101 Adobe Canyon Road
Kenwood, CA 95452
tel. (707) 833-0053; fax (707) 833-1164
Open to the public; est. 1974

When urbanization forced Landmark Vineyards out of the town of Windsor in northern Sonoma County and several of the initial investors in the operation pulled out, Damaris Ethridge rescued this winery by bankrolling a move in 1990 to a new facility in Kenwood. Now sole proprietor, Ethridge is no stranger to the business of agriculture: her great-great-grandfather, John Deere, invented the steel plow over 150 years ago.

In 1980, winemaker Bill Mabry decided to concentrate on what he does best—Chardonnay. All 17 acres of vineyard in Kenwood and another 56 acres in the Alexander Valley are currently planted to Chardonnay, and with additional grapes purchased from Somoma growers, Landmark is now producing 23,000 cases annually. In recent years—notably 1989, 1990, and 1991—both consistency and quality here have improved. The servicable 1990 Sonoma County Chardonnay exhibits clean, lean, and pleasant characteristics with crisp grapefruit notes. The 1990 Damaris Vineyard Chardonay also has grapefruit aromas, but displays more complexity and a range of toasty and peach flavors. The 1991 Sonoma County Overlook Chardonnay is a quality wine at a good price. It's lively with fairly intense green apple and honey flavors with just a hint of vanilla and oak.

Wines/Varietals: Chardonnay, Sonoma County ($), Chardonnay Damaris Vineyard Reserve ($$), Chardonnay, Two Williams Vineyard ($$).

Laurel Glen Vineyard

PO Box 548
Glen Ellen, CA 95442
tel. (707) 526-3914; fax (707) 526-9801
Not open to the public; est. 1980

Patrick Campbell purchased this mountaintop property above Glen Ellen in 1977. For several years he sold his grapes, but grew increasingly eager to make his own statement with the fruit. A musician with a master's degree in philosophy from Harvard, Campbell is self-taught as a winemaker. This is the reason, perhaps, that his Laurel Glen Cabernet is so distinctive: he makes it according to his own taste, packed with fruit but supple in style, accessible sooner than many Cabs of its stature. Consistently cited as one of the top wineries in California, Laurel Glen makes only Cabernet Sauvignon. The principal wine produced here is selected from top lots, a second wine done in some vintages is known as "Counterpoint," and a blended red made from purchased grapes is labeled "Terra Rosa."

Campbell's 30 acres of vineyard on the east-facing slopes of Sonoma Mountain are planted mostly to Cabernet Sauvignon; there are also small plots of Merlot and Cabernet Franc. The vintner leases another eight acres from neighboring growers. Campbell prefers to work the vineyard himself, producing about 4,000 cases of wine annually. He harvests the grapes at full ripeness to maximize flavor but ferments his wines in open-topped fermenters that allow some of the alcohol to dissipate. Laurel Glen Cabernets are powerful and big but never hot, never excessively tannic. They invariably show the richness of fruit Campbell strives for, without any of the heaviness or extract that can require years to mellow. For all their drinkability within three years or so of their vintage, these wines are also ageworthy. The 1989 Laurel Glen has the dark cherry, blackcurrant fruit typical of the vineyard; already appealing, it has potential that only time in bottle can fully reveal and should last well into the the next century. The bracketing vintages of 1988 and 1990 are even finer examples of Campbell's stellar Cabernet. The thoroughly engaging 1989 Terra Rosa, brimming with lively fruit, is a great value for current drinking.

Wines/Varietals: Cabernet Sauvignon ($$$), Terra Rosa ($), Counterpoint ($$).

Marimar Torres Estate

11400 Graton Road
Sebastopol, CA 94572
tel. (415) 331-7741; fax (415) 331-7804
Open to the pubic by appt.; est. 1992

The Torres family of Spain produces a full range of wines, including some of Europe's finest (Milmanda Chardonnay, Gran Coronas Black Label Cabernet Sauvignon) at their home base in the Penedés region of Catalonia, near Barcelona. The family's American venture in Sonoma County began with the purchase of 56 acres in the cool Green Valley region of the Russian River Valley in 1983. The first vines, Chardonnay, were planted here in 1986 and the first wine was made in 1989. In 1993, the state-of-the-art winery in the Sonoma-Green Valley was officially opened. Though Marimar Torres credits her late father Don Miguel as the driving force behind the project, it is she who conceived it and made it happen. Her brother, Miguel, Jr., now head of the Torres firm and one of Europe's best known viticulturalists, also provided his expertise. The winery's Don Miguel Vineyard, 30 acres of Chardonnay, 17 of Pinot Noir, and a small plot of Parellada, a white variety native to Catalonia, is planted and cultivated using the the latest techniques: dense planting of 2,000 vines to the acre, close to the ground on open trellising for maximum ripening.

The first Marimar Torres Estate Chardonnay, made by winemaker Max Gasiewicz in 1989, is excellent, with ripe fruit and crisp acidity nicely rounded with buttery oak flavors. The 1990 shows firmer structure and is fuller in flavor, with fine potential for aging. Barrel fermented, the wine undergoes 100 percent malolactic fermentation, which gives it appealing creaminess and finesse. Produced only from estate grapes, it promises to be among a select group of California Chardonnays that exhibit well-defined character and signature of place. We were highly impressed by the 1991 Chardonnay, a medium-bodied, beautifully balanced wine drinking well young, but with the fruit and acidity to evolve and drink well for years. With the 1992 vintage Marimar Torres will release its first Pinot Noir. Now producing around 5,000 cases annually, the winery's goal is to reach 15,000.

Wines/Varietals: Estate Chardonnay ($$).

Matanzas Creek Winery

6097 Bennett Valley Road
Santa Rosa, CA 95401
tel. (707) 528-6464; fax (707) 571-0156
Open to the public; est. 1978

You've got to admire Sandra MacIver's vision and dedication. As early as 1971 she was thinking about how to produce the finest wine in California. By 1975 she was planting vineyards. In 1978 she established her winery, and a year later released her first wines. Since then, year in and year out, Matanzas Creek has proven its commitment to producing better and better wines, sparing no effort or expense in the process. Blended from Matanzas Creek's own grapes and those purchased from Sonoma suppliers with distinctively complementary vineyards, this winery's Sauvignon Blanc is superb (28 percent of production), its Chardonnay very good (56 percent) and its Merlot world class (16 percent). Sandra MacIver now produces 32,000 cases annually and she doesn't just talk about making premium wine, she delivers.

Matanzas Creek's Merlots are among the handful that are a class apart from the many sound efforts being produced in California and Washington State. The 1989 Merlot is a notable achievement. Critical consensus leaves no doubt that this offering is among the very top (if not *the* top) Merlots produced in America. Aged 17 months in French oak, this wine is drinking well in its youth but will evolve nicely for another decade. Very "French" with tobacco, cedar, berries, cherry, and mint overtones, it is lively, complex, and elegant. Now the bad news: only 6,000 cases are produced. The 1990 Sauvignon Blanc—partially barrel fermented and partially aged in new French oak—is outstanding, too: elegant with floral and fruity (apple, fig, citrus) character.

Wines/Varietals: Chardonnay Sonoma County ($$), Sauvignon Blanc Sonoma County ($$), Merlot Sonoma County ($$$).

The Merry Vintners
3339 Hartman Road
Santa Rosa, CA 95401
tel. (707) 526-4441
Open to the public by appt.; est. 1984

Meredith ("Merry") Edwards was winemaker at such top properties as Mount Eden and Matanzas Creek before fulfilling the long-held dream of starting her own label. She earlier earned a fine reputation for producing rich, powerful Chardonnays, and now concentrates exclusively on this variety (producing a regular bottling and a Reserve) here at The Merry Vintners, her small winery in the Russian River area. Working with purchased grapes, Merry Vintners produces between 5,000 and 7,000 cases of Chardonnay annually. (Edwards keeps herself fully occupied by directing a large wine program for Bronco Wine Company's Domaine Laurier and Grand Cru, as well as by consulting for the new King Estate in Oregon's Willamette Valley.)

Edward's 1989 Reserve is one of the better Chardonnays from that vintage, well-balanced and more concentrated in flavor than most, though rather strongly vegetal. Like most of her Reserves, this one can be expected to age comfortably for at least five years, probably longer. The 1990 Private Reserve is one of the very best of the year, far superior even to the 1989.

Wines/Varietals: Chardonnay, Sonoma County ($$), Chardonnay, Signature Reserve ($$).

Murphy-Goode Estate Winery
4001 Hwy. 128, PO Box 158
Geyserville, CA 95441
tel. (707) 431-7644; fax (707) 431-8640
Open to the public; est. 1985

Tim Murphy and Dale Goode, both already recognized as successful and innovative grape growers in Sonoma County, pooled their resources in 1980. Tim owned the 200-acre Murphy ranch; Dale was vineyard manager for Alexander Valley Vineyards and Hoot Owl Creek Vineyards. By 1984 Murphy and Goode were joined by Dave Ready, founder and president of Winery Associates. Ready's marketing know-how provided the final, essential piece of the puzzle and led to the total team involvement, from planting to pouring, that prevails here today. Quality and innovation are the watchwords at Murphy-Goode. The vineyard's state-of-the-art water management system, which includes neutron probes to measure the soil's moisture content and computer-monitored water allocation is the most sophisticated in Sonoma County. The vineyards are planted in Sauvignon Blanc (70 acres), Pinot Blanc (15 acres), Chardonnay (50 acres), Cabernet Sauvignon (29 acres), and Merlot (4.5 acres).

The 1990 Chardonnay captures the essence of the Murphy-Goode winemaking philosophy: it has distinctive fruit flavors—pineapple, pear, melon—enhanced by French oak and culminating in a long, smooth finish. In short, it's a medium-weight fruity-style wine that delivers good value. Winemaker Christina Benz is doing a good job with Fumé Blanc, which also delivers good value here, especially in 1990 and 1991. The regular 1991 Alexander Valley Fumé Blanc has good balance and ripe, melony flavors with rich honey and peach highlights and with a light dose of typical varietal grass and vegetal tones. The 1991 barrel fermented Reserve Fumé Blanc is a big, young wine with lots of varietal character, ripe tropical fruit and vanillin flavors, and toasty oak barrel; this good wine finishes long and satisfyingly. Among the Cabs, we thoroughly enjoyed the 1989 Alexander Valley with its deep, dark color, beautiful Cabernet nose with hints of violets, and earthy, big body packed with deep hillside grape flavors of blackberries, blueberries, and currants accented with some chocolate and oaky components. Its an interesting wine that we intend to follow in coming years.

Wines/Varietals: Fumé Blanc ($), Reserve Fumé Blanc ($$), Chardonnay ($$), Pinot Blanc ($$), Merlot ($$), Cabernet Sauvignon ($$), Goode & Ready Cabernet Sauvignon ($).

Nalle Winery

PO Box 454
Healdsburg, CA 95448
tel. (707) 433-1040; fax (707) 433-6062
Not open to the public; est. 1984

Doug Nalle was winemaker at Quivira Vineyards in the Dry Creek Valley of Sonoma County when he began making Zinfandel under his own label (He'd previously worked at Chateau Souverain and Balverne Winery). An honest-to-goodness family winery, owned and operated by Doug and his wife, Lee—they're helped out by their adolescent sons when the boys are not in school or playing baseball—Nalle produces some 2,500 cases a year. The family lives at the winery, which was completed in 1990.

Known as a Zinfandel specialist, Nalle owns no vineyards of his own but buys top-grade grapes from older vines with low yields to produce his intensely concentrated, flavorful wines. His winemaking techniques are designed to encourage as much infusion of the grape character into the wine as possible. He uses open-top fermenters and afterwards ages his wines in oak for up to two years. The 1990 Zinfandel, a rich, berryish bottle, will take some time to release its elegant flavors. Nalle now also produces a small quantity of Cabernet Sauvignon.

Wines/Varietals: Zinfandel ($$), Cabernet Sauvignon ($$).

Pedroncelli Winery

1220 Canyon Road
Geyserville, CA 95441
tel. (707) 857-3531; fax (707) 857-3812
Open to the public by appt.; est. 1904

Italian immigrant John Pedroncelli, Sr. purchased 90 acres of Sonoma County land with an exisiting winery on the property in 1927. Throughout Prohibition he sold field-mixed grapes (a jumble of grape varieties planted to each plot) to home winemakers, and following Repeal he started selling in bulk to wineries and distributors. Over the decades, production here has increased to the current 100,000 cases, and this family winery's reputation for good value has grown solid under present owners Jim and John Pedroncelli. The vineyard here, increased in size to 110 acres, is planted mostly to Zinfandel and Cabernet Sauvignon. Purchased grapes (60 percent) all come from within a ten mile radius of the home ranch.

Production here is reliable—plenty of clean, tasty wines are turned out at bottom-dollar prices. We've tasted through the line on several occasions and what we've liked best is the 1990 Dry Creek Valley Chardonnay, fairly light and simple in style and promising more on the nose than the body delivers, but pleasant. We also really liked the 1989 Sonoma County Merlot, medium light with sweet, soft fruit, and nice balance—a pleasant experience. The winery is proudest of its Dry Creek Valley Zinfandel vineyards and wine, which are typical of the area's Zins. The 1990 is a fine one, though thoroughly tannic in its youth. The Pedroncelli family are good, traditional farmers, and we applaud their efforts, and their easy-on-the-pocketbook pricing.

Wines/Varietals: Chardonnay, Dry Creek Valley ($$), Fumé Blanc, Dry Creek Valley ($), Dry Chenin Blanc, Sonoma County ($), White Zinfandel, Sonoma County ($), White Riesling, Sonoma County ($), Zinfandel Rosé, Sonoma County ($), Gamay Beaujolais, Sonoma County ($), Pinot Noir, Dry Creek Valley ($), Zinfandel, Dry Creek Valley ($),

Merlot, Sonoma County ($$), Cabernet Sauvignon, Dry Creek Valley ($$).

Pepperwood Springs Vineyard

1200 Holmes Ranch Road, PO Box 2
Philo, CA 95466
tel. (707) 895-2920
Open to the public by appt.; est. 1981

Gary and Phyllis Kaliher took over Pepperwood Springs in 1987, a few years after its founder, Larry Parsons, died in an automobile accident. (Parsons, who was blind, produced Pinot Noirs which bore distinctive labels printed in Braille). The Kalihers' seven Anderson Valley acres are currently planted equally to Chardonnay and Pinot Noir. Additional grapes are purchased (30 percent) to supply production totaling only 800 cases annually.

Pepperwood Springs' 1990 Pinot Noir caught our attention. It's well-balanced with plenty of deep Anderson Valley fruit. The 1991 Vidmar Vineyards Pinot Noir confirms that this winery is headed in the right direction. Here's another quality Anderson Valley Pinot Noir that bodes well not only for the winery where it is made, but for the region in general.

Wines/Varietals: Chardonnay ($$), Pinot Noir, Estate Bottled ($$), Pinot Noir, Vidmar Vineyard ($$).

Peter McCoy Vineyards

17050 Hwy. 128
Calistoga, CA 94515
tel. (707) 942-0515
Not open to the public; est. 1984

What there is to report about this superb "weekend winery" in Sonoma's Knights

Valley is one sensational Chardonnay. San Francisco businessman Peter McCoy helped out a while at a friend's winery, and then decided he wanted one of his own—a country place where he and his family could spend weekends. So he bought a 15-acre parcel of land and completely replanted it in 1980. Today McCoy's excellent Clos les Pierres vineyard provides the fruit for 1,000 to 2,000 cases of Chardonnay a year.

McCoy follows old-fashioned winemaking practices, barrel-fermenting 100 percent of his wine (20 percent new oak each year) and keeping intervention to a minimum. He looks to suffuse his Chard with as much fruit as possible; with grapes from the vineyard here this approach results in a somewhat minerally-flinty Chablis-style wine. The 1988 Clos Les Pierres Chardonnay is superb: clean and smooth with lush fruit flavors. The 1990 is another star. Both bottles are reasonably priced.

Wines/Varietals: Chardonnay ($$).

Peter Michael
12400 Ida Clayton Road
Calistoga, CA 94515
tel. (707) 942-4459; fax (707) 942-0209
Not open to the public; est. 1987

This 6,800-case winery (its capacity is 10,000-12,000 cases) tends to go to extremes in the pursuit of "quality, quality, quality." The focus here is on small lots of hand-crafted wines from select mountain vineyards. London-born Sir Peter and Lady Michael own 60 acres of vineyards, including property in Sonoma's Knights Valley and the Gauer Ranch in the Alexander Valley. The winery buys in 60 percent of its grapes, from such top sources as the Liparita

Vineyard Company in the heart of the Howell Mountain area. General Manager Bill Vyenielo describes Peter Michael's winemaking as "neo-classical—a marriage between old world tradition and the most advanced vineyard and cellar practices." Many vintners say that, but here they mean it. For example, this winery has separate sections for producing whites and reds, and a special barrel fermentation room, in which temperature and humidity are carefully controlled. Peter Michael's red wines are fined with egg whites, then bottled unfiltered; its whites receive neither heat nor cold stabilization and only the mildest filtration. Plenty of barrel fermentation takes place here in a mix of Allier, Vosges, Tronçais, and Nevers French oak barrels. Wild yeasts are also employed in the winemaking process.

They are making French-style wines here, which probably explains why they give all their wines French names. There are three Chardonnays currently in production: Mon Plaisir, Clos du Ciel and Cuvée Indigène. All are distinctive and first-rate. Mon Plaisir grapes come from a six-acre block on the Gauer Ranch in the Alexander Valley. The 1990, a medium-weight wine, shows honey-roasted nuts and citrus flavors with some softer apple and pear tones. The Clos du Ciel, from Howell Mountain fruit, is a blend of two Chardonnay clones. The inaugural 1990 is striking, with orange blossom and cinnamon-apple aromatics with vanillin, oak, and lemon oil components. Also noteworthy is the 1991 L'Après Midi Sauvignon Blanc, a firm, multi-dimensional, barrel fermented wine (again, from Howell Mountain grapes) with mineral elements and almost wild flower fragrence over melon and honey tones with plenty of barrel vanillin (very sweet on the nose) and oak gained through 9 months of aging. Perhaps it is the

Howell Mountain grapes, but this is not a typically-flavored Sauvignon Blanc. The impressive 1990 has more lemon-lime and melon flavors; the 1991 may evolve. Les Pavots is Peter Michael's estate-grown Cabernet Sauvignon from the volcanic and stoney Les Pavots (The Poppies) Vineyard high on the slopes of Mount St. Helena overlooking Knights Valley. This deeply concentrated wine shows black cherries, cedar and tobacco plus notes of anise and chocolate. It is impressive in 1988, its first release, and again so in 1989. The 1989 is rich, leathery, and has an herbal nose with clear hints of sweet cherry fruit that carries through in a firmly and harmoniously structured medium-big wine showing lots of tannins. This wine should be a delight to drink in a few years.

Wines/Varietals: Chardonnay, Mon Plaisir, Sonoma ($$$), Chardonnay, Clos du Ciel, Howell Mountain ($$$), Chardonnay, Cuvée Indigène ($$$), Sauvignon Blanc, L'Après Midi, Howell Mountain ($$), Cabernet Sauvignon, Les Pavots, Knights Valley ($$$).

tablish a new high-end standard for quality. The Remy-Cointreau Group now owns Piper-Heidsieck and appears to be committed to the Sonoma winery, where only vintage-dated, *méthode champenoise* sparkling wines are produced.

Piper Sonoma was a forerunner in developing Pinot Meunier, the third of the classic Champagne grapes, in Sonoma County. It introduced the grapes in the 1987 Blanc de Noirs. Piper Sonoma owns about 46 acres of vineyards, and so purchases additional grapes to supplement estate-grown fruit. Now integral to this operation's winemaking process is a French oak program consisting of ten 1,600-gallon Foudres (huge wooden barrel-like vats) and two-hundred-and-fifty 57-gallon French oak barrels that have been incorporated to introduce added complexity to the wine. The 1988 Brut (76 percent Pinot Noir, 14 percent Chardonnay, and 10 percent Pinot Blanc) is a clean and fruity bubbly with some slight citrus and some slight cherry aroma highlights. This vintage

Piper Sonoma
11447 Old Redwood Hwy., PO Box 309
Healdsburg, CA 95448
tel. (707) 433-8843; fax (707) 433-6314
Open to the public; est. 1980

France's Piper-Heidsieck Champagne founded Piper Sonoma in 1980 along the successful lines of Domaine Chandon: the winery as tourist center. Since then Piper Sonoma has produced good sparkling wines, especially lately, and has itself inspired a host of European investments in, and ties to, American sparkling wineries. Piper and the newcomers have collectively helped to esis about as good a sparkler as Piper has yet made. The Brut currently accounts for 71 percent of production. Co-winemakers Chris Markell and Rob McNeil are justifiably proud of their 1988 Blanc de Noirs (95 percent Pinot Noir, 5 percent Pinot Meunier) as well. It is creamy and has more pronounced cherry-pop flavors than the regular Brut, but it is clearly its sibling. The Blanc de Noirs accounts for 24 percent of production here.

Wines/Varietals: Brut ($$), Blanc de Noirs ($$), Brut Reserve ($$$), Tête de Cuvée ($$$).

Preston Vineyards

9282 West Dry Creek Road
Healdsburg, CA 95448
tel. (707) 433-3372; fax (707) 433-5307
Open to the public; est. 1975

Preston Vineyards is one of the small family-owned wine estates that spurred the revitalization of Sonoma in the early seventies. In 1973, Susan and Lou Preston bought a prune and pear ranch in Dry Creek Valley. They expanded a venerable Zinfandel vineyard on the property and added Sauvignon Blanc, Chenin Blanc, Cabernet Sauvignon, and Syrah. Today the family's 125-acre vineyard is planted to 16 varieties, including Sémillon, Merlot, Petite Sirah, and Barbera Beginning in 1988, Lou Preston and winemaker Kevin Hamel made a major commitment to Rhône-style wines with additional plantings of Syrah and Petite Sirah, as well as Grenache, Mourvèdre, Cinsault, Viognier, Marsanne, and Carignane. Some 30,000 cases of wine are now produced here annually, all estate-grown.

Initially, Preston Vineyards was best known for its Zinfandel and Sauvignon Blanc, and helped to establish Dry Creek Valley's reputation as a premier growing area for both these varieties. Preston Zinfandel has the typically firm, peppery character of the best Dry Creek Zins; the 1989 and 1990 are excellent examples. The winery's dry, crisp, nicely balanced Cuvée de Fumé is a blend of Sauvignon Blanc, Sémillon, and a splash of Chenin Blanc. Preston is also noted for its Dry Chenin Blanc, made in a lively style with brisk, melon-and-citrus fruit, a well-regarded Gamay Beaujolais, and a solid, full-flavored Barbera. In addition to Marsanne and Viognier, Rhône-style whites that show considerable promise, the Prestons produce a fruity blended red intended for early drinking called "Faux-Castel," and a more ageworthy blend of Syrah and Petite Sirah labeled "Sirah-Syrah." Well-structured and packed with flavor, the 1990 Syrah needs a couple of years in bottle to round off its angles. More Rhône-style wines will be released in the future. In the meantime, don't miss the intriguing dessert white made here. Known as "Muscat Brûlée," it is made from Muscat Canelli grapes.

Wines/Varietals: Cuvée de Fumé ($), Dry Chenin Blanc ($), Viognier ($$$), Cabernet Sauvignon ($$), Syrah ($$), Sirah-Syrah ($$), Faux-Castel ($), Barbera ($$), Muscat Brûlée ($$), Marsanne ($$), Zinfandel ($$).

Quivira Vineyards

4900 West Dry Creek Road
Healdsburg, CA 95448
tel. (707) 431-8333; fax (707) 431-1664
Open to the public; est. 1981

The name comes from a sixteenth-century legend claiming the existence of a sophisticated and wealthy kingdom in the New World. Europeans searched for "Quivira" for 200 years and eventually gave the name to the Northern California region now better known as Sonoma County. Holly and Henry Wendt's Quivira Vineyards is a 90-acre estate in Sonoma's Dry Creek Valley. On their hillside vineyards, the Wendts grow Zinfandel, Petite Sirah, and Cabernet Sauvignon. They've planted valley floor vineyards here to Sauvignon Blanc, Sémillon, Merlot, Cabernet Franc, Grenache, Mourvèdre, and Syrah, as well as additional Petite Sirah and Cabernet Sauvignon. With a total of 76 acres currently under vine, and a supplement of up to 10 percent purchased grapes, Quivira produces 20,000 cases annually. It's hoped for the future that all wines produced here will come exclusively from the estate vineyard.

The state-of-the-art winery here, built in 1987, houses stainless-steel, temperature-controlled tanks with a capacity of 35,550 gallons, and 400 French oak barrels. Quivira is committed to growing only those grape varieties proven to thrive in the Dry Creek Valley, irrespective of market pressures. Grady Wann, the winemaker, embraces the philosophy of emphasizing the importance of fruit character over winemaking techniques in producing quality wines. Zinfandel and Sauvignon Blanc helped put this winery on the map (the Zin was made by Doug Nalle until 1989). The 1990 Sauvignon Blanc is a sound one. A blend with 22 percent Sémillon, it is partially barrel fermented and features figs, melon, and spicy vanilla oak as dominate flavors. The 1990 Zin is very good, too: elegant and firm with dark berry flavors and vanilla aromas. In 1987 this winery began releasing a Cabernet, which has since evolved into "Cabernet Cuvée," a more nearly equal blend of

Cabernet Sauvignon and Cabernet Franc. The 1989 Cabernet Cuvée Dry Creek is Quivira's best release yet, and it is likely to keep with age.

Wines/Varietals: Sauvignon Blanc ($), Zinfandel ($$), Cabernet Cuvée ($$).

Rabbit Ridge Vineyards
3291 Westside Road
Healdsburg, CA 95448
tel. (707) 431-7128
Open to the public; est. 1985

Erich Russell and Darryl Simmons own this 45-acre Russian River Valley vineyard and winery. Russell, an established winemaker who became Belvedere Winery's head enologist in 1988, began developing the vineyard here in the early 1980s with the help of his wife, Catherine. For the first few years he produced only small quantities of varietals under the Rabbit Ridge label, but by 1989, things here were really, well, hopping. Plantings are now divided among Chardonnay (25 percent), Cabernet

Sauvignon (25 percent), Cabernet Franc (20 percent), Sauvignon Blanc (20 percent), and Zinfandel (10 percent). Russell purchases additional grapes (85 percent) to achieve an annual production of 30,000 cases.

The wines here are coming on strong, led by the Chardonnay, which comes in Sonoma County and Rabbit Ridge Vineyard bottlings. These wines are richly fruity with a moderate toasty oak dimension. We recommend the Rabbit Ridge version (it's a tad more complex) in the 1990 and 1991 vintages. The Zinfandel, generally quite good, comes from estate grapes or from other Russian River Valley vineyards. The Cabernet Sauvignon is more than sound and a good value. Two good blended wines have been added to the line here: "Mystique," a white meritage and "Allure," a Rhône-style red. In 1990 Rabbit Ridge produced 600 cases of a Sonoma County Petite Sirah, which is drinking well young with grapey, plummy full flavors. The winery has used the "Clairvaux" and "Meadow Glen " labels for non-estate wines, such as Merlot and Sauvignon Blanc.

Wines/Varietals: Chardonnay, Sonoma ($$), Chardonnay, Rabbit Ridge Vineyard ($$), Mystique ($), Zinfandel ($), Cabernet Sauvignon ($$), Petite Sirah, Sonoma ($), Allure ($), Oddux Red California Reserve ($$).

A. Rafanelli Winery

4685 West Dry Creek Road
Healdsburg, CA 95448
tel. (707) 433-1385
Open to the public by appt.; est. 1938 (in continuous operation since 1974)

Long-time grower David Rafanelli makes two highly regarded red wines: Cabernet Sauvignon and Zinfandel. Both are estate-grown on 50 acres in Sonoma's Dry Creek Valley (18 acres of Zinfandel, 15 of Cabernet Sauvignon, and 5 of Merlot). Located midway between Healdsburg and the Warm Springs Dam on a sunny, non-irrigated hillside that provides stress for the vines, the Zinfandel vineyards yield rich, concentrated fruit. Rafanelli purchases about 5 percent additional fruit when needed, to supply average annual production of 7,500 cases.

The wines here, marked by rugged intensity, with ripe fruit and rich texture, immediately speak of generous California sun. These days Rafanelli seems to be sending these big wines out into the world unfiltered. The Zinfandel is ripe, powerful, and concentrated, full of dark berry fruit that unfailingly enchants lovers of big Zins. The 1989 and 1990, both very fine, are recommended; they are round and spicy with great balance and a tight, raspberry-flavored core. The Cabernet Sauvignon, blended with a little Merlot, shows a bit more restraint but still has that rustic character that we associate with flavorful old-style California reds.

Wines/Varietals: Cabernet Sauvignon ($$), Zinfandel ($$).

Ravenswood

18701 Gehricke Road
Sonoma, CA 95476
tel. (707) 938-1960; fax (707) 938-9459
Open to the public; est. 1976

Although Ravenswood's little 13-acre vineyard grows only Chardonnay (75 percent) and Merlot (25 percent), 65 percent of the 40,000 case annual production here is Zinfandel. Co-owner/winemaker Joel Peterson got his start in the wine business in the early 1970s as an apprentice for Joseph

An Elegantly Orchestrated Hotel
Nestled among the day to evening excitement of San Francisco's
Opera, Ballet, Symphony and dynamic Civic Center.

Classically Designed Accommodations * Complete Guest Services
Specially Selected Amenities * Personalized Attention to Detail
Cocktails & Dining in the Act IV Lounge * Romantic Weekend Packages

333 Fulton St., San Francisco, CA 94102 * 415-863-8400 Toll Free 1-800/325-2708

"La Colombe d'Or is Houston's only European Chateau. Dine in romantic elegance in the nationally acclaimed innovative French restaurant or enjoy a more intimate experience in your own private dining room. La Colombe d'Or is a member of the prestigious Relais & Chateaux."

LA COLOMBE D'OR
HOTEL AND RESTAURANT

3410 Montrose Boulevard
Houston, Texas 77006
Tel: (713) 524-7999
Fax: (713) 524-8923

Fringale
RESTAURANT

From the Southwest of France

FOR LUNCH OR DINNER

**570 FOURTH STREET ■ SAN FRANCISCO ■ 94107
TEL ■ 415 • 543 • 0573 ■ FAX ■ 415 • 905 • 0317**

Gruet Winery
8400 Pam American Fwy,
N. E. Albuquerque
New Mexico 87109

TASTING HOURS:
10 AM - 5 PM
BY APPOINTMENT ON WEEKEND
505.344.4453

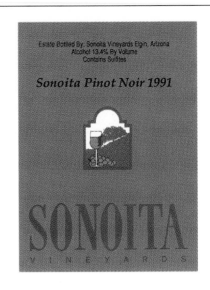

Sonoita Vineyards
Elgin, Arizona
602.455.5893

Bodegas de Santo Tomas,
S.A. de C.V.
Calle Miramar 666
Ensenada, B.C.
011-52-667-83333

PHEASANT RIDGE

TEXAS
CABERNET SAUVIGNON
10th Anniversary
1989

Produced & Bottled by Pheasant Ridge Winery, Lubbock, Texas

Open to the public the second
Saturday of the Month or by
appointment.
Enjoy Complimentary wines at the
picnic tables under the Arbor.
Rt. 3, Box 191
Lubbock, Texas 79401
806.746.6033

Swan of Zinfandel fame. (Swan, who died in 1989, made huge, legendary Zinfandels at his small winery in the 1970s.) By 1976, Peterson was producing 500 cases of his own Zinfandel under the Ravenswood label from rented space in Swan's winery. He entered into partnership with a number of investors in 1987, and moved to his current location.

The "Vintner's Blend" Zinfandel is the volume leader here. Notably strong in 1989, a Cabernet blend called "Pickberry" is the house's best Cab-based wine. For all the emphasis put on Zinfandel here, the wine that Peterson believes best represents Ravenswood's style is its 1989 Sangiacomo Merlot. The quality is indeed outstanding in a rough-and-tumble way, with lots of deep, dark, but dynamic fruit and cedar and spice overtones. For us, though, the 1990 Napa Valley Dickerson Zinfandel still wins all the prizes. Its a superb Zin along big, tannic, flavorful lines with plenty of attractive berry and cherry flavors harmoniously composed. Nor will we soon forget the luscious fruit of Ravenswood's 1989 Zinfandel.

Wines/Varietals: Chardonnay ($$), Zinfandel, Vintner's Blend ($), Zinfandel, Sonoma County ($$), Zinfandel, Dickerson ($$), Merlot, Vintner's Blend ($), Merlot, Sonoma County ($$), Merlot, Sangiacomo Vineyard ($$$), Cabernet Sauvignon, Sonoma County ($$), Cabernet Sauvignon, Gregory ($$), Pickberry Vineyards Proprietary Red ($$$).

Robert Stemmler Winery

3805 Lambert Bridge Road
Healdsburg, CA 95448
tel. (707) 433-6334; fax (707) 433-1531
Open to the public; est. 1977

A native of Germany, Robert Stemmler brought his winemaking skills to the U.S.,

working first for several big-name California wineries including Inglenook, Simi, and Charles Krug. In 1977 he established his own concern with partner Trumbell Webb Kelly. This winery's good reputation, especially for Pinot Noirs, has continued to grow over the years; production is now up to 10,000 cases. In 1988, Stemmler entered into a joint-venture agreement with Racke USA, owner of Buena Vista winery. As a result, all of Stemmler's Pinot Noir, now the only varietal he makes, are produced at Buena Vista in Carneros and marketed exclusively by Racke.

We remember well Robert Stemmler's big, rich Pinots of the mid-1980s: these were wines that provided a reassuring direction for California Pinot Noir. Today, Stemmler's wines are good and solid, full of authentic Pinot Noir flavors. We admire the 1988, the most recent vintage we've tasted.

Wines/Varietals: Pinot Noir, Sonoma County ($$$).

Rochioli Vineyards & Winery

6192 Westside Road
Healdsburg, CA 95448
tel. (707) 433-2305
Open to the public; est. 1982 (vineyard planted in 1933)

The Rochioli family began tending vineyards in the 1930s, selling the grapes from vines planted in the 19th century to a local co-op for bulk wine production. Today Joe Rochioli and his son, Tom, who is the winemaker here, bottle about 6,000 cases of wine annually from their 100 acres of Sonoma vineyards planted to Sauvignon Blanc, Chardonnay, Pinot Noir, and some Cabernet Sauvignon. The family's gravelly benchland and rolling hillside vineyards in the Russian River Valley were some of the first in the county to be devoted to varietal plantings. A small amount of Gewürztraminer, made from purchased grapes, currently augments the Rochioli line of estate-grown wines.

As could be expected, this seasoned farming family doesn't believe in fiddling with what the vineyard provides. Rochioli Vineyards & Winery follows traditional winemaking practices without ignoring modern technology in its effort to produce wines of distinct character and style that speak of their native vineyards. And it is certainly succeeding, especially with Pinot Noir. The 1989 Reserve, luscious with deep cherry and oak flavors, has rose petal and vanilla accents. The 1990 Chardonnay is easily the winery's best ever. It's in the full-bodied style with enough pear, spice, and oak flavor complexities to prove satisfying for years. The 1991 is a bit more lean and acidic but could evolve beyond its already good character. Also strong in 1990 is the Sauvignon Blanc, produced from old vines. This bottle belongs to the class of wines containing leafy, herbal varietal characteristics which overshadow tropical fruit and melon. It also has toasty vanilla accents from barrel aging. The fine 1991 is well-balanced with classic grassiness and melon character in good balance.

Wines/Varietals: Estate Chardonnay ($$), Estate Sauvignon Blanc ($), Estate Sauvignon Blanc, Reserve ($$), Gewürztraminer ($), Estate Pinot Noir ($$), Estate Pinot Noir, Reserve ($$$), Estate Cabernet Sauvignon, Reserve ($$).

Rodney Strong Vineyards

11455 Old Redwood Hwy. (Healdsburg),
PO Box 368
Windsor, CA 95492
tel. (707) 431-1533; fax (707) 433-8635
Open to the public; est. 1959

Rod Strong, an ex-Broadway hoofer, is an important player in California's modern wine industry. He started his first winery in the basement of his Tiburon home in Marin County. When demand outpaced production capabilities there, he headed for Sonoma County, where he purchased vineyards in several appellations. In the 1980s the winery had a series of big corporate owners and in 1989 was purchased by the Kleins, a third-generation California agricultural family. The winemaker here today is Rick Sayre; Strong remains actively involved in marketing the wines. Drawing on 1,200 acres of estate vineyard planted in the cool Russian River Valley, as well as grapes purchased from other Sonoma County growers, Rodney Strong Vineyards produces 130,000 cases annually, about 85,000 cases under the vineyard's own label and additional cases under the "Windsor Vineyards" mail order label.

The vineyard-designated Rodney Strong varietals are generally good to excellent, particularly the crisp Chalk Hill Chardonnay and the River East Pinot Noir (the 1990 Pinot is supple but well-structured with smokey flavors). This winery is perhaps best known for its Alexander Crown Vineyard Cabernet Sauvignon, which comes from a prized hilltop vineyard in the Alexander Valley. The Sauvignon Blanc comes from Charlotte's Home Vineyard—Charlotte is Rod's wife—on the banks of the Russian River. The River West Old Vines Zinfandel is intense, tannic and ripe. Both the Sonoma

County Cabernet Sauvignon and Chardonnay are consistently good, and good values. In outstanding years, the winery also produces a Reserve Cabernet and a Reserve Chardonnay.

Wines/Varietals: Chardonnay, Sonoma County ($), Chardonnay, Chalk Hill Vineyard ($$), Sauvignon Blanc, Charlotte's Home Vineyard ($), Gewürztraminer ($), Cabernet Sauvignon, Sonoma County ($), Cabernet Sauvignon, Alexander's Crown Vineyard ($$), Pinot Noir, River East Vineyard ($$), Old Vines Zinfandel, River West ($$).

Sonoma Chardonnay. The comparatively small quantities of Cabernet Sauvignon made here are usually quality efforts; the 1989 Reserve Cab is noteworthy.

Wines/Varietals: Chardonnay, California ($), Chardonnay, Barrel Select Estate Bottled ($$), Gewürztraminer, Estate Bottled ($), Muscat Canelli, Sonoma Valley ($), Zinfandel, Sonoma Valley ($), Merlot, Sonoma Valley Estate Bottled ($$), Merlot, Sonoma Valley Reserve ($$$), Cabernet Sauvignon, Sonoma Valley ($), Cabernet Sauvignon, Sonoma Valley Reserve ($$$).

St. Francis Winery
8450 Sonoma Highway
Kenwood, CA 95452
tel. (707) 833-4666; fax (707) 833-6534
Open to the public; est.1979

Joseph Martin and Lloyd Canton are the partners behind this 90-acre vineyard in Kenwood, just across the road from Chateau St. Jean. Merlot (68 acres) and Chardonnay (22 acres) are supplemented with additional purchased grapes (65 percent), to bring annual production here to the 42,000 case level.

The Merlots made here, consistently good since the 1983 vintage, are now very good. They are 100 percent varietal, aged in both French and American oak. The 1989 Merlot Reserve, a lush and intense offering bursting with plum and spice flavor components, is certainly the top St. Francis wine we've tasted. The moderately sweet Gewürztraminer may not be quite up to the Merlot, but it's respectable. St. Francis lately seems on track to produce big, rich, buttery Chardonnays of the first rank to go along with its fine reds. We recommend the 1990

Schug Carneros Estate Winery
602 Bonneau Road
Sonoma, CA 95476
tel. (707) 939-9363 or (707) 939-9365;
fax (707) 939-9364
Open to the public; est. 1980

German-born Walter and Gertrude Schug are both descendents of well-known German winemaking families. In California, Walter earned recognition during the 1970s as vice president and winemaker at Joseph Phelps Vineyards. The 38-acre hilltop estate

winery the Schugs now own and operate in Carneros is the realization of Walter's life-long dream. Two-thirds of Schug Carnero's Estate Winery's vineyards are planted to Chardonnay; the remaining third is devoted to Pinot Noir, referred to by Schug as "the grape from Hell." This winery purchases 25 percent of its fruit exclusively from Carneros vineyards to meet the requirements of an-nual production of 8,000-10,000 cases.

Minimal handling, no filtering, and the use of a rotary fermenter (one of only a small number in America) are the techniques Schug employs to produce his Pinot Noir. The 1988 Carneros Pinot Noir is fine. The Pinot Noir, in general, has distinction, especially the Reserve. Chardonnay from the Beckstoffer Vineyard is done in a toasty, earthy, deep green fruit style. Barrel fer-mented but not put through malolactic fer-mentation, the Chards can be expected to live long and evolve nicely in the bottle.

Wines/Varietals: Chardonnay, Carneros ($$), Gamay Beaujolais, Carneros ($), Pinot Noir, Carneros ($$), Pinot Noir Napa Valley Reserve ($$), Rouge de Noir Sparkling Pinot Noir, Carneros ($$).

Seghesio Vineyards

14730 Grove Street
Healdsburg, CA 95448
tel. (707) 433-3579; fax (707) 433-0545
Open to the public by appt.; est. 1902

The Seghesio family—now headed by vine-yard and winery owners Eugene, Edward, and Raymond Seghesio—has been growing grapes and making wine for most of the twentieth century, but only since 1980 have they been producing it under the family name. Prior to that, the Seghesios made wine in bulk. In the late eighties they earned

recognition for their moderately priced and agreeable—occasionally superior—varietals, 95 percent of which were supplied from their own 500 acres of vineyards in the Alexander, Dry Creek, and Russian River valleys. Total annual production here is 120,000 cases.

Winemaker Ted Seghesio places the em-phasis here on producing fruity, immedi-ately accessible wines, like the berryish Zinfandel and fruity, somewhat smokey Pi-not Noir. The 1990 Zin with its voluptuous raspberry flavors is highly drinkable, the 1989 Zinfandel Reserve somewhat more concentrated and deeper in color. The Chardonnay typically has engaging fruit and a pleasing touch of oak. The 1991, rich and unusually well-balanced, is very good and an amazing bargain at $8 a bottle. The Cabernet here is among the lighter ones, with cherry-like fruit and wood accents. Sangiovese may yet prove to be this winery's most interesting red: it's a big, earthy wine with considerable promise. Other Seghesio wines that offer good value are Sauvignon Blanc, white Zinfandel, and a pair of generic blends, Sonoma Red and White.

Wines/Varietals: Chardonnay ($), Sauvignon Blanc ($), White Zinfandel ($), Sonoma White ($), Cabernet Sauvignon ($), Pinot Noir ($), Reserve Pinot Noir ($$), Zinfandel ($), Zinfandel Reserve ($$), Sangiovese ($$), Sonoma Red ($).

Sequoia Grove Vineyards

8338 St. Helena Highway
Napa, CA 94558
tel. (707) 944-2945; fax (707) 963-9411
Open to the public; est. 1980

Jim Allen purchased this 25-acre vineyard site in 1978 intending to grow great Cabernet

Sauvignon. First, though, he had to remove most of the existing vineyard. Joined in 1979 by his brother, Steve, and their mother (known hereabouts as "Granny"), they replanted all but a small plot of Chardonnay. (They now have 11 acres each of Cabernet and Chardonnay). In 1985, Sequoia Grove, named for the circle of redwoods alongside the hundred-year-old horse barn-turned-winery here, received some top awards for its estate-bottled Cabernet, giving the young winery a big boost. Jim and Steve, with other limited partners, subsequently purchased 110 acres in the Carneros area, now planted to Chardonnay, Pinot Noir, and Cabernet Sauvignon, to supplement their smaller Sequoia Grove vineyard.

Sequoia Grove's Carneros Chardonnay (hints of tropical fruit, apples, buttery flavor) has a lower but still abundant acid content than the estate Chardonnay, which, due to warmer growing temperatures, is richer and fruitier. They are good wines, and improving, but we prefer this winery's Cabs. The Bordeaux-style estate Cabernet, blended with Cabernet Franc, Petit Verdot, and Merlot, undergoes extended maceration (2-3 weeks). The non-estate grown Cabernet comes from between six and eight select vineyards. We like the very fine 1989 Napa Valley Estate Cabernet Sauvignon with its accessible, medium-bodied style with ripe and round fruit redolent of plum, black cherry, spicy, and toasty oak flavors.

Wines/Varietals: Chardonnay, Carneros ($$), Chardonnay, Napa Valley Estate ($$), Cabernet Sauvignon, Napa Valley ($$), Cabernet Sauvignon, Napa Valley Estate ($$$).

Simi Winery

16275 Healdsburg Ave., PO Box 698
Healdsburg, CA 95448
tel. (707) 433-6981; fax (707) 433-6253
Open to the public; est. 1876

Founded by the Simi brothers of Tuscany, this winery with its historic stone cellars has been in continuous operation since the nineteenth century. In 1979 Zelma Long was hired as winemaker (she is now president) to recreate Simi as a super-premium winery. Since then, Simi has been as much identified with Long as with the excellent reserve Chardonnay and Cabernets she created. Now owned by LVMH, France's grand luxe products conglomerate, the winery has expanded its vineyard holdings to 300 acres in the Alexander and Russian River valleys. Estate fruit provides 50 percent of the grapes needed for the approximately 150,000 cases produced here annually. Currently, six wines are made from five varietals: Cabernet Sauvignon, Rosé of Cabernet, Chardonnay, Sauvignon Blanc, Chenin Blanc, and (beginning in 1993 with the 1991 vintage)

Sendal, a blend of Sauvignon Blanc and Sémillon.

About half of production here is Chardonnay; about half of it barrel fermented. Only a small percentage of overall Chardonnay production goes into the Reserve Chardonnay, but this is the wine on which Simi's reputation for top quality rests. The regular Chardonnay is consistent, medium-bodied, crisp, fruity, and more than adequate. The Reserve is one of the best: 100 percent barrel fermented, put through a secondary malolactic fermentation, and aged in largely new oak barrels for about six months. The 1988 is superb with classic butter, honey, fruit, and barrel flavors in abundance. The Chenin Blanc and Sauvignon Blanc (blended with about 10 percent Sémillon) are both good, though the Sauvignon Blanc often falls into the pronounced grassy-herbal style. And if you want to know what a Rosé of Cabernet tastes like, Simi makes about the best there is. It's a crisp pink wine with fresh fruit flavors of cherries and raspberries. The regular Cabernet is highly reliable in a somewhat restrained Bordeaux style. The 1987 Alexander Valley wine is typically well-made, attractive and complex. The nose is deeply aromatic and slightly herbal, the body well-shaped and dressed with restrained fruit, spices, and tannins. The finish is reasonably long. The fine 1987 Reserve Cabernet, as can be expected, is all this plus a lot more. Simi's prices are moderate.

Wines/Varietals: Chardonnay ($$), Reserve Chardonnay ($$$), Sauvignon Blanc ($), Chenin Blanc ($), Sendal ($$), Rosé of Cabernet ($), Cabernet Sauvignon ($$), Reserve Cabernet Sauvignon ($$$).

Sonoma-Cutrer Vineyards

4401 Slusser Road (Windsor),
PO Box 9
Fulton, CA 95439
tel (707) 528-1181; fax (707) 528-1561
Open to the public by appt.; est. 1973

This Chardonnay-only winery became a darling of wine lovers in the 1980s by producing very fine American Chardonnays and shipping them to fancy restaurants far and wide. Sonoma-Cutrer is the brain-child of president and principal owner Brice Cutrer Jones, an Air Force Academy and Harvard Business School grad and Vietnam veteran fighter-pilot. Jones has run this business with military precision and winning strategic planning. All of his wines are estate-bottled from his 625 acres in the Russian River Valley and the lower end of the Sonoma Valley. In 1992 he bought a neighboring winery to provide even more fruit for Sonoma-Cutrer Chardonnays. With the help of now-retired winemaker emeritus Bill Bonetti, Jones has adhered to a "no compromise" quality policy and brought Sonoma-Cutrer to the cutting edge—some would say beyond it—of viniculture, viticulture, and research, not to mention marketing.

Bonetti's long-time assistant, Terry Adams, the winemaker here since 1991, was on hand to make the winery's first vintage release, the 1981. This quintessential California winery does everything conceivable to nurture and massage its wines, from taking extra care in transporting and inspecting the fruit, to chilling the grapes before pressing them, to pressing whole-clusters, to the selection of yeasts, to fermenting in barrel, to aging *sur lie*. Three Chardonnays are currently being produced here: Cutrer Vineyards and Les Pierres, two vineyard-designated Chards, and the blended Russian River

Ranches Chardonnay. Les Pierres is the greatest: we'll not soon forget the magnificent 1983, which upon its release struck us, like the Chalone Vineyard Chardonnays of the period, as a breakthrough, world-class, ultra-premium wine that defined a new American standard. Les Pierres Chardonnay, from a vineyard just over the Carneros in Sonoma, tends to be full of finesse with great balance and tight, complex pear, butterscotch, vanillin, and oak creamy flavors. The 1988 is superb, as is the 1990. The Cutrer Vineyards bottling is a bigger, fuller wine, a bit tart and flinty, yet with tropical fruit flavors—fine, even very good, from one year to the next. The Russian River Ranches is also highly reliable and similarly tart but with plenty of pear and peach-like fruit and oak clearly in evidence. Sonoma-Cutrer does not release its production figures, but our "guesstimate" is about 75,000 cases annually, two-thirds or more being the Russian River Ranches bottling.

Wines/Varietals: Chardonnay, Russian River Ranches ($$), Chardonnay, Cutrer Vineyards ($$), Chardonnay, Les Pierres Vineyard ($$$).

Sonoma-Loeb
1695 Geysers Road
Geyserville, CA 95441
tel. (707) 645-7828; fax (707) 645-7839
Not open to the public; est. 1988

John L. Loeb, Jr., a former U.S. ambassador to Denmark and member of the influential family of bankers and philanthropists, has grown grapes on his Russian Riverbend Vineyards in Sonoma since 1973. In 1988 he decided to hold back a small portion of the 600 tons of Chardonnay and Cabernet grapes he harvests annually to vinify a couple of thousand cases of ultra-premium wines bearing his family name. The early results are extremely impressive. Loeb draws from two vineyard parcels: a 47-acre plot planted with Chardonnay and Cabernet Sauvignon that is across the road from the Robert Young Vineyard in the Alexander Valley, and a 69-acre vineyard that borders the Russian River.

Sonoma-Loeb's Chardonnay grapes are crushed at Chappelet Vineyards with Philip Titus serving as winemaker. The 1990 Alexander Valley Chardonnay was 100 percent barrel fermented in French oak (three-quarters new), and left on the lees for seven months. Much of it went through a malolactic fermentation. To add a touch of acidity, Loeb supplements his estate grapes with 15 percent purchased from the Sangiacomo Vineyard in the Carneros district of Sonoma. The result is delicious: rich, buttery, complex with pear, vanilla, and toasty flavor tones. The 1990 Sonoma County Private Reserve Chardonnay, of which there are a mere 50 cases, is even better. It, too, contains 15 percent grapes from the Sangiacomo Vineyard and is a terrifically rich, smooth, and complex wine with smokey, toasty, and powerful multi-dimensional fruit flavors. This is a top-notch Chardonnay, and the 1991 follow-up proves it was no fluke. The

moderately-priced Cabernet here is also good, readily accessible with soft tannins and crisp blackberry flavors. It is made at the Bandiera Winery, with Robert Keeble as winemaker, from Loeb's Alexander Valley fruit supplemented by 18 percent grapes from the Sage Creek Vineyard in the Napa Valley.

Wines/Varietals: Chardonnay, Alexander Valley ($$), Chardonnay, Sonoma County Private Reserve ($$$), Cabernet Sauvignon, Alexander Valley ($).

Steele Wines

4792 Cold Creek
Kelseyville, CA 95451
tel./fax (707) 279-0213
Not open to the public; est. 1990

It is perhaps a stretch to include in our survey of North America's "Best" a brand new winery that owns no vineyards. (Well, this is not exactly a *winery*, either, as Steele wines are made in rented space.) But the owner and winemaker here has quite a history and his first, highly impressive releases have stimulated critical praise and stirred up a lot of interest. We're betting he can keep it up. "He" is Jed Steele, former winemaker at Kendall-Jackson Vineyards & Winery and currently a consultant to several top-quality wineries. His game plan here seems to be to use his talent and experience to buy the best fruit he can identify and produce a range of generally vineyard-designated wines, emphasizing richness and purity of focus in each one.

Steele has so far released five different Chardonnays and one Pinot Noir—all 1991 vintage and all highly recommended. The biggest wine by volume is the blended California Chardonnay (3,300 cases). It is a big wine with lots of oaky, buttery, Chard nose and plenty of ripe fruit and reasonable complexity (pear, honey, spice, vanilla, and oak components), well-balanced with mild acidity. The vineyard-designated Chardonnays have sharper acidity and added complexities, particularly the Sangiacomo (only 80 cases produced!). Steele's oaky, full-blown Chardonnays are the sort that stand out in blind tastings. The Pinot Noir, from Carneros grapes, is also multi-dimensional. It has a complex smokey-spicy nose and is a round and appealing wine with classic cherry and currant flavors amid toasty oak highlights and a long, elegant finish.

Wines/Varietals: Chardonnay, California ($$), Chardonnay, Durrel Vineyard, Sonoma ($$$), Chardonnay, Lolonis Vineyard, Mendocino ($$$), Chardonnay, Du Pratt Vineyard, Mendocino ($$$), Chardonnay, Sangiacomo Vineyard, Carneros ($$$), Pinot Noir, Carneros ($$).

Viansa Winery

25200 Arnold Drive
Sonoma, CA 95476
tel. (707) 996-4726; fax (707) 996-4632
Open to the public; est. 1990

Sam and Vicki Sebastiani established their own brand (the name is a contraction of "Vicki-and-Sam") after Sam left Sebastiani Vineyards, the Sonoma winery started by his grandfather around the turn of the century. Viansa's new winery, a handsome, rustic

Tuscan-style structure, sits on a hilltop overlooking San Pablo Bay to the south and the Carneros district to the north and east. The winery's tasting room is designed along the lines of an Italian marketplace, with long wooden tasting bars at either end. Gourmet take-out food based on Vicki's recipes and prepared in the winery's kitchen is available for sale, making Viansa a popular picnicking spot. The first two acres planted here (out of 76 potentially plantable) are in Sangiovese, Malvasia and Vernaccia, reflecting Sam's interest in Italian varieties. Currently the winery buys virtually all of its grapes to produce 4,500 cases annually.

In its brief existence, Viansa has produced several award-winning wines, notably Chardonnay, Cabernet Sauvignon and Nebbiolo. The 1987 Reserve Cabernet is in the firm-structured style Sebastiani aims for with this variety: solid blackberry fruit in the middle within a sturdy frame of tannin and oak, including some new oak. The owner-winemaker prefers Cabernet Franc over Merlot for blending; the 1988 Cabernet, for example, contains 17 percent Cabernet Franc. Recent Chardonnays are good, too, particularly the 1990. Somewhat on the lean side, it is nevertheless finely balanced with lovely fruit flavors accented with clove and a long creamy finish, clearly an ager. The Reserve Chardonnay, also 1990, is more intensely oaky and somewhat angular, though it may well develop a nice harmony once it has three or four years in the bottle.

Wines/Varietals: Chardonnay ($$), Reserve Chardonnay ($$), Sauvignon Blanc ($), Cabernet Sauvignon ($$), Reserve Cabernet Sauvignon ($$$), Nebbiolo ($$).

William Wheeler Winery

130 Plaza Street
Healdsburg, CA 95448
tel. (707) 433-8786; fax (707) 431-8040
Open to the public; est. 1981

Bill and Ingrid Wheeler purchased their 175-acre ranch situated among the hills of Dry Creek Valley practically on impulse after visiting friends in Healdsburg in 1970. Convinced that the American public was ready for classic European varietals, the Wheelers spent a harvest in Bordeaux, France, to increase their knowledge of grape growing and refine their winemaking skills. Returning to California, they planted their vineyard in Cabernet Sauvignon (20 acres), and have since added Zinfandel (10 acres), Merlot (5 acres), and Cabernet Franc (5 acres). In 1989 the Wheelers formed a joint venture with a major French wine group under the name "Paribas Domaines - USA." The venture failed in 1992 and the winery was sold to the large French negociant Jean Claude Boisset, which also owns Lyeth Vineyards and Christophe Vineyards, both in California. Winemaker Wheeler remains and many of his original plans are still in place and being carried out.

This winery currently produces 20,000 cases annually. Crushing, pressing and fermentation are done in a modern 4,500 square foot fermentation cellar just 150 yards from the Wheeler house. The Chardonnays here are not meant to be blockbuster wines. Rather, harmony and elegance are emphasized. The 1990 Reserve is the best we've tasted from this winery with its ripe pear and honeysuckle flavor highlights on the nose and palate. A slight mineral taste adds complexity. The 1990 Sauvignon Blanc is okay—tangy and light with grapefruit, vanilla, and varietal fruit flavors. The 1987 Cabernet Sauvignon (15 percent Merlot) represents the William Wheeler Winery at its best: full-bodied, it has black cherry, cassis, blackberry and cedar flavors complemented by hints of chocolate and oak with strong tannins and a long finish. The 1988 Cab is also good, again with cherry flavors and softer tannins typical of the vintage.

Wines/Varietals: Sauvignon Blanc ($), Chardonnay ($$), Reserve Chardonnay ($$), White Zinfandel ($), RS [Rhône-style] Reserve ($$), Merlot ($$), Cabernet Sauvignon ($$).

Williams-Selyem Winery
6575 Westside Road
Healdsburg, CA 95448
tel. (707) 433-6425
Open to the public by appt.; est. 1981

If you want a Pinot Noir that can be considered hip, go for one of these. Williams-Selyem's Pinots are the darlings of some critics and collectors, and their limited production (perhaps 3,000 cases a year) and high prices are likely to keep these wines out of the hands of enological hoi polloi. The wines are indeed very good, and moving right up to the head of the class. Owners Ed Selyem and Burt Williams make their wines from small purchased grape lots in a Sonoma winemaking facility owned by Howard Allen.

Winemaking here is very traditional and non-interventionist. The resulting wines are big boys that need some time for their edges to smooth out, yet clearly have definition in an attractive Côte-de-Beaune style. We prefer the 1989 Russian River Pinot Noir, Rochioli Vineyard with its lovely, sweet fruit and firm yet delicate body to the well-regarded 1990 Russian River Olivet Lane Vineyard Pinot. The Summa Vineyard Pinot is even lighter and more delicate. Williams-Selyem also produces a blended Pinot labeled "Sonoma Coast" which is a tad less profound but still a good wine. Of considerable note is the Zinfandel made here with grapes from very old vines from the steepest slopes of the Leo Martinelli Vineyard in the Green Valley AVA. The Zin is intense in color and flavors. The excellent 1989 shows deep purple/ruby colors, jam with sweet berry fruit on the nose, and chunky black cherry flavors laced with herbs and smoky oak on the palate amid plenty of alcohol. Williams-Selyem makes a Chardonnay, too, but not for commercial release, and lately a Muscat Canelli desert wine for distribution.

Wines/Varietals: Pinot Noir, Sonoma ($$), Pinot Noir, Summa Vineyard, Sonoma ($$$), Pinot Noir, Rochioli Vineyard, Russian River ($$$), Pinot Noir, Olivet Lane Vineyard, Russian River ($$$), Zinfandel, Martinelli Vineyard, Green Valley ($$), Muscat Canelli ($$).

The Phylloxera Drama

Indigenous to America, phylloxera is a tiny, aphid-like insect that feeds on grapevine rootstocks. The insect and native North American rootstock are engaged in a millennium-old battle, which both have survived—so far. For a time, it appeared as though the American vines had emerged victorious. But the phylloxera was still alive: for centuries the American rootstock was resistant to the bug's voracious appetite.

Phylloxera traveled to Europe in the nineteenth century and preyed on "virgin" rootstocks unprepared to resist it. As vineyards across the Continent succumbed to the massive attack, scientists searched for a solution to the problem. They discovered that the phylloxera-resistant American rootstocks could serve as a healthy foundation onto which the more fragile European varietal vines could be grafted. Thanks to this wedding, the European vines were saved and the delicate, premium grape varieties were preserved.

As U.S. vintners sought to improve the quality of their wines over the past several decades, cuttings from European vines were imported. All was well until a new strain of phylloxera, known as "Biotype B," appeared in North America. Several rootstocks associated with premium varietals, especially one called "AxR#1," which is widely planted in Northern California, have proved highly vulnerable to this most recent infestation.

The only hope of controlling the present scourge appears to consist of tearing the diseased vines out of plots that have been bled to death by the merciless phylloxera, and replanting them with new, resistant rootstock.

Some experts have estimated that as of mid-1993, half of the vineyards in Northern California must be replanted. The expense involved in replanting (between $15,000 and $30,000 per acre) and the loss of production during the new vines' first three unproductive years are enormous and will place a staggering strain on the effected California wineries. Fighting the current phylloxera infestation is projected to cost vintners in the Napa and Sonoma valleys alone one billion dollars.

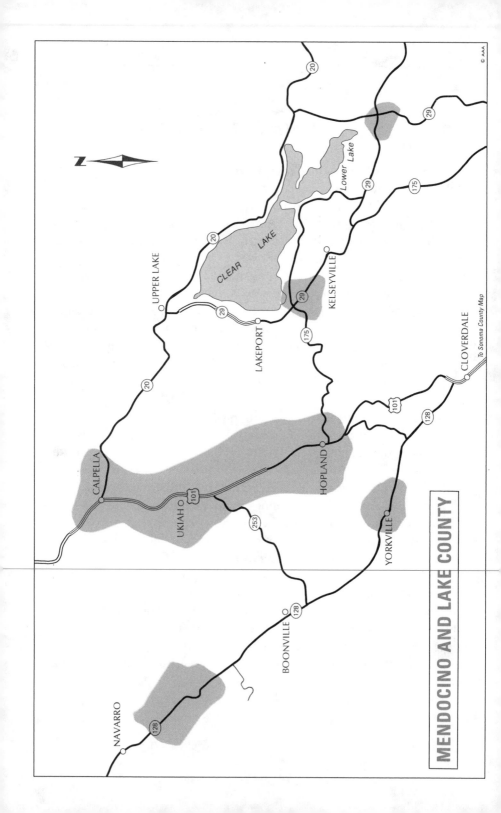

MENDOCINO AND LAKE COUNTY

Mendocino & Lake Counties

Fetzer Vineyards

13601 East Side Road, PO Box 611
Hopland, CA 95449
tel. (707) 744-1250 or (707) 744-1737;
fax (707) 744-1439
Open to the public; est. 1968

One of the largest wineries in America—number six nationwide, and number one in Mendocino County—with three winemaking facilities, and an output of two million cases a year (including second label Arbor Crest), Fetzer has had a strong impact on the wine market in North America. It consistently produces premium wines in the $4-8 range, leading the charge of the "fighting varietals" and delivering excellent value across the board. In the summer of 1992, as sales continued to climb, the family-owned and run winery (11 of the clan worked for the company) was sold to Brown-Forman, the large Kentucky-based spirits and wine company. The Fetzers say they had accomplished what they set out to do and had "seen wineries pull too many families apart." (Leaders in organic farming, they will continue to cultivate 1,000 acres of vineyard and sell the grapes to Brown-Forman.) The new owners are likely to increase production here.

Fetzer's Sundial Chardonnay is a clean, simple, low-priced, star bottling. This house has also enjoyed commercial and critical success with its Gewürztraminer. We've appreciated, too, Fetzer's peachy, spritzy Chenin Blanc. For more serious drinking, the reserve wines, especially the Cabernets

and Zinfandels, are real winners. The Reserve Cabernet (from Mendocino estate grapes) is notable for its cherryish fruit and spicy barrel (new oak), sweet vanilla flavors. The moderately priced Barrel Select Cabernet is the line's best value.

Wines/Varietals: Sundial Chardonnay ($), Reserve Chardonnay ($$), Chardonnay, Barrel Select ($), Fumé Blanc ($), Fumé Blanc, Valley Oak ($), Sauvignon Blanc, Barrel Select ($), Gewürztraminer ($), Chenin Blanc ($), White Zinfandel ($), Premium White ($), Premium Blush ($), Premium Red ($), Reserve Black Muscat ($), Cabernet Sauvignon, Valley Oak ($), Reserve Cabernet Sauvignon ($$), Cabernet Sauvignon, Barrel Select ($), Reserve Pinot Noir ($$), Reserve Petite Sirah ($), Reserve Zinfandel ($), Zinfandel, Barrel Select ($), Johannisberg Riesling, Late Harvest (375 ml, $).

Greenwood Ridge Vineyards

24555 Greenwood Road
Philo, CA 95466
tel./fax (707) 877-3262
Open to the public; est. 1980

Graphic artist Allan Green tends to find unusual ways of combining his interests. For instance, he once commissioned a group of musicians and visual artists to use their respective talents to characterize the essence of Greenwood Ridge wines. Green took the results to Stanford University, and offered them to the public as a live performance art event. Green's 12-acre vineyard, situated 1,200 feet above sea level in the Anderson Valley of Mendocino County, is divided equally among plantings of White Riesling, Cabernet Sauvignon, and Merlot. He purchases about 50 percent of his grapes—Chardonnay from the Redwood Valley,

Sauvignon Blanc from Mendocino County, and Zinfandel from Sonoma County. Total production here is 4,000 cases annually.

Since Van Williamson joined Greenwood Ridge as winemaker in 1988, there has been a steady increase in quality, which is now good across the line. The Anderson Valley Sauvignon Blanc is fine in the grassy herbal style, but light. At first we had doubts about the lean, tart Chardonnay, but we came around on a second tasting of the 1990 as it showed more buttery Chardonnay fruit and some oak. Fine White Riesling with a hint of sweetness, and an even better late harvest Riesling fill out the offerings of white wines. The Merlot in both 1988 and 1989 is good, but the exciting surprise for us is the Pinot Noir. Greenwood Ridge's impressive, medium-bodied 1990 Anderson Valley rendering has lovely color, good Pinot Noir nose, solid fruit and backbone with stalky vegetal hints. This wine drinks well and long. The 1991 proved the previous vintage was no fluke: it's lovely with rich, ripe, almost sweet Pinot Noir fruit fully in character and with great balance and harmony and a good underlying structure of mild acids, tannins, and a hint of barrel pepperiness. (Perhaps it's no surprise that Pinot Noir is good in the Anderson Valley, where the sparkling wine companies are making excellent use of it.) Greenwood is now proving the true potential of Anderson Valley Pinot Noir as a still wine and demonstrating that other vinifera from this area can produce most agreeable wines. Incidentally, Allan Green has put his graphic arts skills to good use in developing his winery's attractive labels and promotional materials.

Wines/Varietals: Sauvignon Blanc ($), Chardonnay ($$), White Riesling ($), White Riesling, Late Harvest (375 ml, $$), Zinfandel ($$), Merlot ($$), Cabernet Sauvignon ($$), Pinot Noir ($$).

Handley Cellars

PO Box 66
Philo, CA 95466
tel. (707) 895-2190 or (707) 895-3876;
fax (707) 895-2603
Open to the public; est. 1982

While Milla Handley was working toward an art degree at U.C. Davis, her interest in wine began to suggest a different picture of the future: in 1975 she graduated with a degree in fermentation science. She spent three years at Chateau St. Jean and another three at Edmeades Winery before she and her husband, Rex McClellan, established their own winery in the basement of their Mendocino home. They moved to larger facilities just down the road in the Anderson Valley in 1987; production here is currently at 15,000 cases. Handley Cellar's 45-acre vineyard is planted to Chardonnay (20 acres), Sauvignon Blanc (10 acres), and Pinot Noir (15 acres). Handley buys in an additional 30 percent of her grapes.

With the contribution of winemaker Dennis Duzick, Handley Cellars is another one of the emerging wineries proving the Anderson Valley's potential as a source for high quality sparkling and still wines. The Gewürztraminer made here (from the Anderson Valley AVA) is consistently good, and with its 1988 Brut and Brut Rosé sparkling wines Handley is showing deftness in handling the area's other established premium wine. The 1988 Brut Rosé is Handley's best effort yet—pale salmon-colored, with a lively mousse and a hint of strawberry on the nose leading to a simple, balanced and crisp sparkling wine. Chardonnay is the big crop here, though, accounting for almost half of production. It comes two ways: an Anderson Valley Chardonnay and a Dry Creek Valley Chardonnay, which, in the 1990 vintage produced from the family's vineyard and barrel fermented in new oak, is impressive. Sauvignon Blanc accounts for another quarter of this winery's output. The 1991 Sauvignon Blanc made from Sonoma County Dry Creek Valley grapes is a light, simple, pleasant and harmonious wine, slightly smokey and melony, with a tinge of varietal vegetal character.

Wines/Varietals: Chardonnay, Dry Creek Valley ($$), Chardonnay, Anderson Valley ($$), Sauvignon Blanc, Dry Creek Valley ($), Gewürztraminer, Anderson Valley ($), Brut, Anderson Valley ($$), Brut Rosé, Anderson Valley ($$).

Jepson Vineyards
10400 So. Hwy 101
Ukiah, CA 95482
tel (707) 468-8936; fax (707) 468-0362
Open to the public; est. 1985

This 125-acre estate winery in Mendocino County is owned by Robert Jepson and run by Gary Woo. It's a distinctive operation, in that 20 percent of production is Jepson Rare Brandy, a Cognac-style, alambic-distilled brandy, made from a single vineyard of French Colombard grapes. The winery also produces still and sparkling wines in quantities averaging 20,000 cases annually.

Everything here starts with white. Forty percent of production is Chardonnay (a regular and a reserve still wine), another 20 percent is a Blanc de Blancs sparkler made from Chardonnay grapes; there is the brandy, and a Sauvignon Blanc that accounts for the final 20 percent of production. The limited

production, 100 percent barrel fermented Chardonnay is the Jepson wine to shop for. The 1988 is a particularly good offering with lots of striking qualities, including very concentrated and complex floral and fruity flavors, good structure and fine length. The Blanc de Blancs sparkler is generally a sound and pleasant one. The brandy, aged in French Limousin oak barrels for 6 or 7 years, is clean, light, and oaky, with lots of fruity, floral aromas.

Wines/Varietals: Chardonnay ($$), Chardonnay, Estate Reserve ($$$), Sauvignon Blanc ($), Blanc de Blancs Sparkling Wine ($$), Jepson Rare Brandy ($$$).

Kendall-Jackson Vineyards & Winery
600 Mathews Road
Lakeport, CA 95453
tel. (707) 263-5299 or (707) 263-9333; fax (707) 544-4013
Open to the public; est. 1982

In a very short time Kendall-Jackson has become one of California's largest producers of premium varietals. Though the winery does not release production figures, its output is estimated at close to a million cases annually. San Francisco lawyer Jess Jackson first bought vineyard land in Lake County, north of the Napa Valley, in 1974. Initially, he sold his grapes to various wineries. When he decided to make his own wines, Jackson expanded his vineyard holdings dramatically, sweeping up two-thirds (1,200 acres) of the Tepusquet Vineyard in Santa Barbara County (*see* Cambria Winery). Kendall-Jackson now owns some 2,500 acres in all, 95 percent planted to Chardonnay, but still buys 60 percent of the grapes needed for

263

production. Jackson feels that the combination of fruit from many different regions brings distinctive components to his Chardonnay, and results in greater finesse and complexity.

Innovative winemaker Jed Steele created K-J's style: richly fruity wines, most of them richly oaked, too, but generally balanced with good acidity in both reds and whites. The white wines here, including the moderately priced Vintner's Reserve Chardonnay, the Sauvignon Blanc, the Muscat, and the Riesling, always have a telltale sweetness that Steele deftly balanced with acidity. Steele left Kendall-Jackson to start his own winery in 1991 and John Hawley took over as winemaker. Steele made some wonderful reds here, including a slew of vineyard-designated Zinfandels that invariably garnered praise and prizes. The DuPratt Zinfandel, with its rich, velvety berry flavors, is always a winner, and is often equalled by K-J's Ciapusci, Lolonis, and Pacini vineyard Zinfandel bottlings. Cabernets are similarly rich in texture and fruit, though never heavy or overly tannic. Top of the line (and so priced at $50) is "Cardinale," a Cabernet-based meritage blended with varying amounts of Merlot and Cabernet Franc. The best Cab value here is the Vintner's Reserve, which in 1989 is supple and fruity but substantial. The Vintner's Reserve Chardonnay was K-J's first major success, a national bestseller vintage after vintage. The Proprietor's Grand Reserve Chardonnay heads the list in breeding and finesse but there are six Chardonnays produced here in all, including specific vineyard attributions (DuPratt, Camelot, Dennison, and Durrell). The Durrell Syrah is one of the best made in California, concentrated without being overly tannic, and well worth cellaring as a Côte Rotie wannabe.

Wines/Varietals: Chardonnay, Vintner's Reserve ($$), Chardonnay, Proprietor's Grand Reserve ($$$), Chardonnay, Durell Vineyard ($$), Chardonnay, DuPratt Vineyard ($$), Chardonnay, Dennison Vineyard ($$), Chardonnay, Camelot Vineyard ($$), Sauvignon Blanc, Proprietor's Reserve ($$), Sauvignon Blanc, Lakewood Vineyard ($$), Sauvignon Blanc, Vintner's Reserve ($), Sémillon, Lakewood Vineyard ($$), Johannisberg Riesling, Vintner's Reserve ($), Johannisberg Riesling, Select Late Harvest (375 ml, $$$), Muscat Canelli ($), Meritage Cardinale ($$$), Cabernet Sauvignon, Proprietor's Grand Reserve ($$$), Cabernet Sauvignon, Lolonis Vineyard ($$), Cabernet Sauvignon, Vintner's Reserve ($$), Merlot, Proprietor's Reserve ($$$), Merlot, Vintner's Reserve ($$), Zinfandel, Ciapusci Vineyard ($$$), Zinfandel, DuPratt Vineyard ($$$), Zinfandel, Pacini Vineyard ($$), Zinfandel, Lolonis Vineyard ($$), Zinfandel, Mariah Vineyard ($), Zinfandel, Vintner's Reserve ($), Syrah, Durrell Vineyard ($$$), Pinot Noir, Julia's Vineyard ($$), Pinot Noir, Vintner's Reserve ($$), Gamay, Dorn Vineyard ($), Grand Finale ($$).

McDowell Valley Vineyards

3811 Highway 175, PO Box 449
Hopland, CA 95449
tel. (707) 744-1053; fax (707) 744-1826
Open to the public for tasting, tours by appt.; est. 1979

Richard and Karen Keehn built their striking solar-powered winery in 1979 in an arid eastern Mendocino Valley named for Paxton McDowell, a Scottish immigrant who ventured west during the Gold Rush and settled in this area. There have been vineyards here since 1890, but the Keehns have the only winery in the valley. They produce 100,000 cases of moderately priced varietals; these are food-friendly wines, light but flavorful. The whites, like the Chardonnay, Fumé Blanc, and Grenache, are a little on the sweet side. The Keehns' own nearly 400 acres of vineyard, including venerable stands of Grenache and Syrah dating to 1919.

The Keehns and John Buechenstein, winemaker here since 1985, have lately focused on Rhône varieties which they bottle under the "Les Vieux Cépage "(The Old Varieties) label. "Le Trésor," a blend of Syrah, Grenache, and Mourvèdre, is an agreeably flavorful red, occasionally a wine of distinction. Syrah is McDowell's most successful effort in the Rhône style, with dark briar-and-berry flavors, and a hint of black pepper. The regular Le Vieux Cépages McDowell Valley Syrah is the house's finest wine. The Grenache is round and robustly fruity with a hint of sweetness in some versions.

Wines/Varietals: Fumé Blanc ($), Chardonnay ($), White Zinfandel ($), Cabernet Sauvignon ($), Zinfandel ($), Cabernet Franc ($$); Les Vieux Cépages label: Syrah ($$), Grenache Rosé ($), Le Trésor ($$), Bistro Red ($), Bistro Syrah ($).

Navarro Vineyards

5601 Hwy. 128, PO Box 47
Philo, CA 95466
tel. (800) 537-9463 or (707) 895-3686;
fax (707) 895-3647
Open to the public; est. 1974

Gewürztraminer is the backbone of this successful Anderson Valley winery owned by Ted Bennett and Deborah Cahn, but the Chardonnays produced here have increasingly turned out to be top quality as well. The 60 acres of vines at the winery in Philo (35 Gewürztraminer, 13 Chardonnay, 10 Pinot Noir, and 2 Muscat), plus some 35 to 40 percent additional purchased grapes, translate into up to 18,000 cases annually. Included are some very fine bottlings, which speak well for both Navarro's owners and its growing area.

Navarro's two Chardonnays, a barrel fermented "Premier Reserve" and the Mendocino Chardonnay, are fermented in stainless steel and oak-aged. Both are consistently good. And if the estate-bottled Gewürztraminer is noteworthy—and it is—the occasionally released *botrytis*-affected late harvest Gewürztraminer is often outstanding. Also good are the house's two Pinot Noirs, one an estate bottling made in the old world style (including the addition of whole clusters during the fermentation process), and the other employing carbonic maceration. The 1990 Gewürztraminer Estate Bottled Dry is a good one; the supple and complex 1990 Sauvignon Blanc is very good; and the appealing 1990 Anderson Valley Première Reserve is this winery's best in years: rich and lively with butterscotch, pear, vanillin, and spice flavor components. The winery's second label, Indian Creek, is off to a good start for quality and value with a pleasant 1991 Chardonnay.

Wines/Varietals: Dry Gewürztraminer, Estate Bottled ($), Chardonnay, Première Reserve ($$), Chardonnay, Mendocino ($$), White Riesling ($), White Riesling, Cluster Select (375 ml, $$; 750 ml, $$$), Edelzwicker ($), Pinot Noir, Méthode à l'Ancienne ($$).

Roederer Estate

4501 Highway 128, PO Box 67
Philo, CA 95466
tel. (707) 895-2288; fax (510) 652-1803
Open to the public; est. 1982

Here's another believer in Anderson Valley sparkling wines. When the people back in Reims, France who make the famous Roederer Cristal and Brut Premier Champagnes decided to produce a sparkling wine in America, they had the knowledge and resources to start up anywhere. In 1982 they invested in the Anderson Valley, becoming a friendly neighbor to Scharffenberger Cellars. Roederer Estate has 500 acres with 400 in vine, 50 percent planted to Chardonnay and 50 percent to Pinot Noir. Spread over 4 separate parcels, these vineyards provide all the fruit required for production here.

What's in every Roederer Estate bottle speaks volumes—distinctive, top-quality wine with lots of finesse. On virtually everyone's list of, say, America's top five sparklers, the Estate Brut is a blend of 70 percent Chardonnay and 30 percent Pinot Noir (almost the inverse of its French cousin, and of the award-winning Brut made next door at Scharffenberger Cellars). Estate Brut is fairly straightforward: good yeasty nose, medium body with clean, clear, creamy flavors with grapefruit, citrus highlights, and sound finish. Late in 1992, Roederer Estate released a sparkling Brut Rosé, only its second wine, and the first addition to its line since the 1988 introduction of Estate Brut. The new Rosé, a 50-50 blend, has a small amount of Pinot Noir with extended maceration, 5 percent by volume, added for color (an unusually faint salmon) before the second fermentation. This wine's bubbles are small and lively with abundant and persistent mousse, and its nose is fresh with slight hints of yeast and earthiness. Its attack is sharp with crisp acidity, not too powerful, more smooth and harmonious with clear, dry, tart Anderson Valley Chardonnay flavors subtly in evidence. The finish is pleasing with a slight echo of bitterness. This first release of Rosé consists of only 450 cases but production will increase to 1,500 cases within two years. We look forward to tracking future releases.

Wines/Varietals: NV Brut ($$), NV Rosé ($$).

Scharffenberger Cellars

8501 Highway 128
Philo, CA 95466
tel. (707) 895-2065; fax (707) 895-1758
Open to the public; est. 1981

Give John Scharffenberger credit for recognizing a very good thing: Northern California's Anderson Valley in Mendocino County offers a superb microclimate for producing top sparkling wines along classic *méthode champenoise* lines. Scharffenberger opened his winery here in 1981, and each year he is seeming wiser and wiser as his wines prove more and more wonderful, and other wineries follow his lead into the area. Today the sparkling wines of Scharffenberger Cellars are easily among the finest sparkling wines produced in America. The French took notice, and in 1989 the venerable Champagne House of Pommery purchased controlling interest in this winery. A huge investment in upgrading of facilities and human winemaking know-how soon followed. A striking 35,000-square-foot, state-of-the-art winemaking facility set on 680 acres of rolling, redwooded hills was built, acres of new vineyards planted (63 acres to date), and, *voilà*, the rave reviews keep piling up. When Champagne Pommery was itself acquired by LVMH, the French-based luxury goods company, Scharffenberger Cellars found itself in some pretty classy company and with even more substantial backing than before.

We're not alone in thinking the 1988 Blanc de Blancs an outstanding bottle, especially among lighter, aperitif-style sparkling wines. (Major competitions and magazines have awarded Scharffenberger Cellars' wines gold medals/top scores; the 1992 American Wine Competition declared the house's 1988 Blanc de Blancs "Best American Sparkling Wine.") Made from 100 percent Anderson Valley Chardonnay handpicked from the winery's top vineyards, the award-winning wine spent over 36 months on the yeast before being riddled and disgorged. The 1988 is crisp yet delicate with lemon-vanilla flavors and a hint of hazelnut, a creamy mouthfeel, and a refreshing finish. The 1989 Blanc de Blanc released mid-year in 1993 is a worthy follow-up. Scharffenberger Rosé is also a winner. Its good color beckons you from inside its clear-glass bottle, inviting you to pop the cork. It has a lovely mousse, full red fruit flavors along strawberry and citrus lines, and a creamy finish. The house's benchmark NV, a blend of 70 percent Pinot and 30 percent Chardonnay, is excellent, with crisp fruit flavors, balance, and complexity. Scharffenberger Cellars also makes still wines under the "Eagle Point" label.

Wines/Varietals: NV Brut ($$), NV Rosé ($$), NV Crémant ($$), Vintage Blanc de Blancs ($$).

Key

$ 750-ml bottle of wine costing less than $10.

$$ Bottle priced between $10 and $20.

$$$ Bottle costing more than $20.

$-$$$ In red indicates excellent value in its class; good relationship between quality and price.

███████████████

Other Areas

Cedar Mountain Winery

7000 Tesla Road
Livermore, CA 94550
tel. (510) 373-6636; fax (510) 373-6694
Open to the public weekends; est. 1990

Earl and Linda Ault's young and tiny (1,600 case) winery resembles an arts and crafts colony with Earl's accomplished sculptures, watercolors, and large-format photographs exhibited in the tasting room and an adjacent gallery. Currently the Aults have 14 acres of vineyards planted, divided equally between Chardonnay and Cabernet, and purchase grapes for their Sauvignon Blanc. They believe in the overriding importance of excellent vineyards to generating fine wines, but finish their wines powerfully in new oak cooperage.

Both the estate Chardonnay and Cabernet Sauvignon are full of promise, making this boutique winery one to watch. The 1990 Chardonnay, obviously an apprenticeship bottling, is all right, with a steely quality over the spicy, pear-like fruit.

Wines/Varietals: Estate Chardonnay ($$), Sauvignon Blanc ($), Estate Cabernet Sauvignon ($$$).

Concannon Vineyard

4590 Tesla Road, PO Box 3231
Livermore, CA 94550
tel. (510) 447-3760; fax (510) 447-2725
Open to the public; est. 1883

We really like the Petite Sirah at this historic winery, which was once one of the stalwarts of the California wine industry. The Concannon family sold the business in 1962 and in 1988 majority interest was purchased by Deinhard, the German wine firm. Then in March 1992, the Tesla Vineyards Limited Partnership, headed by Michael C. Wood, Henry Wilder and the Wente family, became the owners here, returning control of Concannon to Livermore locals. Quality is now inching up at this 65,000-case winery with its 180 acres of vineyards.

A spectrum of wines are produced here by winemaker Tom Lane: Johannisberg Riesling, Sauvignon Blanc, White Zinfandel, Chardonnay, "Assemblage" (a 60 percent Sémillon, 40 percent Sauvignon Blanc reserve wine), and Cabernet Sauvignon. There are also two Petite Sirahs, a lighter style Selected Vineyards bottling released young, and the Estate Bottled Reserve made from old vines and held back for years until it is ready to drink well. The 1985 Sirah, tasted in 1992, had an attractive color and a lovely, fruity nose, balance and structure, with soft, sweet berry fruit and a long and elegant finish. Holding back its release proved a smart move. Next best bets in our experience of Concannon wines are the Assemblage and the Chardonnay. The 1988 Mistral Chardonnay was especially impressive with its lemony and buttery flavors and Chardonnay fruit. The 1987 Livermore Valley Reserve Cabernet is straightforward— a second or third tier bottle.

Wines/Varietals: Johannisberg Riesling ($), Estate Sauvignon Blanc ($), White Zinfandel ($), Chardonnay ($$), Assemblage ($$), Cabernet Sauvignon ($$), Cabernet Sauvignon, Estate Reserve ($$), Petite Sirah, Selected Vineyard ($$), Petite Sirah, Estate Reserve ($$).

Edmunds St. John
4059 Emery Street
Emeryville, CA 94608
tel. (510) 654-1230
Not open to the public; est. 1985

This little Emeryville winery (formerly East Bay Wine Works) aims to make Rhône-style wines from California-grown grapes. Owners Steven Edmunds and Cornelia St. John have about six acres planted to Grenache (25 percent), Syrah (50 percent), Cinsault (16 percent) and Mourvèdre (9 percent), but the 3,000 cases currently produced each year are all from purchased grapes. Finding top quality grapes is a priority for Edmunds, winemaker here and a trendsetting leader of the renowned "Rhône Rangers."

Les Côtes Sauvages (The Wild Hills), a blend of the four grape varieties grown here, is modeled on the wines of Châteauneuf-du-Pape. Experienced tasters have in fact mistaken the 1989 bottling for its French counterpart. It's no wonder this release is Edmunds' personal favorite. We also recommend the 1990 release. Over the years we've enjoyed, too, Edmunds' Syrah and found promising his Viognier.

Wines/Varietals: Viognier ($$), Pinot Grigio ($$), Marchini Bianco ($), Rosé ($), Les Côtes Sauvages ($$), Syrah ($$$), New World Red ($).

E. & J. Gallo Winery
PO Box 1130
Modesto, CA 95353
tel. (209) 579-3111
Not open to the public; est. 1933

One way of looking at Gallo is to view the wine industry of North America in two parts: Gallo and everybody else. Brothers Ernest and Julio (the latter died in an auto-mobile accident in May 1993) produce more than 60 million cases of wine a year under numerous labels such as Tott's, André, Eden Roc and Ballatore sparkling wines, Bartles & Jaymes wine coolers, Carlo Rossi, Thunderbird, etc. Nearly two out of every five bottles of all sparkling wines sold in the U.S., for example, are Gallo's (all made by the Charmat process). The biggest wine company in the world—and the scope of Gallo's operations and the size of its staff are hard to comprehend (for example, they manufacture their own bottles at a clip of about a million a day)—Gallo undoubtedly merits inclusion among the most remarkable wineries in North America. Gallo merits recognition on a couple of other counts: for putting a great deal of wine on people's tables and for leading the educational movement to make wine an everyday part of Americans' lives. Lately the Gallos have become interested in producing estate and premium quality wines. While they own 9,000 acres of vineyards (increasingly farmed organically), the yields of their properties is miniscule compared with the needs of their overall operation.

It is the wines of "The Wine Cellars of Ernest and Julio Gallo" that earn our respect on grounds of quality. The strength of the mass produced Gallo wines (manufactured by an army of Ph.D. enologists) are the generic blends and the varietal blends labeled Reserve Cellars that are the next step up in quality and price. Gallo is the king of $5-$7 varietals. The Sauvignon Blanc can be fresh and simple, as in the 1991, which has pleasant citrus fruit with a touch of varietal herbaceousness in a medium-bodied style. Among the top tier varietal offerings, the Reserve North Coast Chardonnay is respectable in 1990; the Reserve California Cabernet Sauvignon is the house's best offering. When it comes to price, the Gallos certainly deserve praise. With their marketing philosophy and the economies of scale their operation affords them, they've yet to sell a bottle for over $10, save for the 1978 Private Reserve Cabernet. But there are plans afoot to change that. In fact, Gallo has been rearranging some of the Sonoma landscape in order to move into the premium market sector. Expect a few premium Sonoma County varietals to be priced at $10 and up in future. If these new releases are greeted well critically, Ernest Gallo will have met his final challenge.

Wines/Varietals: Chardonnay, White Zinfandel, Sauvignon Blanc, Chenin Blanc, Johannisberg Riesling, Gewürztraminer, White Grenache, Zinfandel, Cabernet Sauvignon (all $).

Kalin Cellars

61 Galli Drive
Novato, CA 94947
tel. (415) 883-3543
Not open to the public; est. 1977

U.C. Berkeley microbiologist Terry Leighton has a good thing going. Out of a Marin County warehouse he produces annually 6,000 cases of handcrafted, artisan wines—notably Chardonnay. He works entirely with purchased grapes (predominately from the Potter, Russian River, and Sonoma valley appellations) and is a believer in the primacy of the vineyard in establishing a wine's pedigree. He seeks out old vines with tiny yields and has taken to labeling his Chardonnay cuvées with letters to indicate the grower. He bucks the California trend to high-tech manufacturing, and manipulates his wines as little as possible; he does not even filter them. To properly appreciate Leighton's wines, you must understand that

they do not necessarily show well when young, but open up beautifully after, say, a half dozen years, and are then ever so true to their varietal character. Leighton seems to really be enjoying himself: in the last couple of years quality here has risen overall.

Kalin Cellars' wines are generally big, intensely flavored, and weighty with fruit and prominent oak components. Both the Cuvée LV and Cuvée W Chardonnays are barrel fermented and go through malolactic fermentation. Cuvée W comes from the gravelly soils of the Livermore Valley and is especially long-lived. The Cuvée LD comes from Sonoma, and like the LV, is a powerful and highly perfumed wine. The 1990s are top examples. In the past Leighton has produced a Sauvignon Blanc (wood-aged); in addition to the Chards he currently makes a Sémillon (barrel fermented), a Pinot Noir, a Cabernet Sauvignon, and a small amount of *méthode champenoise* sparkling wine. The Cabernet is a good wine made from Dry Creek Valley (Sonoma) grapes. It packs lots of dense fruit and wood, but is smooth and elegant, and will develop with time. The 1988 is a good example; we expect the 1990 to be the best bottle yet.

Wines/Varietals: Chardonnay, LD ($$$), Chardonnay, W, Livermore ($$$), Chardonnay, LV, Sonoma ($$$), Sémillon, Livermore ($$), Pinot Noir, Sonoma ($$$), Cabernet Sauvignon, Sonoma Reserve ($$$).

Kathryn Kennedy Winery

13180 Pierce Road
Saratoga, CA 95070
tel. (408) 867-4170
Open to the public by appt.; est. 1979

In 1973, Kathryn Kennedy planted 9 acres of Cabernet vines on land surrounding her surburban Silicon Valley home. She used to sell her Cabernet Sauvignon grapes to Mount Eden Vineyards until she was persuaded to produce the wine under her own label. Though production here is tiny—1,000 cases annually—Kennedy's wines have caught on with Cabernet devotees and are sought after despite steep prices of $45 to $50 a bottle for the estate Cabernet.

Half the production here is from Kennedy's vineyard in Santa Clara County, the rest from purchased grapes. In 1990, winemaker Marty Mathis (Kennedy's son) produced the house's first proprietary blend from Merlot and Cabernet Franc and called it "Lateral." The 1988 Cabernet Sauvignon is ripe, intense, powerful and designed for aging a good ten to twelve years. The 1990 promises good things as well. Mathis recommends giving his dense and chewy wines at least a decade's aging for them to show their best stuff. In part, the extremely low yields of the vineyards around the Kennedy family home (grown in clay and rocky subsoil) provide for the deep and dense varietal character these artisan wines exhibit year after year.

Wines/Varietals: Estate Cabernet Sauvignon ($$$), Lateral ($$).

Mount Eden Vineyards
22020 Mt. Eden Road
Saratoga, CA 95070
tel. (408) 867-5832; fax (408) 867-4329
Open to the public by appt.; est. 1972

Formerly Martin Ray Vineyards (from 1943 through 1971), this winery was born of the splitting up of the eponymous vintner's property. Martin Ray wound up with a small parcel of vineyard, and other investors took over the original winery and the greater

part of the existing vineyards, renaming the operation Mount Eden. This winery has since earned a stellar name for making Chardonnay. Eighteen of the 44 acres here are planted to Chardonnay, another 18 to Cabernet Sauvignon, and the last 8 to Pinot Noir. Mount Eden purchases additional fruit to bring total annual production to 6,200 cases.

Over the years, Mount Eden's hard-to-get Chardonnay and its Cabernet have been consistent performers. Since winemaker Jeffrey Patterson joined the team here in the mid-1980s, the winery's reputation has steadily improved across its product line. The 1989 Estate Bottled Chardonnay is complex and full-blown with all sorts of citrus, spice, and oak flavor complexities packaged in full harmony for the long run. The 1990 Santa Barbara County Chardonnay is earthy with pineapple and oak component flavors in a sharply focused wine. The recent Cabs have been reliably good.

Wines/Varietals: Chardonnay, Santa Cruz Mountain Estate Bottled ($$$), Chardonnay, Santa Barbara County ($$), Pinot Noir, Estate Bottled ($$), Cabernet Sauvignon, Santa Cruz Mountain Estate Bottled ($$$), Cabernet Sauvignon, Lathweisen Ridge, Santa Cruz Mountain ($$).

The R. H. Phillips Vineyard
26836 County Road 12A
Esparto, CA 95627
tel. (916) 662-3215; fax (916) 662-2880
Open to the public; est. 1983

This family-owned estate in the arid Dunnigan Hills west of Sacramento emerged on the scene suddenly in the mid-eighties with its value-priced varietals and varietal blends. Brothers John and Karl Giguiere, grandsons of Robert Hugh Phillips, the Washington wheat farmer for whom the winery is named, were grain and sheep farmers in Yolo County until they and Lane Giguiere planted their first vineyard of Sauvignon Blanc and Chenin Blanc in 1980. Their inaugural release in 1984 was 4,000 cases; within three years production had jumped to an eye-opening 150,000 cases and today it surpasses 250,000 cases. The Giguieres have expanded the vineyards here to over 550 acres, including a 70-acre plot of dry farmed Syrah, Mourvèdre, and Grenache. In Dunnigan Hills, the vineyards get only winter rainfall (and just 18 inches then), which promotes low yields and concentrated grapes.

R. H. Phillips wines, with their bargain-basement prices, offer some of the best values in California. An immediate hit was the Sauvignon Blanc, dry and scintillatingly crisp (Karl harvests the Chardonnay grapes at night to preserve the fruit and its aroma). The off-dry Chenin Blanc here is also quite good, with more character and crispness than the typical California Chenin. Phillips does a creditable job with Chardonnay, producing a dry, fairly lush version with emphasis on fruit over supporting oak. Night Harvest Cuvée Rouge, the winery's nonvintage red, is a sturdy, robust wine. We find most interesting here the move to Rhône-style reds. The 1989 EXP Syrah is a meaty wine, peppery and intense, with good berryish flavors balancing chewy tannins. The 1990 Mourvèdre has even more extract and needs five years or so to tame rough edges. "Alliance," a fruity blend of Rhône varieties, is intended for immediate drinking. R.H. Phillips is a pioneer with 500-milliliter-sized bottles, which the Giguieres feel are just right for two people. The Night Harvest and EXP wines are bottled in these containers.

Wines/Varietals: Chardonnay ($), Cabernet ($), Dry Chenin Blanc ($), Night Harvest Sauvignon Blanc ($), Night Harvest White Zinfandel ($), Night Harvest Cuvée Rouge ($), EXP Syrah ($), EXP Mourvèdre ($$), EXP Viognier ($$), Alliance ($).

Quady Winery

13181 Rd. 24, PO Box 728
Madera, CA 93637
tel. (209) 673-8068; fax (209) 673-0744
Open to the public; est. 1977

To Andy Quady, something of a dessert wine missionary, we say "thanks and amen" for his experimentation with and promotion of a category of wines currently declining in popularity. Quady started out in the 1970s making a fortified America Port wine, mostly from Zinfandel grapes. In 1980, he found some old Orange Muscat vineyards and produced a dessert wine that he called "Essensia." This wine caught the public's imagination with its bold label and appealing flavor and led to more wines, notably a fortified Black Muscat called "Elysium." Quady owns no vineyards of his own, and purchases all of his grapes. There are, however, sixteen acres in Madera (planted to Orange Muscat) and 7 acres in Amador County (a mixture of Tinta Cão, Tinta Amarela, Bastardo, Alvarelhao, and Barocca) planted to Quady's specifications and under long-term contract to him. Annual production here is 11,500 cases; about half is Essensia and a quarter Elysium.

Essensia has been a fairly consistent wine, though lately it seems a tad sweeter than before. Upon release this slightly fortified wine has orange-blossom varietal character, but it darkens considerably with age and picks up more orange-peel flavor overtones. Elysium, which has the rose-like varietal character of Black Muscat, does show vintage effects. The 1990 and the 1987 are best of the recent vintages we've tasted. Quady's first unfortified wine, "Electra," is a light-bodied Orange Muscat wine similar to a Moscato d'Asti but with only 4 percent alcohol (achieved by artifically stopping fermentation by means of chilling and filtering). The Ports here vary some in style and by vintage. The 1989 "Starboard" is very Port-like indeed, with richness and concentrated flavors, fine balance, and a long, fruity finish.

Wines/Varietals: Essensia ($$), Elysium ($$), Electra ($), Port ($$), Vintage Starboard Port ($$$), Spirit of Elysium ($$$), Spirit of Malvasia ($$$).

Renaissance Vineyard & Winery

12585 Rice's Crossing Road,
PO Box 1000
Renaissance, CA 95962
tel. (916) 692-2222; fax (916) 692-2524
Open to the public by appt.; est. 1976

Founded and built by the Fellowship of Friends, a religious group, Renaissance comprises 365 acres of contoured, terraced vineyards stretching across the western slopes of the Sierra Nevada Mountains. This is the only vineyard, in fact, in the North Yuba viticultural area. James Bryant, president of the operation here, believes that it is the largest mountain vineyard anywhere in the world. The 35,000 cases Renaissance produces annually are exclusively from estate-grown grapes. This winery is distinguished by its communal character and by the cooperative arts activities, including arts and crafts fairs, which take place here. There is also a fine arts gallery adjacent to the winery facility.

Winemaker Diana Werner ages all of Renaissance's wines in air-dried white oak barrels or larger wooden ovals. The white varietals, Sauvignon Blanc and White Riesling, are made in both dry and late harvest styles. The 1987 late-harvest Reisling ranked in the top ten at a recent Gault Millau international tasting event in Paris. The 1985, tasted in 1993, is terrific, with classic sweet honey and Riesling flavors in perfect harmony. The regular 1990 Riesling is an impressive wine along Alsatian lines— bone dry with a classic fusil oil nose and the potential to round out appealingly with age. The 1990 Sauvignon Blanc is a good bottle, too, clean and sound but not particularly complex. Sauvignon Blanc used to be the volume leader here, but now 50 percent of production and 45 percent of vineyard plantings are devoted to Cabernet Sauvignon. The Cabernet improves each year: the 1987 is already mature. It has a powerful bouquet with varietal Cabernet aromatics and plenty of red berries, cinnamon, and toasty vanilla flavors in the body. The Sauvignon Blanc is California-classic with banana and grapefruit tropical fruit flavors, plus caramel and vanilla barrel overtones. We first admired it in the 1988 vintage.

Wines/Varietals: Sauvignon Blanc ($$), Sauvignon Blanc, Late Harvest ($$), Dry Riesling ($), Riesling, Late Harvest Special Select ($$), Da Vinci Select White ($), Cabernet Sauvignon, Reserve ($$$), Cabernet Sauvignon ($$).

Rosenblum Cellars
2900 Main Street
Alameda, CA 94501
tel. (510) 865-7007; fax (510) 865-9225
Open to the public; est. 1978

Veterinarian Kent Rosenblum and his team, co-winemaker Tom Coyne, and co-owners Kathy and Roger Rosenblum and Bill Gage, specialize in red wines, focusing on Zinfandel (some five different Zins from favored vineyards along the North Coast), Petite Sirah, Merlot, and Cabernet Sauvignon. The plow on their label symbolizes their "down to earth" winemaking phi-

losophy which means minimal handling, fining, and filtration. Rosenblum owns 31 acres of vineyard planted to Chardonnay (64 percent) and Merlot (36 percent), and purchases an additional 85 percent of its grapes to produce about 9,600 cases annually.

Most of Rosenblum Cellars wines display rich and vigorous character: the 1989 Zinfandel from the George Henry Vineyard in Napa—a Rosenblum personal favorite—is a fine example. Chardonnay grape lots come from Sonoma, Spring Mountain in Napa, and Contra Costa County. Cuvée V, a Chardonnay blend, is softer and fruitier for immediate drinking. The Napa Valley Reserve is more intense and heavy, though the 1990 seems ageworthy. The 1990 Sonoma County Zinfandel is the best of the Rosenblum wines we've tasted: lush with good fruit along deep raspberry and cherry lines and attractively soft, with muted tones and acidity as well as sweet vanilla and toast highlights. It's a good value. The 1989 Sonoma Zin is a near match in quality and value. The non-vintage California Vintners Cuvée is at times a good value as well.

Wines/Varietals: Chardonnay, Carneros ($$), White Zinfandel ($), Sauvignon Blanc, Russian River ($), Dry Gewürztraminer ($), Sparkling Gewürztraminer ($$), Zinfandel, Paso Robles ($), Zinfandel, Contra Costa ($), Zinfandel, Sonoma County ($$), Zinfandel, Samsel Vineyard ($$), Zinfandel, Cuvée V, California ($), Zinfandel, Napa Valley ($$), Zinfandel, Spring Mountain Marston Vineyard ($$), Zinfandel, Napa Valley Reserve ($$), Merlot, Russian River ($$), Cabernet Sauvignon, Napa Valley ($$), Holbrook Mitchell Trio Meritage ($$$), Petite Sirah, Napa Valley ($$), Black Muscat, California ($).

Wente Bros.

5565 Tesla Road
Livermore, CA 94550
tel. (510) 447-3603; fax (510) 447-2972
Open to the public; est. 1883

Wente is practically a winemaking empire in Livermore. With three wineries plus a state-of-the-art sparkling wine facility, Wente dominates this historic region about an hour east of San Francisco. Founded by Hermann and Ernest Wente, German immigrant brothers, Wente Bros. has been one of California's largest family-owned premium wineries for over a hundred years. Since the California wine renaissance of the seventies, this venerable winery has spent much of the past two decades playing catch-up as smaller, younger operations produced increasingly high-quality wines and garnered a good deal of consumer and media attention. The fourth generation of Wentes, however, is now beginning to hit its own stride with well-made, straightforward varietals and occasionally something more exciting (like a 1989 Zinfandel which had wonderfully rich, intense fruit). The grandchildren of co-founder Ernest—Eric (president and winemaker), Philip and Carolyn (executive vice presidents)—are in charge today; their mother, Jean, is chairman of the board. Annual production is 300,000 cases.

As owner of 1,749 acres of vineyard in Livermore and Monterey County (nearly 1,000 in Chardonnay), and with another 2,000 acres mostly in choice regions of Monterey under its control, Wente would seem to be in a position to produce some of California's best wines. Livermore holdings include vineyards owned by historic wine world figures such as Louis Mel and Charles Wetmore, who brought over cuttings from Chateau d'Yquem and Meursault in the 1940s. Wente's Estate Chardonnay is consistently good, and its Zinfandel, Cabernet, and Merlot are occasionally good. Other wines made here are agreeable and serviceable, from the popular off-dry Blanc de Blancs to crisp, fruity Sauvignon Blanc, Riesling, and White Zinfandel. The sparkling wine facilities are most impressive, with separate buildings for various steps of the *méthode champenoise* process as well as storage caves, a visitor and conference center, and one of the East Bay's best restaurants. Wente Brut is clean, crisp and well-balanced.

Wines/Varietals: Chardonnay ($), Chardonnay, Riva Ranch ($$), Chardonnay, Arroyo Seco ($$), Chardonnay, Estate Reserve ($$), Sauvignon Blanc ($), Sémillon ($), Johannisberg Riesling ($), Le Blanc de Blancs ($), White Zinfandel ($), Cabernet Sauvignon, Charles Wetmore Vineyard ($$), Merlot, Crane Ridge ($$), Wente Brut ($$).

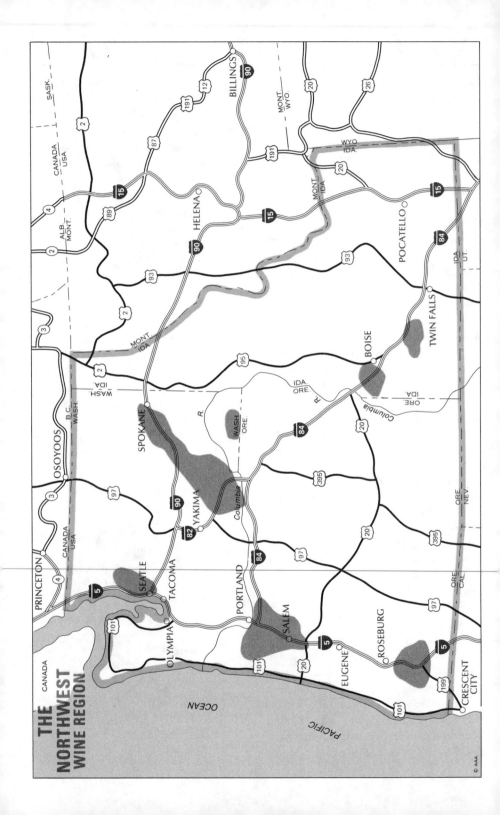

The Northwest & Hawaii

At Home on the 47th Parallel

THE key word for the Pacific Northwest region—Oregon, Washington, and Idaho—is latitude. Vintners and winemakers here like to point out that eastern Washington and the Willamette Valley in Oregon both straddle the 47th Parallel, just like the northern Médoc and Burgundy. As in France, summer days are long in this part of the U.S.: in mid-summer, it is still light at ten in the evening. Temperatures rarely break one hundred degrees, a common occurrence farther south in California's wine regions.

The wine industry here is young, barely a quarter century old really, though wine grapes were brought to the Willamette Valley by the pioneers who traveled the rugged Oregon Trail in the mid-nineteenth century. Eastern Washington, where the majority of this regions' vineyards are today, was a desert back then. Early traders and immigrants planted a number of vineyards in the coves and valleys of western Washington. A handful of these vineyards are still in operation today, but when irrigation transformed the broad Columbia Valley into fertile land, eastern Washington became the leading source of the state's fruit, vegetables, herbs, and hops.

Wine grapes virtually disappeared from the Northwest during Prohibition. From the 1930s to the 1960s, most of the grapes grown in Washington were native labrusca varieties, mostly Concord used for juice and fortified wines. Wine was made from other fruits, too, especially the intensely flavored berries that do so well in the Northwest—

raspberries, blackberries, loganberries, strawberries, even gooseberries. Washington and Oregon still produce some of the country's best fruit wines.

The modern era of grapegrowing in the Northwest began in earnest in the sixties. In Washington, a consortium known as American Wine Growers (later to become Chateau Ste. Michelle) had planted the state's first vinifera, Grenache, in the early fifties. In the early sixties, a group of amateur winemakers, largely composed of professors from the University of Washington in Seattle, formed Associated Vintners, and planted Chardonnay, Pinot Noir, Gewürztraminer, Riesling, and a few other varieties in the Yakima Valley. Riesling was introduced to southern Oregon in 1961, and David Lett of The Eyrie Vineyard planted the first Pinot Noir in the Willamette Valley in 1966.

Today, Oregon has a fine reputation for producing Pinot Noir, and to a lesser extent Chardonnay and Riesling. Washington initially concentrated on such white varieties as Riesling, Gewürztraminer, and Chenin Blanc. But Chardonnay and, increasingly, red varieties such as Merlot and Cabernet Sauvignon are the wines from this state that command attention today. Among the whites, Sauvignon Blanc and Sémillon also do quite well in Washington. Idaho has a climate similar to eastern Washington's, though at higher elevations. The leading—and largest—winery in the state is Ste. Chapelle, which was begun in 1976 by the Symms family, fruit growers in the Snake River Valley near Caldwell where Ste. Chapelle is located. Montana, with a single winery and vineyard near Flathead Lake, does not yet play a meaningful role in the production of wine in the Northwest.

Washington: Mountain and Island-Grown

Of Washington's 11,000 acres of wine grapes, 25 percent are Riesling, the variety which early on proved hardiest in eastern Washington; Chardonnay, Chenin Blanc, Cabernet Sauvignon, Sauvignon Blanc, Merlot, and Sémillon are also cultivated here, along with small amounts of other vinifera. Some Riesling is steadily giving way to other varieties through a process of grafting. The state's principal growing area is the Columbia Valley with its subdistricts, the Yakima Valley and Walla Walla. The Columbia appellation stretches from the foothills of the Cascade Mountains to the plains around Spokane to the southeastern flats that border the Columbia River. Most Washington grapes come from these areas, though there are also a few vineyards scattered along the Columbia Gorge in valleys south of the Cascades, on the eastern Olympic Peninsula, and on a couple of islands (notably Bainbridge and Whidbey) along the coast.

In the early years of winemaking in Washington, most of the vinifera grapes were mixed with native varieties. André Tchelistcheff, wine guru known best for his long association with Beaulieu Vineyards in California's Napa Valley, changed that. On a visit to Seattle, he tasted some homemade Gewürztraminer and recognized the Northwest region's potential for producing fine wine entirely from vinifera varieties. Now there are 85 or so wineries in the state, the largest being Ste. Michelle, Columbia Crest, and Columbia Winery (formerly Associated Vintners). These wineries' products are widely distributed across the U.S.

The eighties was a period in which the state's winemaking industry saw noteworthy improvement in quality and tremendous expansion, as several smaller Washington wineries began to achieve recognition, among them Hogue Cellars, Snoqualmie, Paul Thomas, Covey Run, Arbor Crest, Woodward Canyon, Leonetti, and Quilceda Creek. The surprise here has been the increasing success of red varieties, notably Cabernet Sauvignon and Merlot. Severe winters and cool autumn temperatures can cause problems in some years. In good vintages, like 1985, 1988, 1989 and 1992, Washington reds are firmly structured and long lived, and more Bordeaux-like than their counterparts from California. In white varieties, Chardonnay, Sauvignon Blanc, and Sémillon are rapidly gaining on Riesling in respect to both quality and quantity produced.

Oregon: Dreamers' Paradise

Oregon viticulture has its roots in dreams—dreams of Volnay and La Tâche. That's what such young visionaries as David Lett of The Eyrie Vineyard, Adelsheim Winery's David Adelsheim, and Dick Erath of Knudsen Erath Winery were after in the 1970s: Pinot Noirs with the flavor intensity and graceful proportions of the red Burgundies they so admired. Oregon has none of Washington's giant-sized wineries. The backbone of the industry in this state is small, independent growers—those named above plus Dick Ponzi, Susan Sokol, Blosser, Bill Fuller, Bill Malkmus, Ron Vulysteke, Joe Campbell, and a few others.

These growers' success with Pinot Noir, and to a lesser extent, with Chardonnay and Riesling, has encouraged others. The entrepreneurial eighties saw the rise of newly founded wineries such as Bethel Heights, Rex Hill, Adams, Domaine Drouhin and a dozen or so others. Oregon's Willamette Valley is now the fastest growing area of the Northwest, and Pinot Gris has joined the list of vinifera that are succeeding particularly well there.

Idaho: Snake River Vineyards

Ste. Chapelle is the primary force in Idaho wine; it's the largest winery as well as the only one yet to survive as a viable commercial operation with distribution outside the state. Situated on broad plateaus 2,500 feet above the Snake River, Ste. Chapelle produces Chardonnay, Riesling, and Cabernet Sauvignon. Such young wineries as Indian Creek (Stowe) Winery, Pintler Cellars, and Rose Creek Vineyards are small but increasingly successful; some supplement the yields of their own vineyards with grapes purchased from Oregon and Washington.

Hawaii: Pineapple Wine and Other Pleasures

All right, Hawaii isn't in the Pacific Northwest—more like the South Pacific. And okay, Hawaii isn't the Willamette, Columbia, or some other viticulturally thriving valley. Nevertheless, lots of good wines are consumed in the 50th state, and some of them are from Hawaii's one thriving winery, Tedeschi Vineyard on Maui.

Idaho

an Idaho native and Air Force retiree, and his brother, Mike, even make a white Pinot Noir, described as a "just slightly sweet rosé." As could be expected of a quality Idaho winery, Indian Creek also produces a highly creditable and reliable White Riesling.

Wines/Varietals: White Riesling ($), White Pinot Noir ($), Lemberger ($), Chardonnay ($$), Pinot Noir ($$).

Indian Creek (Stowe) Winery

1000 N. McDermott Road
Kuna, Idaho 83634
tel. (208) 922-4791
Open to the public weekends; weekdays
by appt.; est. 1987

Indian Creek's co-owner and winemaker, Bill Stowe, loves Pinot Noir. Despite the difficulties Idaho growers face with wretched winters, Stowe grows and produces Pinot Noir, which means that when the cold damages the highly climate-sensitive plants back to their roots, he must retrain the vines and accept the loss of a year or two's production. Nevertheless, Stowe owns 20 acres of vineyards (5.3 planted in Pinot Noir), and leases another seven (3 planted in Pinot Noir). Tempering his affection with reason, Stowe has also planted 7.7 acres of White Riesling, 5.5 of Chardonnay (and 4 on the leased land), and 1.5 acres of Cabernet Sauvignon. Moreover, his converted-mule barn-turned-winery in Nampa (near Kuna) makes a nice, reliable, weather-resistant red Lemberger from purchased grapes. Annual production here is 3,000 cases.

The 1988 Pinot Noir is the award-winning wine that fueled Stowe's passion for Pinot. It's big and aromatic and has evolved nicely in the bottle over the years. The 1990 is the follow-up vintage to look for. Stowe,

Pintler Cellar

13750 Surrey Lane
Nampa, Idaho 83686
tel. (208) 467-1200; fax (208) 466-6222
Open to the public; est. 1988

Beginning in 1982, the Pintler family turned 15 south-facing acres on their large farm west of Boise in the Snake River Valley over to grape growing. Six years later, the family established a winery on their property—at an elevation of 2,700 feet and on the same 45th Parallel along which are sited some of the great wineries of France. Today Pintler Cellar is poised to break into the major leagues of fine North American wineries. Co-owner and winemaker Brad Pintler is convinced of the winery's bright future; he talks of "concern for excellence" and plans to "exploit fruit with rich and ripe varietal character." He ferments 3,500 or so cases annually in both small cooperages and stainless tanks.

Although the winery grows and produces Chenin Blanc, White Riesling, Chardonnay (30 percent of production), Sémillon, and Cabernet Sauvignon, Pintler emphasizes Chardonnays, which he says offer "rich varietal grapefruit and apple flavors with a backdrop of toasty, cream oak character."

The Kahala Hilton and its Maile Restaurant
Riding the Crest of Hawaiian Regional Cuisine

Distinctive dining at the Kahala Hilton is as intrinsic to a memorable vacation as the resort's gracious hospitality, flawless service and first-class accommodations. Situated on a secluded beach between Diamond Head and Koko Head in the prestigious Waialae-Kahala district of Honolulu, the Kahala Hilton offers the perfect solution for those seeking the Hawaiian island's quieter side with access to the buzz of Waikiki just ten minutes away.

Currently attracting headlines and the attention of food and wine aficionados from around the world is the Kahala Hilton's innovative Hawaiian Regional Cuisine. Executive Chef Dominique Jamain, a native of the Loire Valley region in France, blends his classic techniques with Pacific Rim flavors and the best local ingredients from land and sea. His imaginative dishes have produced unanimous acclaim from America's most distinguished food and restaurant critics.

The AAA five-diamond award winning Maile Restaurant is the hotel's gourmet showpiece. Readers of Honolulu Magazine named the Maile "Restau-rant of the Year" for the state of Hawaii in both 1992 and 1993 and the Kahala Hilton has also received the DiRONA Award. Highlights from the menu include Roast Duckling Waialae with a Grand Marnier orange sauce, lychees, bananas, oranges and spiced peaches; the Hawaiian Trio with opakapaka,

Maile Restaurant's Hawaiian Trio – opakapaka with mushroom sauce, mahimahi with spinach sauce and onaga with chardonnay sauce – accompanied by Seared Scallops on Balsamic Mango Coulis.

mahimahi and onaga; and Seared Rare Ahi with enoki mushrooms, radish sprouts and red bell peppers in a pickled ginger and shoyu mustard sauce.

The Maile has also garnered the Wine Spectator's Best of Award of Excellence for its exten-sive wine list. Sommelier Leighton Hatanaka over-sees the wine collection which is one of the largest in Hawaii. The list includes an impressive selection of champagnes and sparkling wines, rare vintages of Bordeaux, hard to find wines of the Vosne-Romanée village, and a wide selection from California in addition to Germany, Italy, Australia and other regions of France.

In between meals the Kahala Hilton is famous for indulging its guests with gracious hospitality and large, amenity-filled rooms. This world class resort offers sunbathers the choice of a golden sandy beach or a beautifully landscaped pool plus various water-sports. Tennis, aerobics classes and a gym are available at the exclusive Maunalua Bay Club. Popular with visitors of all ages is the resort's lagoon which houses a variety of marine life including three bottlenose dolphins.

A selection of vacation packages are offered during most of the year. Reservations can be made through any travel agent or by calling the Kahala Hilton toll-free at 1-800-367-2525 in the U.S. or direct at 808-734-2211.

Blackwood Canyon Vintners
Benton City, WA
509.588.6249

Wine Tasting Daily
Noon to 5 pm
Route 2, Box 2169E
Benton City, Washington 99320
509.588.6716

Oregan's most beautiful winery site, in
the hills overlooking the Willamette
Valley. Tasting room and picnic facility
open Spring through Thanksgiving. An
hour from Portland on the way to the
Oregan Coast. Call for brochure.
503.843.3100
Fax 503.843.2450

PORTLAND'S FINEST

As one of Gault Millau's "Top 40" places to dine in the U.S., you are assured a superior experience featuring the finest and freshest cuisine in the Pacific Northwest.

As winner of Restaurant Hospitality's 1992 Best International Wine List Award, you are assured that our 10,000 bottle cellar's 560 labels are of the highest caliber.

No other Portland restaurant can claim these distinctions. Visit us soon. You'll agree with Gault Millau and Restaurant Hospitality…

Atwater's is Portland's finest.

Atwater's
RESTAURANT & LOUNGE

115 SW 5th Avenue • 30th Floor, •
U.S. Bancorp Tower • Portland, Oregon •
503-275-3600 For Reservations.

HOTEL

Hana-Maui

AT HANA RANCH

In Hana, Maui, the Hawaii that used to be still exists. In the sound of the surf on her beaches. In the laughter of her Hawaiian children. In the dramatic unspoiled vistas of her secluded, privileged location...The adventure and enchantment of Hana. The warm Hawaiian spirit of her small, charming community. The intimate luxuries of the hotel itself. It's no wonder why guests return to Hotel Hana-Maui again and again.

An exquisite, coveted gem on the exclusive east coast of Maui. The intimate Hotel-Maui offers 96 rooms and suites located on 66 acres of tropical beauty. The amenities and services are luxurious, yet the feeling is pure Hawaii. This is the way the islands used to be, with warm Hawaiian hospitality and guest rooms located in one story "plantation-style" cottages, reflecting Hana's rich ranching heritage. Activities like tennis and hiking and picnicking on stunning, secluded beaches make for an unforgettable stay. It's no wonder "Lifestyles of the Rich and Famous" ranked the Hotel Hana-Maui as the #1 resort in America...and that our guests return again and again.

To plan your escape...please call your travel planner or
1-800-321-Hana.

Warmest Aloha...the World's Most romantic Hideaway.

To our palate, he's not far off: the 1990 Pintler Vineyard Reserve Chardonnay is a lively, balanced wine with additional butterscotch overtones. The Riesling and Cabernets we've tasted are very creditable renderings as well.

Wines/Varietals: Chardonnay, Vickers Vineyard ($$), Chardonnay, Pintler Vineyard Reserve ($$), White Riesling ($), Dry White Riesling ($), Sémillon ($), Dry Chenin Blanc ($), Pinot Noir, Tiegs Vineyard ($$), Cabernet Sauvignon, Pintler Vineyard ($$).

Rose Creek Vineyards

111 W. Hagerman Avenue,
PO Box 606
Hagerman, Idaho 83332
tel. (208) 837-4413; fax (208) 837-6405
Open to the public; est. 1984

The original three acres of Chardonnay grapes that Jamie Martin planted here in 1980 had to be torn out early in the 1990s, because they were in a frost pocket. Opting out of grape-growing altogether, this one-time potato farmer and his family continue to produce wines deserving of the fine reputation Rose Creek Vineyards has earned in recent years. In 1988, *The Times* of London named this winery among the "New World Top 20."

Martin, who once worked for Ste. Chappelle Winery, purchases Chardonnay grapes from Washington and Idaho; Riesling and Merlot vinified here come from Idaho, Cabernet Sauvignon and Chenin Blanc from Washington, and Pinot Noir from Oregon. Rose Creek's 7,000-case annual output includes crisp, fruity Rieslings (50 percent of production), smooth, Bordeaux-style

Cabernet Sauvignon (10 percent), and pleasant Chardonnays (30 percent). The Martins are especially proud of their barrel fermented 1990 Idaho Chardonnay. The 1990 Johannisberg Riesling Idaho is a fine, off-dry rendering with floral and melon flavors and good value. In the tasting room here, they sell a lot of Rose Creek Mist, a blush wine usually blended of mostly Riesling with some Cabernet. In the past, the Martins have also made Pinot Noir from Oregon grapes and a late-harvest Riesling from local fruit.

Wines/Varietals: Idaho Chardonnay ($$), Idaho Johannisberg Riesling ($), Rose Creek Mist ($), Thousand Springs ($), Basque Red ($), Cabernet Sauvignon ($$).

Ste. Chapelle Winery, Inc.

14068 Sunny Slope Road
Caldwell, Idaho 83605
tel. (208) 459-7222; fax (208) 459-6932
Open to the public; est. 1976

Idaho's big-time winery, located 35 miles from Boise in the southwestern part of the state, turns 100,000-125,000 cases of wine annually, proving to the world that there's a very good future in wine production in the Pacific Northwest. Ste. Chapelle's modern facility is located in a desirable microclimate and overlooks an expanse of fertile valleys and lush knolls known as Sunny Slope. It's an area renown for producing fine fruit, and the Symms family that owns the winery here supplies over 40 percent of the required grapes from their own Symms Fruit Ranch.

Generally, the wines here are sound and good values, fairly fruity and crisp, if a tad sweet (this seems to suit consumers just fine, especially considering the winery's low prices). Director of winemaking Mimi Mook, who trained in California, and winemaker Kevin Mott are proving to be a dynamic duo committed to advancing the cause of winemaking in Idaho. Johannisberg Rieslings (44 percent of production) reign here, and the Dry Johannisberg Riesling is probably the winery's single best offering: in 1990, it was clean and aromatic, with plenty of citrus and apricot fruit flavors to go around. Despite its name, it is only semi-dry. The 1990 Vineyard Select Dry Riesling is indeed dry and very good—crisp, fresh, lively, and full flavored. The winery has had some success with Chardonnay (20 percent of production) as well; the best bottles/vintages are re-released in the aptly-named Collector's Series. The Cabs, including the 1989 Washington Cabernet Sauvignon, tend toward a tomato-vegetable-herbal style and pack a lot of distinctive flavors on top of the varietal fruit.

Wines/Varietals: Johannisberg Riesling, Special Harvest ($), Johannisberg Riesling ($), Dry Johannisberg Riesling ($), Dry Riesling, Vineyard Select ($), Dry Chenin Blanc ($), Soft Chenin Blanc ($), Gewürztraminer ($), Fumé Blanc ($), Chardonnay ($), Canyon Chardonnay ($), Reserve Chardonnay ($$), Canyon Blush ($), Cabernet Sauvignon ($), Merlot ($), Pinot Noir ($), Pinot Noir Blanc ($), Pinot Noir Sparkling Wine ($), Brut Sparkling Wine ($), Johannisberg Riesling Sec Sparkling Wine ($), Johannisberg Riesling Demi-Sec Sparkling Wine ($).

Oregon

Adelsheim Vineyard

22150 NE Quarter Mile Lane
Newberg, Oregon 97132
tel. (503) 538-3652; fax (503) 638-2248
Not open to the public; est. 1978 (vineyard planted in 1971)

Credit Dave and Ginny Adelsheim with helping to nurse the infant Oregon wine industry on its way. The Adelsheims admit they entered the wine business on something of a romantic whim, but things seem to have worked out quite well. From the beginning, they had their priorities straight: In 1971, they purchased 19 acres and the first thing they did was build a house. Then they planted vineyards—today totaling 43 acres (18 Pinot Noir, 16 Pinot Gris, 7 Chardonnay, 2 Riesling). Next, Adelsheim humbly sought out information on winegrowing from all quarters, France included. Over the years, he has selflessly shared the expertise gained through his self-education and tirelessly promoted Oregon wines, in Europe as well as at home (his French and German aren't half bad). With the aid of winemaker Don Kautzner and with brother Michael handling business matters, Adelsheim bottles and sells 10,000 cases annually. Of special note are the winery's labels: all are based upon Conté crayon portraits of friends and family by Ginny Adelsheim.

Needless to say, Adelsheim wines have improved markedly from their early days, and now are consistently good, especially the Pinot Noir (the winery's main focus) and the Pinot Gris. Three different Pinot Noirs are produced here, the finest being

"Elizabeth's Reserve," named after Dave and Ginny's daughter. It's made from the best lots of estate-grown grapes. In 1989, only 340 cases were produced, but they were great ones—big, elegant, rich in black cherry fruit, wonderfully harmonious, perhaps the best bottle of Adelsheim ever. The 1990 is good. The Chardonnays are much improved and quite good, especially the reserve, which in 1990 is a complex, concentrated, toasty bottle. A limited amount of Pinot Blanc, Dry Riesling, and Merlot are also produced and marketed only in the Pacific Northwest. The winemaking technique here merits note. Red grapes are rarely crushed and sometimes not even destemmed prior to fermentation "in order to keep the wines rich and fruity," according to Adelsheim. Whites never see skin contact and are often pressed as whole clusters to prevent tannins from getting into the wine. Thereafter, there is a minimum of pumping, stirring, fining, and filtering. In addition, fruit is picked as late as possible to overcome the tendency in this region for grapes to yield thin and austere wines.

Wines/Varietals: Pinot Gris, Oregon ($$), Chardonnay, Oregon ($$), Chardonnay, Yamhill County Reserve ($$$), Pinot Blanc, Oregon ($$), Dry Riesling, Oregon ($), Pinot Noir, Oregon ($$), Pinot Noir, Seven Springs Vineyard, Polk County ($$$), Pinot Noir, Elizabeth's Reserve, Yamhill County ($$$), Merlot, Oregon ($$).

Amity Vineyards

18160 Amity Vineyards Road
Amity, Oregon 97101
tel. (503) 835-2362; fax (503) 835-6451
Open to the public; est. 1974

Amity's president and winemaker, Myron Redford, found his way to the Willamette Valley and the world of wine from Cedar City, Utah, where he was born in 1945. He came to the Northwest via Antioch College in Ohio, stopping first in Seattle. In 1974, he purchased a 70-acre site with a small vineyard (now 13 acres) in Oregon and established a winery named after the nearby town. With his long-lived Pinot Noirs, he has earned a solid reputation and an important place as one of the pioneering pundits of Pinot in Oregon. Production here is 7,000-10,000 cases annually, with purchased grapes accounting for a bit more than half of the required fruit.

In the Northwest, Amity has a good reputation for Riesling, Gewürztraminer, drier whites, and Gamay Noir, the clone of Pinot Noir found in France's Beaujolais district. With the 1991 vintage, Amity went national with this light, fresh, and inexpensive red. Still, it is Pinot Noir that forms the foundation of the winery's reputation. Currently, there is a range of releases: Oregon Pinot Noir (red label), Willamette Valley Pinot Noir (black label), and Estate Pinot Noir Willamette Valley (black label, only marketed at the winery). In very good years, there's also a Winemaker's Reserve Oregon Pinot Noir (gold label). In addition, there's a Pinot Noir labeled Eco Wine (organic grapes, no sulfites added) for its environmentally-conscious packaging (the label is printed on recycled paper). To our palate, these are all good wines—a bit lighter and thinner in fruit than some powerhouse Pinots. There's no quality difference between the 1988s and 1989s we tasted; the 1988 Winemaker's Reserve, released in September 1992, suggests that Amity's Pinots need a few years in the bottle to fully emerge. This one is reasonably concentrated, with a concentration of fruit reminiscent of cherries and cloves.

Wines/Varietals: Riesling, Oregon ($), Dry Gewürztraminer, Oregon ($), Chardonnay, Willamette Valley ($$), Gamay Noir ($), Pinot Noir, Oregon ($$), Pinot Noir, Willamette Valley ($$), Pinot Noir, Oregon, Winemaker's Reserve ($$$), Eco Wine ($$), Riesling, Oregon, Late Harvest (375 ml, $$).

Argyle

PO Box 280
Dundee, Oregon 97210
tel. (503) 538-8520; fax (503) 538-2055
Open to the public; est. 1987

The Dundee Wine Company, a partnership between Brian Croser and Cal Knudsen, bottles under the Argyle label and specializes in sparkling wines. The company, with the guidance of viticulturist Allen Holstein, manages 200 acres of Oregon vineyards. The winery here, formerly a hazelnut processing plant located in the Willamette Valley, produces 18,000 cases annually.

Argyle's vintage sparkling wines include Brut, Blanc de Blancs, and Rosé. Limited quantities of still wine are also produced, including a Riesling and a barrel fermented Chardonnay. We tasted the 1987 Brut, an equal blend of Oregon-grown Chardonnay and Pinot Noir grapes aged on yeast lees for three years, and found it strong in fruit flavors, rich, and complex. Is it damning with faint praise to say that Argyle's are the best sparkling wines yet produced in Oregon? We wish the stiff prices had more to do with Oregon—or even California—than Champagne. The bone-dry Riesling is a quality bottle, reminiscent of a good Alsatian Riesling, at an attractive price.

Wines/Varietals: Riesling ($), Brut ($$), Blanc de Blancs ($$$), Rosé ($$$), Chardonnay ($$), Reserve Chardonnay ($$$).

Arterberry Winery

905-907 East 10th Street, Box 772
McMinnville, Oregon 97128
tel. (503) 472-1587
Open to the public; est. 1979

Fred and Margaret Arterberry own no vineyards of their own, but buy grapes from some of the top growers in the Willamette Valley. At their winery in the little town of McMinnville, at the heart of the Willamette Valley, the Arterberrys concentrate mostly on Pinot Noir and Chardonnay, producing smaller amounts of Riesling, Pinot Blanc, Gewürztraminer, and Sauvignon Blanc. What we especially like about this 8,000-case winery is the consistent quality it achieves across all varietals.

Arterberry Pinot Noir has big, berryish flavors; the Reserve is often quite deep in color, as with the 1989 Winemaker Reserve. The 1990, though, is much lighter. The 1985 Pinot Noir was a break-through wine for Arterberry. The Chardonnays made here are also laden with fruit, surprisingly tropical and fairly rich in big vintages like 1989 and 1990. The White Riesling, somewhat off-dry and fruity, is easy drinking. There's also a White Riesling Vintage Sparkling Wine as well as a Red Hills Brut Sparkling Wine. Both are made using the traditional Champagne method. Indeed, in this winery's early years, its sparkling wines were its leading products.

Wines/Varietals: Oregon Chardonnay ($$), White Riesling ($), Sauvignon Blanc ($), Pinot Noir ($$), Pinot Noir Winemaker Reserve ($$), Red Hills Sparkling Wine ($$), White Riesling Sparkling Wine ($).

Ashland Vineyards

2775 East Main Street
Ashland, Oregon 97520
tel./fax (503) 488-0088
Open to the public; est. 1988

Bethel Heights Vineyard

6060 Bethel Heights Road NW
Salem, Oregon 97304
tel. (503) 582-2262; fax (503) 581-0943
Open to the public; est. 1984

One of Oregon's youngest wineries, Ashland has 26 acres of vineyard in southern Oregon's Rogue Valley. Its vines are just coming into bearing, so we expect quality here to continue to rise. Owner Bill Knowles currently purchases most of the grapes he requires; this amount will gradually decrease as his vineyards become established. Production here is 4,000 cases annually, including Cabernet Sauvignon (30 percent), Merlot (20 percent), Chardonnay (30 percent), and Sauvignon Blanc (20 percent). This part of Oregon is Bordeaux rather than Burgundy country, and over half the acreage in this part of the state is devoted to Bordeaux varieties: Cabernet Sauvignon, Merlot, and Cabernet Franc.

Knowles is proudest so far of his barrel fermented Chardonnay, particularly the 1989 and 1990 Reserve, which is impressive with toasty, oaky, tropical fruits. It is interesting to note, however, that in the land of Pinot Noir, his aim is to excel with the Bordeaux varieties, including Sauvignon Blanc, which in Ashland's 1991 vintage has a sugar candy nose with sweet fruit and a round, balanced body. The 1989 Cabernet shows the winery's potential. The 1989 Merlot is more accomplished, with lots of berry flavors in the nose and palate and a good fruit and acid structure; it is well balanced and pleasant to drink.

Wines/Varietals: Reserve Chardonnay ($$), Sauvignon Blanc ($), Cabernet Sauvignon ($$), Merlot ($$).

The Casteel brothers, twins Ted and Terry, and their wives, Marilyn Webb and Pat Dudley, planted vineyards in the Eola Hills of the Willamette Valley in 1978. (Ted and Pat had caught the wine bug while living in France and Italy; both were doing doctoral research in history.) For the first few years, the Bethel Heights owners sold the grapes they grew (they still sell some of them), but in 1984, the barn on their property was converted to a winery and tasting room. Bethel Heights released its first wines in 1986 and currently produces 7,000 cases annually. Ted, a clinical psychologist by training, manages the 52-acre vineyard planted mostly to Pinot Noir and Chardonnay. Terry, the winemaker here, does a great job of bringing out the best in the Eola Hills fruit. The brothers receive advice and support from the rest of their family, all of whom are actively involved both with Bethel Heights and the Oregon wine industry-at-large.

Pinot Noir shines here, as is evident in the 1989 Pinot Reserve; it's richly colored, packed with fruit, and well-balanced with a touch of new oak. The 1988 was even better, more tightly knit, though, it must be noted, not quite up to the very highest level of Oregon Pinot Noirs. A fruity First Release Pinot is quite good served cool and is a good value, particularly the 1990. The Chardonnay is a bit austere in some vintages, but in the better ones, the Reserve exhibits fine structure and a nice touch of oak: the 1990 is an excellent example.

Wines/Varietals: Estate Chardonnay, First Release ($$), Reserve Chardonnay ($$), Chenin Blanc ($), Gewürztraminer ($), Pinot Noir, First Release ($), Reserve Pinot Noir ($$).

Cameron

PO Box 27
Dundee, Oregon 97115
tel. (503) 538-0336
Not open to the public; est. 1984

This 3,500-case, high-quality winery is owned by three families. Their collective aesthetic and stylistic focus is strictly Burgundian vis-à-vis the two principal wines made here, Pinot Noir and Chardonnay. Partners Bill and Julia Wayne settled in the Dundee hills in 1977 and are the sole owners of 20 highly prized acres, known as the Abbey Ridge Vineyard. Cameron also draws upon four acres of its own estate vineyard, divided equally between plantings of Pinot Noir and Chardonnay. John Paul, another partner, serves as Cameron's president and winemaker. Paul came to the Willamette Valley from California, where he had worked as an enologist at Carneros Creek Winery. He also worked for a stretch in New Zealand, and passed considerable time in Burgundy.

Cameron, best known for its Pinot Noir made in the traditional Burgundian manner, uses small open-top fermenters. Their finest wine is the Abbey Ridge Pinot Noir. The Unfiltered Reserve is the most potent; in 1989, it is full-bodied, with vanillin, herbs, and berries on the nose, and is deep in oak and rich in currant flavors. The 1990 is at the same level. Chardonnay is also produced here in the Burgundian tradition, barrel fermented with 100 percent malolactic fermentation ("as with the wines of the Côte de Beaune," says John Paul) and aged

in Nevers and Alliers barrels. The 1990 is tightly knit with toasty, buttery Chardonnay flavors that will please easily until the mid 1990s. The 1991 Pinot Blanc is a pleasant surprise, well balanced with clear, appley flavors.

Wines/Varietals: Chardonnay ($$), Reserve Chardonnay ($$$), Pinot Blanc, Abbey Ridge ($$), Pinot Noir, Abbey Ridge ($$$), Pinot Noir ($$).

Domaine Drouhin Oregon

PO Box 700
Dundee, Oregon 97115
tel. (503) 864-2700; fax (503) 864-3377
Not open to the public; est. 1987

The day Robert Drouhin, third-generation patriarch of the renowned Maison Joseph Drouhin in Burgundy, decided to produce wine in Oregon was perhaps the proudest day yet in the history of the still-young Oregon wine industry. That a man whose name is synonymous the world over with top Pinot Noir wines would purchase 130 acres of land (32 now planted in Pinot Noir), and invest four million dollars in a four-level, state-of-the-art, gravity-fed winery seemed to confirm Oregon's position as the promised wineland, at least for Burgundy aficionados. It must surely have looked that way to Drouhin: he had made many visits to the area, finding the Willamette Valley's soil and microclimate ideally suited to Pinot Noir. He bet that his future lay in Oregon—indeed, he even sent his daughter, Véronique, first to apprentice in the state and later to serve as winemaker at his new facility. The winery's capacity is 15,000 cases.

Amid much anticipation, 1,875 cases of 1988 Domaine Drouhin Oregon Pinot Noir were released in March 1991. The suggested retail price of $32 surprised some people: this was Oregon Pinot Noir at Burgundy prices. The 1988 shows a good, smokey, oaky nose with a palate center of clear cherry-flavored fruit and a medium body. The follow-up 1989 is a good bottle, a tad better than its predecessor; possessing medium fruit (black cherries) and body, and spicy oak flavors, it is balanced, easy drinking, with crisper acids and sharper tannins (which should fall away nicely in 1993 and 1994) than the 1988. The 1990 is also rich and complex. Domaine Drouhin seems a good bet; its promise may be confirmed in the coming years. We'll have to wait at least until the 1991 and 1992 vintages—made from estate-grown grapes, cultivated in Burgundian fashion with low-training and high-density—to see.

Wines/Varietals: Pinot Noir ($$$).

Elk Cove Vineyards

27751 NW Olson Road
Gaston, Oregon 97119
tel. (503) 985-7760; fax (503) 985-3525
Open to the public; est. 1977

What is it with these M.D.'s whose passion is for making fine wine? Count Dr. Joe Campbell among them. Back in 1974, with his wife, Pat, he planted 10 acres of grapes and founded Elk Cove Vineyards. The acreage is now up to 45, planted over to Pinot Noir (approximately 18 acres), Pinot Gris

(8), Chardonnay (9), Riesling (7), and Gewürztraminer (4). The Campbells buy in another quarter or so of their grape supply to produce 12,000 cases annually, some of which is bottled under their second label, La Bohème Vineyard. In 1981, they moved their winemaking operations from a farm building to a new winery built on a splendid hilltop amid their vineyards. In the vineyards, they were among the first growers in Oregon to use the French system of close vine spacing; generally, conservative winemaking practices are adhered to here.

Over the years, Elk Cove has had most success with Pinot Noir, followed by Riesling, though we were quite taken with the 1990 Pinot Gris with its fragrant sensory components and lush feel. The *botrytis*-infected late-harvest Rieslings made here are usually full of sweet, tropical fruit flavors; they go nicely with fruit, cheeses, or by themselves, and are probably the winery's star bottling (The dry 1988 Riesling Estate is a real winner). While the Chardonnays still need work (the 1989 was sound), the 1985 Pinot Noirs set a standard of excellence for the winery to work to sustain. The 1989 Pinots were also good efforts: the lower-priced Estate bottling, full of spicy and fruity flavors (berries and cherries), with a hint of oak and good balance, has a silky texture. We preferred it slightly over the pricier, more peppery, tea-like, and complex Wind Hill Vineyard bottling.

Wines/Varietals: Chardonnay ($$), Pinot Gris ($), Gewürztraminer ($), Riesling ($), Riesling, Late-Harvest ($$), White Pinot Noir ($$), Pinot Noir, Estate ($$), Pinot Noir, Wind Hill Vineyard ($$$), Pinot Noir, Dundee Hills Vineyard ($$).

The Eyrie Vineyards

PO Box 697
Dundee, Oregon 97115
tel. (503) 472-6315; fax. (503) 434-5038
Open to the public by appt.; est. 1970

This winery is synonymous with quality Oregon winemaking. Its missionary owner and winemaker, David Lett, is acknowledged as the respected father (now grandfather) of the Oregon wine industry. This bearded pioneer came to the Willamette Valley in 1965 (with a viticulture degree from U.C. Davis) and, contrary to the advice he was consistently given, decided the following year to plant vinifera grapes, focusing his efforts on Pinot Noir. For a while, he was considered a maverick (some might say eccentric), toiling on an isolated path. Then came his 1975 Pinot Noir. Its thundering, good quality and the acclaim it received sent shock waves through not only the American, but also the French (read: Burgundian), winemaking communities. After that, the wine game was played at a new level in Oregon's Willamette Valley. Lett is now producing about 5,000-7,000 cases annually from his 46 acres of vineyards; currently planted are 16 acres of Pinot Noir, 15 of Pinot Gris, 4 of Chardonnay, 1.4 of Pinot Meunier, and 1.3 of Muscat Ottonel. The obvious commitment at Eyrie (pronounced eye-ree) to Pinot Gris marks the second front the Letts' (David's wife, Diana, is an important player here) have formed in their battle to produce world-class wines in Oregon. And they are succeeding splendidly.

David Lett's winemaking style is noninterventionist: he interferes as little as possible with the processes of nature. He uses no herbicides or insecticides, and employs only elemental sulfur and copper sulfate as fungicides. For his Reserve Pinot Noir, he ferments in small bins and hand punches down from 50 percent to 70 percent uncrushed, completely destemmed grapes. The wine ages 23 months in barrels, permitting natural (uninoculated), malolactic fermentation. Fining and filtering? No way! (Even Lett's whites are not fined and only very lightly filtered.) What is surprising about the resultant Pinot Noirs is that they are light in color and medium in body, yet full of fruit, spice, and oak. The 1985 is great, the 1988 almost as good, and the 1989 very good, as it is expected the 1990 will be upon release. The Chardonnay is well made, too, Burgundian in style, but shorter on complexity than the great ones. When the Pinot Gris is right, as in 1990 and 1991, its dryness, balance, and apple-like fruit render it a refreshing, moderately priced treat that goes well with food. Warning: it could become habit-forming!

Wines/Varietals: *Pinot Gris ($$), Chardonnay ($$), Reserve Chardonnay Reserve ($$$), Muscat Ottonel ($$), Pinot Noir ($$), Reserve Pinot Noir ($$$), Pinot Meunier ($$$).*

Henry Estate Winery

Highway 6, PO Box 26
Umpqua, Oregon 97486
tel. (503) 459-5120; fax (503) 459-5146
Open to the public; est. 1978

Aeronautical engineer Scott Henry returned to his family homestead in 1972 with his wife, Sylvia, and took up winemaking as a sort of avocation. Well, you know how consuming "hobbies" can be: Scott Henry IV, who works as vice president of operations/marketing, has become caught up in pursuing Dad's (increasingly remunerative) pastime. Today, the Henrys' 31 acres of vineyards in the Umpqua Valley, planted over to Pinot Noir (12.5 acres), Chardonnay (12), Gewürztraminer (4), and Riesling (2.5), provide 95 percent of the grapes required for the 12,000 cases their winery produces annually (The purchased 5 percent is Cabernet Sauvignon).

All of the wines made here are sound and are a bit controversial in style owing to Henry's exclusive use of American oak, which leaves a strong impression on the Pinot Noir and Chardonnay. Nevertheless, the Pinot Noirs are good efforts, as is the barrel fermented Chardonnay. The 1987 Chardonnay is a bit lean and tart but finished well. The 1988 Barrel Select Pinot Noir is distinctively good with raisins and dried cherry flavors, a seductive manner, and an almost sweet finish. We give the prize here to Henry Estate's Select Cluster, Botrytis-Affected White Riesling, a much-admired dessert wine with a honey, apricot, and apple quality and without an overbearing or cloying character.

Wines/Varietals: Riesling ($), Gewürztraminer ($), Chardonnay, Early Harvest ($), Chardonnay, Barrel Fermented Chardonnay ($$), Reserve Chardonnay ($$$), Pinot Noir Blanc ($), Pinot Noir, Early Harvest ($), Estate Pinot Noir ($$), Reserve Pinot Noir ($$$), Pinot Noir, Barrel Select ($$), Cabernet Sauvignon ($$), Gewürztraminer, Late Harvest ($), Riesling, Late Harvest ($$).

Hidden Springs Winery, Inc.

9360 S.E. Eola Hills Road
Amity, Oregon 97101
tel. (503) 835-2782
Open to the public; est. 1980

This estate winery produces 3,000 cases a year of Riesling and Pinot Noir, selling off its 8 acres of Chardonnay grapes to another winery. Owner Donald R. Byard, a home winemaker-gone-commercial, is seemingly loving every minute of it, especially since he and his wife, Carolyn, became sole owners here in 1990. With a little professional winemaking consultation along the way, and a pruning back of the house's offerings—Cabernet Sauvignon was eliminated; the Chardonnay grapes sold off—Hidden Springs is no longer so hidden, nor are its wines as rough around the edges as they were in the early years. The winery facility itself is located up in the Eola Hills, on the crest of a hillside covered with vineyards, cherry and Brook prune trees, and holly.

As with many other Oregon wineries, the 1985 vintage was the breakout year here. Hidden Springs' 1985 Pinot Noir is still its best to date, but the 1989 seems to us very modestly priced. It has clean, clear cherry flavors and is reasonably elegant, if not too complex. This winery's Pinot Noirs age well. Its Rieslings are fine, too, both the dry and the dessert Riesling. The Byards also make a blush wine, called "Pacific Sunset," from 70 percent Riesling and 30 percent Pinot Noir. It has 2 percent residual sugar and, if served chilled, is a fun sort of picnic beverage. If some of the wines made here are simple and straightforward, so are their modest prices.

Wines/Varietals: Dry White Riesling ($), Reserve White Riesling ($), NV Pacific Sunset ($), Pinot Noir ($, older vintages, $$), Dessert White Riesling ($).

Knudsen Erath Winery

Worden Hill Road, PO Box 667
Dundee, Oregon 97115
tel. (503) 538-3318; fax (503) 538-1074
Open to the public; est. 1972 (vineyard planted in 1968)

Winemaker Richard Erath, a former electrical engineer, with the investment of Seattle's Cal Knudsen, built one of the pioneering wineries in Oregon. With an annual production of 25,000-30,000 cases, it is now also the largest. Forty-six acres are under vine here (Pinot Noir 63 percent, Chardonnay 17 percent, White Riesling 15 percent, and Pinot Gris 5 percent) and another 20 acres are leased under a long-term agreement. Still, the winery buys about half the grapes it requires, all from within the state.

The Vintage Select bottlings age beautifully and are usually of good quality. The 1985 Vintage Select Pinot Noir is excellent; the regular 1989 vintage Pinot is also attractive. The 1990 Barrel fermented Chardonnay, with *sur lie* aging, constitutes a quality effort in a lighter style with good fruit. The dry Riesling here (as evidenced by the 1990 vintage) is exemplary of the tart, lean style that goes so well with food.

Wines/Varietals: Chardonnay ($$), Riesling ($), Gewürztraminer ($), Pinot Noir ($$), Pinot Noir, Vintage Select ($$).

Lange Winery

18380 NE Buena Vista, PO Box 8
Dundee, Oregon 97115
tel./fax (503) 538-6476
Open to the public; est. 1987

Don and Wendy Lange, impressed by Oregon's success with Pinot Noir, came to the Willamette Valley from California, where they were involved in the wine industry in Santa Ynez Valley. Six of their 27 acres in the Red Hills above Dundee are presently planted solely to Pinot Noir, but the Langes purchase grapes to produce the three wines that interest them most: Pinot Noir, Chardonnay, and Pinot Gris.

Lange's 3,200-case production makes it one of Oregon's smallest wineries. Chardonnay here is fermented in barrel, and in 1990, was fairly rich in oak: its tart, lemony flavors veered toward sharpness because of high acidity. Nevertheless, this wine shows Chablis-like potential. Pinot Gris, now also barrel fermented and aged *sur lie*, is one of the best in the state and is the wine that distinguishes the Lange Winery. It tends to be fresh and fruity, and we rather liked the roundness and depth (credit the barrel aging?) in the brisk 1991, with its exotic pineapple nose. We think there's good potential for Pinot Noir here, too. If the noteworthy progress made since 1987 can be taken as precedent, Lange should be delivering quality wines for years to come. The 1990 Reserve, for example, seems to move the winery up a notch in class.

Wines/Varietals: Chardonnay ($), Chardonnay, Canary Hill Vineyard ($$), Pinot Gris ($$), Pinot Noir, Dundee Hills ($$$), Pinot Noir, Canary Hill Vineyard ($$).

Oak Knoll Winery

29700 SW Burkhalter Road
Hillsboro, Oregon 97123
tel. (503) 648-8198; fax. (503) 648-3377
Open to the public; est. 1970

One of Oregon's larger (25,000-plus cases annually) and older wineries, Oak Knoll owns no vineyards. Nevertheless, it produces consistently enjoyable, generously fruity wines year in and year out. Founded as a fruit and berry winery by Ron Vuylsteke, yet another "defrocked" electrical engineer, Oak Knoll is still renowned for its sweet raspberry wine and its blackberry wine, and also produces loganberry and rhubarb wines. Many members of the big Vuylsteke family currently work at the winery, now 90 percent focused on vinifera.

The winery attributes the complexity of its Pinot Noirs (15 percent of production) and Chardonnays (40 percent) to good fruit, cultivation within special microclimates which results in specific flavor characteristics, and the blending of carefully selected vineyard lots. Winemakers here also blend with an eye on the marketplace. The 1988 Pinot Noir is the best of this winery's efforts we've tasted recently: big, rich, and earthy, with plum and spicy flavors. The 1989 bottlings are almost as good, the 1990 as good. The Vintage Select designation is given to a small lot, highly selective blend that tends to be a bit more tannic, need more bottle age, and cost more. The 1989 and 1990 Chardonnays are fruity with a hint of sweetness, ready to be drunk young and well. The 1991 lighter whites—Riesling (30 percent of production), Pinot Gris (5 percent), and Müller-Thurgau (10 percent)— are clean, fresh, and balanced offerings.

Wines/Varietals: Chardonnay ($$), White Riesling ($), Pinot Gris ($), Müller-Thurgau ($), Pinot Noir ($$), Pinot Noir, Vintage Select ($$$).

Panther Creek Cellars

455 N. Irvine
McMinnville, Oregon 97128
tel. (503) 472-8080; fax (503) 472-5667
Open to the public by appt.; est. 1986

Meet one of the rising stars. Founded in 1986, and producing its 3,000 cases annually from purchased grapes, Panther Creek already stands apart from the pack with its distinctively handsome label, extra-heavy bottle, and highly concentrated wines. Co-owner, general manager, and winemaker Ken Wright (he's got lots of good California experience) is driven by a desire for quality. Fruit yields here are kept low; grapes are hand sorted before crushing; fermentation is in 500-gallon vessels with up to six yeast strains employed for each vintage; maceration is long; cooperage is in French barrels; racking and fining are limited; and filtering is nonexistent.

Panther Creek began production in 1989 with Melon, the little known white Muscadet of France's Loire Valley that is sometimes mistaken for Pinot Blanc. The 1990 Melon is a crisp, dry, fruity wine with lots of character along butterscotch and pineapple, butter, and citrus lines. The Chardonnay here tends to be crisp, too, well-balanced with full, tropical fruit flavors and toasty, oaky-vanillin overtones. It's a keeper, especially the excellent 1989. As good as the whites produced here are, the Pinot Noirs are even better. So far there's a first release and a late release Pinot Noir. As could be expected, the late release is superior: deep in color and flavors, with highly concentrated Pinot Noir fruit, smokey, spicy, ripe-cherry/black cherry accents, and a chewy, medium-full body. The 1989 will drink well for years. The first release of the 1990 Pinot is a worthy successor to the 1989; it is full of ripe flavors, more forward than the 1989, appealingly seductive. The unfiltered 1990s, with their Reserve designation, maintain this winery's track record for top quality. Prices for Panther Creek wines are still very reasonable.

Wines/Varietals: Chardonnay ($$), Melon ($$), Pinot Noir, First Release ($$), Pinot Noir, Late Release ($$).

Ponzi Vineyards

14665 SW Winery Lane
Beaverton, Oregon 97007
tel. (503) 628-1227; fax (503) 628-0354
Open to the public; est. 1970

In 1970, Dick and Nancy Ponzi planted 12 acres of vineyards just 10 minutes outside Portland. They produced their first vintage (Pinot Noir) in 1974, thus qualifying theirs as one of the oldest wineries in Oregon. It is also one of the state's very best, and Dick Ponzi, son of Italian immigrants and possessor of a degree in mechanical engineering, is one of the finest winemakers in America. The vineyards here have grown to 100 acres, and today additional grapes are purchased to produce 10,000-plus cases a year. A second generation of Ponzi family winegrowers is now on hand, working with their parents, continuing to lead the Oregon wine industry out of the realm of "potential" into "reality," and onward to greater renown.

The Ponzis believe in allowing their wines to speak—to make themselves, as it were—and there is little intervention in the vineyards or in the winery. They use an absolute minimum of SO$_2$ (commonly employed to prevent oxidation and act as a preservative) and the Pinot Noirs are unfiltered. Ponzi makes good Chardonnay (15 percent of production), and Pinot Gris (30 percent),

and an exemplary Riesling (5 percent); most of the production of these whites is consumed locally. However, this house primarily caters to Pinot Noir (50 percent), and *these* wines have gained respect and fame across America and in England. The 1988 Pinot Noir Reserve, for example, is outstanding: big, lush, and complex with deep cherry, smokey, and earthy flavors—as good as it currently gets in Oregon Pinot Noirs. The 1989 Reserve nearly equals it, and the 1990 "20th Anniversary Edition" is arguably the state's top Pinot of the vintage.

Wines/Varietals: Chardonnay, Willamette Valley ($$), Reserve Chardonnay ($$), Pinot Gris ($$), Dry White Riesling ($), Pinot Noir, Willamette Valley ($$), Reserve Pinot Noir ($$$).

Rex Hill Vineyards

30835 N. Highway 99W
Newberg, Oregon 97132
tel. (503) 538-0666; fax (503) 538-1409
Open to the public; est. 1982

Paul Hart sold his insurance business in 1981 and a year later, with his wife and partner, Jan Jacobsen, bought an old farm on Rex Hill, 20 miles south of Portland. A 1920s prune and nut dryer, partially tunneled into the hill, was renovated and converted to a handsomely rustic stone and wood winery. The Harts own 140 acres of vineyard, which supply grapes for a quarter of their 14,000-case production. Half of the wine made here is Pinot Noir, 30 percent Chardonnay, 10 percent Riesling, and 8 percent Pinot Gris. Small quantities of Sauvignon Blanc are also produced.

Rex Hill's first Pinot Noirs were big, powerful wines, impressive for their intensity early on, but lacking the balance to age. Since 1988, when Lynn Penner-Ash became winemaker, the Pinots have shown much greater finesse without sacrificing intensity of flavor. Overall, the wines here are good and we see the potential for even higher quality. Rex Hill produces four Pinots, including two vineyard-designated wines chosen from best lots and aged almost entirely in new oak. The 1989 Maresh Vineyard is tougher and tighter in structure than the 1989 Dundee Hills Vineyard, which is more generous in fruit, but both seem poised to age with distinction. The winery's second label Pinot Noir, King's Ridge, is an excellent value: the 1990 has spicy, cherryish fruit, with faintly smokey accents. Rex Hill hasn't quite hit its stride with Chardonnay. The 1991, admittedly a lesser vintage, is quite mild in character. The 1991 Pinot Gris is more appealing, fresh and stylish; an excellent choice with salmon.

Wines/Varietals: Chardonnay, Willamette Valley ($$), Chardonnay, Dundee Hills Vineyards ($$$), Pinot Gris ($$), Sauvignon Blanc ($), Pinot Noir, Willamette Valley ($$), Pinot Noir, Maresh Vineyards ($$$), Pinot Noir, Dundee Hills Vineyards ($$$), Pinot Noir, King's Ridge ($).

Sokol Blosser Winery

PO Box 399
Dundee, Oregon 97115
tel. (800) 582-6668 or (503) 864-2282;
fax (503) 864-2710
Open to the public; est. 1977

Things here start in the vineyards: they were planted years before any winemaking operations began, they "own" the winery. There are three vineyard sites in Yamhill County: 45 acres of Sokol Blosser Vineyards in the Red Hills area of Dundee, planted in 1971; 90 acres of Hyland Vineyards in the Sheridan Hills, planted in 1972; and 26 acres of Durant Vineyards in Red Hills, planted in 1973. These 161 acres provide all the fruit for Sokol Blosser Winery's four varietal wines: Chardonnay (34 percent of production), White Riesling (25 percent), Müller-Thurgau (11 percent), Pinot Noir (30 percent). Under Susan Sokol Blosser's direction as president, this has become one of Oregon's best known wineries, and with an annual production of 25,000 cases, one of its largest.

The wines made here are consistently good in an easy-drinking, fruity style. In 1988, John Haw joined as winemaker; quality has recently picked up a bit from that of some dubious mid-'80s vintages. The 1988 and 1989 wines are very good across the board. The 1989 Chardonnay is exuberant, with melons and honeysuckle on the nose, spicy oak, and round, elegant flavors. The 1989 Chardonnay Redland (75 percent of which is fermented in new oak barrels and left on the lees for six months), is at the same level of quality but more concentrated, with bigger, rounder flavors and more pronounced new oak. The 1989 Redland Pinot Noir is a particularly strong effort: moderately big, earthy, cinnamon-spicy, with ripe black-cherry Pinot Noir fruit flavors.

Wines/Varietals: Chardonnay, Yamhill County ($$), Chardonnay, Redland ($$), White Riesling, Yamhill County ($), Pinot Noir, Yamhill County ($$), Pinot Noir, Redland ($$$) White Riesling, Late Harvest ($).

Tualatin Vineyards

10850 N.W. Seavey Road
Forest Grove, Oregon 97116
tel. (503) 357-5005; fax (503) 357-1702
Open to the public; est. 1973

Tualatin's winemaking philosophy is much like its name, the Native American word meaning "gentle and easy flowing." Bill Fuller has been making the wine here since 1973, when he left his winemaking position in the Napa Valley to start Tualatin Vineyards with Bill Malkmus, an investment banker from San Francisco. Their large spread, comprising 85 acres of vineyards, is located thirty miles west of Portland, toward the western end of the Tualatin Valley. Fruit here ripens a week or so earlier than at the mass of wineries to the south in the Dundee Hills, which for the Chardonnay seems to mean an added layer of depth and richness. On the other hand, the Pinot Noir can get a bit jammy and plummy. All 20,000 cases produced annually at Tualatin come from estate grapes: Riesling (32 percent), Chardonnay (20 percent), Pinot Noir (19 percent), Gewürztraminer (13 percent), Müller-Thurgau (1 percent), and Sauvignon Blanc (1 percent).

Stainless steel tanks are used for cool fermentation of the fruity wines here, and French oak barrels are utilized for the Pinot Noir and Chardonnay. Make no mistake about it: Chardonnay is the star here, excellent in 1988, 1989, and in earlier years as well. It comes in two styles, regular and "premium." The regular Chardonnay is forward, ripe, and slightly oaky. In 1989, it was crisp and elegant with apple and pear highlights. The 1989 Private Reserve Chardonnay is rich, round—powerful even—with hazelnut and honey aromas, and pear and toasty oak flavors leading to a long, graceful finish.

The 1985 Pinot Noir is brilliant; the 1989 is typically light and soft, with some spiciness and Pinot flavors, very much a wine that is "gentle and flowing." The pleasant 1990 follows suit.

Wines/Varietals: Chardonnay ($$), Reserve Chardonnay ($$), White Riesling ($), Müller-Thurgau ($), Sauvignon Blanc ($), Gewürztraminer ($), Pinot Noir ($).

Yamhill Valley Vineyards

16250 SW Oldsville Road
McMinnville, Oregon 97128
tel. (503) 843-3100; fax (503) 843-2450
Open to the public; est. 1985

Yamhill County has the largest concentration of wineries in the Willamette Valley. Set in a grove of handsome oaks in the western hills of the Pacific Coast Range, Yamhill Valley Vineyards produces 10,000 cases annually, half of it Pinot Noir. A group of partners, headed by Denis Burger, started Yamhill in 1982 and had 100 acres under vine by 1987 (Pinot Noir, 60 percent; Pinot Gris, 25 percent; Chardonnay,10 percent; Riesling, 5 percent). Burger is winemaker here; he works with associate winemaker Stephen Carey, a veteran Oregon vintner, who came aboard in 1991.

Yamhill scored big with its very first Pinot Noir in 1985, a firm, muscular wine of powerful proportions. The style here has evolved in recent vintages, taking on greater elegance to counter the wines' intensity. Yamhill Estate Reserve Pinots continue to be among the bigger versions of this varietal available, with plenty of black cherry fruit; restrained tannins make for better balance and aging potential. The winery also makes a lighter style Pinot, like the attractively fruity 1990, which is for current drinking. Yamhill's 1991 Pinot Gris is fresh and stylishly racy. The 1991 Riesling is just off-dry and very appealing.

Wines/Varietals: Chardonnay ($$), Pinot Noir ($), Estate Pinot Noir ($$), Pinot Gris ($), Riesling ($), Gewürztraminer ($).

Washington

Arbor Crest Wine Cellars
N. 4705 Fruithill Road
Spokane, Washington 99207
tel. (509) 927-9463
Open to the public; est. 1982

With its spectacular setting, Arbor Crest sets high expectations. The estate rises 450 feet above the Columbia River and culminates in the spectacular Cliff House, the winery's home (and a national historic landmark), perched on a steep cliff. The panoramic views from the winery are sensational, taking in meticulously landscaped grounds, vineyards, and orchards. Owners David and Harold Mielke come from a family that has been in the fruit growing and processing business since 1910. They produce 30,000 cases of wine a year here, drawing on 80 acres of estate vineyards and supplemental purchased grapes.

Arbor Crest produces a full house of classic varietal wines under the supervision of U.C. Davis-trained winemaker Scott Harris. Using state-of-the-art equipment and techniques, he has turned out wines that have won medal after medal in national competitions. The Sauvignon Blanc is perhaps the best of the best (at least it was in

1989), but quality here is high across the board with good balance, clear flavors, and reasonable prices being the winery's trademarks. Overall, the whites tend toward a sweet style, especially the Sauvignon Blanc. The oak-aged Chardonnay and the full-bodied Cabernet have both shown sharp improvement in recent years.

Wines/Varietals: Chardonnay ($), Dry Riesling ($), Johannisberg Riesling ($), Sauvignon Blanc ($), Merlot ($$), Cabernet Sauvignon ($).

Blackwood Canyon
Rt. 2, Box 2169H, Sunset Road
Benton City, Washington 99320
tel. (509) 588-6249
Open to the public; est. 1982

You've got to admire the drive of Blackwood Canyon's one-man band, owner-winemaker, M. Taylor Moore. In the early 1980s, he established his winery in the eastern end of the Yakima Valley, planting 51 acres of vinifera: Chardonnay (20 acres), Cabernet Sauvignon (15), Sémillon (10), Merlot (5), and Cabernet Franc (1). His early vintages were sound and pleasing efforts; he trained with Doug Meador at Ventana Vineyards in California. Then, on October 1, 1985, in the middle of the crush, the Blackwood Canyon winery burned down. Lost with the facility was most of the winery's stock and equipment. Moore wasted no time in building new facilities—and boosting production! Now, with the addition of 20 percent purchased grapes, he produces the planned for 15,000 cases annually. The 176-acre estate has room for another 75 acres of vineyards; who can guess what will ultimately be the future of

Blackwood Canyon under the unsinkable, energetic Moore?

The winemaking here tends toward the experimental: Moore is a great believer in extended oak and *sur lie* aging. He is also a wizard with *botrytis*-affected grapes. For Blackwood Canyon's reds, Moore leaves the wine on the skin for six or more weeks after fermentation, letting the alcohol extract all it can. The wines are neither overly oaked (old barrels are used) nor overly tannic (much of the tannins polymerize and fall out with the sediment). And Moore achieves good quality across the board. The house Chardonnay is of the big, toasty sort; the Sémillon is less oaky but still clearly yeasty from its stay on the lees. Among Moore's excellent but oh-so-high-priced late-harvest wines, we favor "Pinnacle," a 100 percent *botrytisized* Riesling.

Wines/Varietals: Dry White Riesling ($), NV Chardonnay ($), Chardonnay, Columbia Valley ($$), Sémillon ($), Meritage ($$), Pinot Noir ($$$), NV Cabernet Sauvignon ($), Cabernet Sauvignon, Yakima Valley ($$$), White Riesling, Late Harvest ($), Botrytisized Sémillon (375 ml, $$), Pinnacle (375 ml, $$$), Penultimate (Gewürztraminer Ice Wine, 375 ml, $$$).

Chateau Ste. Michelle

PO Box 1976, One Stimson Lane
Woodinville, Washington 98072
tel. (206) 488-1133; fax (206) 488-4657
Open to the public; est. 1967 (origins to 1934)

Meet the behemoth of the Washington wine industry. This large winery produces 500,000-plus cases of still wines annually. It is the undisputed flagship of all Washington wineries—just ask any winemaker in the state. Chateau Ste. Michelle's phenomenal growth in recent years has been accompanied by moderate pricing and a rededication to top quality, which is evident in the wines produced from the 1990 vintage onward—in both what is being bottled and in what is not any longer being bottled, such as Cabernet Blanc and Grenache Rosé. The winery's growth and commitment to quality are being funded by its owner since 1974, the well-heeled U.S. Tobacco Company; Chateau Ste. Michelle's direct parent is Stimson Lane Wine & Spirits, Ltd., a wine holding company. (In recent years, U.S. Tobacco Company has been buying Washington and California wineries for Stimson Lane. In the past four years, additional vineyard acreage, including a 1,900 acre site under development at Canoe Ridge, 150 miles up the Columbia River from Portland, Oregon, has also been purchased.)

Mike Januik is the winemaker at Chateau Ste. Michelle; he was hired in 1990 to upgrade the winemaking process at every stage. He's moving to make the wines here warmer and broader in character (earlier efforts tended to be crisp and tart). He is also adding a signature wine called "Chateau Reserve," a Meritage offering. Though quality and consistency are now sound up and down the line, we tend to prefer the winery's results with white wines. The 1990 Columbia Valley Sauvignon Blanc, for example, is an excellent wine, with citrus and floral flavors, a crisp but creamy body, satisfying through its long finish. The price is right, too. Ditto the 1990 Columbia Valley Sémillon, with its melon and fig flavors and classy balance. We also like the 1991 Sauvignon Blanc and the 1991 Sémillon. Among the reds, the 1989 Columbia Valley Cabernet Sauvignon is impressive: firm, fruity, and tannic, with good balance and flavors of ripe black cherries, currants, and spices.

Wines/Varietals: Chardonnay, Columbia Valley ($$), Chardonnay, Cold Creek ($$), Chardonnay, River Ridge ($$), Chenin Blanc ($), Dry White Riesling, Columbia Valley ($), Sauvignon Blanc, Columbia Valley ($), Sauvignon Blanc ($), Sémillon ($), Pinot Noir ($$), Merlot ($$), Merlot, Cold Creek ($$), Cabernet Sauvignon, Columbia Valley ($$), Cabernet Sauvignon, River Ridge ($$), Cabernet Sauvignon, Cold Creek ($$), White Riesling, Late Harvest ($$).

Chinook Wines

PO Box 387
Prosser, Washington 99350
tel. (509) 786-2725
Open to the public; est. 1983

Producing only 1,800 cases annually, all from purchased grapes—save what they can blend from their .75 acre of Cabernet Franc—wife and husband Kay Simon and Clay Mackey truly are in the handmade wine business. Both have significant backgrounds in the California wine industry. Viticulturalist Clay headed north in 1979, attracted by the pioneering spirit ablaze in the Yakima Valley wineries. He met Kay Simon, an accomplished winemaker, while both were working at Château Ste. Michelle. They married and subsequently released their first wine in August 1984. Original farm buildings, surrounded by plum and cherry trees and the little vineyard, serve as Chinook's winery, storehouse, and popular tasting room.

Simon and Mackey produce Chardonnay, Sauvignon Blanc, Sémillon, and Merlot, all

to consistent acclaim and for a loyal following, which includes many of Seattle's leading restaurants and retailers. The 1990 Sémillon, a blend of grapes from two very different vineyards, is a dry, flavorful wine with complex levels of melon, citrus, and light herbaceous varietal flavors with a touch of oak. The 1989 Proprietor's Reserve Chardonnay is rich in vanilla-oak and buttery flavors, owing, in part, to its barrel fermentation; it possesses a relatively soft mouthfeel, 50 percent of the wine's having undergone malolactic fermentation. The Merlot, also a blend of grapes from two vineyards, is a strong example of how well Merlot can be handled in Washington. The style in this case is full of herbal, cherry-ripe berry qualities.

Wines/Varietals: Sémillon ($), Sauvignon Blanc ($), Chardonnay ($$), Merlot ($$).

Columbia Crest

Highway 221, PO Box 231
Paterson, Washington 99345
tel. (206) 488-1133; fax (206) 488-4657
Open to the public; est. 1983

One of the pleasant surprises of the many, many blind tasting sessions that went into researching this book, was the repeated fine showing of the wines of Columbia Crest. This wholly-owned subsidiary of Stimson Lane Wine and Spirits (*see* Château Ste. Michelle) produces nearly 500,000 cases of wine annually. All of it is relatively low priced ($6-$9), and most of it relatively high quality. Many would say that's a winning combination—and it is here.

Winemaker Doug Gore produces a wide range of wines, drawing from the estate's 2,000 acres of vineyards and an additional 50 percent of purchased grapes. Columbia

Crest's Merlot is our favorite. In 1987, for example, it has a deep, deep color, some varietal herbal character, but plenty of good fruit. Well balanced with tannins that promise a good life, it finishes extremely long. The 1987 Cabernet Sauvignon was almost as compelling, with its deep color and clear Cabernet-berry nose and fruit flavors. Of more recent releases, the 1989 Merlot was lovely with generous, ripe flavors along plum and cherry lines. The 1988 Cabernet further proved that quality (and value) here is no fluke; it is firm and balanced with vanilla, cedar, and berry flavors with a touch of tannins. Among the whites, the Riesling is perhaps the most interesting. It comes in various degrees of sweetness, accommodating a broad range of personal preferences. In 1990, the Columbia Valley bottle was fine in the semi-dry (sweet) range, while the 1990 Dry Riesling has good flavors and balance, and a good, clean attack and finish. Our notes for the other white wines show consistently sound, if not thrilling, efforts. The 1990 Chardonnay was especially pleasing with good, young Chardonnay citrus flavor. The Sémillon is perhaps less interesting but still a pleasant bottle, and the combination of Sémillon-Chardonnay has interesting layers of complexity: in 1990, it drinks easily, with crisp citrus and buttery flavors. The Sauvignon Blanc is sound as well. As part of an upgrading of quality, in 1989, 1990, and 1991, Gore put more wine in Barrel Select bottlings of Merlot and Cabernet Sauvignon. The time spent in new French oak barrels addresses the chief criticism one can make of Columbia Crest wines—that they are simple. The added oak successfully increased the richness and nuances of the wines.

Wines/Varietals: Columbia Valley White ($), Johannisberg Riesling ($), Dry Riesling ($),* *Blush Riesling ($), Gewürztraminer ($), Dry White Grenache ($), Sauvignon Blanc ($), Sémillon ($), Sémillon-Chardonnay ($), Chardonnay ($), Chardonnay, Barrel Select ($$), Gamay Beaujolais ($), Merlot ($), Merlot, Barrel Select ($$), Cabernet Sauvignon ($), Cabernet Sauvignon, Barrel Select ($$).

Columbia Winery

14030 N.E. 145th St., PO Box 1248
Woodinville, Washington 98072
tel. (206) 488-2776; fax (206) 488-3460
Open to the public; est. 1962

As the state's oldest premium winery, Columbia deserves credit for inspiring the burgeoning Washington State wine industry to the pursuit of excellence. Started up as something of an amateur endeavor by mostly University of Washington academics, this winery has grown into a significant commercial enterprise producing about 100,000 cases of wine annually. The turning point came in 1979 with the hiring of David Lake, an Englishman, as winemaker. This Master of Wine (a prestigious British certification), and U. C. Davis-educated enologist is greatly respected and is committed to producing distinctive wines with rock-steady natural balance. It could be argued that a second turning point came in 1988 with the move to an enlarged, up-to-date winery in Woodinville, adjacent to that of Chateau Ste. Michelle. Continuity comes from maintaining close, long-term associations with a few important growers.

The focus here is on the classical varietals, particularly Cabernet Sauvignon (15 percent of production), though in volume,

298

Chardonnay (30 percent) tops production. Other varietals made here include Merlot (15 percent), Sémillon (15 percent), Johannisberg Riesling (12 percent), Gewürztraminer (12 percent), Pinot Noir (4 percent), and Syrah (2 percent). Columbia's wines age particularly well: both the 1983 Cabernet and the 1983 Chardonnay, Wyckoff Vineyard, tasted in 1992, were drinking well. The Cab has a classic leathery, cedar nose and deep cherry-berry flavors; the Chardonnay is toasty and buttery, still with good fruit, but just starting to show oxidation. Among more recent releases, the 1990 Chardonnay from Wyckoff Vineyard is a good one (and sports a new label). It is French barrel fermented and went through malolactic fermentation. Its nose is of pineapple and lemon, with typical hazelnuts, vanillin, and butterscotch carrying through into the clean and lively palate and long finish. The 1989 Merlot from Milestone Vineyard, with its gobs of black-cherry fruit (the Red Willow Vineyard bottling is about as good), or the 1989 Cabernets are also recommended. The long-gone 1989 Pinot Noir Washington Woodburne Cuvée was a revelation, a shockingly fine, complex, and elegant Pinot Noir that wasn't expected to—but did—surpass the best of Oregon and California.

Wines/Varietals: Sémillon ($), Chevrier ($$), Chardonnay ($), Chardonnay, Wyckoff Vineyard ($$$), Johannisberg Riesling ($), Johannisberg Riesling, Cellarmaster's Reserve ($), Gewürztraminer ($), Pinot Noir ($$), Syrah ($$$), Merlot ($$), Merlot, Milestone Vineyard ($$$), Cabernet Sauvignon ($$), Cabernet Sauvignon, Red Willow Vineyard ($$$), Cabernet Sauvignon, Otis Vineyard ($$$), Cabernet Sauvignon, Sagemoor Vineyard ($$$).

Domaine Ste. Michelle

PO Box 1976, One Stimson Lane
Woodinville, Washington 98072
tel. (206) 488-1133 or (206) 488-4657
Open to the public; est. 1974

Spunoff as a separate business entity in 1989 and now with its own, independent label, its own winemaker, and its own winemaking facility, this sparkling wine division of Château Ste. Michelle and Stimson Lane Wine & Spirits, Ltd., deserves its own entry. Like all the wines in the Stimson Lane group, it is poised for aggressive growth. Domaine Ste. Michelle's production is up to about 200,000 cases annually. All the wines here are produced by the *méthode champenoise* and over the years have been subject to much experimentation and modification.

Winemaker Allan Pangborn's current releases incline to the crisp and lean side. The Blanc de Blancs bottling, which we know from the 1986 vintage as a sound, dry Chardonnay sparkler with lots of fruity flavors, is now available in a non-vintage version which has apple and pear flavors and ample freshness but with a hint of sweetness. The NV Brut and the vintage Blanc de Noirs are acceptably straightforward in style, flavors, and quality.

Wines/Varietals: NV Brut ($), NV Blanc de Blancs ($$), Vintage Blanc de Noirs ($$).

The Hogue Cellars

Lee Road and Mead Avenue,
PO Box 31
Wine Country Road
Prosser, Washington 99350
tel. (509) 786-4557; fax (509) 786-4580
Open to the public; est. 1983

Hogue Cellars' remarkable success is testimony to the old adage that good wine is made in the vineyard. The Hogue family, a big farming clan, knows how to grow things. On their 1,500 acre farm and ranch, patriarch Mike Hogue decided to establish a small vineyard of vinifera and to produce some wine (the first releases were Chenin Blanc and Riesling, then came Cabernet Sauvignon). Hogue Cellar's high quality was recognized immediately and its subsequent growth has been geometric. There are now 292 acres here planted over to Chardonnay (24 percent), Riesling (22 percent), Merlot (19 percent), Cabernet Sauvignon (17 percent), Chenin Blanc (7 percent), Sauvignon Blanc (4 percent), Sémillon (2 percent), Gewürztraminer (2 percent), and Cabernet Franc (1.5 percent). Nevertheless, son Gary, who runs the wine company as president, still has to purchase 60 percent of the grapes required to produce the 170,000 cases of quality wines Hogue now handles annually. (Talk about rapid growth!) Hogue Cellars has developed a fairly strong market in Japan that consumes a large portion of its annual production.) Needless to say, the old shed on the ranch that first served as the winery has been replaced by a modern facility in an industrial park.

The Hogue Cellars has an excellent reputation for producing quality wines all across the spectrum. Winemaker David Forsyth sees to the ultimate expression of the excellent Hogue estate-grown and Washington State grapes. The house's white wines, especially Riesling, Fumé Blanc (Sauvignon Blanc), and Chardonnay are its big volume items, though its reds are massive, full-flavored affairs of extremely impressive quality. Fifteen percent of the Riesling is in a medium-dry style, 6 percent is vinified dry, and 2 percent goes into a rich, late-harvest wine. For Chenin Blanc fans, the 1990

effort here in an off-dry, floral style is one to try. For us, Hogue's top wine is the Merlot. The regular 1989 displays wonderful concentrated fruit (strawberry, blueberry, currant flavors), smooth texture, a touch of oak, good moderate tannins, and great value. It is a fine, fine wine with plenty of bottle life in it for the 1990s. The 1990 Merlot is also good, and the 1989 Reserve is exceptionally good, complex and age-worthy.

Wines/Varietals: Chenin Blanc ($), Johannisberg Riesling, Yakima Valley ($), Dry Johannisberg Riesling ($), Reserve Dry Riesling ($), White Riesling, Late Harvest ($), Fumé Blanc ($), Sémillon ($), Chardonnay ($), Reserve Chardonnay ($$), Blush ($), Cabernet Sauvignon ($$), Reserve Cabernet Sauvignon ($$), Merlot ($$), Reserve Merlot ($$).

Kiona Vineyards and Winery
Route 2, Box 2169E
Benton City, Washington 99320
tel./fax (509) 588-6716
Open to the public; est. 1979

Back in 1972, Jim and Pat Holmes and John and Ann Williams purchased 86 acres of raw land, literally—no fences, no structures or roads to demarcate the arid rangeland—in the most eastern and unsettled portion of Southeastern Washington's Yakima Valley. The fitting name they gave their vineyard, Kiona, derives from the Yakima Indian word meaning "brown hills." Deep irrigation wells had to be drilled, electricity brought in, and roads graded, before the first vineyard could be planted in 1975. Now there are 32 acres here devoted to Chardonnay, White Riesling, Chenin Blanc, Lemberger, Cabernet Sauvignon, and

Merlot. The partnership has been successful and today 20 percent of the grapes required to provide for the annual production of 12,000 cases is purchased from other growers.

The flavorful Kiona wines fared well repeatedly in our blind tastings, especially the Chardonnay, Merlot and Lemberger. The barrel fermented Chardonnay has lively acids, butter, lemon, and oak flavors, complexity, balance, and a long finish. The 1989 Columbia Valley Merlot is a good example of the sort of high quality Merlots Washington State wineries are now turning out with increasing regularity: deep, full purple-garnet color, fruit flavors buried under the tannins when first released, well-knit and well made. The Columbia Valley Lemberger, an unusual red from an uncommon grape, is worth trying. Kiona first released this variety in 1980. The 1989 Lemberger, medium deep in color with tinges of purple, possesses an unusual, fruity, sweet nose. It's medium-bodied with spices, blackberry, currant, sweet fruit flavors, and moderate oak. The 1989 Yakima Valley Tapteil Vineyard Cabernet Sauvignon is a fine, brilliantly flavored wine that suggests that Cab, too, is becoming a quality offering for Kiona.

Wines/Varietals: Chardonnay, Yakima Valley, Barrel Fermented ($$), Estate Dry White Riesling, Yakima Valley ($), Estate Chenin Blanc, Yakima Valley ($), White Riesling, Columbia Valley ($), Merlot Rosé, Columbia Valley ($), Lemberger, Columbia Valley ($), Merlot, Columbia Valley ($$), Estate Cabernet Sauvignon, Yakima Valley ($$), Cabernet Sauvignon, Taptiel Vineyard, Yakima Valley ($$), White Riesling, Columbia Valley, Late Harvest ($), Estate Ice Wine, Yakima Valley ($$).

Leonetti Cellar

1321 School Avenue
Walla Walla, Washington 99362
tel. (509) 525-1428
Not open to the public; est. 1977

If Washington has a cult winery, this is it: only red wines are made here, half Merlot, and half Cabernet Sauvignon, in a volume of just 3,000 cases a year. And when Leonetti Cellar's wines are good (they usually are), they are extremely good. Gary Figgins has been making wine literally out of his cellar for 25 years—okay, now he has a little winery out back. Though he owns a one-acre vineyard of Merlot, Figgins uses purchased grapes, and this Walla Walla native who learned winemaking from his Italian grandfather, a home winemaker, is on a quest to discover the secret of sacred red wine.

Figgins is known to introduce a little Merlot into his Cabernet—and a little Cabernet into his Merlot. Leonetti Cellar's Merlot is among the very best in the Northwest. Great in 1988, 1989, and 1990, with mouthfuls of lush, complex flavors, these wines need some bottle age. The Cabernet, especially from the Seven Hills Vineyard, is among the very best in America. It's classic Cabernet, with cedary, cigar-box scents, toasty oak, and blockbuster chocolately-berry flavors. The 1988 Seven Hills Vineyard Cab is excellent. It, too, needs five or 10 years before it peaks. The 1989 is simply great.

Wines/Varietals: Merlot ($$$), Cabernet Sauvignon ($$$), Cabernet Sauvignon, Seven Hills Vineyard ($$$).

Paul Thomas Winery

1717 136th Place Northeast
Bellevue, Washington 98005
tel. (206) 747-1008; fax (206) 747-1138
Open to the public by appt.; est. 1979

Quilceda Creek

5226 Machias Road
Snohomish, Washington 98290
tel. (206) 568-2389
Open to the public by appt.; est. 1978

Paul Thomas made his name initially with fruit wines: a stylish Crimson Rhubarb, a luscious Raspberry, a scintillating Bartlett Pear—all dry. Then he became known for making a very berryish Cabernet Sauvignon (His 1983 Cab is one of the wines that first focused attention on premium Washington Cabernet Sauvignon). He also produced one of the first—and best—Dry Rieslings in the Northwest. Since 1986, winemaker Mark Cave, formerly of Jekel Vineyards in California, has been in charge of making the wines at Paul Thomas Winery. The following year, Paul and his wife, Judy, sold their winery to John Stoddard, who is now president.

Production here from 100 percent purchased grapes has increased to 20,000 cases annually, and still includes the dry fruit wines. The emphasis on Chardonnay, Cabernet, and Merlot is now much intensified, however, and these wines, especially the red Reserves, demonstrate that quality here is high. The Chardonnays have been most consistent, in 1988, 1989 and 1990. The 1989 Reserve Merlot is one of the winery's best efforts, a dark and plummy wine with potential for further aging.

Wines/Varietals: Chardonnay ($), Reserve Chardonnay ($$), Sauvignon Blanc ($), Dry Johannisberg Riesling ($), Cabernet Sauvignon ($), Reserve Cabernet Sauvignon ($$), Reserve Merlot ($), Crimson Rhubarb ($), Raspberry ($), Bartlett Pear ($).

Quilceda Creek makes only Cabernet Sauvignon, in frustratingly small amounts: a thousand cases maybe, some years even less. The winery, owned by Alex P. Golitzin, burst on the scene in 1982 with its first release, the 1979 Cabernet Sauvignon. The wine immediately created a stir, thrusting Golitzin, the shy winemaker (a nephew of André Tchelitscheff), into the limelight. This specialist in deep, concentrated, but extremely well-balanced and complex Cabernets buys his grapes from vineyards in eastern Washington (Kiona, Alderdale, and Klipsun in Yakima Valley) and makes his wines in Snohomish, a small town in the mountains, 25 miles north of Seattle.

Aged in used French oak barrels (on the advice of Tchelitscheff), Quilceda Cabernets put the emphasis on fruit, dark and cassislike; these wines are not overly big, but are deep and long in the finish. The 1988 is particularly rich and berryish with spice and toast flavor, tight focus, and a good finish. With the 1989 vintage, Golitzin began using a bit of new oak in the Reserve Cabernets. Pleased with the results, he now uses about a third new French oak each year. "We came to the conclusion that the structure of our wines can handle more oak," Golitzin explains, "but not enough to obscure the fruit." He has also experimented with blending in some Merlot, though 1991 and 1992 will be 100 percent Cabernet again. Golitzin feels that the 1989 Reserve is his most outstanding wine to date; the 1992 appears very promising. You must find Quilceda Cabernet quickly when it comes on the market because collectors snap it up on release. It is first class and long-lived.

Wines/Varietals: Cabernet Sauvignon ($$), Reserve Cabernet ($$$)

Salishan Vineyards

305011 NE North Fork Avenue
La Center, Washington 98629
tel. (206) 263-2713
Open to public weekends by appt.; est. 1982 (vineyards planted in 1971)

This 11-acre, 1,500-case winery has something of a split personality. Geographically it's in Southwestern Washington State (the only winery operating in the area), but climatically it is part of Oregon's northern Willamette Valley. Thus, while its wines and growing season resemble those of Oregon, its Pinot Noirs, which account for about half of the winery's production, cannot be marketed as Oregon Pinot Noir. Joan and Lincoln Wolverton, who planted the vines here in 1971 and took over the winemaking operation from another winery in 1982, are nevertheless doing all right.

Joan, the winemaker, buys in about 10 percent of her grapes and produces relatively light but balanced wines. She makes an acceptable dry Riesling (20 percent of production), a passable dry Chenin Blanc (10 percent), and a barrel fermented Chardonnay (20 percent) that goes through complete malolactic fermentation. The Cabernets (5 percent) are light, with peppery and vegetal characters. It is the Pinot Noirs (50 percent), however, upon which the reputation of the winery rests, and here Salishan is a bit at the mercy of the climate. In hot years, with their grapes on the vine, the Wolvertons have perhaps a week's advantage over Oregon

Pinot Noirs, if there's no rainfall. But in cooler years, they can run up against poor grape set (as temperatures inhibit growth and, in the extreme, result in damaging frost) and be at the mercy of late October weather. The 1987 Salishan Pinot Noir is representative of the style and philosophy of this winery at its best: it's an impressive wine with an attractive Pinot Noir nose, delicate, fruity, and balanced on the palate with a medium-long, fruit-filled finish with underlying acid, and capable of living longer and better than its light style might at first suggest. Salishan produced an under $10 "Washington Lot 1" Pinot Noir in 1989 with black cherry and plum flavors. It's sound though simple.

Wines/Varietals: Pinot Noir ($$), Chardonnay ($$), Riesling ($), Chenin Blanc ($), Cabernet Sauvignon (blended with Merlot, $$).

Snoqualmie Winery

1000 Winery Road
Snoqualmie, Washington 98065
tel. (206) 888-4000; fax (206) 888-9847
Open to the public; est. 1985

Snoqualmie was founded by Joel Klein, one of the Northwest's most innovative winemakers in the seventies and eighties. Klein made wines at Chateau Ste. Michelle for several years. Then, restless and headstrong, he left to pursue his own vision, starting Snoqualmie in 1985, and acquiring F. Langguth, a large German-owned winery, in 1986. The purchase of Langguth, noted for late harvest Riesling, boosted Snoqualmie's annual production to over 30,000 cases. In 1991, Klein was bought out by Stimson Lane, owners of Chateau Ste. Michelle, Columbia Crest, and other wineries. Production is now at about 26,000 for the Snoqualmie label, with another 42,000 cases bottled as Saddle Mountain wine.

Winemaker Joy Andersen produces 10 wines from purchased grapes. Best among them are the Dry Riesling and Fumé Blanc, both crisp and well balanced. Other whites—Riesling, Gewürztraminer, Muscat Canelli—are lightly sweet and light in character as well, but nicely balanced. Even Snoqualmie's Chardonnay and Sémillon, styled for broad appeal, have a hint of residual sweetness. The house's two reds, Cabernet Sauvignon and Lemberger, are soft and fruity, drinkable early. With Stimson Lane now behind it, we anticipate an evolution in style here and even better wines at affordable prices.

Wines/Varietals: Chardonnay ($$), Fumé Blanc ($), Sémillon ($), Dry Riesling ($), Gewürztraminer ($), Johannisberg Riesling ($), Muscat Canelli ($), Cabernet Sauvignon ($$), Lemberger ($).

Stewart Vineyards, Inc.
1381 West Riverside Avenue
Sunnyside, Washington 98944
tel. (509) 854-1882
Open to the public; est. 1983

Back in the sixties, as an early grower of vinifera in Washington State, Dr. George Stewart helped point up the Yakima Valley's potential for winegrowing. He now cultivates 50 acres in the northern Willamette Valley, on the Wahluke Slope near the mouth of the Columbia (the river moderates winter cold in the area). Most of the vineyard here is devoted to Chardonnay (28 percent), Riesling (22 percent), and Cabernet Sauvignon (16 percent), together with smaller amounts of Merlot, Muscat Canelli, Sémillon, Sauvignon Blanc, and Gewürztraminer. The winery's annual production of 7,000 cases is supplied entirely by estate-grown grapes.

Under the guidance of winemaker Scott Benham, Stewart Vineyards has gained a good reputation for producing lushly-fruited Riesling and ripe, toasty Chardonnay. One of the house's best recent releases is the 1990 Dry Riesling, which is well balanced and highly fragrant. Some vintages of Stewart's late harvest Rieslings have merited praise, too, for opulent apricot fruit and intensity. The 1988 Chardonnay is crisp with hard-edged, appley flavors that are settling down nicely. Unquestionably, all of the right resources—vineyards, winery, and winemaker—are here. With a tad more effort, Stewart should be able to maintain its reputation.

Wines/Varietals: Chardonnay ($$), Reserve Chardonnay ($$), Dry Riesling ($), Johannisberg Riesling ($), White Riesling , Late-Harvest ($$).

Waterbrook Winery

Route 1, Box 46
Lowden, Washington 99360
tel. (509) 522-1918; fax (509) 529-4770
Open to the public by appt. only; est.
1984

Eric and Janet Rindal worked the crush at
a winery in Walla Walla and decided to start
a winery of their own. Until recently, they
purchased grapes from growers around Walla
Walla and Pasco; now they've got their own
32 acres of vineyard (26 in Chardonnay, 4 in
Cabernet Sauvignon, and 1.5 in Cabernet
Franc). The Rindals will continue to purchase Merlot and Sauvignon Blanc as well as
other grape varieties to supplement current
annual production of 10,000-11,000 cases
of wine.

Walla Walla Valley in southeast Washington has produced some good Cabernets
that show real potential for aging.
Waterbrook's 1989 Cabernet, for example,
has spicy, currant-like fruit with considerable spicy oak and berries in the nose. It may
be a little tart for some palates, but we like
the fruit/acid/tannins components and look
for this bottle to age with some complexity.
The 1989 Merlot is softer, with excellent,
very appealing plummy fruit—an outstanding wine. Waterbrook whites are dry, aimed
at complementing food, with none of the
residual sugar that mars some Washington
Chardonnays and Sauvignon Blancs. The
Rindals point to their 1990 Chardonnay as
an example of what they strive for; we found
their 1990 Reserve a little heavy on oak,
which may affect the fruit.

*Wines/Varietals: Chardonnay ($), Reserve
Chardonnay ($$), Sauvignon Blanc ($), Merlot
($), Cabernet Sauvignon ($$).*

Woodward Canyon Winery

Route 1, Box 387
Lowden, Washington 99360
tel (509) 525-4129; fax (509) 522-0927
Open to the public; est. 1981

There must be something to the Walla
Walla appellation. Besides being home to
the stellar Leonetti Cellar, this valley in
Southeastern Washington provides the base
of operations for Woodward Canyon Winery, another of the state's quality leaders.
This small winery produces 6,000 cases annually, including some extraordinarily fine
Chardonnays and Cabernets. Rick Small
started the winery here in 1981, after helping Gary Figgins make his Walla Walla
wines at Leonetti. Small is doing fine on his
own, purchasing 90 percent of his grapes but
drawing distinctive Chardonnay from his
10-acre plot.

As Woodward Canyon's winemaker,
Small was one of the first in the state to work
with barrel fermented Chardonnays with
extended aging on the lees. The Chardonnays
here are big, round, and buttery. The 1990
is a complex, Burgundy-style wine with butterscotch, honey, pear, and hazelnut flavor,
and layers of overtones in the finish. It's
exceptional, but then so are the 1988 and
1989 Chardonnays. The 1987, 1988 and
1989 Cabernets are equally remarkable:
oozing ripe plum flavors, big-bodied, spicy,
firmly structured, and exhibiting variations
on the fruit theme throughout the experience into the long finish. Small is very fond
of his 1988 Charbonneau Red, a Walla
Walla County proprietary wine made of
mostly Merlot with Cabernet added, and
we've admired his white proprietary
Charbonneau, a blend of Sauvignon Blanc
and Sémillon that's smooth, smokey, and

varietally herbal with additional toasty flavors and impressive depth.

Wines/Varietals: White Riesling ($), Chardonnay ($$), Chardonnay, Barrel Fermented ($$), Charbonneau White ($$), Merlot ($$), Charbonneau Red ($$$), Cabernet Sauvignon ($$$).

Hawaii

Tedeschi Vineyards, Ltd.
Highway 37
Ulupalakua, Hawaii 96790
tel. (808) 878-6058; fax (808) 878-2178
Open to the public; est. 1974

Wine grapes in Hawaii? The very idea is a surprise to many people, but Tedeschi Vineyards on Maui has survived the skeptics for nearly two decades. The slopes that wind toward Haleakala, Maui's spectacular volcano, are part of the ancient royal lands sacred to Hawaii monarchs. Acquired by a whaler in 1856, some 2,000 acres in the Ulupalakua district of Maui first were used as a sugar plantation, and later were turned into a working cattle ranch. Then, in the early seventies, the land's current owner, C. Pardee Erdman, met up with Napa Valley winegrowers, Emil and Joanne Tedeschi. When early efforts with wine grapes proved successful here, they formed a partnership and launched Tedeschi Vineyards. Planted to 23 acres of Carnelian, a red grape bred in California to thrive in warm climates,

Tedeschi produces table and sparkling wines. The first wine produced here, however, in 1977, before the young vineyard bore grapes, was a dry white made from pineapple and called "Maui Blanc."

Tedeschi still makes 20,000 cases of pineapple wine every year, of the original Maui Blanc as well as of a sparkling "Maui Brut," which was introduced in 1984. These house specialities are standouts: distinctive, and refreshing, with clean fruit aromas and flavors, and only a touch sweet. Another 8,000 cases of wine are made from plantation-grown grapes, supplemented by grapes grown on 60 leased acres nearby. Wines produced include a crisp Maui Brut Blanc de Noirs, a Rosé Ranch Cuvée, and a Brut Rosé. In 1991, the winery produced "Maui Nouveau Hawaii," a red nouveau style with lots of tannins and berry flavors.

Wines/Varietals: Maui Blanc Pineapple Wine ($), Maui Blush ($), Maui Nouveau ($$), Maui Brut ($), Rosé Ranch Cuvée ($$$), Maui Vintage Brut ($$$).

North and South of the Borders

H ISTORIANS note that the first name given to the North American continent in the year 1001 by the Viking Leif Eriksson was Vinland. Sailing his longboat somewhere off the shores of Newfoundland, Eriksson and his crew discovered wild grapes growing in abundance (Some believe he ventured farther south, possibly as far as Delaware and the Chesapeake). Canadian Tony Aspler, author of *Vintage Canada*, observes that a Norwegian archaeologist has pinpointed the spot where Eriksson put ashore as L'Anse aux Meadows in northern Newfoundland. It was summer, of course, the only time of year feasible to cross the north Atlantic back then, and late enough in the season that the grapes were ripe. One of Eriksson's men, according to an eleventh-century account of the voyage, emerged from the woods, unsteady on his feet and eyes aglow, slightly inebriated, having eaten fermented wild grapes. Some of this story may be apocryphal; the vines certainly are not. Perhaps the "grapes" were wild cranberries, but the point—the very historic nature of the event—and the fruit's potency remain the same.

Some nine hundred years later, Canada is finally realizing its potential for winegrowing. It has taken this long for Canadian winegrowers to find the right climate—not only in the meteorological-geographical sense, but in the political sense as well. Early on, Canada's wine industry suffered the same setbacks that winegrowers in the U.S. once encountered. Imported vines couldn't survive the cold winters; wines from native grapes were sweet and often fortified (i.e., with brandy or neutral alcohol added, raising the alcohol content to approximately 20 percent), which made them inappropriate as table wines. And once a Canadian wine industry was at last established, Prohibition all but obliterated it (Unlike U.S. Prohibition, Canadian law permitted domestic wine production to continue but severely limited its sale to five gallons per person). Only a few of the largest Canadian wineries survived, Brights and Jordan-Ste. Michelle (now owned by Brights) among them. Prohibition lasted 11 years in Canada, ending in 1927 (it continued until 1933 in America).

It is only within the last few decades that Canadian wines, like their American counterparts, have begun to show the quality and palatability to compete with imported wines. Earlier, the Canadian public, accustomed to fortified wines, was not receptive to milder domestically produced table wines, most of which were sharp and tart. The public's exposure to European wines during and after World War II, however, encouraged efforts to upgrade the quality of Canadian wines. French hybrid grape varieties, such as Seyval Blanc, Maréchal Foch, and Vidal were introduced here during the late 1940s and 1950s. Several wineries even experimented with such vinifera varieties as Pinot Noir and Chardonnay, but yields were too low to be economically viable, particularly for the larger wineries. The "Big Four" Canadian wineries—Andres, Brights, Jordan-Ste. Michelle, and London—today produce the full spectrum of wine types including as many as fifty products or more, from low-alcohol spritz to hybrid table wines to sparkling, dessert, and fortified wines.

It was left to the small growers, who could dedicate the time and painstaking effort required, to ferret out the microclimates most conducive to vinifera. These intrepid grape farmers gave the vines the attention and care necessary to enable them to survive. During the seventies and eighties, wineries such as Inniskillin, Château des Charmes, Hillebrand, Colio, and Vineland Estates in Ontario and Sumac Ridge, Gray Monk, Uniacke and Gehringer in British Columbia literally laid the groundwork for the successful vinifera bottlings of today.

Wines and spirits consumed in Canada, domestic and imported, are controlled and disseminated through state-owned stores operated by the Liquor Control Board of Canada. Each province has its own board (LCBO, for example, is the Ontario unit) which operates local stores and regulates the sale of alcoholic beverages. The Liquor Control Board has always been controversial here because of the tremendous control it exercises over sales and distribution and for the rather loose standards it has established for quality wine. Canadian law, for instance, permits wines to be mixed with water, sugar, imported juice, concentrate, and flavor additives. In other ways, the LCB is quite strict: every single wine, Canadian or imported, sold in the country is tested for any kind of contamination. Though this militates for sound wines, it does little to promote quality. So, consortiums of producers have come into being, such as the Vintners Quality Alliance in Ontario, to set standards for quality along the lines of those in the Chianti Classico appellation in Italy.

Canada has some 18,000 acres of vineyard today, with more than 60 wineries producing just under 30 million gallons annually. There are two principal growing regions: on the shores of the Niagara River and Lake Erie in Ontario, and in the Okanagan Valley of British

Columbia. There are also vineyards in the Annapolis Valley of northern Nova Scotia, fairly near Halifax, and a dozen tiny, quite young vineyards in Quebec.

Ontario: Secured by the Great Lakes

Most Canadian wine is produced in Ontario, which now has three officially designated appellations: Niagara Peninsula, Pelee Island (located in Lake Erie), and Lake Erie North Shore. Two of the huge Great Lakes, Ontario and Erie, temper winter cold and summer heat in this region and provide air flow that protects against frost and excessive humidity. On the Niagara peninsula, further protection is offered by the Niagara Escarpment, a ridge just south of Lake Ontario that creates an excellent microclimate for winegrowing. Here, near Niagara Falls, are some of Ontario's best small wineries. Most grow a mix of vinifera and hybrids, which Ontarians refer to as "resistant varieties." These winery's strong suits are in plantings of Chardonnay, Riesling, Pinot Noir (especially for sparkling wines), Pinot Auxerrois, Gewürztraminer, and Cabernet Franc. There is potential for Gamay and Pinot Gris as well. Most of Ontario's wineries make wines from the reliable, higher-yielding hybrids: Seyval Blanc or Vidal, reds from De Chaunac (named for a Canadian who pioneered farming hybrids in the forties), Maréchal Foch and Chelois.

In 1990, Ontario producers formed the Vintners Quality Alliance (VQA) which today sets standards of quality for all wines bearing the organization's seal. VQA wines with an Ontario appellation must be 100 percent from Ontario grapes and made only of hybrids or vinifera that reach minimum sugar levels set by the VQA board. Wines bearing a "Designated Viticultural Area" must meet even more stringent requirements: only vinifera wines may apply, and varietals must contain 85 percent of the grape variety for which they are named (75 percent is required for the Ontario province appellation). All wines produced in Ontario must be submitted to a tasting panel that includes members of the LCBO, viticulturalists, and vintners.

British Columbia: Toughing It Out in Western Canada

Western Canada's wine industry, considerably younger than Ontario's, is centered in the picturesque Okanagan Valley, a sort of wide glacial crevice, with steep slopes and high bluffs, overlooking Lake Okanagan. The narrow glacial lake, still of unfathomed depth, runs south to north a hundred kilometers through corridors of orchards and vineyards. Without its lakes, this region, which receives extremely low rainfall (six inches a year in the southern town of Oliver), would likely be high desert, both too hot and too cold to grow fruit, and certainly not grapes.

Fruitgrowing, mostly peaches, apples, and apricots, began here after 1860, when the valley was settled by French and German immigrants. A few vineyards were planted then, but winegrowing on a commercial basis was not established here until the 1930s. Due to the area's northern latitude, summer days are long, as in the winegrowing valleys of Germany. But days in the Okanagan Valley get extremely hot, too—well over 100 degrees. The deep lake here helps, absorbing heat during summer nights; from dusk to dawn, temperatures can drop 30 to 50 degrees. The cool nights maintain grape acidity and in good years help develop intense flavor in the fruit. Though autumns are mild, early freezes can occur to prevent full ripening of the grapes. The lake, too deep to freeze over, tempers winter cold, but in some years, winters in these parts are so severe the vines suffer winterkill. Only the hardiest vinifera can survive here, and then only in the most protected spots. After harvest, growers must water the vineyards profusely to protect vine roots against the dry winter cold.

A dramatic change recently occurred in the British Columbia wine industry as a result of Free Trade and GATT decisions. Grapes previously used for making blended wines were uprooted and are now being replanted. Before Free Trade, the British Columbia wine industry, at its peak in 1988, consisted of over 200 vineyards with 3,400 acres under vine. Today, the industry is rebuilding by planting higher quality grapes. And through the efforts of the British Columbia Vintners Quality Alliance (VQA), a new dedication to premium winemaking has emerged. Some 115 vineyards now account for about 1,500 acres under vine.

Despite political difficulties and its challenging weather conditions, the Okanagan Valley nevertheless produces some very appealing wines, including hybrid varieties such as Seyval, Vidal, and the locally developed Okanagan Riesling. Many wineries in the area, especially large ones like Brights, Jordan-Ste. Michelle, and even the smaller Mission Hill, imported huge quantities of grapes from California and Washington. It is the smaller growers who have made the greatest strides in improving wines produced from locally grown grapes.

In an effort to upgrade the quality of their wines, local vintners enlisted the help of Professor Helmut Becker, a renowned grape scientist from the Research Institute at Geisenheim on the Rhine. In the late seventies, Professor Becker introduced to this region such grape varieties as Gewürztraminer, Pinot Noir, Pinot Gris, and Lemberger. Since then, there has been some success here with Pinot Blanc, Chenin Blanc, Pinot Auxerrois, Perle of Zala, Muscat Ottonel, Kerner, and Bacchus. Okanagan growers, aided by the very active research station in the town of Summerland, are constantly experimenting with other varieties. There have been some very promising batches of red wines produced from experimental plots of Cabernet, Syrah, and Nebbiolo, but the Okanagan Valley is best known for its white wines and will probably continue to be so.

Mexico: The Cradle of New World Wine

It's conceivable that Mexico could one day rival Chile in the production of good table wine. Home winemakers already make some attractive wines. At the moment, however, the country produces more brandy and beer than wine. Most of Mexico's grapes are varieties of neutral character, like Thompson Seedless, St. Emilion, Perlette, and others that can be picked early to make a high-acid wine that is then distilled and used in the manufacture of brandy. Some of the world's largest brandy producers, including Martell, Pedro Domecq, and Osborne, make brandy here.

A few years ago, at a time when some wineries had begun to produce table wines from the better varieties of grapes, Mexico dramatically reduced tariffs on imported wines. A flood

310

of quality European and American wines followed. Unable to compete with imports, some vintners on the Mexican mainland have stopped making wine or turned to selling their wines to brandy distillers. As many as 50 percent of Mexico's vintners may have shut down altogether. Nevertheless, Baja's wineries are doing well. And throughout Mexico's several growing regions, vigorous pockets of such vinifera grapes as Cabernet Sauvignon, Merlot, Chardonnay, Sauvignon Blanc, Zinfandel, Barbera, and Pinot Noir offer proof that Mexico can indeed produce sound, appealing table wines—perhaps even great ones some day.

Certainly the Spanish thought it possible. Mexico's wine history is the oldest in the New World, dating back some 470 years old to when Hernando Cortès was governor of the vast territory first christened "New Spain." In 1524, Cortès decreed that henceforth, recipients of major land grants would be required to plant vines every year for five years based on the number of native "Indians" available to work the land—1,000 acres of vines for each 100 Indians. The vineyards, planted to Spanish varieties including the Mission grape that was the first leading grape to be cultivated in California, did so well that the early growers put themselves out of business in short order. By the late sixteenth century, New Spain was exporting so much wine to Spain that King Philip II, at the behest of Spanish vintners, ordered the halt of all grape planting in the New World. This policy was enforced over the next two centuries, effectively destroying a promising industry. After the Revolution of 1910 and the ten-year Mexican civil war that followed, vineyard planting went mainly in the direction of high-yield grape varieties suited for brandy production. It is only in the last 25 years that there has been serious effort given to the production of grapes for table wine here.

Mexico would seem to be much too close to the equator to grow wine grapes—so much of the country is warm and arid—but there are moderating factors. Baja, the most successful region so far, is cooled by Pacific breezes. In the hinterlands, the central plateaus are much cooler at these latitudes, especially at night. In fact, temperatures here drop dangerously low at times, threatening the vines even in summer. There tends to be precious little rainfall; in areas remote from sources of irrigation, precipitation can be life-threateningly scarce. In some years, however, sudden torrential rains during the summer or at harvest can be ruinous to the grape crop.

The Mexican wine industry has also faced tough economic challenges, the largest perhaps being lack of domestic demand. Most Mexicans drink beer and *pulque*, the fermented drink made from maguey juice. (A beverage low in alcoholic content that looks something like coconut milk, it's an acquired taste, to be sure. But myriad *pulquerias* across Mexico sell oceans of the stuff.) In the last two decades, soft drinks have grown faster than any other segment of the beverage market here. Each Mexican drinks, on average, a little more than one quart of wine annually, while in the U.S., the average is 1.8 gallons per person. In France, per capita annual consumption is 18 gallons.

Despite all the problems, there are many in Mexico who believe that, as the Mexican economy improves, wine will prove to be the drink of the future. Restaurants in the major cities have begun to offer better wines from quality Mexican producers such as Monte Xanic and a few other wineries that can now compete well with top shelf imports from Europe and California. Not even a substantial reduction in the stiff import tariff that once made imported wines four times more costly than domestic wines has dampened the enthusiasm of those restaurateurs determined to support their country's vintners. With the advent of the North American Free Trade Agreement, however, the availability of even more good quality, moderately priced wines, especially from California, will surely soar. There remains cause for cautious optimism nevertheless: in the current, developing Mexican economy, wine sales are up sharply. And a younger generation of Mexican winemakers, trained in Europe and California to improve domestic grapegrowing and winemaking techniques, is working hard to insure that the trend to consumption of Mexican-made wine continues.

The wines of Baja remain the best known in the United States. Ensenada, a fishing and beach community 50 miles south of the California border, and the Guadalupe Valley, where many European immigrants came in the late 1800s, are today principal areas for thriving commercial vineyards and wineries in Mexico (A graduate program in enology is now offered at university in Baja). Pedro Domecq's operation, Vides de Guadalupe in the Calafia Valley, about an hour northeast of Ensenada, produces good, well-balanced Cabernet and Zinfandel. This valley is also home to the vineyards of Luis Cetto, who has wineries in Tijuana and Tecate and has the largest market share of any Mexican producer, and the small but excellent Monte Xanic. Just south of Ensenada, the vineyards of Santo Tomas, Baja's oldest winery, produce very drinkable Barbera and Cabernet as well as Chenin Blanc, Chardonnay, and Riesling. Santo Tomas also produces *espumoso*, sparkling wines made by the Charmat process. Baja's other young wineries, San Antonio and Valmar, though small, both show considerable promise.

Only a few years ago, the inland highlands of central Mexico were thought to offer the greatest potential for the future growth of Mexico's wine industry. Successful experiments with better varieties of grapes resulted, a short time ago, in the expansion of vineyards in places like Aguascalientes, Zacatecas, Saltillo, and Parras. But these areas have recently come up against severe competition from imported wines, and, as noted, have seen wineries close down, or their annual wine production sold off for brandy making. In Queretaro, just northeast of Mexico City, though, grapes are grown on plateaus at elevations of over 6,000 feet. Here, Martell of Mexico has a large vineyard of Ugni Blanc (for brandy) as well as Bordeaux varieties, including Cabernet Sauvignon, Merlot, and Sauvignon Blanc.

Canada

Cave Spring Cellars, Ltd.
3836 Main Street, Box 53
Jordan, Ontario, Canada LOR 1SO
tel. (416) 562-7797; fax (416) 682-9171
Open to the public; est. 1986

The success some Ontario growers have had recently with vinifera has encouraged other vintners in the region to increase their acreage planted to vinifera varieties or even, in the case of a few young wineries, to devote themselves exclusively to cultivating these grapes. Cave Spring Cellars currently produces 90 percent of its annual output of 21,000 cases from 60 acres of vinifera. Riesling makes up the majority of the plantings here, at 32 acres (comprising 50 percent of production), and Chardonnay is next, with 15 acres (30 percent of production). Smaller amounts of Gamay, Cabernet Sauvignon, Cabernet Franc, Merlot, and Pinot Noir are also grown. Cave Springs is located somewhat inland from the lake and up the Niagara escarpment. This wine area, known as the "Bench" region, produces fruit with pronounced acidity.

Cave Spring Cellars makes four Rieslings and four Chardonnays; the Chardonnay Reserve points to the real potential here. With barely a half dozen vintages out, this winery has already made an impression on us: overall, its wines showed best in our blind tastings of Ontario wines. We had consistently flattering notes on the Rieslings, Chardonnays, and the Cabernet-Merlot produced here. All are well made with clear varietal character, though a bit light and

simple. The 1990 Chardonnay Reserve has an attractive floral nose and a crisp, peppery oaked, medium body over the fruit. The most pleasing wine here, however, is the dessert Riesling, "Indian Summer" (the 1990 is significantly better than the 1989). Deep gold-colored, this wine has a honey-toned nose. On the palate, it displays complex honey and melon flavors, a lush texture, and lots of natural sweetness.

Wines/Varietals: Chardonnay, Musqué ($$), Reserve Chardonnay ($$), Chardonnay, Bench ($$), Chardonnay, Barrel Fermented ($$), Dry Riesling ($), Off-Dry Riesling ($), Reserve Riesling ($), Riesling, Indian Summer (375 ml, $$), Ice Wine (375 ml, $$$), Gamay Rosé ($), Gamay ($), Cabernet Merlot ($$), Pinot Noir ($$).

Cedarcreek Estate Winery
5445 Lakeshore Road
Kelowna, B.C., Canada V1Y 7R3
tel. (604) 764-8866; fax (604) 764-2603
Open to the public; est. 1986

This 20,000-case estate winery, with 30 acres of vineyards on lake view property in the Okanagan Valley, is the dream-come-true of Canadian businessman Ross Fitzpatrick. The emphasis here is decidedly on quality rather than quantity, and the arrival of Ann Sperling as winemaker in 1991 only helped the cause. Sperling's family has been growing grapes and making wine in this Valley for three generations; she came to Cedarcreek with seven years experience and impressive credentials.

The big seller here is "Proprietor's White" (45 percent of production), a blend of 100 percent Okanagan Valley white wines. The most interesting wines are the Pinot Blanc (dry with citrus and banana overtones and a

313

touch of oak) and the Gewürztraminer (soft and spicy). Also worth tasting is Cedarcreek's 1990 Pinot Auxerrois (a grape that appears well suited to the Okanagan Valley), which displays a prominent floral nose, dryness, and a medium-light body redolent with melon and pear flavors that finishes with more citrus highlights. The winery's own vineyards yield Pinot Noir, Merlot, Chardonnay, Auxerrois, Riesling, and Gewürztraminer grapes. Additional fruit (50 percent) is purchased.

Wines/Varietals: Proprietor's White ($), Riesling Blanc ($), Pinot Blanc ($), Pinot Auxerrois ($), Reserve Auxerrois ($$), Sémillon ($), Chardonnay ($), Dry Riesling ($), Johannisberg Riesling ($), Gewürztraminer ($), Reserve Gewürztraminer ($$), Ehrenfelser ($), Proprietor's Blush ($), Proprietor's Red ($), Chancellor ($), Reserve Merlot ($$).

Château des Charmes

PO Box 280
St. Davids, Ontario, Canada L0S 1P0
tel. (416) 262-4219; fax (416) 262-5548
Open to the public; est. 1978

Paul Michel Bosc, founder and co-owner of Château des Charmes and a fifth genera-tion French winegrower trained at the Uni-versity of Dijon in Burgundy, attributes the quality of the wines he produces to Niagara-on-the-Lake's excellent growing conditions. Indeed, Niagara Peninsula wineries with their VQA (Vintners Quality Alliance) stan-dards are leading the drive for high quality winemaking in Canada. Château des Charmes was the first winery to plant an all-vinifera vineyard in Ontario (in 1978), and today its 160-acre vineyard is planted to

Chardonnay, Riesling, Pinot Noir, and Gamay Noir. Sixty thousand cases are cur-rently produced here annually.

The 1990 Estate Chardonnay is a sound effort, showing this winery's promise. It has a sweet, perfume nose, and a medium-light body with clear flavors, though a nutty fin-ish. The 1988 Cabernet, a blend of Cabernet Sauvignon, Cabernet Franc, and Merlot, will not set the hearts of California winemakers to beating rapidly in fear, but it is okay, with a somewhat dry, barnyard character.

Wines/Varietals: Riesling ($), Chardonnay ($), Gamay Blanc ($), Sauvignon Blanc ($), Estate Chardonnay ($$), Estate Aligote ($), Gamay Noir ($), Pinot Noir ($), Estate Pinot Noir ($$), Cabernet Sauvignon ($), Estate Cabernet ($$), Riesling Ice Wine ($$$).

Gray Monk Cellars Estate Winery

Box 63
Okanagan Center, B.C., Canada
V0H 1P0
tel. (604) 766-3168; fax (604) 766-3390
Open to the public; est. 1982 (vineyards planted in 1972)

Gray Monk, the northern-most estate win-ery in North America, is a premium winery using 100 percent vinifera estate-grown varietals to produce award-winning, top-quality wines. True enough, though strictly speaking, this winery supplements its own 23 acres of vineyards with numerous acres of vines grown especially for it. George and Trudy Heiss are the owners here. Their winery takes its name from an old European grape variety: in Austria (George's home-land), Pinot Gris is called the "Gray Monk" grape. According to winemaker George, Heiss, Jr., the "Gray Monk grape, like the winery, is known for consistent, superior quality." Gray Monk Cellars is indeed known and respected in the Canadian wine industry for its fine efforts.

The Heiss family works with vines that originated in Europe and now thrive in the growing conditions of the Okanagan Valley, notably Pinot Gris, Pinot Auxerrois, Bacchus, Kerner, and Johannisberg Riesling. The winery draws upon seven other grape varieties as well: Ehrenfelser, Gewürztraminer, Müller-Thurgau, Pinot Chardonnay, Pinot Noir, Rotberger, and Siegerrebe. Gray Monk makes good, clean white wines and prices them modestly. The Pinot Gris here has a strong character and a medium-to-full body. The Kerner is an interesting offering: a German variety that's a cross between Riesling and Trollinger, it ripens earlier than Riesling and possesses floral aromas and a crisp body with unique fruit flavors. The award-winning Ehrenfelser made here is fragrant, lightly sweet and good.

Wines/Varietals: Johannisberg Riesling ($), Bacchus ($), Ehrenfelser ($), Gewürztraminer, Kabinett ($), Reserve Gewürztraminer ($), Kerner, Dry ($), Kerner, Late Harvest ($), Müller-Thurgau ($), Pinot Auxerrois ($), Pinot Blanc ($), Chardonnay ($), Pinot Gris ($), Pinot Noir ($), Rotberger ($), Siegerrebe ($), Latitude Fifty ($).

Gehringer Brothers Estate Winery

R.R. No. 1, Road 8, Site 23
Oliver, B.C., Canada V0H 1T0
tel. (604) 498-3537; fax (604) 498-3510
Open to the public; est. 1985

The Gehringer family started the vineyards and winery here in 1981 and released their first wines in 1985. The family's German heritage is apparent in the kind of wines

it produces: mostly whites, off-dry to lightly sweet in style. Ice Wines are also made here when nature provides vine-frozen grapes. Gehringer Brothers' 25-acre vineyard, set on a high bluff overlooking the southern end of the Okanagan Valley, is planted primarily to such German varieties as Riesling and Ehrenfelser. Also included are six acres of the rather austere French hybrid known as Verdelet and a small plot of Schönburger, a German hybrid.

The Gehringers purchase up to 50 percent of the grapes required for an average annual production of 15,000 cases. Gordon and Walter Gehringer, both trained at Geisenheim in Germany, share winemaking duties here. Their father, Helmut, and their uncle, Karl, are the senior partners in the operation. Gehringer produces some of the most attractive wines made in the region. The 1991 Johannisberg Riesling, 1991 Pinot Auxerrois, and 1991 Verdelet are all three especially recommended.

Wines/Varietals: Verdelet ($), Johannisberg Riesling ($), Pinot Auxerrois ($), Ehrenfelser ($), Cuvée Noir ($), Müller-Thurgau, Dry ($), Riesling Ice Wine (375 ml, $$$), Ehrenfelser Ice Wine (375 ml, $$$), Chancellor Ice Wine (375 ml, $$$).

Jost Vineyards Limited

Malagash, Nova Scotia, Canada
B0K 1E0
tel. (902) 257-2636; fax (902) 257-2248
Open to the public; est. 1984

The former owner of vineyards and a winery in Germany's Rhine Valley, Hans Jost immigrated to Canada in 1970, where today he carries on his family's 300-year tradition of winemaking. The easternmost estate winery in North America, Jost Vineyards' 22-acres enjoy the protection of the warm waters of Canada's Northumberland Strait. Its vineyards further benefit from the Malagash Peninsula's long summers and frost-free fall seasons. Average annual production here is 22,000 cases, 60 percent from purchased grapes (some from as far as British Columbia). Estate plantings include Maréchal Foch (6 acres), Habitant Blanc (3 acres), Geisenheim (10 acres), and De Chaunac (2 acres).

Most of the large assortment of wines produced by Jost are big, modestly priced blends of passable quality, such as liters of "Chablis House" and "Comtessa Red." The Riesling-Vidal bottling—light and slightly off-dry—is a commendable effort, as is the Maréchal Foch, which here is a fresh and fruity red wine. The winery is especially proud of its 1991 Habitant White.

Wines/Varietals: Riesling-Vidal ($), Riesling, Gold ($), Sonnehof Vidal ($), Gewürztraminer ($), Muscat ($$), Habitant White ($), Chardonnay ($), Chablis, House ($), Geisenheim ($), Sweet Muscat Alexandria ($), Blush ($), Maréchal Foch ($), Comtessa Red ($), Cuveé Rouge ($), St. Nicolaus Ice Wine (375 ml, $$$).

Inniskillin Wines, Inc.

Niagara Parkway, RR 1
Niagara-on-the-Lake, Ontario, Canada
LOS 1JO
tel. (416) 468-2187; fax (416) 468-5355
Open to the public; est. 1974

Ken Kaiser and Donald Ziraldo can be credited with being the bold leaders of the Niagara Peninsula, Ontario's—indeed all of Canada's—quest to be recognized as a quality wine producer by the international wine market. Their Inniskillin Wines was granted the first Ontario wine license since 1929. From the time they opened up shop in 1974, they have dedicated themselves to producing and bottling fine wines from select grapes grown in the Niagara Peninsula. Their first winery was in a barn at the Ziraldo Nurseries site once known as Inniskillin Farm. They've since built a new facility and grown production to 120,000 cases annually. Wines here are made from vinifera grapes such as Chardonnay, Riesling, Gamay Beaujolais, Pinot Noir, and such hybrids as Vidal, Maréchal Foch, and Seyval Blanc.

Winemaker Kaiser (Ziraldo is the winery's president and chairman of Ontario's VQA) believes Chardonnay and Pinot Noir are the wines of the future here, owing to the region's cool climate, long growing season, and the *terroir* along the lakeside plain. Be that as it may, it is his splendid ice wines that have thus far brought the winery acclaim. The 1990 Ice Wine (Vidal from the Braeburn Vineyard), with 13 percent residual sugar, is big, round, lush, and oozingly sweet with a mild acid backbone, reminiscent of lychee nuts and tropical fruits. This wine has plenty of dedicated fans dating back to the 1984 vintage and extending right up through the release of the 1991 bottling. In general, the whites show best here. The Reserve

Chardonnay has reasonable varietal character, tending toward melon flavors with some buttery and sweet citrus under added oak complexities, as in the 1989 release. The Auxerrois (crisp and aromatic with acacia and green apple overtones) and the Riesling (with naturally high residual sugar) are both interesting offerings. The easy-drinking 1991 Auxerrois with its good acid structure, nice body, and slightly sweet fruit stands out for its pleasing personality and good quality.

Wines/Varietals: Chardonnay ($), Reserve Chardonnay ($$), Chardonnay, Schuele Vineyard ($$), Chardonnay, Montague Vineyard ($$), Chardonnay, Seeger Vineyard ($$), Riesling/Chardonnay, Proprietor's Reserve ($), Reserve Riesling ($), Riesling, Late Harvest ($), Blanc de Noir Gamay Noir ($), Gewürztraminer ($), Auxerrois ($), Seyval Blanc ($), Vidal ($), Vidal, Late Harvest ($), Cabernet Franc ($), Pinot Noir ($), Reserve Pinot Noir ($$), Gamay Noir ($), Cabernet Sauvignon, Proprietor's Reserve ($), Cabernet Sauvignon/Cabernet Franc ($$), Maréchal Foch ($), Reserve Maréchal Foch ($), Millot-Chambourcin ($), Baco Noir ($), L'Allemand Sparkling Wine ($), Ice Wine (375 ml, $$$).

LeComte Estate Winery

Box 498, Green Lake Road
Okanagan Falls, B.C., Canada V0H 1R0
tel. (604) 497-8267; fax (604) 497-8073
Open to the public; est. 1986

The home, former winery and current tasting room of Albert LeComte, president and winemaker of LeComte Estate Winery, are today set in an historic structure, complete with stone surround, built in the early 1900s by the original settlers of this property on the western hillside of the Okanagan Valley. LeComte and his family purchased

the vineyard here in 1983, planted many new grape varieties, and expanded over time to their current holdings of about 50 acres under vine. They also built a new winery just in back of the old stone house. The views from the winery—of the full valley, Shaha Lake, and the estate's vineyards—are special.

The LeComtes' primary goal here is to develop premium wines, and they have made good progress, especially with their Gewürztraminer. They are justly proud of the 1990 vintage and consider it a benchmark wine for their winery. LeComte, who watches over his vineyards during the sometimes harsh winters and throughout the long growing season here, is keen on optimizing the natural fruit qualities of each specific grape variety. Among red wines made here, LeComte has had success with Maréchal Foch and Chelois, which bear the VDQ symbol of quality, signifying they have met appellation and wine-making standards, and have been tasted and approved by the British Columbia Wine Institute.

Wines/Varietals: Riesling, Okanagan ($), Johannisberg Riesling ($), Pinot Blanc ($), Chardonnay ($), Bacchus ($), Pinot Gris ($), Müller-Thurgau ($), Gewürztraminer ($), Gewürztraminer, Late Harvest ($), Chelois ($), Chelois, Private Reserve ($), Maréchal Foch ($), Pinot Noir ($).

Mission Hill

PO Box 610
Westbank, B. C., Canada V0H 2A0
tel. (604) 768-5125; fax (604) 768-2044
Open to the public; est. 1966 (in continuous operation since 1981)

There are family wineries and family wineries. This one, owned by Anthony von

Mandl and managed by Swiss-born winemaker Daniel Lagnaz, produces a mere 900,000 cases of wine per year, all from purchased grapes. The winery here crowns Mission Hill in British Columbia's Okanagan Valley, where wine has been produced since the mid-nineteenth century. The 20 percent of the vinifera grapes that are purchased to supplement estate fruit come primarily from British Columbia growers, though Washington State grapes are not strangers here.

Among its wide range of bottlings, including eau-de-vie and brandy (both produced at the winery), Mission Hill's oak-aged Chardonnay is its strongest effort. The Maréchal Foch merits special attention, too, as does the Verdelet-Riesling. Both are made from organically-grown grapes cultivated in Hans Buchler's vineyards. These very limited-production wines are noteworthy in the 1991 vintage. The 1990 "Bin 33" barrel fermented Chardonnay has an extra layer of flavors adding to its appeal. With a Swiss winemaker running the show here, it's no surprise that Mission Hill produces an interesting private reserve Chasselas, the grape known in Switzerland as "Fendant," which yields a fresh, crisp, youthful red wine, here a little spritzy. This winery's prices across the board are modest and its quality agreeable; wines here are generally soundly and cleanly made. The 1990 Private Reserve Barrel Aged Cabernet Sauvignon, for example, is without flaws, though the style, with the addition of Merlot, leans toward sweet fruit on the nose and palate and a softness that runs counter to what we might expect from the wine's barrel aging.

Wines/Varietals: Chardonnay ($), Chasselas ($), Chenin Blanc ($), Dry Chenin Blanc ($),

Gewürztraminer ($), Johannisberg Riesling ($), Dry Riesling ($), Dry Botrytis Affected Optima ($), Bacchus ($), Pinot Blanc ($), Sauvignon Blanc ($), Sémillon ($), Sémillon/ Chardonnay ($), Cabernet Sauvignon ($), Cabernet Sauvignon/Merlot ($), Merlot ($), Botrytis Affected Optima ($$), Johannisberg Riesling, Late Harvest ($), Muscat of Alexandria ($), NV Port ($), NV Sherry ($), Organic Maréchal Foch ($), Organic Verdelet Riesling ($).

Please see Mission Hill Color label adjacent to page 280.

Reif Estate Winery

R.R. #1, Niagara Parkway
Niagara-on-the-Lake, Ontario, Canada
L0S 1J0
tel. (416) 468-7738; fax (416) 468-5878
Open to the public; est. 1982

The Reif family moved to Niagara from the Rhine region of Germany in 1977 and immediately started planting vineyards. They arrived with a century of family experience in winemaking and soon began importing equipment from the Reif winery in Neustadt to continue working in their Old World tradition. Five years later, President Klaus Reif opened the winery's doors. Situated in the Niagara plains area along the Niagara Parkway with lovely views of the Niagara River, Reif Estate Winery uses 100 percent estate-grown grapes.

Reif, who holds top German degrees in both enology and viticulture, works closely with winemaker Roberto D. DiDomenico to turn out some highly attractive wines. The Rieslings and the Chardonnays stand out here; both the premium unfiltered Merlot and the Cabernet Sauvignon are also intriguing efforts. This winery's

Gewürztraminer has an unusual tea-leaf character on the palate that follows a big, floral nose. This flavor element is evident in the 1990 Dry Gewürztraminer as well as in the 1990 Medium Dry (demi-sec), though in the latter, it is toned down by the overlying sugar and is a bit more attractive (This tea flavor is no doubt a characteristic of the *terroir,* as we've also found it in some of the Rieslings from the area). The 1990 Chardonnay, at under $10, is a good value. It is aged in small French oak barrels and German oak casks and is well defined and dry with buttery tones.

Wines/Varietals: Chardonnay ($), Reserve Chardonnay ($$), Johannisberg Riesling, Dry ($), Johannisberg Riesling, Medium Dry ($), Rheingold ($), Seyval Blanc ($), Vidal ($), Vidal, Select Harvest Dry ($$), Gewürztraminer, Dry ($), Gewürztraminer, Medium Dry ($), Gamay Rosé ($), Pinot Noir ($), Cabernet Sauvignon ($), Cabernet Sauvignon, Non-Filtered ($$$), Merlot, Non-Filtered ($$$), Baco Noir ($), Vidal, Late Harvest ($), Riesling, Late Harvest ($), Vidal Ice Wine ($$$), Riesling Ice Wine ($$$), Vidal, Select Harvest Sweet ($$).

Sumac Ridge Estate Winery
Highway 97, PO Box 307
Summerland, B.C., Canada V0H 1Z0
tel. (604) 494-0451; fax. (604) 494-3456
Open to the public; est. 1981

Sumac Ridge was officially founded in 1981, though the partnership that then owned it was already at work in the late seventies, converting a golf course clubhouse into a winery and transforming portions of adjacent fairways into vineyards.

The vineyards here have now expanded to 20 acres, but work on the vines still turns up a stray golf ball now and then. Summerland, home of peach orchards as well as vineyards, is midway up the long, narrow Okanagan Valley. Bob Wareham bought out the last remaining partner in 1991 (Harry McWatters remains aboard as president). Sumac Ridge's vineyards have been planted carefully, with a concentration of vines best able to withstand winter cold and damaging frost. Initial plantings included white varieties such as Gewürztraminer (currently 25 percent of production), Chardonnay, Pinot Blanc, and Riesling, plus hybrids like Chancellor and Verdelet. Annual production is 20,000 cases.

Sumac Ridge has won the most recognition for its Gewürztraminer and Chancellor. The Gewürztraminers, ranging in style from dry to late-harvest, are spicy and well-balanced, similar to good Alsatian versions. The winery is particularly proud of its 1990 Private Reserve Gewürztraminer. Chardonnay and Pinot Blanc are somewhat more austere in style, but well-made. The Chancellor Private Reserve, a firm, flavorful, oak-aged red, is best with three to five years of age on it. In recent years, the vineyard has been expanded to include vinifera varieties, including such reds as Pinot Noir, Merlot, and Cabernet Franc that show promise for the future. Sumac Ridge also makes a limited quantity of highly regarded *méthode champenoise* sparkling wine.

Wines/Varietals: Gewürztraminer ($), Gewürztraminer, Private Reserve ($), Chardonnay ($), Pinot Blanc ($), Chancellor ($), Riesling ($), Stellar's Jay Cuvée (méthode champenoise, $$).

Vineland Estates Winery

3620 Moyer Road
Vineland, Ontario, Canada LOR 2CO
tel. (416) 562-7088; fax (416) 562-3071
Open to the public; est. 1983

Riesling reigns here at one of Ontario's finest wineries. Eighty percent of Vineland Estate's 75 acres of vineyards are devoted to Riesling; the remainder are planted to Chardonnay (10 percent), Vidal (5 percent), and Pinot Noir (5 percent). With the addition of 10 percent purchased grapes, owners Herman Weis, a German vintner with vineyards in the Mosel region, and Allan Schmidt, general manager and winemaker here, produce 10,000 cases a year. Schmidt, a third-generation grape grower from British Columbia, learned winemaking in Germany and in the Napa Valley with Joseph Heitz of Heitz Wine Cellars. Vineland Estate's vineyards are on the rolling hills between the Niagara escarpment and the lake in an area known as the "Bench" region that is reputed to be one of the top grape-growing spots in Canada.

Half of the production here consists of dry Riesling, another 5 percent of dessert wine, 3 percent of Riesling, and 2 percent of Vidal Ice Wine. These bottlings are Vineland's quality leaders. The Premium Dry St. Urbain, Niagara-on-the-Lake Rieslings in 1989 and 1990 are all floral with clean, balanced flavors. In the dessert wine category, we prefer the late harvest Riesling, which is a fairly lean and attractive sweet wine, displaying some tea leaf flavor highlights that seem characteristic of this region,

to the only bottle of the Vidal Ice Wine we tasted. We also rather like the Gewürztraminer and the Chardonnay. The 1991 Gewürztraminer is semi-dry, fresh, with high natural sugars, good front fruit on the palate, and an acceptable finish with a touch of final bitterness that is not glaring. The surprise here is the Chardonnay, which received top ratings in our tastings of Canadian Chards. The 1990 has classic flavors, nice balance and medium body, and is clearly well made. Its natural fruit sugars render it just slightly sweet.

Wines/Varietals: Riesling, Dry ($), Riesling, Semi-Dry ($), Riesling, Late Harvest ($$), Chardonnay ($), Gewürztraminer ($), Seyval Blanc ($), Baco Noir ($), Pinot Noir ($).

See page 34-35 for map of wine growing regions of Canada and Mexico and see adjacent page 249 for color label of Santo Tomas Winery in Mexico.

Mexico

Monte Xanic

Avenida Marina 10
Ensenada, Baja, Mexico 22800
tel. (526) 678-3146
Open to the public by appt.; est. 1987

A five-member partnership founded Monte Xanic ("Xanic" is a Cora Indian name meaning "the first flower that blooms after the rain") and produced their first vintage in 1987. One of the partners, Hans Backhoff (grandson of a German immigrant), is winemaker here. This winery's 125 acres of vineyard are about 25 miles northeast of Ensenada, in the Guadalupe Valley, a vine-laden area devoted mostly to viticulture, but also to olive and citrus farming. Already, Monte Xanic (pronounced SHA-nic) produces some of Mexico's best wines: Bordeaux-style reds from the five classic varieties (Cabernet Sauvignon, Cabernet Franc, Merlot, Malbec, and Petit Verdot), and dry, crisp whites from Sauvignon Blanc and Chardonnay. This young operation is highly prized by those who have long waited for Mexico to realize its potential for producing wines capable of achieving international levels of quality and style.

Monte Xanic is poised to do just that with its current production of 16,000 cases annually (on the way to its 25,000 capacity). "We compete head-on with imported wines," says sales director Tomas Fernandez, "including Bordeaux, White Burgundy, and Chardonnays from California." Indeed, at top restaurants in Mexico City, Monte Xanic's wines command $40 to $50 a bottle. The 1989 Cabernet Sauvignon, concentrated and well balanced with an impres-

sively long finish, won a gold medal in the Los Angeles County Fair's judged competition in 1992; the winery's Cabernet/Merlot took the silver medal in this same competition. We also admire Monte Xanic's 1990 barrel fermented Chardonnay.

Wines/Varietals: Chenin Blanc ($), Sauvignon Blanc ($$), Chardonnay ($$$), Cabernet Sauvignon ($$$), Cabernet/Merlot ($$$).

Santo Tomas Winery

Avenida Miramar, 666
Ensenada, Baja, Mexico 22800
tel. (667) 83333
Open to the public; est. 1888

Santo Tomas was founded in 1888 by a Spanish family in the Santo Tomas Valley, about 25 miles south of Ensenada. The property was known then as "Rancho de los Dolores," but in the 1920s, it was acquired by General Abelardo Rodriguez, president of Mexico. The estate was in wretched shape, and General Rodriguez was reluctant to pour money into it. Fortunately, he hired the energetic Esteban Ferro to do what he could, promising him 40 percent of the business if it succeeded. The strong and determined Señor Ferro and his sons labored long hours to restore the vineyards and winery. They turned the poor wine then coming from the vineyard into port, using honey to sweeten it (because they had no money to buy sugar) and fortifying it with brandy; it sold well to American tourists during Prohibition. With the proceeds from port sales, Ferro was able to begin replanting the vineyard. The climate for wine grapes is very good in Baja, the arid terrain cooled by its proximity to the Pacific. By the early 1940s, Ferro had the place thriving. He eventually planted 250 acres in Santo Tomas

Valley and another 250 acres east of Ensenada in the Guadalupe Valley, including blocks of a number of Italian varieties such as Barbera, Nebbiolo, Freisa, Dolcetto, and Brachetto. In 1952, Ferro sold Santo Tomas to Pedro Domecq, who later sold it to the Pandro corporation.

Today Santo Tomas remains a large winery with an annual production of 100,000 cases (Ten percent of its production is exported). The winery's tasting room in Ensenada is one of the city's major tourist attractions. Fourteen wines are currently produced here, the best of which are red, notably Barbera, Cabernet Sauvignon, and good everyday blends labeled "Tinto San Emilion" and "Tinto Mision." The most popular Mexican white wine is Chenin Blanc, which makes up the largest part of Santo Tomas' production. The winery also makes Sauvignon Blanc and Chardonnay, as well as several blends. Santo Tomas wines are inexpensively priced and agreeable for everyday drinking.

Wines/Varietals: Chenin Blanc ($), Sauvignon Blanc ($), Chardonnay ($$), Blanc de Blancs ($$), Blanco Seco ($), Blanco San Emilion ($), Calvine ($), Cabernet Sauvignon ($$), Barbera ($), Rosado ($), Tinto San Emilion ($), Tinto Mision ($), Oporto ($$), Jerez ($).

Vides de Guadalupe, S.A. [L.A. Cetto]

Calle Eusebio Kino s/n
Entre Fray Mayorga y La Linea Internacional
Tijuana, B.C.N. 292
tel. (91) 66-238-386; fax (91) 66-238-237
Open to public by appt.; est. 1972

Owned by Pedro Domecq, the Spanish sherry and brandy firm, this winery in Baja comprises 1,500 acres of vineyard set in a small valley about an hour inland from the Pacific. Dry and arid, with reddish soil, the vineyards here are largely dry-farmed. Calafia Valley (also known as Guadalupe Valley) once boasted two wineries, Domecq and L.A. Cetto, but they have long since merged, creating this, the largest winery in Mexico by far, with about a 50 percent share of the market for domestically produced wines (10 percent of production is currently exported, and this number is rising). Winemaking facilities are still in the valley, but this operation's corporate headquarters and marketing activities are now located in Tijuana. The vineyards here are planted entirely to vinifera varieties—mostly French—such as Cabernet, Sauvignon Blanc, Chenin Blanc, Colombard, Petite Sirah, Ruby Cabernet, and Zinfandel. Wines made here are marketed under the "L.A. Cetto" label.

Domecq has done a good job of producing sound, medium-weight wines with good fruit and balance, if little character or complexity. Production is enormous—750,000 cases annually; the winery purchases about 60 percent of the grapes needed to attain that level. We prefer this winery's reds to its whites, particularly the consistently good Cabernet, Zinfandel, and blended everyday reds labeled "Los Reyes" and "Calafia," which represent fine values. The better Cabernet, vintage-dated and labeled "Château Domecq," is usually given extra aging before release, rather like red Rioja in Spain.

Wines/Varietals: Los Reyes (red, white, and rosé, $), Calafia (red and white, $), Riesling ($), Blanc de Blancs ($), Cabernet Sauvignon ($), Zinfandel ($), Château Domecq ($$).

PART III

If You Want To Know More

Glossary of Wine Terminology

A

ACETIC Vinegary smell caused by an excessive amount of acetic acid, a natural element in all wines.

ACID A natural component of all wine, which, when present in the proper degree, produces liveliness. Too much acid makes a wine sharp, tart or sour; too little makes it flabby and flat. Principal acids in wine are malic, tartaric, succinic, lactic, and citric.

AFTERTASTE The taste left in the mouth after a wine is swallowed or, in the case of a tasting, expectorated. The longer a pleasant aftertaste remains in the mouth, the finer the quality of the wine. Also known as finish.

AGGRESSIVE Characterized by high acid and/or harsh tannin content.

AGEABILITY Wine is a living thing that changes in the bottle with age. Most wines, especially white wines,

are at their best within a few years of bottling. Some wines, however, especially big-bodied, ultra-premium reds, improve with age because of various varietal characteristics and winemaking techniques. Balance is all important. A young wine that is out of balance will almost certainly evolve into a clumsy, out-of-balance mature wine, often with tannins softening to reveal no fruit or dried-out fruit. How long to age a wine is subject to debate, taste and especially storage conditions. Color is an indicator of maturity, though you can't see the color of red wines through the dark glass of the bottle to determine if the purple-red of youth has mellowed to the reddish-brown of maturity (that hint of brown signals the turning point in a quality wine's evolution). Five years, ten years, twenty years from the vintage date are perhaps the moments to open an expensive bottle deemed ageworthy, in order to monitor its growth. But that practice is only meaningful if you've held back an additional couple of bottles so you can apply the

newly-acquired knowledge of the wine's health. Otherwise, ask the experts.

ALCOHOLIC High in alcohol, which can cause a burning sensation and is often described as hot.

ANGULAR Lacking roundness and depth.

APPELLATION Designation of geographical origin of a wine.

AROMA The smell derived from grapes. Often used to describe the smell of a young wine, as contrasted with bouquet, the smell of an older wine.

ASTRINGENT Describes wines that make the mouth pucker, usually associated with an excess of tannin. Not necessarily indicative of a flaw in the wine—many red wines, for example, tend to mellow with age, and astringency in a young red wine may indicate that it will be long-lived.

ATTACK The first impression of a wine upon tasting.

324

AUSTERE   Hard; dry; lacking richness or softness.

AVA (AMERICAN VITICULTURAL AREA) Regions officially designated by the U.S. Bureau of Alcohol, Tobacco, & Firearms, the government agency responsible for regulation of alcoholic beverages. Use of an AVA on a label requires that 85 percent of the wine come from the region named.

B

BALANCE   Harmony among all the taste and odor components of a wine, i.e., acid, sugar, alcohol and extract.

BARNYARD   Descriptive of a farmyard smell and, although it can be picked up from unclean barrels or winemaking conditions, it is also naturally inherent in some wines/grapes and can be a distinguishing characteristic. Also excessively earthy.

BARREL A wooden container, generally made of oak, used for the storage, aging, shipping and occasionally fermenting of wines. The most common-sized barrel holds 55 gallons.

BARREL FERMENTED Wines that are fermented in small wooden casks, as opposed to large tanks. Advocates believe it leads to greater harmony in a wine, especially a more natural balance between oak and wine.

BERRYLIKE   Describes the intense aroma and/or flavor reminiscent of any of a wide variety of berries— raspberries, blackberries, cranberries, strawberries and cherries; common in red wines.

BIG Full-bodied, intense, powerful wines; a wine of weighty proportions, including alcoholic content and grape extracts.

BITTER One of the four basic elements of taste (with sour, salt, and sweet). Stems, seeds, and tannins from other sources can contribute to a bitterness in the aftertaste of a wine, and some grapes, notably Gewürztraminer and Muscat, have slight elements of bitterness as part of their natural flavor.

BLACK CURRANT Distinctive smell of red wines, notably Cabernet Sauvignon and Merlot, varying in intensity from faint to very rich.

BLANC DE BLANCS French term for sparkling or white wine made entirely from white grapes.

BLANC DE NOIRS French term for sparkling white wine made from black grapes. Pressing the grapes quickly allows the juice to separate from the skins before it can be colored with the pigment.

BODY   Substance; fullness; weight. *See* full-bodied.

BOTRYTIS CINEREA Beneficial mold that forms on the skin of ripe grapes under alternating conditions of moist and dry heat, causing the grapes to shrivel and retain a high concentration of sugar. Essential for some sweet white wines.

BOUQUET   The smell of a wine developed with bottle aging, essentially the result of the interaction among alcohol, acids, fruit, oak, and oxygen.

BRAWNY Describes particularly full-bodied, tannic wines.

BREATHING The practice of uncorking a bottle a half-hour or more before serving, or of decanting it (*see* decanting), or of simply pouring it into a glass 10 minutes or so before consumption, in order to introduce air into the oxygen-starved wine. Allowing the wine to "breathe" may "improve" it by releasing flavor complexities and toning down angularities. Applied almost exclusively to red wines.

BRIARY Woodsy; stemmy; earthy.

BRILLIANT Describes clear, unclouded wines.

BRIX Measurement used to determine the sugar content of grapes and unfermented grape juice. An aid in determining the degree of ripeness. Most table wine grapes are picked at between 20 and 25 degrees Brix.

BROWNING Describes the color of a wine which has matured beyond the point of improvement and is in an advanced stage of oxidation.

BRUT French term describing the driest of Champagnes or other sparkling wines (though in rare in-stances there are some sparkling wines made with no sugar added at all, and thus are absolutely "bone dry"). Sugar content in brut wines is generally between .8 and 1.2 percent. In the U.S., the term is sometimes used a bit freely to suggest relative dryness of a sparkling wine, even when the sugar content might suggest otherwise. Top-quality sparkling wines adhere to the standard (and all French sparkling wines do so by law).

BUD BREAK Term used to describe the unfurling of the grape buds on the vine.

BULK PROCESS Mass-production method for sparkling wines wherein the secondary fermentation, which transforms still wines into sparkling wines, takes place in large tanks rather than individual bottles.

BUNG Plug used to stopper the bungholes in barrels or casks used for aging wine. Traditionally wooden, now the bung can be plastic or fiberglass.

C

CARBON DIOXIDE (CO_2) Gas produced by fer-mentation. In still wines, the gas is released; in sparkling wines, it is captured in the bottle to create bubbles.

CARBONIC MACERA-TION Method of fermentation for some red wines using whole grapes rather than crushed ones. The result is suppler, lighter, more aromatic wines with less acidity than if made traditionally.

CARBOY A glass container, generally of five gallon capacity, used in fermentation and storage of wines.

CASK A wooden container, usually made of oak, used for storing, aging, and sometimes shipping wines.

CEDAR Describes the aroma of some reds (e.g., Cabernets, Rhône blends) which often resembles that of cedarwood.

CELLARING Although this refers to the practice of putting wines away in a cavernous, underground hideaway, in contemporary wine practices, cellaring is merely the act of putting wines away in an evenly-temperatured (preferably cool), dark, still, and somewhat humid spot for proper storage and aging. An average temperature of 55 degrees Fahrenheit is deemed ideal, but any temperature comfortable for a human being is okay for a living wine. The key to temperature is stability: there should not be significant fluctuations. Keeping the wine out of direct and harmful light, and away from unsettling vibrations, is also essential. Wine must be stored horizontally so the cork will remain moist and so that fresh air, which causes oxidation, will be kept out of the bottle. Temperature-controlled storage units are available in every size and shape; a recalibrated refrigerator works nicely. Even an out-of-the-way closet functions well.

CHAPTALIZATION Procedure of adding sugar to the grape juice before fermentation to increase the alcohol content of wines. Prohibited by law in California and Italy.

CHARACTER Taster's term used to describe a wine with distinctive qualities relating to geographical origin, grape variety, etc.

CHEWY Describes dense, concentrated red wines resulting from a high extract of tannin and flavor content.

CLEAN Term for wines that have no off-color, aroma or taste.

CLONE A vine that is asexually reproduced from cuttings or graftings to retain the same character of the parent vine. Many clones can be developed from a single variety, for adaptation to particular climates or soils.

CLOSED Generally refers to a young wine that is not yet revealing fruit or flavor.

COLD FERMENTATION Low temperature process of fermentation using stainless steel, temperature-controlled tanks to preserve the aroma and character of the grape.

COMPLEX Describes a wine that has an interesting combination of flavors and scents.

CONCENTRATED Describes a wine that is rich and full of extract; deep.

COOKED An odor similar to baked that signals a flawed wine.

CORKED; CORKY Describes a wine that has been flawed by taking on the flavor of the cork. Usually attributed to a cork that is defective or unclean.

CORKSCREWS The screw's the thing: it should be a reasonably thin coil that comes to a definite point that can work its way firmly into the cork. Any number of corkscrews will open a bottle adequately, from the almost fool-proof, teflon-coated screwpull model, to the levered butterfly design, whose arms are lowered as the cork rises, to the trusty waiter's corkscrew with its small knife and single-levered action, to a screw-less variety with two thin prongs that remove a cork intact with a pulling-twisting motion.

CROSS Similar to a hybrid, a cross is the result of cross-pollination between vines of the same species.

CROWN GALL Bacterium that attacks the vine at points of trunk injury, preventing nutrients from passing and causing the vine to die.

CRUSH Harvest; the crushing of the grapes.

CUTTING Stalk cut from the vine used in reproduction.

CUVÉE A blend of wines, usually sparkling ones. Most commonly used in North America to identify a specific lot of wine. From the French *cuve*, the tank in which wines are fermented.

D

DECANTING The process by which a wine is transferred from its original bottle to another container. This age-old ritual is performed for two reasons: to aerate oxygen-starved wine and release sleepy aromas and flavors, and to remove sediment. This procedure is usually necessary only with older red wines that have thrown sediment. However, it is sometimes carried out with young wines if they are unfined or unfiltered and show a sediment. A big, young red wine that is "closed" may benefit from being decanted a few times; aerating the wine aggressively helps it "open" up, more so than simply letting it "breathe" in an open bottle. To decant a wine, hold the open bottle directly above a light source (traditionally a candle, but a flashlight also works well) and position the bottle horizontally so that the light shines through the neck. Pour gradually, in one continuous motion, into a clean, dry decanter until a dark arrow of sediment begins to appear in the neck. The idea is to trap all sediment in the shoulder of the bottle, as it muddies the wine and can impart a bitter taste. It is not, however, harmful. Regardless of whether or not a decanter is stoppered, wine inside it is being exposed to oxygen, and a judgment must be made with regard to when the wine is ready to drink. For a very old, frail wine, over-aeration can lead to a rapid death. On the other hand, some hearty red wines benefit from a good deal of air to bring out their inherent bouquets and other charms. Smell the wine, and perhaps taste it as well, at intervals to determine its evolution and readiness for optimal consumption.

DEEP Rich; concentrated.

DELICATE Light; subtle; elegant.

DEMI-SEC "Sec" is French for "dry." Demi-sec means "half-dry." When applied to sparkling wines, the term actually indicates a relatively sweet wine—sweeter than extra dry—which is appropriate with dessert.

DIFFUSE Describes wines with unfocused taste and smell; opposite of focused.

DRY Opposite of sweet. Dry wines have had most of their sugar converted into alcohol.

DUMB A wine not yet showing much in terms of flavor and character; used to describe a wine that is expected to improve.

E

EARTHY Describes a wine in which tastes or scents are characteristic of the soil in which the grapes were grown.

EASY Smooth; pleasant; supple.

ELEGANT Well-balanced, graceful; characterized by poise and finesse. A high compliment for a wine.

ENOLOGY The study and science of wine production.

ESTATE-BOTTLED Indicates the grapes have been grown, vinified and bottled under the supervision of a single winery.

EXTRA DRY Term used to describe sparkling wines that are not as dry as brut (though still not pronouncedly sweet). A wine containing between 1.2 and 2 percent sugar is considered extra dry.

EXTRACT Flavor substances (acids, pigment) extracted from the grape during fermentation and/or maceration.

EXUBERANT Generously fruity and vigorous.

F

FAT Describes a wine with mouth-filling flavor and texture.

FERMENTATION The process by which sugars are converted into alcohol and carbon dioxide gas, turning grape juice into wine.

FILTER To clarify wine (removing dead yeast cells and other suspended matter) by passing it through a filtering machine prior to bottling.

FINING A method of clarifying wine by the use of such agents as gelatin, egg white, or bentonite.

FINISH The tastes and smells that remain with the senses after swallowing.

FIRM Describes tightly-structured wine, which usually has fairly high acidity or astringency.

FLABBY Lacking structure; flat in taste due to low acidity.

FLESHY Describes a wine full of substance; chewy; meaty.

FLORAL Describes a wine with a flowery bouquet.

FOCUSED Describes wines with well-defined bouquet and flavor; opposite of diffuse.

FORTIFIED WINES Wines to which brandy has been added, usually containing between 16 percent and 21 percent alcohol. Ports and Sherries are examples of fortified wines.

FORWARD Describes a young wine that reveals character sooner than expected.

FOXY Applied to wines with a pronounced wild grape flavor, particularly Labruscas species such as Concord, Catawba, Niagara, etc. grapes. Probably origi-

nating from the native American Fox grape, the distinctive flavor and aroma have been traced to the presence of methyl anthranilate.

FREE RUN The part of the juice that runs freely from wine grapes before pressing.

FRESH Generally applied to a young wine, a term indicating liveliness and fruity acidity.

FRUIT SET The new fruit formed after a vine has flowered.

FRUITY Describes a wine, usually young, with a flavor and aroma of fresh, ripe fruits—grapes, naturally, but fruity wines can also display berrylike or appley overtones.

FULL-BODIED Describes wines in which high alcohol content produces a mouth-filling sensation.

G

GENERIC WINES Blended wines with names unrelated to their origin or grape variety.

GLASSWARE Glasses can make a big difference in

the experience of wine. Cleanliness (no detergent residue, please) and appropriate shape (to capture the pleasurable bouquet and to gently release the wine over the taste centers in the mouth) are the keys. Much has been made of the myriad of glasses that have been developed for precision tasting—from the luxurious and traditional Baccarat crystal designs, to scientifically-engineered Reidel glassware, to the unorthodoxly-shaped, but highly effective, Les Impitoyables. At the root of all this fuss is the simple idea that different wines require differing amounts of space. Time and experience have proven that a fragrant Pinot Noir, for instance, benefits from a large, bulbous glass with a tapered opening at the top to allow the bouquet to collect in the bowl. In general, a clear, smooth-surfaced, stemmed glass has proven best. And although there are glasses made for virtually every style of wine, a set of medium-large, so-called Bordeaux-style or egg-shaped INAO (International Standard Organization) all-purpose glasses that hold about six ounces when two-thirds full is functional for most wines, with the exception of sparkling wines. A tall, tulip- or flute-shaped glass with a tapered body and relatively small opening best releases the bubbly charms of these wines.

GRASSY Describes a wine with characteristic flavor and aroma resembling grass or herbs, particularly associated with Sauvignon Blanc.

GREEN Describes wines made from unripe grapes, resulting in a raw, acidic taste. The color green is sometimes prevalent in young, white wines.

H

HARD Describes wines with high acidity or tannic astringency; opposite of lush. Young wines may lose their hardness with time.

HARSH Excessively hard.

HERBACEOUS Possessing a distinctively grassy or herbal smell, particularly associated with some Cabernet Sauvignons, Merlots and Sauvignon Blancs. Sometimes erroneously used to describe vegetal character.

HOLLOW Used to describe a wine that lacks depth; shallow; empty.

HOT Causing a burning sensation when swallowed as a result of high alcohol content.

HYBRID The result of cross-breeding two species of grapes.

I

IMPERIAL Oversized bottle capable of holding the equivalent of eight standard 750 ml bottles.

J-K

JAMMY Characterized by a very high concentration of ripe fruit and natural grapey and berrylike flavors. Often used negatively to characterize hot-climate red wines.

JEROBOAM A large bottle which has the capacity of six ordinary bottles (750 ml). When applied to Champagne, indicates a bottle with the capacity of four 750 ml Champagne bottles.

L

LABELING In North America, wine labels are remarkably straightforward and reliably informative. The U.S. Bureau of Alcohol, Tobacco & Firearms (BATF) subjects each and every wine label, indeed each and every item that appears on the outside of the bottle, from the capsule to the back label to the main label and its design, to a rigorous review and approval process, insuring that everything meets the Bureau's strict regulations. For a varietal name (e.g., Cabernet Sauvignon) to be listed on a label, for example, a minimum of 75 percent of the wine must be comprised of that grape. If no varietal is listed, but a special proprietary name is given, the wine is likely to be a blend of several grapes (*see* Meritage). The vintage and vintner are always prominently displayed on each label, as well as the area of origin (as specific as an individual vineyard, or as general as a large growing area) and the percentage of alcohol in the wine, although this may vary a degree or two in either direction.

LABRUSCA   *See* Vitis labrusca

LATE HARVEST Term used to indicate wine made from extra-ripe grapes that have been purposely left on the vine beyond normal picking time, generally to enhance sugar content.

LEAFY   Describes wine with a smell characteristic of leaves. Very leafy wines are considered green.

LEAN Lacking fatness or mouth-filling flavor, though perhaps pleasant.

LEES   Heavy sediment, including dead yeast cells, that falls to the bottom of a wine vat during fermentation.

LENGTH The duration of flavors and aromas remaining in the mouth after swallowing; finish. Good length is a characteristic of most quality wines.

LIGHT WINES   Wines low in alcohol content. Also used legally to describe a wine with fewer calories than standard table wine.

LIVELY Describes a wine with good acidity and freshness.

LONG Having flavors or aromas that remain in the mouth after swallowing.

LUSH   Fat; rich; opposite of hard.

M

MADERIZED   Turned amber in color as a result of oxidization and possessing an aroma and flavor like that of Madeira, indicating that a white wine is past its prime.

MAGNUM The equivalent of two regular bottles, or 1.5 liters (50.7 oz.).

MALOLACTIC FERMENTATION A secondary fermentation process which transforms malic acid, found in many fruits, into lactic acid (and releases carbon dioxide), producing a wine that is milder, less tart and, to some, more complex.

MEATY Describes wine which is chewy; fleshy.

MELLOW Smooth; not hard; sometimes used for reds that aren't fully dry.

MERITAGE A portmanteau term ("merit" plus "heritage") developed in the 1980s because of U.S. government labeling regulations to categorize red and white wines blended from traditional Bordeaux grape varieties. Cabernet Sauvignon, Cabernet Franc, Merlot,

Petit Verdot and Malbec for red wines; Sauvignon Blanc, Sémillon and Muscadelle for whites. There are no percentage or Bordeaux varietal rules for the blending formula except that no grape may represent 75 percent of the total blend (in which case the varietal name takes precedence).

MÉTHODE CHAMPENOISE Classic method of producing Champagne and sparkling wines by inducing a secondary fermentation after bottling, which releases the carbon dioxide that creates bubbles.

METHUSELAH Oversized Champagne bottle equal to eight regular 750 ml bottles, or 203 oz.

MICROCLIMATE An area where soil conditions and such factors as altitude, inclination/slope, drainage, and exposure to the sun influence the quality and distinctiveness of the wine produced. A few feet of distance can mean a different microclimate and suitability for a grape variety.

MILDEW A fungus that is extremely detrimental to vines and grapes, controllable to some degree through the use of powdered sulfur or copper sulphate.

MOUTH-FILLING Describes wines that have a high concentration of fruit extract and alcohol; chewy.

MUST Crushed grapes or grape juice ready to be fermented into wine.

N

NEBUCHADNEZZAR The largest of oversized bottles, equal to 20-750 ml bottles, or 507 oz.

NEMATODE Parasite that feeds on vine roots.

NOSE The aroma or smell of a wine. After color, the most readily apparent indication of a wine's character and quality.

NOUVEAU French word for "new," used to indicate a wine that has been released within a few weeks of the harvest.

O

OAKY Describes a wine that smells and/or tastes of the oak barrel in which it was aged. Vanilla, as well as toasty flavors, can be derived from the barrel.

OFF Flawed; bad or in any way unpleasant.

OFF-DRY Slightly sweet or semi-sweet.

OVERCROPPING Allowing the vine to produce more fruit than it is capable of bringing to maturity, resulting in an inferior wine and causing damage to the vine.

OVERRIPE Term applied to wines made from overripe fruit, resulting in high alcohol content, heaviness, and imbalance.

OXIDIZED Applies to wines that are in the final stage of life, resulting in a brownish color and loss of freshness; may occur prematurely in wines that are exposed to oxygen.

P-Q

PEPPERY Describes the aroma of black pepper found in many red wines.

PERFUMED Highly fragrant; aromatic.

pH Measure of hydrogen ions, indicating the level of acidity in a wine — the lower the pH, the higher the acid level.

PHYLLOXERA Plant louse that feeds on vine roots and was responsible for the near destruction of Europe's vineyards in the late nineteenth century. Since then, virtually all European vines have been grafted onto native American roots, which are tougher and until recently thought phylloxera-resistant. Currently vast vineyards in California have varying degrees of phylloxera and are being replanted with more resilient root stocks.

PLUMMY Describes a wine having the taste or aroma of ripe plums.

POMACE Grape residue after pressing, consisting of skins, stems, and seeds.

POURRITURE NOBLE French for "noble rot." *See* Botrytis cinerea.

PRESS WINE That part of the wine produced from the final pressing of the grapes, as contrasted with free run, which, as the name implies, runs freely without pressing. Richer in tannin and extracts, the press wine

is sometimes added back to the free run.

PROPRIETARY Name or brand that a producer uses exclusively for his or her own wines, e.g., Rubicon, Opus One, etc.

PRUNEY Describes the taste or smell of wines flawed by overripe grapes.

R

RACKING Method of clarifying wine by siphoning the clear wine into barrels or tanks, leaving behind the sediment and lees.

RAISINY Having a taste characteristic of raisins, usually a flaw, though desirable in some Ports or sherries.

RESIDUAL SUGAR Sugar remaining in a wine after fermentation.

RICH Describes a wine with highly-concentrated flavor or texture.

RIDDLING The method of turning bottles (by hand or machine) of sparkling wine to accumulate the sediment (mostly dead yeast cells) in the neck of the bottle for removal before final corking.

RIPE Describes a wine made from grapes at their optimum point of maturity.

ROBUST Used to describe a sound, full-bodied wine.

ROUGH Describes a wine with unpleasantly high levels of acidity and tannin.

ROUND Describes a well-balanced wine with smooth contours and no angularities.

S

SALMANAZAR Oversized bottle equal to twelve 750 ml bottles.

SHALLOW Applies to a weak or watery wine.

SHARP Describes a wine that is hard or highly acidic.

SHORT A commonly used negative term for describing a wine with a finish that lacks distinction and disappears too quickly.

SILKY Describes a wine that is soft, smooth, fine-textured and velvety.

SMOKEY Describes wines that have the flavor or aroma of smoke, which can come from the soil in which the grapes were grown or from the barrels used in aging.

SOFT Describes a wine that is round and low in acidity; not hard or harsh.

SOLERA Spanish system used for blending and aging fortified wines by progressively adding younger wines to older ones.

SOUR Denotes a wine that has spoiled to the point of becoming undrinkable. Often used incorrectly to mean the opposite of sweet.

SPICY Describes wines that have flavors and aromas characteristic of certain spices, such as clove, nutmeg, pepper and cinnamon.

SPRITZY Describes wines with a tiny amount of sparkle—specks of carbonation left over from vinification. Usually undesirable, though sometimes adds liveliness to light, simple white wines.

STALKY Describes wines that have a green or vegetal flavor or aroma due to contact with the stems.

STORAGE *See* Cellaring.

STRUCTURE Term used to mean the way in which a wine is held together in regard to its components (fruit, tannins, acids, etc.).

STYLISH Applied to young, well-structured wines that show a certain dash and verve or personality.

SULFUR DIOXIDE (SO$_2$) Chemical used to prevent wines from oxidizing. The gas can give an unpleasant odor to a wine if it becomes noticeable. Often it will "blow off" quickly after a bottle is opened.

SUPPLE Term of praise used to indicate that a wine is velvety and round.

SUR LIE Practice of aging wines "on the lees," in contact with dead yeast cells and other sediments left over from vinification. Increasingly common practice with fine white wines, sparkling wines, Chardonnay and Sauvignon Blanc to add complexity to the wine.

T-U

TABLE WINE Wines of between 7 percent and 14 percent alcohol, generally intended to be consumed with food.

TANNIN A group of organic compounds found in the bark, roots, stems and seeds of many plants which gives wine astringency, structure and flavor, and which assists in the aging process. The source of the "puckeriness" of many young red wines.

TART Describes a wine high in acid content. A sharp-and-sour taste description used with both positive and negative connotations.

TARTARIC ACID The primary acid in wine which forms crystals of potassium bitartrate, harmless flakes or deposits frequently found in bottled wine.

TEINTURIER Highly-pigmented grapes often used to deepen the color of red wines.

THICK Describes highly-concentrated wines often high in tannins and with low acidity.

TOASTY Describes smells and flavors derived from dead yeast cells and sediments the wine has been in contact with, but primarily is associated with the oak barrel in which the wine is aged. Often an attractive flavor component in white wine.

V

VARIETAL Describes a wine that takes its name from the primary grape variety from which it was made. By U.S. law, 75 percent of the total blend of the wine.

VARIETAL CHARACTER Describes wines that have the flavor and bouquet characteristic of the grape variety used in making the wine.

VEGETAL Describes tastes and smells of bell pepper and asparagus as well as other plants and vegetables. In small amounts adds to complexity and character, and in larger amounts signals flaws and out-of-balance and undesirable flavors.

VINICULTURE The science of making wine; winemaking. *See* viticulture.

VINIFERA *See* Vitis vinifera.

VINIFICATION The process of making grape juice into wine.

VITICULTURE The science of growing grapes.

VITICULTURAL AREAS A grape growing region recognized by the U.S. Bureau of Alcohol, Tobacco, & Firearms, the government agency responsible for the regulation of alcoholic beverages. When used on a label, 85 percent of the wine must come from that area. Also AVA (American Viticultural Area).

VITIS LABRUSCA Native North American grape species, of which Concord is best known. Characterized by a distinctive grapey aroma. *See* additional reference glossary on North American grape varieties.

VITIS VINIFERA The primary species of wine grapes—derived from the European-Middle Eastern vine from which most of the world's fine wines are made, including Cabernet Sauvignon, Chardonnay, Riesling, and Pinot Noir, among many others. *See* additional reference glossary on North American grape varieties.

WELL BALANCED A wine that has all the desired components in good proportion.

W

WOODY Describes the taste of a wine that has been left too long in the barrel used for aging, or, in general, for the taste of a wine that is wooden beyond stalky.

X-Y-Z

YEASTS Plant organisms that cause grapes to ferment, converting sugar into alcohol and carbon dioxide. Different strains of natural and cultivated yeasts are selected and employed by various wineries during vinification.

North American Wine Grapes

ALEXANDER   Also known as the Cape grape, the Alexander is believed to have originated from crossing wild native grapes with the vinifera planted by William Penn's gardener, John Alexander, in the Philadelphia vineyard he established in 1684.

ALICANTE BOUSCHET. v. vinifera Grown primarily in California's San Joaquin Valley. A thick-skinned variety with purple juice, it can be used to add color to red wines and by itself is popular with do-it-yourself winemakers.

ALIGOTE. v. vinifera A secondary white variety grown in Burgundy. Less distinctive than Chardonnay, the leading white Burgundy, it nevertheless produces good, though simple, white wines. Limited plantings in California and the Pacific Northwest.

AURORE   French hybrid which produces white and sparkling wines, often with foxy (wild grape) flavors. Grown in New York and other eastern states.

AUXERROIS   *See* Pinot Auxerrois.

BACCHUS. v. vinifera A vinifera hybrid white developed in Germany from Riesling, Sylvaner, and Müller-Thurgau. Grown in Canada, mainly in the Okanagan Valley of British Columbia.

BACO NOIR   French hybrid which produces vivid red wines. Mainly grown east of the Rocky Mountains.

BARBERA. v. vinifera Red variety originating from the Piedmont region in northern Italy. Grown in California's Central Valley—and a few decades ago, California's fourth leading grape grown—and more recently in Texas and New Mexico.

BLANC DUBOIS   White Muscadine variety introduced by Florida plant geneticists in 1987. Named for French grape breeder, Emile Dubois, who worked in Tallahassee in the 1880s.

BLUE EYE   An American hybrid grape developed to resist cold weather. Grown in Ohio, where it produces a dry red wine.

BURGER. v. vinifera   Lesser white variety with large yield used primarily in blending jug whites or low-priced sparkling wines in California.

CABERNET FRANC. v. vinifera   Red variety from Bordeaux, where it is grown significantly in Saint-Emilion vineyards. Now grown increasingly in California and other states, with notable success in New York's Long Island region. Sometimes used for blending with Cabernet Sauvignon. Also occasionally seen as a varietal.

CABERNET SAUVIGNON. v. vinifera The primary red variety in the Médoc region of Bordeaux and on the California coast, Napa and Sonoma in particular. Now grown increasingly in other states, including Washington, Idaho, Texas, Virginia, Arkansas, and Georgia. Recognized worldwide as the top reigning red grape.

CARDINAL A vinifera cross developed for warm climates at the University of California at Davis. Mainly grown in the inland valleys of California.

CARIGNANE. v. vinifera Black variety which produces hearty red wines used primarily for blending. Grown in southern France and California's inland valleys.

CARLOS. v. rotundifolia White Muscadine grape developed in North Carolina. Grown primarily in the Southeast: Florida and Mississippi in particular.

CARMINE. v. vinifera Red vinifera hybrid developed from Carignane, Cabernet Sauvignon and Merlot at the University of California at Davis for warm climates.

CARNELIAN. v. vinifera Red vinifera hybrid developed in California for high yield in warm climates, from Carignane, Cabernet Sauvignon, and Grenache. Also grown in Texas.

CASCADE French hybrid red used for blending. Grown in the East: New York in particular.

CATAWBA. v. labrusca One of the earliest American grapes. Proliferated in Ohio until it was attacked by black rot. Now grown primarily in New York, and used to produce sweet or off-dry white wines with marked Labrusca flavor.

CAYUGA Hybrid producing fruity, off-dry whites developed at New York's Geneva experimental station.

CENTURION. v. vinifera Red hybrid developed in California. Limited plantings in the San Joaquin Valley.

CHAMBOURCIN French hybrid which produces claret-like reds or rosés. Grown in the East and Midwest.

CHAMPANEL. v. riparia Native American red variety used as rootstock, and occasionally for blending.

CHANCELLOR French hybrid red which produces well-balanced, flavorful red wines. Widely grown east of the Rocky Mountains and in Canada.

CHARDONNAY. v. vinifera Leading noble grape for dry white wines. Grown widely in North America and wine regions around the world, particularly with great success in Burgundy and California.

CHARDONNEL A relatively new American hybrid grape developed in New York with input from Michigan grape scientists. A cross between Chardonnay and Seyval Blanc, it withstands cold better than Chardonnay and produces a dry, full-bodied white wine.

CHASSELAS. v. vinifera Lesser white variety used mainly for blending. Also known as Golden Chasselas and as Fendant in Switzerland.

CHELIOS French hybrid producing a fruity, medium-bodied red wine. Grown in the East and Midwest.

CHENIN BLANC. v. vinifera White variety producing fruity, lightly sweet or sometimes dry wines. Used for France's Loire

Valley whites, notably Vouvray, as a varietal, and for blending in California, the Northwest, and Texas.

CHEVRIER   Old Bordeaux name for Sémillon (q.v.).

COLOBEL   French hybrid teinturier (color grape) used to deepen color in red wines. Not widely planted in North America.

COLOMBARD   *See* French Colombard.

CONCORD. v. labrusca   Native American grape variety with pronounced foxy flavor, now used more for juice and jams than for wine, though still used for some sweet kosher wines. Developed in the mid-1800s by Ephraim Bull of Concord, Massachusetts. Still widely planted outside California.

CONQUISTADOR. v. rotundifolia   Red Muscadine developed at Florida State University and released in 1983. Grown mainly in the South.

COUDERC NOIR   French hybrid which produces hearty reds and rosés. Not widely grown.

CYNTHIANA. v. aestivalis   Grown in the Ozark highlands of Arkansas and Missouri, producing a claret-like red with no foxy flavor and some aging potential. Controversy exists as to whether this is the same variety as the Norton grape.

DE CHAUNAC   Red hybrid which is disease resistant and produces a large yield, though the reds and rosés it has yielded are typically mediocre. Developed in Ontario and grown in Canada and the eastern U.S.: particularly in the Finger Lakes region of New York.

DELAWARE. v. labrusca   Native pink variety with some aestivalis in its parentage, traditionally used to make American Champagne (sparkling wine). Bred for cold climates, it produces crisp, usually sweet pink or white wines.

DIAMOND. v. labrusca   Neutral white with Labrusca overtones usually used for sparkling wines. Not widely planted. Also known as Moore's Diamond.

DUTCHESS. v. labrusca   Developed in the Hudson Valley in the 1860s, this variety produces light, crisp white wines with little of the foxy Labrusca flavor. Grown primarily in the Northeast.

EHRENFELSER. v. vinifera   Vinifera hybrid developed in Germany which produces a lightly sweet white wine. Grown in Canada.

ELVIRA   White variety used primarily for blending. Developed in Missouri from Labrusca and Riparia. Not widely planted.

EMERALD RIESLING. v. vinifera   White variety developed at the University of California at Davis from Riesling and Muscadelle. Grown primarily in the San Joaquin Valley and West Texas.

FLORA. v. vinifera   Cross between Gewürztraminer and Sémillon. Mainly used to produce sweet wines or for blending.

FOCH   *See* Maréchal Foch.

FOLLE BLANCHE. v. vinifera Known as Gros Plant in the coastal region of the Loire Valley, this white variety has limited plantings in California, though Louis M. Martini makes a crisp white varietal with it.

FOX Certain native American varieties were dubbed "fox grapes" by early American growers including Thomas Jefferson. Probably the origin of the term "foxy," referring to the wild grape flavor of native Labrusca varieties.

FRANKEN RIESLING *See* Sylvaner.

FRENCH COLOMBARD. v. vinifera White variety grown in California and the Southwest with high yield. Used primarily for blending, but also bottled as a varietal.

FUMÉ BLANC *See* Sauvignon Blanc.

GAMAY BEAUJOLAIS. v. vinifera A clone of Pinot Noir originally thought to be related to the true Gamay of Beaujolais. Used in California to produce fruity, light red wines.

GAMAY NOIR À JUS BLANC. v. vinifera The true Gamay of Beaujolais. Limited plantings in the U.S., though on the increase in California, the Southwest, and New York, among other areas.

GEWÜRZTRAMINER. v. vinifera Spicy white variety originating in Germany and Alsace, which produces dry or off-dry aromatic whites, and occasionally sweet late-harvest wines. Grown in cool regions of California, in the Northwest and elsewhere.

GRAY RIESLING. v. vinifera This lesser-known white variety is not the true German Riesling. Known in France as Chauche Gris, it is used in California mainly for blending. Also spelled Grey Riesling.

GRENACHE. v. vinifera Red variety which grows best in warm climates, such as the Rhône Valley. Used in central California primarily for blending and to make rosé. Also seen occasionally as a varietal.

GRIGNOLINO. v. vinifera Italian grape grown in the Piedmont region, which produces light red and dry wines. Not widely planted in the U.S., though Heitz Cellars makes a Grignolino rosé.

GUTEDEL *See* Chasselas.

HERBEMONT Rare native red variety which has some vinifera parentage as a result of cross-pollination. Initially grown by Huguenot Nicolas Herbemont in South Carolina around 1788, it died out with the exception of the Val Verde Winery in southern Texas. New plantings have been introduced in central Tennessee.

HORIZON New French hybrid white variety resembling Cayuga, which produces a fruity white wine. Developed at the experimental station in Geneva, New York.

ISABELLA. v. labrusca Red grape with strong, fruity Labrusca flavor. Named for Isabella Gibb of Brooklyn, it is grown primarily in New York, though the acreage is in decline.

IVES NOIR. v. labrusca Native red grape which was widely planted in Ohio and New

York, though strong foxy flavors have greatly decreased its popularity.

JACQUEZ *See* Lenoir.

JOHANNISBERG RIESLING *See* Riesling.

KAY GRAY New white hybrid developed to withstand extreme cold.

KERNER. v. vinifera Extremely cold- and disease-resistant white vinifera cross developed in Germany. Limited plantings in the Okanagan Valley of British Columbia.

LANDOT Red French hybrid with limited plantings in the Northeast and Midwest.

LENOIR American hybrid known in the late 1800s for the spicy, sturdy red wines it produced. Grown almost exclusively at the Val Verde Winery in Texas. (Also called Jacques, Jacquez, or Black Spanish.)

LEON MILLOT Black French hybrid developed by Eugene Kuhlmann which produces concentrated red wines. Similar to Maréchal Foch.

MAGNOLIA. v. rotundifolia Muscadine hybrid with a bronze color, developed in North Carolina in 1961. Mainly grown in the Southeast, it produces sweet white or varietal wines.

MALBEC. v. vinifera Red variety traditionally grown in Bordeaux and used for blending. Limited plantings in California where it is used for the same purpose.

MALVASIA. v. vinifera One of the oldest varieties in the world. Grown in Spain, Yugoslavia, Madeira, and parts of Italy mainly to produce sweet white wines and a few dry ones. Limited plantings in warm inland areas of California.

MARÉCHAL FOCH Also called simply Foch. Red French hybrid developed for cold climates by Eugene Kuhlmann. Produces concentrated or light, fruity red wines, depending on the vinification procedure. Primarily grown in the Northeast and the Midwest.

MATSVANI Russian variety experimentally grown in the Okanagan Valley of British Columbia. Brights Wines produces it as a dry white varietal.

MELON. v. vinifera The white Muscadet of France's Loire Valley. In California, sometimes mistaken for Pinot Blanc. Has been produced by Beaulieu Vineyard in Napa Valley as a varietal.

MERLOT. v. vinifera Primary red variety from Bordeaux, notably from the Pomerol district. Soft textured with a berrylike flavor, it has become important in California for blending with Cabernet Sauvignon and as a varietal. Also grown successfully in Virginia, on Long Island, New York, and in Washington.

MICHURNIT. v. amurensis Red variety from the Amur Valley in the former Soviet Union imported to Canada. Now grown in Nova Scotia at the Grand Pré Winery.

MISSION. v. vinifera Originally from Spain, the first European variety to be brought to the New World in the 1500s. Named for the California missions where it was first planted by Franciscan friars. Limited plantings remain in California, where it is used for blending, usually in fortified dessert wines.

MISSOURI RIESLING. v. labrusca Native white grape bred in Hermann, Missouri in the late nineteenth century; no relation to the true German Riesling. Popular in Missouri, it is used to produce sweet or off-dry white wines.

MOURVEDRE. v. vinifera Also known in the U.S. as Mataro, this is a major grape in French Rhône-style blends, both in France and now in California.

MULLER-THURGAU. v. vinifera Vinifera cross of Riesling and Sylvaner which produces a crisp off-dry white wine. Developed in Germany, it has limited plantings in the Pacific Northwest and Canada.

MUNSON Group of American hybrids developed by a nineteenth-century breeder named T.V.Munson. Originally planted in Missouri and later in Texas. The red variety known as Munch continues to be grown in Missouri.

MUSCADELLE DE BORDELAIS. v. vinifera White grape grown in Bordeaux for occasional use in Sauternes. Limited plantings in California.

MUSCAT BLANC (CANELLI). v. vinifera The preferred muscat for dessert wines and sparkling wines, such as the Italian Asti Spumanti. Occasionally used to produce a crisp dry white wine.

MUSCAT HAMBURG. v. vinifera Produces sweet red dessert wines (Quady's Elysium in California). Also known as Black Muscat.

MUSCAT OF ALEXANDRIA. v. vinifera White variety used to produce dessert wines with spicy aromatic flavors. Grown in California's Central Valley, with limited plantings elsewhere.

MUSCAT-OTTONEL. v. vinifera Primarily known in Eastern Europe, notably Alsace and Hungary. Produces white wines with wild Muscat character and aroma. Limited plantings in Oregon, British Columbia, and New York.

MUSTANG. v. candicans Native American red grape originally from Texas and the Southeast. Limited plantings exist today, though nineteenth-century grape breeder T.V. Munson considered it an excellent variety for producing potent, sturdy red wines.

NAPA GAMAY. v. vinifera Recently identified as the Valdiguié grape of the Midi region of France, this variety was long believed to be related to the true Gamay. Used in California to produce Beaujolais-type wines.

NIAGARA. v. labrusca Native white variety originally grown in New York and Ohio. Strong Labrusca flavor has limited its current use, though still popular as a table wine. Also known as the "white Concord."

NOAH. v. labrusca Native American white grape planted in France after the phylloxera blight of the late 1800s. Because of its strong Labrusca flavor, it never gained popularity in Europe.

NOBLE. v. rotundifolia Black Muscadine bred in North Carolina and introduced in 1971. Produced in the Southeast as a red varietal or rosé, usually sweet.

NORTON. v. aestivalis Some growers consider this to be the same as the Cynthiana grape. Developed by Dr. Daniel Norton of Richmond, it was originally known as the Virginia Seedling. Now grown in Missouri and Arkansas, where it is used to make a sturdy and appealing claret-like red wine.

OKANAGAN RIESLING. v. vinifera No relation to the true Riesling, this old Hungarian variety produces a mild, neutral-flavored white wine. Widely grown in the Okanagan Valley of British Columbia, though it is being phased out in many of the better vineyards.

ORANGE MUSCAT. v. vinifera This muscat, which is grown in Southern Italy and Sicily, has an orange aroma and flavor. San Joaquin Valley has very limited plantings.

ORLANDO SEEDLESS New American hybrid developed as a seedless table variety in Florida. May also be desirable for producing white wine.

ORTEGA Vinifera cross between Müller-Thurgau and Siegerrebe developed in Germany and experimentally grown in the Okanagan Valley in British Columbia. Named for philosopher Jose Ortega y Gasset.

PERLE OF CSABA. v. vinifera Hungarian variety not widely known. Characterized by a wild muscat aroma and flavor, it produces a lightly sweet, delicate white wine. Only significant plantings in North America are in the Okanagan Valley of British Columbia.

PETIT VERDOT. v. vinifera Red variety grown in Bordeaux for use in blending. Limited plantings in California and Long Island, New York.

PETITE SIRAH. v. vinifera A grape with a checkered history in the U.S. First brought to the continent in the nineteenth century as Syrah (the great red grape of France's Rhône Valley), later clones were identified as Durif, a minor red variety of the Rhône. Recent DNA mapping technologies in California indicate that various varietals are among those grapes identified as Petite Sirah. Depending upon a given vineyard's location and age, various clones of Durif, Peloursin, Mondeuse, Grenache, Zinfandel, Carignane and Syrah may be present. In practice, the so-called Petite Sirah generally produces wines of deep red color and lusty character that require aging.

PINOT AUXERROIS. v. vinifera White grape belonging to the Pinot variety from France's Alsace, which shows promise as a cold-climate white with delicate fragrance.

PINOT BLANC. v. vinifera White grape popular for the dry white wines it produces. Increasingly grown in California, the Northwest, Northeast and Canada.

PINOT GRIS. v. vinifera Pinkish-white variety producing a very crisp white wine.

Grown in Oregon and the Okanagan Valley of British Columbia, it shows promise for other cool climates. Also known as Tokay d'Alsace in France, Rulander in Germany, and Pinot Grigio in Italy.

PINOT MEUNIER. v. vinifera Known primarily as a minor red variety from France's Champagne region. Limited plantings in California and Oregon.

PINOT NOIR. v. vinifera The noble red variety of France's Burgundy. Difficult to grow in North America, though plantings in Oregon, California, and North Carolina have recently shown promise of success. May also be suitable for growing in parts of the Southwest and New York.

PINOT ST. GEORGE. v. vinifera Lesser red variety sometimes produced in California as a varietal.

RAVAT NOIR French hybrid crossed with Pinot Noir to make a light red wine. Primarily grown in northern states.

RAYON D'OR White French hybrid which produces spicy, fruity wines. Used mainly in the Northeast for blending in table wines and sparkling wines.

RIESLING. v. vinifera Also known as White or Johannisberg Riesling. One of the noble wine grapes of the world, the true German Riesling of the Rhine and Mosel valleys. Produces a variety of white wines, from dry and tart (Alsace), to lightly sweet, to very sweet, rare and expensive late-harvest wines. Grown widely in North America, though the wines it produces here are often quite ordinary. At its best in cool climates

like those of New York, the Northwest and Canada.

ROSETTE French hybrid red used mainly to produce rosé. Limited plantings in Canada, New Mexico, and a few other areas.

ROUGEON French hybrid red grown in the colder climates of the Northeast and in the Midwest. Good color but not much structure.

ROUSSANNE. v. vinifera White grape associated with France's Northern Rhône, yielding wines of great delicacy and perfume. Introduced experimentally in California, notably at Bonny Doon Winery.

RUBY CABERNET Vinifera hybrid cross between Cabernet Sauvignon and Carignane, developed by the University of California at Davis. Bred for warm climates, it is grown mainly in the San Joaquin Valley and in Texas.

RULANDER *See* Pinot Gris.

SAINT-ÉMILION *See* Ugni Blanc.

SANGIOVESE Red variety that is the dominant grape in Italy's Tuscany region. Currently being planted on an experimental basis in California and elsewhere.

SAUVIGNON BLANC. v. vinifera Popular white wine grape of France's Loire Valley and Bordeaux which produces a crisp, dry, full-bodied white with fruity, herbaceous, or "grassy" character. Used exclusively for the wines of Sancerre and Pouilly-Fumé, it is known locally as Blanc Fumé. It is grown in California, the Northwest, Texas and the Southwest and is increasingly blended with Sémillon.

SCHEUREBE. v. vinifera Vinifera cross between Riesling and Sylvaner which produces mostly sweet, often late-harvest white wines. Developed in Geisenheim, Germany, it has limited plantings in California, Canada, and New York.

SCUPPERNONG Original wild Muscadine grape, the first of the Muscadines to be made into wine in Colonial days. Still grows in both wild and cultivated forms in the South, though newer Muscadine varieties such as Carlos, Magnolia, and Noble are achieving equal popularity.

SÉMILLON. v. vinifera White variety widely grown in southwestern France. It is the principal grape in Sauternes, and an important component of white Graves in Bordeaux, where it is used for blending with Sauvignon Blanc. It is increasingly grown in California and the Northwest for this purpose. Seen also as a varietal.

SEVERNYI. v. amurensis Dark red variety with spicy flavor from the Amur Valley in eastern Siberia. Now grown at Grand Pré in Nova Scotia.

SEYVAL BLANC The leading French hybrid white, producing a crisp, dry to off-dry white wine. Widely grown east of the Rockies, notably in the Northeast, Maryland, Virginia, and eastern Canada.

SIEGERREBE. v. vinifera Experimental hybrid with Gewürztraminer parentage, bred for early ripening. Brought to the Okanagan Valley of British Columbia from Germany and planted in small trial plots.

SOUZAO. v. vinifera Portuguese grape used in Port production in the U.S., principally California, because of its ripe, raisiny character.

STEUBEN American Muscadine originally used to produce table wines. Occasionally produces a sweet, spicy rosé with slight muscat aroma.

STOVER White variety hybridized in Florida and used for blending with stronger Muscadines.

SUWANNEE White hybrid developed in Florida which produces wines with a muscat character. Grown in the South, it shows promise as a blending grape.

SWENSON Group of American hybrids mainly bred for cold climates. Developed by Elmer Swenson of Minnesota.

SYLVANER. v. vinifera White wine grape widely planted in Germany. Similar to but not as distinguished as Riesling, it is grown in California as Franken Riesling, Monterey Riesling or Sonoma Riesling. Also grown in Canada.

SYMPHONY. v. vinifera Vinifera cross of Muscat of Alexandria and Grenache, developed in California. The wines it produces are mostly sweet. Limited plantings to date.

SYRAH. v. vinifera The primary red variety of the northern Rhône Valley, used to produce Hermitage. Limited plantings in North America, though California and the Southwest show some promise.

THOMPSON SEEDLESS One of the most widely planted grapes in California,

Ask us for a glimpse of France before you've even landed.

AIR FRANCE, SERVICE À LA FRANÇAISE.

AIR FRANCE ///
ASK THE WORLD OF US

best known as a white table variety. Used in tremendous quantities for bulk wines in the San Joaquin Valley and in the Southwest. Also used for distilling brandy.

UGNI BLANC. v. vinifera One of the most widely planted grapes in the world; used in California mainly for bulk or jug wines. Also known as Saint-Émilion and Trebbiano.

VERDELET White French hybrid grown in the Northeast and the Midwest.

VIDAL BLANC French hybrid white descended from Ugni Blanc. Increasingly grown east of the Rocky Mountains, notably in the Midwest, where it shows promise as a fruity, dry white wine, or a late-harvest dessert wine when *botrytis*-affected.

VIGNOLES Also known as Ravat 51. A Pinot Noir hybrid that produces a dry, crisp, spicy white wine, as well as a fine dessert wine. Promising grape for colder climates. *See also* Ravat.

VILLARD BLANC French hybrid white widely planted in southern France. Suited to warmer climates, it is used primarily for blending.

VILLARD NOIR French hybrid red which produces a light, fruity red wine. Suited to warmer climates.

VIOGNIER. v. vinifera Rare and hard-to-grow white grape producing strongly-perfumed, elegant wine, principally in the Northern Rhône at Condrieu. Introduced in a limited but successful effort in California.

VIRGINIA SEEDLING The original name for the Norton grape.

WEISSBURGUNDER *See* Pinot Blanc.

WHITE RIESLING *See* Riesling.

ZINFANDEL. v. vinifera A widely-planted red grape in California. Often referred to as California's mystery grape, because its European origins are uncertain, though it is now believed to be from southern Italy. Produces hearty, flavorful red wines and appealing rosés, though more white Zinfandels than reds have been produced in recent years. Limited plantings outside of California, notably in Texas.

Vintage Notes & Chart

A T their best, vintage charts offer the consumer a bit of protection. When someone has doubts about a wine, a chart can point that person toward (or away from) a wine for immediate consumption (or for long-term cellaring). Knowing a couple of top vintages can help make choosing a wine safer than guessing or perhaps even listening to a salesperson. However, vintage charts are not all they are cracked up to be, especially when it comes to California wines.

Like so much in the world of wine, vintage charts owe their origin to France and England and directly to the vintages of Bordeaux. Over the years, they have made some sense for Bordeaux and subsequently Burgundy, because these are relatively small areas with uneven records of annual harvests. Some years produce decidedly better wines than others. Throughout Bordeaux's Médoc or Burgundy's Côte des Nuits, the weather (the amount of sunshine and rain) is generally consistent; certainly the climate is the same; the elevations and even the basic soils are the same (excluding for the moment minor hills, and thus important soil and exposure variations that make one vineyard better than another). It is safe to generalize and say if the vintage is good for one Bordeaux château, and it is generally good for a neighbor a mile or five miles away. Not so in California.

It is something of an exercise in futility to try to characterize a vintage covering, say, both Napa and Sonoma counties with all their variations in weather, soil, elevations and growing areas. How about a number rating to cover all of California? Is that helpful? In 1989, for example, Chardonnays on the Napa Valley floor suffered from rain and were often light and weak, while a couple of miles away, up on Howell Mountain (still a Napa appellation), conditions and quality were markedly different. The range of quality in 1989 Napa Cabernets also ran the gamut. What can one number mean, then, except a vague acknowledgment of general merit? And a danger of making such broad assessments is in dismissing a great wine because the wines produced ten, fifty or a hundred miles away weren't very good that year.

Vintage ratings work better for smaller and more uniform areas, such as Long Island or the Willamette Valley. There are still exceptions, especially in off years when, in spite of the vintage, someone or another produces a wine (thanks to the specific vineyard, viticulture, viniculture and chance) that is uncharacteristically strong compared with his or her neighbors. If the price for the better wine in this lesser vintage is lower, then that wine might well represent a good value. In Bordeaux, they usually lower the prices for lesser vintages. In America, they never do.

Vintage charts can also serve as a consumer guide to how wines from a particular vintage are evolving in the bottle. We've done our best to present this information as well, yet as winemaking styles vary so greatly, this information too cannot be taken as the blanket truth. For the past decade there has been a trend toward early maturing (cost-effective) wines, or at least toward wines that drink well young, such as so-called "restaurant wines." Some age well; most fade quickly. These are curve balls in the game of estimating a vintage wine's evolution in the bottle. There are still plenty of winemakers who believe in big, long-lived wines that take years to peak. If the winery is rich enough, then it will age vintages for years before releasing the wine. Others hold back a portion of their production, age the wines in bottles in their cellars until they are drinking well, and then release them as library reserves.

In putting this chart together, we have tasted and retasted vintages, polled dozens of wineries and winemakers, consulted a wealth of published sources, and been as specific as possible (narrowing our areas much more than is common) to provide meaningful and helpful guidelines. Remember, though, that vintage charts are by nature ever so general, and that we place much greater value on recommending a producer rather than a vintage for American wines. And, of course, there is never any substitute for tasting a wine and making one's own assessment.

	CA: Napa Chardonnay	CA: Sonoma Chardonnay	CA: Central Coast Chardonnay	CA: Napa Sauvignon Blanc	CA: Sonoma Sauvignon Blanc	CA: North Coast Cabernet S.	CA: Central Coast Cabernet S.	CA: North Coast Pinot Noir	CA: Central Coast Pinot Noir	CA: Napa Merlot	CA: Sonoma Merlot	CA: North Coast Zinfandel	NY: Long Island Reds	NY: Long Island Whites	OR: Pinot Noir	WA: Cabernet Sauvignon	WA: Whites
1991	**18b**	17b	17b	16b	**18b**	17b	16b	16a	16a	17a	16a	17b	16a	**18b**	16b	15a	16b
1990	**18b**	17b	**18b**	18c	**18b**	15b	17b	17b	14b	17b	17b	**18b**	17a	17b	**18b**	17b	16c
1989	14c	16b	16b	16c	17c	16c	15b	15c	15c	16b	**19b**	14b	14c	16c	14c	17b	15c
1988	16c	17b	16b	15c	17c	14c	15b	17c	16c	14b	**18b**	13b	**19b**	17c	17c	17c	15c
1987	14c	17b	15b		17d	17c	15b	14c		17b	17b	17b	12b	12d	12c	15c	13c
1986	**18c**	**18b**	16c		**18b**	17c	13b	15c		14c	**18b**	15c	16c	17c	13c	12c	14c
1985	17c	17c	15c		**18c**	**19b**	17b	16c		15c	**18b**	17b	12d	13d	**19b**	16b	
1984	14d	15c	14b		**18c**	**18c**	17b	15c		13d	15b	15c	12c	13d	9d	11d	
1983	13d	13d	13c		17d	12d	13b	14d		14d	14d	13c	15c	16d	**18c**	**18c**	
1982	12d	17d	13c		13d	13c	11c	15d		13d	14d	12d	16c	**18d**	14d	11d	
1981	15d	14d	13d		14d	14c	15c	12d		13d	14d	14c	16c	**18d**	13d	11d	
1980	15d	14d	15d		15c		14c			13d		13c	15c		14d	11d	

TOP VINTAGES

MI: 1991
OH: 1988
PA: 1991
RI: 1990
TX: 1991 (white),
   1989, 1990 (red)
VA: 1991, 1988,
   1986, 1985

KEY

Exceptional	19/20
Excellent	18/20 & 17/20
Very Good	16/20 & 15/20
Good	14/20 & 13/20

Best vintages are highlighted in **bold** red type.

a Needs more time
b Drinking fine now but
   may improve with age
c Drink now
d Drink now; may be too
   old

How Wine is Made

WINE is one of the most natural and simple food beverages on earth; one that will, literally, make itself. Yeast cells, one of the key components in the winemaking process, are naturally present on the outside of grape skins. Once the skins are broken, the yeasts convert the natural sugars in the fruit to alcohol and carbon dioxide gas, beginning the process of fermentation.

Still Wine

All wines begin in the vineyard. Soil, climate, weather, and cultural practices directly affect the quality and character of the grapes. Harvest in North America usually begins in late August to early September and can last through November depending on the weather and grape variety. Once the grapes are harvested, they are placed in a destemmer/crusher which separates the stems from the fruit and breaks up the berries. The stems are then discarded leaving a "must," a combination of juice, seeds, pulp, and skins. At this point, the processes for red and white wine production begin to differ.

White Wine

The juice from both red and white winegrapes is without color. In red wine production, the skins are fermented with the crushed juice to give it color and flavor. Unless a full-bodied white wine is desired, the skins and seeds are usually removed from the must after only a few hours leaving juice known as "free-run." The skins are pressed to extract all the remaining juice, called "press juice." The free-run and press juice are then filtered in preparation for fermentation. At some point in production, the press juice may be blended back into the free-run. Next, the juice is placed in stainless steel tanks or oak barrels where the wine will ferment following the addition of yeast. White wine fermentation lasts from three days to three weeks.

When fermentation has run its course, the vintner will stop the process and filter the wine to remove solids and yeast remnants. The wine is then aged for a period of one week to a year in stainless steel, oak, or redwood containers, or it can be aged in the bottle. After aging, the wine may be blended with other wines with different characteristics to create the desired style. The next step is "finishing," a process by which the wine is stabilized and filtered before bottling. Substances such as egg whites or gelatin are added to remove astringent substances or proteins which can cloud the wine and give it "off" flavors. Sulfites may also be added to prevent oxidation and bacterial spoilage.

Red Wine

Red wines are fermented with the grape skins and seeds at warmer temperatures than white wines. The skins float to the top forming a cap during fermentation and must be moistened regularly with juice to extract color and flavors. Red wines are usually fermented for a period of five to ten days and then are filtered, clarified and preserved with the addition of sulfites.

It is common for red wines to be aged in oak barrels for a period of about one to two years. As with whites, the vintner may choose to blend at this stage. The wine is then finished, filtered, and clarified before bottling. In some rare but important instances, generally among small, ultra-premium wineries, no or only minimal fining and filtering is carried out in an effort to capture the maximum amount of natural flavor components.

Blush Wine

Blush wines, such as White Zinfandel, White Grenache, or White Cabernet, are in contact with the skins for a very short period—usually six to eight hours. Fermentation is halted before all of the sugars can be converted to alcohol, giving these wines a slightly sweeter or off-dry taste.

Sparkling Wine

Sparkling wines are made from still wines, such as Chenin Blanc, French Colombard, Chardonnay, or Pinot Noir, which serve as a base wine for the next stage of this unique winemaking process. (Among premium sparkling wines, Chardonnay and Pinot Noir grapes are used almost exclusively.) A "triage"—a blend of the base wine, yeast nutrient, and a source of sugar—is added to the base wine and the mixture is fermented a second time in a sealed container which traps carbon dioxide producing the effervescence or bubbles.

There are two basic methods of secondary fermentation: *méthode champenoise*, or bottle fermented; and the *charmat* or bulk process. Each process produces a different style of sparkling wine. In *méthode champenoise* production, the more time-intensive of the two processes, the triage and the base wine are bottled and cellared for a period of six months to two years or more. The yeast cells break down during the second fermentation giving the wine unique aromas and flavors. When fermentation is complete, the sediment is collected and removed before a "dosage," a blend of wine and sweetener, is added to replace any wine lost during sediment removal. All premium sparkling wines are made using the *méthode champenoise*. This process is identified on the label, sometimes by the phrase "fermented in the bottle."

The bulk or *charmat* process is similar except the wine undergoes fermentation in a large tank, instead of the bottle, and is fermented for a shorter period of time.

Dessert Wine

Grapes for dessert wines are harvested at slightly higher sugar levels than those for table wines. Fermentation is stopped before all the sugar can be converted to alcohol by the addition of brandy. The wines are often aged in oak or stainless steel.

Calendar of Wine Events

This is only a selective listing of wine-related events held across North America each year. Many others could not be included due to space limitations. Contact your local wine shop or a nearby winery for information on wine festivals or tastings in your area.

January

•Connoisseur Ski Invitational: The Wine Summit of Health and Fitness; Vail, CO. Benefit for The American Institute of Wine and Food. Call (212) 447-0456.

•Dallas Morning News National Wine Competition; Dallas, TX. Call (214) 319-7000.

•Winter Wineland; Healdsburg, CA. Wine tastings and winery tours hosted by Sonoma county vintners. Call (707) 433-6935.

February

•Albany American Wine Festival; Albany, NY. Call (518) 452-0707.

•Wineries Unlimited Annual Seminar and Trade Show; Philadelphia, PA. Call (607) 535-7133.

•Masters of Food & Wine; Highlands Inn, Carmel, CA. A prestigious annual gathering of international chefs and winemakers celebrating great cuisine and wine. Call (408) 624-3801.

•American Wine Appreciation Week. The last week of February has been proclaimed "American Wine Appreciation Week" by a resolution of the U.S. Congress. The intention of this commemoration is to recognize the contributions of winegrape fruit growers and vintners to the U.S. economy and to the nation's cultural, religious and family traditions. Look for corresponding celebrations, wine tastings and other activities to be sponsored by wineries and wine retailers across the country.

March

•Cincinnati International Wine Festival; Cincinnati, OH. Benefit for Public Radio station WGVC. Call (513) 556-4444.

•Wine America International Wine & Spirits Trade Show; New York, NY. Call (310) 271-3200.

•Monterey Wine Festival; Monterey, CA. The largest celebration of California wines in the U.S. Call (800) 925-FEST.

April

•Texas Hill Country Wine and Food Festival; Austin, TX. Benefit for Public Television station KLRU and Public Radio station KMFA. Call (329-0770).

•Intervin International Wine Competition; Buffalo, NY. Call (716) 634-2456.

•Florida Winefest and Auction; Sarasota, FL. Benefit for the New College Foundation and the University of Southern Florida at Sarasota. Seminars, winemaker dinners, a Suncoast tasting showcase and major wine auction. Call (813) 366-0007.

•Winefest; Ypsilanti, MI. Benefit for the Ann Arbor Art Association Community Arts Program. Call (313) 994-8004.

•Yakima Valley Spring Barrel Tasting; Yakima Valley, WA. Call (509) 882-1223.

May

•Santa Barbara Wine Auction; Santa Barbara, CA. Benefit for the Santa Barbara Museum of Natural History. Call (805) 682-4711).

•Paso Robles Wine Festival; Paso Robles, CA. Call (805) 467-2343.

•KQED Wine & Food Festival; San Francisco, CA. Call (415) 553-2200.

•San Francisco Wine Market Week; San Francisco, CA. The most comprehensive international wine show held on the West Coast. Call (800) 497-3376.

•Old Mesilla Wine Festival; Mesilla, NM. Call (505) 646-4543.

June

•Napa Valley Wine Auction; St. Helena, Ca. Benefit for local healthcare facilities. This four-day food and wine festival is highlighted by numerous special events and winery open houses. Call (707) 963-0148.

•Aspen Food & Wine Classic; Aspen, CO. Seminars, demonstrations and winemaker dinners highlight this renowned annual event. Call (212) 382-5885.

•Telluride Wine Festival; Telluride, CO. Benefit for Alcohol Awareness Program for Telluride Youth. Call (303) 728-4708.

July

•Kapalua Wine Symposium; Maui, HI. A weekend of tastings, seminars and fine dining. Call (800) 527-2582.

•The New Orleans Wine & Food Experience; New Orleans, LA. Benefit for Crescent City cultural organizations. Call (504) 522-5730.

•Los Angeles County Fair Wine Judging; Pomona, CA. Call (909) 623-3111.

•Cuisines of the Sun; Mauna Lani Bay Hotel, Honolulu, HI. An annual event celebrating the bold-flavored, healthful foods of sunny climates with cooking demonstrations, seminars and special meals prepared by guest chefs. Call (800) 367-2323.

August

•Sonoma County Wine Showcase & Charity Wine Auction; Santa Rosa, CA. Benefit for Sonoma County charities. Call (707) 579-0577.

•Festival of Northwest Wines; Seattle, WA. Call (206) 833-2631.

•Tri-Cities Wine Festival; Pasco, WA. Call (509) 375-0211.

•Prosser Food & Wine Festival; Prosser, WA. Call (509) 786-3177.

September

•Central Coast Wine Festival; San Luis Obispo, CA. Benefit for the Arthritis Foundation. Call (805) 541-1721.

•Livermore Valley Harvest Wine Celebration; Livermore, CA. Benefit for the Livermore Valley Education and Museum Fund. Call (510) 370-9777.

•The Auction of Northwest Wines; Woodville, WA. Benefit for Children's Hospital and Medical Center. Call (206) 488-4617.

•International Wine Showcase and Auction on the Hudson; Staatsburg, NY. Benefit for Autistic Children. Call (800) 322-8194.

•Nevada County Winefest & Grape Stomp; Miner's Foundry, NV. Benefit for the Miner's Foundry Cultural Center. Call (916) 477-2097.

•American Wine & Food Festival; Los Angeles, CA. Benefit for Meals on Wheels. An "All-American Cook-Out" themed tasting party, hosted by Wolfgang Puck and Barbara Lazaroff. Call (310) 652-4025.

October

•Sonoma County Harvest Fair; Santa Rosa, CA. Call (707) 545-4203.

•Midwest International Wine Exposition; Chicago, IL. Benefit for Roosevelt University Hospitality Management Program and Washburne Trade School Chef Training Program. Call (312) 372-0771.

•Capitol Food & Wine Festival; Lacey, WA. Benefit for St. Martin's College. Call (206) 438-4366.

•The Wine Spectator New York/California Wine Experience. A tasting extravaganza alternating annually between Manhattan and San Francisco. Call (212) 684-4224.

November

•Bucks County Wine and Food Festival; Hollyhedge, New Hope, PA. Call (215) 345-4552.

•"World of Wines, A Celebration of Food and Wine"; Ritz Carlton Laguna Niguel, Laguna Niguel, CA. A premier food and wine event comprising seminars, tastings and a gala dinner. Call (714) 240-5008.

•Thanksgiving in Wine Country; Grandview, WA. Call (509) 882-1223.

•Winter Wine Escape; Mauna Kea Beach Hotel, Hawaii, HI. Hawaii's best chefs join in a celebration of Hawaiian Regional Cuisine. Many Northern California winemakers also participate. Call (800) 882-6060.

December

•Livermore Valley Christmas Wine Trails; Livermore, CA. Call (510) 370-9777.

Food & Wine Pairings

CONSIDER the myriad foods available at our grocers and food preparations that can be enjoyed in our restaurants. Then consider the number of varietal wines available and all their styles. It quickly becomes clear that the enterprise of pairing food and wine can be as complicated as you wish to make it. If you'd like some rules of thumb to help you sort out the possibilities, here are two that have stood the test of time. Rule One: Drink red wine with meat, and white wine with fish and poultry. Rule Two: Forget about Rule One and marry any food with any wine you wish; when it comes to personal preferences, there are no rights and wrongs.

There are, of course, some classic food and wine matches that satisfy again and again. And there are exciting new standards being discovered daily as the range of foods and wines available continues to expand. Based on our experience, the following matches of widely available dishes and cuisines with the wines of North America are worthy of special consideration. One caveat: Sauces can change everything, so ask the cook or a waiter for a flavor forecast.

Appetizers & First Courses

ANTIPASTO

Pinot Gris, (Dry) Chenin Blanc, Sauvignon Blanc, Pinot Blanc, Gamay Beaujolais, Barbera

ASPARAGUS

Sauvignon (Fumé) Blanc, (Dry) Riesling, Vidal Blanc

CARPACCIO (BEEF)

Barbera, Cabernet Rosé, Rhône Blends

CARPACCIO (TUNA)

Sauvignon (Fumé) Blanc, Vin Gris

CAVIAR

Brut Sparkling Wine

CLAMS (RAW OR CASINO)

Sauvignon (Fumé) Blanc, Brut Sparkling Wine, (Dry) Chenin Blanc, Pinot Blanc, Seyval Blanc

COLD MEATS

Vin Gris, Riesling, Gamay Beaujolais, Barbera, Seyval Blanc, (Dry) Vignoles, Chambourcin Rosé

CRUDITÉS

Pinot Blanc, Chenin Blanc, Chardonnay, Gamay Beaujolais

FOIE GRAS

Brut Sparkling Wine, Late-Harvest Riesling, Sauvignon Blanc, Gewürztraminer, Muscat, Pinot Noir

NIÇOISE SALAD

Sauvignon (Fumé) Blanc

NUTS AND/OR OLIVES

Brut Sparkling Wine

OYSTERS (RAW)

Sauvignon (Fumé) Blanc, Brut Sparkling Wine, Pinot Gris, Chardonnay, (Dry) Riesling, Pinot Blanc, Chenin Blanc

PASTA SALAD

Sémillon, Sauvignon (Fumé) Blanc, (Dry) Chenin Blanc, (Dry) Riesling

PASTA WITH CREAM SAUCE

Chardonnay, Pinot Blanc

PASTA WITH SHELLFISH

Sauvignon (Fumé) Blanc, Chardonnay

PASTA WITH TOMATO SAUCE

Barbera, Sangiovese, Zinfandel, Rhône Blends

PASTA WITH VEGETABLES

Pinot Blanc, Dry Riesling, Sauvignon Blanc, Viognier, Gamay Beaujolais, Barbera

PATÉS

Gewürztraminer, Seyval Blanc, Gamay Beaujolais, Riesling, Brut Sparkling Wine, Cabernet Franc, Vin Gris

PROSCIUTTO AND MELON

Pinot Blanc, Riesling, Late Harvest Riesling or Gewürztraminer, Muscat

QUICHE

Riesling, Chenin Blanc, Chardonnay, Viognier, Gamay Beaujolais

SCALLOPS

Sauvignon (Fumé) Blanc, Chardonnay, Brut Sparkling Wine, Pinot Noir, Sémillon

SMOKED FISH (trout, herring)

Riesling, Gewürztraminer, Pinot Blanc, Brut Sparkling Wine

SOUPS

Usually none, or (Solera) Sherry

Fish & Shellfish

CRAB

Sauvignon (Fumé) Blanc, Brut Sparkling Wine, Chardonnay

LOBSTER

Brut Sparkling Wine, Chardonnay

MUSSELS

Chenin Blanc, Pinot Blanc, Pinot Gris, Sauvignon (Fumé) Blanc

RED SNAPPER

Chardonnay, Sauvignon (Fumé) Blanc

SALMON

Pinot Noir, Sauvignon Blanc, Pinot Gris, Sémillon, Vin Gris

SALMON TARTARE

Brut Sparkling Wine, Pinot Gris

SASHIMI, SUSHI

Brut Sparkling Wine, Semi-Dry Riesling

SCALLOPS, OYSTERS, CLAMS

(See Appetizers*)*

SHRIMP

Pinot Blanc, Chenin Blanc, Sauvignon (Fumé) Blanc, Chardonnay, Colombard, Vidal Blanc

STRIPED BASS

Chardonnay, Pinot Blanc, Viognier, (Dry) Vignoles

SWORDFISH

Sauvignon (Fumé) Blanc, Brut Sparkling Wine, Vin Gris, Pinot Noir

TUNA

Sauvignon (Fumé) Blanc, Pinot Noir, Merlot, Vin Gris, Chardonnay

OTHER WHITE FISH

Chardonnay, Viognier, Dry Riesling, Sémillon

Meat & Poultry

CHICKEN

Chardonnay, Vin Gris, Riesling, Merlot, Gamay Beaujolais, Chenin Blanc, Pinot Noir, (Lighter) Cabernet Sauvignon

CHICKEN SALAD

Riesling, Chenin Blanc, Gewürztraminer, Pinot Blanc

CHICKEN (SMOKED)

Vin Gris, Pinot Noir, Zinfandel

DUCK

Pinot Noir, Merlot, Rosé Sparkling Wine, Cabernet Sauvignon, Zinfandel

FRANKFURTER

Riesling, (Chilled) Gamay Beaujolais

HAM

Vin Gris, Gamay Beaujolais, Merlot

HAMBURGER

Cabernet Sauvignon, Gamay, Syrah, Chancellor, Barbera, Zinfandel, Rhône Blends

LAMB (GRILLED, BROILED)

Meritage, Cabernet Sauvignon, Merlot, Pinot Noir, Marechal Foch, Chancellor, Zinfandel

PHEASANT

Pinot Noir, Syrah

QUAIL

Pinot Noir

RABBIT

Riesling, Pinot Noir, Barbera, Merlot, Zinfandel

SAUSAGE

Riesling, Brut or Rosé Sparkling Wine, Barbera, Gamay Beaujolais, Norton or Cynthiana, Syrah, Zinfandel

STEAK (GRILLED, BROILED)

Cabernet Sauvignon, Merlot, Rhône Blends, Zinfandel, Meritage, Norton or Cynthiana, Brut Sparkling Wine

TURKEY

Zinfandel, Merlot, Chardonnay, Gamay Beaujolais

VEAL

Chardonnay, Barbera, Merlot, Cynthiana

VENISON

Syrah, Rhône Blends, Petite Sirah, Zinfandel, Pinot Noir, Norton, Chancellor, Cabernet Sauvignon

Other Main Courses

COUSCOUS

Cabernet Franc, Merlot, Petite Sirah, Rosé Sparkling Wine, Syrah, Vin Gris,

CURRY, FISH OR CHICKEN

Riesling, (Chilled) Gamay Beaujolais, Sauvignon (Fumé) Blanc, Zinfandel

MOUSSAKA

Merlot, Sangiovese, Barbera, Zinfandel

PIZZA

Barbera, Zinfandel, Sangiovese, Brut or Rosé Sparkling Wine, Cabernet Rosé

SPICY CHINESE

Dry (and off-dry) Riesling, Pinot Gris, Pinot Blanc, Brut or Rosé Sparkling Wine, Merlot

SPICY MEXICAN

Dry (and off-dry) Riesling, Vin Gris, Chenin Blanc, (Chilled) Gamay Beaujolais

THAI

Chenin Blanc, Pinot Blanc, Riesling, Gewürztraminer, Brut or Rosé Sparkling Wine

Cheeses

GOAT

SOFT: Brut or Rosé Sparkling Wine, Sauvignon (Fumé) Blanc, Cabernet Sauvignon, Merlot, Pinot Noir

HARD: Pinot Noir, Merlot, Syrah, Cabernet Sauvignon

COW & SHEEP

MEDIUM: Pinot Noir, Petite Sirah

HARD: Cabernet Sauvignon, Petite Sirah, Zinfandel, Port Blue, Late-Harvest Riesling, Chenin Blanc, Gewürztraminer, Muscat, Zinfandel

Desserts

APPLE PIE, TART & BAKED

Late-Harvest Riesling, Various Ice Wines, Muscat, Demi-sec Sparkling Wines, Blueberry Wine

BERRIES

Brut Sparkling Wines, Demi-sec Sparkling Wines, Late-Harvest Riesling, Muscat, Zinfandel

CHOCOLATE

Late-Harvest Riesling, Raspberry Wine, Black Muscat, Cabernet Sauvignon

CAKES

Demi-sec Sparkling Wines, Late-Harvest Riesling, Muscat, Various Ice Wines

CREAMS, CUSTARDS, PUDDINGS

Demi-sec Sparkling Wines, Late-Harvest Riesling, Muscat, Various Ice Wines

FRESH FRUIT

Late-Harvest Chenin Blanc, Riesling, Gewürztraminer, Muscat

ICE CREAMS, SORBETS

Usually none, perhaps fruit wine or fruit liqueurs

NUTS

Port, Brut Sparkling Wine, Angelica

TIRAMISU

Angelica

Listing of Wineries by Country and State

THE following geographical check list of wineries illustrates the breadth and vitality of the North American wine world in the 1990s. We believe it is the most thorough and comprehensive listing yet compiled, but we know there are still more wineries that belong on it—wineries are opening and popping into the wine-drinking public's collective consciousness all the time.

We have checked and rechecked our entries. In a few instances, a winery's second-label wine has taken on an identity and life of its own. In such cases, we have given the second label its own listing, and placed in brackets the name of the parent winery. In a handful of instances, we identified a winery or wine label through the variety of published sources we consulted in our research (including the results of competitions), but were unable to track down the winery's location beyond its home state. We suspect that these, too, are second-label or negociant wines or, perhaps, are from new, small wineries not yet widely documented. In these few instances, we have included the name in our listing and simply noted "unknown" for the location of the winery.

Sometimes the business office of a winery is not in the same town as the winery itself; throughout these listings we have tried to give the location of the winery. In sum, we believe that this list offers an excellent overview of the geographical distribution of winery and vineyard activity in North America and provides leads for people wishing to know more.

Alabama

ALISTAIR VINEYARDS (New Market)
BRASWELL'S WINERY (Dora)
BRYANT VINEYARD (Talladega)
PEACOCK VALLEY WINERY (Perdido)

Arizona

ARIZONA VINEYARDS (Nogales)
CALLAGHAN VINEYARDS (Soñoita)
SAN DOMINIQUE (Scottsdale)
SAN XAVIER VYDS. & WINERY, INC. (Coyote Springs)
SONOITA VINEYARDS (Elgin)
R.W. WEBB WINERY, INC. (Vail)

Arkansas

CONCERT VINEYARDS, INC. (Lakeview)
COTNER VINEYARDS, INC. (Altus)
COWIE WINE CELLARS, INC. (Paris)
EUREKA SPRINGS WINERY, THE (Eureka Springs)
MOUNT BETHEL WINERY (Altus)
POST FAMILIE VINEYARDS & WINERY (Altus)
WIEDERKEHR WINE CELLARS, INC. (Altus)

California

ABBEY D'OR (San Miguel)
ACACIA WINERY (Napa)
ADELAIDA CELLARS (Paso Robles)
ADLER FELS (Santa Rosa)
AETNA SPRINGS WINE RANCH (Pope Valley)
AHLGREN VINEYARD (Boulder Creek)
ALAMBIC, INC. (Ukiah)
ALDERBROOK VINEYARDS (Healdsburg)
ALEXANDER VALLEY FRUIT & TRADING CO. (Geyserville)
ALEXANDER VALLEY VINEYARDS (Healdsburg)
ALPEN CELLARS (Trinity Center)
ALTA VINEYARD CELLAR (Calistoga)
ALTAMURA WINERY AND VINEYARDS (Napa)
AMADOR FOOTHILL WINERY (Plymouth)
AMIZETTA VINEYARDS (St. Helena)
ANDERSON'S CONN VALLEY VINEYARDS (St. Helena)
S. ANDERSON VINEYARD (Yountville)
ANDERSON WINE CELLARS (Exeter)
ANNAPOLIS WINERY (Annapolis)
ANTELOPE VALLEY WINERY (Lancaster)
ANTHONY D. MATERA WINE CELLAR (Calistoga)
ARCIERO WINERY (Paso Robles)
ARGONAUT WINERY (Ione)
ARIEL VINEYARDS (Napa)
ARMIDA WINERY (Healdsburg)
ARROWOOD VINEYARDS & WINERY (Glen Ellen)
ASV WINES, INC. (Delano)
ATLAS PEAK VINEYARD (Napa)
AU BON CLIMAT (Santa Maria)
AUDUBON CELLARS, INC. (Berkeley)
AUSTIN CELLARS (Los Alamos)
BABCOCK VINEYARDS (Lompoc)
BACIGALUPI VINEYARDS (Healdsburg)
BAILY VINEYARD & WINERY (Temecula)
BALDINELLI VINEYARDS (Plymouth)

BALLARD CANYON CORP. WINERY (Solvang)
BALLONA CREEK WINERY (Culver City)
BALVERNE WINERY & VINEYARDS (Windsor)
BANDIERA WINERY (Cloverdale)
BANNISTER (Healdsburg)
BARGETTO'S SANTA CRUZ WINERY (Soquel)
BARON KOLB WINERY (Paso Robles)
BAY CELLARS (Berkeley)
BEAUCANON (Healdsburg)
BEAULIEU VINEYARD (Madera)
BEL ARBORS VINEYARD (Hopland)
BELLA NAPOLI WINERY (Manteca)
BELLEROSE VINEYARD (Healdsburg)
BELVEDERE WINERY (Healdsburg)
BENZIGER OF GLEN ELLEN (Glen Ellen)
BERGFELD WINERY (St. Helena)
BERINGER VINEYARDS (St. Helena)
BERNARD PRADEL CELLARS (Napa)
BERNARDO WINERY (San Diego)
BEVERAGE SOURCE, INC., THE (Sanger)
BIANCHI VINEYARDS (Kerman)
BLACK MOUNTAIN / MORRIS (Healdsburg)
BLACK SHEEP VINTNERS (Murphys)
BLACKWELL WINE COMPANY (Lost Hills)
BOEGER WINERY, INC. (Placerville)
BOGLE VINEYARDS, INC. (Clarksburg)
BONNY DOON VINEYARD (Santa Cruz)
BORDONI VINEYARDS (Vallejo)
BORRA'S CELLAR (Lodi)
BOUCHAINE VINEYARDS, INC. (Napa)
BOUNTY HILL VINEYARD (Berkeley)
BOYER (Soledad)
BRANDBORG CELLARS (Fairfax)
BRANDER VINEYARD, THE (Los Olivos)
BRAREN PAULI WINERY (Petaluma)
BRICELAND VINEYARDS (Redway)
J.F.J. BRONCO WINERY (Ceres)
BRUTOCAO CELLARS (Hopland)
BUEHLER VINEYARDS (St. Helena)
BUENA VISTA CARNEROS (Sonoma)
BURGESS CELLARS (St. Helena)
BUTTERFLY CREEK WINERY (Mariposa)
BUTTONWOOD FARM WINERY (Santa Ynez)
BYINGTON WINERY & VINEYARDS, INC. (Los Gatos)
BYRON VINEYARD & WINERY (Santa Maria)
CACHE CELLARS (Davis)
CACHE CREEK WINERY (Woodland)
CADENASSO WINERY (Suisun)
CAFARO CELLARS (St. Helena)
CAIN CELLARS (St. Helena)
CAKEBREAD CELLARS (Rutherford)
CALAFIA CELLARS (St. Helena)
CALERA WINE COMPANY (Hollister)
CALIFORNIA FRUIT PRODUCTS COMPANY (Fresno)
CALLAWAY VINEYARD AND WINERY (Temecula)
CAMBRIA WINERY & VINEYARD (Santa Maria)
CANYON ROAD [Geyser Peak, Geyserville]
CANTERBURY [Stratford Winery, St. Helena]
CAPARONE VINEYARD (Paso Robles)
CAPORALE WINERY (Napa)
CARCO VALLEY WINERY (Napa)
CAREY CELLARS (Solvang)
CARNEROS CREEK WINERY (Napa)
CARRARI VINEYARDS (Buellton)
CARROUSEL CELLARS (Gilroy)
CASA DE FRUTA (Hollister)
CASA NUESTRA (St. Helena)
CASTORO CELLARS (Paso Robles)
CASWELL VINEYARDS (Sebastopol)
CAYMUS VINEYARDS, INC. (Rutherford)
CECCHETTI-SEBASTIANI CELLAR (Sonoma)
CEDAR MOUNTAIN WINERY (Livermore)

CHALK HILL WINERY (Healdsburg)
CHALONE VINEYARD (Soledad)
CHAMISAL VINEYARD (San Luis Obispo)
CHANDELLE OF SONOMA (Glen Ellen)
CHANNING RUDD CELLARS (Middletown)
CHANSA CELLARS (Santa Maria)
CHANTER WINERY (Napa)
CHAPPELLET WINERY (St. Helena)
CHARIS VINEYARDS (Geyersville)
CHARLES F. SHAW VINEYARD AND WINERY, LTD. (St. Helena)
CHARLES KRUG WINERY (St. Helena)
CHARLES SPINETTA WINERY (Plymouth)
CHATEAU BOSWELL (St. Helena)
CHATEAU CHEVALIER WINERY (St. Helena)
CHATEAU CHEVRE WINERY (Yountville)
CHATEAU DE BAUN (Santa Rosa)
CHATEAU DE LEU WINERY (Suisun)
CHATEAU DIANA (Healdsburg)
CHATEAU JULIEN (Carmel)
CHATEAU MONTELENA WINERY (Calistoga)
CHATEAU NAPA BEAUCANON (St. Helena)
CHATEAU POTELLE (Napa)
CHATEAU ST. JEAN, INC. (Kenwood)
CHATEAU SOUVERAIN (Geyserville)
CHATEAU WOLTNER (Angwin)
CHATOM VINEYARDS (Douglas Flat)
CHAUFFE-EAU CELLARS (Geyserville)
CHICO CELLARS (Chico)
CHIMERE (Santa Maria)
CHIMNEY ROCK WINERY (Napa)
CHOUINARD VINEYARDS (Castro Valley)
CHRIS A. FREDSON WINERY (Healdsburg)
CHRISTIAN BROTHERS, THE (St. Helena)
CHRISTINE WOODS WINERY (Philo)
CHRISTOPHE (San Francisco)
CIENEGA VALLEY WINERY (Hollister)
CILURZO VINEYARD & WINERY (Temecula)
CINNABAR VINEYARD & WINERY (Saratoga)
CLAIBORNE & CHURCHILL VINTNERS (San Luis Obispo)
CLAIRVAUX [Rabbit Ridge Vineyards Winery, Healdsburg]
CLAUDIA SPRINGS WINERY (Philo)
CLINE CELLARS (Oakley)
CLONINGER (unknown)
CLOS DU BOIS (Healdsburg)
CLOS DU LION (Healdsburg)
CLOS DU MURIEL (Temecula)
CLOS DU VAL WINE CO., LTD., THE (Napa)
CLOS PEGASE WINERY (Calistoga)
CLOUDSTONE VINEYARDS (Los Altos Hills)
CLOVERDALE RANCH [Pellegrini Bros. Wines, Inc., South San Francisco]
COBB MOUNTAIN WINERY (Middletown)
CODORNIU NAPA, INC. (Napa)
B. R. COHN WINERY (Glen Ellen)
COLBY VINEYARDS (Napa)
CONCANNON VINEYARD (Livermore)
CONGRESS SPRINGS VINEYARDS (Saratoga)
CONN CREEK WINERY (St. Helena)
CONN VALLEY VINEYARDS (St. Helena)
CONRAD VIAND WINERY (Martinez)
A. CONROTTO WINERY, INC. (Gilroy)
R. & J. COOK (Clarksburg)
COPENHAGEN CELLARS (Solvang)
CORBETT CANYON VINEYARDS (San Luis Obispo)
CORISON (St. Helena)
COSENTINO (Yountville)
COSTELLO VINEYARDS (Napa)
COTTONWOOD CANYON (San Luis Obispo)
H. COTURRI & SONS, LTD. (Glen Ellen)
CREEKSIDE VINEYARDS (Suisun)
CRESCINI WINES (Soquel)

CRESTON VINEYARDS (Creston)
CRIBARI VINEYARDS, INC. (Fresno)
CRONIN VINEYARDS (Woodside)
CULBERTSON WINERY (Temecula)
CUVAISON (Calistoga)
CYGNET CELLARS (Hollister)
CYPRESS [J. Lohr Winery, San Jose]
D'AGOSTINI WINERY (Sobon)
DALLA VALLE VINEYARDS (Napa)
DANFIELD CREEK (unknown)
DAUME WINERY (Camarillo)
DA VINCI VINEYARD (Renaissance)
DAVID ARTHUR VINEYARDS (St. Helena)
DAVID AND MERYL SALTER WINERY (Somerset)
DAVID BRUCE WINERY, INC. (Los Gatos)
DAVIS BYNUM WINERY (Healdsburg)
DECANTER CORPORATION / ROYCE VINEYARDS (Talmage)
DEER PARK ESCONDIDO (Escondido)
DEER PARK WINERY (Deer Park)
DEER VALLEY (Monterey)
DEER VALLEY (Gonzales)
DEHLINGER WINERY (Sebastopol)
DELANO GROWERS GRAPE PRODUCTS (Delano)
DELICATO VINEYARDS (Manteca)
DE LOACH VINEYARDS (Santa Rosa)
DE LORIMER WINERY (Geyserville)
DE MOOR WINERY (Oakville)
DENATALE VINEYARDS (Healdsburg)
DEVLIN WINE CELLARS (Soquel)
DIAMOND CREEK VINEYARDS (Calistoga)
DIAMOND OAKS VINEYARDS (Cloverdale)
DOLAN VINEYARDS (Redwood Valley)
DOMAINE BRETON [Guenoc Winery, Middletown]
DOMAINE CARNEROS, LTD. (Carneros)
DOMAINE CHARBAY WINERY & DISTILLERY (Ukiah)
DOMAINE CHANDON, INC. (Yountville)
DOMAINE DE CLARCK (Carmel)
DOMAINE KARAKASH WINERY AND DISTILLERY (Ukiah)
DOMAINE LAURIER (Forestville)
DOMAINE MICHEL (Healdsburg)
DOMAINE MONTREAUX (Napa)
DOMAINE NAPA WINERY (St. Helena)
DOMAINE ST. GEORGE WINERY (Healdsburg)
DOMAINE SAINT GREGORY (Ukiah)
DOMINUS ESTATE (Yountville)
DONATONI WINERY (Inglewood)
DRY CREEK VINEYARD, INC. (Healdsburg)
DUCKHORN VINEYARDS (St. Helena)
DUNCAN PEAK VINEYARDS (Hopland)
DUNN VINEYARDS (Angwin)
DUNNEWOOD VINEYARDS (Lodi)
DURNEY VINEYARD (Carmel)
DUTCH HENRY WINERY (Calistoga)
DUXOUP WINE WORKS (Healdsburg)
EAGLE RIDGE WINERY (Penngrove)
EAST-SIDE WINERY (Lodi)
EBERLE WINERY (Paso Robles)
EDMUNDS ST. JOHN (Emeryville)
EDNA VALLEY VINEYARD (San Luis Obispo)
ED OLIVIEIRA WINERY (Arcata)
ELDORADO VINEYARDS (Camino)
ELLISTON VINEYARDS (Sunol)
EL MOLINO (St. Helena)
EMERALD BAY WINERY (Carmel)
EMILIO GUGLIELMO WINERY (Morgan Hill)
ENDGATE VINEYARDS (Novato)
ENZ VINEYARDS (Hollister)
EQUINOX (Boulder Creek)
ESTANCIA ESTATES (Rutherford)
ESTRELLA RIVER WINERY (Paso Robles)
EVENSEN VINEYARDS (Oakville)
EVEREST VINEYARDS (unknown)

FALCONER CELLARS (St. Rafael)
FALLBROOK WINERY (Fallbrook)
FALLENLEAF WINERY (Napa)
FARELLA-PARK VINEYARDS (Napa)
FAR NIENTE WINERY (Oakville)
FARVIEW FARM VINEYARD (Templeton)
FELLOM RANCH VINEYARDS (Cupertino)
FELTON EMPIRE (San Francisco [merchant label])
FENESTRA WINERY (Livermore)
FERRARA WINERY (Escondido)
FERRARI-CARANO WINERY (Healdsburg)
FESS PARKER WINERY (Los Olivos)
FETZER VINEYARDS (Redwood Valley)
FICKLIN VINEYARDS (Madera)
FIDDLE FARM (Buena Vista)
FIELDBROOK VALLEY WINERY (Fieldbrook)
FIELD STONE WINERY & VINEYARD, INC. (Healdsburg)
FILIPPI VINTAGE CO., J. (Fontana)
FILSINGER VINEYARDS AND WINERY (Temecula)
FINKELSTEIN VINEYARDS / JUDD'S HILL (St. Helena)
FIRESTONE VINEYARD (Los Olivos)
FISHER VINEYARDS (Santa Rosa)
FITZPATRICK WINERY AND LODGE (Somerset)
FLAX VINEYARDS (Sonoma)
FLORA SPRINGS WINE CO. (St. Helena)
FOLIE À DEUX WINERY (St. Helena)
FOPPIANO VINEYARDS (Healdsburg)
FOREST HILL WINERY (St. Helena)
FOREST GLEN WINERY (Ceres)
FORMAN VINEYARDS (St. Helena)
FORTINO WINERY, INC. (Gilroy)
FORTUNA CELLARS (Davis)
FOXEN VINEYARD, INC. (Sisquoc)
FRANCISCAN OAKVILLE ESTATE (Rutherford)
FRANUS (Napa)
FRANZIA BROS. (Ripon)
FRASCETTI WINERY (Sacramento)
FRATELLI PERATA (Paso Robles)
FREEMARK ABBEY (St. Helena)
FRENCH VALLEY VINEYARDS (Murrieta)
FREY VINEYARDS, LTD. (Redwood Valley)
FRICK WINERY (Geyserville)
FRISINGER CELLARS (Napa)
FRITZ CELLARS (Cloverdale)
FROG'S LEAP WINERY (St. Helena)
GABRIELLI WINERY, INC. (Redwood Valley)
GAINEY VINEYARD, THE (Santa Ynez)
GALLEANO WINERY, INC. (Mira Loma)
E. & J. GALLO WINERY (Modesto)
GAN EDEN WINERY (Sebastopol)
GARRIC-LANGBEHN WINERY (Santa Rosa)
GARY FARRELL WINES (Forestville)
GAUER ESTATE VINEYARD (Healdsburg)
J. H. GENTILI WINES (Redwood City)
GEORIS WINERY (Carmel)
GERWER WINERY (Somerset)
GEYSER PEAK WINERY (Geyserville)
GIBSON WINE CO. (Sanger)
GIRARD WINERY (Oakville)
GIUMARRA VINEYARDS CORP. (Bakersfield)
GLASS MOUNTAIN [Markham Vineyards, St. Helena]
GLEN ELLEN VINEYARDS & WINERY (Glen Ellen)
GLORIA FERRER (FREIXENET SONOMA) CHAMPAGNE
    CAVES (Sonoma)
GOLDEN CREEK VINEYARD (Santa Rosa)
GOLD HILL VINEYARD (Colma)
GOLDEN STATE VINTNERS (Cutler)
GOOSECROSS CELLARS (Yountville)
GRACE FAMILY VINEYARDS (St. Helena)
GRAND CRU VINEYARDS (Glen Ellen)
GRANITE SPRINGS WINERY (Somerset)

GRAPE LINKS WINE PRODUCTIONS & BAREFOOT CELLARS (Healdsburg)
GREEN & RED VINEYARD (St. Helena)
GREENSTONE WINERY (Ione)
GREENWOOD RIDGE VINEYARDS (Philo)
GRGICH HILLS CELLAR (Rutherford)
GROTH VINEYARDS & WINERY (Oakville)
GROVER GULCH WINERY (Soquel)
GUENOC WINERY (Middletown)
GUILD WINERIES AND DISTILLERIES (Woodbridge)
GUNDLACH-BUNDSCHU WINERY (Vineburg)
HACIENDA WINE CELLARS, INC. (Sonoma)
HAFNER (Healdsburg)
HAGAFEN CELLARS (Napa)
HAHN ESTATES (Soledad)
HALLCREST VINEYARDS (Felton)
HANDLEY CELLARS (Philo)
HANNA WINERY (Santa Rosa)
HANNS KORNELL CHAMPAGNE CELLARS (St. Helena)
HANS FAHDEN WINERY (Calistoga)
HANZELL VINEYARDS (Sonoma)
HARBOR WINERY (West Sacramento)
HARMONY CELLARS (San Miguel)
HART WINERY (Temecula)
HAVENS (Napa)
HAYWOOD WINERY (Sonoma)
HECKER PASS WINERY (Gilroy)
HECK'S CELLARS (Di Giorgio)
HEITZ WINE CELLARS (St. Helena)
HERITAGE CELLARS (Fresno)
HERON LAKE WINERY (unknown)
HESS COLLECTION WINERY (Napa)
HIDDEN CELLARS (Ukiah)
HMR ESTATE WINERY (Paso Robles)
HOMEWOOD WINERY (Sonoma)
HOP KILN WINERY, GRIFFIN VYD. (Healdsburg)
HOPE FARMS (Paso Robles)
HORIZON WINERY (Santa Rosa)
HORNE VINEYARDS (Middletown)
HOUTZ VINEYARDS (Los Olivos)
HUNTINGTON (Geyserville)
HUSCH VINEYARDS (Philo)
IMAGERY VINEYARDS (Philo)
INDIAN ROCK VINEYARDS (Murphys)
INDIAN SPRINGS VINEYARDS (Penn Valley)
INGLENOOK NAPA VALLEY (St. Helena)
IRON HORSE VINEYARDS (Sebastopol)
IVAN TAMAS (San Jose)
JADE MOUNTAIN (Geyserville)
JAEGER FAMILY WINE CO. (St. Helena)
JAMES FRASINETTI AND SONS (Sacramento)
JANKRIS (Templeton)
JEKEL VINEYARD (Greenfield)
JEPSON VINEYARDS (Ukiah)
JOANNA VINEYARD (Yountville)
JOHN PICONI WINERY, LTD. (Temecula)
JOHNSON TURNBULL VINEYARDS (Oakville)
JOHNSON'S ALEXANDER VALLEY WINES (Healdsburg)
JORDAN VINEYARD AND WINERY (Healdsburg)
JORDAN SPARKLING WINE CO. (Healdsburg)
JORY WINERY (Los Gatos)
JOSEPH PHELPS VINEYARDS (St. Helena)
JOSEPH SWAN VINEYARDS (Forestville)
JOULLIAN VINEYARDS (Carmel Valley)
JUDD'S HILL (Napa Valley)
JUSTIN WINERY & VINEYARD (Paso Robles)
KALIN CELLARS (Novato)
KARLY (Plymouth)
KATE'S VINEYARD (Napa)
KAUTZ VINEYARDS, INC. (Murphys)
KATHRYN KENNEDY WINERY (Saratoga)
KENDALL-JACKSON VINEYARDS (Lakeport)

KENT RASMUSSEN WINERY (Napa)
KENWOOD VINEYARDS (Sonoma)
KENWORTHY VINEYARDS (Plymouth)
J. KERR WINERY (unknown)
KIRIGIN CELLARS (Gilroy)
KIRKPATRICK CELLAR WINERY (Eureka)
KISTLER VINEYARDS (Glen Ellen)
KOHNAN, INC. (Napa)
KONOCTI WINERY (Kelseyville)
F. KORBEL & BROS. (Guerneville)
KORYO WINERY COMPANY (Gardena)
KUNDE ESTATE WINERY (Kenwood)
LA CREMA VINERA (Sebastopol)
LA JOTA VINEYARD CO. (Angwin)
LAKE SONOMA WINERY, INC. (Geyserville)
LAKESPRING WINERY (Napa)
LAMBORN FAMILY VINEYARDS (Angwin)
LANDMARK VINEYARDS (Kenwood)
LA REINA WINERY (Gonzales)
LAS MONTANAS (Glen Ellen)
LAS VINAS WINERY (Lodi)
LA TOURNELLE (Monterey)
LATROBE CELLARS (Shingle Springs)
LAUREL GLEN VINEYARD (Glen Ellen)
LAURIER VINEYARDS (Forestville)
LAVA CAP (Placerville)
LA VIEILLE MONTAGNE (St. Helena)
LAZY CREEK VINEYARD (Philo)
LEEWARD WINERY (Oxnard)
LE MONTPELIER WINERY (Waterford)
LIBERTY SCHOOL [Caymus, Rutherford]
LIBERTY WINERY, INC. (Acampo)
LIMUR WINERY (St. Helena)
LIVE OAKS WINERY (Gilroy)
LIVERMORE VALLEY CELLARS (Livermore)
LIVINGSTON VINEYARDS (St. Helena)
LLORDS & ELWOOD WINERY (Yountville)
LOCKWOOD VINEYARDS (San Lucas)
J. LOHR WINERY (San Jose)
LOLONIS WINERY (Redwood Valley)
LONG VINEYARDS (St. Helena)
LOST HILLS WINERY (Acampo)
LOUIS CORTHAY WINERY (St. Helena)
LOUIS HONIG CELLARS (Rutherford)
LOUIS M. MARTINI (St. Helena)
LUCAS WINERY, THE (Lodi)
LYETH VINEYARDS (Geyserville)
LYTTON SPRINGS WINERY, INC. (Healdsburg)
MACAULEY VINEYARD (St. Helena)
MACROSTIE WINERY (Sonoma)
MADDELANA VINEYARD (Los Angeles)
MADRONA VINEYARDS (Camino)
MAISON DEUTZ WINERY (Arroyo Grande)
MANZANITA RIDGE (unknown)
MARCASSIN WINES (Calistoga)
MARIMAR TORRES ESTATE VINEYARDS (Sonoma)
MARIETTA CELLARS (Healdsburg)
M. MARION & CO., INC. (Geyserville)
MARIO PERELLI-MINETTI WINERY (Rutherford)
MARK WEST VINEYARDS (Forestville)
MARKHAM WINERY (St. Helena)
MARTIN RAY VINEYARDS, INC. (Palo Alto)
MARTSON VINEYARDS (St. Helena)
MARTIN BROTHERS WINERY (Paso Robles)
MARTINELLI WINERY (St. Helena)
MARTINI & PRATI WINES, INC. (Santa Rosa)
MARTZ VINEYARDS (Yorkville)
MASTANTUONO (Templeton)
MASTER CELLARS (DiGiorgio)
MATANZAS CREEK WINERY (Santa Rosa)
MATSON VINEYARDS (Redding)
MAURICE CARRIE WINERY (Temecula)

MAYACAMAS VINEYARDS (Napa)
MAZZOCCO VINEYARDS (Healdsburg)
McCALL WINERIES & DISTILLERIES (Sanger)
McDOWELL VALLEY VINEYARDS & CELLARS (Hopland)
McHENRY VINEYARD (Santa Cruz)
MEADOW GLEN [Rabbit Ridge Vineyards Winery, Healdsburg]
MEEKER VINEYARD, THE (Healdsburg)
MELIM / MAACAMA CREEK VINEYARD (Healdsburg)
MENGHINI WINERY (Julian)
MERIDIAN VINEYARDS (Paso Robles)
MERLION WINERY (Napa)
MERRY VINTNERS (Santa Rosa)
MERRYVALE VINEYARDS (St. Helena)
MICHTOM VINEYARDS (Healdsburg)
MILANO WINERY (Hopland)
MILAT VINEYARDS (St. Helena)
MILL CREEK VINEYARDS (Healdsburg)
MILLIAIRE WINERY (Murphys)
MIRAMONTE (Palos Verdes)
MIRASSOU VINEYARDS (San Jose)
MISSION VIEW ESTATE VINEYARDS AND WINERY (San Miguel)
MOCERI CELLARS (Geyserville)
C. K. MONDAVI (St. Helena)
MONT ST. JOHN CELLARS, INC. (Napa)
MONTEREY PENINSULA WINERY (Sand City)
MONTEREY VINEYARD, THE (Gonzales)
MONTEVINA WINES (Plymouth)
MONTICELLO CELLARS (Napa)
MONTPELLIER (Ceres and Woodbridge)
MORESCO VINEYARDS (Stockton)
MORGAN WINERY (Salinas)
J. W. MORRIS WINERY/BLACK MOUNTAIN VINEYARD (Healdsburg)
MOSBY WINERY (Bulleton)
MOSS CREEK WINERY (Napa)
MOUNTAIN VIEW VINTNERS (Mountain View)
MOUNT EDEN VINEYARDS (Saratoga)
MOUNT PALOMAR WINERY (Temecula)
MOUNT VEEDER WINERY (Napa)
MUMM NAPA VALLEY (Napa)
MURPHY-GOODE ESTATE WINERY (Geyserville)
NALLE WINERY (Healdsburg)
NAPA CREEK WINERY (St. Helena)
NAPA RIDGE [Beringer Vineyards, Asti]
NAPA VALLEY PORT CELLARS (Napa)
NAPA VALLEY WINE CO. (Napa)
NAVARRO VINEYARDS (Philo)
NELSON ETATE VINEYARDS VINWOOD CELLARS (Gesyerville)
NERVO WINERY (Geyserville)
NEVADA CITY WINERY (Nevada City)
NEWLAN VINEYARDS & WINERY (Napa)
NEWTON VINEYARD (St. Helena)
NICASIO VINEYARDS (Soquel)
NICHELINI WINERY (St. Helena)
NICHOLAS G. VERRY, INC. (Parlier)
NIEBAUM-COPPOLA ESTATE (Rutherford)
NOBLE CREEK VINEYARDS (Cherry Valley)
NOBLE HILL WINERY (Felton)
A. NONNINI WINERY, INC. (Fresno)
NORDMAN OF CALIFORNIA (Fresno)
OAKFORD (Oakville)
OAKVILLE RANCH (Napa)
OAK RIDGE VINEYARDS (Lodi)
OAK SPRINGS VINEYARD (San Anselmo)
OBESTER WINERY (Half Moon Bay)
OCEANIA CELLARS (Arroyo Grande)
OJAI VINEYARD, THE (Oakview)
OL BLUE JAY [Girard Winery, Oakville]
OLD CREEK RANCH WINERY (Oakview)
OLIVER (unknown)

OLIVET LANE ESTATE [Pellegrini Bros. Wines, Inc., South San Francisco)
OLSON WINERY, INC. (Redwood Valley)
OPICI WINERY, INC. (Alta Loma)
OPTIMA WINE CELLARS (Healdsburg)
OPUS ONE (Oakville)
ORGANIC WINE WORKS (Felton)
ORION [Sean H. Thackery Vintner, Bolinas]
ORLEANS HILL VIN. ASSN. (Woodland)
OSGOOD WAREHOUSE CO. (San Francisco)
OZEKI SAKE (U.S.A.), INC. (Hollister)
PACHECO RANCH WINERY (Ignacio)
PACIFIC STAR WINERY (Westport)
PACIFIC WESTERN SYSTEMS, INC. (Mountain View)
PAGE MILL WINERY (Los Altos Hills)
PAHLMEYER (Napa)
PALOS VERDES WINERY (Inglewood)
PAPAGNI VINEYARDS (Madera)
PARADISE VINTNERS (Paradise)
PARAISO SPRINGS VINEYARDS (Soledad)
PARDUCCI (Ukiah)
PARSONS CREEK WINERY (Ukiah)
PASO ROBLES WINERY (Paso Robles)
PASTORI WINERY (Cloverdale)
PAT PAULSEN VINEYARDS (Cloverdale)
J. PATRICK DORE (Mill Valley)
PATZ & HALL (Napa)
PAUL MASSON (Gonzales)
PEACHY CANYON WINERY (Paso Robles)
PEDRIZZETTI WINERY (Morgan Hill)
J. PEDRONCELLI WINERY (Geyserville)
PEJU PROVINCE (Rutherford)
PELLEGRINI BROS. WINES, INC. (South San Francisco)
PENDLETON WINERY (Santa Clara)
PEPPERWOOD GROVE [Cecchetti-Sebastiani, Sonoma]
PEPPERWOOD SPRINGS VINEYARD (Philo)
PESENTI WINERY (Templeton)
PETER McCOY (Sonoma)
PETER MICHAEL WINERY (Calistoga)
PHILLIPS FARMS VINEYARDS (Lodi)
R. H. PHILLIPS VINEYARD, THE (Esparto)
PHILIP TOGNI VINEYARD (St. Helena)
PICONI WINERY (Temecula)
PIEDRA CREEK WINERY (San Luis Obispo)
PINA CELLARS (Rutherford)
PINE RIDGE WINERY (Napa)
PINNACLES WINERY (Monterey)
PIPER SONOMA CELLARS (Healdsburg)
PLAM VINEYARDS & WINERY (Yountville)
PLEIADES [Sean H. Thackery Vintner, Bolinas]
POMMERAIE WINERY (Sebastopol)
POPPY HILL (Napa)
PORTER CREEK VINEYARDS (Healdsburg)
PRAGER WINERY & PORT WORKS (St. Helena)
PRESTON VINEYARDS (Healdsburg)
QUADY WINERY (Madera)
QUAFF WINERY (Windsor)
QUAIL RIDGE (St. Helena)
QUIVIRA VINEYARDS (Healdsburg)
QUPE (Santa Cruz)
RABBIT RIDGE VINEYARDS WINERY (Healdsburg)
RADANOVICH VINEYARDS & WINERY (Mariposa)
A. RAFANELLI WINERY (Healdsburg)
RANCHITA OAKS WINERY, INC. (San Miguel)
RANCHO DE PHILO (Alta Loma)
RANCHO PALOMA WINERY (Inglewood)
RANCHO SISQUOC WINERY (Santa Maria)
RAPAZZINI WINERY (Gilroy)
RAVENSWOOD (Sonoma)
RAYMOND VINEYARD & CELLAR (St. Helena)
RENAISSANCE VINEYARD & WINERY, INC. (Renaissance)
RETZLAFF VINEYARDS (Livermore)

REVERE VINEYARD AND WINERY (Napa)
RICHARD L. GRAESER WINERY (Calistoga)
L. W. RICHARDS WINERY (Somerset)
RICHARDSON VINEYARDS (Sonoma)
RIDGE VINEYARDS (Cupertino)
RITCHIE CREEK VINEYARDS (St. Helena)
RIVER ROAD VINEYARDS (Forestville)
RIVER RUN VINTNERS (Watsonville)
RIVERSIDE FARM [Foppiano Vineyards, Healdsburg]
RMS VINEYARDS (Napa)
ROBERT KEENAN WINERY (St. Helena)
ROBERT MONDAVI WINERY (Napa Valley)
ROBERT MONDAVI WOODBRIDGE (Woodbridge)
ROBERT PECOTA WINERY (Calistoga)
ROBERT PEPI WINERY (Oakville)
ROBERT SINSKEY VINEYARDS (Napa)
ROBERT STEMMLER WINERY (Healdsburg)
ROBERT TALBOTT VINEYARD AND WINERY (Carmel Valley)
ROCHE WINERY (Sonoma)
J. ROCHIOLI VINEYARDS (Healdsburg)
RODNEY STRONG VINEYARDS (Healdsburg)
ROEDERER ESTATE (Philo)
ROLLING HILLS VINEYARDS (Camarillo)
ROLLING RIDGE WINERY, LTD. (San Miguel)
ROMBAUER VINEYARDS (St. Helena)
ROSENBLUM CELLARS (Alameda)
ROSS KELLER WINERY (Nipomo)
ROSS VALLEY WINERY, THE (San Anselmo)
ROUDON-SMITH VINEYARDS, INC. (Santa Cruz)
ROUMIEGUIERE VINEYARDS (San Rafael)
ROUND HILL WINERY (St. Helena)
ROYCE VINEYARDS & WINERY (Ukiah)
RUST RIDGE VINEYARD & WINERY (St. Helena)
RUTHERFORD HILL WINERY (Rutherford)
RUTHERFORD RANCH (St. Helena)
RUTHERFORD VINTNERS (Rutherford)
SADDLEBACK CELLARS (Oakville)
SAGE CANYON WINERY (Rutherford)
ST. AMANT WINERY (French Camp)
ST. ANDREW'S WINERY (Napa)
ST. CLEMENT VINEYARDS (St. Helena)
ST. FRANCIS VINEYARDS & WINERY (Kenwood)
ST. GEORGE SPIRITS (Alameda)
ST. SUPERY VINEYARDS & WINERY (Rutherford)
SAINTSBURY (Napa)
SALAMANDRE WINE CELLARS (Aptos)
SALMON CREEK VINEYARDS [Peter McCoy, Napa-Sonoma]
SALTER WINERY, DAVID & MERYL (Somerset)
SAN ANTONIO WINERY, INC. (Los Angeles)
SAN MARTIN WINERY (San Martin)
SAN PIERRO VARA VINEYARD & WINE CO. (Calistoga)
SANFORD WINERY (Buellton)
SANFORD & BENEDICT VINEYARDS (Lompoc)
SANTA BARBARA WINERY (Santa Barbara)
SANTA CRUZ MOUNTAIN VINEYARD (Santa Cruz)
SANTA MARGARITA VINEYARD & WINERY (Temecula)
SANTA YNEZ VALLEY WINERY (Santa Ynez)
SANTINO WINES (Plymouth)
SARAH'S VINEYARD (Gilroy)
SATIETY (Davis)
V. SATTUI WINERY (St. Helena)
SAUCELITO CANYON VINEYARD (Arroyo Grande)
SAUSA WINERY (Oakland)
SAUSAL WINERY (Healdsburg)
SCHARFFENBERGER CELLARS (Philo)
SCHRAMSBERG VINEYARDS CO. (Calistoga)
SCHUG CARNEROS ESTATE WINERY (Sonoma)
SEA CLIFF WINE CO., INC. (Carmel)
SEAN H. THACKERY VINTNER (Bolinas)
SEA RIDGE WINERY (Occidental)
SEAVEY VINEYARD (St. Helena)

SEBASTIANI VINEYARDS (Sonoma)
SEGHESIO WINERY, INC. (Healdsburg)
SELLARDS WINERY (Sebastopol)
SEQUOIA GROVE VINEYARDS (Napa)
SERAFORNIA [StoryBook Mountain, Calistoga]
SHADOW BROOK WINERY (St. Helena)
SHADOW CREEK CELLARS [Domaine Chandon, Yountville]
SHAFER VINEYARDS (Napa)
SHENANDOAH VINEYARDS (Plymouth)
SHERRILL CELLARS (Palo Alto)
SIERRA VISTA WINERY (Pleasant Valley)
SIERRA WINE (Tulare)
SIGNORELLO VINEYARDS (Napa)
SILVER FAMILY VINEYARD (Mariposa)
SILVER MOUNTAIN VINEYARDS (Los Gatos)
SILVER OAK WINE CELLARS (Oakville)
SILVERADO HILL CELLARS (Napa)
SILVERADO VINEYARDS (Napa)
SILVER RIDGE VINEYARDS (Ceres)
SIMCHA [Gan Eden Winery, Sebastopol]
SIMI WINERY, INC. (Healdsburg)
SIRUS [Sean H. Thackery Vinter, Bolinas]
SKY VINEYARDS (Napa)
SMITH & HOOK WINERY (Soledad)
SMITH-MADRONE VINEYARDS (St. Helena)
SMITH VINEYARD & WINERY (Grass Valley)
SMOTHERS BROS. WINES (Kenwood)
SOBON ESTATE (Plymouth)
SODA CANYON VINEYARDS (Napa)
SOLIS WINERY (Gilroy)
SOLITUDE (Windsor)
SONOMA CREEK WINERY (Sonoma)
SONOMA-CUTRER VINEYARDS, INC. (Windsor)
SONOMA-LOEB (Gayersville)
SONORA WINERY AND PORT WORKS (Sonora)
SOTOYOME WINERY (Healdsburg)
SOUZAO CELLARS (San Rafael)
SPECIALITY BEVERAGES, INC. (Visalia)
SPOTTSWOODE WINERY (St. Helena)
SPRING MOUNTAIN VINEYARDS (St. Helena)
STAG'S LEAP WINE CELLARS (Napa)
STAG'S LEAP WINERY, INC. (Napa)
P. AND M. STAIGER (Boulder Creek)
STAR HILL WINES, INC. (Napa)
STEARNS WHARF VINTNERS (Santa Barbara)
STELTZNER VINEYARDS (Napa)
STEPHEN ZELLERBACK (Healdsburg)
STERLING VINEYARDS (Calistoga)
STEVENOT WINERY (Murphys)
STONE CREEK [negociant label, San Francisco]
STONEGATE, INC. (Calistoga)
STONE HILL [Geyser Peak, Geyserville]
STONERIDGE (Sutter Creek)
J. STONESTREET & SONS VINEYARD & WINERY (Healdsburg)
STONY HILL VINEYARD (St. Helena)
STONY RIDGE WINERY (Livermore)
STORRS WINERY (Santa Cruz)
STORY VINEYARD (Plymouth)
STORYBOOK MOUNTAIN VINEYARDS (Calistoga)
STRATFORD WINERY (St. Helena)
STRAUS (St. Helena)
STRINGER'S ORCHARD (Modoc County, CA, south of New Pine Creek, OR)
STUERMER WINERY/ARCADIA (Lower Lake)
SUGARLOAF RIDGE WINERY (Glen Ellen)
SULLIVAN VINEYARDS (Rutherford)
SUMMIT LAKE VINEYARDS AND WINERY (Angwin)
SUNRISE WINERY (Cupertino)
SUTTER HOME WINERY, INC. (St. Helena)
SWAN VINEYARDS, JOSEPH (Forestville)
SWANSON VINEYARDS & WINERY (Rutherford)
SYCAMORE CREEK VINEYARDS, INC. (Morgan Hill)

TAFT STREET (Sebastopol)
TAKARA SAKE USA, INC. (Berkeley)
TALLEY VINEYARDS (Arroyo Grande)
TAURAS [Sean H. Thackery Vinter, Bolinas]
TAYLOR CALIFORNIA CELLARS (Gonzales)
TEJON MARKETING COMPANY (Lebec)
TELLUS INDUSTRIES, INC. (Napa)
TENLE CREEK ASSOCIATES (Calistoga)
THOMAS FOGARTY WINERY (Woodside)
THOMAS JAEGER WINERY (Escondido)
THOMAS KRUSE WINERY (Gilroy)
TIFFANY HILL (Arroyo Grande)
TIJSSELING VINEYARDS (Ukiah)
TIVOLI [S. Anderson Vineyard, Yountville]
TKC VINEYARDS (Plymouth)
TOPAZ (Napa)
TOPOLOS AT RUSSIAN RIVER (Forestville)
TOYON WINERY & VINEYARD (Healdsburg)
TRADER JOE'S WINERY (South Pasadena)
TRAULSEN VINEYARDS (Calistoga)
TREFETHEN VINEYARDS (Napa)
TRENTADUE WINERY (Geyserville)
TRIBAUT DEVAVRY, INC. (Hayward)
TRUCHARD VINEYARDS (Napa)
TRUCKEE RIVER WINERY (Truckee)
TUDAL WINERY (St. Helena)
TULOCAY WINERY (Napa)
TWIN HILLS RANCH WINERY (Paso Robles)
TYLAND VINEYARDS (Ukiah)
VALLEY OF THE MOON WINERY (Glen Ellen)
VAN DER HEYDEN VINEYARDS WINERY (Napa)
VEGA VINEYARDS WINERY (Buellton)
VENTANA VINEYARDS WINERY, INC. (Soledad)
VERDUGO VINEYARDS, INC. (Acampo)
VIADER VINEYARDS (Deer Park)
VIANO VINEYARDS (Martinez)
VIANSA WINERY (Sonoma)
VICHON WINERY (Oakville)
VIE-DEL COMPANY (Fresno)
VILLA BIANCHI WINERY (Kerman)
VILLA HELENA WINERY (St. Helena)
VILLA MT. EDEN WINERY (Oakville)
VILLA ZAPU (Napa)
VINA VISTA WINERY (Geyserville)
VINCENT ARROYO WINERY (Calistoga)
VIRGINIATOWN WINERY (Newcastle)
VITA NOVA (Santa Maria)
VON STRASSER VINEYARDS (Calistoga)
WALKER WINES (Felton)
WATSON VINEYARDS (Paso Robles)
WEIBEL VINEYARDS (San Jose)
WEINSTOCK CELLARS, INC. (Healdsburg)
WELLINGTON VINEYARD (Glen Ellen)
WENTE BROS. (Livermore)
WERMUTH WINERY (Calistoga)
WEST WIND WINERY (Suisun)
WESTWOOD WINERY (Shingle Springs)
WHALER VINEYARD WINERY (Ukiah)
WILLIAM HILL WINERY (Napa)
WHITE OAK VINEYARDS (Healdsburg)
WHITE ROCK VINEYARDS (Napa)
WHITEHALL LANE WINERY (St. Helena)
WHITCRAFT WINES (Santa Maria)
WHITFORD CELLARS (Napa)
WILD HOG VINEYARDS (Between Fort Ross and Cazadero)
WILDCAT WINES (Sonoma)
WILD HORSE WINERY (Templeton)
WILDWOOD (Sonoma)
J. WILE & SONS (St. Helena)
WILLIAM HILL WINERY (Napa)
WILLIAMS-SELYEM WINERY (Healdsburg)
WILLIAM WHEELER WINERY (Healdsburg)

WINDSOR VINEYARDS (Healdsburg)
WINTERBROOK WINERY / JACKSON VALLEY VINEYARDS (Ione)
WINTERS WINERY (Winters)
WOODBRIDGE (Lodi)
WOODEN VALLEY WINERY (Suisun)
WOODSIDE VINEYARDS (Woodside)
YANKEE HILL WINERY (Columbia)
YAYIN CORP. (Sebastopol)
YORK MOUNTAIN WINERY (Templeton)
YVERDON VINEYARDS (St. Helena)
Z MOORE WINERY (Windsor)
ZACA MESA WINERY (Los Olivos)
ZAYANTE VINEYARDS (Felton)
ZD WINES (Napa)

Colorado

CARLSON VINEYARDS (Palisade)
COLORADO CELLARS (Palisade)
MINTURN CELLARS (Minturn)
PIKES PEAK VINEYARDS (Colorado Springs)
PLUM CREEK CELLARS, LTD. (Palisade)
VAIL VALLEY VINTNERS (Vail)

Connecticut

BISHOP FARMS WINERY (Cheshire)
CHAMARD VINEYARDS, INC. (Clinton)
CROSSWOODS VINEYARDS, INC. (Stonington)
DI GRAZIA VINEYARDS & WINERY (Brookfield Center)
HAMLET HILL WINES CO. (Pomfret)
HOPKINS VINEYARD (New Preston)
NUTMEG VINEYARD (Coventry)
ST. HILARY'S VINEYARDS (North Grovenordale)
STONINGTON VINEYARDS, INC. (Stonington)

Florida

CHAUTAUQUA VINEYARDS & WINERY, INC. (DeFuniak Springs)
EDEN VINEYARDS WINERY & PARK (Alva)
LAFAYETTE / LAKERIDGE VINEYARDS & WINERY (Tallahassee & Clermont)
TODHUNTER INTERNATIONAL, INC. (Auburndale)

Georgia

CAVENDER CASTLE WINERY (Dahlonega)
CHATEAU ELAN (Braselton)
CHESTNUT MOUNTAIN (Braselton)
FOX VINEYARDS (Social Circle)
GEORGIA WINES, INC. (Chickamauga)
HABERSHAM VINEYARDS AND WINERY (Baldwin)
MONARCH WINE CO. OF GEORGIA (Atlanta)
B. & B. ROSSER WINERY (High Shoals)

Hawaii

TEDESCHI VINEYARD, LTD. (Ulupalakua, Maui)

Idaho

CAMAS WINERY (Moscow)
CANA VINEYARDS (Wilder)
CARMELA WINERY (Glenns Ferry)
COCOLALLA WINERY, INC. (Athol)
FAMILI PUCCI WIN (Sandpoint)
HEGY'S SO. HILLS VINEYARD & WINERY (Twin Falls)
HELL'S CANYON VINEYARDS (Caldwell)

INDIAN CREEK (STOWE) WINERY (Kuna)
PINTLER CELLARS (Nampa)
ROSE CREEK VINEYARDS (Hagerman)
STE. CHAPELLE WINERY, INC. (Caldwell)
WESTON (Caldwell)

Illinois

ALTO VINEYARDS (Northwest Alto Pass)
BAXTER'S VINEYARDS (Nauvoo)
CHATEAU RA-HA (Grafton)
GALENA CELLARS, INC. (Galena)
LYNFRED WINERY (Roselle)
THOMPSON WINERY CO. (Monee)
WATERLOO WINERY (Waterloo)

Indiana

BROWN COUNTY WINE CO., LTD. (Unionville)
BUTLER WINERY (Bloomington)
CHATEAU POMIJE WINERY & RESTAURANT (Guilford)
CHATEAU THOMAS WINERY (Indianapolis)
EASLEY ENTERPRISES, INC. (Indianapolis)
HUBER ORCHARD WINERY (Borden)
OLIVER WINE COMPANY, INC. (Bloomington)
SCOTELLA WINERY & RESTAURANT (Madison)
VILLA MILAN VINEYARD (Milan)

Iowa

ACKERMAN WINERY, INC. (South Amana)
CHATEAU SAN MARIE, INC. (Marion)
EHRLE BROS, INC. (Homestead)
GRAPE VINE WINERY, THE (Amana)
HERITAGE WINE & CHEESE HAUS (Amana)
LITTLE AMANA WINERY, INC. (Amana)
OLD WINE CELLAR WINERY (Amana)
PRIVATE STOCK WINERY, INC. (Boone)
SANDSTONE WINERY, INC. (Amana)
VILLAGE WINERY (Amana)
VOLLBEHR CELLARS, LTD. (Tipton)

Kanasas

BALKAN WINERY (Girard)
FIELDS OF FAIR (Paxico)
LUDWIGSHOF WINERY (Eskridge)

Kentucky

PREMIUM BRANDS, LTD. (Bardstown)

Louisiana

CHURCH POINT WHOLESALE GROCERY CO., INC. (Church Point)
LES ORANGERS LOUISIANAIS, LTD. (New Orleans)

Maine

BARTLETT MAINE ESTATE WINERY (Gouldsboro)
DOWNEAST COUNTRY WINES (Trenton)

Maryland

BASIGNANI WINERY LTD. (Sparks)
BERRYWINE PLANTATIONS WINERY (Mt. Airy)
BOORDY VINEYARDS (Hydes)
BYRD VINEYARDS (Myersville)
CATOCTIN VINEYARDS, INC. (Brookeville)

ELK RUN VINEYARDS, INC. (Mt. Airy)
FIORE WINERY, INC. (Pylesville)
LOEW VINEYARDS, INC., THE (Mt. Airy)
MONTBRAY WINE CELLARS, LTD. (Westminster)
MONTEBELLO BRANDS, INC. (Baltimore)
WHITEMARSH CELLARS (Hampstead)
WOODHALL VINEYARDS & WINE CELLARS, INC. (Sparks)
ZIEM VINEYARDS (Fairplay)

Massachussetts

CHICAMA VINEYARDS (West Tisbury)
INN WINES (Hatfield)
MALLEA FARM VINEYARDS (Dudley)
NASHOBA VALLEY WINERY (Bolton)
PLYMOUTH COLONY WINERY (Plymouth)
VIA DELLA CHIESA VINEYARDS (Raynham)
WESTPORT RIVER VINEYARD & WINERY (Westport)

Michigan

BERRIEN VINTNERS, INC. (Harbert)
BOSKYDEL VINEYARD (Lake Leelanau)
CHATEAU GRAND TRAVERSE (Traverse City)
FENN VALLEY VINEYARDS, INC. (Fennville)
FENN VALLEY WINES OF ROCKFORD (Rockford)
GOOD HARBOR VINEYARDS (Lake Leelanau)
LAKESIDE VINEYARD (Harbert)
LEELANAU WINE CELLARS, LTD. (Omena)
LEMON CREEK WINERY, LTD. (Berrien Springs)
LOAF AND MUG (Saugatuck)
L. MAWBY VINEYARDS (Suttons Bay)
MADRON LAKE HILLS (Buchanan)
MOERSCH'S VINEYARD & WINECELLAR (Baroda)
NORTHVILLE WINERY (Northville)
PETERSON & SONS WINERY (Kalamazoo)
ST. JULIAN WINE CO., INC. (Paw Paw)
SEVEN LAKES VINEYARD (Fenton)
SHARON MILLS WINERY, LTD. (Manchester)
TABOR HILL/CHI CO. (Buchanan)
TARTAN HILL WINERY, LTD. (New Era)
TILL MIDNIGHT, INC. (Holland)
WARNER VINEYARDS (Paw Paw)

Minnesota

ALEXIS BAILLY VINEYARD (Hastings)
J. BIRD WINES, INC. (Hanover)
CHATEAU DEVENOIS (Rice)
NORTHERN VINEYARDS (Stillwater)
PHILLIPS & SONS CO. (Minneapolis)
SCENIC VALLEY WINERY, INC. (Lanesboro)

Mississippi

ALMARLA VINEYARDS & WINERY, INC. (Matherville)
CLAIBORNE VINEYARDS (Indianola)
OLD SOUTH WINERY (Natchez)
WINERY RUSHING, THE (Merigold)

Missouri

ADAM PUCHTA WINERY (Hermann)
AMERICAN WINERY, INC. (St. Louis)
AUGUSTA WINERY (Augusta)
BARDENHEIER'S WINE CELLARS (St. Louis)
BIAS VINEYARDS & WINERY (Berger)
BLUMENHOF VINEYARDS COMPANY (Dutzow)
BOONE COUNTRY WINERY, INC. (Defiance)
BRISTLE RIDGE VINEYARD (Nob Noster)
BYNUM WINERY (Lone Jack)
ECKERT'S SUNNY SLOPE WINERY (Chesterfield)

K. FARMS PTY., LTD. (Weston)
FERRIGNO VINEYARDS & WINERY (St. James)
GLORIA WINERY & VINEYARD (Mountaingrove)
HEINRICHSHAUS VINEYARDS & WINERY (St. James)
HERMANNHOF (Hermann)
LES BOURGEOIS VINEYARDS (Rocheport)
McCORMICK DISTILLING CO. (Weston)
MISSION CREEK WINERY (Weston)
MONTELLE WINERY AT OSAGE (Augusta)
MOUNT PLEASANT VINEYARDS (Augusta)
MOUNT PLEASANT WINERY/ABBEY VINEYARD (Cuba)
O'VALLON WINERY (Washburn)
OZARK VINEYARDS (Chestnut Ridge)
PEACEFUL BEND VINEYARD (Steelville)
PIRTLE'S WESTON VINEYARDS (Weston)
REIS WINERY (Licking)
ROBLLER VINEYARD (New Haven)
ST. JAMES WINERY (St. James)
SAINTE GENEVIÈVE WINERY (Ste. Geneviève)
SPRING CREEK WINERY, LTD. (Blue Springs)
STONE HILL WINERY (Hermann)
WINERY OF THE LITTLE HILLS (St. Charles)

Montana

MISSION MOUNTAIN WINERY (Dayton)

Nevada

PAHRUMP VALLEY VINEYARDS (Pahrump)

New Hampshire

THE NEW HAMPSHIRE WINERY (Laconia)

New Jersey

ALBA VINEYARD (Milford)
AMALTHEA CELLARS (Atco)
AMWELL VALLEY VINEYARD (Ringoes)
BALIC WINERY (Mays Landing)
BUCKS COUNTRY VINEYARDS, INC. (Bordentown)
CAPE WINE (Cape May Courthouse)
CREAM RIDGE VINEYARDS & CHAMPAGNE CELLARS (Cream Ridge)
DELVISTA VINEYARDS (Frenchtown)
FOUR SISTERS WINERY (Belvedere)
KINGS ROAD VINEYARD (Asbury)
LA FOLLETTE VINEYARD & WINERY (Belle Mead)
POLITO VINEYARDS (Vincentown)
POOR RICHARDS WINERY (Frenchtown)
REGINA WINE CO. (Newark)
RENAULT WINERY, INC. (Egg Harbor City)
SYLVIN FARMS (Germainia)
TAMUZZA VINEYARDS (Hope)
TOMASELLO WINERY, INC. (Hammonton)
UNIONVILLE VINEYARDS (Ringoes)

New Mexico

ALAMOSA CELLARS (Elephant Butte)
ANDERSON VALLEY VINEYARDS (Albuquerque)
BALAGNA WINERY CO. (Los Alamos)
BINNS VINEYARDS & WINERY (Las Cruces)
CHATEAU SASSENAGE (Engle)
DOMAINE CHEURLIN (Truth or Consequences)
GALLUP SALES COMPANY (Gallup)
GRUET WINERY / DEVALMONT VINEYARDS, INC. (Albuquerque)
HURST VINEYARDS (Bosque)
LA CHIRIPADA WINERY AND VINEYARDS (Dixon)
LA VINA WINERY (Chamberino)

LAS NUTRIAS VINEYARD (Corrales)
MADISON VINEYARD (Villa Nueva)
MONTANA DEL SOL VINTNERS, INC. (Deming)
MOUNTAIN VISTA VINEYARDS & WINERY (Albuquerque)
NEW MEXICO WINERY, INC. (Lordsburg)
SANDIA SHADOWS VINEYARD & WINERY (Albuquerque)
SANTA FE VINEYARDS (Espanola)
TULAROSA VINEYARDS (Tularosa)
VINA MADRE (Dexter)

New York

ADAIR VINEYARDS, INC. (New Paltz)
AMBERG WINE CELLARS (Clifton Springs)
AMBERLEAF VINEYARDS (Wappingers Falls)
AMERICANA VINEYARDS (Interlaken)
ANTHONY ROAD WINE COMPANY, INC. (Penn Yan)
ARBOR HILL GRAPERY (Naples)
ASHKOL WINE CO., INC. (Middletown)
BALDWIN VINEYARDS, INC. (Pine Bush)
BANFI VINTNERS (Old Brookville)
BARRINGTON CHAMPAGNE CO. (Dundee)
BARRY WINE CO., THE (Conesus)
BATAVIA WINE CELLARS, INC. (Batavia)
BEDELL CELLARS (Cutchogue)
BENMARL WINE CO., LTD. (Marlboro)
BIANCALANA & LA GAMMA WINE CELLARS (Newburgh)
BIDWELL VINEYARDS (Cutchogue)
BRIDGEHAMPTON WINERY, THE (Bridgehampton)
BRIMSTONE HILL VINEYARDS (Pine Bush)
BROTHERHOOD WINERY (Washingtonville)
BULLY HILL VINEYARDS, INC. (Hammondsport)
CANA VINEYARDS (Hammondsport)
CANANDAIGUA WINE COMPANY, INC. (Canandaigua)
CASA LARGA VINEYARDS, INC. (Fairport)
CASCADE MOUNTAIN VINEYARDS (Amenia)
CASTEL GRISCH WINERY (Watkins Glen)
CHATEAU DE RHEIMS (Hammondsport)
CHATEAU FRANK, INC. (Hammondsport)
CHATEAU GEORGES WINERY/RIVENDELL WINES (New Paltz)
CHATEAU LAFAYETTE RENEAU (Hector)
CLINTON VINEYARDS, INC. (Clinton Corners)
CROWN REGAL WINE CELLARS / JOSEPH ZAKON WINERY (Brooklyn)
DELMONICO'S (Brooklyn)
DOVER WINERY, INC. (Dover Plains)
DR. FRANK'S VINIFERA WINE CELLARS (Hammondsport)
EAGLE CREST VINEYARDS, INC. (Conesus)
EAST BRANCH WINERY, INC. (Dundee)
EATON VINEYARDS, INC. (Pine Plains)
EL PASO WINERY (Ulster Park)
FOUR CHIMNEYS FARM WINERY (Himrod)
FREDERICK S. JOHNSON VINEYARDS (Westfield)
FRONTENAC POINT VINEYARD (Trumansburg)
FULKERSON WINERY (Dundee)
GIASI WINERY, INC. (Rock Stream)
GLENORA WINE CELLARS, INC. (Dundee)
GOLD SEAL VINEYARDS (Hammondsport)
GREAT WESTERN WINERY (Hammondsport)
GRISTINA VINEYARDS (Cutchogue)
HARGRAVE VINEYARD (Cutchogue)
HAZLITT'S 1852 VINEYARD (Hector)
HERMANN J. WIEMER VINEYARD (Dundee)
HERON HILL VINEYARDS, INC. (Hammondsport)
HOSMER (Ovid)
HUNT COUNTRY VINEYARDS (Branchport)
ISLAND WINE COMPANY, THE (Sag Harbor)
JAMESPORT VINEYARDS (Jamesport)
KEUK SPRING VINEYARDS (Penn Yan)
KING FERRY WINERY (King Ferry)
KNAPP VINEYARDS (Romulus)

KONSTANTIN D. FRANK & SONS VINIFERA WINE CELLARS (Hammondsport)
LAKESHORE WINERY (Romulus)
LAKEWOOD VINEYARDS, INC. (Watkins Glen)
LAMOREAUX LANDING WINE CELLARS (Lodi)
LARRY'S VINEYARDS & WINERY (Altamont)
LEIDENFROST VINEYARDS (Hetor)
LENZ WINERY (Peconic)
LONG ISLAND VINEYARDS, INC. (Cutchogue)
LUCAS VINEYARDS (Interlaken)
MAGNANINI FARM WINERY (Wallkill)
MATTITUCK HILLS WINERY (Mattituck)
McGREGOR VINEYARD (Dundee)
MERRITT ESTATE WINERY, INC. (Forestville)
MILLBROOK VINEYARDS (Millbrook)
MOGEN DAVID WINE CORP. (Westfield)
NEWLAND VINEYARD (Geneva)
NIAGARA WINE CELLARS (Ransomville)
NORTH SALEM VINEYARD, INC. (North Salem)
PALMER VINEYARDS (Aquebogue)
PAUMONOK VINEYARDS (Aquebogue)
PECONIC BAY VINEYARDS (Cutchogue)
PINDAR VINEYARDS (Peconic)
PLANE'S CAYUGA VYD. (Ovid)
POPLAR RIDGE VINEYARDS (Valois)
PREJEAN WINERY, INC. (Penn Yan)
PUGLIESE VINEYARDS (Cutchogue)
REGENT CHAMPAGNE CELLARS, INC., THE (Highland)
RIVENDELL WINERY (New Paltz)
ROBERIAN VINEYARDS, LTD. (Forestville)
ROLLING VINEYARDS FARM WINERY (Hector)
ROYAL KEDEM WINE CORPORATION (Marlboro)
ST. WALTER DE BULLY WINE CO. (Hammondsport)
SCHAPIRO'S WINE CO., LTD. (Brooklyn)
SCHLOSS DOEPKEN WINERY (Ripley)
SIGNORE WINERY (Brooktondale)
SIX MILE CREEK VINEYARD (Ithaca)
SOUNDVIEW VINEYARDS, INC. (Peconic)
SOUTHHAMPTON WINERY (Water Mill)
SQUAW POINT LAND & WINE CO., INC. (Dundee)
SWEDISH HILL VINEYARD (Romulus)
TAYLOR WINE CO., THE (Hammondsport)
THORPE VINEYARD, INC. (Wolcott)
TRANSAMERICA WINE CORP. (Brooklyn)
VERAISON WINE CELLARS, INC. (Millbrook)
VETTER VINEYARDS (Westfield)
WAGNER VINEYARDS (Lodi)
WALKER VALLEY VINEYARDS (Walker Valley)
WEST PARK WINE CELLARS (West Park)
WIDMER'S WINE CELLARS, INC. (Naples)
WINDSOR VINEYARDS & GREAT RIVER WINERY (Marlboro)
WOODBURY VINEYARDS (Dunkirk)
WOODSTOCK WINERY, INC. (West Shokan)

North Carolina

BILTMORE ESTATE WINERY (Asheville)
CHATEAU à COEUR OVERT (Union Mills)
DUPLIN WINE CELLARS (Rose Hill)
GERMANTON VINEYARD & WINERY, INC. (Germanton)
LaROCCA WINE COMPANY (Fayetteville)
PLOGER VINEYARDS & WINERY (Arden)
SOUTHLAND ESTATE WINERY (Selma)
VILLAR VINTNERS OF VALDESE, INC. (Valdese)
WESTBEND VINEYARDS, INC. (Lewisville)

Ohio

BREITENBACH WINE CELLARS (Dover)
BRUSHCREEK VINEYARDS (Peebles)
BUCCIA VINEYARDS (Conneaut)
CANTWELL'S OLD MILL WINERY (Geneva)

CHALET DEBONNÉ VINEYARDS (Madison)
COLONIAL VINEYARDS (Lebanon)
DANKORONA WINERY, INC. (Aurora)
DIAMOND ISLAND CELLARS (Cincinnati)
DOVER VINEYARDS, INC. (Westlake)
FERRANTE WINE FARM (Geneva)
FIRELANDS WINERY (Sandusky)
GRAND RIVER WINE CO. (Madison)
GRECO, ANTHONY M. (Middletown)
HAFLE VINEYARDS (Springfield)
HAMMER COMPANY, THE (Cleveland)
HARPERSFIELD VINEYARD (Geneva)
HEINEMAN WINERY (Port Clinton)
HERITAGE VINEYARDS (Milton)
JOHLIN CENTURY WINERY (Oregon)
JOHN CHRIST WINERY (Avon Lake)
KELLEY'S ISLAND WINE CO. (Kelley's Island)
KLINGSHIRN WINERY, INC. (Avon Lake)
LIMPERT, CARL M. (Westlake)
LONZ WINERY (Middle Bass Island)
MANTEY VINEYARDS, INC. (Sandusky)
MARKKO VINEYARD (Conneaut)
McINTOSH'S OHIO VALLEY WINES (Bethel)
MEIER'S WINE CELLARS, INC. (Cincinnati)
MON AMI CHAMPAGNE CO. (Port Clinton)
MOYER VINEYARDS, INC. (Manchester)
OLD FIREHOUSE WINERY (Geneva-on-the-Lake)
POMPEI WINERY, INC. (Cleveland)
PORTAGE HILLS VINEYARDS (Suffield)
RAINBOW HILL VINEYARDS (Newcomerstown)
RINI WINE COMPANY (Cleveland)
ROLLING HILLS WINERY (Conneaut)
RONSARA WINERY (Lebanon)
SHAMROCK VINEYARD (Waldo)
STEUK WINE COMPANY (Sanduslky)
STILLWATER WINERIES, INC. (Troy)
WARREN J. SUBLETTE WINERY CO. (Cincinnati)
TANNERY HILL WINERY (Ashtabula)
TROY WINERY, INC. (Troy)
VALLEY VINEYARDS WINERY (Morrow)
VINOKLET (Cincinnati)
WICKLIFFE WINERY (Wickliffe)
WILLOW HILL VINEYARDS (Johnstown)
WOLF CREEK VINEYARDS, INC. (Norton)
WYANDOTTE WINE CELLARS (Gahanna)

Oklahoma

CIMARRON CELLARS (Caney)

Oregon

ABERG VINEYARDS / KRISTIN HILL WINERY (Amity)
ADAMS VINEYARD WINERY (Portland)
ADELSHEIM VINEYARD (Newberg)
AIRLIE WINERY (Monmouth)
ALPINE VINEYARDS (Alpine)
AMITY VINEYARDS (Amity)
ANKENY VINEYARDS WINERY (Salem)
ARGYLE (Dundee)
ARTERBERRY, LTD. (McMinnville)
ASHLAND VINEYARDS (Ashland)
AUTUMN WIND VINEYARD (Newberg)
BELLFOUNTAIN CELLARS (Philomath)
BETHEL HEIGHTS VINEYARD, INC. (Salem)
BRIDGEVIEW VINEYARDS (Cave Junction)
BROADLEY VINEYARDS (Monroe)
CALLAHAN RIDGE (Roseburg)
CAMERON WINERY (Dundee)
CHATEAU BENOIT (Carlton)
CHATEAU BIANCA (Dallas)

CLEAR CREEK DISTILLERY (Portland)
COOPER MOUNTAIN VINEYARDS (Beaverton)
CUVEE NORTHWEST, INC. (Tigard)
DAVIDSON WINERY (Tenmile)
DOMAINE DROUHIN OREGON, INC. (Dayton)
DUCK POND CELLARS (Crawporo)
DUNDEE WINE CO. (Dundee)
ELK COVE VINEYARDS (Gaston)
ELLENDALE VINEYARDS, INC. (Dallas)
EOLA HILLS WINE CELLARS (Rickreall)
EVESHAM WOOD VYD. & WINERY (Salem)
EYRIE VINEYARDS (Dundee)
FORGERON VINEYARD (Elmira)
FORIS VINEYARDS (Cave Junction)
GIRARDET WINE CELLARS (Roseburg)
GLEN CREEK VINEYARDS & WINERY (Salem)
GOLDENLEAF VINEYARDS (Umpqua)
HENRY ESTATE WINERY (Umpqua)
HIDDEN SPRINGS WINERY (Amity)
HILLCREST VINEYARD (Roseburg)
HINMAN VINEYARDS (Eugene)
HONEYWOOD WINERY, INC. (Salem)
HOOD RIVER VINEYARDS (Hood River)
JAMES SCOTT WINERY (Sherwood)
JONICOLE VINEYARDS (Roseburg)
KNUDSEN-ERATH WINERY (Dundee)
KRAMER VINEYARDS (Gaston)
LA CASA DE VIN (Boardman)
LANGE WINERY (Dundee)
LAUREL RIDGE WINERY (Forest Grove)
LESTER MARTIN AND MERTON DOUGLAS (Parkdale)
LOOKINGGLASS WINERY (Roseburg)
MARQUAM HILL VINEYARDS (Molalla)
McKINLAY VINEYARDS (Portland)
MIRASSOU CELLARS OF OREGON (Salem)
MONTINORE VINEYARDS, LTD. (Forest Grove)
MT. HOOD WINERY (Government Camp)
NEHALEM BAY WINE CO. (Nehalem)
OAK GROVE ORCHARDS WINERY (Rickreall)
OAK KNOLL WINERY, INC. (Hillsboro)
OREGON CELLARS WINERY (Cheshire)
OREGON ESTATES WINERY (Eugene)
PANTHER CREEK CELLARS (McMinnville)
PONDEROSA VINEYARDS (Lebanon)
PONZI VINEYARDS (Beaverton)
REDHAWK VINEYARDS (Salem)
REX HILL VINEYARDS (Newberg)
ROGUE RIVER VINEYARDS, LTD. (Grants Pass)
SAGA VINEYARDS (Cotton)
ST. INNOCENT, LTD. (Salem)
ST. JOSEF'S WINECELLAR (Canby)
SCWARZENBERG VINEYARDS, INC. (Dallas)
SERENDIPITY CELLARS WINERY (Monmouth)
SEVEN HILLS WINERY (Milton-Freewater)
SHAFER VINEYARD CELLARS (Forest Grove)
SHALLON WINERY (Astoria)
SILVER FALLS WINERY (Sublimity)
SISKIYOU VIINEYARDS (Cave Junction)
SOKOL BLOSSER WINERY (Dundee)
SPRINGHILL CELLARS (Albany)
TEMPEST VINEYARDS (Portland)
THREE RIVERS WINERY (Hood River)
TUALATIN VINEYARDS, INC. (Forest Grove)
TYEE WINE CELLARS (Corvallis)
UMPQUA RIVER VINEYARDS (Roseburg)
VALLEY VIEW WINERY (Jacksonville)
VERITAS VINEYARD (Newberg)
WASSON BROTHERS WINERY (Sandy)
WEISINGER OF ASHLAND (Ashland)
WILAMETTE VALLEY VINEYARDS (Turner)
WITNESS TREE VINEYARD (Salem)
YAMHILL VALLEY VINEYARDS (McMinnville)

Pennsylvania

ADAMS COUNTY WINERY (Orrtanna)
ALLEGRO VINEYARDS (Brogue)
BRANDYWINE VINEYARDS (Kemblesville)
BROOKMERE VINEYARDS (Belleville)
BUCKINGHAM VALLEY VINEYARDS (Buckingham)
BUCKS COUNTY VINEYARDS, INC. (New Hope)
CALVARESI WINERY (Bernville)
CEFALO'S WINE CELLAR (Pittston)
CHADDSFORD WINERY (Chadds Ford)
CHERRY VALLEY VINEYARDS (Saylorsburg)
CLOVER HILL VINEYARDS & WINERY (Breinigsville)
CONESTOGA VINEYARDS, INC. (Lancaster)
CONNEAUT CELLARS (Conneaut Lake)
COUNTRY CREEK VINEYARD & WINERY (Telford)
FOX MEADOW FARM (Chester Springs)
FRANCESCO WINERY (Wexford)
FRANKLIN HILL VINEYARDS, INC (Bangor)
FRENCH CREEK VALLEY WINERY, LTD. (Elverson)
HERITAGE WINE CELLARS, INC. (North East)
HILLCREST WINERY, LTD. (Greensburg)
HUNTERS VALLEY WINERY (Liverpool)
IN & OUT VINEYARDS (Newtown)
JAMES MORONEY, INC. (Philadelphia)
KOLLN VINEYARDS (Bellefonte)
LANCASTER COUNTY WINERY, LTD. (Lancaster)
LAPIC WINERY (New Brighton)
LAUREL HEIGHT'S WINERY (Landenberg)
LITTLE VINEYARD, THE (Quakertown)
MOUNT HOPE ESTATE & WINERY (Cornwall)
MT. NITTANY VINEYARD & WINERY (Centre Hall)
NAYLOR WINE CELLARS, INC. (Stewartstown)
NISSLEY VINEYARDS & WINERY ESTATE (Bainbridge)
OAK SPRING WINERY (Altoona)
OREGON HILL WINE CO., INC. (Morris)
PEACE VALLEY WINERY (Chalfont)
PENN SHORE VINEYARDS, INC. (North East)
PREATE WINERY (Old Forge)
PRESQUE ISLE WINE CELLARS (North East)
QUAKER RIDGE WINERY (Washington)
ROBERT MAZZA, INC. (North East)
SAND CASTLE WINERY, INC. (Erwinna)
SARA COYNE WINE CELLARS (Erie)
SARA'S WINERY (Erie)
SHUSTER CELLARS, INC. (North Huntingdon)
SKEW VINEYARDS, INC. (Zionsville)
SLATE QUARRY WINERY (Nazareth)
SMITHBRIDGE CELLARS (Chadds Ford)
STEPHEN BAHN WINERY, INC. (Brogue)
STRASBURG CELLARS, LTD. (Gap)
SUSQUEHANNA VALLEY WINERY (Danville)
TRACH CELLARS, INC. (Allentown)
TWIN BROOK WINERY (Gap)
VICTORIAN WINE CELLARS (Rohrerstown)
VYNECREST WINERY (Brenigsville)
WINDGATE VINEYARDS (Smicksburg)
YORK SPRINGS (York Springs)

Rhode Island

DIAMOND HILL VINEYARDS (Cumberland)
PRUDENCE ISLAND VINEYARDS, INC. ((Prudence Island)
SAKONNET VINEYARDS (Little Compton)
SOUTH COUNTY VINEYARDS, INC. (Slocum)
VINLAND WINE CELLARS (Middletown)

South Carolina

KENNETH L. CRUSE (Chester)
FOXWOOD WINE CELLARS (Woodruff)
MONTMORENCI VINEYARDS (Aiken)

TENNER BROTHERS, INC. (Patrick)
TRULUCK VINEYARDS & WINERY (Lake City)

Tennessee

BEACHAVEN VINEYARDS & WINERY (Clarksville)
CORDOVA CELLARS (Cordova)
COUNTRYSIDE VINEYARDS WINERY (Blountville)
GRAPE PATCH WINERY (Jonesbourgh)
HIGHLAND MANOR WINERY, INC. (So. Jamestown)
LAUREL HILL WINERY (Memphis)
LOUDON VALLEY VINEYARDS (Loudon)
MARLOW WINE CELLARS, INC. (Monteagle)
MOUNTAIN VALLEY VINEYARDS, INC. (Pigeon Forge)
ORR MOUNTAIN WINERY (Madisonville)
SMOKY MOUNTAIN WINERY, INC. (Gatlinburg)
STONEHAUS WINERY, INC. (Crossville)
TENNESSEE MT. VIEW WINERY (Charleston)
TENNESSEE VALLEY WINERY (Loudon)

Texas

ALAMO FARMS WINERY & VINEYARD (Adkins)
AVERY FARMS (Odessa)
BELL MOUNTAIN WINERY (Fredericksburg)
BELL MOUNTAIN/OBERHELLMANN VYDS. (Fredericksburg)
BIEGANOWSKI CELLARS, INC. (El Paso)
CAP*ROCK WINERY (Lubbock)
FALL CREEK VINEYARDS (Tow)
GRAPE CREEK VINEYARDS, INC. (Stonewall)
GUADALUPE VALLEY WINERY (New Braunfels)
HOMESTEAD VINEYARD & WINERY, INC. (Ivanhoe)
LA BUENA VIDA VINEYARDS (Springtown)
LA ESCARBADA XIT VINEYARD & WINERY, INC. (Amarillo)
LLANO ESTACADO WINERY, INC. (Lubbock)
MESSINA HOF WINE CELLARS (Bryan)
MOYER WINERY (New Braunfels)
PEDERNALES VINEYARDS (Fredericksburg)
PHEASANT RIDGE WINERY (Lubbock)
PINEY WOODS COUNTRY WINES (Orange)
PRESTON TRAIL WINERY (Gunter)
STE. GENEVIEVE / CORDIER ESTATES, INC. (Ft. Stockton)
ST. LAWRENCE WINERY (Garden City)
SANCHEZ CREEK VINEYARDS (Dallas)
SCHOPPAUL HILL WINERY (Ivanhoe)
SISTER CREEK VINEYARDS (Sisterdale)
SLAUGHTER LEFTWICH VINEYARDS (Austin)
TEJAS VINEYARD & WINERY (Mesquite)
VAL VERDE WINERY (Del Rio)
WIMBERLEY VALLEY WINERY (Driftwood)

Utah

ARCHES VINEYARDS (Spanish Fork)
SUMMUM (Salt Lake City)

Vermont

JOSEPH CERNIGLIA WINERY (Proctorsville)
NORTH RIVER WINERY (Jacksonville)

Virginia

ACCOMACK VINEYARDS (Painter)
AFTON MOUNTAIN VINEYARD CORP. (Afton)
AUTUMN HILL VINEYARDS (Stanardsville)
BARBOURSVILLE VINEYARDS (Barboursville)
BLENHEIM WINE CELLARS, LTD. (Charlottesville)
BURNLEY VINEYARDS (Barboursville)
CHATEAU MORRISETTE WINERY (Floyd)

CHATEAY NATUREL VINEYARD (Rocky Mount)
CHERMONT WINERY (Esmont)
DEER MEADOW VINEYARD (Winchester)
DOMINION WINE CELLARS (Culpeper)
FARFELU VINEYARD (Flint Hill)
GUILFORD RIDGE VINEYARD (Luray)
HARTWOOD WINERY, INC. (Fredericksburg)
HOUSE OF MARQUIS (Charlottesville)
INGLESIDE PLANTATION VINEYARDS (Oak Grove)
LA ABRA FARM & WINERY, INC. (Lovingston)
LAIRD & COMPANY (North Garden)
LAKE ANNA WINERY, INC. (Spotsylvania)
LINDEN VINEYARDS (Linden)
LOUDOUN VALLEY VINEYARDS (Waterford)
MEREDYTH VINEYARD (Middleburg)
MISTY MOUNTAIN VINEYARDS, INC. (Madison)
MONTDOMAINE CELLARS (Charlottesville)
MOUNTAIN COVE VINEYARDS (Lovingston)
MT. HERMON VINEYARDS WINERY (Basye)
NAKED MOUNTAIN VINEYARD & WINERY (Markham)
NORTH MOUNTAIN WINERY, INC. (Mauertown)
OAKENCROFT VINEYARD & WINERY CORP. (Charlottesville)
OASIS VINEYARDS (Hume)
PIEDMONT VINEYARDS (Middleburtg)
PRINCE MICHEL VINEYARD (Leon)
RAPIDAN RIVER VINEYARDS, INC. (Culpeper)
REBEC VINEYARDS (Amherst)
RIVERSIDE WINERY (Rapidan)
ROSE BOWER VINEYARD & WINERY, THE (Hampden-Sydney)
ROSE RIVER VINEYARDS (Syria)
SALZBURG VINEYARDS AND WINERY (Columbia)
SHENANDOAH VINEYARDS (Edinburg)
SIMEON VINEYARDS (Charlottesville)
STONEWALL VINEYARDS (Concord)
SWEDENBURG WINERY (Middleburg)
TARARA (Leesburg)
TOMAHAWK MILL WINERY (Chatham)
TRI-MOUNTAIN WINERY, INC. (Middletown)
VIRGINIA WINERY C0-OP (Culpeper)
WILLIAMSBURG WINERY LTD., THE (Williamsburg)
WILLOWCROFT FARM VINEYARDS (Leesburg)
WINCHESTER WINERY (Winchester)
WOOLWINE WINERY (Floyd)

Washington

ANDREW WILL CELLARS (Seattle)
ARBOR CREST/WASHINGTON CELLARS (Spokane)
BADGER MOUNTAIN VINEYARD (Kennewick)
~~BAINBRIDGE ISLAND VINEYARDS & WINERY~~
(Bainbridge Island)
BARNARD GRIFFIN WINERY (Kennewick)
BISCUIT RIDGE WINERY (Dixie)
BLACKWOOD CANYON VINTNERS (Benton City)
BONAIR WINERY (Zillah)
BOOKWALTER WINERY (Pasco)
CAMARADERIE CELLARS (Port Angeles)
CASCADE ESTATES WINERY (Sunnyside)
CASCADE MOUNTAIN CELLARS (Ellensburg)
CAVATAPPI WINERY (Kirkland)
CHAMPS DE BRIONNE WINERY (Quincy)
CHARLES HOOPER FAMILY WINERY (Husum)
CHATEAU GALLANT WINERY CO. (Burbank)
CHATEAU STE. MICHELLE (Woodinville)
CHINOOK WINES (Prosser)
COLUMBIA CLIFFS (Wishram)
COLUMBIA CREST WINERY (Woodinville)
COLUMBIA WINERY (Woodinville)
COVENTRY VALE WINERY, INC. (Grandview)
COVEY RUN VINTNERS (Zillah)

DELILLE CELLARS (Woodinville)
DOMAINE WHITTLESEY MARK, LTD. (Seattle)
EATON HILL WINERY (Granger)
FACELLI WINERY (Woodinville)
E. B. FOOTE WINERY (Seattle)
FRENCH CREEK CELLARS (Seattle)
GORDON BROS. CELLARS (Pasco)
HEDGES CELLARS (Zillah)
HINZERLING WINERY (Prosser)
HOGUE CELLARS (Prosser)
HOODSPORT WINERY, INC. (Hoodsport)
HORIZON'S EDGE WINERY (Zillah)
HUNTER HILL VINEYARDS (Othello)
HYATT VINEYARDS WINERY (Zillah)
JOHNSON CREEK WINERY (Tenino)
KNIPPRATH CELLARS (Spokane)
KIONA VINEYARDS WINERY (Benton City)
LATAH CREEK WINE CELLARS (Spokane)
LEONETTI CELLAR (Walla Walla)
LOPEZ ISLAND VINEYARDS (Lopez Island)
LOST MOUNTAIN WINERY, INC. (Sequim)
L'ECOLE NO. 41 (Lowden)
MANFRED VIERTHALER WINERY (Sumner)
Mc CREA CELLARS (Lake Stevens)
MERCER RANCH VINEYARDS (Prosser)
MONT ELISE VINEYARDS, INC. (Bingen)
MOUNT BAKER VINEYARDS, INC. (Deming)
MOUNTAIN DOME WINERY (Spokane)
NEELEY & SON WINERY (Kennewick)
NEUHARTH WINERY, INC. (Sequim)
OAKWOOD CELLARS (Benton City)
PACIFIC CREST WINE CELLARS (Fircrest)
PATRICK M. PAUL VINEYARDS (Walla Walla)
PAUL THOMAS WINES (Bellevue)
PONTIN DEL ROZA WINERY (Prosser)
PORTTEUS VINEYARD & WINERY (Zillah)
PRESTON CELLARS (Pasco)
QUARRY LAKE VINTNERS (Pasco)
QUILCEDA CREEK VINTNERS, INC. (Snohomish)
REDFORD CELLARS (Seattle)
RUCKER MEAD (Bremerton)
RICH PASSAGE WINERY (Bainbridge Island)
SALISHAN VINEYARDS (La Center)
SETH RYAN WINERY (Benton City)
SILVER LAKE WINERY (Bothell)
SNOQUALMIE WINERY (Snoqualmie)
SOOS CREEK WINE CELLARS (Renton)
STATON HILLS WINERY CO., LTD. (Wapato)
STEVEN THOMAS LIVINGSTONE WINERY (Spokane)
STEWART VINEYARDS, INC. (Granger)
TAGARIS WINERY (Othello)
TEFFT CELLARS (Outlook)
THURSTON WOLFE WINES (Yakima)
TUCKER CELLARS (Sunnyside)
VASHON WINERY (Vashon Island)
VIN DE 'L'QUEST WINERY (Toppenish)
WASHINGTON HILLS CELLAR (Sunnyside)
WATERBROOK WINERY, INC. (Lowden)
WENATCHEE VALLEY VINTNERS (Wenatchee)
WHIDBEY ISLAND VINEYARDS (Langley)
M. W. WHIDBEYS, LTD. (Greenbank)
WHITE HERON CELLARS (George)
WOODWARD CANYON WINERY (Lowden)
WORDEN'S WASHINGTON WINERY (Spokane)
WYCKOFF FARMS, INC. (Grandview)
YAKIMA RIVER WINERY, INC. (Prosser)
ZILLAH OAKES WINERY (Zillah)

West Virginia

FISHER RIDGE WINE CO. (Liberty)
FORKS OF CHEAT WINERY (Morgantown)

A. T. GIFT COMPANY (Harpers Ferry)
LAUREL CREEK WINERY, INC. (Lewisburg)
LITTLE HUNGARY FARM WINERY (Buckhannon)
ROBERT F. PLISKA & CO. WINERY (Purgitsville)
SCHNEIDER'S WINERY (Romney)
VANDALIA WINES (Colliers)
WEST-WHITEHILL WINERY, LTD. (Keyser)

Wisconsin

BERRYLEA FARM WINERY (Sturtlevant)
BOUNTIFUL HARVEST WINERY (Lodi)
CEDAR CREEK WINERY (Cedarburg)
CHRISTINA WINE CELLARS (LaCrosse)
DOOR-PENINSULA WINERY (Sturgeon Bay)
FRUIT OF THE WOODS WINE CELLAR, INC. (Three Lakes)
KETTLE MOUNTAIN VINEYARDS (Cascade)
MINERAL SPRINGS WINERY (Mineral Point)
ORCHARD COUNTRY WINERY (Fish Creek)
SPURGEON VYDS. & WINERY (Highland)
VON STIEHL WINERY (Algoma)
WOLLERSHEIM WINERY (Prairie Du Sac)
WOODLAND TRAIL BEVERAGE COMPANY, INC., THE (Lakewood)

Canada

A & H VINEYARDS (Peachland, B.C.)
ANDRES DU QUEBEC, LTEE., LES VINS (St. Hyacinth, Quebec)
ANDRES WINES, LTD. (Winona, Ontario)
ANDRES WINES, LTD. (Calgary, Alberta)
ANDRES WINES, LTD. (Truro, Nova Scotia)
ANDRES WINES, LTD. (Port Moody, B.C.)
ANDRES WINES, LTD. (Morris, Manitoba)
ANDREW WOLF CELLARS, LTD. (Stony Plain, Alberta)
BRIGHT & CO., LTD. (Niagara Falls, Ontario)
BRIGHTS WINES (Oliver, B.C.)
CALONA WINES, LTD. (Kelowna, B.C.)
CARTIER WINES (Penticton, B.C.)
CAVE SPRINGS CELLARS (St. Catharines, Ontario)
CEDARCREEK ESTATE WINERY (Kelowna, B.C.)
CELLIERS DU MONDE, INC. (Longueuil, Quebec)
CHATEAU DES CHARMES WINES (St. David's, Ontario)
CHATEAU STE. CLAIRE WINES, LTD. (Peachland, B.C.)
CLAREMONT ESTATE WINERY (Peachland, B.C.)
COLIO WINES OF CANADA, LTD. (Harrow, Ontario)
CULOTTA WINES, LTD. (Oakville, Ontario)
D'ANGELO VINEYARDS ESTATE WINERY (Amherstburg, Ontario)
DIVINO ESTATE WINERY,LTD. (Oliver, B.C.)
DOMAINE DE CHABERTON (Langley, B.C.)
DUMONT WINES & SPIRITS, INC. (Rougemont, Quebec)
GASPEREAU VALLEY VINEYARDS, LTD. (Wolfville, Nova Scotia)
GEHRINGER BROS. ESTATE WINERY (Oliver, B.C.)

GRAND MASTERS WINE AGENCY (Enfield, Nova Scotia)
GRAND PRE WINES CO., LTD. (Grand Pré, Nova Scotia)
GRAY MONK CELLARS, LTD. ESTATE WINERY (Okanagan Center, B.C.)
HAINLE VINEYARDS ESTATE WINERY (Peachland, B.C.)
HENRY OF PELHAM ESTATES WINERY (St. Catherines, Ontario)

HILLEBRAND ESTATES WINERY, LTD. (Niagara-on-the-Lake, Ontario)
HILLSIDE CELLARS (Penticton, B.C.)
INNISKILLIN WINES, INC. (Niagara-on-the-Lake, Ontario)
J. & STE. M., SURREY, B. C. DIVISION T. J. BRIGHT (Surrey B.C.)
JOST VINEYARDS, LTD. (Malagash, Nova Scotia)
JULAC, INC. (Dolbreau, Quebec)
KONZELMANN VINEYARDS, INC. (Niagara-on-the-Lake, Ontario)
LA MAISON SECRESTAT (Dorval, Quebec)
LANG VINEYARDS (Naramata, B.C.)
LE COMTE ESTATE WINERY (Okanagan Falls, B.C.)
LES VIGNOBLES DU QUEBEC, INC. (Hemmingford, Quebec)
LES VINS LA SALLE, INC. (Hyacinthe, Quebec)
LEWIS BROTHERS WINERY (Grand Prairie, Alberta)
LONDON WINERY, LTD. (London, Ontario)
MAGNOTTA WINERY (Vaughan, Ontario)
MISSION HILL VINEYARDS (Westbank., B.C.)
MONTRAVIN CELLARS (Beamsville, Ontario)
OKANAGAN VINEYARDS (Oliver, B.C.)
PAUL MASSON & CIE LTEE. (Dorval, Quebec)
PELEE ISLAND VINEYARDS, INC. (Kingsville, Ontario)
QUAILS' GATE ESTATE WINERY (Westbank, B.C.)
REIF WINERY (Niagara-on-the-Lake, Ontario)
RIDOUT WINES LIMITED (Mississauga, Ontario)
RIEDER DISTILLERY, LTD. (Grimsby, Ontario)
SAINTE FAMILLE WINES, LTD. (Falmouth, Nova Scotia)
ST. LASZLO VINEYARDS (Keremeos, B.C.)
SOCIETE DE VIN INTERNATIONALE, LTD. (Leman, Quebec)
STONECHURCH VINEYARDS (Niagara-on-the-Lake, Ontario)
STONEY RIDGE CELLARS (Winona, Ontario)
SUMAC RIDGE ESTATE WINERY, LTD. (Summerland, B.C.)
UNIACKE FARMS/ESTATE WINERY, LTD. (Kelowna, B.C.)
VALLEY WINE MERCHANT, LTD., THE (Vancouver, B.C.)
VINE GELOSO, INC. (Laval, Quebec)
VINELAND ESTATE WINES, LTD. (Vineland, Ontario)
VINOTECA, INC. (Woodbridge, Ontario)
WILD GOOSE VINEYARDS (Okanagan Falls, B.C.)
WILLOWBANK ESTATE WINES (Virgil, Ontario)

Mexico *

ANTONIO FERNANDEZ Y CIA., S.A. (Tlalnepantla)
BODEGAS CALIFORNIA, S.A. (Mexico City)
BODEGAS CAPELLANIA, S.A. (Mexico City)
BODEGAS CRUZ BLANCA, S.A. (Mexico City)
BODEGAS DE SANTO TOMAS, S.A. DE C.V. (Ensenada, B.C.)
BODEGAS FERRINO, S.A. (Cuatro Cienegas)
BODEGAS SAN CARLOS, S.A. (Veracruz)
BODEGAS SAN LUIS REY (San Luis de la Paz)
BODEGAS SAN PABLO, S.A. (Mexico City)
CAFES DE VERACRUZ, S.A. DE C.V. (Mexico City)
CASA MADERO, S.A. (Monterey)

CASA PINSON HERMANOS, S.A. (Mexico City)
CAVAS BACH, S.A. (Tlalnepantla)
CAVAS DE MONTOROY Y FONTENAC (Aguascalientes)
CAVAS DE SAN JUAN, S.A. DE C.V. (Mexico City)
CAVAS VALMAR (Ensenada)
CHARMONT, S.A. (Mexico City)
CIA. DESTILADORA, S.A. (Mexico City)
CIA. MEXICANA DUBONNET, S.A. (Mexico City)
CIA. VINICOLA BORDEGAS DE REFUGIO, S.A. (Aguascalientes)
CIA. VINICOLA DE AGUASCALIENTES, S.A. (Mexico City)
CIA. VINICOLA DE ENSENADA, S.A. (Ensenada)
CIA. VINICOLA DE LA LAGUNA, S.A. (Mexico City)
CIA. VINICOLA DEL VERGEL, S.A. DE C.V. (Gomez Palacio)
CIA. VINICOLA DE SALTILLO, S.A. (Mexico City)
CIA. VINICOLA DIAZ DE LEON HERMANOS, S.A. (Pabellon de Arteaga)
CIA. VINICOLA EL MILAGRO, S.A. (Pabellon de Arteaga)
CIA. VINICOLA FRUITILANDIA, S.A. (Aguascalientes)
CIA. VINICOLA LA VIOLETA, S.A. (Aguascalientes)
CIA. VINICOLA REGIONAL, S.R.L. Y V.E.V. (Tijuana)
CINZANO DE MEXICO, S.A. (Mexico City)
DERIVADOS DE FRUTA, S.A. (Aguascalientes)
DERIVADOS DE UVA DE SONORA, S.A. (Hermosillo)
DESTILADORA DE CARBORCA , S.A. DE C.V. (H. Caborca)
DIAZ GOENAGA, S.A. (Mexico City)
EXCLUSIVAS BENET, S.A. (Mexico City)
FORMEX-YBARRA, S.A. (Ensenada)
FREIXENET DE MEXICO, S.A. DE C.V. (Mexico City)
FRUCOVIN, S.A. (Mexico City)
GONZALEZ BYASS DE MEXICO, S.A. DE C.V. (Mexico City)
INDUSTRIAS AGROPECUARIAS DE DELICIAS, S.A. (Delicias)
INDUSTRIAS DE LA FERMENTACION, S.A. DE C.V. (Aguascalientes)
LA BORDALESA, S.A. DE C.V. (Aguascalientes)
LA MADRILENA, S.A. (Mexico City)
LAS CAVAS DE AGUASCALIENTES, S.A. (Aguascalientes)
MARTINI & ROSSI DE MEXICO, S.A. (Mexico City)
MEZCLAS FAVORITAS, S.A. (Mexico City)
OSBORNE DE MEXICO, S.A. DE C.V. (Naucalpan de Juarez)
PEDRAGES Y CIA., S.A. (Mexico City)
PEDRO DOMECQ MEXICO, S.A. DE C.V. (Mexico City)
PRODUCTOS DE UVA DE AGUASCALIENTES, S. DE R.L. (Tijuana)
PRODUCTOS DE UVA, S.A. (Tijuana)
SAN ANTONIO (Ensenada)
SOFIMAR, S.A. (Mexico City)
SUNTORY DE MEXICO, S.A. (Mexico City)
UNION VINICOLA DE AGUASCALIENTES, S.A. (Aguascalientes)
UNION VINICOLA ZAZATECANA, S.A. DE C.V. (Zacatecas)
VALMAR (Ensenada)
VIDES DEL GUADALUPE, S.A. DE C.V. (Tijuana)
VINDESSA, S.A. Y VINICOLA DEL SAUCITO (Fresnillo)
VIDES DEL GUADALUPE (Calafia)
VINICOLA DE TECATE, S. DE R.L. (Tecate)
VINICOLA DE TIJUANA, S.A. (Mexico City)
VINICOLA PITIC (Hermosillo)
VINICOLA SELLER, S.A. (Mexico City)
VINICOLA VITALI (Cuatro Cienegas)
VINIFICACION Y TECNOLOGIA, S.A. (Delicias)
VINOS VALLE REDONDO, S.A. (Mexico City)

---

* It should be noted that most grape growers and wine producers in Mexico do not produce table wines, but rather vinify grapes for sale in bulk to Mexico's large brandy producers, who distill the wine into spirits. The recent economics of wine production in Mexico have made this an increasingly common practice; there is little reliable information on which wineries—beyond a handful of well-established wine producers—may also make and market a table wine in any given year. *See* Introduction to Mexico Winery Profiles in Part Two.

Index

S

T

U-V

W

Y

Z

BE SMART. BOOK US.
"BEST OF" GUIDES

André Gayot Publications bring you the best of major U.S., European and Asian destinations. The guidebooks include full details on the best of everything that makes these places special: the restaurants, diversions, nightlife, hotels, shops and arts. The guides also offer practical information on getting around and enjoying each area. Perfect for visitors, residents and also make great long-lasting gift ideas.

> "Gault Millau is provocative and frank."
> – *Los Angeles Times*

> "Witty, breezy, opinionated."
> – *New York Times*

> "You will enjoy their prose."
> – *US News & World Report*

Please send me the "Best of" books checked below:

☐ Chicago	$15.95	☐ Italy	Sold out	☐ Paris	$20.00
☐ Florida	$17.00	☐ London	$16.95	☐ San Francisco	$16.95
☐ France	$20.00	☐ Los Angeles	$18.00	☐ Thailand	$17.95
☐ Germany	$18.00	☐ New England	$15.95	☐ Toronto	$17.00
☐ Hawaii	$16.95	☐ New Orleans	$1700	☐ Washington D.C.	$16.95
☐ Hong Kong	$16.95	☐ New York	$16.95	☐ Wines of America	$18.00

Mail to:
Gault Millau, Inc., P.O. Box 361144, Los Angeles, CA 90036

Or, order toll free: *1 (800) LE BEST 1*
In the U.S., include $3 (shipping charge) for the first book, and $2 for each additional book. Outside the U.S., $10 and $7.

☐ Enclosed is my check or money order made out to: Gault Millau, Inc. for $ _____ .

☐ Please charge my credit card: ☐ MC   ☐ VISA   ☐ AMEX

Card Number _____ Exp. ___/___

Signature _____ Telephone _____

Name _____

Address _____

City _____ State _____ Zip _____

Country _____

318/93

TASTES

THE WORLD DINING & TRAVEL CONNECTION

Want to keep current on the best bistros in Paris? Discover that little hideaway in Singapore? Or stay away from that dreadful and dreadfully expensive restaurant in New York? André Gayot's Tastes newletter gives you bimonthly news on the best and worst in restaurants, hotels, nightlife and shopping around the world.

☐ YES, please enter my subscription to **TASTES** newsletter for 6 bimonthly issues at the rate of $40 per year. (Outside U.S. and Canada, $45.)

Name_____

Address_____

City_____State _____

Zip_____Country _____

CHECK ENCLOSED FOR $ _____.

CHARGE TO:

____ MASTERCARD ____ VISA ____ AMEX Exp. ___/___

Acct. # _____

Signature _____

318/93

FOR FASTER SERVICE CALL 1 (800) LE BEST 1